W9-BVZ-721

Current Issues
in Biblical
and Patristic Interpretation

Merrill C. Tenney, 1974

Current Issues
in Biblical
and Patristic Interpretation

**STUDIES IN HONOR OF MERRILL C. TENNEY
PRESENTED BY HIS FORMER STUDENTS**

**Edited by
Gerald F. Hawthorne**

William B. Eerdmans Publishing Company
Grand Rapids, Michigan

Library of Congress Cataloging in Publication Data

Main entry under title:

Current issues in Biblical and patristic interpretation.

"Select bibliography of the writings of Merrill C.
Tenney": p. 19
  1. Bible—Addresses, essays, lectures.
2. Theology—Early Church, ca. 30-600—Addresses,
essays, lectures. 3. Tenney, Merrill C. I. Tenney,
Merrill Chapin, 1904-   II. Hawthorne, Gerald F.,
1925-   ed.
BS413.C8   220.6'6   74-19326
ISBN 0-8028-3442-6

Contents

Preface, *Gerald F. Hawthorne* 7
Introduction, *F. F. Bruce* 9
In Appreciation, *Hudson T. Armerding* 13
Merrill C. Tenney: A Brief Biography, *Thomas A. Askew* 17
Select Bibliography of the Writings of Merrill C. Tenney, *Thomas A. Askew* 19
Tabula Gratulatoria 21
Abbreviations 26

I. HISTORICAL

The Extent of the Old Testament Canon, *Norman L. Geisler* 31
The Development of the Concept of "Orthodoxy" in Early Christianity, *Robert A. Kraft* 47
The Power of Giving and Receiving: Reciprocity in Hellenistic Benevolence, *Stephen Charles Mott* 60

II. BIBLICAL AND PATRISTIC

Were David's Sons Really Priests?, *Carl Edwin Armerding* 75
The Significance of the Delay of the Parousia for Early Christianity, *David E. Aune* 87
A Note on Colossians 1:27a, *W. Paul Bowers* 110
Paul's "Cutting" Remarks about a Race: Galatians 5:1-12, *Carl E. De Vries* 115
The Composition of Luke 9 and the Sources of Its Christology, *E. Earle Ellis* 121
Wisdom, Torah, Word: The Johannine Prologue and the Purpose of the Fourth Gospel, *Eldon Jay Epp* 128
A New English Translation of Melito's Paschal Homily, *Gerald F. Hawthorne* 147
The Weightier and Lighter Matters of the Law: Moses, Jesus and Paul, *Walter C. Kaiser, Jr.* 176
Bultmann's Law of Increasing Distinctness, *Leslie R. Keylock* 193
The Holy Spirit in Galatians, *George Eldon Ladd* 211

5

Literary Criteria in Life of Jesus Research: An Evaluation and Proposal, *Richard N. Longenecker* 217

Sins Within and Sins Without: An Interpretation of 1 John 5:16-17, *David M. Scholer* 230

Multiple Meanings in the Gospel of John, *Russell Shedd* 247

The Limits of Ecstasy: An Exegesis of 2 Corinthians 12:1-10, *Russell P. Spittler* 259

Charismatic Theology in the *Apostolic Tradition* of Hippolytus, *John E. Stam* 267

"Love" in the Old Testament: Some Lexical Observations, *Larry L. Walker* 277

The Greek "Verbal Genitive," *G. Henry Waterman* 289

III. THEOLOGICAL

The Deity of Christ in the Writings of Paul, *Walter Elwell* 297

Some Reflections on the Mission of the Church, *David M. Howard* 309

Some Reflections on Evangelism in the New Testament, *Paul E. Little* 318

Christology and "The Angel of the Lord," *William Graham MacDonald* 324

A Study of the New Testament Concept of the Parousia, *W. Harold Mare* 336

The Metaphorical Language of Theology: Its Experiential Base—Biblical and Contemporary, *A. Berkeley Mickelsen* 346

Some Comments on Hebrews 6:4-6 and the Doctrine of the Perseverance of God with the Saints, *Roger Nicole* 355

Historical Explanation and Barth on Christ's Resurrection, *Stanley R. Obitts* 365

Preface

GERALD F. HAWTHORNE

Without commenting on the quality of the articles in this volume, I will say that the quantity of them testifies to the esteem in which Professor Tenney's former students hold him. Cautious by nature, I composed a list of contributors longer than advisable for a *Festschrift* of reasonable size. I was certain, in those early stages of this project, that many of the invited would be unwilling or unable to undertake such a venture or to complete it on time. Quite the reverse was true. Almost to a man, each responded with alacrity, glad for such an opportunity to honor their professor. Hence, the length of the present volume.

The variety of titles, on the one hand, reflects the wide-ranging curiosity of Dr. Tenney's own mind, even though his area of specialization is the New Testament. The diversity of viewpoints, on the other hand, reflects the vigor of his scholarship—a catapult, never a cage, for the thinking of his followers.

Dr. Tenney's teaching career has spanned almost half a century. His former students therefore number in the hundreds. They fill places of responsibility in the home, in the church, in seminaries, and in colleges and universities, both in the United States and in foreign countries. Some of these will be disappointed because they were not asked to write an essay in his honor. To these I offer my apology, pleading the limitations of my own knowledge, and that of the size of a single book. May these articles, however, represent the whole of his students and reflect vicariously the talents and willingness of all not chosen.

In honoring Dr. Tenney, our ultimate goal is to honor the God whom he serves. Therefore, our prayer of presentation is a paraphrase of one made by St. Augustine: "O Lord, whatever has been written in this book that comes by thy prompting, may thy people recognize it; for that which is written only of ourselves, we ask of thee and of thy people pardon."

In preparing a volume like this, many people besides the editor play important and crucial roles. Consequently, I want to thank Mr. William B. Eerdmans, Jr., President of William B. Eerdmans Publishing Company, who enthusiastically accepted my proposal and who has been most kind and cooperative from the inception to the realization of this project. My thanks, too, to each contributor, who so readily responded when asked to write, to Dr. Donald Mitchell and Dr. Robert Baptista, administrative officers of Wheaton College, who gave encouragement at every turn, enabling me to resolve difficulty after difficulty, and to Dr. Richard Gross, Dean of Gordon College. My wife, Jane Elliot Hawthorne, has spent many hours at the typewriter. I owe her much.

Special thanks, however, must go to Professor Donald Hagner, Wheaton College, who read all of the edited copy, caught many of my mistakes, and offered excellent suggestions along the way, and to the Wheaton College Alumni Association, which made possible a reduced teaching load for me so that I could meet my deadlines.

Introduction

F. F. BRUCE

The invitation to write this introduction to a volume of essays in honor of Dr. Merrill C. Tenney is one which I accept with pleasure. I am conscious, indeed, that any one of the contributors could in many ways have written a more adequate introduction than I can. They are former pupils of Dr. Tenney, and as such they know their teacher with an immediacy denied to others. But for that very reason their appraisal of him might be thought to be insufficiently objective. The editor has therefore cast his net more widely for this particular contribution, reckoning that an assessment of Dr. Tenney's place in the world of biblical and theological scholarship could best be made by someone less closely associated with him.

Dr. Tenney had been well known to me by name for several years when I first met him at Chicago in 1958 at a meeting for theological students convened by the Inter-Varsity Christian Fellowship. A few days after that first meeting I visited him at Wheaton, where he entertained me generously and showed me around the campus of the College and Graduate School. I think we have actually met face to face on only one other occasion. But we have been associated in a variety of ways. We have been fellow-contributors to a number of dictionaries and symposia, and I have contributed to works of reference produced under his editorship. In all these associations I have been impressed by his sober, exact and trustworthy Christian scholarship.

It will not be surprising if the verdict of posterity is that his most solid contribution has been made as a teacher—first at Gordon and then for thirty years at Wheaton. The quality and fame of many of his pupils will suffice to establish his reputation in this regard. Some of them stand today in the van of international New Testament study. With one of them I have had an especially close association. Robert A. Kraft, having taken his Master's degree in Wheaton Graduate School, went on to pursue his doctoral studies at Harvard, as Dr. Tenney had done before him, and came straight from there, with the highest commendation from his New Testa-

---

F. F. Bruce, Rylands Professor of Biblical Criticism and Exegesis at the University of Manchester, Manchester, England.

ment teachers, to lecture with me in the Department of Biblical Criticism and Exegesis at the University of Manchester. Of all the candidates for that lectureship he was incomparably the most outstanding, and it was inevitable that he should be quickly enticed back to his native land (to our great loss at Manchester) to the post which he continues to hold at the University of Pennsylvania and to a career of ever increasing distinction in his chosen field. I sometimes tell my students that, as Paul expected the standard of his apostolic labors to be assessed on the last day by the quality of his converts, so I expect my teaching to be assessed by the way in which they acquit themselves. I guess that Dr. Tenney has sometimes felt the same. And he may well rest confident: with pupils such as his, his reputation stands secure.

Some of his literary works are by-products of his teaching activity. His excellent *New Testament Survey* belongs to this category. Others have made the fruits of his study and teaching available to a wider public; such are his volumes on *John, Galatians, Philippians* and *Revelation*. While his works fall uniformly within the conservative school of biblical criticism, his fame is not confined within that school. When, a few years ago, the editors of a popular encyclopedia of the supernatural entitled *Man, Myth and Magic*—by no means a conservative, and not even a distinctively Christian, production—looked around for someone to write the article on the book of Revelation, it was on Dr. Tenney that their choice fell. His theological position was (very properly) of no concern to them; what mattered was that he was a recognized authority on this particular subject. If his own line of conservatism is not followed by all his pupils, that simply shows that he has not trained them to be carbon copies of himself; like all good teachers, he has encouraged them to think for themselves.

He has always insisted on the historical resurrection of Christ as the basic fact for Christian thought and life. His first published book dealt with this subject, and he returned to it twenty years later in a contribution to Carl Henry's symposium *Jesus of Nazareth: Saviour and Lord.* While he might have gone farther than he does in the tradition- and redaction-criticism of the resurrection narratives, he presents a telling case for the objectivity of the event. "The Easter faith must logically presuppose an historical event which underlies it" (*Jesus of Nazareth: Saviour and Lord,* p. 144). This is a conclusion which, I think, cannot be upset.

Dr. Tenney's biblical scholarship is marked by no cheap gimmicks, nor is he prone (like some other scholars) to indulge in brilliant guesswork with a fifty-fifty chance of being right. He proceeds on the conviction that nothing can take the place of an analytic study of the text, in which due regard is paid to the natural structure of the document under examination. Only so can a firm foundation be laid.

Again, he has never considered it part of the exegete's duty to give the current climate of opinion a determinant role in the prosecution of his task. One will look in vain in his writings for any trace of the influence of that existentialist hermeneutic which has dominated so much New Testament scholarship for a generation and more. In his view, the message of the New Testament writers for today can be learned only by considering what they intended by their words and what their words would naturally have been understood to mean by the people for whom they wrote. "The word for this century" is materially identical with the word for the first century. "The Bible may say nothing about airplanes," he once wrote, "but its precepts apply as well to men who fly planes as they did to men who drove chariots. . . . God has spoken His final word to men through the historical Christ, and because Christ still lives His truth is applicable to our age" (*The Word for This Century,* Introduction, pp. xiv-xv).

To bear consistent witness to this Christian fact, in teaching and in writing, for so many years is a noble achievement for any man, a valuable service to render in any age. Because I appreciate so highly what Dr. Tenney has accomplished through his witness, I am glad to be associated with his pupils in paying this tribute of esteem and gratitude to him.

In Appreciation

HUDSON T. ARMERDING

The popular conception of higher education is a curious mixture of myth and fact. It is the product of a series of impressions drawn from fragments of information that are not necessarily the most significant or the most important. Particularly in recent days the dramatic incidents on the college campus have tended to attract attention to the unusual or the unfortunate and have largely obscured the basic campus functions. These are noticed only if they are associated with a successful athletic program or a scientific discovery perceived to have immediate usefulness in society.

This perception of higher education has been further complicated by the uncertainty that has characterized the search by the colleges and universities to discover what their major purposes really are. Not too many years ago it was generally agreed these were to preserve and transmit culture and to extend the frontiers of knowledge. It was also assumed these legitimately included the certification of vocational skills, particularly in the graduate schools.

More recently, there has been a growing uneasiness about what really constitutes the content of education and equally about what produces real learning. One result of this is a new pedagogical goal, that of student self-realization or self-fulfillment. The precedence given this objective and the persistent uncertainty about content and method have combined to produce a centrifugal force that has tended to propel the student into encounters with circumstances rather than professors. The role of the teacher increasingly is one of director or critic rather than educator.

At the same time, the rapidly increasing use of machines as aids to learning has reinforced the autonomous stance of the student. These devices have been employed to perform an evaluative function. The result has been to place the college professor in the uncomfortable position occupied by others in earlier eras of the industrial revolution. "You can be replaced by a machine" seems today to have more significance than simply an attempt at sardonic humor.

Hudson T. Armerding, President of Wheaton College, Wheaton, Illinois. B.A., Wheaton College; M.A., Clark University; Ph.D., The University of Chicago; D.D., Gordon-Conwell Theological Seminary.

Yet despite this apparent realignment of educational priorities and procedures, what remains of a college education years later is far more personal than statistical. Even the imperfections of various educational programs have failed to obscure the discipling dimension of teaching. It continues to be recognized and appreciated by the overwhelming majority of college graduates.

This is splendidly true of Dr. Merrill C. Tenney. Throughout his long and distinguished career, in which he pursued scholarship and pedagogy with equal vigor, he never failed to give priority to his relationship to his students. Indeed, it was his research and writing that reinforced his classroom work. Conversely, it was his meaningful interaction with his students that enabled him to communicate successfully to a wide spectrum of the Christian world through his publishing and lecturing.

Such involvement was in no sense at the expense of scholarship. His devotion to excellence has become a legend among his students. They correctly perceived that what he demanded of them was simply a reflection of that which he first expected of himself. Throughout his life he has sought for economy and efficiency in the use of time and opportunity. This reflects both his New England heritage and his mature conception of Christian stewardship.

He was fortunate to be reared in an atmosphere of Christian piety that combined personal self-discipline with a love of books. His father enjoyed a wide reputation for his remarkable bibliographical knowledge. On one occasion my father visited Mr. Tenney's bookstore after an absence of some years. Immediately Mr. Tenney recognized him and recalled that on the previous occasion he had requested a particular volume. He announced that he had procured it for my father and was ready to sell it to him. Such perspicacity was happily inherited by his son and splendidly manifested in both his undergraduate and graduate studies and in his academic life thereafter.

When Dr. Tenney was asked to assume administrative responsibilities in the Wheaton Graduate School, he undertook these with a characteristic sense of duty. While he continued to give substantial portions of his time to teaching and writing, he faithfully responded to the demands of administration as an opportunity to serve for the glory of God as well as for the best interests of the Graduate School. Into its program he infused his own ideals and convictions. These combined an uncompromising commitment to the entire trustworthiness of the Holy Scriptures with a clear-eyed vision of the need for well-prepared and dedicated graduates to serve in all parts of the world.

It is sometimes said that it is the institution which furnishes a reputation to those who are associated with it. In Dr. Tenney's case he has enhanced the reputation of Wheaton because of the recognition he has earned as a diligent Christian scholar. Prominent among the significant aspects of this reputation is his fervent love for Christ and for those who share his devotion for the Lord. To his colleagues he has provided a splendid example of service for others even when personal needs were very real. It can correctly be said of him that the focus of his life has been upward and then outward rather than inward.

The Scriptures speak of the path of the just as shining more and more unto the perfect day. At a time when even Christian higher education has been visibly affected by the confusion and paradoxes of contemporary culture, Dr. Tenney has shown himself capable of being both resolute and adaptable. His reputation is secure as one who is at once mature in outlook and youthful in spirit.

As a friend and colleague I can testify to the contributions he has made to my own perspective. I recognize that this same contribution has been made to scores of colleagues and students. I speak for them as well as myself in expressing appreciation for the witness and service of Dr. Merrill Tenney. We thank our God upon every remembrance of him. This is why it is altogether fitting that a volume should be published in his honor. This will permit many others to glimpse something of the remarkable ministry of this servant of Jesus Christ.

Merrill C. Tenney

A Brief Biography

THOMAS A. ASKEW

Merrill Chapin Tenney was born of New England stock in Chelsea, a suburb of Boston, in 1904. His father, Wallace Fay Tenney, managed the religious book department at Goodspeed's Bookstore in Boston. From his boyhood Merrill displayed an avid interest in books and language, a precocity recognized by his classmates at Needham High School. Many years later Professor Tenney remarked that as a youth he could become as excited over running down a Latin verb root as many boys do in chasing after a football.

Early in life Merrill Tenney felt God's call to service. Subsequent to his conversion in a tent meeting, he was especially influenced by the appeals of a missionary from Africa. Upon his graduation from Needham High School, an interest in foreign missions led the earnest youth to Nyack Missionary Training Institute from which he received a diploma in June, 1924. The next fall he began twenty years of association with Gordon College of Theology, then located on the Fenway in Boston.

At Gordon Tenney soon surfaced as a clever wit and brilliant student; so outstanding, in fact, that he was drafted to teach Greek courses during his senior year because of the illness of the professor. At the same time he pastored the Storrs Avenue Baptist Church in Braintree. He received the Th.B. from Gordon in 1927; the following year he was ordained at the First Baptist Church of Needham, joined the Gordon faculty, and began graduate study in theology at Boston University.

In 1930 he received the M.A. from Boston University and married Helen M. Jaderquist, an alumna of Gordon, '28, and the daughter of the Gordon Greek professor. Mrs. Tenney, who held a B.A. from Wheaton College and an M.A. from Northwestern University before earning a B.D. from Gordon, was an able student in her own right. Her literary talents would later prove invaluable in Tenney's writing career.

By 1935 Merrill Tenney was pursuing doctoral studies at Harvard

---

Thomas A. Askew, Professor of History at Gordon College, Wenham, Massachusetts. B.A., Wheaton College; M.A., Wheaton College Graduate School; M.A. and Ph.D., Northwestern University.

University while serving as Professor of New Testament and Greek at Gordon. He was respected at Gordon as a teacher who demanded excellence from those he taught, and also at Harvard as a student who demanded the same from himself. Submitting a dissertation supervised by Professor Cadbury on the text of Tertullian, Merrill Tenney received the Ph.D. degree in Biblical and Patristic Greek from Harvard in 1944. By this time the Tenneys had two sons, Robert Wallace and Philip Chapin.

In 1943 Tenney accepted a full-time appointment at Wheaton College after teaching in two summer sessions there. Named full Professor of Bible and Theology in 1945 and Dean of the Graduate School in 1947, he embarked on a productive twenty-five-year Wheaton career distinguished by administration, teaching, lecturing, preaching and writing. From 1943 to 1949 he pastored the United Gospel Tabernacle in Wheaton. Under the Tenney leadership the Wheaton College Graduate School grew in both numbers and stature. By the 1950's Dean Tenney was lecturing and preaching across the country as well as overseas. A member of numerous honorary and professional societies, he was the second president of the Evangelical Theological Society. Despite a heavy schedule on and off campus, he maintained a vigorous flow of publications, as the following bibliography demonstrates. In 1971 Dr. Tenney retired from the deanship of the Graduate School, but he has continued to teach classes and keep an active writing regimen at Wheaton.

Select Bibliography of the Writings of
Merrill C. Tenney

THOMAS A. ASKEW

BOOKS:

Resurrection Realities. Los Angeles: Bible House of Los Angeles, 1945. Out of print.

John: The Gospel of Belief. Grand Rapids: Wm. B. Eerdmans, 1948.
> British edition—in *New London Commentary on the New Testament.* London: Marshall, Morgan & Scott, 1954.
> Japanese translation—Sendai, Japan: Seisho Tosho Kankokai, 1958.

Galatians: The Charter of Christian Liberty (first edition, 1951; second edition, 1957). Grand Rapids: Wm. B. Eerdmans, 1957.
> Spanish translation—*Galatas: La Carta de la Libertad Cristiana.* Tradicido per Samuel Vila. Grand Rapids: TELL, n.d.
> Portuguese translation—*Galatas: Escritura du Liberdade Crista.* Traducao po Joao Bentes. São Paulo, Brasil: Edicees Vida Nova Soc. Ltda., 1967.
> Japanese translation—Sendai, Japan: Seisho Tosho Kankokai, 1968.

The New Testament: An Historical and Analytical Survey. Grand Rapids: Wm. B. Eerdmans, 1955.
> British edition—London. Inter-Varsity, 1954.
> Portuguese translation—*O Nove Testamente: Sua Origem e Analise.* Leiria e Lisboa, Portugal: Vida Nova Edicoes, 1960.
> Revised edition—*New Testament Survey.* Grand Rapids: Wm. B. Eerdmans, 1961.
> Japanese translation—*Shinyako Seisho Gaikan.* Sendai, Japan: Seisho Tosho Kankokai, 1962.

The Genius of the Gospels. Grand Rapids: Wm. B. Eerdmans, 1956. Out of print.

Philippians: The Gospel at Work. Grand Rapids: Wm. B. Eerdmans, 1956. Out of print.

Interpreting Revelation. Grand Rapids: Wm. B. Eerdmans, 1957.

The Reality of the Resurrection. New York, Evanston, London: Harper & Row, 1963. Reprinted Chicago: Moody, 1972.

The Book of Revelation in Proclaiming the New Testament. Grand Rapids: Baker, 1963.

New Testament Times. Grand Rapids: Wm. B. Eerdmans, 1965.

The Vital Heart of Christianity. Reprint of *Resurrection Realities* (1954). Grand Rapids: Zondervan, 1964. Out of print.

EDITED WORKS:

The Word for This Century (symposium). New York: Oxford University Press, 1960.
> English edition—London: Lutterworth, 1960.

The Pictorial Bible Dictionary. Grand Rapids: Zondervan, 1963.

The Bible: The Living Word of Revelation (symposium). Grand Rapids: Zondervan, 1968.

The Pictorial Bible Encyclopedia (4 vols.). Grand Rapids: Zondervan, 1975.

BIBLE STUDY GUIDES:

John (2 vols.); *I and II Corinthians* (2 vols.); *Revelation.* Wheaton: Scripture Press, 1961-62; 1964; 1959.

CONTRIBUTIONS TO OTHER WORKS:

"Reversals of New Testament Criticism" in *Revelation and the Bible*. Ed. C. F. H. Henry. Grand Rapids: Baker, 1958. Pp. 351-67.

"Luke" in *Wycliffe Bible Commentary*. Eds. Pfeiffer and Harrison. Chicago: Moody, 1960. Pp. 1027-70.

"Pentecost," "Persecution," "Sanhedrin," "Zealot" in *Dictionary of Theology*. Eds. Harrison, Bromiley and Henry. Grand Rapids: Baker, 1960.

"Revelation" in *The Biblical Expositor*, Vol. III. Pp. 463-86. Ed. C. F. H. Henry. Philadelphia: A. J. Holman, 1960.

"Baptism and the Lord's Supper" in *Basic Christian Doctrines*. Ed. C. F. H. Henry. New York: Holt, Rinehart and Winston, 1962. Pp. 255-61.

"Science Operates Within Fixed Limits" in *Science and Religion*. Ed. John Clover Monsma. New York: G. P. Putnam's Sons, 1962. Pp. 179-86.

"Outline for Revelation" in *The Holman Bible*. Philadelphia: A. J. Holman, 1962. Pp. 1153a,b.

"The Importance and Exegesis of Revelation 20:1-8" in *Truth for Today*. Ed. John Walvoord. Chicago: Moody, 1963. Pp. 175-86.

"The Focus of Faith" in *88 Evangelistic Sermons*. Ed. Charles L. Wallis. New York, Evanston and London: Harper & Row, 1964. Pp. 11-13.

"The Historicity of the Resurrection" in *Jesus of Nazareth, Saviour and Lord*. Ed. C. F. H. Henry. Grand Rapids: Wm. B. Eerdmans, 1966. Pp. 133-55.

"The Expansion of the Church" in *Pictorial Bible Atlas*. Ed. E. M. Blaiklock. Grand Rapids: Zondervan, 1969. Pp. 321-49.

"The Glorious Destiny of the Believer" in *Fundamentals of the Faith*. Ed. C. F. H. Henry. Grand Rapids: Zondervan, 1969. Pp. 273-91.

PAPERS AND ARTICLES:

"Books," *Eternity* (Nov. 1958), pp. 20, 21, 34.

"Eschatology and the Pulpit," *Bibliotheca Sacra*, 116 (Jan. 1959), 30-42.

"God's Word Today," *Christian Life* (Dec. 1959), pp. 14, 15.

"The Great Alternative," *Alliance Witness*, 104 (5, 1960), 3-5.

"The Limits of Biblical Criticism," *Christianity Today* (Nov. 21, 1960), pp. 5-8.

Lectures on "The Footnotes of John's Gospel," *Bibliotheca Sacra*, 117 (Oct.-Dec. 1960), 350-64.

"One Voice; Many Translations," *Christian Life* (Nov. 1961), pp. 42-44.

Lectures on "The Symphonic Structure of JOHN," "The Author's Testimony to Himself," "The Old Testament and the Fourth Gospel," and "The Imagery of John" in Nos. 478, 479, 480 and 481 respectively of *Bibliotheca Sacra*, 1963-64. (Lectures given at Dallas Seminary on "Literary Keys to the Fourth Gospel," 1962.)

"The Return of Christ," *Christian Life* (Jan. 1964), pp. 20-24.

"The Revelation of God," *The Alliance Witness*, 101 (Feb. 4, 1966), 5, 4, 6-8.

"Jesus Christ: His Relevance Today," *The Alliance Witness*, 101 (March 7, 1966), 5, 6, 18.

"A New Approach to the Book of Hebrews," *Bibliotheca Sacra*, 491 (July-Sept. 1966), 230-36.

Lectures on "The Relevance of the Book of Revelation": (1) "Revelation and the Church"; (2) "Revelation and History"; (3) "The Christology of Revelation" in *The Seminary Review*, 13 (Fall 1966), 3-5. Cincinnati Bible Seminary.

"The Centrality of the Resurrection," *Sunday School Times* and *Gospel Herald*, 66 (April 7, 1968), 8-9.

Tabula Gratulatoria

Wallace Alcorn
Robert L. Alden
Harold Alexander
Ralph H. Alexander
Dennis L. Allen
Ronald Barclay Allen
Gilda Altman
Neil Altman
Ismael E. Amaya
Howard G. Andersen
Donald E. Anderson
Frances Fairchild Anderson
George A. Anderson
John C. Anderson
N. Duane Anderson
Stanley E. Anderson
Roger J. Andrus
Hideo Aoki
Herbert Apel
Samuel K. Arai
John Armstrong
Norman H. Arnesen
William M. Arnett
Daniel A. Augsburger
H. Wilbur Aulie
Hermann J. Austel

Robert E. Bailey
Thomas I. Bailey
James D. Bales
Andrew J. Bandstra
Steven Barabas
Cyril J. Barber
Louis A. Barbieri, Jr.
Kenneth L. Barker
David Barnes
Vivian Barnett
Earl E. Barrett
John Barrier
Robert J. Bartel
Stan Barthold
Clarence B. Bass

Beatrice Batson
James R. Battenfield
Paul A. Beals
Joseph Bean
Paul M. Bechtel
Marleen Beck
John D. Bennett
Esther Koch Benziger
Harold M. Best
William H. Bicksler
George B. Biggs, Jr.
Gilbert Bilezikian
Caryl Bjorklund
LaVern Bjorklund
Ed Blakely
Vivienne Blomquist
Donald C. Boardman
Richard Allen Bodey
John M. Boice
John C. Bonson
William Harllee Bordeaux
Andrew Bowling
Neal O. Brace
J. Kenneth Brand
Raymond H. Brand
William B. Brewer
Mollie Brien
Wick Broomall
Martha Dilling Brown
Nancy H. Brown
W. Gordon Brown
Don Brugmann
David Bryant
Chris R. Bullard
C. Hassell Bullock
Donald W. Burdick
Edith Buss
Siegfried A. Buss
Vertis R. Butler, Jr.

Henry J. Cadbury
P. Joseph Cahill

Earle Cairns
R. J. Campbell
Charles W. Carpenter
Charles W. Carter
John Carter
Vernon Caston
Louise C. Wright Cerling
Robert H. Chandler
David Chapman
Gwendolyn Charles
Robert B. Chase
Pauline Ip-Heung Chien
Gladys Christensen
H. C. Chrouser
Ernest Chun
Ann Church
Donald L. Church
Kenneth E. Churchill
Alfred A. Cierpke
Howard H. Claassen
Gordon H. Clark
Christie Claypoole
Howard Z. Cleveland
Arthur M. Climenhaga
George W. Coats
Carter H. Cody
Asa J. Colby
Robert E. Coleman
Gordon Coles
C. E. Colton
Charles E. Cook
Robert A. Cook
Ronald J. Cook
Robert E. Cooley
Edward A. Coray
Robert H. Countess
Albert E. Cramer
George H. Cramer
Raymond D. Creer
Barbara Ann Crenshaw
Kent W. Creswell
Malcolm Cronk
Moses C. Crouse

21

Virgil Cruz
Robert D. Culver
Melvin D. Curry, Jr.

W. J. Danker
Evangeline Davidson
Jack Davidson
Paul E. Davies
D. Clair Davis
John J. Davis
Kenneth R. Davis
Leroy Davis
Eugene E. Dawson
Larry Day
Wilber T. Dayton
Lloyd F. Dean
Willis P. DeBoer
Glenn D. Deckert
Sterling R. Demond
A. Robert Denton
Wayne Detzler
Helen deVette
Robert O. deVette
David A. DeVries
Dale S. DeWitt
Mariano Di Gangi
Locke E. Dillard
Gil Dodds
Jack B. Dougherty
Marion Dougherty
Donald K. Drake
Wesley L. Duewel
Donald A. Dunkerley
Roberta Dunkle
Betty Dunnam
Walter McGregor Dunnett
Gary A. Dusek

Ralph Earle
Jack Stewart Early
Kermit A. Ecklebarger
Siev Eckmann
John E. Eggleton
William R. Eichhorst
C. William Eidenire
James F. Engel
Millard Erickson
Norman R. Ericson
Elisa M. Espineli
M. P. Estabrooks
Robert P. Evans
W. Glyn Evans
David Ewert

Albert Fadenrecht
Frank E. Farrell
Hobert K. Farrell
Donald H. Fee
Gordon D. Fee

Charles Lee Feinberg
Paul D. Feinberg
Rosalinda Ison Ferguson
Virginia Fey
Harold A. Fiess
Warren Filkin
Floyd V. Filson
Norman Finke
Herman A. Fischer
Gloria C. Flosdorf
Leslie B. Flynn
David H. Forbes
Janet E. Ford
Lewis Foster
William R. Foster
Richard B. Foth
Phillip Ross Foxwell
Wayne Frair
Gloria C. France
Robert G. France
Walter Frank
Max L. Frazier, Jr.
Doris A. Freese
Paul Fromer
Jim Frost
Edward Fudge
David Otis Fuller
Sherman B. Fung
Clarence (Barney) Furman
Ruth Furman

Russell A. Gabler
Frank E. Gaebelein
H. Lynn Gardner
W. Ward Gasque
Lawrence T. Geraty
Reginald R. Gerig
Richard E. Gerig
Wesley L. Gerig
Gene A. Getz
George Giacumakis
Kay Gieser
P. Kenneth Gieser
Gerald W. Gillaspie
Ralph E. Gillette
Bobby Lee Gilley
Victor C. Glavach, Jr.
Burton L. Goddard
J. Howard Goddard
Paul L. Goodman
Louis Goldberg
Benny D. Gore
Billy Graham
David Granskou
Earl E. Grant
Robert M. Grant
John D. Grassmick
John A. Gration

Robert D. Gray
Greater Europe Mission
  Paul E. Parker, Chm.
  David Barnes
  Don Brugmann
  Malcolm Cronk
  Wayne Detzler
  Robert P. Evans
  Warren Filkin
  Norman Finke
  Walter Frank
  Wilbur Haas
  Basil Jackson
  J. Herbert Kane
  Irwin Killian
  James Reapsome
  Bill Reed
  David L. Roberts
  Robert Watson
Floyd Green
Frank O. Green
Leonard Greenway
Thomas M. Gregory
Joseph A. Grispino
Robert Gromacki
Allen R. Guenther
Robert H. Gundry

Wilbur Haas
Stuart C. Hackett
Donald A. Hagner
Clarence B. Hale
Bert H. Hall
Kenneth W. Hall
Alfred C. Hambly
Mariel Hampton
H. A. Hanke
Kenneth N. Hansen
Harry Hardwick
E. Harold Harper
R. Laird Harris
Everett F. Harrison
Gerhard F. Hasel
Joyce Van Zanten Haspels
Martin H. Heicksen
Paul Heidebrecht
Andrew K. Helmbold
Julia S. Henkel
William A. Henning
Carl F. H. Henry
Ronald Henson
Humberto Hernandez
D. Edmond Hiebert
Harold W. Hoehner
Anthony A. Hoekema
Ben Hoeppner
Alfred J. Hoerth
Donald E. Hoke

22

Stephen T. Hoke
Arthur F. Holmes
Ardith Hooten
Barbara J. Hopwood
Charles Horne
Stanley M. Horton
Joyce Houggy
Philip G. Houghton
Arne T. Howard
Betty Howard
J. Grant Howard, Jr.
Jeanette Lowe Hsieh
Donald L. Hughes
Robert J. Hughes III
Charles E. Hummel
Joseph I. Hunt
Larry W. Hurtado
David Huttar
Ruth Fancher Hutton

Morris A. Inch
John R. Ingram
Philip C. Irabon
Rufina G. Irabon
Gordon S. Ivey
Olin M. Ivey
Hiroyasu Iwabuchi
Motoko Iwai

Basil Jackson
Herbert K. Jacobsen
Edgar C. James
Ferrell Jenkins
James E. Jennings
Irving L. Jensen
John H. Johansen
Colleen Johns
Alan F. Johnson
A. Robert Johnson
Deryl F. Johnson
Edward A. Johnson
Gilbert II. Johnson
Gordon G. Johnson
Stuart P. Johnson
Walter H. Johnson
Constance Ainsworth Jones

David A. K. Kaapu
Masaki Kakitani
Earl S. Kalland
Lloyd A. Kalland
J. Herbert Kane
Satoru Kanemoto
Kenneth S. Kantzer
Robert J. Karris
Joyce Hughes Karsen
Wendell P. Karsen
Charles C. Kary

Thomas O. Kay
Homer A. Kent, Jr.
William Nigel Kerr
Erich H. Kiehl
Clyde S. Kilby
Irwin W. Killian
R. M. Kincheloe
Dennis F. Kinlaw
Lee V. Kirkpatrick
Simon J. Kistemaker
Georgina Kladensky
William C. Klem
Donald R. Knauer
D. Wayne Knife
George W. Knight III
Betty Knoedler
Gunther H. Knoedler
Dorothy L. Knox
Manfred W. Kohl
James H. Kraakevik
Edgar Krentz
Sakae Kubo
Fred Carl Kuehner
Harold B. Kuhn
J. Kenneth Kuntz
Andrew Kwong

Harriet Borg LaBorde
Beverly G. Lacey
John W. Lackey
Donald M. Lake
William L. Lane
Louise M. Lazaro
Lois LeBar
Mary LeBar
Won He (Daniel) Lee
John L. Leedy
Marlene D. LeFever
Werner E. Lemke
Walter H. Leveille, Jr.
Frank M. Levi
Gordon R. Lewis
Jack P. Lewis
LeMoine G. Lewis
Paul N. Lewis
Walter L. Liefeld
Joy Paget Lilley
Larry W. Lindblade
Harold Lindsell
David E. Lindvall
Wilhelm C. Linss
James M. Lower
Philip E. Lueck
Orville Lyttle

Douglas B. MacCorkle
Don MacCullough
Martha MacCullough

Kenneth E. MacDonald
Ronald A. MacDonald
Polly Machin
Allan A. MacRae
Gordon Magney
Eugene H. Maly
Lynn A. Riefler Mansfield
Benson T. Maple
Alvin Martin
Loyal J. Martin
Marvin K. Mayers
Ronald B. Mayers
Helene McCauley
Larry McCauley
Joe McClatchey
Tom McComiskey
Dorothy A. McCullough
Margaret M. McCullough
Francis P. McGivern
Gerald E. McGraw
C. Donald McKaig
Graham D. McKelvie
John L. McKenzie
Raymond W. McLaughlin
J. Robertson McQuilkin
John McRay
Paul R. McReynolds
Belden Menkus
William W. Menzies
Eugene H. Merrill
Beatrice Metcalf
David Metcalf
Robert P. Meye
J. Ramsey Michaels
Terry L. Miethe
Albert H. Miller
John E. Miller
Lloyd E. Miller
Neva F. Miller
William C. Miller
Patricia Milligan
Akiko Minato
Donald R. Mitchell
Russell L. Mixter
John Warwick Montgomery
Margaret Montgomery
David Morey
Lela Morgan
Bill Moss
John Mostert
Robert H. Mounce

Ronald H. Nash
Bernard A. Nelson
Delburt H. Nelson
Henry W. Nelson
Bob Neuman
Paul Nevin

23

Franklyn W. Nevosad
George B. Newitt
Robert C. Newman
Howard W. Newsom
Tai A. Nguyen
Robert E. Nicholas
Thomas A. Nicholas
Roy S. Nicholson
Dwight H. Noé
Elaine Nordstrom
Donald L. Norbie
H. Wilbert Norton

Joseph O'Hanlon, Jr.
Linda Okerstrom
John W. P. Oliver
Barry Olson
Ivy Olson
Earl G. Osborn
Isaya Guy Otemba
Lois M. Ottaway

Stephen W. Paine
G. Joseph Palangattil
Roberta Ludington Palangattil
Kathleen Blowers Palansky
Edwin H. Palmer
William H. Pardee
Paul E. Parker
Robert D. Parlotz
Frank W. Parsons
Priscilla Patten
Rebecca Patten
Leroy (Pat) Patterson
J. Barton Payne
Ruby M. Peckford
Archie F. Penner
Pablo Perez
E. Robert Petersen
Gilbert A. Peterson
Lee Pfund
Richard V. Pierard
Kenneth L. Pike
John H. Pilch
Wesley M. Pinkham
Clark H. Pinnock
Wesley G. Pippert
Glenn E. Platt
C. W. Pollard
Austin H. Potts
Gerald E. Price
Eugene A. Priddy
Neale Pryor

Guttorm Raen
Torhild Raen
Marcos A. Ramos
Herbert M. Randall

Walter E. Rast
Ella Rathod
Samuel R. Rathod
Robert G. Rayburn
John Rea
James Reapsome
Bill Reed
John T. Reed
Lenice F. Reed
Lyman E. Reed
Gareth L. Reese
R. A. Reider
Irwin Reist
J. Berkley Reynolds
Shirley Reynolds
H. Robert Rhoden
Linda Tenjack Rice
M. Jill Pape Rieck
Ronald W. Ritchey
R. Vernon Ritter
David L. Roberts
Jack Robinson
Theo Robinson
Louis O. Robles
Brian E. Roe
Lianne Roembke
Delbert R. Rose
Judah M. Rosenthal
Arthur M. Ross
Virginia Meier Roth
Erwin P. Rudolph
Jean Rumbaugh
Dee Ann Rupp
Arthur Rupprecht
Jon Ruthven
Lucile Damon Ryckman
Leland Ryken

Ernest W. Saunders
Millard Scherich
Daniel Schibler
Marla Schierling
Steve Schierling
Alvin J. Schmidt
Calvin H. Schmitt
Carl Schultz
Samuel J. Schultz
Lillian Scobie
Douglas H. Scott
J. Julius Scott, Jr.
Marilyn Scribner
William P. Scully
O. R. Sellers
Richard J. Shakespeare
Larry D. Sharp
Bruce Shelley
Royce M. Shelton
Irvin J. Shook

John H. Skilton
Elmer B. Smick
James W. Smith
Jerry E. Smith
P. Paul Snezek
Dorothy Soderholm
Marjorie Solderholm
Chandra L. Solomon
Walter F. Specht
Carl Spence
Joseph L. Spradley
Bertley N. Springer
Inez Springer
Ralph Sprunk
Frank Bateman Stanger
Joan Richards Stark
Zada E. Stevens
Beverly B. Stieglitz
Bill L. Stieglitz
Samuel J. Stoesz
John H. Stoll
Carolyn Bartholomew
    Stonehocker
D. Keith Stonehocker
Richard L. Stoppe
Sadie Strachan
Samuel Strachan
Harriet Stroh
Robert C. Strubhar
Carroll Stuhlmueller
Delores McAvey Suárez
Linda Lou Sully
Daniel Sun
Ruth Sun
Jack Swartz
Mark O. Sweeney
Leonard Sweetman, Jr.

James F. Talbot
Yoshiyuki Tamura
J. D. Tangelder
Carrie A. Tarbell
Gladys E. Taylor
John F. Taylor
Francis C. R. Thee
Balachandra Theodore
Rosella Thiesen
Arden Thiessen
Robert L. Thomas
William C. Thomas
Ellen Thompson
W. Ralph Thompson
Terrance Tiessen
Lyman Rand Tucker, Jr.
Bob Tuttle, Jr.

Merrill F. Unger

Fred M. Valdez

24

Carolyn H. Van Dermark
Gerard Van Groningen
Dorothy Van Kampen
Robert C. Van Kampen
Bruce Vawter
Peter Veltman
Habel G. Verghese
Eldin Villafañe
Ceferino D. Villegas
Lina Villegas
Lamberta Voget
Arthur H. Volle

William M. Wachtel
Bill Wallace
Wilber B. Wallis
John Walmert
John F. Walvoord
Linda Wanaselja
Roy Bowen Ward
Elmo Warkentin
Virgil Warren

David L. Waterman
Patricia Waterman
Bruce Watkins
Elaine Watkins
Robert Watson
Carl Philip Weber
Charles W. Weber
Robert Webber
Vance Wegner
Francis Marion Wheeler
John C. Whitcomb, Jr.
Curtis Whiteman
Paul Wieland
Allen Wikgren
George (Bud) Williams
Charles E. Williams, Jr.
Arthur Williamson
Donald L. Wise
John A. Witmer
Herbert M. Wolf
Chester E. Wood
Clinton L. Wood

Joy C. Wood
Leon J. Wood
Wanda L. Woodruff
William J. Woodruff
Clyde M. Woods
Paul Woolley
Jerry W. Worsham
Marten H. Woudstra

Edwin Yamauchi
Kimie Honda Yamauchi
Ruth Anne Yoakam
J. Otis Yoder
Alda Young
Warren Young
Ronald F. Youngblood
Fumiko Suzuki Yui

Jack Zandstra
Edward J. Zenchina
John M. Zinkand

25

Abbreviations

OT Apocrypha

Add Esth	Additions to Esther
Bar	Baruch
Bel	Bel and the Dragon
1-2 Esdr	1-2 Esdras
Jdt	Judith
Ep Jer	Epistle of Jeremiah
1- 4 Mac	1- 4 Maccabees
Pr Azar	Prayer of Azariah
Pr Man	Prayer of Manasses
Sir	Sirach
Sus	Susanna
Tob	Tobit
Wis	Wisdom of Solomon

Pseudepigrapha, etc. and Apostolic Fathers

Asc Isa	Ascension of Isaiah
As Mos	Assumption of Moses
1-2-3 Enoch	Ethiopic, Slavonic, Hebrew Enoch
1QS	Rule of the Community, Manual of Discipline
Jub	Jubilees
Odes Sol	Odes of Solomon
Pss Sol	Psalms of Solomon
T 12 Patr	Testaments of the Twelve Patriarchs
T Levi	Testament of Levi, etc.
Gos Pet	Gospel of Peter
Gos Thom	Gospel of Thomas
Barn	Barnabas
1-2 Clem	1-2 Clement
Did	Didache
Herm Man	Hermas, Mandate

Herm Sim	Similitude
Vis	Vision
Ign Eph	Ignatius, Letter to the Ephesians
Magn	Magnesians
Phld	Philadelphians
Pol	Polycarp
Rom	Romans
Smyrn	Smyrnaeans
Trall	Trallians

Periodicals, Reference Works and Serials

AB	Anchor Bible
ACW	Ancient Christian Writers
ASV	*American Standard Version*
AV	*Authorized Version (KJV)*
ATR	*Anglican Theological Review*
AUSS	*Andrews University Seminary Studies*
BA	*Biblical Archaeologist*
Bib	*Biblica*
BJRL	*Bulletin of the John Rylands Library*
BS	*Bibliotheca Sacra*
BZ	*Biblische Zeitschrift*
BZNW	Beihefte zur *ZNW*
CAD	*The Assyrian Dictionary of The Oriental Institute of the University of Chicago*
CBQ	*Catholic Biblical Quarterly*
CNT	Commentaire du Nouveau Testament
ConNT	*Coniectanea Neotestamentica*
EA	*Tel el Amarna Tablets*
ETL	*Ephemerides theologicae lovanienses*

EvQ	Evangelical Quarterly	RSR	Recherches de science religieuse
ExpT	Expository Times		
HNT	Handbuch zum Neuen Testament	RSV	Revised Standard Version
		SBT	Studies in Biblical Theology
HTKNT	Herders theologischer Kommentar zum Neuen Testament	SC	Sources chrétiennes
		SJT	Scottish Journal of Theology
HTR	Harvard Theological Review	Str-B	H. Strack and P. Billerbeck, Kommentar zum Neuen Testament
ICC	International Critical Commentary		
JB	Jerusalem Bible	TDNT	G. Kittel and G. Friedrich (eds.), Theological Dictionary of the New Testament
JBL	Journal of Biblical Literature		
JETS	Journal of the Evangelical Theological Society	TLZ	Theologische Literaturzeitung
JHS	Journal of Hellenic Studies	TS	Theological Studies
JR	Journal of Religion	TT	Theology Today
JTS	Journal of Theological Studies	TWNT	G. Kittel and G. Friedrich (eds.), Theologisches Wörterbuch zum Neuen Testament
NAB	New American Bible		
NASB	New American Standard Bible	TZ	Theologische Zeitschrift
		UBSGNT	United Bible Societies' Greek New Testament
NIC	New International Commentary		
		UUA	Uppsala universitetsårsskrift
NIV	New International Version	VC	Vigiliae Christianae
NovT	Novum Testamentum	VT	Vetus Testamentum
NovT Sup	Novum Testamentum Supplements	VTSup	Vetus Testamentum Supplements
NTS	New Testament Studies	WMANT	Wissenschaftliche Monographien zum Alten und Neuen Testament
PW	Pauly-Wissowa, Realencyclopädie der classischen Altertumswissenschaft		
		ZAW	Zeitschrift für die alttestamentliche Wissenschaft
RB	Revue biblique		
RGG	Religion in Geschichte und Gegenwart	ZNW	Zeitschrift für die neutestamentliche Wissenschaft

I. HISTORICAL

The Extent of the Old Testament Canon

NORMAN L. GEISLER

I. The Importance of the Old Testament Apocrypha Today

The question as to which books belong in the OT canon has surfaced anew in the latter part of the twentieth century for several reasons. First, there is the popularity of the Roman Catholic *Jerusalem Bible* which contains the apocryphal books canonized at Trent in A.D. 1546. Many readers, unaware of the history and controversy over the Apocrypha (= Apoc from here on), are assuming without question that these books are part of the inspired Scriptures.

Second, the publishing of ecumenical Bibles containing the Apoc occasions the same naive assumption by the theologically uninitiated that these books must belong in the Bible or else they would not be included in the Bible he possesses.

Third, one could have hoped that the Roman Catholic Church would have mitigated its stand on the Apoc in Vatican II. But, on the contrary, the Church only repeated the decision of Trent to count these apocryphal books as inspired as the other biblical books. We read in *The Documents of Vatican II* ("Revelation," II, 8; III, 11) that "Through the same tradition the Church's full canon of the sacred books is known . . ." and that the "Holy Mother Church . . . holds that the books of both the Old and New Testament *in their entirety, with all their parts,* are sacred and canonical because, having been written under the inspiration of the Holy Spirit. . . ." (The emphasized phrases are in reference to the apocryphal books, repeating in substantially the same words what the Council of Trent said when these books were first officially added to the Bible in 1546.)

Fourth, with the mention of Trent there arises another reason for the importance of this topic. In debate against Luther and in support of the Roman Catholic doctrines of purgatory and prayers for the dead, the representatives of the Church would quote with authority from these apocryphal books. "It is therefore a holy and wholesome thought to pray

Norman Geisler, Chairman of Department of Philosophy of Religion at Trinity Evangelical Divinity School, Deerfield, Illinois. B.A., Wheaton College; M.A., Wheaton College Graduate School; Th.B., Detroit Bible College; Ph.D., Loyola University.

for the dead, that they may be loosed from their sins" (2 Mac 12:46). The footnote in the Catholic (Douay) Bible says, "Here is an evident and undeniable proof of the practice of praying for the dead under the old law. . . ." The appeal to the Apoc to support such doctrines as praying for the dead and justification by works (cf. Tob 12:9) raises very serious questions for the evangelical Christian.

Fifth, if the Apoc is considered inspired, then the question may legitimately be raised as to how one can hold the doctrine of inerrancy in view of the glaring historical errors in it. It is claimed that Tobit was alive when the Assyrians conquered Israel (722 B.C.) as well as when Jeroboam revolted against Judah (931 B.C.), even though his total life span was only 158 years (cf. Tob 14:11 and 1:3-5). Jdt 1:1 speaks of Nebuchadnezzar as reigning in Nineveh instead of Babylon. William Green noted, "The books of Tobit and Judith abound in geographical, chronological, and historical mistakes, so as . . . to make it doubtful whether they even rest upon a basis of fact."[1]

It is with these problems in mind that we must examine afresh the alleged basis on which some sectors of Christendom have given quasi or full canonical status to these apocryphal books.

II. Various Defenses of the Apocrypha

A. Some Preliminary Distinctions

What Protestants call the Apoc consists of 15 (or 14) books, depending on whether Bar (chaps. 1-5) and the Ep Jer (chap. 6) are counted together or as separate books: 1-2 Esdr (called 3-4 Esdr by Roman Catholics since they give the names 1-2 Esdr to Ezra and Neh), Tob, Jdt, Add Esth, Wis, Sir, Bar, Ep Jer, Pr Azar, Song of the Three, Sus, Bel, Pr Man and 1-2 Mac. With the exception of 2 Esdr (ca. A.D. 100), all the apocryphal books were written between 300 B.C. and the time of Christ.[2] Only 12 (11) of these books were canonized by the Council of Trent (1546), 1 and 2 Esdr and Pr Man being excluded. Of these 12 (11) only 7 appear in a table of contents in Roman Catholic Bibles because Add Esth is made Esth 10:4-16:24, Pr Azar is inserted between Dan 3:23 and 3:24, Sus is made Dan 13, Bel is Dan 14 and Ep Jer is made Bar 6. Hence, only the remaining seven books have a listing in the table of contents, making a total of 39 + 7 or 46 OT complete books listed in the Roman Catholic Bible.

One further word of clarification is needed. What Protestants call the Apoc, Roman Catholics call deutero-canonical as opposed to proto-canonical books—the 39 books agreed upon by both Protestants and Catholics. By labeling these books "primary" and "secondary" Roman Catholic scholars are quick to point out that no lesser inspiration or authority is intended.[3] The "primary" or "first" canon is so called because it was undisputed and ac-

---

[1] William H. Green, *General Introduction to the Old Testament Canon*, New York, 1899, p. 195.
[2] See B. M. Metzger, *An Introduction to the Apocrypha*, New York, 1957, *passim*.
[3] *New Catholic Encyclopedia* (hereafter *NCE*), 3, 386 (cf. p. 29).

cepted first. "Books whose canonicity was once doubted or disputed but later defined and accepted are called deutero-canonical (belonging to the 'second' or later-defined canon)."[4] With these distinctions in mind, we turn now to the justification given for considering these books of the Second Canon or Apoc as being inspired and normative for the Christian church.

B. The Early "Palestinian Canon" Theory

It has been fashionable to argue that there were two canons, one of Palestinian origin (with only 39 books) and the other of Alexandrian origin (with the extra apocryphal books). However, some Roman Catholic scholars have insisted that the Apoc also formed part of an early Palestinian canon. "The Catholic writers, Nickes, Mowers, Danko, and more recently Kaulen and Mullen, have advocated the view that originally the Palestinian Canon must have included all the deutero-canonicals, and so stood down to the time of the Apostles."[5] This view was based on Justin Martyr's statement that the Jews had a mutilated Scripture plus the fact that a few deutero-canonical books were venerated and even quoted as Scripture by the Jews. The discovery of apocryphal books at Qumran could be used as further support of this early Palestinian canon theory. However, even the dominant strain of Catholic scholarship is forced to admit that Justin's quote is "a statement that rests on no positive evidence" and that "the private utterances of a few rabbis cannot outweigh the consistent Hebrew tradition of the canon [against these books]...."[6] There is simply no evidence that official Judaism in Palestine accepted the Apoc as canonical.

The reason Catholics are willing to grant this point is that, unlike Protestants, they do not feel that Jewish rejection of a book is definitive for the Christian church. The Christian criterion for canonicity, they argue, is Christian usage, not Jewish usage of a book. Catholic scholars speak of "the self-sufficiency of the Church in establishing the canon; its independence of the Synagogue in this respect."[7] In more technical language, "Catholics hold that the proximate and ultimate criterion is the infallible decision of the Church in listing its sacred and canonical books."[8] In this they believe they are following Augustine who said, "I would not believe the Gospel, if the authority of the Church did not move me." Admittedly, this leaves open the question as to what *means* the church used to decide which books are canonical. In view of Vatican II it is common among Catholic writers to stress "that the Church's recognition and determination of the canon is, primarily, an example of the gradual operation of the common *sensus fidei* shared by pastors and people, to which Vatican II has restored the emphasis due to it as a theological source."[9] Hence, it is in effect the growing usage of and attitude toward the Apoc by Christians

---

[4] *Ibid.*, 3, 29.
[5] *The Catholic Encyclopedia* (hereafter *CE*), 3, 270.
[6] *Ibid.*
[7] *NCE*, 3, 271.
[8] *Ibid.*, 3, 387.
[9] Cf. R. Murray, "How did the Church Determine the Canon of Scripture?" *Heyth Journal*, 11 (2, 1970), 115-16.

down through the centuries culminating in their final adoption of it at Trent that forms the basis of Roman Catholic acceptance of the Apoc.

Of course the original and primary usage was by Jesus and the apostles. It is their usage and attitude that passed on to the church an implicit, though not formal, recognition of the Apoc. As for Trent, "being dogmatic in its purport, it implies that the Apostles bequeathed the same canon to the Church, as a part of the *depositum fidei.* But this was not done by way of any formal decision; we should search the pages of the NT in vain for any trace of such action."[10] That there was anything like an early Palestinian canon that was bequeathed to the Christian church is, admittedly, without any historical support. Catholic scholarship is willing, in general, to grant this and to look elsewhere for support of its acceptance of the Apoc.

C. "Alexandrian Canon" Theory Basis for Accepting Apocrypha

Granting the assumption that the Palestinian Jews did not accept the Apoc but that NT writers did quote some 300 or 350 times from the Septuagint Version (LXX) which allegedly contained the Apoc, it seems only natural that scholars would use the so-called broader Alexandrian canon to support the acceptance of the Apoc.

One recent scholar contends that from the many quotations made by early Christian writers from the LXX and the deutero-canonical books it is clear that the LXX with its wider canon was the normative edition of the OT in the early church.[11] Even though the Alexandrian thesis is now being called into question, it has been defended in recent years by scholars like F. V. Filson, B. W. Anderson and N. K. Gottwald.[12] Professor R. H. Pfeiffer gave a cautious presentation of factors favoring the Alexandrian canon: (1) Since the Law, the Prophets and other sacred books had been translated from Hebrew into Greek at Alexandria, it was natural that all writings translated from Hebrew or Aramaic into Greek were considered sacred in Alexandria. (2) Further, the view of inspiration found in Philo, which may have been held in Alexandria, did not limit inspiration chronologically (as Palestinian Judaism did) to the time from Moses to Ezra. (3) There was no division between Prophets and Hagiographa in Alexandria. Even Josephus completely disregarded this division and used the LXX, which contained Add Esth as well as 1 Esdr and 1 Mac. Hence, concludes Pfeiffer, the Hellenic Jews had a wider canon that corresponds to the great Vaticanus MS (except that 3 and 4 Mac are added), namely, all of the 12 (11) apocryphal books accepted by Trent as canonical.[13]

---

[10] *CE,* 2, 270; cf. also *NCE,* which says, "The NT writers knew and used a fuller collection that included the so-called deutero-canonical books," but "the Council of Trent definitively settled the matter of the OT canon" (2, 390).

[11] J. N. M. Wijngaards, "The Apostolic Church and the So-called Apocrypha," *Clergy Monthly,* 34 (1970), 55-63.

[12] See F. V. Filson, *Which Books Belong in the Bible?,* Philadelphia, 1957; B. W. Anderson, *Understanding the Old Testament,* Englewood Cliffs, N. J., 1957; N. K. Gottwald, *A Light to the Nations,* New York, 1959.

[13] R. H. Pfeiffer, *Introduction to the Old Testament,* New York, 1941, pp. 65-70.

Summarizing the evidence in favor of an Alexandrian canon theory, A. C. Sundberg says, "[1] this theory was posited on the assumption that the books of the Apoc were composed originally in Greek. [2] It was assumed, also, that the Hebrew canon had been closed by Ezra and the men of the Great Synagogue. [3] However, the Christian Church had received and used a larger collection of Jewish scripture than the Hebrew canon. . . . [4] And, since early Christian codices of the Greek OT included the books of the Apoc, the theory came to be posited that Alexandrian Judaism used an enlarged canon of scripture, a usage the church adopted. [5] Having, then, postulated an Alexandrian canon, the discussions and usage of Josephus were urged in support of this hypothesis."[14]

Sundberg, however, rejects the hypothesis that there was any Alexandrian canon, saying, "there is a lack of any primary evidence for this hypothesis, so that, even when it is presented to its best advantage, Pfeiffer considers the theory incapable of proof."[15] Sundberg lists several reasons for rejecting the existence of an Alexandrian canon: (1) Alexandria was not the "mecca" for non-Palestinian Jews; Jerusalem was. Hence, even the non-Palestinian Jews looked to Palestine as normative for the Jews of the diaspora. (2) There is no exact correlation between the supposed "Alexandrian canon" and Christian usage. The Greek MSS and Western Fathers varied widely as to which additional books were received. Sometimes they included the Pss Sol, 2 (4) Esdr, Enoch, the As Mos, 4 Mac and the Asc Isa. Other times they included less than those accepted at Trent.[16] (3) Furthermore, the apocryphal books were not composed in Greek, as was once supposed in support of the Alexandrian canon thesis.[17] And the shift of scholarship favoring Hebrew originals for the Apoc "does carry a consequent shift of locale of writing from diaspora and Alexandrian Judaism to Palestinian Judaism."[18]

Several other points might be added in rejection of an "Alexandrian canon." (1) Philo, the spokesman of Alexandrian Judaism, did not accept the apocryphal books as inspired. Even Catholic scholarship admits that "there is a natural presumption that if he had regarded the additional works as being quite on the same plane as the others, he would not have failed to quote so stimulating and congenial a production as the [deutero-canonical] Book of Wisdom."[19] After all, Philo's writings are filled with hundreds of quotations from almost all of the proto-canonical books. (2) Further, as Catholic authorities point out, "the independent spirit of the Hellenists could not have gone so far as to set up a different *official* canon from that of Jerusalem, without having left historical traces of such a rupture." Hence, the best one may infer is that "while the deutero-canonicals were

---

[14] A. C. Sundberg, *The Old Testament of the Early Church*, Cambridge, Mass., 1964, p. 78.

[15] *Ibid.*, p. 79.

[16] H. B. Swete, *An Introduction to the Old Testament in Greek*, New York, repr. 1968, has shown, by contrast, that the Jewish OT canonical lists are identical in contents.

[17] Sundberg, *Old Testament of the Early Church*, pp. 52-53, 60-62.

[18] *Ibid.*, p. 62.

[19] *CE*, 3, 270.

admitted as sacred by the Alexandrian Jews, they possessed a lower degree of sanctity and authority than the longer accepted books. . . ."[20]

D. Sundberg's "Open Canon" Theory Basis for Apocrypha

A recent alternative defense for the acceptance of the Apoc by the Christian church has been offered by A. C. Sundberg.[21] He argues: (1) that there was no Alexandrian canon containing the Apoc in contrast to a Palestinian canon without it; (2) that the Jewish canon had closed only the divisions of the Law and the Prophets by NT times; (3) that a wide third section of Jewish books was open and circulating before Jamnia (A.D. 90); (4) that the Christian church inherited this open third section and decided for itself which ones would be accepted into its canon; (5) that the Jewish canon was closed later in polemics with Christians, and (6) that this closing of the Jewish canon influenced later Christians to limit the OT canon by excluding apocryphal books.

Sundberg's thesis fits in well with the current Catholic "Christian Usage" basis for canonicity. A brief examination of the evidence that early Jewish and Christian usage of the Apoc supports its acceptance as part of the inspired canon of Christian Scriptures is now in order.

E. Jewish and Christian Usage of the Apoc

It is claimed that there is evidence from the NT period onward to the Council of Trent that Christians revered and/or held as inspired some or all of the Apoc. The following is a brief summary of the evidence offered in support of Christian acceptance of these books.

(1) The NT makes direct quotes from some deutero-canonical books (e.g. Jude 14 quotes from Enoch 1:9) and makes many allusions to others (e.g. Heb 11:35 alludes to 2 Mac 6:18-19). Nestle's edition of the Greek NT lists some 132 different NT passages that allude to books beyond the 39 proto-canonical books.

(2) Some first-century Jews quoted the Apoc as inspired. Philo is said to have quoted as Scripture a phrase not in the OT.[22] Some have even argued that Bar was considered canonical by Jews as late as the fourth century, on the basis that they sang a song from Bar in their synagogue. [23] And the existence of some apocryphal books at Qumran in Hebrew along with other OT books is argued by some in favor of their acceptance by first-century Jews.

(3) Jews continued to quote and revere the Apoc after Jamnia (A.D. 90). Sir, for example, is quoted twice in the Talmud with the formula "for so it is written in the Book of Ben Sira" (cf. also Bar 12:15).[24]

---

[20] Ibid.

[21] Sundberg, Old Testament of the Early Church, pp. 102-3, 128-29, 159-60.

[22] De praem et poenis 19.111; cf. also De vita contemp 3.28.

[23] This is the thesis of H. J. Thackeray, The Septuagint and Jewish Worship, London, 1921. Sundberg objects to this view since the quote comes from a Christian sermon merely suggesting that the Jews sang from Bar, not declaring that they did in fact do this (Old Testament of the Early Church, p. 76).

[24] The Babylonian Talmud, ed. by I. Epstein, London, 1935-53, Hagigah 13a.

(4) Early Christian Fathers quoted apocryphal books as Scripture. According to Sundberg's compilation, in the Eastern Church Origen (A.D. 185-253) listed the Ep Jer in the OT. Athanasius (A.D. 293-373) included Bar and the Ep Jer. So did Cyril of Jerusalem (A.D. 315-386). Epiphanius (A.D. 315-402) lists Bar and the Ep Jer as well as Wis and Sir. Pseudo-Chrysostom listed Sir, Tob, Jdt and Wis. The Council of Laodicea counted Bar and the Ep Jer among the OT books. In the Western Church there were Fathers who also included the apocryphal books. Hilary (A.D. 300-367) included the Ep Jer and noted that some include Tob and Jdt. Augustine (A.D. 354-430) listed all of the 12 (11) books accepted later by the Council of Trent. Codex Vaticanus (A.D. 325) includes all the apocryphal books canonized by Trent except 1 and 2 Mac. Codex Sinaiticus (A.D. 350) lists Tob, Jdt and 1 and 2 Mac. Codex Alexandrinus (A.D. 450) lists all the books accepted at Trent plus 3-4 Mac and the Pss Sol.

(5) In view of the above usage, Roman Catholic scholars point to the following local conciliar actions, prior to Trent, which support the Apoc: (a) the Synod by Pope Damasus (382); (b) the canon of Innocent I (405); (c) the Synod of Hippo (393); (d) three synods at Carthage (393, 397, 419); (e) Pope Adriani I sent a list of books including the Apoc to Charlemagne, who adopted it as the law of the church in the Frankish Empire (802); (f) Nicholas I enjoined the same decree on the bishops of France (865), and (g) the Council of Florence (1442) lists the apocryphal books as inspired but does not use the word canon nor pass on their canonicity.

(6) This long line of Christian usage and acceptance of the Apoc culminated in the official recognition of their canonicity by the Roman Church at the Council of Trent (1546). According to Roman Catholics, "The Council of Trent definitely settled the matter of the OT canon."[25] The decision reads as follows:

> The Synod . . . receives and venerates . . . all the books [including the Apoc listed by name] both of Old and of the New Testament . . . as having been dictated, either by Christ's own word of mouth or by the Holy Ghost. . . . if anyone receives not as sacred and canonical the said books entire with all their parts, as they have been used to be read in the Catholic Church . . . let him be anathema.[26]

(7) Even non-Catholics after Trent continued to accept the Apoc. The Eastern Church, it is argued, did not begin to question the Apoc until the seventeenth century and the Russian Orthodox did not reject it until the nineteenth century. The first Protestant to reject the authority of the Apoc was Andreas Bodenstein von Karlstadt in his *De canonicis scripturis* (1520). Luther placed the Apoc between the Old and New Testaments with the title, "Apoc, that is, books which are not held equal to the sacred Scriptures, and nevertheless are useful and good to read." Despite the fact that Protestants continued to include the Apoc in the Bible with titles that "seem to indicate a growing rather than diminishing regard for the books," by 1629 the Apoc was omitted in the English editions. Hence, to date, "the

---

See Sundberg, *Old Testament of the Early Church*, pp. 160-61 for other usages of the Apoc by Jews after the first century A.D.

[25] *NCE*, 2, 390.

[26] *The Creeds of Christendom*, ed. by Philip Schaff, New York, 1919, 2, 81.

confessions of Lutheran and Reformed Churches agree substantially with Article VI of the English Church (Lat. 1562, Eng. 1571), which ... explains: 'And the other books (as Jerome saith) the Church doth read for example of life and instruction of manners; but yet doth it not apply them to establish any doctrine.' " Through gradual pressure in England by the Puritans, the Apoc came to be rejected from Protestant Bibles. By 1648 the Westminster Confession stated: "The books commonly called Apoc, not being of divine inspiration, are no part of the Canon of Scripture; and therefore are of no authority in the Church of God, not to be in any otherwise approved, or made use of, than other human writings."[27] Thus the Puritans demanded the exclusion of the Apoc from the Bible and from use in their services in 1689. By 1827 the Foreign Bible Society decided to exclude the Apoc from all its publications.

Despite the modern rejection of the Apoc one must agree with Catholic scholars that *if* select Christian usage, attitude and acceptance over the centuries before Trent and the Reformation are definitive, then one can make out a plausible case for accepting the Apoc as canonical. However, that is precisely the problem. Is Christian usage and attitude the basis for the canonicity of OT books? Protestants think not for reasons that will now be elaborated.

III. Critique of the Christian Usage Theory

There are several serious flaws in the theory that Christian usage determines the canonicity of OT books. Three basic objections may be addressed to the theory in general.

A. Christian Usage Is Indecisive and Inconclusive

At best Christian usage of the Apoc, especially early Christian usage, is a double-edged sword. (1) On the basis of early Christian usage a strong case can be built for not including the Apoc in the canon: (a) Not one of the 12 (11) apocryphal books is quoted in the NT as Scripture.[28] (b) Many of the early Fathers, including Melito, Origen, Cyril of Jerusalem and Athanasius, rejected the apocryphal books. (c) No important Father before Augustine accepted all of the apocryphal books adopted by Trent. (d) Augustine's acceptance of the Apoc is confuted by his contemporary Jerome, who was the best biblical scholar of the church of that day.[29] (e) Not even a local church council listed the apocryphal books as canonical until almost 400 years after Christ. (f) Even after the Reformation, Cardinal Cajetan, who .opposed Luther at Augsburg in 1518, published a *Commentary on all*

---

[27] James Hastings, ed., *Dictionary of the Bible,* 5 vols., New York, 1898-1904, 1, 122-23.

[28] *CE,* 3, 270, speaks of "the admitted absence of any explicit citation of the deutero writings . . ." in the NT.

[29] In opposition to Sundberg, *Old Testament of the Early Church,* p. 149, we suggest that the highly circumstantial evidence that Jerome was secretary to the Council of Bishop Damascus (382), which included apocryphal books, does not imply that Jerome himself agreed with this local opinion.

the Authentic Books of the Old Testament (1532) which excluded the Apoc.[30]

(2) Furthermore, Christian usage vacillated, sometimes accepting more than 12 (11) apocryphal books and sometimes less. (a) A survey of Sundberg's charts shows that most Fathers both East and West before Augustine accepted only a fraction of the apocryphal books, sometimes only one or two complete books. (b) The great LXX MSS are equally indecisive. The earliest one, Vaticanus, omits 1 and 2 Mac, which Trent accepts. Alexandrinus adds three which Trent does not have, namely, 3 and 4 Mac and Pss Sol, and Sinaiticus lacks Bar. In fact, no important Greek MS has the exact number of books accepted by Trent. Furthermore, since these copies date from the fourth century A.D. they cannot be used to prove that a canon other than the Hebrew canon was the acknowledged view of Christians in earlier centuries. Nor, indeed, does the fact that they are included prove conclusively they were held to be canonical. The Apoc was sometimes included in Protestant Bibles without being held canonical.

(3) Finally, the level of "acceptance" varied from place to place and from Christian scholar to scholar. Many Church Fathers would "quote" and "use" and even "read" in church apocryphal books that they would not include in their canonical lists. The best explanation for this seems to be that the homiletical collection and even the ecclesiastical readings were not in all cases identical with the doctrinal canon, i.e. with the books considered normative and definitive for doctrine and practice. Hence, the fact that an apocryphal book was "used" in a sermon or select reading in church did not automatically grant it canonical status by that group. As is evident from the OT (Josh 10:13) and NT practice (cf. Jude 14), a much wider range of religious literature was used than that which was considered canonical

We conclude, then, that Christian usage alone is indecisive in determining the canonicity of the Apoc for three reasons. First, early historical evidence is strong for rejecting the Apoc. Second, if "usage" is measured by the listing of books in early Greek Bibles, then there was no set group of apocryphal books held to be canonical by early Christians. Finally, the fact that Christians "used" apocryphal books in sermons and readings does not demonstrate that they held them to be canonical. In fact, often it is demonstrable that they clearly did not.

B. Trent Was Inconsistent in Canonizing Only Some Apocryphal Books

(1) In view of the vacillating Christian usage, the Council of Trent was, at best, on shaky historical grounds in choosing just 12 (11) of the 15 (14) apocryphal books. Why not 1 and 2 Esdr (which were very popular books) and the Pr Man? What about 3 and 4 Mac or the Pss Sol? (2) In the case of 2 Esdr the reason would appear to have been arbitrary and dogmatic. For 2 Esdr 7:105, in contrast to 2 Mac 12:46 (45), has a strong passage against praying for the dead. Speaking of one's death it reads, "so

---

[30] See N. L. Geisler, *General Introduction to the Bible*, Chicago, 1968, pp. 170-71.

no one shall ever pray for another on that day. . . , for every one shall bear his own righteousness or unrighteousness." That some medieval cleric cut this whole section out of the then sole extant Latin MS does not at all detract from the suspicion that dogma dictated the limits of the canon.[31] (3) Furthermore, it is theologically suspect to add to the official list of Scripture for the *first* time after 1500 years the very books that support the extrabiblical teachings of salvation by works (Tob 12:9) and prayers for the dead (2 Mac 12:46), teachings that had been challenged by Luther 29 years earlier (in 1517). Even as late as 1532, 14 years before Trent and 15 years after Luther's "95 Theses," Catholic scholars like Cajetan excluded the Apoc from the "authentic" books of the OT.

We conclude, then, that the Council of Trent, in canonizing the Apoc, was wrong both historically and theologically. The Christian church had no substantial historical grounds for accepting these books as canonical, and their theological teaching on good works (cf. Eph. 2:8-9; Tit 3:5; Rom 4:5) and prayers for the dead (cf. 2 Sam. 12:19; Heb. 9:27; Luke 16:25-26) was contrary to Scripture.

C. The Christian Church Is Not the Custodian of the Old Testament Canon

Perhaps the most fundamental error of the Catholic position is the principle of canonization which says that Christian attitude and usage determine canonicity. This seems clearly wrong on several counts.

(1) According to Rom 3:2 the Jews were the custodians of OT Scripture: "the Jews are entrusted with the oracles of God." Contrary to Catholic scholars, we must hold that the Christian church has no right to determine the Jewish canon. And certainly no right to do it, more than 1500 years later, on the questionable basis of Christian "usage." Judaism must determine its own canon, and Judaism did exactly that in the equivalent of our 39 books. As Swete showed, Jewish canonical lists are identical.[32]   And regardless of the question of when this was finally determined (by 400 B.C. by the Great Synagogue or in A.D. 90 by the Jamnia scholars or later), the point remains that Judaism is the custodian of their Scriptures and not Christendom.

(2) The fact that nothing but the most isolated and questionable references from Jewish sources can be elicited to confute the unanimous Jewish testimony to a canon exclusive of the Apoc is testimony to the solidarity of Jewish opinion on the canon. (a) Philo's alleged quote from the Apoc is uncertain, stands alone, and is contrary to his clear statements and otherwise unanimous usages of only the 39 (24 or 22 by Jewish numbering) canonical books (*De vita contemp* 3.25). That Josephus did not accept Cant and Eccl is a gratuitous assumption. The evidence is to the contrary. Josephus lists 22 OT books, "five belonging to Moses . . . the.

---

[31] See Metzger, *Introduction to the Apocrypha*, p. 23. It was not until 1874 that Robert L. Bentley found a Latin MS with this section (2 Esdr 7:36-105) in it. Before this time it was known only from Syriac, Ethiopian, Arabic and Armenian versions. Since 1895 it has been printed in the Apoc with double numbering (e.g. 36 [106], 37 [107]).

[32] Swete, *Introduction to the Old Testament in Greek*, p. 32, n. 15.

prophets, who were after Moses . . . in thirteen books. The remaining four books containing hymns to God and precepts for the conduct of human life" (*Against Apion* 1.8). This latter category probably includes Pss, Prov, Eccl and Cant. Ruth was no doubt appended to Judg and Job was probably counted among the historical books, since there would be only twelve without it (namely, Josh, Judg-Ruth, 1-2 Sam, 1-2 Kgs, 1-2 Chr, Ezra-Neh, Esth, Isa, Jer-Lam. Ezek, Dan and the Twelve). The *Mishnah* (completed ca. A.D. 200) declares that "No man in Israel ever disputed about the Song of Songs" as to its canonicity.[33]

That apocryphal books were written in Hebrew and known in Qumran at the time of Christ is admitted, even by Catholic scholars, not to be evidence of their canonicity. No commentaries on apocryphal books were found. "The Qumran scribes apparently adhered to a particular script and format in copying unquestioned canonical works."[34] The canonical books were copied on special parchment and in a special script. No apocryphal books were found in this form. Hence, even in this Jewish sect there is no reason to believe their canon differed from the official Jewish OT canon. The Jews have apparently been unanimous concerning the extent of their canon. And since Rom 3:2 grants them custodianship over their canon, we must conclude that Christian usage, however extensive, cannot retroactively canonize Jewish writings into the status of Scripture when they were never accepted as such by the Jews. Hence, the Jewish canon and the Protestant canon, both excluding the Apoc, constitute the true canon of the OT.

(3) Further, Jewish teaching is very explicit as to when its canon ended. Josephus (*Against Apion* 1.8) declared the Jewish succession of prophets ended by the time of Artaxerxes (fourth century B.C.). The Talmud teaches that "After the latter prophets Hag, Zech . . . and Mal, the Holy Spirit departed from Israel."[35] Since all the apocryphal books were written after this time (namely, between 300 B.C. and A.D. 100), they are automatically excluded by Jewish teaching from the canon. Jewish usage is in complete agreement with this teaching.

D. The Misdirection Given by Augustine[36]

It would seem a fair assessment to say that the key figure in misdirecting Christian understanding on the canon was the "medieval monolith" himself, St. Augustine. In his *On Christian Doctrine* (2.8, A.D. 397), Augustine listed the 39 books of the OT, and then he listed the names of (1) Jdt, (2) Tob, (3 and 4) two books of Mac, (5) Wis and (6) Sir. Reviewing the list in his *Retractions* (A.D. 427) Augustine makes no changes except on his view that Solomon is the author of Wis, not Sirach as he held earlier. It seems that Augustine also counted (7) Bar with the Ep Jer since

[33] Yadaim 3:5, *The Mishnah*, trans. by H. Danby, p. 782.

[34] *NCE*, 2, 390. See also M. Burrows, *More Light on the Dead Sea Scrolls*, New York, 1958, p. 178, who said, "There is no reason to think that any of these works were venerated as Sacred Scripture."

[35] *Babylonian Talmud*, Sanhedrin 7-8, 24.

[36] For an excellent article on Augustine's misdirection on the canon see Samuel J. Schultz, "Augustine and the Old Testament Canon," *BS*, 112 (1955), 225-34.

he quotes Bar 3:35-37 as the words of Jer.[37] That Augustine accepted the other three additions to Dan and the one to Esth may be argued from his quotations. For instance, he quotes Dan 3:35 from The Song of the Three as "Holy Scripture" in *City of God* (11.9). This, then, would make Augustine's 11 books the same as those 11 (12) accepted by Trent (assuming the Ep Jer is with Bar).[38]

Although Augustine was not Bishop, but only an invited teacher at the Council of Hippo (393), his influence here and his domination of the Carthage councils (397, 414) clearly explain the acceptance of the Apoc by these councils and those through the Middle Ages right up to Trent. It will be instructive, therefore, to inquire into Augustine's basis for accepting the Apoc.

(1) Speaking of the Apoc, Augustine wrote, "These are held as canonical, not by the Jews, but by the Church, on account of the extreme and wonderful suffering of certain martyrs who . . . contended for the law of God even unto death. . . ."[39] This seems like a strange justification for canonicity. On this basis we should canonize Foxe's *Book of Martyrs!* Furthermore, his acknowledgment that the Jews did not accept the Apoc is revealing. In view of God making the Jews custodians over their own Scriptures (Rom 3:2), Augustine should have acknowledged that the Jewish canon of sacred writings is the true canon.

(2) Probably the real key to Augustine's acceptance of the Apoc was its inclusion in the Greek (LXX) translation of Scripture, which he considered to be inspired. Both in *On Christian Doctrine* (2.15) and in *The City of God* (18.43) 20 years later, Augustine considered the LXX inspired. In the latter passage he wrote, "And they received so wonderful a gift of God, in order that the authority of these Scriptures might be commended not as human but divine, as indeed it was, for the benefit of the nations who should at some time believe, as we now see them doing." Now on the basis that the Apoc was found among these inspired Greek writings one can see how Augustine could hold them to be inspired. But in the *Retractions* Augustine withdrew his previous view on the inspiration of the LXX in favor of Jerome's view of the inspiration and superiority of the Hebrew text. In view of this Augustine should also have changed his view on the canon in favor of the Hebrew canon. For if the LXX is not inspired, then what grounds does he have left for accepting the Apoc supposedly contained in it as inspired?

(3) Since Augustine even retracted the Solomonic origin of the book of Wis and since he held that only books written by a prophet of God under inspiration are canonical,[40] then he ought to have rejected the apocryphal books since they lack any claim to divine inspiration. 1 Mac records that "there was great distress in Israel, such as had not been since the time that prophets ceased to appear among them" (9:27). Other

---

[37] Augustine, *City of God* 23.33.

[38] Augustine does think that 3 Esdr may be a prophecy about Christ which would make it an inspired and canonical book according to the criteria he laid down in *City of God* 18.38 (see also 18.36).

[39] Augustine, *City of God* 18.36.

[40] *Ibid.*, 18.38.

passages concur in the lack of a prophetic witness in the days of the Maccabees (1 Mac 4:46; 14:41). There is indeed a striking absence in the Apoc of the "thus saith the Lord" found hundreds of times in the prophetic books of the Hebrew canon. Indeed, there is neither an explicit nor implicit claim to inspiration in any of the apocryphal books,[41] and there is no addition to the messianic prophecy found in the Hebrew canon.

IV. A Protestant Basis for Canonicity

The Catholic principle of canonicity is too broad. It is not Christian usage that determines the canonicity of the OT. Even on Catholic theological grounds this conclusion is unwarranted.

A. Inspiration Determines Canonicity

Canonicity is not determined by the church but by God. Vatican I pronounced that the books of the Bible are held by the church to be "sacred and canonical, not because ... they were afterwards approved by her authority ... but because, having been written by the inspiration of the Holy Ghost, they have God for their author, and have been delivered as such to the Church herself." *The Documents of Vatican II* repeat the same point. The church "holds that the books of both Old and New Testament in their entirety, with all their parts, are sacred and canonical *because, having been written under the inspiration of the Holy Spirit* ... they have God as their author. . . ." Further, "this teaching office [of the church] is not above the word of God, but *serves* it. . . ."[42]

But if the church is only the servant and depository of the canon, holding only those books which were inspired of God, how can the church include the Apoc which possess neither the claim nor credentials of being inspired prophetic writings? That is, if the church does not *determine* canonicity but merely *discovers* it in the books which God by inspiration has determined to be canonical, how can confessedly non-prophetical writings be considered canonical? This leads naturally to the next point.

B. Propheticity Is the Principle of Canonicity

According to the NT, inspired books came only through Spirit-moved prophets (2 Pet 1:20, 21). Now every biblical author was a prophet or mouthpiece for God by function, if not by occupation (cf. Amos 7:14). And within the traditional time period (ca. 1500 to 400 B.C.), that of the traditional OT authors (Moses to Nehemiah), there is little problem of identifying the 39 books as prophetic. Moses was a prophet (Deut 18:15),

---

[41] Sir 50:27 is not a claim to divine revelation. At best it is a claim to illumination into divine truth. He wrote, "Instruction in understanding and knowledge I have written in this book. . . ." Vs. 29 seems to confirm that the claim is for no more than light or illumination when it says "for the light of the Lord is his path." Indeed the Prologue of the book says only that "those who love learning should make even greater progress in living according to the law."

[42] *Documents of Vatican II*, chaps. 3.11 and 2.10 (italics mine).

as was his successor, Joshua (Deut 34:9, 10). Samuel, Nathan and Gad were all writing prophets (1 Chr 29:29), as were Isaiah, Jeremiah, Ezekiel and the Twelve. Daniel is called a prophet by Jesus (Matt 24:15), and even Solomon received prophetic revelations from God (1 Kgs 11:9). The rest of the proto-canonical books are prophetic both by their own claim and by the claim of other prophetic writings about them (cf. 2 Pet 1:20, 21). But this is not so with the Apoc. There is neither a claim in them, nor for them by Scripture, to be prophetic Scripture. Indeed, they themselves disclaim inspiration (1 Mac 4:46; 14:41). Hence, on the grounds of the lack of propheticity the Apoc should be excluded from the OT canon.

C. Prophetic Continuity

There is another argument that follows closely upon the former, namely, that the OT was formed as a growing collection of prophetic books, added as they were written by prophets to the prophetic writings.[43] For instance, Moses' books were stored alongside the ark (Deut 31:24-26). Joshua's book was also laid in the sanctuary (Josh 24:26). Samuel wrote a book and "laid it up before the Lord" (1 Sam 10:25). According to Ezekiel there was an official register of prophets and their writings in the temple (13:9 *ASV*). Daniel refers to a collection of prophetic books (9:2-3). The fact that later prophets quote earlier prophetic writings is further evidence of this growing canon of prophetic writings. Moses' books are cited from Josh (1:7) to Mal (4:4), including most major books in between (cf. 1 Kgs 2:3; 2 Kgs 14:6; 2 Chr 14:4; Jer 8:8; Ezra 6:18; Neh 13:1, and Dan 9:11). Joshua is referred to in Judg (1:1). 1 Kgs (3:14; 5:7; 8:16; 9:5) cites the life of David as recorded in Sam. Chr reviews Israel's history recorded from Gen through Kgs including the genealogical link mentioned only in the book of Ruth (1 Chr 2:12, 13). Nehemiah reviewed Israel's history as recorded in Gen through Ezra. 1 Kgs (4:32) makes reference to Solomon's writings, Daniel (9:2) cites Jer, Jonah (2) quotes many Pss and Ezekiel (14:14, 20) refers to Job.

Since prophetic writings were collected and even used as part of a growing prophetic canon of the OT, and since this OT prophetic collection is known to exclude the Apoc (cf. the Talmud, Josephus and the lack of NT quotations), then it would follow that the Apoc was not part of any prophetic canon. In fact, the apocryphal books were written after Mal (ca. 400 B.C.) when there were no prophets in Israel, as both Josephus and the Apoc (1 Mac 9:27) acknowledge.

D. The Canon of Law and Prophets

Whatever evidence may be offered for an alternate threefold division of the Hebrew OT, the most frequent way to refer to the entire OT (of 39 [22] books) is as "Law and Prophets." As Laird Harris has ably pointed out, it is odd to assume (as Sundberg and others do) that the fifth-century

---

[43] See Laird Harris, *Inspiration* and *Canonicity of the Bible*, Grand Rapids, 1957, pp. 168-69.

Talmud's threefold division of Law (5), Prophets (8) and Writings (11) is the basis of the first-century Jewish OT. The best Jewish evidence we have from the first century is the NT and Josephus. Josephus does list four books (probably Pss, Prov, Eccl and Cant) in a third section, but of the 22 early Christian canonical lists, 16 associate these 4 books together and almost all of them point to a twofold division of the OT.[44]

The earliest and most repeated way to refer to the OT canon was twofold, Law of Moses and Prophets after him. (1) The exilic Daniel (9:2, 6, 11) referred to "the law of Moses" and "the prophets." (2) Post-exilic Zechariah mentioned "the law and ... the former prophets" (7:12). (3) Nehemiah makes the same distinction (9:14, 29-30). (4) During the intertestamental period 2 Mac (15:9) speaks of "the law and the prophets." (5) The Qumran Manual of Discipline refers to the OT several times as "the law and the prophets" (1:3; 8:15; 9:11). (6) In the NT there are at least a dozen references to a twofold Law and Prophets division of the OT (see below).

What is most significant about these NT references is that the phrase "Law and Prophets" is obviously intended (1) to contain the *whole* OT canon including books in the so-called third division of "Writings." (2) Hence, the "Law and Prophets" by both biblical and extrabiblical usage did not contain the Apoc, since it is nowhere either listed or quoted as part of "Law and Prophets."

First, Jesus said, "*all* the law and the prophets prophesied until John" (Mark 13:11; cf. Luke 16:16, 29, 31). Matt 22:40 carries the same implication: "on these two [love commandments] depend *all* the law and the prophets." Likewise, in Luke 24 Jesus spoke of the Law and Prophets as "*all* the scriptures" (vs. 27). The Law and Prophets were read in the first-century synagogues (Acts 13:15). The Apostle Paul defended his complete orthodoxy by stressing his belief in "*everything* laid down in the law or written in the prophets" (Acts 24:14; cf. 26:22). In his Sermon on the Mount Jesus stressed that he had come to fulfill "*all*" that was written in the "law and the prophets" (Matt 5:17, 18; cf. Rom 1:2). There can be no question that the first-century Jews, as well as Jesus and the apostles, believed that the "Law and Prophets" were a complete Jewish canon containing "all" that must be fulfilled, "all" that was prophesied before John the Baptist, "everything" about the coming Messiah, indeed, "the whole council of God" (Acts 20:27).[45]

Second, it can be specifically demonstrated by NT usage that the eleven OT books later classified as "Writings" are quoted as among the second section known as "Prophets." (1) Jesus uses the phrase "the law of Moses and the prophets and the psalms" (Luke 24:44) as parallel to "Moses and *all* the prophets" (vs. 27). Elsewhere the Pss are quoted as part of the Torah (John 10:34, 35). Indeed the Pss are authoritatively quoted as Scripture more than any other OT book. Job is quoted as "Scripture" in 1

[44] Laird Harris, "Was the Law and the Prophets Two Thirds of the Old Testament Canon?" *JETS*, 9 (1966), 163-64.

[45] See N. L. Geisler, *Christ, The Key to Interpreting the Bible*, Chicago, 1975, chap. 1.

Cor 3:19. Dan is cited as Scripture and its author called a "prophet" by Jesus (Matt 24:15). Prov is probably cited by Jesus (Luke 14:8-10) and clearly by Jas 4:6.

Now since the *whole* OT Scripture is referred to as "Law and Prophets" and since the NT clearly cites books, later classified as a third section of "Writings," as part of the "Scriptures," then it necessarily follows that the NT viewed these books as part of the canon of OT Scripture which it most commonly called "Law and Prophets." This evidence is sufficient to lay to rest the thesis of Sundberg and others that the third section of OT "Writings" was not canonized until A.D. 90 or later. Jesus and the apostles quoted from these books as an accepted part of the complete OT canon of "Law and Prophets" between 27 and 85 A.D. The later discussion of Jews at Jamnia (A.D. 90) and afterwards did not decide the canon. Josephus (ca. A.D. 90) lists the 22 books of the OT as being long established, saying, "It is become natural to all Jews, immediately and from their very birth, to esteem these books to contain divine doctrines . . . " (*Against Apion* 1.8). The "open" or "flexible" canon theory fails on the witness of Josephus, Jesus and the apostles.

Finally, the fact that no apocryphal book appears among "the Law and Prophets" is ample testimony to the exclusion of the Apoc from the canon by the Jews and apostolic Christianity. First, no Jewish canonical list of B.C. or A.D. contains apocryphal books among the inspired OT books. Second, there is no NT quotation of any of the Apoc as Scripture.[46] This, in view of the obvious awareness of these books on the part of Christian writers (Nestle's Greek Testament lists some 132 allusions to the Apoc), their presence in the first century in Hebrew MSS, and even the popularity of some of these books, is ample testimony to the fact that Jesus and the apostles did not merely omit but *excluded* them from canonicity. Some 18 of the 22 books of the OT Scriptures are cited by the NT (all but Judg, Chr, Esth and Cant), but never once is an apocryphal book quoted as Scripture.

Furthermore, when the apocryphal books did come to be counted by some Christians as canonical, it was as a part of a broader third section of "Writings" but never as part of the complete OT canon of "Law and Prophets." The fact that there is no testimony to indicate that from the time of Jesus or before there was any open group of "Writings" containing 11 canonical books along with a number of other books not yet decided upon by the Jews is evidence enough that the Apoc was never listed among the canonical "Law and Prophets," and that the two divisions of Law and Prophets included all 39 (22) books of the OT.[47]

---

[46] Both Catholics and Protestants agree that Jude's citation of Enoch does not support Enoch's canonicity since (1) Enoch is not quoted as "Scripture," (2) no Christian list, canon or council ever considered it canonical (including Trent), and the citation of Enoch makes it no more canonical than Paul's quote from Aratus' work (Acts 17:28) makes it inspired.

[47] The third section in the Prologue to Sir may refer to non-inspired writings. Josephus' third division may be an alternate division for liturgical reasons, as indeed the latter Talmud division may have been.

The Development of the Concept
of "Orthodoxy" in Early Christianity *

ROBERT A. KRAFT

By the year 400 of the common era, there had developed what can be called "classical Christian orthodoxy." This type of Christianity became mainstream Christianity in both the eastern and the western world prior to the time of the Protestant Reformation. It not only defined its *beliefs* in terms of standard creeds, such as the so-called "Apostles' Creed" and the so-called "Nicene Creed," but it judged the *conduct* of its adherents in terms of certain prescribed rules and practices for worship and for private life. It not only appealed to a standard collection of religious *writings* as authoritative, but it also acknowledged the presence of institutional authority in the leaders of the church, an authority believed to have been passed down from generation to generation in a line of spiritual transmission that could be traced back to Jesus Christ himself. It not only actively sought to bring non-Christians into the fold, but it also actively *fought* to exclude so-called "heretics" and to prohibit such "heretics," insofar as that was possible, from providing competition for so-called "orthodoxy." This classical Christian orthodoxy called itself by such names as "the holy catholic and apostolic church," and by the end of the fourth century had already gained the full support of the Roman government in establishing itself as the only *legitimate* type of Christianity in existence in the Roman world, both eastern Greek and western Latin. To resist this orthodoxy was to resist the Roman Empire and its laws.

Things had not always been that way; nor would they always remain so. For several years now, I have been amazed, if not amused, to discover what an ambivalent attitude my conservative Protestant tradition has unconsciously taken to this classical Christian orthodoxy. We seem willing to die, almost, in defense of its collection of Scriptures and its awesome reverence for these Scriptures, but we scoff at the concept of transmitted institutional authority, or "apostolic succession," as it is called. We vigor-

*This is a revised form of an address delivered to the students and faculty of Eastern Baptist College (St. Davids, Pennsylvania) on February 20, 1969.

Robert A. Kraft, Graduate Chairman of the Department of Religious Thought at the University of Pennsylvania, Philadelphia. B.A., Wheaton College; M.A., Wheaton College Graduate School; Ph.D., Harvard University.

ously maintain, although often from ignorance, the doctrinal formulations of classical orthodoxy—like the concept of the Trinity—but we pick and choose among other matters also held dear by these same formulators of orthodoxy, such as formalized liturgy or sacramental theology, or the separation between ordinary church members (laity) and the (celibate) clergy leading them, or, in our day and age, their rather strict ideas on such matters as birth control or on women having their heads covered in church.

In most cases, we are not conscious that any problem exists. We know only what we have been taught, and modern Protestant Christianity has *not* been known for its attention to the details of early church history beyond the so-called NT period, despite the real relevance of such a broader awareness.

What follows is an attempt to outline briefly how "classical orthodoxy" developed in the first three centuries of Christian history. Hopefully, an awareness of this material will be of value for a contemporary Christian in assessing his present position and attitudes, as well as for understanding whence his Christian traditions have come. Such a survey might even have some immediate relevance for the question, "Where do we go from here?"

I

The Greek word *orthodoxia,* which means "correct belief" or "right opinion," does not occur at all in the NT writings, nor for that matter in the Greek Jewish scriptures used by early Christians. It is frequent in the literature from the fourth century, when Christianity became the leading religion of the Mediterranean world and the Roman Empire.[1] But to say that the *word* "orthodoxy" (or even the adjective "orthodox") does not occur in the earliest Christian writings is not to deny that some early Christians believed themselves to be "right" while they considered others to be "wrong." The related term "heresy," for example, is already found in the letters of Paul—the oldest Christian writings preserved for us—with a somewhat negative thrust. It should be noted that in the early period of Christian history, the Greek word *hairesis* (from which we get our word "heresy") also could be used in an entirely neutral sense to designate a subgrouping or a school of thought within a larger designated unity—for example, the Jewish *"haireseis"* of the Pharisees, Sadducees and Essenes.[2] In fact, in the NT book of Acts early Christianity is sometimes described as a subgroup, or *hairesis,* within the Jewish framework! But in his letters, Paul uses the word to refer to subfactions existing in places like the Corinthian Christian community (1 Cor. 11:19), and comments (probably sarcastically) that it is necessary for such subgroupings to exist so that God's approved representatives might stand out the more clearly! Again in Gal, Paul includes "factions, divisions, *haireseis*" among the "works of the flesh" to be avoided by God's Spirit-led children (5:20). When the author of the letter to Titus, whom many scholars do *not* think was Paul,[3] warns

[1] See the relevant entries in *A Patristic Greek Lexicon,* ed. by G. W. H. Lampe, Oxford, 1961.

[2] This terminology is used by Paul's younger Jewish contemporary, Josephus, in *Antiquities* 13.171 (see also *War* 2.119), and by the author of Acts (5:17; 15:5).

[3] Cf. M. S. Enslin, *Letters to the Churches,* Bible Guides, 18, London and New

his readers to avoid a person who is *hairetikos* (3:10), this may represent the technical negative use of the term that later becomes standard, or it might refer less technically to a "factious" person in general. In 2 Pet, which most scholars doubt was written by the "apostle" Peter,[4] the reference to "false teachers" who bring "*haireseis*" of destruction (2:1) also borders on the polemic technical use that seems to appear more clearly in the writings of Ignatius of Antioch (Eph 6:2; Trall 6:1), a Christian bishop who died as a martyr before the year 120, as well as in other Christian documents of the second century.[5]

But to return to our earliest preserved evidence, we find Paul making very strong claims for what he calls *his* gospel message, in contrast to what certain "others" are proclaiming about Jesus the Messiah. To the Galatians he writes: "I am amazed that you have gone over so quickly from the one who called you in the grace of Messiah to another gospel, although there is no other! But there are certain people stirring you up and trying to turn you from the gospel of Messiah. But even if we ourselves, or an angel from heaven, proclaim something other than what I proclaimed to you, let him be *anathema*" (1:6-9). Paul seems to have a rather firm idea of what might be called "right belief"! It is what *he* claims to believe and to have preached among the Galatians. Elsewhere he makes similarly strong statements. In combating what he feels are false or inadequate approaches at Corinth, he claims that he knows the "mind of Christ" (1 Cor 2:16; cf. 7:10, 12, 40; etc.) and has the "Spirit of the Lord." Of course the problem remained for Paul's listeners whether to accept such weighty claims or to accept the claims of his Christian rivals. To put it another way, *by what criteria* are such claims of correctness or authority to be evaluated? Should we accept a man simply on his own word? We will return to this issue later.

Paul is not alone among NT authors in claiming to have "right" on his side. The writer of the short tractate known as Jude contends against "ungodly men" in behalf of "the faith once for all delivered to the saints" (3-4), and 2 Pet has a similar thrust. A claim of "truth" is also made by and for the Johannine witness (see 1 John 4:6; 3 John 12; Gospel of John

York, 1963, pp. 32-35; C. K. Barrett, *The Pastoral Epistles*, Oxford, 1963, pp. 4-12; R. M. Grant, *Historical Introduction to the New Testament*, New York, 1963, pp. 208-15; P. Feine and J. Behm, *Introduction to the New Testament*, rev. by W. G. Kümmel, trans. by A. J. Mattill, Jr., Nashville and New York, 1965, pp. 261-62 for a summary of other scholars who reject Pauline authorship. For a relatively recent discussion of the problem of the Pastorals which argues for Pauline authorship from a scholarly point of view, see chap. 3 of E. E. Ellis, *Paul and His Recent Interpreters*, Grand Rapids, 1961. Pauline authorship is also defended by D. Guthrie, *The Pastoral Epistles*, New York, 1964, and *New Testament Introduction: The Pauline Epistles,* Chicago, 1961; and by J. N. D. Kelly, *The Pastoral Epistles*, New York, 1964.

[4] But for a scholarly presentation of the arguments for Petrine authorship, see D. Guthrie, *New Testament Introduction: Hebrews to Revelation*, London, 1962, and the detailed 1960 Tyndale Lecture by E. M. B. Green, *2 Peter Reconsidered*, London, 1961. This was even a disputed point among some Christians in the period when classical orthodoxy became established; see Eusebius, *Ecclesiastical History* 3.25.3-4, following Origen, *Comm in John* 5.3 (*Eccl Hist* 6.25.8); see also n. 8 below.

[5] Especially Justin Martyr, Irenaeus and Clement of Alexandria; see Lampe, *Lexicon*, under the relevant entries.

21:24). The apocalyptic spokesman of Rev cryptically condemns various objectionable positions in Asia Minor—beware of the "teaching of Balaam" (2:14), the "Nicolaitans" (2:15), and the "followers of Jezebel" (2:20). Other Christian writings from the same period, which for various reasons were not included in the collection known as the NT, sometimes also exhibit this defensive attitude of an "orthodox" outlook in opposition to positions with which they disagree.[6]

It is clear, then, that from as far back as we are able to go in Christian history, the claim "I am right," "God (or truth) is on my side," was made by various people in various connections. It is equally clear that such a claim necessarily stands over against some alternative claim by the opposition! Paul was opposing and was being opposed by others who doubtless also claimed to be correct! From his opponents' point of view, *Paul* is wrong and *they* are "orthodox," if I may use that concept in this anachronistic manner! But Paul's words have been preserved for us with approval, while theirs have not. From as close to the beginning as we can get—for Paul's letters seem to have been actually written before the Gospels were edited in their present forms—I repeat, from our earliest available evidence, we find diversity of approach in Christianity! This raises the vital question of whether there ever was a *single, pure,* and *authentic* Christian position, as later "orthodoxy" would have us believe.[7]

How is it, then, that Paul and certain other early Christian authors and documents stand out for us as "orthodox," to the exclusion of others? That is, why have *some* early Christian writings been preserved for us in a special collection dubbed the "New Testament," and have traditionally come to be treated as a *special* category of literature, not subject to the same questions and criticisms we might offer of other literature (including Christian literature) from the ancient world? (To bring it closer home, why is it that some of us automatically react rather negatively when it is suggested that Paul might *not* have written the letter called Titus, and that Peter might *not* have penned 2 Pet, although it probably would not bother us in the least if it were claimed that the apostle Barnabas did not write the letter attributed to him, or that Thomas did not write the gospels preserved in his name?) Is it that Paul's writings are "Apostolic" (with a capital *A*), which very claim somehow rescues them for "orthodoxy"? The later church is fond of playing such games with words and labels, but it is startling to find that some of Paul's opponents made an even *stronger* claim to being "apostles," and of presenting the message of Christianity in the form closest to that taught by Jesus' earliest Jewish followers in Jerusalem!

---

[6] For example, 1 Clem laments the "schism" that has occurred at Corinth (1:1); Ignatius is continually warning against positions he considers "false" (e.g. Magn 8-10; Trall 6-8; Smyrn 6-7); Polycarp exhorts the Philippians to oppose those who "pervert" the Christian truths (7.12). For convenient treatments of the "Apostolic Fathers" see *The Apostolic Fathers: A New Translation and Commentary,* ed. by R. M. Grant, 6 vols., New York, 1964-68.

[7] On this general problem, see W. Bauer, *Orthodoxy and Heresy in Earliest Christianity,* ed. with added appendices by G. Strecker, trans. and ed. by R. A. Kraft and G. Krodel, Philadelphia, 1971, and especially the appendix on "The Reception of the Book."

Paul, in fact, has to defend himself as being just *as "apostolic" as they were* or as they claimed to be (see 1 Cor 9; 2 Cor 11). But elsewhere he also argues that his essential message was *not* "apostolic" in the sense that it was *passed down* directly from Jesus' earliest followers but that it came to him directly from God by revelation; and the so-called "leading apostles" in Jerusalem did not, he claims, significantly modify his approach (Gal 1-2).

But as time went on, such subtle and basic distinctions and problems as these came to be forgotten or ignored, and Paul's claim to be an "Apostle" came to be taken at face value by Christians who for various reasons were sympathetic to his person and message. For the emerging mainstream church, "apostolicity" came to signify a *chain of transmission,* from *God* to Jesus the Messiah, from *Jesus* to his appointed "apostles," and from the "apostles" to approved successors, and so on (see 1 Clem 42-44; cf. Ign Smyrn 8). This pattern became known as the doctrine of "apostolic succession"—a forceful and convenient tool in the struggle with people considered to be non-authorized. In some ways, however, this was in striking contrast to the kind of thing Paul had *claimed about himself,* namely, that his true apostleship stood independent of, and even sometimes in opposition to other "apostles," even when these other "apostles" claimed to have derived their authority from Jesus' "apostolic" companions. To put it most forcefully, some of Paul's opponents seem to have been in an excellent position to appeal to "apostolic succession" in defense of their approach, in opposition to Paul! Paul did not, and almost surely could not make the same appeal!

But the later church came to accept as "apostolic" most of those letters bearing the name of Paul. It would also have us believe that such anonymously published documents as our first and fourth gospels, 1 John and the tractate known as Hebrews originated with the "apostolic" figures of Matthew, John and Paul. And other books that vaguely mention their authors, like James ("a servant of God"), or Jude ("a servant of Jesus Messiah and brother of James"), or 2-3 John and Rev (John the presbyter and John the seer/prophet), came to be considered "apostolic" in some sense, while the anonymous second and third gospels (Mark and Luke) and Acts were attributed to the allegedly "close associates of the apostles." But these are surely, to some degree, rationalizations despite what we are sometimes told in books on the NT canon. The churches wanted to accept these writings as authoritative *for other reasons,* and after doing so, found justification through the category of "apostolic" origin or association. Why does this seem likely? There are several reasons: for example, there were *other* equally ancient documents known to the churches and used in some Christian communities which also came to bear "apostolic" names—documents such as the Gospel of Peter, the Gospel of Thomas, the Acts of Paul, the letters attributed to Clement (a name mentioned favorably as a coworker with Paul in Phil 4:3), and the letter attributed to Barnabas (who is called an apostle twice in Acts [14:4, 14], and who was a companion of Paul). But none of these ultimately was included in the orthodox NT collection despite their claim to "apostolicity." Further, the "apostolicity" of some of the writings presently contained in the NT was highly suspect by some leading church authorities at various times and places, but they finally came to be included anyhow—for example, 2 Pet, Rev, Heb.[8] Thus, while apostolic connection may have been a *factor* in some of the selection, it certainly does not seem to have been *the actual determining criterion* in the gradual selection of the orthodox NT collection as we have inherited it! Many other more important factors seem to have been at work.[9]

II

What, then, were some of the high points—or some might prefer to say "low points"—in the development of classical Christian orthodoxy with its attendant (1) collection of literature, (2) set of beliefs, and (3) prescriptions for conduct? Human history is made up of real people and their relationship to their own worlds. It reflects situations just as complex as are met today in your life and mine. I cannot hope to sketch here the whole process of early Christian history in detail, and to the extent that I tend to generalize about history, I am in danger of falsifying its complexity—of unintentionally lying a little bit. Nevertheless, certain periods and events stand out as we look back over early Christian history—periods and events of crucial importance for the development of certain ideas and attitudes and practices that came to be known as "orthodox." I will mention a few of those which seem most important for the present discussion.

Paul represented a radically non-traditional approach to both the Judaism and the Christianity of his world, if the impression left by his writings is accurate. His emphatic personal attachment to his message, and his emphasis on its origin directly from God, by revelation, speak loudly from his writings: "my gospel" (Rom 2:16; 16:25) and "the mystery now made known" (Rom 16:25) are phrases representative of this concern (see also Gal 1:6-12; 2 Cor 4:3, etc.). Further, much of his violent opposition is directed against Christians who operated in a traditional Jewish framework of circumcision, calendar, food laws, and the like—the way Peter is pictured in the early part of Acts, and the Jerusalem community led by James in Acts 21. Paul's main point is that the resurrection of Jesus, which proclaims him to be God's Messiah, heralds the start of the long-expected last times (the "eschaton"). This view was probably accepted also by his opponents, but what Paul urges against them is that the new situation created by Messiah's coming opens the door of salvation to *every* human, regardless of

---

[8] Most of the evidence of such discussions is preserved by Eusebius, the early fourth-century compiler of Christian traditions—see his *Ecclesiastical History* 2.23. 24-25 (James and Jude), 3.3.1-5 (2 Pet, Heb), 3.25.2-5 (Rev, Jas, Jude, 2 Pet, 2-3 John), 6.20.3 (Heb). See also above, n. 4. The absence of Jude, 2 Pet, 2-3 John and Rev from the fifth-century (?) Syriac Peshitta revised version of the NT (and presumably from the older Syriac version[s] on which it was based) is also noteworthy. For a useful comprehensive (if old) discussion of canon, see B. F. Westcott, *A General Survey of the History of the Canon of the New Testament,* London, 1896.[7] Briefer, more up-to-date treatments are readily available in encyclopedias, NT Introductions, etc.; see especially R. M. Grant, *The Formation of the New Testament,* New York, 1965.

[9] For a general discussion of the category "apostolic" as it relates to early Christian literature, see W. Schneemelcher's introduction to Vol. 2 of Hennecke-Schneemelcher, *New Testament Apocrypha,* ET ed. by R. McL. Wilson, Philadelphia, 1963-64, pp. 25-31.

nationality, cultural background, economic status or gender (see Gal 6:15; 2 Cor 5:17; 1 Cor 12:13, etc.). For Paul, God no longer accepts only law-observing Jews—if indeed that was ever the case! Salvation is now determined without reference to the traditional Jewish legal system. Paul surely shocked many of his contemporaries with such an approach, including Christian contemporaries! Here is a *good* example of what was referred to so vividly by Professor Morton S. Enslin in his book on *Christian Beginnings:*

> Many of those in the early and formative years whom men today regard as the pillars of orthodoxy must have seemed far from the light to many of their fellow saints. What a debt every religion—and Christianity perhaps most of all—owes to its heretics, for notions dubbed heresy at bedtime often arise the next morning with a halo of orthodoxy firm upon their brows.[10]

Clearly Paul deserved to be considered "heretical" in the eyes of many of his Christian contemporaries!

Especially among non-Jews who embraced Christianity, however, this startlingly new approach represented by Paul (and some others) became an "orthodoxy" of sorts. And in the process, the older, more traditionally Jewish-oriented forms of Christianity themselves came to be considered non-orthodox (heterodox, heretical) and gradually fell by the wayside. [11] But Paul's "liberalism," if I may call it that, bred new problems. Some Christians seemed to act without any ethical constraint whatsoever—"Christ has set us free," they echoed from the message of Paul. Paul himself attempted to counter this position by appealing to a sort of (Christian) relativism and pragmatism in which the ideal is to proclaim the eschatological news ("gospel") most widely by becoming "all thing to all men" (1 Cor 9:22). As he put it elsewhere, although he realized that all things are lawful, not all things are constructive (1 Cor 10:23). Such a policy of realistic Christian relativism of action, for the sake of the message, never became the official position of later classical orthodoxy. At the same time, Paul also appealed to certain *moral* and ethical standards that he doubtless felt were universal "by nature," but which clearly derive from his own Jewish heritage and cultural ideals (see e.g. Rom 1-2; Gal 5:16-26). These came to be emphasized (and institutionalized) more and more by developing orthodoxy.

But Paul had helped to start something he could hardly finish. God gives his children a special wisdom, he maintained, a spiritual insight that is sometimes called "gnosis" in Greek. Paul himself remained a Jew—freed from bondage to Jewish Torah (law), and led by special "gnosis," but a Jew nonetheless for whom Messiah had come. Others found that *their* special insight ("gnosis") led them to conclude that the Jewish *creator* God could hardly be the *true* God—the God of Jesus and of enlightened men through

---

[10] M. S. Enslin, *Christian Beginnings,* New York, 1938, repr. 1956, 1, 147.

[11] Justin, the second-century heresiologist, apologist and martyr, attests such a shift when he discusses the problem of Christians who still observe Jewish cultic law—he does not condemn them as long as they do not require Gentiles so to act; but Justin admits that some Christians do indeed condemn them regardless (*Dial* 47).

the ages. Had not the philosophers of old shown that this physical world along with this material body is a tomb (*"sōma sēma,"* as some philosophical Greeks sloganized), imprisoning the divine spark—the immaterial spirit—which seeks for reunion with the ultimate source (deity) from which it originally derived? The *creator* God forged the prison. This is why he prohibited Adam and Eve from eating the tree of "gnosis"—the tree of the knowledge of good and evil (Gen 2:17). Man would become divine, he would escape his prison; so the creator God expelled Adam and Eve from the garden and blinded them all the more! This is not the God of Jesus, who has come down from heaven to bring salvation to man. Jesus is a divine *redeemer,* a celestial agent, not another walking prison of material substance! His importance is in the secret, timeless, heavenly *teachings* he brings and in the resulting salvation for those who have true "gnosis" about these matters. So these "enlightened" Christians believed and taught.[12]

Whether Paul ought to be described as "gnostic" I leave for others to debate. I find no evidence that he abandoned the creator God of his Jewish tradition, although "fleshly existence" certainly was characterized by Paul as the major hindrance to salvation. Nor was Paul particularly concerned with the problem of Jesus' historical activity *as a man*—rather, the indwelling and redeeming figure of the resurrected Messiah obsesses Paul (see 2 Cor 5:16 and 17). But about two generations after Paul's death, a Christian leader named Marcion arose, who claimed to be a true follower of Paul and even collected ten Pauline letters (not including the Pastorals). These, along with an edited version of the Gospel of Luke, formed for Marcion an authoritative collection—a primitive NT canon, if you like. But Marcion's Paul preached a message suspiciously like that of the anti-creation gnostics, as did his Jesus! After all, for Marcion this consituted the true interpretation of reality, and if Paul and Jesus were true representatives of the true God, they would necessarily be in agreement with Marcion's position! Marcion won many followers and wrote a major work, called the "Antitheses," about his two Gods—the loving God of Jesus and the inferior creator God. Some scholars suspect that a representative of emerging classical orthodoxy may have edited or composed the letters of 1-2 Tim and Tit *in Paul's name* precisely in order to combat the allegedly Pauline Marcionites and rescue Paul for "orthodoxy." Notice the closing words of 1 Tim— "guard the tradition, turning from empty babblings and *antitheses* of the falsely called gnosis; by proclaiming it, certain ones have missed the mark concerning the faith."[13]

Several later Christian leaders also took a clear stand against the developing "gnostic" positions, and emphasized the *historical* aspects of

---

[12] Discussions of the origins and developments of early Christian "gnosis" and "gnosticism" are numerous, and have been spurred on recently by the discovery of a "gnostic library" in the Coptic language at Nag Hammadi (Chenoboskion) in Egypt. See J. Doresse, *The Secret Books of the Egyptian Gnostics,* New York, ET 1960, for an extensive, if in some ways now outdated, account. For a more recent survey and prospectus, see J. M. Robinson, "The Coptic Gnostic Library Today," *NTS,* 14 (1967-68), 356-401.

[13] For a general discussion of Marcion and his impact on second-century Christianity, see E. C. Blackman, *Marcion and His Influence,* London, 1948. On Pauline authorship of the Pastorals, see n. 3 above.

Jesus' existence—he was *really* a man who did this and went there, etc.; lived in a Jewish setting, and spoke of the Jewish creator God as his Father; his first followers (who come more and more to be called the "apostles" as a technical designation) were of the same background. The Gospels that came to be accepted by emerging "orthodoxy" in this struggle with "gnosis" also emphasize the *historical* connections of Jesus, even when they tend to picture him as a timeless redeemer, as in the Gospel of John. This is no coincidence. A major factor in selecting these documents as "orthodox" documents was their usefulness in the argument against "gnosis." Not that they were necessarily written or edited with that problem in mind, although the Fourth Gospel may have been. But their emergence as "orthodox" literature *is conditioned in this way*. The "gnostic" problem provided a catalyst and also provided certain criteria for selection. This also is the situation that produced the opening words of the traditional "orthodox" creeds:[14]

> I believe in God the Father almighty, maker of heaven and earth. . . ;
>
> We believe in *one* God, almighty Father, *maker* of heaven and earth and all things visible and invisible. . . —

not in *two* gods, the creator and the true, but in *one* true God who created!

Around the same time, a century after Paul's death, a less serious crisis (from our modern point of view) but equally influential in many ways, arose in some of the churches. A man named Montanus took seriously the idea which we find in early authors like Paul, that in these last times God gives his true children spiritual gifts, one of the most desirable of which is ecstatic, prophetic utterance. Montanus was not at all happy with what he saw taking place in emerging mainstream Christianity, where the measure of a leader's spirituality was his relation to a growing institution that passed authority along through formal ordination in an increasingly hierarchical structure. It is the *Spirit* that gives life, he would have echoed from Paul (2 Cor 3:6); and Montanus even came to see himself as personifying the "advocate" or paraclete promised by Jesus in the Gospel of John—"the paraclete will lead you into all truth, for he will speak of my things," said the Jesus of that Gospel (John 14:26; 16:13). For Montanus, God's man is a stringed instrument over which the Spirit hovers and watches; an instrument strummed by the Spirit, so that through a Spirit-filled man, God speaks directly to other men.

Montanus tried to recapture the atmosphere of fervent expectation of God's impending judgment—an atmosphere that Paul also clearly breathed. Montanus spoke of the Lord's return, of judgment, of reward. But he was too late—or perhaps too *early!* His "new prophetism" and its fervor were rejected by growing "orthodoxy"—expectation of the end had long since given way to *institutional* procedures and concerns for the *continuity* of the Christian community in the often hostile Greco-Roman world. Legitimate ordination had become more important than Spirit-filled ecstasy. And

---

[14] For a convenient general survey of Christian creedal developments, see J. H. Leith, *Creeds of the Churches,* Garden City, New York, 1963; also J. N. D. Kelly, *Early Christian Creeds,* London, 1950.

to ensure that the literature produced by Montanists which claimed divine authority and content should not sway the faithful, an increasing emphasis is put by emerging "orthodoxy" on the ancient texts that are most revered and most defensibly "apostolic," from the perspective of anti-Montanistic and anti-gnostic "orthodoxy." Whether the book of Revelation ought to be read and circulated was hotly debated in this period to a large extent because it was so similar to the Montanist approach. Montanism and Rev alike presented a prophetic seer, who sometimes spoke directly for Jesus, who talked of the last times, the descent of the new Jerusalem, and similar matters. That Rev finally won canonical status some two centuries later should not blind us to the very real problems it faced at this earlier period. Also instructive is the figure of Tertullian, of North Africa, who is remembered as one of the leading spokesmen for emerging Latin orthodoxy around the end of the second century, but who actually spent the last decades of his life as a supporter of Montanist Christianity! History plays some strange tricks.[15]

By the year 200, more or less, a rather clearly defined tendency to "orthodoxy" had emerged with its collection of "apostolic" books, its allegedly "apostolic" confessions or creeds, and its institutionalized hierarchical continuity based on "apostolic" succession. It had been a long and hard battle to come this far. But the defenses could hardly be abandoned since opponents such as Montanism and various sorts of Marcionism and "gnosticism" continued to flourish in various parts of the world. Pockets of more cultically Jewish Christianity were also prospering, especially in Palestine and Syria. Nor were the adherents of "orthodoxy" in any position to consolidate their forces openly, since Christianity, of whatever brand, was not a legally recognized religious option in the Roman world and was looked on with disfavor by the Roman officials in general, as well as by the more culturally sophisticated Roman intelligentsia. There was considerable contact and interchange between like-minded churches, but open, wide-scale cooperation and consolidation still was not possible. Nevertheless, for most of the third century an uneasy peace permitted Christianity to flourish and to reflect upon its practices and ideas, while sporadic persecution—usually local in nature—served to remind the various Christian communities not to become overly complacent.

But the various internal crises already described had caused some Christian thinkers to attempt defining more precisely the relationship between God the Father and Jesus the Christ, whom every type of Christianity, whether "orthodox" or heterodox, acknowledged to be in some unique relationship to deity. Words and concepts were adopted *both* from (1) Jewish and Christian scriptures *and* from (2) the Greek philosophical heritage in general. Arguments were formulated in such a way as to be true *both* to accepted logic *and* to accepted religious vocabulary.[16] One could

---

[15] On the influence of the "Montanist crisis" on emerging orthodoxy, see Bauer, *Orthodoxy*, pp. 132-46. For a translation of preserved "oracles" of Montanus, see R. M. Grant, *Second Century Christianity*, London, 1946.

[16] For an illuminating treatment of early Christian scriptural interpretation in relation to its Hellenistic background and setting, see R. M. Grant, *The Letter and the Spirit*, London, 1957.

not choose willy-nilly from an undefined and unlimited expanse of writings; the authoritative collection existed, for the most part, and thus *imposed* certain limitations on the discussion. But how can one logically synthesize such statements as "the Logos (or Word) was in the beginning with God and was divine" (John 1:1) with titles like "first-born of all creation" (Col 1:15) or "only begotten of God" (John 1:18), or indeed, with such sayings as "the Father is greater than I" (John 14:28; see 10:29) and its near neighbor in the Fourth Gospel, "I and the Father are one" (John 10:36)? The scriptural passages *had* to be retained because the Scriptures were considered authoritative. Their words constituted *fixed* elements of the definition that was being sought. But what *could* be adjusted were such things as definitions of the wording, conceptual framework of understanding, and the like. Whereas the very Johannine passage in which Jesus says that "the Father is greater than I" must have been very useful in arguing against those hypermonotheists who refused to make any real distinction between Jesus and the Father—indeed, some went so far as to claim that the Father died on the cross[17] —it nevertheless presented a problem for those who rejected the idea that the Son was really subordinate to the Father! A wide variety of ideas and nuances flourished within the general stream of "orthodoxy," and characteristic attitudes gradually developed in particular churches and areas, while all the time the political situation in which the churches existed made it extremely difficult if not impossible for such issues as these to be discussed at a sufficiently wide level to be resolved satisfactorily for "Christendom" at large.

Then the roof fell in and the castle was built, so to speak, almost at the same time, viewing things from our comfortable perspective of more than 1600 years later. Shortly after the year 300, the Roman emperor decided to try to stamp out Christianity throughout his domains.[18] Official persecutions were sanctioned and organized; Christians were faced with the alternative of reverence to the traditional Roman emperor-cult, which was considered by many Christians as pagan idolatry, or severe punishment or even death. Churches were closed or destroyed, property was confiscated, books were burned. But the result was not what the emperor expected. The program failed to break the hold Christianity was gaining on the people. Then a new Roman emperor gained control—an emperor whose sympathies were with the Christians, the emperor Constantine "the Great." Not only did he grant official amnesty to Christians, restoring their property and rights, but he sponsored a council that would draw together leaders of churches throughout the empire, at government expense, so that the knotty problem of the relation between Father and Son, as well as other problems, could be solved once and for all, to bring unity to the churches. Constantine let it be known that he wanted unity. He sat at the council in the year 325 at Nicea. He made suggestions, although he was neither a trained theologian nor an ordained cleric. He enforced the decisions of the council.

---

[17] This claim became known as the "patripassion heresy." See the encyclopedias and general church history surveys.

[18] On the persecution by Diocletian (as well as earlier persecutions), see W. H. C. Frend, *Martyrdom and Persecution in the Early Church*, Garden City, New York, 1967.

In all this he set a precedent for what would happen in the next century or two of Christian councils—the so-called "ecumenical" councils of classical orthodoxy. The ultimate result was a clear and official creedal "orthodoxy," with political power to back up its ideas and decisions. For reasons that are not always easy to grasp, much less to explain or defend, it now became the creedal cornerstone of classical Christianity to believe that the Jewish carpenter-preacher of Nazareth, who had been executed for treason but came to be considered Messiah by his resurrection-believing earliest followers—this Messiah who in the understanding of Paul had ushered in the new age of (1) free access to God and (2) spiritual life in what Paul believed were the last times—was indeed, as the creed says,

> only begotten offspring from the Father,
> that is, from the very being of the Father,
> God of God, Light of Light, true God of true God,
> begotten not made, of the same being as the Father.

And if anyone *dares* claim that the Son of God did not exist before he was begotten, or that he came into existence out of non-existence, or that he was from something other than the divine essence or being, or that he is a creature or subject to change, the classical orthodox catholic and apostolic Christian church after the Council of Nicea declares that person to be *anathema*.

III

Perhaps we are so used to hearing this classical orthodox formulation that we fail to realize how long a route it has been from Paul and his predecessors to Constantine's Nicene Council and its successors. It is a long route indeed from Paul's problem with "another gospel" to the Nicene definition of the Son. We have come quite a way from Paul's struggles to plant his message among the non-Jewish populace of his world, to the emerging Christian *state-church* of the later fourth century! But whether we like it or not, and whether we claim to understand it or not, if we stand in the stream of historical Christianity, this fourth-century crystallization of orthodoxy also has remained part of our heritage and has left a deep impact on our various outlooks and presuppositions. For most of Christendom, neither Luther nor the Protestant Reformation he sparked renounced this part of early Christian history, whatever else may have happened to other aspects. What constitutes a satisfactory contemporary attitude to these developments doubtless requires further exploration and discussion, but that is ultimately a personal decision.

I have attempted to outline here the development of classical "orthodoxy" in the early Christian period. We are all heirs of these developments, although in Protestant Christianity there has been a strong tendency to pick and choose among the different aspects of the heritage. We sometimes seem to build our theological structures on the scriptural *canon* developed by emerging orthodoxy, and on its creedally defined Jesus and Trinity, but we neglect, or even willfully ignore, other matters like the developing hierarchical-institutional structures or various other liturgical and theological developments. I would suggest that our reasons for such an "eclectic" approach are not always clear or consistent, at least not from a historical perspective. By what *principles* do we accept, or perhaps reject, this or that aspect of the heritage? Closer attention to the matters so briefly presented above might prove fruitful for anyone who attempts to maintain a self-consciously consistent "Christian" position in our contemporary world.

The Power of Giving and Receiving:
Reciprocity in Hellenistic Benevolence

STEPHEN CHARLES MOTT

Introduction

The need to receive welfare in our society is often accompanied with the frustration of a basic inner need to reciprocate a gift. The state of indebtedness has attendant feelings of guilt and of threat to one's status and power. It has been demonstrated that people who do not anticipate being able to return a favor are less willing to ask for and receive needed help.[1] Public assistance in the United States is not conceived in terms of reciprocity, and the result is reluctance to receive it for some and loss of self-esteem when it is received for others. In contrast, in ancient Greek and Roman society reciprocity was at the heart of benevolence.

An important societal bond in the Hellenistic and Roman periods was the relationship between benefactor and beneficiary. The formal obligations of rendering appropriate honor and gratitude to one's benefactor at once motivated and controlled personal, political and diplomatic conduct.

The dynamic factor in this phenomenon of benefactor and beneficiary relationships, the factor that gave it social impact, was its reciprocal character. The act of benefitting set up a chain of obligations. The beneficiary had an obligation to respond to the gift with gratitude; his expression of gratitude then placed the original benefactor under obligation to do something further. "Every service (*officium*) which consists of two men just as much places demands on both" (Sen., *De beneficiis* 2.18.1, speaking specifically of benefitting).[2]

Such a cycle is contained in a report by Polybius. King Attalos

[1] M. Greenberg and S. Shapiro, "Indebtedness: An Adverse Aspect of Asking for and Receiving Help," *Sociometry*, 34 (1971), 290-301, with references to other studies of reciprocity.

[2] M. Gelzer, *The Roman Nobility*, Oxford, 1969, pp. 66-67, renders *officium* itself as "reciprocal personal relationship"; often *officium* is the performance of an action arising out of such a relationship and involves a social and, ultimately, a moral duty.

Stephen Charles Mott, Assistant Professor of Christianity and Urban Society at Gordon-Conwell Theological Seminary, South Hamilton, Massachusetts. B.A., Wheaton College; B.D., Wheaton College Graduate School; Ph.D., Harvard University.

ransoms Sicyonian land consecrated to Apollo. In response the Sicyonians set up a statue of him next to that of Apollo. After this, he gives them ten talents and 10,000 medimnoi of wheat, and they in return decree a gilded portrait of him and annual sacrifices (Polyb. 18.16).

The reciprocal giving could appear to be a contest. Seneca speaks of the most honorable contest (*contentio*) of conquering benefits with benefits (*Ben.* 1.4.4). Isocrates describes the shame of being defeated in benevolence by a friend (1.26).[3] One who has a debt of gratitude (*referre gratiam debet*) can never repay it unless he goes beyond his benefactor (Sen., *Ben.* 1.4.3; cf. Diod. Sic. 1.70.6).

When such a repayment is made, the benefactor in a sense becomes the beneficiary with the resulting obligation of gratitude.

The dynamic, reciprocal character of the benefactor relationship consists, then, of two factors: the obligation a benefit placed on its recipient and the demand the recipient's expression of gratitude in turn placed upon the benefactor.

The Obligation of Gratitude

Cicero considered no duty to be more important than returning gratitude (*Off.* 1.47). So strong was this obligation that some sources describe it as a law. Dio Chrysostom states that the law (*nomos*) repays gratitude to all for the things in which they have benefitted others. Those who are benefactors of things in the private sphere receive from those who have received benefits (cf. Liddell-Scott, πάσχω, III1b); those who publicly strive for honor receive from the city (Dio Chrys. 75.6). In *Dec.* 165-67, Philo speaks of laws dealing with the relationship between benefactor and beneficiary; here the beneficiaries are commanded to repay gratitude. In an inscription, *Michel* 312.15-16 (third century B.C.), the bestowal of the title *euergetēs* is concluded with the formula "according to the law"; cf. *GDI* 1505 (second century, B.C.).[4] Seneca, however, tends to cast uncertainty on the degree to which the traditional obligation is codified. He states that only Macedonia has made ingratitude a crime since it is too hard to assess the penalty—that will have to be reserved for the judgment of the gods (*Ben.* 3.5.2).

Seneca states that a proper expression to use in receiving a benefit is, "You have obligated me more than you think" (*Ben.* 2.24.4). The benefactor expects repayment (*Ben.* 1.1.4-8; 2.11.6), and his benefaction can be viewed as a loan (*Ben.* 1.1.3; cf. 4.12.1). This attitude toward benevolence, however, represents a prevalent view that Seneca throughout his treatise takes pains to correct. The beneficiary, not the benefactor, is the one to emphasize the obligations entailed in a benefit. The latter is not supposed to give with a view toward receiving (1.1.9-10; cf. Philo, *Dec.* 167). Seneca continually presents the receiver as regarding the benefaction as a debt

---

[3] Cf. H. Bolkestein, *Wohltätigkeit und Armenpflege im vorchristlichen Altertum*, Utrecht, 1939, p. 107. (The numerous classical abbreviations in this article conform to the abbreviations listed in the well-known and easily accessible *Oxford Classical Dictionary* [Ed.]).

[4] Cf. J. Oehler, "Εὐεργέτης," PW (1907-9), 6, 980.

(1.4.5 *et al.*). The relationship is that of *obligantium obligatorumque* (1.4.5). "He who does not repay a benefit sins" (*Ben.* 1.1.13).

Dio Chrysostom's rhetoric carries him to the more mercenary view of benefaction that Seneca resists. By their actions the benefactors have in effect paid a price for the statues which have been made of them in their honor. If the city should take away their statues by inscribing other names on them, it should give them back the value of their payment; in the case of a deliverer, this would mean ceding the city itself (Dio Chrys. 31.59, 61).

The certainty of a response of gratitude rising out of this obligation influenced the choice of the recipient of benevolence (cf. Cic., *Off.* 1.48). "One is supposed to help not the poor but the good, not so much as to avoid serving the wicked, but because one can only expect the recompense of *charis (thanksgiving)* or *charis (friendly help)* from good men."[5]

Since gratitude to benefactors is an important obligation, ingratitude to benefactors becomes a serious offense. Philo places it beside failure to give honor to parents and to fatherland, all being a result of not worshipping God (*Mos.* 2.198; cf. *Spec. leg.* 2.174).

On ingratitude to human (for divine, see below) benefactors one notes Philo, *Jos.* 99; LXX Esth 8:12c; Wis 19:14; 2 Mac 9:2; 3 Mac 3:19; 6:24 (ingratitude to benefactors is the dominant theme of the use of *euergetēs* in the LXX [all in Hellenistic books]); 4 Mac 8:17 with 9:10; Horapolla, *Hieroglyphics* 1.57.[6] The Egyptians use the dove to symbolize him who is ungrateful to his benefactors since the male, when it grows strong, drives out the father. Cicero states that nothing so violates our humanity as ingratitude (*Planc.* 81).

Because of the demands that accompany benevolence and the offensiveness of ingratitude, one should be particular from whom he receives benefits (Sen., *Ben.* 2.18.3). So the Achaeans rejected Eumenes' offer of 120 talents. They reasoned that their acceptance of such a gift could be followed by gifts from the kings, Prusias and Seleucus, and that they would be torn between letting the kings' interests take precedence or appearing to be ungrateful (Polyb. 22.8.7).

Being grateful or expressing gratitude itself can adequately meet the obligation (Sen., *Ep.* 73.9; Cic., *Off.* 2.69; *Leg. agr.* 2.22). The proper response was to assume the posture of being under obligation. Seneca states that we do not need wealth, but only our will, to be free from our obligation to a benefit: "He repays a benefit, who owes" (*Ben.* 1.1.3). In fact, material return without crediting the giver as a benefactor changes the nature of the gift. If a wicked man paid a ransom on Seneca's life, Seneca would pay the money back; but he would not enter into friendship (*amicitia*) with the man nor credit him as being his deliverer (*servator*). He would accept the gift as a loan, not as a benefit (*Ben.* 2.21.2). Yet it would

---

[5] Bolkestein, *Wohltätigkeit und Armenpflege*, p. 107. Cicero recognized giving in proportion to individual need—but only if other things, such as moral character and closeness of relationship, were equal (*Off.* 1.49).

[6] T. Hopfner, *Fontes historiae religionis aegyptiacae*, Fontes historiae religionum, 2, Bonn, 1922-25, p. 588.

be expected that gratitude be manifested. "He who receives a benefit with gratitude pays his first payment" (2.21.6); to refuse to express the gratitude in public is a form of denying a claim (*infitiandi genus, Ben.* 2.23.2).

The Obligation to a Grateful Beneficiary

The other dynamic factor in the reciprocal benefactor relationship was the fact that the expression of gratitude placed a valid claim for further benefits upon the benefactor. The subordinate, in effect, could now become the benefactor of someone more powerful than he. Receiving a benefit thus was a source of power, not only from the boon of the initial gift, but also because it gave the recipient the fortunate opportunity of placing a person from a more advantageous position in society under obligation to himself.

That a beneficiary can in fact become a benefactor is seen in Seneca. One who is in the position of receiving benefits should learn how he may give more benefits and be more grateful (*beneficentior gratiorque*) to his benefactors (*Ben.* 1.4.5). He may even place his benefactor under a greater obligation: "No one can be beaten with respect to benefitting if he knows how to owe, if he wishes to pay back; if he is not able to be equal in substance, he can be in spirit" (5.4.1). The reception and expression of gratitude for a benefit can set up a relationship of formal friendship (*amicitia*) in which the subordinate, too, will be expected to take the initiative (2.18.5). The benefactor on his part should be willing to receive benefits from those to whom he gives (2.18.3).

In the cultic honors set up to show gratitude to rulers of Greek cities for their role as benefactors, there are numerous examples where the thanksgiving is rendered in order to demand something else.[7] For example, *SIG*³ 493 (230-20 B.C.) reads, ὅπως οὖν εἰδῶσιν πάντες ὅτι ὁ δῆμος ὁ τῶν Ἱστιαιέων ἐπίσταται τιμᾶν τοὺς εὐεργετοῦντας αὐτὸν καὶ πλείους ἀγωνισταὶ γινῶνται ὑπὲρ τῶν συμφερόντων τῆι πόλει ὁρῶντες τοὺς ἀξίους τιμ[ω]μένους (cf. Welles[8] 15.10-12 [261-46 B.C.]; 22.15-17 [ca. 246 B.C.]). Larfeld provides a large collection of similar decrees.[9] "Gratitude for one favor is the best method of securing another."[10] When the benefactor responded to this request, the cycle would be in operation all over again. After the cities received the response granting them their request, they not only published the response by inscription, but also often added decrees of their own in honor of their benefactor (Welles 1 [311 B.C.], 14 [262/1 B.C.], 23 [260-40 B.C.], 45 [186 B.C.], 65-67 [142-35 B.C.], p. x1). Both social clubs and political assemblies honor a donor with a formula which states that the honors that they are conferring are more

---

[7] C. Habicht, *Gottmenschentum und griechische Städte*, Zetemata 14, München, 1956, pp. 164-65.

[8] C. B. Welles, *Royal Correspondence in the Hellenistic Period. A Study in Greek Epigraphy*, New Haven, 1934.

[9] W. Larfeld, *Griechische Epigraphik*, Handbuch der Altertumswissenschaft 1, 5, 1914³, München, pp. 377-81, 422-23.

[10] Welles, *Royal Correspondence*, p. 108.

than the equivalent of his gift; thus the donor is obligated for further generosity.[11]

Diodorus Siculus comments on the phenomenon of giving honors in hope of further benefits. He states that to the Egyptians,

> the return of gratitude to the benefactors is the greatest ally in life. For it is clear that everyone hastens to the benefit of those from whom they especially see that acts of gratitude will be treasured up the best (1.90.2-3).

In the following texts a benefit is made in response to an expression of gratitude: Welles 15.15-16; 14.8-10; 22.2-6; 25.26-33; 31.16-20; 45.9; 66.11; 71.6; Dio Chrys. 20.21; 50.4; Dio Cass. 72.31.3; 1 Mac 11:30; 2 Mac 6:22; 11:19; 12:30.

Benefactor Relationships with the Gods

The concepts of the benefactor relationship were very early applied to the gods. Since religious experience taught that the gifts of life flow from the gods, it was natural that they came to be viewed as the greatest benefactors (Arist., *Eth. Nic.* 1162a.6; cf. Sen., *Ben.* 2.30.1). Relating to them as benefactors was a basic approach. Gods were beings or powers who, if treated properly, brought blessings and gave benefits.[12] Benefitting was an essential characteristic of deity in Stoicism (cf. Sen., *Ep.* 95.48 and Bolkestein, p. 173). Philo defines the relationship clearly; God benefits, his creation gives thanks (*Plant.* 130).

The relationship with the gods as benefactors has the same reciprocal character as with human benefactors.

As the essentiality of gratitude was emphasized even in response to human benevolence, so the moralists often stress that honor and gratitude rather than material gifts are the proper repayments of obligation for divine benefaction. The gods do not need anything, but we can offer them gratitude (Sen., *Ben.* 2.30.2). Reverence and paying gratitude to the gods constitute piety and religion (Cic., *Planc.* 80). It is not possible to express gratitude to God through buildings, votive offerings, or sacrifices, for if the whole world were a temple, it would not be sufficient for honoring him; adequate honor of God comes through recounting his works, by eulogies in prose and poetry, by eloquent speech or song (Philo, *Plant.* 126-31; cf. *Ebr.* 117-18).

Worship is the response of gratitude to divine benevolence. God's benevolence creates in us the proper response of gratitude. His beneficial mercy produces in us the good will and friendship that go out to a benefactor (Philo, *Plant.* 90). The Greek cities render thanks to the gods for specific acts of deliverance similar to that which they give to the rulers, primarily through the institution of new festivals.[13]

---

[11] A. R. Hands, *Charities and Social Aid in Greece and Rome, Aspects of Greek and Roman Life,* Ithaca, 1968, pp. 50-51.

[12] M. P. Charlesworth, "Some Observations on Ruler-Cult, Especially in Rome," *HTR,* 28 (1935), 7.

[13] Habicht, *Gottmenschentum und griechische Städte,* pp. 231-32, presents several examples.

The response to a benefactor is personal and warm. Jacob desired to fear God no longer as a ruler, Philo states, but to honor him lovingly as a benefactor (*Som.* 1.163). Correspondingly, the violation of this relationship is the greatest evil of ingratitude to the benefactor of all the world (Philo, *Leg.* 118; cf. *Op.* 169; *Q.G.* 2.50; *Q.E.* 2.49).

The other part of the reciprocal relationship, the claim that gratitude places upon the benefactor, also is important to religious experience. Julian composes a hymn to recount his gratitude to Helios and prays that the god will be well disposed (*eumenēs*) to him for this zeal (*Or.* 4.158).

In this connection two characteristics of Greek sacrifice are important: sacrifices are honors of gratitude; sacrifices produce an effect.

A standard way of honoring a benefactor is through sacrifice (Arist., *Rhet.* 1.1361a). Nock states that, to both laymen and theorists among the Greeks (and Romans), sacrifice was primarily a matter of gift, first fruits, or tribute.[14]

The character of sacrifice as gratitude for benefits is clear in Philo. Even the earliest men used sacrifice as the means for thanksgiving and prayer in order to give honor to God (*Spec. leg.* 1.195). We sacrifice to the beneficent power of God

> because we who, when hope wavers, are unexpectedly saved from the evil that comes upon us, consider only the benefactions (of God), and in our joy ascribe this to the Benefactor. . . . But the Benefactor inclines to us. . . , Himself accepting (our sacrifice) and honouring the gratitude of the good man lest He seem to make a halting return (*Q.G* 2.53, Marcus).

Sacrifice is to be performed "with care and thought as if rendering thanks to God, the saviour and benefactor of all (men)" (*Q.E.* 1.2, Marcus).

For sacrifice as gratitude and honor in Philo see also the following: *Q.G.* 3.3; *Q.E.* 1.13; *Spec. leg.* 1.224, 229, 286, 297-98; 2.146. First fruits: *Spec. leg.* 1.152; *Sac.* 117. Altar of incense: *Spec. leg.* 1.276.

Sacrifice was not only oriented toward the past as gratitude for favors; it also was oriented toward the future as a means of securing favor from the gods. Sacrifice was primarily not only a matter of gifts but also of "effective action by the offering of these: 'gifts persuade the gods, gifts persuade revered kings' " (Nock, p. 149; cf. p. 154). Philo, in discussing the motives for sacrifice, states:

> One is either giving thanks for benefits previously received or as security for those which are present or to request acquisition of good things in the future or removal of present or anticipated evils; because of these motives one should procure health and welfare for his reason. For, if he is giving thanks for past benefits, let him not become evil (because the acts of favor are given to the good); if he is securing present gracious and good things or expecting those in the future, let him show himself worthy of such fortunate success by being good; if he is requesting escape from certain evils, let him not do things worthy of punishment and penalty (*Spec. leg.* 1.283-84).

[14] A. D. Nock, "The Cult of Heroes," *HTR*, 37 (1944), 149.

The following passages are also relevant: *Spec. leg.* 2.187 (*charistēria tou mellontos*); *Virt.* 159 (first fruits offered as *elpida tēs eis to mellon eukarpias*).

The side of the reciprocal relationship in which gratitude produces a gracious response from the benefactor thus has an anticipatory aspect that renders the benefactor-beneficiary phenomenon useful as symbolism for worship. Apart from the high evaluation of the honor contained in the terms, there is an element of expectation in the relationship which is appropriate for expressing the confidence worship affords. Philo thus fears that the obscure and humble folk, because of their despairing lack of hope, will shrink back from becoming grateful supplicants of God (*Mut.* 222).

There are indications of the other side of this reciprocity in a conception that if men did not provide honors, the gods would not fulfill their task either, nor were they expected to do so.[15] From the viewpoint of Porphyry, Asclepius stopped protecting a city when honors ceased to be offered to him:

> They are amazed that disease has held the city for so many years because Asclepius and the other gods no longer reside here. For, since Jesus is honored, none of the gods have enjoyed one public benefit (*Apud* Theodoret, *De curandis graecorum affectionibus* 12.96-97; Edelstein, 1, no. 506 and 2, 181).

Pseudo-Plutarch, *De fluv.* 16.1 (Hopfner, *Fontes,* p. 397), humorously presents the moral that feigned honors to the gods effect only apparent gratitude. Garmathone, queen of Egypt, lost her son and mourned. When Isis suddenly appeared, the queen simulated a pretended joy and welcomed the goddess in a generous manner. To repay her, Isis persuaded Osiris to bring the woman's son up from the underworld. The dogs of Hades, however, barked so loudly that they frightened the queen's husband to death.

The worship of the gods in relation to deliverance from peril illustrates the place of this reciprocal relationship in piety. For the Greeks prayer in distress and thanksgiving after deliverance belong to the highest expression of piety.[16] The gods were worshipped and received sacrifices and other honors both in the face of peril and after the deliverance.

The gratitude after deliverance, of course, is common to religious expression. So Pausanias explains that the statue of Artemis, the Deliverer, in Megara had been erected out of gratitude for a miraculous defeat of the army of Mardonius (1.40.2-3; cf. 2.31.1; 3.22.12). Aelius Aristides, *SD* 4.32, and Philo, *Mig.* 25; *Vit.* 87, provide similar examples.

More striking are the texts where honor is given to the gods as *sōtēres* (deliverers) in the face of peril with the assumption that this may secure deliverance or with an actual statement that the deliverance was in response to this worship. When severe earthquakes were destroying villages in the province of Asia, Aelius Aristides in response to a command of Asclepius publicly sacrifices an ox to Zeus, the Deliverer. The earthquakes stopped, Aristides relates, "by the care and power of the gods and by my necessary

---

[15] E. Edelstein and L. Edelstein, *Asclepius. A Collection and Interpretation of the Testimonies,* Baltimore, 1945, 2, 181.

[16] P. Wendland, "Σωτήρ," *ZNW,* 5 (1904), 347.

service" (*SD* 3.39-40). Similarly, the Dioscuri deliver Simonides in gratitude for his praise (Ael., *VH,* frg. 63 [but not here called *sōtēres*]).[17] In addition see Aelius Aristides, *SD* 4.4, 8 (of Asclepius), and a text where Isis says in response to a petition of a woman facing the death of her expected infant, "You will not complain that you have worshipped an ungrateful deity" (Ovid, *Met.* 9.700-1).

Criticism of Mercenary Benefactor Relationships

The more mercenary aspects of such a relationship with both divine and human benefactors did not escape the criticism of the moralists. Their criticism, however, can be taken as further evidence of the prevalence of the custom. Already notice has been made of Seneca's efforts to resist the idea of benevolence as strictly a loan (p. 61). He also protests a mercenary outlook on behalf of the beneficiary: "He is ungrateful who returns gratitude with his eyes on a second gift, who hopes while he repays" (*Ben.* 4.20.3). Philo perhaps is voicing a similar criticism when he urges those who love God to honor him for his own sake alone (*Quod Deus* 69; cf. *Abr.* 128). "The thanksgiver finds in thanksgiving itself an all-sufficient reward" (*Plant.* 136 [translation of Whitaker in *LCL*]).

In another sphere a prosecutor attempts to show that the defendant was buying the privilege of "undemocratic" conduct by his gifts, i.e. he was invoking gratitude for his benefits to citizens and the city in order to gain acquittal from crime (Lysias 26.3-4; cf. 27.9-12; 29.4; 30.26).[18] In Pliny, *Pan.* 28.2, Trajan is praised for avoiding such a misuse of benefits.

Charis (favor) in political and judicial life was often frowned upon as favoritism (Arist., *Ath. Pol.* 41; Theoc. 5.39). The Greek citizen swore that he would act neither because of favor *(charitos)* nor enmity (Dem. 57.63; Arist., *Eth. Nic.* 1137a; cf. Plut., *De rect. rat. aud.* 44e).[19] For *gratia* as favoritism see Cicero, *QFr.* 1.1.20; 1.2.10.

Pliny offers to pay but a third of a foundation for teachers' salaries "in order that my money might not be corrupted by ambition" (*Ep.* 4.13.6). He apparently is trying to avoid the appearance of nepotism.[20]

Bond of Society

This possibility of producing favorable action toward oneself from a political unit or from an individual by granting a benefit or by expressing gratitude for a benefit was an important factor binding Greco-Roman society together, especially vertically between units possessing different degrees of power. Throughout this essay evidence from the late Classical

[17] A. Furtwängler, "Dioskuren," Roscher, *Lex.,* 1884-90, 1, 1158.

[18] W. P. Clark, "Private and Public Benefactions in Athenian Litigation," *Classical Weekly,* 23 (1929), 33 n. 1.

[19] Cf. J. Moffatt, *Grace in the New Testament,* New York, 1932, pp. 34-36, who also cites Acts 24:27; 25:3, 9.

[20] A. N. Sherwin-White, *The Letters of Pliny. A Historical and Social Commentary,* Oxford, 1966, p. 288; cf. H. Marrou, *A History of Education in Antiquity,* New York, 1956[3], p. 305.

period appears beside evidence from Imperial times, as do Latin and Greek sources. This juxtaposition is conscious. The broad lines of the benefactor relationship are characteristic of the whole period, including the Roman world at least from Republican times on. The arduous task of tracing a historical development does not appear fruitful, and the distinctions that can be drawn do not appear to contribute to the development of the thesis (cf. Hands, *Charities,* p. 15).

The central importance of gifts in the Homeric writings, so tremendously influential themselves on later culture, lies behind the relationships that later became formulated in terms of benefactors and beneficiaries. Moses Finley states that no single detail in the life of the heroes receives so much attention in the *Iliad* and the *Odyssey* as the gift. "The word 'gift' [*dōron*] was a cover-all for a great variety of actions and transactions which later became differentiated and acquired their own appellations."[21] Here too the factor of self-interest and reciprocity was fully involved. With the attention to gifts, there is frank reference to adequacy and recompense. As among many primitive people, gift-exchange was the basic exchange mechanism; and no one gave anything in goods, services, or honors without proper recompense to himself or his kin. The act of giving was the first half of a reciprocal action, the second half of which was a counter-gift. Gifts described that which functioned as fees, rewards, prizes, bribes, taxes, dues, amends with penal overtones. Peaceful foreign relations were conducted by gift-exchange (Finley, pp. 62-64).

The high value that later was placed on being publicly honored as a benefactor was anticipated in the prestige that public gifts had in the Homeric world. Public gifts are signs of pre-eminence and where the "point of honor" lies.[22]

The dowry is an example of the social importance of the reciprocal gift. In the Homeric period gifts of wooing had their counter-gift in the dowry, without which there was no marriage (Finley, p. 64). The dowry continued to receive an enormous amount of public attention in Classical and Hellenistic times. It had a basic reciprocal function. Its purpose was to protect the woman from frivolous desires of divorce or lack of support on the part of her husband. Thus, when the husband's duty of reciprocity for the gift of the dowry was not fulfilled, or could not be, the dowry was returned to the house of the wife's father. To preserve the element of reciprocity, she was the possessor of the materials that belonged to the dowry; and upon divorce the husband lost all powers over them, even when adultery on the part of the wife was the cause. It had to be used to support her and was returned if she died without sons from the marriage or if the husband died even with sons.[23]

In later times (by the fifth century B.C.) the phenomenon of benefaction was a specific manifestation of important aspects of this reciprocity of giving.

Seneca called benefits the greatest bond of human society (*maxime*

[21] M. I. Finley, *The World of Odysseus,* New York, 1954, pp. 63-64.
[22] W. Leaf, *A Companion to the Iliad,* London, 1892, pp. 24, 58, 110, 139.
[23] H. J. Wolff, "Προίξ," PW (1957), 23, 147, 151-53, 163-64.

humanam societatem adligat, Ben. 1.4.1). To Cicero, *justitia* and *beneficentia* or *benignitas* are the two factors maintaining *societas* (*Off.* 1.20.1; cf. 1.50, 56). Gelzer convincingly demonstrates the importance of social relationships established on this basis in the Republic and cites Sallust's description of Roman society: "A few powerful men to whose favor the masses had committed themselves" (Sallust, *H.* 1.12).[24]

Social relationships based on the exchange of benefits had no less a role in Hellenistic or Imperial society (cf. Hands, 33). Dio Chrysostom satirizes the craving for honor that would drive a man into benevolence to the public. He speaks of those who sell their houses and land and go about hungry that their name may be heralded by their fellow citizens; some even die to get leaves (66.2). Crowns, public proclamations, seats of honor are worth everything to those who obtain them (75.7). The force driving a man to public benefactions was not just the power and material advantages that the resulting obligations placed on the beneficiary but also the high value placed on being honored as a benefactor. A word for the *love of honor, philotimia,* became a name for public benefactions (cf. L & S I.4). As Hands notes, in private transactions in upper society essential services were obtained through such reciprocity without implying one person to be the employee of another; thus when money was passed, it was described as gratitude, not as a fee (Hands, pp. 33-34). Practicality suggested investing wealth in friends rather than hoarding it (Cic., *Planc.* 81; *Amic.* 55).

The importance of establishing such relationships was evident in the courts. The defendant worked hard to demonstrate his past benefactions which had put the city or the jurors in debt to him. The prosecutor, in turn, had to show that he deserved only anger and hatred because he never had done them any kindness.[25] The practice was criticized but apparently was prevalent and basic. Thus the orator involved in prosecution and defense is instructed to show how he had benefitted the judges or those for whom the judges care and to show that now is the time to return gratitude for what was done at his initiative (Ps.-Arist., *Rh. Al.* [beginning of the third century B.C.] 1444b.39-1445a.2).[26] Cicero suggests that orators should appeal to the leniency (*mansuetudo*) of the jury that in response to his many benefits to them the defendant be pardoned for one error (*Inv. Rhet.* 2.104).

The obligations between benefactor and beneficiary were especially important in politics. "Candidature for a magistracy could not rely on the support of an organized party, but was based on a system of personal relationships of all kinds, reaching both upwards and downwards in society" (Gelzer, p. 62). Cato exasperated the common people by making candidates for office personally canvass the people, neither soliciting nor

---

[24] Gelzer, *Roman Nobility,* p. 76 n. 130. Fustel de Coulanges (*Histoire des institutions politiques de l'ancienne France,* Vol. 5: *Les origines du système féodal. Le bénéfice et le patronat pendant l'époque mérovingienne,* Paris, 1890, pp. 205-47 and 65-110) first demonstrated that these relationships of mutual obligation were the decisive element in the structure of late Republican society (cf. Gelzer, p. 62).

[25] Clark, "Private and Public Benefactions," pp. 33-35, primarily using materials from Lysias, Isocrates and Isaeus.

[26] For the criticism of this practice, cf. above, p. 67.

conferring with the citizens through the agency of another; he thus deprived the common folk of the opportunity of bestowing favor (Plut., *Cat. Min.* 49.5 [783d]; cf. *Nicias* 2.3). When Cicero ran for consulship in 63 B.C., he was told by his brother that he would have to bind to himself his numerous distinguished friends by every means and would have to make it clear to them all that the moment had come for them to show their gratitude to him or to put him under an obligation. Most important was the good will of the *nobiles* and especially the consulars. The obligation created by his service as a defending counsel was an essential factor. These debts must be collected and new connections established (Cicero [Quintus], *Comment. Pet.* 4-5, 19, 21-22; cf. Gelzer, 56, 139). Kindness (*benignitas*) wins the favor of the multitude and thus advantage for the candidate (*Comment. Pet.* 44.1; cf. 41.4; Cic., *Off.* 2.32).

Social and political units too needed to establish such relationships. The various trade guilds had their patrons (*ILS* 7216-22 [second and third centuries A.D.]) for lawsuits to speak for them in the senate, for the good will of the provincial governors (Gelzer, p. 92). Benefactors were needed by cities as well, and honor was a sufficient prize to induce the wealthy to hold public office without remuneration (cf. Hands, pp. 37-38). It is important to exercise zeal in honoring benefactors because having many who are kindly disposed and who lend aid when there is opportunity leads to a more secure life for a city (Dio Chrys. 31.7; cf. 31.22). It can become an important basis for relationships between cities. Such relationships are the wealth of the city (Dem., *Chersonese* 8.66). In Isocrates it became a real and systematic creed that ties between cities should be based on *eunoia* (good will) rather than on fear as in Thucydides (e.g. *Antidosis* 122). Isocrates uses the term 25 times to refer to relations between cities.[27] In later times it was important for a city to have benefactors in its dealings with Rome. Abdera had no patrons in Rome; so to avoid the giving of its land to the Thracian king, Cotys, it secured the help of two patrons of Teos, who achieved its aim (*SIG*[3] 656[ca. 166 B.C.]). In 54 B.C. Tenedos lost its autonomy because it had not attached enough influential senators for its interests (Cicero, *QFr.* 2.9.2).[28]

The bestowal of divine honors on rulers had the same social and political function. Deissmann calls this expression "the crown and summit of the culture of the ruling classes."[29] In Bowersock's words, "The highest honor was worship, disclosing little about the religious life of the Hellenic peoples but much about their ways of diplomacy.... Mutual interest buttressed the system of honors, and therefore underlay the worship of benefactors, magistrates, and kings." Bowersock describes how in the imperial cult, the initiative came from politically alert segments of the subordinate political units, from the Roman partisans, who were precisely the ones who could underwrite the cost of the cults; thus the diplomatic relationship that had worked so well in the Republic was established. The

[27] J. de Romilly, "Eunoia in Isocrates or the Political Importance of Creating Good Will," *JHS*, 78 (1958), 92-101.

[28] Gelzer, *The Roman Nobility*, p. 89.

[29] A. Deissmann, *Light from the Ancient Near East*, New York, 1927[4], p. 338.

friends of Rome paid for elaborate games in honor of the emperor, and their names adorn the lists of high priests. It was to be expected that the honors spread to members of Augustus' family: "These people were avenues to the great patron himself, the Princeps."[30]

The office of *Augustales* provides illustration of the social and political functions involved in the imperial cult. This office was in charge of the imperial cult in Italian towns, particularly with regard to games in honor of the Princeps. It was created in the Augustan system as one of the ways to find a special function within the state for all classes; the office was occupied by freedmen, to whom other public offices were closed. It also gave their fellow townsmen an opportunity to use the ambition of the freedmen for the municipal advantage; the holders of the office had to express their gratitude for the honor by providing sacrifices, repairing public works, or paying a *summa honoraria*.[31] One form in which their gratitude was expressed was in foundations (Laum[32], 2.15, 18, 37 [also called patrons], 55; cf. Vol. 1, p. 21).

Rulers too needed stronger social ties than merely the political tie of allegiance to sovereignty. According to Philo, *Praem.* 97, dignity (*semnon*), terror (*phobos*), and benevolence (*eunoia*) are three qualities that keep a government from being overthrown. The same three virtues appear in Diotogenes' discussion of the proper appearance that the king should present to the multitude except that kindness (*chrēstos*) appears in the place of benevolence (Stob. 4.7.62 [W-H 4.267.5-11]). Plutarch states that the greatest task of government is to produce ready obedience through good will (*Cp. of Luc. and Cim.* 2.3 [522a]). The *Augustales*, for example, helped to cement the bond of unity and loyalty with the class of freedmen (Nock, "Seviri and Augustales," p. 636).

The kings of Pergamon are outstanding examples of the use of the benefactor role for political purposes. Mention already has been made (p. 62) of Eumenes II's offer of a grant of 120 talents to the Achaeans in 187 B.C. to remunerate the members of the legislature. His purpose was to regain, with the aid of his friendship with Rome, the lost sympathy of the Greek and Hellenistic powers (Polyb. 22.7.3; Laum, Vol. 1, pp. 35-36). Other examples are cited by Laum, Vol. 1, pp. 36-37: Attalos' gifts to Sicyon (Polyb. 18.16); the great gifts to Rhodes (Polyb. 5.88ff.); Rhodes' reception of a grant for teachers' salaries from Eumenes (Polyb. 31.31.1).

Pliny in discussing Trajan in his role of *bene faciendi* (*Pan.* 28.2) states that he provided educational foundations to educate the children from infancy so that they might know him as parent. This meant that when they pass to soldiers' pay they would owe as much to him as to parents (Pliny, *Pan.* 26.3-4; similarly, in 26.6-7 the benevolence functions to prevent revolution). Dio Chrysostom demonstrates the ruler's need for beneficiary relationships: since the king has no recourse to law, when his trust is

---

[30] G. W. Bowersock, *Augustus and the Greek World,* Oxford, 1965, pp. 112-19. Quotations are from pp. 112 and 119.

[31] A. D. Nock, "Seviri and Augustales," in *Mélanges Bidez,* Annuaire de l'institut de philologie et d'histoire orientales, 2, Brussels, 1934, pp. 630-31, 635-36.

[32] B. Laum, *Stiftungen in der griechischen und römischen Antike,* Berlin, 1914.

betrayed, he must depend on *eunoia*. He maintains happiness by the loyalty (*pistis*) of his friends; thus *philia* is the most sacred of all his possessions (3.86).[33]

Summary and Conclusion

The relationship between a benefactor and his beneficiary was extremely important throughout the Classical and Hellenistic periods and in both Latin and Greek regions; it affected almost every relationship in the life of the upper classes, including the relationship to the gods. It consisted of reciprocal obligations, composed of gratitude of the recipient to his benefactor and a resulting obligation of the benefactor to the beneficiary who had expressed gratitude. The reciprocal benefactor relationship formed a most basic bond of society. By giving, or responding to, a benefit, a person gained power in the judicial and political system; and states gained internal and international support.

Marx and Engels correctly saw the destruction of this tradition in the rise of the bourgeoisie.[34] Money became the impersonal medium to express the obligation and value of the exchange of goods and services in society. In our society welfare recipients are commonly regarded as a drain on bourgeois enterprise. A simple return to the Hellenistic pattern of benevolence, however, is no solution. Hellenistic benevolence was voluntary, paternalistic, and made little penetration into the lower classes. Moreover, the greater correction to wrong thinking about welfare would be to present it in terms of justice—society's response to the rights of the needy—rather than in terms of benevolence. Yet, given the present prevalent attitudes regarding welfare as public charity, efforts could be made to bring more ideas of reciprocity into the welfare picture. What opportunities the welfare people have to contribute to society should be understood as adequate return—a welfare mother's care of her children or participation in efforts to govern and improve one's community. Even more so, poverty programs must be conceived with the goal of increasing the recipients' economic, political and social ability to reciprocate so that their response to society is a reality and is power.

---

[33] As a type of force supplementing the legitimacy of the ruler's power, compensation is more stable and reliable than deprivation since at the heart is a conscious reciprocity in which both rulers and subjects believe that they are benefitting from the relationship. Cf. M. Olsen, "Power as a Social Process," in *Power in Societies,* ed. by M. Olsen, New York, 1970, pp. 6-7.

[34] K. Marx and F. Engels, "The Manifesto of the Communist Party," in K. Marx and F. Engels, *Basic Writings on Politics and Philosophy,* ed. by L. Feuer, New York, 1959, p. 9. Ernst Troeltsch missed this characteristic of Hellenistic society in his invalid contrast of authority-submission relationships in the ancient world with mutual service-loyalty relationships in the Middle Ages (*The Social Teachings of the Christian Churches,* New York, 1960 [1911], pp. 248-50). For an example of the medieval retention of this tradition, cf. Thomas Aquinas, *De regimine principum* 1.10.

II. BIBLICAL AND PATRISTIC

Were David's Sons Really Priests?

CARL EDWIN ARMERDING

In the *New American Standard Bible's* translation of 2 Sam 8:18b, a classic problem of OT studies is skirted by the substitution of the phrase "chief ministers" for the Hebrew text, which plainly says that David's sons were "priests" (*koh^{a}nîm*). A marginal note does give the literal rendering, but it is obvious that the plain meaning was an embarrassment to the committee. Inasmuch as it is characteristic of the life and work of Professor Tenney that problems should be faced rather than avoided, I have chosen, in his honor, to attempt in this short study an exoneration of the unambiguous text of 2 Sam 8:18. In so doing, I hope to show that there is in the reference another link in a strong chain that ultimately supports the essential theological truth of the royal priesthood of our Lord Jesus Christ.

Of course, the translators of the *NASB* are not the first to have found a solution other than taking the clear meaning of the word. The translators of the *King James (Authorized) Version* many years ago preferred "chief rulers" to "priests." The Chronicler, writing about six hundred years after David's time, states only that David's sons were "the chiefs beside the king" (*hāri'šōnîm l^{e}yad hammelek*, 1 Chr 18:17), and it is undoubtedly from this reference that both the *KJV* and the *NASB* made their harmonization. Likewise, the LXX text of 2 Sam 8:18 avoids the problem, using *aularchai* instead of *hiereis* for the word *koh^{a}nîm* (or some other word, which may have been in the *Vorlage*). But the problem will not go away so easily. In a second list of David's court officials (2 Sam 20:23-26) there is, in addition to the official Levitical priesthood, a reference to Ira the Jairite as the priest *l^{e}dāwîd*. Finally, in a Solomonic list in 1 Kgs 4:1-5 there are again two official Levitical priests, plus the statement *w^{e}zābûd ben-nātān kōhēn rē'eh hammelek*. The *RSV*, following the more usual interpretation, translates this as "Zabud the son of Nathan was priest and king's friend," making Zabud the holder of the dual office. Zabud apparently succeeded Ira the Jairite as priest. The *KJV* retains the grammatical structure of the *RSV* but

Carl Edwin Armerding, Associate Professor of Old Testament at Regent College, Vancouver, British Columbia, Canada. B.A., Gordon College; B.D., Trinity Evangelical Divinity School; graduate study at Wheaton College Graduate School; M.A. and Ph.D., Brandeis University.

translates *kōhēn* as "principal officer," in keeping with the avoidance of the priestly terminology in 2 Sam 8:18. The *NASB* here finds another way out of the difficulty. The text is clearly problematical, so the *NASB*, while retaining the translation "priest" for *kōhēn*, says, "Zabud the son of Nathan, a priest, (was) the king's friend"![1] Here are three references, two of them fairly unambiguous, that point to a second order of priests within the court of early Israel. In the first case, those so designated are definitely non-Levitical (David's sons), while in the case of Ira the Jairite and Zabud ben Nathan, there is nothing to indicate Levitical background.

Classical solutions to the problem (in addition to altering the translation) are not wanting. These are listed by Aelred Cody in his very useful monograph.[2] Cody rightly comments, however, "These hypotheses have nothing to support them and they attempt to solve a problem that lies not in the text but in an assumption *a priori* that David's sons, Nathan's son, Zabud, and Ira the Jairite could not have been priests as the text says they were." The fact is, the texts do say they were priests and no amount of explaining away will rid us of that fact.

I am going to assume that both text and normal translation for each passage are correct, since all signs point in this direction. There were then priests in early Israel who were (1) connected with the royal house, (2) not of the Levitical order, and (3) serving a function that is still largely unknown to us. Rather than try to speculate on the function of these priests, I want to re-examine the concept of a non-Levitical, royally connected priesthood in early Israel, and then draw out the theological implications of what is found.

First, it is clear that there is a strong tradition of a royal priesthood within the OT itself. Most important, of course, is the Melchizedek reference in Gen 14:17-24 with its application to a Davidic king (or ultimately to the Messiah) in the enthronement Ps 110.[3] For our purposes it does not matter whether the tradition was originally connected with Shechem, Shiloh or Jerusalem, though it is apparent that later biblical and post-biblical writers, especially Josephus, identified Salem with Jerusalem. The idea of a king who was also specifically designated a priest is clear, and it is this factor that looms so large in the discussion of Ps 110. In normal Canaanite fashion, he was designated a priest *le* ("with respect to") a deity, in this case El Elyon, who is identified (in Gen 14:22) with Yahweh. Cody makes the point that normally the Israelite *kōhēn* was priest with respect to (*le*) some human authority (e.g. Micah, Judg 17:5, 10, 12; 18:4, 19; or the Danites, Judg 18:19, 30; or David, 2 Sam 20:26)[4] but here there is a direct

---

[1] Cf. R. deVaux, "Melange," *RB*, 48 (1939), 403, n. 3, for discussion of the textual problem here.

[2] A. Cody, *A History of Old Testament Priesthood*, Rome, 1969, p. 103, n. 55.

[3] That these two passages are very early and reflect a Canaanite background is now generally though not universally held. A survey of the material is available in I. Hunt, "Recent Melchizedek Study," *The Bible in Current Catholic Thought*, ed. by J. L. MacKenzie, New York, 1962, pp. 21-33. A more recent discussion is by J. A. Emerton, "The Riddle of Genesis XIV," *VT*, 21 (Oct. 1971), 403-39.

[4] Cody, *History*, p. 101. I see no reason to deny the authenticity of the references in 1 Sam 1:3 and 1 Kgs 2:27 where Hophni and Phinehas and then

relationship between the king-priest and his God. He himself is both the vice-regent under God, and the mediator between his people and God.

Here the pattern is set. The royal priest, unlike the other priests mentioned, served directly under God, a fact that is corroborated in Ps 110:1, where the one to whom the psalm is addressed is seated at the right hand of Yahweh. Additional functions performed which fit into a priestly role are the blessing of Abraham *and* God (Melchizedek is the mediator, who can turn both ways), and the receiving of tithes.[5] The context in which the "tenth" is given (whether given *to* or *by* Melchizedek) is clearly connected with Melchizedek's role as priest of El Elyon, and is not simply tribute money to a local king. Abram's relations with Canaanites, both his allies (*ba'alê berît*, Gen 14:13) and the local kings (Gen 14:21-24), are carried out quite differently from his encounter with Melchizedek, and it is plain that the difference lay in Melchizedek's role as a priest of El Elyon. In fact, the distinction drawn between Melchizedek and the king of Sodom should give us caution, lest any sweeping generalizations about the nature of Canaanite royal priesthood be made from the role of Melchizedek. Even if we are to date Abraham in the beginning of the Middle Bronze Age (rather than Late Bronze, as several scholars do who write on this subject) and thus take our model of Canaanite kingship from sources reflecting that period, we still have to recognize that there were many petty kings in the land. But Abram neither gives tithes to nor accepts blessing from all. Melchizedek stands as a lone example of a royal figure whose priesthood is recognized by the biblical writer as a genuine position of mediatorship before a true God.

There is no hint in the biblical record that the patriarchs ever thought of themselves as kings, either in the Canaanite "petty-king" sense or in the sense of later empire-builders like David and Solomon. Gen 36 does refer to kings (*melākîm*) of Edom, but the part of the chapter that undoubtedly reflects the earliest designation of Edomite patriarchal figures (Gen 36:10-30, 40-43) uses the term *'allûp* rather than *melek* for the clan head. However, it is clear that Israelite patriarchal clan heads Abraham, Isaac and Jacob also functioned as the family priest. Each one built altars, sacrificed, offered prayers directly to God, and received revelations and thus teaching directly from the Lord. But since there is no hint of royalty in the record, their priestly activities are not relevant to this discussion.

With the rise of Moses we come to a time when a royal function is clearly attached to the leader of Israel, though again no royal title is ever given. But Moses is pictured in the Exodus narratives as much more than a

---

Abiathar are called "priests to Yahweh," but Cody's point is not materially affected by these exceptions to the rule. The case of others designated Levitical priests is ambiguous because in no clear case is the Levitical priest called a priest "with respect to" (*le*) anyone.

[5] The recent attempt by R. H. Smith, "Abraham and Melchizedek," *ZAW*, 77 (1965), 129-53, to find in the passage a suzerainty treaty in which Melchizedek gives tribute money to Abraham in a fashion analogous to the action of King PBL with the victorious KRT, I find unconvincing. Unless Gen 14:21-23 is to be separated from the rest of the section, it is clear that Abram would *not* be made rich by acquisition from Canaanite, or even Mesopotamian, kings.

clan leader; he assumes all the prerogatives of a monarch.[6] Thus, his relation to the priesthood, and his function as such, becomes of interest, even if only to support or deny conclusions from other data. Cody discusses both the passage in the Book of the Covenant (Exod 24:3-8) and the narrative in Exod 18 in which Moses is somehow involved (the text is not clear) in a sacrificial meal and receives oracles from God.[7] In the former passage, Moses built an altar and manipulated the blood, but as Cody points out, the ritual is quite different from that prescribed for Levitical offerings. Cody argues that the text has to do with covenant-making rather than sacrifice and concludes that Moses is less a priest than a leader. He finally affirms that "whether we call his activity priestly or not depends on what we understand by 'priestly.' "[8]

Of course, Moses is presented in the early chapters of Exod as functioning prior to the designation of a special Levitical priesthood, and as such he partakes of the character of priest for his people, in addition to his kingly and prophetic roles. When Aaron is initially introduced (Exod 4:14) he is called "Aaron the Levite," a text that might lead us to expect priestly functions on his part. However, Aaron, throughout the remainder of the time in Egypt, is simply Moses' spokesman or prophet (Exod 7:1) and never performs as a priest. It is the elders of Israel (Exod 12:21) who perform the Passover sacrifice, and thus the first-born are set apart to God, seemingly for some priestly purpose, in the narrative of Exod 12. Exod 19:6 pictures the entire nation as ideally a "kingdom of priests" (*mamleket kōh^{a}nîm*), although in the same chapter (Exod 19:22 and 24) priests and people are separately designated, and neither has anything like direct access to God.

Coming back to Exod 24:5 we find "young men of the sons of Israel" offering burnt offerings and peace offerings, as part of Moses' covenant ceremony, and in the latter part of the chapter (Exod 24:9-11) Moses, Aaron, Nadab and Abihu, together with seventy elders of Israel, are granted a special vision of God. Finally, in Exod 28, Aaron and his sons are set apart to serve as priests, though in light of the special ordination of the Levites in Exod 32 most critics have concluded that the instructions of Exod 28 must be from a later period.[9] At any rate, the role of Moses vis-à-vis the Levitical order is not our concern. What should be noted is that, both before and after Sinai, Moses the leader performed priestly acts, particularly in the sense that he, more than any other, had direct access to God and was the direct representative of God among the people. In this sense his role is analogous to that of the royal priest, though to say that he was such would be stretching the analogy.

[6] E.g. legislator and executor of a developed legal system, commander-in-chief of a standing army, chief architect of foreign policy, recipient of taxes and tithes, etc.

[7] Cody, *History,* pp. 42-44.

[8] *Ibid.,* p. 43.

[9] It should be noted that nowhere in Exod 28 is there a proscription of non-Levitical or non-Aaronic priestly activity. Exod 25-31 concerns the worship at the sanctuary in Israel, and in this there seems to be no provision for non-Levitical participation. Relegation of the entire section to a putative "P" document need not be resorted to in order to explain non-Levitical priestly acts *outside of* the sanctuary.

Joshua, though presented as an absolute ruler like Moses, seems much more dependent upon the Levitical orders. His covenant-making function (Exod 24:13) and his direct access to God could be called priestly activities, but there the similarities end. When we come to the book of Judges, the situation is very different. The silence of Judges concerning legitimate priesthood (apart from Judg 20:27-28) has long intrigued scholars and various solutions to the critical problems have been proposed.[10] Judg, however, is not generally a good source for studying the royal element in priestly function, because there is little evidence of any truly royal figure within that book. Gideon, like Moses before him, built an altar and offered sacrifices (6:24-26), but this was before he was even a judge, and furthermore it fits the normal pattern of family sacrifices of the early period. Gideon, like the editor of Judg, has a clear antipathy toward the whole idea of kingship (Judg 8:22-23), and the pathetic account of the Shechemite reign of Gideon's son Abimelech only fortifies the impression. Similar to Gideon's is the sacrifice made by Samson's father, Manoah (Judg 13), while the strange story of the Levite who signed on as Micah's priest (in place of, and obviously preferred to, Micah's son) raises more questions than it answers. The major point of interest here, in light of our initial reference in 2 Sam 8:18, is the fact that Micah, like David later, had his son as priest. Had Micah himself served in this way, it would be simply another example of patriarchal priesthood, but the installation of the son as *kōhēn* lends another dimension. However, the entire incident is considered most abnormal (Judg 17:6). If Micah's son had continued to function after the arrival of the Levite, and if Micah had made any pretension of kingship, the accounts would be more analogous, but Micah clearly preferred a Levite to his son, and the text explicitly states that kingship had not yet arrived in the land (Judg 17:6). Finally, the account in Judg 20 and 21 tells us nothing about unusual priestly functions and even less about kingship.

The next great judicial figure is Samuel, and here we come to the transition between a local judge and a genuine king, though certainly Samuel partakes much more of the character of the former.[11] Although it was he who united Israel, and it was he who apparently attempted to establish some hereditary succession (1 Sam 8:1-3), he never claimed the title of king and obviously found the concept distasteful. But that Samuel functioned as a priest is without question. Although his lineage is given in 1 Sam 1:1 as from Ephraim, the Chronicler (1 Chr 6:27 and 33-34) ties him to the Levitical tribe. His early training is as an assistant to Eli in the Shiloh shrine, and 1 Sam 2:27-36 seems to see in him the legitimate successor to the fallen line of Eli. Whether in fact Samuel is intended to be the "faithful priest" of 1 Sam 2:35, and, if so, who the "anointed" of God might be, is not entirely clear. Christians have always seen in the prophecy a pointer to relationships between king and priest in the development of a messianic consciousness.

[10] Cf. Edward Robertson, *The Period of the Judges*, Manchester, 1946, pp. 22-24.

[11] Like Moses, he controls legal, political and military institutions for an increasingly centralized state, but the centralization and bureaucracy did not reach the levels of the earlier or later times.

But that Samuel functioned as a priest (in addition to his functions as prophet and king-figure) is clear. To exactly which role each of his acts should be assigned is not so obvious, as there is much role-overlap at this time, but we should note the following: Samuel received oracles (1 Sam 3:21—this was a priestly function; cf. 1 Sam 22:10; 23:6-12). He interceded in prayer for Israel, offered burnt and other offerings to Yahweh (1 Sam 7:8-9), and even after a king had been appointed he reserved for himself certain sacrificial functions (1 Sam 13). Finally, he appeared in the sanctuary service wearing a linen ephod (1 Sam 2:18). 1 Sam 22:18 would seem to indicate that wearing a linen ephod was synonymous with being a priest, but Cody questions the legitimacy of this text as it is traditionally understood.[12] This would leave only 2 Sam 6:14 where David wore an ephod for his dance before Yahweh, and since the question is one of proving a priestly act by the actor's wearing an ephod we cannot use this as evidence. However, in light of the Massoretic Text of 1 Sam 22:18 and the general context of Samuel's position, both while in training under Eli and in subsequent days, I would suggest that the evidence points overwhelmingly to his having functioned as a priest. When Cody claims that "he was not, in fact, a priest in any genuine sense,"[13] I would question his conclusions. It is precisely the fact of a priesthood operating outside of the normal sanctuary that I wish to establish, and its tie with royalty and the royal order is the key point at issue. Of course, the Chronicler does testify to Samuel's Levitical heritage, and Ps 99:6 groups him with the priests, Moses and Aaron, but this is not crucial for our study. What is important is that, in Samuel, we have another prototype of the royal-priestly figure, though his priesthood is presented as closer to the Levitical than the Melchizedek model. In fact, it is Samuel who dominates the priestly role in his own time, even though there is at least a functioning remnant of an old Levitical order. That old order, weakened through the almost simultaneous death of Eli and his two sons, resurfaced in the person of Ahijah (1 Sam 14:3), apparently a grandson of Eli, who is found as a retainer in Saul's rustic court at Gibeah. Later (apparently after the destruction of Shiloh) members of the same family are found in the sanctuary at Nob near Jerusalem (1 Sam 21-23), and the tragic story of their destruction by Saul and the transfer of the line's allegiance to David is well known. Therefore, although there was never lacking some kind of continuity in the Levitical priesthood (activities of the alternate line of Zadokites descended from Eleazar and Phinehas are not even considered in our texts), it is not until David finally raises Zadok and Abimelech to the level of court priests that the Levitical order again predominates in the religious life of Israel. In all this period it is the civil or royal head who acts as priest.

Saul presents an exception to the civil head functioning as priest, and it is tempting to say that the only reason his priestly pretenses are rejected

---

[12] Cody, *History*, p. 75, where it is suggested that since the word linen is absent in the B text of the LXX, and since the verb *nasa'* is never really attested in Hebrew with the sense of "wearing," we should properly translate the verse, "carrying the (oracular) ephod." Cody does not cite 1 Sam 14:3, but this might be an example of *nasa'* with ephod in the sense of "wear."

[13] *Ibid.*, p. 78.

is that the editors of Samuel regard everything Saul does as irregular. Such a claim would leave the biblical editors open to the charge of gross inconsistency, however, and we should expect them to have harmonized the negative attitude toward Saul's attempt at sacrifice with their apparent approval of the same activity on the part of David and Solomon. Samuel's priestly activity is not as much of an issue as Saul's, for Samuel was a legitimate Levitical figure. Nevertheless, there is no hint that David's or Solomon's sacrifices or other priestly acts were not perfectly in order. During Saul's tenure, the Levitical priests, represented by Ahijah ben Ahitub, a descendant of Eli, are represented in the court at Gibeah (1 Sam 14:3). In the same chapter we find Saul using Ahijah as an oracular functionary in connection with the ark,[14] though later Saul builds an altar himself with no mention of priestly help (1 Sam 14:35). Again in the same chapter a priest appears (1 Sam 14:36), and again it is in his role as chief oracle, though this time it is Urim and Thummim that are used (1 Sam 14:41). Finally, the Levitical priesthood is represented in 1 Sam 21-23, this time in the shrine at Nob (not far from Gibeah) and in the person of Ahimelech, another son of Ahitub (1 Sam 22:20). Here is a shrine complete with holy bread (the Bread of the Presence, 1 Sam 21:4), an ephod (1 Sam 23:9) and the sword of Goliath (1 Sam 21:9; cf. 1 Sam 17:54). Neither Saul nor David, however, asks the priests to conduct sacrifices (though presumably they did), and again the major interest seems to be in the oracular use of the ephod.

During this entire period there are but two references to sacrifice. One, recorded in 1 Sam 20:29, indicates with apparent approval that David's family would conduct a clan sacrifice in Bethlehem, and it would not seem unusual if Saul's clan had conducted the same kind of sacrifices at Gibeah in connection with their new moon feast. The other reference is to Saul's condemned act at Gilgal (1 Sam 13:8-15), where that monarch, facing the exigencies of an impending battle, took it upon himself to offer the burnt offering and presumably, had time permitted, the peace offering. Since both David and Solomon offered burnt offerings, and of course Samuel was authorized to do the same, we are forced to certain conclusions. There seems to have been no prohibition of family sacrifices (either in the period of the Judges or in Saul's time), but here either the occasion (beginning of a battle) or the shrine (Gilgal) or Saul's lack of credentials (perhaps he was not ordained for that priestly role) demands that Saul refrain from the priestly act.

David, like Saul, used the remnants of the priesthood at Nob to inquire of Yahweh (2 Sam 23:6; 30:7 and possibly 2 Sam 2:1 and 5:19, 23). However, when the ark is brought up to Jerusalem (2 Sam 6) there is no reference to any special priesthood. The Chronicler makes it clear that the reason for the abortive first attempt—the ark being brought then only as far as the house of Obed-edom, the Gittite—was that there were no Levites in charge (1 Chr 15:2). Certainly David supervised the movement of the ark both times, and the journey was accomplished amidst singing,

---

[14] According to 1 Sam 7:2 the ark was then at Kiriath-jearim; possibly the LXX reading "ephod" should be substituted in 1 Sam 14:18, as the *Jerusalem Bible* does.

sacrificing and dancing (2 Sam 6:12-15), in all of which David (clothed in a linen ephod) takes his place as the religious leader of the people. In the tent pitched for the ark, David offered burnt offerings and peace offerings (2 Sam 6:17) and dispensed the blessing of Yahweh, together with (ritual?) portions of bread and raisins (2 Sam 6:19). It is interesting to note that the Chronicler, with his concern to give the Levites their due, supplements but does not contradict this picture. Although Levites enter the picture as porters of the ark (1 Chr 15:2), and perform sacrifices (1 Chr 15:26; 16:1), it is still David who is dressed in the ephod (1 Chr 15:27), blessing the people and distributing the portion (1 Chr 16:2) and even offering the burnt offerings and peace offerings (1 Chr 16:2).[15] The role of Zadok and Abiathar is supervisory, but only in a secondary sense (1 Chr 15:11), and after the ceremonies Zadok is sent back to the high place at Gibeon where, according to the Chronicler, were the tabernacle,[16] the altar of burnt offering, and much of the Levitical machinery (1 Chr 16:39-42).[17]

Zadok and Abiathar appear together, but with Zadok apparently taking the lead, in carrying the ark out of Jerusalem when David escaped before Absalom (2 Sam. 15:24-29). Both are also counted in David's two lists of officials (2 Sam 8:17 and 20:25), but neither is named as having participated in David's final sacrifice at the threshing floor of Araunah, whether in the 2 Sam 24:25 account or in its parallel in 1 Chr 21:26-28.

In summary, it seems plain that David himself was the chief sacrificial and priestly intermediary between Yahweh and the people during his reign. The Levitical priests were used for determining the will of God, and apparently kept equipment for that purpose, such as an ephod and the Urim and Thummim. The Zadokites seem to have been centered at the

---

[15] Some may feel I have built a case for royal priesthood based on texts that speak of David or Solomon offering sacrifice while, in truth, neither of them actually sacrificed. Levites were always there, but they are just not mentioned. It is as though the reporter states in the evening news, "The President today has called up an additional fifty thousand soldiers." Any listener knows that the President does such a thing only through his agents; so with the sacrifices of David and Solomon it is not necessary to mention the Levitical functionary, but in light of material in the Mosaic law it is obvious that the Levites would have done the actual sacrificing. I can only say that, from my knowledge of the texts, there is too much that points to personal sacrificial acts on the part of kings. Furthermore, sacrifice is only one of the priestly activities of David and Solomon, and it is consistent with the other activities they perform.

[16] It is true, as the marginal note in *NASB* suggests, that the word *miškan* can mean simply "dwelling place." However, its use in cultic terminology as a technical term for the tent-dwelling of Yahweh is well established and there is no reason to doubt such a use here. If there were any doubt, the reference in 1 Chr 21:29 should remove it. The problem arises because there is no other unambiguous reference to the tabernacle after the destruction of Shiloh. Many scholars of an earlier day surmised that the tabernacle in the wilderness was a literary reconstruction, based on Solomon's temple and, secondarily, on David's tent in Jerusalem, but on this question there is no unanimity currently.

[17] There is no information about the whereabouts of Abiathar and the former priests of Nob. It may be that they attended the ark in its new tent in Jerusalem. The reference to the high place in Gibeon, with its tabernacle, has long intrigued scholars but little is known about it, except the Chronicles reference and the fact that Solomon prayed there—1 Kgs 3:4.

shrine in Gibeon with its tabernacle, while the Abiathar line may originally have served David more directly in Jerusalem, possibly having been eventually attached to his new shrine after being detached from Nob. But David himself is the chief priest of the Jerusalem tent, a role that seems to have created no conflicts with his royal and non-Levitical status.

This brings us to the matter of David's two lists of officials. In the first one (2 Sam 8:18) David's two sons are listed as priests, along with Zadok and Abiathar, while in the second list (2 Sam 20:26) Ira the Jairite is listed, again with Zadok and Abiathar, as David's priest. Since there is no indication that either David's sons or Ira were Levites, I can only surmise that they were part of another order, perhaps partaking of the royal order connected with the Jerusalem shrine, which David himself served as monarch under Yahweh in his country. This could be argued more conclusively with the sons of David, because of the nature of the relationship, but it may have been true of Ira as well.

At the close of David's life we see the same sacrificial role being undertaken by his son Adonijah (1 Kgs 1:9, 18), the latter activity with the assistance of Abiathar. The sacrificial act of Adonijah, moreover, is most significant, as it was conducted before all of the important men of Israel by the Serpent's Stone by the spring Rogel (En-Rogel, 1 Kgs 1:9). It seems highly suggestive of the fact that Adonijah was proclaiming himself the new "priest-king" in place of his father, or at least it was interpreted as such by Bathsheba, Nathan, and eventually David. Later the same day Solomon is anointed at another spring, this time by the priest Zadok (1 Kgs 1:38-40), but there is no mention of sacrifice in the hastily prepared ceremony. It is only from Solomon's later activities that we may conclude that he too considered himself the chief intermediary between his people and Yahweh.

Solomon's priestly activities parallel those of his father David. He prays at Gibeon (1 Kgs 3:15), after which a major effort is given to the construction of the temple and the setting in motion of its ritual. In the actual dedication of the temple the priests are involved (1 Kgs 8:3-4), but it is Solomon himself who leads the procession, sacrificing (1 Kgs 8:5, 62-64), blessing the assembly (1 Kgs 8:12-21, 55-61), interceding before God (1 Kgs 8:22-53), and making covenant with Yahweh (1 Kgs 9).[18]

In a summary of his activities, the author of Kings (1 Kgs 9:25) notes that Solomon would offer burnt offerings and peace offerings on the altar three times a year. The following chapter (1 Kgs 10:5) cites the number and splendor of Solomon's burnt offerings as part of that which amazed the Queen of Sheba.

Finally, Solomon, like David, had a list of court officials.[19] Together with the usual reference to Zadok and Abiathar (though the latter is ultimately deposed), there is reference, mentioned above, to one Zabud ben

[18] These chapters, 1 Kgs 8-9, are generally considered post-exilic by literary critics, so it is especially interesting to note that they in no way deny Solomon's central role in the priestly activity. The post-exilic book of Chronicles, which likewise gives the king the most prominent priestly role, is here simply a touched-up version of the Kings account.

[19] A definitive study of this material is now available in T. N. D. Mettinger, *Solomonic State Officials*, Lund, 1971.

Nathan, who was the King's Friend. The textual problem has already been discussed, but either Zabud or his father Nathan is called a priest (*kōhēn*), and it is difficult to escape the conclusion that we have here the same order of priesthood noted earlier in David's time. If the father of Zabud is the same Nathan the prophet who was David's adviser (1 Kgs 1:10, etc.) there is no indication that he had a Levitical background. Again, it is difficult to know whether such men as Ira and Zabud had any connection with the royal priesthood, but obviously both served in a special way in the Jerusalem court.

Throughout the time of the monarchy various examples of royal-priestly activities could be given, but the examples noted should be sufficient. They hold special significance in light of Ps 110, an enthronement hymn, which ties together the old Canaanite Melchizedek royal priesthood with the Judean monarchy of David, Solomon and their successors. Although some evangelical Christians through the years have shown a notable reticence to apply Messianic Psalm terminology to OT individuals,[20] it seems obvious to me that there was a strong sense of royal-priestly ideology that existed in early Israel, and a psalm like Ps 110 simply shows us the chain of thinking by which this ideology was expressed. Melchizedek provides the prototype, and it is after his "order" (*'al dibrātî*) that David and Solomon are to be thought of as priests. This order is different from the Aaronic one, and it would require a full exegesis of the Ps to elucidate the matter.[21] The royal priest is not such by human investiture, and his commission is irrevocable. He sits (figuratively) at God's right hand, unlike Levitical priests who are not so directly in God's presence, and he rules in the midst of all his foes. His scepter, coming forth from Zion, will ultimately judge all nations.

It is easy to see why later interpreters have been loath to see in these so-called "enthronement" Pss any reference to a human king. But I am convinced that we need not accept popular ideas about annual re-enthronement feasts[22] or excessive conclusions of the myth and ritual school[23] to appreciate the valid growth and development of this idea in the ongoing history of Israel. I submit that the concept of royal priesthood, which began with Melchizedek, continued to grow, though unconsciously, in the non-royal figures of Moses and Samuel, and came to full flower when the monarchy was established in Zion under the covenant God gave to David (2 Sam 7). If such hymns as Pss 2 and 110 were indeed used in the enthronement of Judean monarchs, it was with the continued hope that each subsequent king would be "the one who would come." That none of the Judean kings ever fully lived up to the expectation made the longing for

[20] See E. W. Hengstenberg, *Christology of the Old Testament*, Grand Rapids, 1847, repr. 1970.

[21] Such an exegesis has been done by R. Tournay, "Le Psaume CX," *RB*, 67 (1960), 5-41.

[22] Cf. A. R. Johnson, *Sacral Kingship in Ancient Israel*, Cardiff, 1967, or S. Mowinckel, *The Psalms in Israel's Worship*, 2 vols., Nashville, ET 1962.

[23] Cf. S. H. Hooke, *Prophets and Priests*, London, 1938, pp. 8-10, for a typical statement of royal priesthood based on the place of the king in (1) the death and resurrection of a god ceremony, and (2) a sacred ritual marriage. Hooke does note some valid distinctions between the king-priest and his function, and the Levitical or cultic priests and theirs.

one who would do so all the more intense. Thus, when John the Baptist puts his very poignant question to our Lord (Matt 11:3), it is with these years of expectation and longing, and constant frustration, in mind.

Returning to the history of royal priesthood, it is my belief that Ps 110 was used in early times, and that both David and Solomon were conscious of holding a priestly investiture that was different from that of the Levitical order. After their time the picture of an ideal priest-king becomes less, rather than more, credible, until finally in the course of history the line of David seems to have disappeared completely in Babylonian exile. But even then, a few sparks of hope (e.g. the Jehoiachin survival and restoration, 2 Kgs 25:27-30) appeared, and after the exile the priest-king ideology is clearly a part of the prophetic message of Zechariah (especially Zech 6:9-14)[24] and possibly Haggai. Again, hopes were dashed, and no ideal priest-king appeared. In the Hasmonean line of Judas Maccabeus, the priest-king ideology becomes a reality, but by the time of the actual investiture of Simon Maccabeus or more properly his son John Hyrcanus with the dual office, many pious observers had lost their hopes for any truly messianic figure to come from the line. It is in light of this long history of the idea that the NT writer of the letter to the Hebrews has developed the concept of our Lord's priestly ministry "after the order of Melchizedek." To deny that David and Solomon were priests, or that David's sons could have been priests, is to break one of the important links in this chain.

In conclusion I would like to suggest that we have evidence for several "orders" of priesthood operative in early Israel, possibly connected with the status of the individual priest (Levite, royal figure, prophetic figure) and possibly relating to particular shrines (Gilgal, Shiloh, Gibeon, Nob, Jerusalem). Samuel seems to have functioned as a priest both of the Gilgal shrine (1 Sam 13:8-15) and at Ramah (1 Sam 9:12-14). Whether he was a Levite or not remains debatable. The Levitical orders, represented in Davidic times by Zadok and Abiathar, were variously connected with Shiloh, Bethel,[25] Nob (until Saul's time), Gibeon, and later, Jerusalem. The royal priesthood, patterned after Melchizedek, who was certainly believed to have been connected with earlier kingship in Jerusalem, evidently did not function in Saul's court at Gibeah, but did become operative in David's Jerusalem. Whether there was any connection between a continuing Jebusite priesthood in Jerusalem or not has been debated at length, but usually in relation to Zadok. I would suggest that, inasmuch as Zadok is related to the cult at Gibeon and not originally Jerusalem, a more fruitful search would be for links between the Davidic royal priesthood and Jebusite priests from the line of Melchizedek. David's son Solomon became a priest after this order and his elder son Adonijah attempted to function as such. Whether Ira the Jairite and Zabud ben Nathan were also of this order must remain a mystery.

The question of why Saul, of all the civil leaders of his era, is denied

[24] Emerton, "The Riddle of Genesis XIV," pp. 414-20, argues that there is no real evidence for a priest-king before the Hasmonean period and Zech 6:9-11 is a corrupt text.

[25] In the Judg 20:26-27 reference, Bethel may not refer to the city by that name but rather should be translated "house of God."

priestly functions remains an intriguing one. Possibly Saul's rejection at Gilgal was for attempting to violate the perquisites of another order. On the other hand, it is possible that, since Jerusalem was the seat of the Melchizedek tradition, Saul's court at Gibeah never did have any claim to a royal priesthood.

Another question that inevitably comes to mind is where, besides from an old Melchizedek tradition, did David get his concept of kingship, especially in light of other Canaanite traditions on the subject. I have not gone into this matter, not because I believe it to be unimportant or irrelevant, but rather because much of the work in this area has been done. Aelred Cody is only the latest in a series of scholars who have suggested links with Canaanite (or Egyptian or Babylonian) royal ideology, and his study merits consideration.[26] That David's priesthood has legitimate analogies with, and possibly roots in, Canaanite practice I would not deny. But I believe that the basic sense of David's royal priesthood comes from the Melchizedek concept and that this in the ongoing revelation of God picks up the thread that is so beautifully woven into the tapestry of our Lord's life and work in the letter to the Hebrews.

[26] Cody, *History*, pp. 98-107.

The Significance of the Delay of the Parousia for Early Christianity

DAVID E. AUNE

I. Introduction

The expectation of the Parousia of Jesus, in varying degrees of intensity and emphasis, permeates the literature of early Christianity.[1] The ubiquitous character of this eschatological hope underscores its structural and functional significance within the belief systems of the various phases of early Christianity. Since the influential work of Johannes Weiss and Albert Schweitzer at the turn of the century, eschatology has become widely regarded, not only as the matrix in which early Christian life and thought developed, but more significantly as an inseparable feature of the very essence of early Christianity itself. The rediscovery of eschatology has produced a series of important breakthroughs in the modern understanding of both Jesus and earliest Christianity. One important result of the concentrated study of early Christian eschatology has been the general recognition of the truth of two propositions: (1) primitive Palestinian Christianity lived and worked in the fervent expectation of the imminent return of Jesus as Son of Man in power and glory from heaven to bestow salvation and execute judgment, and (2) with the passage of time and the expansion of Christianity into the world of Roman Hellenism, the fervency of this eschatological expectation began to fade and the significance that it once held for the belief systems of early Christian communities began to lessen.[2]

---

[1] Mention of the Parousia is fortuitously missing from Gal and Phlm. The claim that it is absent from Eph has been ably refuted, in my opinion, by Markus Barth, "Die Parusie im Epheserbrief, Eph 4, 13," *Neues Testament und Geschichte,* ed. by H. Baltensweiler and B. Reicke, Zürich and Tübingen, 1972, pp. 239-50. For an excellent discussion of the term, its background and use in the NT, see A. Oepke, "parousia, pareimi," *TDNT,* 5, 858-71. All of the writings classified as Apostolic Fathers mention the Parousia hope.

[2] One rather general factor that supports the validity of this process of "de-eschatologization" is the decline of apocalyptic as a literary genre. The Shepherd of

---

David E. Aune, Chairman of the Department of Religion and Theology at St. Xavier College, Chicago, Illinois. B.A., Wheaton College; M.A., Wheaton College Graduate School; M.A., The University of Minnesota; Ph.D., The University of Chicago.

NT scholars have not failed to relate these important insights to other aspects of the early Christian belief systems and to the changes and developments these systems inevitably experienced. More specifically, it has been theorized that the problematic involved in the early Christian experience of the delay of the Parousia was the *conditio sine qua non* (i.e. the necessary condition) accounting for the radical transformation of early Christian life and thought. The major purpose of this essay, written in honor of my esteemed teacher, Dean Merrill C. Tenney, has both a positive and a negative aspect. Negatively I intend to demonstrate the weaknesses inherent in any theory that regards the delay of the Parousia as a causal factor in the theological transformation of early Christianity. Positively, I wish to make several suggestions regarding the structural and functional significance of the Parousia hope during the first century of early Christianity. Those discussions will be prefaced by a brief treatment of the major modern approaches to the role the delay of the Parousia might have played in early Christian thought.[3]

II. Interpretations of the Delay of the Parousia

With the rediscovery of eschatology, four major "schools" of thought on the subject of the significance of eschatology in the NT have arisen.[4] Since each of them deals in one way or another with the problem of the delay of the Parousia, or the larger problem of the de-eschatologization of early Christianity, each deserves consideration.

1. If, following the approach of "consistent" eschatology advocated by Johannes Weiss and Albert Schweitzer, eschatology is regarded as inseparable from the very essence of both the teaching of Jesus and the beliefs of the post-Easter community, the process of de-eschatologization presents modern scholarship with a theological problem of significant dimensions. Since Schweitzer in particular regarded the eschatological structure of early Christian thought as wholly temporal in its expectation of an imminent future consummation, the de-eschatologization of early Christianity could only be regarded as the abandonment of its original essence. Although the results of these presuppositions are theologically disastrous for modern Christianity, Schweitzer boldly applied them to the NT and early Christian literature generally. Schweitzer placed the problem of de-eschatologization at the center of all theological development throughout early Christianity, and regarded it as a key to unlocking the logic of that development:

Hermas and the Apocalypse of Peter are examples of the transformation of the apocalyptic genre.

[3] With regard to methodology, I approach the subject of this essay with the descriptive purpose of a historian, not the normative intent of a biblical theologian. This clear distinction of the roles of historical and theological methodology is properly advocated by Richard H. Hiers, "Eschatology and Methodology," *JBL,* 85 (1966), 170-84.

[4] An excellent review article on the subject is that by Otto Knoch, "Die eschatologische Frage, ihre Entwicklung und ihr gegenwärter Stand," *BZ,* new series, 6 (1962), 112-20. See also Oscar Cullmann, *Salvation in History,* trans. by S. G. Sowers, New York, 1965, pp. 28-64.

The whole history of "Christianity" down to the present day, that is to say, the real inner history of it, is based on the delay of the Parousia, the non-occurrence of the Parousia, the abandonment of eschatology, the progress and completion of the "de-eschatologising" of religion which has been connected therewith.[5]

Schweitzer suggests that the recognition of the delay of the Parousia produced a series of embarrassing crises necessitating a matching series of theological adjustments until a long-term solution to the problem of de-eschatologization was reached coincident with the complete Hellenization of early Christianity. The first crisis was experienced by Jesus himself when the prediction of his own Parousia failed to materialize; Schweitzer regarded Matt 10:23 as evidence for this first eschatological disappointment. The next crisis occurred when the death of Jesus failed to compel the arrival of the Kingdom of God, and the disciples were forced to accommodate this further delay of the Parousia to their belief system. While Schweitzer suggested the major theses for interpreting the delay of the Parousia as the *conditio sine qua non* for the radical theological transformation of early Christianity, it remained for his spiritual disciples, Martin Werner and Fritz Buri, to apply them in a vigorous and thoroughgoing way to the history of Christian theology.[6] Erich Grässer, a pupil of W. G. Kümmel, has applied Schweitzer's thesis to the Synoptic Gospels and Acts with equal vigor.[7]

2. C. H. Dodd's formulation of "realized" eschatology is primarily concerned with the mission and message of Jesus. Reacting against the completely future orientation of Jesus' teaching regarding the Kingdom of God espoused by Schweitzer and Weiss, Dodd argued that Jesus taught the essential presence of the Kingdom of God in and through his words and works. All of the imagery and conceptualizations of apocalyptic eschatology, such as predictions of the Parousia, must therefore be regarded as "re-eschatologizations" of Jesus' message, since Jesus himself had de-eschatologized the traditional eschatological framework of contemporary Judaism. In Dodd's view, the almost total absence of future eschatology from the teaching of Jesus radically differentiates him from both contemporary Judaism and major phases of earliest Christianity. The major problem with which Dodd and his followers are concerned, therefore, is not with the non-occurrence of the Parousia of Jesus, nor the general problem of the de-eschatologization of earliest Christianity, but rather with the problem of how the Parousia expectation became such an integral feature of the belief system of primitive Christianity at all.[8] At this point Dodd

---

[5] Albert Schweitzer, *The Quest of the Historical Jesus,* trans. by W. Montgomery, New York, 1961, p. 360. The original German edition appeared in 1906, and this translation has been based on it.

[6] Cf. Martin Werner, *The Formation of Christian Dogma: An Historical Study of Its Problem,* trans. by S. G. F. Brandon, New York, 1957. This book is the translation of a condensed version of the author's more extensive work, *Die Entstehung des christlichen Dogmas,* Bern-Leipzig, 1941.

[7] Erich Grässer, *Das Problem der Parusieverzögerung in den synoptischen Evangelien und in der Apostelgeschichte,* BZNW, 22, Berlin, 1960[2]. A thorough critique of this book is found in Oscar Cullmann, "Parusieverzögerung und Urchristentum: der gegenwärtige Stand der Diskussion," *TLZ,* 83 (1958), 1-12.

[8] N. A. Dahl rejects the delay of the Parousia as the principal problem of early

and his followers think they perceive two trends of thought on the subject developing in early Christianity. One trend, represented by the Synoptic Gospels, Acts, the Pauline letters and the Apocalypse of John, exemplifies the re-entry of apocalyptic eschatology into Christianity in the post-Easter period. The other trend, represented by the Fourth Gospel and the letter to the Hebrews, is thought to retain the original emphasis on realized eschatology taught by Jesus.[9]

3. For all practical purposes, Rudolf Bultmann and his students have effected a marriage between the form-critical method and the existential interpretation of the NT kerygma. While Bultmann appears to accept the futurity of the Kingdom of God in the teaching of Jesus (in continuity with Weiss and Schweitzer), in reality he stresses the existential dimensions of Jesus' eschatological message to the neglect of the temporal dimensions. In a manner reminiscent of older Protestant liberalism's attempt to remove the husk of temporal eschatology from the kernel of Jesus' moral teachings, Bultmann has removed the husk of eschatological temporality from the kernel of the existential call to decision. In the words of one of his more noted students, Hans Conzelmann,

> From the beginning, eschatology is not primarily an apocalyptic conception, but an understanding of being in faith. Hope remains prior to waiting. Once that has been understood, the delay of the parousia is not a problem for existence in faith.[10]

Since the real significance of eschatology lies not in its temporal but in its existential dimensions, the inevitable process of de-eschatologization accompanying the Hellenization of early Christianity does not necessarily result in a radical transformation of its essential character. Bultmann traces two major theological developments in the history of early Christianity, both of which have their roots in the kerygma of the primitive Palestinian community.[11] The *conditio sine qua non* for both of these developments lies in the negative factor of the non-occurrence of the Parousia against the larger background of the de-eschatologization of the kerygma. In the authentic development, the process of de-eschatologization prompted the abandonment of the temporal features of eschatology while the existential dimension was retained. This process had already begun with Paul and was

---

Christian eschatology, and in agreement with Dodd and his school finds the genesis of the Parousia hope as the real problem; "Eschatology and History in the Light of the Dead Sea Scrolls," *The Future of Our Religious Past*, ed. by J. M. Robinson, trans. by C. E. Carlston and R. P. Scharlemann, New York, 1971, p. 25, n. 52.

[9] In continuity with older Protestant liberalism, Dodd views the theological teachings of Jesus as normative for all subsequent Christian theologizing. Thus the near obliteration of realized eschatology in phases of early Christianity is viewed as an aberration from the essence of Christianity. Those followers of Dodd who have attempted to work out his insights in a more systematic way include J. A. T. Robinson, *Jesus and His Coming*, New York, 1957, and T. F. Glasson, *The Second Advent*, London, 1963³ and *His Appearing and His Kingdom*, London, 1953.

[10] Hans Conzelmann, *An Outline of the Theology of the New Testament*, trans. by John Bowden, New York, 1969, p. 308.

[11] What follows is a succinct summary of the basic theological structure of his *Theology of the New Testament*, trans. by Kendrick Grobel, 2 vols., New York, 1951-55.

carried out in a more radical way by the Fourth Evangelist. Subsequently, apart from the lonely exception of Ignatius of Antioch, the authentic Christian understanding of existence became progressively more obscured.

The other line of development, which Bultmann would certainly characterize as "inauthentic," and which many of his students designate as "early Catholicism," is also brought about by the inexorable process of de-eschatologization. Here the earliest community's awareness of itself as an eschatological community, i.e. as a non-historical phenomenon, was gradually transformed into an awareness of itself as a worldly-historical phenomenon.[12] Bultmann and many of his *Schüler* insist that primitive Palestinian Christianity was essentially non-cultic in orientation, largely because its understanding of itself as an eschatological community was diametrically opposed to sacralization in any form.[13] Thus the emerging emphasis on sacramentalism, the preservation of church tradition, the appointment of church officials and the formulation of church discipline and law—in short, the institutionalization of early Christianity—are all inauthentic adjustments to the problem of de-eschatologization. In Bultmann's words, the church was transformed from a community of the saved to an institution of salvation.[14] The theological justification for this radical reformulation of early Christianity was primarily the conceptual framework of "salvation history" (*Heilsgeschichte*), articulated in a relatively sophisticated form by the author of Luke-Acts.[15] Later research by adherents to the Bultmann school has identified more rudimentary forms of this historical-theological framework in the later strata and final redactions of each of the Synoptic Gospels.

Bultmann is somewhat critical of Werner's attempt to trace the radical transformation of Christian theology as wholly attributable to the crises caused by the non-occurrence of the Parousia, and regards this thesis as "greatly over-estimated," since it is only one factor among a number of others.[16] As a historian, Bultmann is sensitive to several qualifications that make it difficult to regard the delay of the Parousia as *the* centripetal force responsible for *all* centrifugal developments in early Christianity. He recognizes the facts (1) that disappointment over the non-occurrence of the Parousia did not take place everywhere at the same time, (2) that the Parousia was never, in the early period, expected to occur at a fixed date,

---

[12] Rudolf Bultmann, *History and Eschatology: The Presence of Eternity*, New York, 1957, pp. 35-37, 51-55.

[13] Bultmann offers a very strict definition of "cult," and is thereby able to sustain his thesis of the non-cultic orientation of primitive Christianity; *Theology of the New Testament*, 1, 121. This thesis is emphasized by Ferdinand Hahn, *The Worship of the Early Church*, trans. by D. E. Green, Philadelphia, 1973, pp. 32-52, esp. pp. 35-39, and Conzelmann, *Outline of the Theology of the New Testament*, pp. 254-56.

[14] Bultmann, *History and Eschatology*, p. 53 and *Theology of the New Testament*, 2, 113f.

[15] Bultmann, *Theology of the New Testament*, 2, 116ff. The classic work on this subject is of course Hans Conzelmann's *The Theology of St Luke*, trans. by G. Buswell, New York, 1960. Motivated by the delay of the Parousia, Luke places the period of the church before the relatively distant Parousia.

[16] Bultmann, *Theology of the New Testament*, 2, 138.

and consequently (3) that adjustment to the continuing non-occurrence of the Parousia never occurred in crises, but rather gradually.[17]

A few words of criticism are appropriate at this point. First of all, while Bultmann regards the delay of the Parousia as the *conditio sine qua non* in a negative sense for subsequent theological developments within early Christianity, the positive causes behind theological change are never articulated nor drawn into Bultmann's depiction of the progress of early Christian thought.[18] Thus despite his qualifications, the historical factor of the disappointment over the non-occurrence of the Parousia remains for Bultmann the single necessary factor determining subsequent theological developments within early Christianity.

Bultmann's lack of concern for the positive factors that produced changes in early Christianity are traceable, I believe, to the basic weakness of major sections of his *Theology of the New Testament.*[19] This basic weakness lies in the fact that the model Bultmann uses to provide coherence to the history of early Christian thought is that of the phenomenological analysis of human existence derived from Martin Heidegger. This becomes particularly clear when Bultmann speaks of the self-understanding of the church, undoubtedly based on the model of individual man's self-understanding. The reason that this existential model for conceptualizing the developments in early Christian theological thought is inappropriate for the task assigned to it is that theological development is intimately connected with the phenomenon of socio-cultural change experienced by early Christianity. All models for analyzing social systems or social change, when based on the life of an individual organism (whether viewed biologically or existentially), have proven to be overly simplistic in the face of the complex task they must perform.[20]

Thus, for Bultmann and his school to speak of the "non-cultic" life-style of the primitive Palestinian Christianity as a reflection of its self-understanding as an eschatological community is more a logical inference based on the existential model used than on the historical data that have survived. Comparative religion knows of no eschatologically-oriented religious sect that has a non- or anti-cultic attitude analogous to Bultmann's interpretation of earliest Christianity.[21] On the contrary, even inchoate sectarian developments within major religious systems are characterized by

---

[17]*Ibid.*; Bultmann, *History and Eschatology*, p. 51.

[18]These positive causes could all probably be summed up under the general rubric "Hellenization"; cf. Rudolf Bultmann, *Primitive Christianity in Its Contemporary Setting*, trans. by R. H. Fuller, New York, 1956, pp. 175ff.

[19]The large sections on the theologies of Paul and John must be excluded from the above criticism since they are treated individually and not primarily with regard to their place in the development of early Christianity.

[20]Cf. Francis R. Allen, *Socio-Cultural Dynamics: An Introduction to Social Change*, New York and London, 1971, and Walter Buckley, *Sociology and Modern Systems Theory*, Englewood Cliffs, New Jersey, 1967, pp. 7-40.

[21]Montanism is an ancient example of an eschatological Christian sect that lived in imminent expectation of the Parousia, and yet had a very fully developed cult, ethical system and mythical world view. All the examples of modern "doomsday" cults known to me do not contradict this tendency; cf. Leon Festinger, Henry W. Riecken and Stanley Schachter, *When Prophecy Fails*, Minneapolis, 1956; John Lofland, *Doomsday Cult: A Study of Conversion, Proselytization, and Maintenance*

the three constitutive features of all religions: cult, behavior and belief-myth system.[22] This viewpoint has crucial significance for the final section of this essay.

4. Oscar Cullmann and others have forcefully suggested that the historical-theological framework of salvation history is the most appropriate model for interpreting the belief system and message of the NT authors.[23] For Cullmann, the framework of salvation history is endemic to the theology of early Christianity, and indeed forms the very essence of the Christian gospel. In contrast to Bultmann, he refuses to absolutize the present secular viewpoint of "modern man," but rather (in effect) absolutizes the biblical revelation viewed in terms of salvation history.[24] For Cullmann, the appearance of Jesus in A.D. 1-30 was and remains the decisive salvation event and the center of history. At one end of this "linear" conception of time lies Creation and at the other the Parousia of Jesus. The Christ-event therefore constitutes the essential achievement of salvation. According to a vivid metaphor that he not infrequently adduces, the decisive battle has been won (through the Incarnation), though minor skirmishes remain until the inauguration of Victory Day (the future Parousia of Jesus). The Parousia, therefore, must remain an integral feature of the history of salvation. In Cullmann's words,

> . . . in spite of the delay of the *parousia*, the eschatological expectation in primitive Christianity loses none of its intensity. The only explanation for this is that the root of all New Testament eschatology lies not in the expectation in and of itself that the end is imminent, but in the tension characteristic of the New Testament's salvation history, and that this is already present in Jesus.[25]

In disagreement with Bultmann, Cullmann—together with other scholars such as W. G. Kümmel—maintains an emphasis on both the temporal and existential dimensions of the eschatological message of Jesus and earliest Christianity.[26] Both the "already" of realized eschatology and the

---

of Faith, Englewood Cliffs, New Jersey, 1966. Bultmann's theory is obviously predicated in part by a pejorative attitude toward the phenomenon of the religious cultus.

[22] Cf. the observation by Sigmund Mowinckel, *The Psalms in Israel's Worship,* New York and Nashville, 1962, 1, 15: " . . . the cult is . . . a general phenomenon appearing in all religions, even in the most 'anti-cultic' Protestant sects and groups. It is indeed an essential and constitutive feature of a religion, that in which the nature and spiritual structure of a religion is most clearly manifested."

[23] Oscar Cullmann's most important contribution to this subject is his *Salvation in History,* trans. by S. G. Sowers, New York, 1965.

[24] From the viewpoint of the sociology of knowledge, Peter Berger makes the following relevant observation: "I am not concerned for the moment with either the viability of the translation process or the empirical validity of the premise about modern man, but rather with a hidden *double standard,* which can be put quite simply: The *past,* out of which the tradition comes, is relativized in terms of this or that socio-historical analysis. The *present,* however, remains strangely immune from relativization. In other words, the New Testament writers are seen as afflicted with a false consciousness rooted in their own time, but the contemporary analyst takes the consciousness of *his* time as an unmixed intellectual blessing"; *A Rumor of Angels,* Garden City, New York, 1969, p. 51.

[25] Cullmann, *Salvation in History,* p. 38.

[26] W. G. Kümmel, *Promise and Fulfilment: The Eschatological Message of Jesus,* trans. by D. M. Barton, London, 1961[2].

"not yet" of future eschatology were already present in the teaching of Jesus in a combination of temporal and existential significance. If early Christianity (or modern Christianity, for that matter) were to depart from this salvation-historical framework, that departure would constitute an illegitimate departure from the very essence of the perennially normative theology of the NT revelation.

As a historian, Cullmann is convinced that while primitive Christianity did not expect the immediate dawn of the Kingdom of God through the Parousia of Jesus, neither did the church expect the Parousia to be delayed by several centuries. This failure of the Parousia to occur within the broad time limits set for its occurrence, however, does not bring us face-to-face with an insoluble theological problem. According to Cullmann, a series of new saving events was experienced by the church (i.e. various workings of the Spirit in the church) enabling it to extend the period of time prior to the event of the Parousia without sacrificing the ultimately temporal significance of that expectation.[27]

In brief, let us succinctly summarize each of the modern interpretations of the significance of the delay of the Parousia expectation within early Christianity: (1) The viewpoint of consistent eschatology sees Jesus' expectation of the inauguration of the Kingdom of God coincident with his own Parousia as exclusively a future occurrence. The non-occurrence of the Parousia, therefore, interpreted solely in terms of its temporal significance, resulted in a series of embarrassing crises necessitating a radical transformation of the essence of early Christianity, as it increasingly came to terms with Hellenism. (2) The realized eschatology of C. H. Dodd finds the inception or genesis of the Parousia expectation of early Christianity as exclusively a post-Easter phenomenon. The question of the delay of the Parousia, therefore, is essentially an irrelevant problem, since both its presuppositions and solutions have nothing to do with the essential nature of Christianity, which must only regard the teachings of Jesus as normative. (3) For Bultmann and his school, early Christian eschatology together with its focus in the Parousia expectation is interpreted not in a temporal, but rather in an existential sense as a call to decision. The husk of temporality is therefore separated from the kernel of abiding existential significance. The delay of the Parousia and related problems form the *conditio sine qua non* for subsequent developments within early Christian theological thought. Growing awareness of the problems connected with a temporal expectation of the end make it possible for an authentic continuation of the existential call to decision to emerge in Paul, John and Ignatius as the mythical trappings of temporal eschatology were increasingly abandoned or demythologized. An inauthentic interpretation attendant upon the de-eschatologization of early Christianity resulted in the movement toward "early catholicism" with its supportive theological framework of salvation history. (4) For Oscar Cullmann, on the other hand, salvation history belongs to the essence of the early Christian eschatological proclamation in which both temporal and existential dimensions are maintained in tension. The delay of the Parousia caused no major crisis with the early church since

---

[27]Cullmann, *Salvation in History,* p. 125.

the basis for eschatological expectation within the NT lies in the basic core of the eschatological hope, namely, that the saving event has already occurred in Christ. The Christ-event, therefore, is the centripetal force in NT theological thought, while the Parousia is a necessary but contingent datum whose primary significance lies in its implicit relationship to the occurrence of salvation coincident with Christ's first advent.

III. The Delay of the Parousia and the Transformation of Early Christianity

Those schools of thought which attribute great significance to the delay of the Parousia as a *conditio sine qua non* in the theological transformation of early Christianity generally locate this process within the context of the broader problem of the de-eschatologization of early Christianity attendant upon its Hellenization. This process is not infrequently stereotyped by adherents to these schools, as well as by a great many NT scholars who hesitate to identify themselves with any particular "school"[28] in terms of the linear development of early Christianity from the cultural-linguistic phase of primitive Palestinian Christianity to that of Hellenistic Christianity.[29] Since the time of W. Heitmüller it has not been uncommon to suggest a third cultural-linguistic phase, that of Hellenistic Jewish Christianity, as mediating between those two phases mentioned above. On the basis of this typological framework the theological transformation of early Christianity is depicted in approximately the following manner: The first generation of Aramaic-speaking Palestinian Christians lived in feverish expectation of the imminent return of Jesus as Son of Man to establish the Kingdom of God forever. Through the delay and disappointment connected with the continued non-occurrence of the Parousia, the fervor of this expectancy cooled both with Jewish Christianity because of the unsettling fact of non-occurrence, and within Hellenistic Christianity both because of the fact of the delay and because of the general foreign nature of eschatology to Hellenistic religious thought. Because of the critical significance eschatology had for primitive Christianity, de-eschatologization had a profound effect in expediting the transformation of other closely related doctrines such as Christology, ecclesiology and soteriology.[30] While not all NT scholars who regard the problem of the delay of the Parousia as a significant factor in the theological development of early Christianity will agree with all aspects of the paradigm articulated above, it

[28] I have heard it said, not without some degree of truth, that when two or three Teutonic theologians agree on any one thing, there is a *Schule* in their midst.

[29] In a very informative article, I. Howard Marshall traces the history of this periodicization of early Christianity and levels severe criticisms against its usefulness; "Palestinian and Hellenistic Christianity: Some Critical Comments," *NTS*, 19 (1973), 271-87.

[30] Reginald H. Fuller, for example, traces the distinctive christological developments of Hellenistic Jewish Christianity to the delay of the Parousia and the experience of the presence of the Spirit; *The Foundations of New Testament Christology*, New York, 1965, pp. 182-202, 244. The significance of the delay also permeates the influential book by Ferdinand Hahn, *The Titles of Jesus in Christology*, New York and Cleveland, 1969.

will nevertheless serve as a satisfactory basis for a number of critical issues I wish to raise.

1. The paradigm speaks with some confidence about the character of the eschatological expectation of the primitive Palestinian community, a phase of early Christianity about which we know little indeed, although Wilhelm Thüsing is one scholar who is convinced that the intensive expectation of the Parousia belongs to the very earliest stages of Palestinian Christianity. He suggests the following arguments in support of this contention: (1) the messianic-apocalyptic thought structure was characteristic of contemporary Judaism, (2) there is a strong future-orientation in the Logia source (Q), (3) the location of the earliest church in Jerusalem and not Galilee is based on eschatological presuppositions, (4) the Aramaic ejaculatory prayer *marana tha* ("our Lord, come!") has undoubtedly a Palestinian provenance, (5) there are references to futuristic eschatology in the Eucharistic words of Jesus, and (6) the Pauline letters contain traditions of imminent eschatological expectation stemming ultimately from Palestinian Christianity.[31] These varied arguments have a cumulative effect and tend to confirm the thesis that imminent eschatological expectation characterized the outlook of earliest Palestinian Christianity.

2. A related problem concerns the possibility of more precisely defining the somewhat vague expression "imminent expectation" (*Naherwartung*). In his discussion of the eschatological expectation of Jesus, Robert Morgenthaler carefully distinguishes "erfüllte Erwartung," "Nächsterwartung," "Naherwartung" and "Fernerwartung."[32] Erich Grässer, on the other hand, dismisses the first and fourth distinctions as foreign to the oldest strata of the Synoptic tradition and finds the distinction between "Naherwartung" and "Nächsterwartung" both academic and exegetically useless. According to Grässer (and here one senses the subtle elimination of temporality), "the greater or lesser nearness of the crisis is not the essential thing, but only the thought that it is the last hour."[33] I would suggest that "imminent expectation" is comprised of two interrelated and essentially inseparable aspects, the quantitative (the temporal aspect) and the qualitative (the existential aspect). With regard to the specificity of the qualitative aspect, NT scholars are agreed that neither Jesus nor earliest Christianity fixed specific dates for the eschatological consummation.[34] Thus at no point in the historical experience of early Christianity could the imminent expectation of the Parousia be regarded as empirically disconfirmed through its non-occurrence.[35] The reality constructions of sectarian religious movements are frequently not disconfirm-

---

[31] Wilhelm Thüsing, "Erhöhungsvorstellung und Parusierwartung in der ältesten nachösterlichen Christologie," *BZ*, new series, 12 (1968), 224f.

[32] Robert Morgenthaler, *Kommendes Reich*, Zürich, 1952.

[33] Grässer, *Das Problem der Parusieverzögerung*, p. 5.

[34] David Flusser has collected references to the specific fixing of dates for the eschaton by movements within Christianity that flourished during the late first and early second centuries in an article entitled "Salvation Present and Future," *Types of Redemption*, Studies in the History of Religions (Supplements to *Numen*), Vol. 18, ed. by R. J. Zwi Werblowsky and C. Jouco Bleeker, Leiden, 1970, pp. 53ff.

[35] It is therefore a priori improbable that a *crisis* or series of crises over the non-occurrence of the Parousia would have occurred at all. In this sense Bultmann's criticism of Werner (above, p. 91) is pertinent. It is also inappropriate, in my

able, i.e. they have formidable capacities for "rationalizing" (both consciously and unconsciously) cognitions of reality that are in apparent conflict with primary cognitions derived from their reality construction.[36]

Several scholars, most notably W. G. Kümmel, have attempted to demonstrate that Jesus' expectation of the eschaton was not immediate but rather that he envisaged a continuation of the present age for a short period after his death.[37] Such texts as Mark 9:1; 13:30, and Matt 10:23 indicate that such a period was bounded by the lifetime of those in his own generation.[38] The many attempts to interpret these and other crucial texts in other ways, in Kümmel's opinion as well as that of the present author, can only be regarded as unsuccessful.[39] I would therefore concur with Kümmel's conclusion that " . . . all these texts confirm that Jesus did indeed count on a shorter or longer period between his death and parousia, but that he equally certainly proclaimed the threatening approach of the Kingdom of God within his generation."[40]

In their analyses of the so-called Logia Source (Q), which most scholars think took shape in Palestine during the period A.D. 40 to 60, D. Lührmann and A. P. Polag find the *Parusieverzögerungsproblem* as a basic concern of the Q-redaction of Jesuanic logia.[41] If their opinion is correct, it means that early Palestinian Christianity understood the "imminent" expectation of the Parousia in such a way that its non-occurrence at this early period was already producing a cognitive crisis in their belief system.[42] According to them, this crisis is already evident in the Q-redaction of some of the Q parables: Luke 12:39-40/Matt 18:43-44; Luke 12:42-

---

opinion, to characterize the changing foci of eschatological thought as a crisis as does the church historian Carl Andresen: "Bereits die ersten Generationen hatten die Krise ihrer eschatologische Naherwartung hinnehmen und theologisch bewältigen müssen"; *Die Kirchen der alten Christenheit,* Die Religionen der Menschheit, Bd. 29, 1/2, Stuttgart, 1971, p. 28.

[36] Cf. Lofland, *Doomsday Cult,* p. 195. In an intriguing empirical study of a modern millennial movement or doomsday cult, Leon Festinger and his colleagues have shown that even in instances where a specific date has been predicted for the occurrence of a cosmic crisis, the experience of empirical disconfirmation of the expected event produces no radical changes in the belief system of the sect; *When Prophecy Fails: A Social and Psychological Study of a Modern Group That Predicted the Destruction of the World,* Minneapolis, 1956. We shall have occasion below to discuss the significance of this and other studies in analogical relationship to early Christian eschatological expectation.

[37] Kümmel, *Promise and Fulfilment,* pp. 54-87.

[38] Oscar Cullmann, "The Return of Christ," *The Early Church,* ed. by A. J. B. Higgins, abridged ed., Philadelphia, 1966, pp. 150ff. Kümmel has provided an excellent review article on the general subject entitled "Eschatological Expectation in the Proclamation of Jesus," *The Future of Our Religious Past: Essays in Honour of Rudolf Bultmann,* ed. by J. M. Robinson, trans. by C. E. Carlston and R. P. Scharlemann, New York, 1971, pp. 29-48.

[39] One such recent attempt is that of Stephen S. Smalley, "The Delay of the Parousia," *JBL,* 83 (1964), 41-54.

[40] Kümmel, *Promise and Fulfilment,* p. 87; cf. G. R. Beasley-Murray, *A Commentary on Mark Thirteen,* London, 1957, pp. 9, 99.

[41] D. Lührmann, *Die Redaktion der Logienquelle,* Neukirchen, 1969, pp. 85f., 93; A. P. Polag, "Die Christologie der Logienquelle," unpublished dissertation, Trier, 1968, p. 185.

[42] Since Lührmann uses the typology of the linear succession of cultural-linguistic phases of Christianity briefly discussed above (p. 95), he uses the sup-

46/Matt 18:45-51; Luke 19:12-27/Matt 25:14-30.[43] The general thrust of these parables is to exhort the hearers to vigilance in view of an impending crisis. Imminent eschatological expectation is an integral feature in each of these parables, and there are no signs of any lessening of the expectation as a result of awareness of the delay of the Parousia. Further, I see no justification whatsoever for regarding the theme of watchfulness or vigilance in view of an impending eschatological crisis that may occur at any time as a corollary of the problematic of the delay of the Parousia.[44]

In summary it may be said that the imminent expectation of earliest Christianity anticipated neither the immediate inauguration of the Kingdom of God momentarily, nor the delay of that consummation beyond the generation contemporaneous with Jesus. However, the lack of specificity with regard to the exact date of the Parousia made it impossible for its non-occurrence to become a critical problem at any point in the subsequent history of early Christianity. While redaction criticism has had some success in reconstructing the contours of that phase of Palestinian Christianity out of which the collection of Q logia arose, there is no indication that imminent eschatological expectation was being dampened by the supposed influence of the delay of the Parousia.[45]

3. Since the paradigm traces radical theological developments back to increasing awareness and anxiety over the delay of the Parousia, it is important that we examine those texts in early Christian literature prior to ca. A.D. 150 in which the problem apparently comes to the surface. The following list includes every reference known to me, though I cannot claim it to be exhaustive: (1) Luke 12:42-46/Matt 24:45-51, (2) 2 Pet 3:1-10, (3) Jas 5:8ff., (4) Heb 10:36-39, (5) 1 Clem 23:3, (6) 2 Clem 11-12, (7) Asc Isa 3:21-30, (8) Herm Vis 3.8.9.[46] In view of the fact that several modern reconstructions of the development of early Christian thought place such emphasis on the anxiety and disappointment caused by the delay of the Parousia, it is amazing to observe how infrequently the supposed problem comes to expression in early Christian literature.[47]

---

posed presence of *Parusieverzögerung* in Q as a major basis for suggesting the composition of Q within Hellenistic Christianity, ca. A.D. 50-60 (Lührmann, *Die Redaktion der Logienquelle*, p. 88).

[43] Lührmann, *Die Redaktion der Logienquelle*, pp. 69ff.

[44] In a stimulating chapter entitled "Die Naherwartung in der Logienquelle," Paul Hoffmann successfully argues, in my opinion, that the "Naherwartung" rather than the "Parusieverzögerung" is of central importance in the eschatology of Q, and that imminent expectation was an integral feature of the message of the "Q-group"; *Studien zur Theologie der Logienquelle*, Münster, 1972, pp. 34-50. Hoffmann presents a very convincing reconstruction of the *Sitz im Leben* of the Q tradition.

[45] The particular relevance of the Q parable found in Luke 12:42-46/Matt 18:45-51 will be discussed in some detail below.

[46] In limiting the consideration to these texts, I am rejecting the supposition not infrequently expressed (cf. Bultmann, *Theology of the New Testament*, 2, 114) that exhortations to watchfulness in view of the possible sudden occurrence of the eschatological crisis are a kind of "whistling in the dark" that reflects disappointment over the non-occurrence of the Parousia.

[47] According to L. W. Barnard, "Justin Martyr's Eschatology," *VC*, 19 (1965), 86f., "Justin has a vivid belief in the Second Advent of Christ, *yet it is remarkable how little the delay in the Parousia seems to have worried him.*"

While the limitations of space forbid the exegesis of each of these texts, several are of such importance that they deserve individual treatment, and general observations may be made regarding the others. In the parable of the Servant Entrusted with Supervision found in Luke 12:42-46/Matt 24:45-51 (located within a group of Parousia parables in Matt 24:32-25:46/Luke 12:35-59), we find the phrase "my lord delays his coming" (Luke 12:45) or "my lord is delayed" (Matt 24:48). While the early church undoubtedly understood this phrase in terms of the Parousia of Jesus, it is less clear whether the term "delay" reflects the supposed early Christian preoccupation with the non-occurrence of the Parousia.[48] In the most original form of the parable, no particular emphasis was given to the fact of the delay of the master,[49] a circumstance that put the trusted servant to a sudden test.[50] Within the context of contemporary Judaism the phrase could be understood as an oblique reference to the eschatological expectation of God's visitation.[51] There is no exegetical evidence to suggest that the mention of "delay" is anything more than a circumstantial feature of the original parable, nor to suggest that this "delay" is in any way connected with the hypothetical problem of the delay of the Parousia.[52]

One of the primary texts used to indicate an awareness within early Christianity of the problems involved in the non-occurrence of the Parousia is 2 Pet 3:4, where heretics are quoted as saying: "Where is the promise of his coming? For ever since the fathers fell asleep, all things have continued as they were from the beginning of creation." In an incisive article Charles H. Talbert demonstrates that those who deny the Parousia are Gnostics.[53] The basis for their denial, however, is not the fact of the *delay* of the

[48] Grässer, *Das Problem der Parusieverzögerung*, pp. 90ff., affirms with Lührmann and Polag that this parable presupposes an anxious awareness of the delay of the Parousia.

[49] Joachim Jeremias, *The Parables of Jesus*, trans. by S. H. Hooke, rev. ed., New York, 1963, p. 57; C. H. Dodd, *The Parables of the Kingdom*, rev. ed., New York, 1961, p. 126.

[50] Jeremias, *The Parables of Jesus*, p. 57.

[51] Glasson, *The Second Advent*, pp. 167-71 and *His Appearing and His Kingdom*, pp. 9-11; cf. A. Strobel, *Untersuchungen zum eschatologischen Verzögerungsproblem aufgrund der spätjüdisch-urchristlichen Geschichte von Habakuk*, Leiden, 1961, 2, 2ff.

[52] Joachim Jeremias, in my opinion, has concluded too uncritically that the delay of the Parousia had a primary influence in the redaction of the five "Parousia parables" (Matt 24:43-44/Luke 12:39-40; Matt 25:1-13; Mark 13:33-37/Luke 12:35-38 (cf. Matt 24:42); Matt 24:45-51/Luke 12:41-46; Matt 25:14-30/Luke 19:12-27). Originally, he thinks, these were crisis parables in which the necessity of vigilance in view of the impending catastrophe is enjoined. According to Jeremias, "it was the primitive Church which first interpreted the five parables in a christological sense and as addressed to the community, warning them not to become slack because of the delayed *Parousia*" (*The Parables of Jesus*, p. 63). I am unable to see the connection between exhortations to watchfulness for a Parousia that will occur suddenly and unexpectedly and the problem of non-occurrence of that event; both imminent expectation and enjoinders to vigilance were advocated, for example, by Paul (1 Thess 5:1ff.).

[53] C. H. Talbert, "II Peter and the Delay of the Parousia," *VC*, 20 (1966), 137-45. This is also the view of Ernst Käsemann, "An Apologia for Primitive Christian Eschatology," *Essays on New Testament Themes*, SBT, 41, Naperville, Illinois, 1964, pp. 170ff.

Parousia (an *ad hoc* argument used against the Christian community standing behind 2 Pet), but rather the typical Gnostic presuppositions of spiritualized eschatology that made it impossible for them to accept an actual, objective future Parousia expectation involving the final bestowal of salvation and judgment. Talbert concludes that 2 Pet cannot be used ". . . as evidence for the thesis that the delay of the Parousia caused a crisis of major proportions in the life and thought of early Christianity."[54]

In line with Talbert's interpretation of 2 Pet 3:4, it would appear that several of the texts listed above that are said to reflect the crisis caused by the non-occurrence of the Parousia seem rather to be directed against aberrant forms of Christianity that eliminated apocalyptic-eschatological expectations on principle. This may apply to 1 Clem 23:3,[55] 2 Clem 11-12, and Asc Isa 3:21-30. Certainly the imminent expectation of the Parousia is prominent within the immediate contexts of each of these supposed "delay" texts (1 Clem 23:5; 2 Clem 12:1, 6; Asc Isa 4:1)[56] —unless we are to assume that each author formally acquiesces to the truth of a traditional doctrine that is no longer structurally or functionally significant for his belief system.[57]

One recurring life-situation in early Christianity that provoked periodic intensifications of the expectation of the Parousia was the experience of sporadic persecution,[58] a fact that makes hypotheses of the gradual and linear decline of the Parousia hope problematic. In these situations, one not infrequently finds exhortations to patience and endurance, not because of an awareness of the continuing delay of the Parousia, but rather because the occurrence of the Parousia will bring an end to suffering.[59] Of the several "delay" texts we have listed, this would apply to Heb 10:36-39 and Herm Vis 3.8.9. The experience of poverty and oppression of those to whom the letter of James was addressed makes it probable that Jas 5:8ff. should also be viewed against this general background.

In summary, it must be observed that even if all of these texts are viewed as direct expressions of the anxiety caused by the delay of the Parousia, the infrequency with which the problem comes to the surface may be taken to indicate how generally unimportant the matter actually was. If our suggestions regarding the ways in which many of these texts ought to be interpreted are accepted, the theory that the problem of the delay of the Parousia was either critical (Schweitzer, Werner, Grässer) or gradual (Bultmann, Conzelmann) in early Christian thought appears to be

---

[54] Talbert, "II Peter," p. 145.

[55] *Ibid.*, p. 144.

[56] Asc Isa 4:14 fixes a more precise date for the Parousia, which is set (somewhat ambiguously) at 1,332 days.

[57] This is essentially the position of Käsemann regarding 2 Pet ("An Apologia for Primitive Christian Eschatology," pp. 183ff.).

[58] Cf. B. H. Streeter, *The Four Gospels*, London, 1924, p. 475; W. D. Niven, "After Fifty Years: VI. 'Eschatology and the Primitive Church,' " *ExpT*, 50 (1938-39), 330; Bultmann, *Theology of the New Testament*, 2, 114.

[59] With this statement we begin to see important aspects of the functional role of the Parousia expectation within early Christianity. Other important features of the structural position of the Parousia together with its functional significance will be dealt with in the final section of this essay.

even less viable. The possibility arises that the "problem" might have been latent rather than manifest; in this case the hands of the historian are tied, for he has neither the tools nor the inclination to psychoanalyze early Christianity.

4. A final problem emerging from the paradigm, and one that I regard as the most significant of all, lies in the fact that there is no demonstrable causal relationship between the oscillating functional significance of the Parousia expectation on the one hand, and various changes and developments in early Christian life and thought on the other.

In a provocative article entitled "Salvation Present and Future," David Flusser has examined the thesis with which we are dealing in this essay, namely, that the non-occurrence of a predicted eschatological event would produce profound changes in the message and structure of early Christianity.[60] Since crises over the non-occurrence of predicted eschatological events are almost inevitable in the case of sects that precisely fix the date for such occurrences, Flusser limits his study to several sectarian movements within late first- and early second-century Christianity as well as to several millennial movements of modern times. Even though a fixed date of redemption was the focal point of the movements Flusser discusses, the crisis of the non-occurrence of their predictions generally fails to spell the end of the movement, or to alter (in any essential way) either the eschatological tension or the original meaning of their religious message. [61] Flusser concludes that

... even if a religious movement originates in acute eschatological expectation, its structure does not fundamentally change if this expectation is not fulfilled. If a religious movement is based upon eschatological expectation but had also a strong faith in the present, past or extra-historical salvation, the weakening of acute eschatological expectation can find its more or less complete substitute in strengthening of the idea of present salvation of its members. But this does not mean that this theological feature came into existence only in the stage of weakening eschatological tension. It is an organic part of the religious group from its very origins.[62]

The significance of Flusser's conclusions is that they indicate that even among religious groups for whom eschatological deliverance is constitutive, the crisis over the non-occurrence of the expected event does not appear to be a major factor in the subsequent developments and changes in the belief systems of these groups. If that is true for sects that fix a specific eschatological chronology, how much more is it true for movements (such as early Christian communities) that resist fixing specific dates for the impending eschatological crisis and thus never find themselves confronted with the empirically undeniable fact of disconfirmation. If this argument from analogies drawn from comparative religions is valid, it strongly militates against the theory that the delay of the Parousia is the *conditio sine qua non* for the radical reformulation of the life and thought of early Christianity.

Another major difficulty with the hypothesis that the problem of the

[60] Flusser, "Salvation Present and Future," pp. 46-61.
[61] *Ibid.*, p. 59.
[62] *Ibid.*, p. 61.

delay of the Parousia, or the broader problem of de-eschatologization, was a major causal factor in the development of early Christian theology is the simplistic notion of socio-cultural change that such a theory presupposes. [63] Indeed, since the progress of thought, whether viewed in terms of intellectual history, belief systems or reality constructions, is intimately (even dialectically) related to the phenomenon of socio-cultural change, I seriously doubt whether developments within a particular belief system may be accounted for apart from the socio-historical context in which such change occurs.[64] In view of the paucity of appropriate empirical data from the early years of Christianity, the present author is highly doubtful of the success of attempts to comprehensively account for the phenomenon of theological change within that period. The dynamics of socio-cultural change are sufficiently complex that the isolation of one cognitive factor from many as the *sine qua non* for the phenomenon of change is inherently improbable.[65] We are therefore presented with two possibilities: (1) either the general de-eschatologization of early Christianity or the specific problem of the delay of the Parousia is to be viewed as either a primary or integral factor productive of theological change, or (2) the centripetal force that produced theological development within early Christianity lies elsewhere and the volatile expectation of the Parousia of Jesus is but one centrifugal result among others of the exertion of these socio-cultural forces. The latter position is far more probable than the former.

In summary, let us briefly recapitulate each of the four points made in this section: (1) While evidence of the precise nature and character of the Parousia expectation of earliest Palestinian Christianity is very scanty indeed, it may be said that the imminent (as opposed to immediate) expectation of the Parousia of Jesus and the coincident dawn of the Kingdom of God occupied a structurally significant position within the belief system. Awareness of the delay of the Parousia has in no demonstrable way muted, altered or transformed imminent eschatological expectation. (2) The "imminent" expectation of early Christianity must be generally defined in such a way that the Parousia was expected either immediately (at any moment), or in the distant future. Because the precise date of the consummation was never fixed, no crisis could occur since the empirical disconfirmation of the Parousia expectation was thereby made

---

[63] Following the definition of Kroeber and Parsons, I would define "social" as "the specifically relational system of interaction among individuals and collectivities," and "cultural" as the "transmitted and created content patterns of values, ideas, and other symbolic-meaning systems as factors in the shaping of human behavior and the artifacts produced through behavior", quoted in Francis R. Allen, *Socio-Cultural Dynamics: An Introduction to Social Change,* New York and London, 1971, p. 40.

[64] See Robert K. Merton, *Social Theory and Social Structure,* rev. ed., Glencoe, Illinois, 1957, pp. 439-88; Peter L. Berger and Thomas Luckmann, *The Social Construction of Reality: A Treatise in the Sociology of Knowledge,* Garden City, New York, 1966.

[65] Allen, *Socio-Cultural Dynamics,* pp. 66f.: "A fundamental proposition is, at any rate, that no one explanation has been found adequate for the panoramic range of socio-cultural change. . . . One-factor explanations tend to oversimplify (if they do not do gross violence to the empirical data of situations)."

impossible. Even in instances when specific dates for the Parousia were fixed, beginning with the late first century, the non-occurrence crises that inevitably came did not result in any observable transformation of the constituent structural elements of the particular belief system involved. (3) Of the specific texts that are often adduced in support of the theory that the delay of the Parousia was a critical problem within early Christianity, some reinforce the "orthodox" view of imminence over against the "heretical" denials, denials that stem from Gnostic presuppositions of spiritualized eschatology. Yet other texts enjoin patience and endurance in situations of persecution in view of the imminent Parousia since that event will bring an end to persecution and suffering. The very paucity of references to a supposed delay of the eschaton is indicative of the fact that the delay of the Parousia was largely a non-problem within early Christianity. (4) Finally, there is no compelling evidence to suggest a causal relationship of even the most casual nature between the supposed perception of the delay of the Parousia and the radical reformulation of other doctrinal elements of the belief systems of early Christian communities. On the contrary, the increased knowledge of the complexities involved in the process of socio-cultural change militates against the isolation of one factor as a *conditio sine qua non* in the transformation of early Christian religious thought.

We have therefore returned to the place from which we started, namely, the generally held validity of two propositions: (1) earliest Christianity lived in fervent expectation of the imminent return of Jesus, and (2) this fervency was subject to considerable oscillation, and with the passage of time and the expansion of Christianity into the world of Roman Hellenism the structural significance of the earlier Parousia expectation began to lessen. It is now important for us to turn our attention to the functional significance that the expectation of the Parousia of Jesus had in early Christian belief systems, having laid to rest the problem of its supposed delay.

IV. The Function of the Parousia in Early Christianity

The central religious concern of early Christianity, in all of its variety and phases, was salvation or deliverance, a characteristic of religion in general.[66] This basic concern for salvation which is so characteristic of man's religious quest undoubtedly proceeds from an individual and social self-awareness in terms of incompleteness or "fallenness." Perceptions of salvation or deliverance are normally conceptualized in terms closely corresponding to the particular modes of incompleteness of which man is aware. Thus "salvation" is conceptualized by such ideas as wholeness, completeness, perfection, health, strength, vigor, welfare, well-being and bliss in one or another religious system.[67] The experiences of life generally contradict (to varying degrees) the full or permanent realization of this salvific ideal,

[66]G. van der Leeuw, *Religion in Essence and Manifestation*, trans. by J. E. Turner and H. H. Penner, New York and Evanston, 1963, 2, 681f.
[67]*Ibid.*, 1, 101.

making it necessary for religion to direct man away from life to, in the words of van der Leeuw, the "Other."[68]

Eschatology within late Judaism and early Christianity is integral to the belief systems of both religions in that it envisions the full, future implementation of salvation (i.e. the restoration of man to his pre-Fall perfection and bliss). A more common perception of man in an ideal state of completeness and perfection found in countless religions focuses on the present re-creation or re-actualization of the ideal conditions of the mythical past within the context of religious ritual.[69] Protological conditions are the source of salvation for religions with a mythical orientation, while eschatological conditions are the focus of the salvific expectations of Judaism and Christianity, both of which have a historical orientation. No religion, however, is content to leave salvation in the distant mythical past or in the distant historical future. Rather by various modalities, but primarily that of religious ritual, the idealized conditions of the past are "re-presented" or the idealized conditions of the future are "pre-presented" in the cult. Thus the primordial victory of Marduk over Tiamat was re-presented in the annual Babylonian Akitu festival much as the Exodus was re-presented and experienced anew in a realistic way by later Israel in the dramatic ritual of the Passover celebration. Similarly the Gnostic sacrament of mystical marriage functions as a pre-presentation of the future union of the Gnostic with his angelic counterpart in the heavenly Pleroma. It is of crucial importance to realize that the particular mode in which the ideal salvific conditions of either the past or future are conceptualized is precisely that mode which determined the cultic or ritualistic appropriation of salvation.

The significance of the Parousia expectation of earliest Palestinian Christianity lay primarily in the fact that it stood for the full bestowal of salvation upon the Christian community, and as such it was a functional equivalent of the eschatological expectation of the visitation of God anticipated by such first-century Jewish groups as the Qumran Community. For early Christians the full enjoyment of salvation was to a large measure identical with the experience of the presence of God. Thus the expected Parousia of Jesus was looked upon as the occasion upon which the full benefits of salvation would be attained in combination with the everlasting experience of God's presence, whether on a renovated earth or in heaven. The visitation of God in Judaism, as the Parousia of Jesus in early Christianity, was conceptualized as a public event in which salvation would be dispensed to the righteous and judgment to the wicked.

The purpose of the foregoing remarks has been twofold: (1) to suggest that salvation in its full dimensions lies outside the grasp of man in either the mythical past or the historical future, but that (2) the central purpose of the religious cult is to partially actualize the experience and benefits of "salvation" either through re-presentation of the salvific past or pre-presen-

---

[68] *Ibid.*, 1, 206.

[69] On this religious phenomenon, see Mircea Eliade, *Cosmos and History: The Myth of the Eternal Return*, trans. by W. R. Trask, New York, 1959; S. G. F. Brandon, *History, Time and Deity: A History and Comparative Study of the Conception of Time in Religious Thought and Practise*, Manchester, 1965.

tation of the salvific future.[70] Applying this insight from religious phenom-
enology to early Christianity we are led to the a priori hypothesis, subject
to the necessity of verification through exegesis, that the Parousia, viewed
as a primary way in which the future implementation of Christian salvation
would be achieved, would have a decisive effect on the way in which
salvation was experienced and appropriated in the cultic ritual of earliest
Christianity.[71] If this in fact was the case,[72] then *at no time was the
experience of salvation placed wholly in the future within the belief system
of earliest Christianity*. The experience of the presence of the Spirit (i.e. the
presence of God) within the collective and individual experience of the
earliest community carries with it the unavoidable implication that the
benefits of salvation, in at least some of their dimensions, were part of the
present experience of early Christians. The present experience of salvation,
therefore, stands in tension with the future and complete realization of it in
greatly varying proportions. It is probable, for example, that the earliest
Palestinian Christians gave greater emphasis to the future experience of
salvation, expressed through their hope of an imminent Parousia, than they
did to its present realization.[73] On the other hand, it is clear that the
Johannine community placed a greater emphasis on the present experience
of salvation than they did on its future consummation.[74] Thus it is
theoretically probable that these two foci of early Christian belief systems
stand in a relationship of dynamic equilibrium, i.e. greater emphasis on the
present results in a lessened emphasis on the future, and the contrary. To
suggest that either the present experience of salvation or the expectation of
its full realization in the future could become merely a formal, non-func-
tional[75] doctrine maintained solely for the sake of its venerable pedigree
would be an inaccurate analysis of the structures of early Christian belief

[70] Not infrequently NT scholars have suggested that, in contrast to Christianity,
the salvific hope of contemporary Judaism was wholly directed to the future. At
the other end of the spectrum, it is proposed, the various Gnostic movements are
viewed as religious movements that wholly locate the attainment of "salvation" in
the present. Elsewhere I have sought to demonstrate that this stereotyped charac-
terization does not agree with what we know of either religious movement; cf.
David E. Aune, *The Cultic Setting of Realized Eschatology in Early Christianity*,
NovT Sup, 28, Leiden, 1972, pp. 6ff., 29-44 (on the Qumran Community),
195-219 (on Marcion of Sinope).

[71] This is the reason that I attempted, however briefly, to question Bultmann's
supposition that the earliest Palestinian community was "non-cultic" (above, pp.
92ff.).

[72] This is the central thesis of my monograph, *The Cultic Setting of Realized
Eschatology in Early Christianity*, esp. pp. 1-28.

[73] Cf. Flusser, "Salvation Present and Future," pp. 60f.

[74] Aune, *The Cultic Setting*, pp. 45-135.

[75] For the purposes of this kind of analysis, I accept the definition of religion
viewed functionally by Milton Yinger: "Religion, then, can be defined as a system
of beliefs and practices by means of which a group of people struggles with these
ultimate problems of human life. . . . The quality of being religious, then, from the
individual point of view, implies two things: first, a belief that evil, pain, bewilder-
ment, and injustice are fundamental facts of existence; and, second, a set of
practices and related sanctified beliefs that express a conviction that man can
ultimately be saved from those facts"; *The Scientific Study of Religion*, New York,
1970, p. 7.

systems. On the basis of these rather lengthy introductory remarks, I would now like to suggest several functional aspects of the expectation of the Parousia and the effects of that expectation on the religious experience of the early Christians.

1. The Parousia of Jesus had a bivalent function within early Christianity: salvation and judgment. On the basis of our remarks indicating that one of the major functions of the religious cult is to actualize either (or both) the past or future in the present, one could antecedently expect to find the metaphorical use of Parousia imagery applied in a multiplicity of ways to the corporate and individual experience of Christians as well as to the theological articulation of that experience. I hasten to add that under no circumstances does the figurative use of concepts drawn from the Parousia expectation imply either the diminution or the extinction of that future hope. Indeed the very validity of the application of Parousia language to present religious experience lies in the actuality of that expectation. I would like at this point to suggest several examples of the application of Parousia imagery to present religious experience: (1) The resurrection, though a collective event, is the indispensable factor necessary for the individual's full enjoyment of salvation in the thought of both late Judaism and early Christianity. The final resurrection is, of course, intimately connected with the Parousia of Jesus. Despite the futurity of this salvific event, it is metaphorically applied to the present experience of Christians, both collectively and individually, by Paul (Rom 6-8; Col 3:1-3), by the author of Ephesians (Eph 2:1-10) and by the Gnostics (2 Tim 2:18; Epistle to Rheginos). (2) The language that describes the gathering of the elect from the four winds in the Parousia expectation (Did 10:5) is applied to the gatherings of Christians for purposes of worship in Heb 12:18-24 and Did 9:4. (3) The angelic host that accompanies Christ upon his return is also regarded as present in the midst of the worshipping Christian community according to 1 Cor 11:10; Heb 12:22; 13:2; Col 2:18; Herm Sim 9.27.2. (4) The final cosmic victory of Christ, at which time all creation will submit to his Lordship (Phil 2:5-11), is also anticipated by the confession of Jesus' Lordship within the context of worship (1 Cor 12:3). (5) The verb "come" is an important feature of the Parousia expectation that is used figuratively for the coming of the Paraclete in John 14:18-24, and the "coming" of Jesus to judge unfaithful churches in Rev 2:5, 16 (the literal Parousia cannot be meant in these passages).[76] (6) Judgment is an indispensable feature of the Parousia expectation, and this conception is also drawn into the orbit of Christian worship in terms of unworthy participation in the Lord's Supper (1 Cor 11:27-32), the pronouncement of judgment "in the name of the Lord Jesus" in the case of an immoral Christian (1 Cor 5:2-5), and for the purpose of keeping the community generally pure (1 Cor 5:12-6:6; 11:31f.).[77] While these examples are only suggestive, and in no way exhaustive, they do indicate that the expectation

---

[76] This has been pointed out in an excellent article by G. R. Beasley-Murray, "The Relation of the Fourth Gospel to the Apocalypse," *EvQ*, 18 (1946), 173-86.

[77] See Calvin J. Roetzel, *Judgment in the Community: A Study of the Relationship between Eschatology and Ecclesiology in Paul*, Leiden, 1972.

of the future Parousia was functionally drawn into the present experience of early Christians.

2. It is common knowledge that many of the writings of early Christians that most emphatically deal with the imminent expectation of the Parousia in the full dress of apocalyptic conceptions were composed in the midst of the experience of sporadic or general persecutions. The Gospel of Mark, with its apocalyptic expectation emphasized in Mark 13, is generally regarded as having been written in Rome during the Neronian persecutions. An analogous life-situation is the background of Rev, 1 Thess, 1 Pet and the Shepherd of Hermas, to name only a few. In such situations of stress, both the salvific and juridical aspects of the Parousia take on greater significance and importance than they might during periods of relative peace and tranquility. While Paul, for example, is able to view the Parousia hope almost exclusively in terms of its salvific function in one context (1 Thess 4:13-18), he can also articulate the expectation of the Parousia almost exclusively in terms of its juridical function (2 Thess 1:5-10). This juridical view of the Parousia was important in situations wherein Christians were experiencing the hostility of their pagan neighbors or of the state, since it assured them that those who caused their suffering would in turn experience suffering and punishment at the hands of the coming Judge.[78] Both the expectation of deliverance from untoward present circumstances (Heb 10:32-39; Jas 5:8-10; Rom 8:18-25; 1 Pet 4:12-13; Rev 2:13, 17) and the comfort that the justice of God would be visited upon the persecutors (1 Thess 1:6) are important functions of the Parousia hope of early Christians within the context of situations of stress. Thus the periodic intensification of the apocalyptic hope of early Christians cannot profitably be viewed apart from the socio-cultural situation within which it occurred.

3. The popularity of the apocalyptic genre of literature and pattern of writing was borrowed from Judaism by early Christians. The distinctively Christian view of the Parousia of Jesus was completely and easily integrated into the eschatological framework of apocalyptic. Christian apocalyptic, with its focus on the glorious return of Jesus, was primarily directed toward the community's collective experience of salvation at the close of history (an identical orientation of Jewish apocalyptic). This reflects the basic anthropology that the earliest Christians derived from Judaism, namely, the conception of man-in-community.[79] On the other hand, within Hellenistic religious thought (after the decline of the city-state coincident with the rise of "individualism") the conception of a collective experience of salvation that would occur at some future point in time had absolutely no place. While it would be a falsification of the evidence to suggest that individual-

---

[78] Donald Riddle looks upon this apocalyptic emphasis as a form of social control in that the assurance that God would punish the oppressors of the Christians made it unnecessary for them to consider taking up arms to avenge themselves; *The Martyrs: A Study in Social Control*, Chicago, 1931.

[79] On this subject see R. P. Shedd, *Man in Community: A Study of St Paul's Application of Old Testament and Early Jewish Conceptions of Human Solidarity*, London, 1958. (Russell Shedd is a contributor to this *Festschrift* [Ed.]).

ism was exclusively Hellenistic while the communal emphasis was exclusively Jewish (since Hellenism had penetrated Judaism beginning with Alexander's conquest of Palestine), nevertheless these two typologies of man-in-himself and man-in-community, and various combinations of the two, are helpful for analyzing the structure of early Christian religious thought, though necessarily divested of their supposed cultural loci.

Along lines more conducive to Hellenistic religious thought, early Christianity began to think in terms of a more complete experience of salvation that would occur subsequent to the death of individual believers. While it would be inaccurate to suppose that the individual acquisition of immortality upon death was foreign to late Judaism, it cannot be disputed that such a conception was more fully a part of the reality construction of the world of Roman Hellenism. Within the NT itself there are signs of an oscillation between individual immortality upon death and collective reception of salvific blessings at the appearance of Jesus. Thus the Christian community at Thessalonica, to whom Paul addressed 1 Thess, had been re-socialized to expect the imminent Parousia at which time all Christians would enter into the fullness of salvation. Their doubts regarding believers who had died before the eschaton were probably caused by an inchoate attitude toward personal death and immortality. In general it may be observed that the NT is ambiguous regarding individual eschatology, and it was precisely this ambiguity which needed theological clarification as Christianity matured in a world that had definite views on the subject. We should not turn to another phase of the subject without noting that Parousia language is occasionally used to describe the death of such martyrs as Stephen (Acts 7:55f.) and James the Just (as described by Hegesippus in Eusebius, *Eccl Hist* 2.23.13), a fact that seems to suggest the conflation of the conception of individual immortality with the collective experience of salvation at the Parousia.

Since the attempt was generally made to re-socialize Hellenistic converts to the Christian reality construction (a construction that continued to perpetuate a strong Judaic orientation), the Hellenistic interest and concern with personal immortality upon death became gradually integrated with the collective interest in the Parousia as full implementation of salvation. It is therefore true that early Christianity never lost its eschatological orientation. While the personal immortality acquired upon death was generally viewed as a more complete acquisition of salvation than that which could be experienced in life, nevertheless the expectation of the Parousia with the coincident resurrection of the dead continued to be regarded as the necessary event that would enable man to enjoy the benefits of salvation to the fullest extent possible.

The experience of salvation as conveyed by the doctrine of the immortality of the soul upon personal death became, therefore, a functional substitute for the experience of salvation that was expected to occur upon the event of the Parousia of Jesus. The decline of apocalyptic and the rise in popularity of the martyrology is one important literary indication of this transposition of functions.[80]

[80] D. W. Riddle, "From Apocalypse to Martyrology," *ATR*, 9 (1927), 260-80.

In summary, I have suggested in this section of the essay that early Christianity had a primary interest in religious salvation, which it conceptualized in a number of ways. The primary way of conceptualizing the full realization of man's divinely intended but hitherto frustrated potential was through the imminent expectation of the Parousia of Jesus. However, earliest Christianity could not but draw this future reality into the present in the experience of the community at worship and in the individual who participated in that worship. The remarkably varied use of Parousia imagery underlines the salvific and existential significance which that future event had. At various times, and usually under situations of stress, more intensive emphasis was placed on the Parousia expectation, which functioned in such a way that Christians were able to persevere and find meaning in the most extreme conditions. Finally, the gradual diminution of the Parousia expectation may be attributed to the fact that it was functionally replaced within the belief systems of early Christian communities.

V. Summary

The purpose of the foregoing article has been to question the theory that the awareness of the delay of the Parousia in early Christianity was a necessary factor in the radical reformulation of early Christian life and thought. We found no evidence to suggest that the so-called problem of the delay of the Parousia was in fact perceived as a problem by early Christians. Turning our attention to the functional significance that the Parousia had within the belief system of early Christians, we found it to be an important source of language that was used to describe salvation as at least partially present within collective and individual experience. It was further suggested that at various times and places when the Parousia hope was intensified, the reasons for this arose out of the socio-historical situation. The gradual diminution of emphasis on the Parousia may be ascribed to the fact that it was functionally replaced by the conception of personal immortality upon death. Nevertheless, regardless of an oscillation of emphasis and intensity of the expectation of the Parousia, it remained for early Christianity an indispensable event whereby the complete possession of the benefits of salvation could be realized by the believer and the community.

A Note on Colossians 1:27a

W. PAUL BOWERS

I

The intent of this note is to sketch out for consideration a possible alternative to the usual rendering of Col 1:27a. The context, Col 1:24-29, bears particular interest in discussion of Paul's vocational consciousness, a discussion which, however, is hampered by exegetical uncertainties throughout the passage. In the process of a not altogether lucid accumulation of clauses, one reads of Paul's task to fulfill the word of God, the mystery long hidden but now disclosed "to his saints." Attached to the mention of "his saints" is the relative clause that is the subject of this note:

... τοῖς ἁγίοις αὐτοῦ, οἷς ἠθέλησεν ὁ θεὸς γνωρίσαι τί τὸ πλοῦτος τῆς δόξης τοῦ μυστηρίου τούτου ἐν τοῖς ἔθνεσιν—

which normally is taken to read:

... to his saints, to whom God willed to make known how rich the splendor of this mystery among the Gentiles.

I wish to suggest for consideration that the initial relative, *hois,* be taken as an accusative, attracted to the dative of its antecedent *tois hagiois,* functioning as the subject of the infinitive *gnōrisai.* The resultant rendering would be:

... to his saints, whom God willed to make known how rich the splendor of this mystery among the Gentiles,

in the sense: God willed that they, his saints, make this known among the Gentiles.

II

Distaste for pressing obscure grammatical possibilities into exegetical service is appropriate, especially where a perfectly natural reading is avail-

W. **Paul Bowers,** Igbaja Theological Seminary, Igbaja, Nigeria. B.A., Columbia Bible College; M.A., Wheaton College Graduate School; B.D., Trinity Evangelical Divinity School; Ph.D. candidate, University of Cambridge, Cambridge, England.

able. But is such a reading here available? Though it initially appears natural enough to take the *hois* as an indirect object, "to whom," this produces odd complexity if not ambiguity when the connection of thought is pursued to the end of the clause. One instinctively expects the concluding *en tois ethnesin* to represent, as elsewhere in the Pauline corpus,[1] the disclosure's audience. But the initial *hois* taken as the indirect object firmly relegates the *en tois ethnesin* to some unclear qualifying function. Is the point of *en tois ethnesin* that the saints in view are among the Gentiles? Or is it that the divulgence is intended to take place in a Gentile setting? Is it a Gentile-sited mystery which is indicated? Is it the mystery's splendor that the Gentile context serves to focus? The sense is by no means immediately apparent.[2]

It is not here necessary for our purposes to offer a critique of such solutions to the problem of Col 1:27a, much less to imply the inadequacy of any. It is enough to indicate the difficulty in the text and thereby to account for the wish to test grammatical possibilities for alternate renderings.

III

Thelō frequently takes an infinitive and object, as would be the case in the usual reading of Col 1:27a (e.g. Phlm 14: *ouden ethelēsa poiēsai*). If, however, the desire is for activity by a subject other than the wisher, *thelō* may be accompanied by (1) the aorist subjunctive (e.g. Mark 10:51: *ti soi theleis poiēsō*, or by (2) *hina* (e.g. Mark 9:30: *ouk ethelen hina tis gnoi*), or by (3) an accusative with the infinitive (e.g. Mark 7:24: *oudena ethelen gnōnai*). This last arrangement is common enough in the Pauline literature.[3] There would be nothing syntactically remarkable in Col 1:27a if it read: οὓς ἠθέλησεν ὁ θεὸς γνωρίσαι τί . . . ἐν τοῖς ἔθνεσιν. This structure may be compared with Acts 16:3: τοῦτον ἠθέλησεν ὁ Παῦλος σὺν αὐτῷ ἐξελθεῖν.[4]

The attraction of an accusative relative to the case of its antecedent as here proposed is a common phenomenon. One might of course question whether, about to express the clause *hous ethelēsen ho theos gnōrisai ti . . .*, with *tois hagiois* as the relative's intended antecedent, a writer would have acquiesced in the attraction of the relative to *hois*. The resulting formulation is indeed not only ambiguous but misleading, as—this rendering for the moment granted—the history of exegesis illustrates. Would a writer have let pass an attraction bearing such deceptive possibilities? The objection of course merits attention. One can only point out that in Paul one does not observe habitual concessions to clarity: witness the clause as it

---

[1] E.g. Gal 1:16; 2:2; 1 Tim 3:16; cf. Rom 1:5, 13; 15:9.

[2] Other solutions might be to take the *en* as indicating (1) instrument (or example): by the Gentile experience God wishes to unveil the richness of his mysterious plan to his saints; or possibly as indicating (2) advantage: God wished to disclose it to his saints for the Gentiles.

[3] E.g. Rom 1:13; 11:25; 16:19; 1 Cor 7:7, 32; 10:20; 11:3; 12:1; 14:5; 2 Cor 1:8; Gal 6:13; Phil 1:12; Col 2:1; 1 Thess 4:13; 1 Tim 2:4, 8; 5:14; Tit 3:8.

[4] Cf. Ep Jer 45; Luke 19:14; John 21:22; 2 Pet 3:9; 1 Clem 8:5; 36:2.

stands—not to mention the whole paragraph. In any case the alternative proposed does fall within the range of grammatical possibilities.

IV

The effects of this rendering would be that (1) *gnōrisai* becomes not a revelatory action in elaboration of the mystery's disclosure just mentioned in Col 1:26b, but rather a proclamatory action in sequence to it;[5] (2) *hoi hagioi* are the agents rather than recipients of that *gnōrismos;* and (3) *en tois ethnesin* indicates the audience of the *gnōrismos*. Not the mystery's divulgence to his saints but its diffusion by them among the Gentiles is the divine intent specified. Such a shift of meaning in the clause offers several potentially significant implications.

If Col 1:27a does indeed speak of a proclamation to the nations rather than revelation to saints, then an unusual accord opens up between Col 1:26-27 and the doxology of Rom 16:25-27. Scholars have long been aware of the community of thought shared among such passages as Eph 3:1-13, Col 1:24-29 and Rom 16:25-27.[6] But so long as the *gnōrisai* of Col 1:27a denotes a revelation to saints, any extended parallel of the Colossian context with the pattern of the Roman doxology is ruled out. If, however, by means of the reading proposed, it is possible instead to see at Col 1:27a a proclamation to the Gentiles, then a tripartite pattern emerges for Col 1:26-27 of a mystery hidden, revealed, *and* proclaimed, precisely corresponding to the pattern in Rom 16:25-26. The texts in parallel appear thus:

Col 1:26-27	Rom 16:25-26
τὸ μυστήριον	. . . μυστηρίου
τὸ ἀποκεκρυμμένον ἀπὸ τῶν αἰώνων καὶ ἀπὸ τῶν γενεῶν—	χρόνοις αἰωνίοις σεσιγημένου
νῦν δὲ ἐφανερώθη (τοῖς ἁγίοις αὐτοῦ, οἷς)	φανερωθέντος δὲ νῦν (διά τε γραφῶν προφητικῶν) κατ᾽ ἐπιταγὴν τοῦ αἰωνίου θεοῦ
ἠθέλησεν ὁ θεὸς γνωρίσαι (τί τὸ πλοῦτος τῆς δόξης τοῦ μυστηρίου τούτου) ἐν τοῖς ἔθνεσιν	(εἰς ὑπακοὴν πίστεως) εἰς πάντα τὰ ἔθνη γνωρισθέντος

The conceptual, structural, and even linguistic concurrences permitted these two sequences by the proposed rendering are remarkable, and suggest further questions in the study of the pre-histories of these two literary units.

Another accord, of an entirely different nature, is also made possible for Col 1:27 by the shift of meaning suggested. Given the usual exegesis of

---

[5] The verb *gnōrizō* is as appropriate for describing the mystery's dissemination as its disclosure; cf. Eph 3:3, 5 with 6:19 (so also *phaneroō* in Col 1:26 with 4:4) and Luke 2:15 with 2:17. Cf. also Rom 16:26; 1 Cor 15:1; Eph 3:10; 2 Pet 1:16.

[6] Also 1 Cor 2:6-10; 2 Tim 1:9-11; Tit 1:2-3; cf. 2 Cor 3:12-4:6; 1 Tim 3:16.

the Colossian clause, Isa 66:19b provides only a meager linguistic parallel and no conceptual similarity. But if it is a proclamation and one directed specifically toward the nations in view in Colossians, then the measure of conceptual accord with Isa 66:19, attended by the linguistic parallels, becomes sufficient to hint at conscious allusion:

Col 1:27a	Isa 66:19b
οἷς ἠθέλησεν ὁ θεὸς γνωρίσαι τί τὸ πλοῦτος τῆς δόξης τοῦ μυστηρίου τούτου ἐν τοῖς ἔθνεσιν	καὶ ἀναγγελοῦσίν μου τὴν δόξαν ἐν τοῖς ἔθνεσιν

The possibility of allusion is especially raised in that the setting of the Isaianic clause would seem to be one of the very few places in the OT where one might recognize human agents employed in pursuing a divinely superintended eschatological mission to the Gentiles:

> I am coming to gather all nations and tongues, and they shall come and shall see my glory; and I will set a sign among them. And from them I will send survivors to the nations, . . . and they shall declare my glory among the nations (Isa 66:18-19).

If the suggested reading of Col 1:27a should prove reasonable and thereby the allusion to Isa 66:19 become perceivable, one may be provided with perhaps the most direct Pauline identification of the current mission with an OT eschatological missionary outreach to Gentiles.

But if the proposal is possible, then an even more significant implication for Pauline mission thought develops—namely, that the divinely intended agency for the Gentile mission is *hoi hagioi*. It is a puzzle of some moment that a Paul so preoccupied with Gentile mission nowhere specifies a common Christian responsibility in that mission. There are hints and debatable allusions but no expression of a clarity comparable, for example, to the post-Easter commissions of the Gospels and Acts. If the position suggested in this note is possible, then the issue would need to be reexamined, for here it is affirmed that a Gentile mission carried out by the saints is in fact God's own will. One must indeed discuss who "the saints" are, but it seems likely that the referent is broader than any previously identified agency for the mission in the Pauline literature.

The novelty is such that one could argue that we here have an un-Pauline conception—which could be for some indicative of a non-Pauline origin for the letter, and for others of the improbability of this rendering. But it should be noted that in any case Col 1:26 has already broadened the reception of the revelation to "un-Pauline" proportions by granting it not alone to Paul nor only, as in Ephesians, to God's prophets and apostles (Eph 3:5), but to *hoi hagioi*. The "un-Pauline" extension has already taken place in the text; the proposed reading only consolidates the breakthrough by assigning the broadened participation not only to the reception but also to the dissemination of the mystery.

No doubt there are other implications that could be developed. Certainly not all features of the clause have been illuminated; neither have the possible arguments both for and against such a shift in rendering been fully explored; especially there has been no attempt to argue that the reading represents the best choice among the options available. The intent of this note has been fully served if the alternative proposed for Col 1:27a has been shown to be a possibility, and one with implications of sufficient import to justify its airing thus for wider critical consideration.

Paul's "Cutting" Remarks about a Race: Galatians 5:1-12

CARL E. DeVRIES

In paying tribute to Merrill C. Tenney on the occasion of his seventieth birthday, I return to the area of our closest academic connection, NT Greek. During my years at Wheaton he and I had many associations: he was one of my instructors in Greek; he was pastor of the Tabernacle, which I attended, and he traveled to rural Minnesota to preach my ordination sermon. We were also colleagues—he teaching in the NT department, and I in the departments of Physical Education and Bible Archeology. With a degree of nostalgia and with warm admiration, this brief study combining athletics and NT exegesis is dedicated to Merrill C. Tenney, teacher, minister and friend.

The object of this paper is to investigate the meaning of a word employed by Paul in Gal 5:7 and to point out a possible clever play on words on the part of the Apostle in Gal 5:1-12. In doing this I appear to be running counter to the contemporary current in conservative Bible study, in which the emphasis seems to be on a preference for paraphrastic translations; grammatical elements, etymologies and original meanings contemporary with NT times apparently have lost their validity or at least their importance. The motives of those who paraphrase are legitimate and good, but the methodology is suspect and the results unreliable. This stands in marked contrast to the accuracy and precision demanded by translators working in the field of ancient Near Eastern studies.

The interest in sports and athletics in Greek culture has been the subject of much specialized discussion over the years, and a considerable body of secular literature treating this subject has appeared.[1] All of the NT commentators have had to familiarize themselves to a degree with the athletics

[1] For a useful, though perhaps in part outdated, bibliography covering the area of the Greek festivals and related NT works, see C. E. DeVries, "Pauline Athletic Terminology," unpublished M.A. thesis, Wheaton College (1944).

Carl E. DeVries, Research Associate (Associate Professor) at the Oriental Institute, The University of Chicago, responsible for the publication of the Nubian materials. B.S., Wheaton College; M.A. and B.D., Wheaton College Graduate School; Ph.D., The University of Chicago.

of the Greeks, for Paul's use of athletic terms is one of the striking features of his writings.

Archeology, the handmaiden of history, has continued to provide information for the understanding of the celebration of the Grecian festivals, among whose primary elements was a series of athletic competitions. Paul frequently uses the figure of running to describe the Christian life. From the excavations undertaken by the University of Chicago at Isthmia, the site of the Isthmian games, near the city of Corinth, has come welcome light as to the means by which the starting of a race was effected. Remains of two stadia at Isthmia were unearthed. At the Early Stadium, located at the southeast corner of the sanctuary of Poseidon, were found mechanisms that Oscar Broneer, director of the Isthmian dig, refers to as "very intricate starting gates, called *balbides*,[2] unlike those found in other athletic buildings of this kind."[3] The *balbides* have been reconstructed in their original position and a photograph of them in use is published in Broneer's article.[4] These starting gates did not consist of the more ordinary posts with a rope drawn between them but were composed of wooden elements, including a sort of bar that dropped away in front of the runner at the start of the race.

All that we can learn of the ancient physical contests should be of concern to us in our aim to understand the background of Paul's figures of speech. To students of the history of athletics, knowledge of the starting of races is of particular interest, but perhaps strangely to the thinking of some, Paul never used any specialized term relating to the beginning of a race. He never employed any figure analogous to joining the track team or signing up for wrestling. His metaphors were taken primarily from the actual participation in the athletic event and from its successful culmination in victory. There were no empty "moral victories" for the spiritual athlete.

But here we must recognize that the figure of speech breaks down, for when the Christian runs the race he does not win by making someone else a loser. There is no competition for the crown in this running, but each participant strives to help his fellow-runners also attain the prize. In short, the basic urging of the Apostle is best conveyed by his exhortation to his youthful colleague, Timothy, in a passage whose meaning is obscured for many people because of the archaic rendering of the Greek text by the translators of the *King James Version.* Paul pressed on Timothy this encouragement: "Do your best to present yourselves approved unto God." He also pointed out that the man of God was to handle God's Word in a right and acceptable manner (2 Tim 2:15). The figure of utmost exertion is not without its corollary, for Paul also stressed the fundamental concept that one's best is not enough; the overcoming power must come from God himself and actually is supplied by the living presence of the Holy Spirit. "It is God who both wills and puts forth power within you" (Phil 2:13).

---

[2] Plural of *balbis*, "prop. rope drawn across the race-course at the starting and finishing point"; mostly in plural, "posts to which this rope was attached." H. Liddell and R. Scott, *A Greek-English Lexicon,* Oxford, 1940, p. 304.

[3] O. Broneer, "The Apostle Paul and the Isthmian Games," *BA,* 25 (1962), 10. For other reports on excavations at Isthmia, see *ibid.,* p. 7, nn. 4-6. For more on starting-gates, see H. A. Harris, *Sport in Greece and Rome,* 1972, pp. 27-31.

[4] Broneer, "The Apostle Paul and the Isthmian Games," Fig. 6, p. 11.

The Christian engages in life with the same intensity that the Greek runner had when he strove for the one prize given in the contest, but he recognizes that his power to win in the spiritual life is the indwelling Christ (cf. Gal 2:20; Col 1:27).

Before commenting on Gal 5; it is important to examine the goal-oriented emphasis Paul gives to his figures of speech from athletics. In Phil 3 Paul speaks of pressing on toward the goal for the prize of the upward call of God in Christ (3:14). Earlier in the same chapter he talked about similar and related goals—to know him (Christ) and the power of his resurrection; to share his sufferings, and, finally, to attain the resurrection from the dead (3:10-11). In a somewhat different context he declares that his goal in life is to please God (2 Cor 5:9).

In view of such goals, Paul describes how the Christian is to conduct himself in life. In spite of the ever present antinomians, i.e. those who break the rules, Paul avers that one must participate lawfully or legally (*nomimōs,* 1 Tim 1:8). Though a person is not saved by keeping regulations and observing precepts, life, like a race, is patterned after certain rules, which cannot be broken except at the cost of disqualification and the loss of an award. Sometimes the rules of an athletic contest are stringently interpreted, and even an Olympic medalist may be deprived of his award. At other times the breaking of a rule is not noticed or the rule is not enforced. Such is not the case in the Christian life, for the Lord knows everything and will mete out judgment that is fair and not susceptible to question or cavil.

Paul also was aware of the hazards of athletic competition and brought this parallel to bear on the life of the Christian. He was concerned about the possibility that after having preached ("served as a herald") to others, he himself might be disapproved (*adokimos,* 1 Cor 9:27). At times he wondered if he had run in vain, i.e. if his work for the Lord would prove to be empty or valueless (Gal 2:2).

In writing to the believers in Galatia, Paul was basically concerned with what he considered was a corrupting of the doctrine of salvation, an insistence on legalism that had become a hindrance to progress in faith.

It was typical of the legalists to argue that Christianity was an adjunct to Judaism and that all male believers among the Gentiles should be forced to submit to the rite of circumcision, since this had been a physical badge of faith since the time of Abraham. (Although long before the time of the patriarch the operation had been practiced in Egypt and was shown in the relief sculpture of the Old Kingdom.)

As a Hebrew Christian, Paul was not opposed to the observance of circumcision as a rite or symbol among the Jews and was very careful not to offend the Jews unnecessarily with respect to this ancient custom. When Paul chose as his fellow-worker and traveling-companion the young man, Timothy, who was born of a Jewish mother and a Greek father, he circumcised Timothy so as not to offend the Jews (Acts 16:1-3). But when Judaizing teachers tried to force circumcision on Gentile believers as a condition for salvation, Paul became very much aroused and accused the Galatians of having turned aside to "another gospel," one that was based not on faith alone, but on faith plus the practice of a rite that now belonged to a past dispensation and had no relevance to saving faith in Jesus, the Messiah (Gal 1:6-9; 5:1-12).

The demand that the Gentile Christian observe all the tenets of Judaism was not new to Paul; this problem had arisen earlier in the church and had come to a head at Antioch in Syria. Paul and Barnabas then went to confer with the elders at Jerusalem and a practical and workable compromise had been reached. But in the Galatian churches the matter had reached such proportions that a living faith was itself endangered.

As a consequence Paul wrote boldly against the false teachers. In addressing the members of the Galatian churches in Gal 5:7, he first complimented them on their previous progress and then posed a rhetorical question: "You were running well; who cut in on you that you do not continue to obey the truth?"

Trechō means "to run," and its usage parallels that of its English equivalent. Here in Gal 5:7 the important grammatical element is the imperfect tense, which must be rendered "you *were running* well." Without any additional statement on the part of Paul, it is evident that there is an unfavorable contrast between the past and the present. The clear implication is that at present the running is not so good. This conclusion is confirmed when Paul asks, "Who cut in [*enekopsen*] on you?"[5] The answer is obvious and is the same as that required by another rhetorical question in 3:1, "Who has bewitched you?" In both cases it is the Judaizers who are at fault.

In any running competition one of the considerations of fairness and sportsmanship is that all contestants must have an open and unimpeded course. Their progress must not be hindered, restricted, or interfered with by any other runner. Years ago E. Norman Gardiner pointed out that in the foot races of the Greek festivals there were rules against tripping or otherwise interfering with an opponent.[6] Comparable rules apply to present-day competition in track: a runner must be a full running stride ahead before he is permitted to cut in front of another runner. If the stride of a

---

[5] It is interesting to observe how various translators and exegetes handle this and associated passages, but it is unnecessary to list their many views, for a correct interpretation is not necessarily determined by majority vote.

E. D. Burton, *Epistle to the Galatians*, ICC, New York, 1920, p. 282, says of *enekopsen*: "if the figure is that of a race, the word suggests a breaking into the course, getting in the way, or possibly a breaking up of the road."

W. F. Arndt and F. W. Gingrich, *A Greek-English Lexicon of the New Testament*, Chicago, 1957, p. 215, give for the entry *emkoptō* only the derived meaning, "hinder, thwart."

For an example of how a commentator can garble a figure of speech, see F. Rendall in the *Expositor's Greek Testament: The Epistle to the Galatians*, Grand Rapids, 1961, p. 184. Though he correctly identifies the running, he changes the figure in the question and interprets: "who had thrown obstacles in their way?" missing the point of the kind of hindrance Paul is describing. Perhaps he was thinking of *skandalizō*. The same confusion appears in R. T. Stamm, *The Epistle to the Galatians, Interpreter's Bible*, New York, 1953, 10, 551.

[6] E. N. Gardiner, *Greek Athletic Sports and Festivals*, Oxford, 1955, p. 146; DeVries, "Pauline Athletic Terminology," p. 99.

competitor is broken because someone has fouled him by cutting in prematurely, the offender is liable to disqualification.

The result of cutting in on a runner may be physical injury or it may be only the impeding of his progress, slowing him down by breaking his stride and the rhythm of his pace. Intellectually and spiritually, this is what had happened in Galatia. The Judaizers had cut in on the Galatians, and as a result the Galatian believers were thrown off stride and were hindered in their faith by being doctrinally confused.

As Ernest DeWitt Burton points out,[7] the tenses used in Paul's question are significant. *Enekopsen* is aorist, indicating that "he is thinking of what his opponents have already accomplished in their obstructive work," but the infinitive, *peithesthai,* dependent on it is present, showing progression or continuation. Burton translates, *tis hymas enekopsen alētheia mē peithesthai,* "Who has succeeded in preventing you from continuing to obey the truth?"

The figure of "cutting in," in connection with a race, in Gal 5:7, is paralleled by references to circumcision in the previous verses of this chapter, particularly vs. 6. Circumcision is a "cutting around," a "cutting off." *Peritomē,* "circumcision," is derived from *peritemnō,* a compound of *temnō,* "to cut," and *peri,* "around." The operation is graphically depicted in the Old Kingdom mastaba of Ankh-mi-hor,[8] just to the north of the Step Pyramid of Djoser at Sakkarah. On the right-hand side of the thickness of the doorway into Room 6, several youths are shown undergoing this surgical procedure. The boys are in a standing position; behind one of them is a man who restrains the lad by holding his arms. The boy has one hand placed on the head of the "surgeon," while his other hand is at his side. The men who are doing the operating are squatting before the patients. Each "doctor" holds a boy's penis with his left hand and wields the flint knife[9] with his right.

The Galatians had been "cut in" on by those who in a religious-physical sense demanded that all male converts to Christianity should also be "cut around," circumcised, in conformity with Judaic practice. In contending with the Judaizers Paul concludes his argument with a "cutting" remark. In vs. 12 he thunders, "I wish that all of those who upset you would mutilate themselves." The word here translated "mutilate" is *apokoptein,*[10] which the *King James Version* renders quite literally "cut off." Some commentators have interpreted this text in a religious sense and have thought that Paul meant only that he wished they would take leave of the congregations that they had confused by their doctrinal aberrations.[11]

[7] Burton, *Galatians,* p. 282.

[8] See Jean Capart, *Une rue de tombeaux a Saqqarah,* Brussels, 1907, Plate 66. The scene is published also in J. B. Pritchard, *The Ancient Near East in Pictures Relating to the Old Testament,* Princeton, 1954, Fig. 629, p. 206.

[9] For the use of a stone instrument for circumcision in the OT, see Exod 4:5.

[10] Arndt and Gingrich, *Lexicon,* give two meanings, opting for the second in this passage: (1) "cut off limbs or parts of the body"; (2) "make eunuchs of, castrate" (p. 92).

[11] John Calvin states that here Paul "prays for destruction on the impostors by whom the Galatians had been deceived"; *Calvin's Commentaries: The Epistles of*

In this context, however, where Paul speaks much of circumcision, it is more likely that by his use of "cut off" (5:12), he is expressing a wish that the trouble-makers not stop with a mere cutting away of their prepuce, or foreskin, but that they would carry the operation further and cut off the whole of their male organ![12]

Exegetes have suggested that the reference is to emasculation. The city of Pessinus was the center of the worship of Cybele, the Anatolian mother-goddess and goddess of fertility, whose priests castrated themselves in her honor.[13] Since this practice was a recognized form of devotion to Cybele such a reference would not be prohibited from common speech. Marvin R. Vincent regards Paul's vehement wish as perhaps the most severe statement in all of Paul's writings.[14] Similarly, George S. Duncan comments: "And with regard to circumcision we may set alongside this passage the equally brutal language of Phil iii 2 ff., which suggests that while the Christians have spiritualized circumcision, the Jews (by limiting it to a physical act) have made it no better than 'incision,' mutilation."[15] Sounding like an extremist, Paul was faced with a serious problem involving the Galatian converts and the situation required strong words and drastic measures.

The "cutting in" of the foot race, the "cutting around" of circumcision, and the "cutting off" of mutilation (with a possible allusion to a practice in honor of a false deity) are combined by Paul in this vivid and telling argumentation against false doctrine in the Galatian churches. Set for the defense of the gospel, Paul sought to strongly impress his followers with the necessity for maintaining purity of doctrine and holiness of living.

Paul the Apostle to the Galatians, Ephesians, Philippians and Colossians, trans. by T. H. L. Parker, Grand Rapids, 1965, p. 99.

[12] Many commentators indicate that a person so mutilated would be excluded from the Jewish congregation (see Deut 23:1). For discussion of this OT passage, see C. F. Keil and F. Delitzsch, *Commentary on the Old Testament: Pentateuch,* trans. by James Martin, Grand Rapids, 1949, 3, 413-15.

[13] See, for example, H. N. Ridderbos, *The Epistle of Paul to the Churches of Galatia,* Grand Rapids, 1956, pp. 194-95; Stamm, *Galatians,* pp. 554-55; K. S. Wuest, *Word Studies from the Greek New Testament: Galatians,* Grand Rapids, 1944, pp. 146-47.

[14] M. R. Vincent, *Word Studies in the New Testament,* New York, 1900, 4, 162. In similar vein Burton speaks of "the element of deep disgust which the language of Paul suggests"; *Galatians,* p. 289.

[15] G. S. Duncan, *The Epistle of Paul to the Galatians,* London, 1934, p. 161.

The Composition of Luke 9
and the Sources of Its Christology [1]

E. EARLE ELLIS

The application of composition criticism to Luke 9 can contribute to understanding the purpose of St. Luke, both within this passage and also for the Gospel as a whole. The application, in turn, of source criticism to the passage leads us toward the origins of the traditions and of the Christology expressed in them.

I

Herod's words, "Who is this?" (Luke 9:9), pose a question that the following episodes then answer, both in explicit titles given to Jesus and in the thrust of the narratives. [2]

However, Herod is only one of a series of persons who ask of Jesus, "Who is this?" The theologians and churchmen (5:21), John the Baptist (7:20), the guests of Simon the Pharisee (7:49), the disciples in the storm (8:25), the Sanhedrin (22:67, 70), and Pilate (23:3) make essentially the same query. In each case, the question arises because of Jesus' miracles and/or his assertion of messianic or divine prerogatives, for example, his claim to forgive sin. [3] The question sets forth a basic theme of the Gospel, that is, the meaning of Jesus' messiahship and person. And it appears that Luke, as far as his traditions allow, selects representative figures to raise it. In Herod, Luke sees such a figure and, as we hope to show, has traditions that occasion and justify his use of Herod in this way.

The episodes in Luke 9:10-50 give Luke's response to Herod's question. Jesus is the one who imparts life-giving nourishment (16), is the

---

[1] This essay is a revised form of a paper given at the Society of Biblical Literature, Los Angeles, Sept. 1-5, 1972, and at Journées Bibliques, Louvain, August 22-24, 1973.

[2] E. E. Ellis, *The Gospel of Luke*, London, 1966, pp. 135, 136-45.

[3] Also, the term Son of God (22:70; 9:20d) sometimes carries more than messianic connotations in Luke (cf. 1:35; 10:22).

E. Earle Ellis, Professor of Biblical Studies at New Brunswick Seminary, New Brunswick, New Jersey. B.S., University of Virginia; M.A. and B.D., Wheaton College Graduate School; Ph.D., University of Edinburgh.

Messiah of God (20), the chosen and unique "Son" who alone brings God's saving word (35),[4] the teacher whose works manifest the majesty of God (43), and the Son of man who will enter his glory through suffering (22, 29ff., 44). This is not only Luke's response but also that of the postresurrection community, who truly have come to know who Jesus is. But these episodes present another answer that retains, I suggest, the perspective of the preresurrection mission: no one except God (35) and Jesus himself knows who Jesus is. The crowds think he is the Baptist, or Elijah, or a resurrected OT prophet. Only Peter understands, and he misunderstands. His misunderstanding is evident in the Transfiguration story where he, "not knowing what he said" (33), wrongly places Jesus on a level with Moses and Elijah[5] and is rebuked by the heavenly voice. It is confirmed again in Luke's comment on the Passion prediction: the disciples "did not understand this saying, and it had been hidden from them in order that they might not perceive it" (45). Finally, it underlies the last episode of the section (46-50): the disciples' idea of greatness and legitimacy reflects their ignorance of the meaning of Jesus' mission and, therefore, of who Jesus is. No less than Mark, Luke presents Jesus' messiahship as something that is concealed[6] but, with reference to the disciples, his emphasis is somewhat different. Mark (8:32) and Matthew (16:22) call attention to the disciples' opposition to Jesus' conception of a suffering Messiah. Luke stresses only their incomprehension and misunderstanding. In this the disciples are one with the crowds and with Herod.

Running through the episodes, then, is a double answer to Herod's question, with accompanying notes of exaltation (6, 17, 20, 32, 43) and rejection (9, 22, 44). When this is observed, the role of these episodes as a prelude to the central section may be more fully appreciated. Jesus is God's glorious Messiah, but he is a messiah destined to be abandoned and rejected. This rejection forms the context in which Jesus sets his face to go to Jerusalem. Thus, the central section of Luke is framed by two episodes underscoring this fact, the rejection in Samaria (9:51-56) and the rejection in Jerusalem (19:41-44).[7]

II

A second issue in Luke 9:1-50 concerns the source of the Lukan variations from Mark, both in Herod's question and in the episodes following. Each of the episodes has a Markan parallel and, apart from the omission of Mark 6:45-8:26 at Luke 9:17, each follows the Markan order. Therefore, if one accepts the traditional two-document hypothesis,[8] one must ascribe the non-Markan variations either to Lukan editorial or to his use of oral traditions. However, if Luke used written sources in addition to

[4] See n. 3 above.
[5] Luke (1:17, 76; 7:26-28) already has identified John the Baptist with Elijah. He does not, therefore, use (repetitiously) the Elijah saying of Mark 9:9-13.
[6] Cf. Luke 4:34f., 41; 5:14.
[7] Cf. Ellis, *Gospel*, pp. 224f.
[8] So, recently, J. A. Fitzmyer, "The Priority of Mark and the 'Q' Source in Luke," *Jesus and Man's Hope*, ed. by D. G. Buttrick, Pittsburgh, 1970, 1, 131-70.

Mark, the traditional character of the variations would make it more probable that the resultant Lukan formulation also was based on or influenced by traditional antecedents.[9] In this situation one can see the importance of source criticism for the tasks of redaction and composition criticism.

It is unfortunate but true that after two hundred years of historical analysis no agreement about the sources of the Gospels has been achieved. One can here only offer a considered opinion that for Luke the most probable working hypothesis remains one that includes at least three types of written sources: Mark, extra-Markan traditions in common with Matthew (=Q), and traditions peculiar to Luke (=L). In the case of Q the hypothesis of a single document, a sayings source consisting of "a collection of precepts, parables and discourses," was first advanced 174 years ago (under the symbol ב) by Herbert Marsh of Cambridge.[10] However, attempts to demonstrate this—recently from the common order in Matthew and Luke of some Q episodes[11] —show at most only the unity of several smaller sections of Q material.[12] The relative order of a number of Q episodes or sections is predetermined by the Markan model or by the commonly received sequence of Jesus' mission (e.g. the accounts of the Baptism, Temptation, Eschatological Discourse). The remaining (one-third of) Q episodes that *may* have been arranged on the model of a Q document would form in any case only a minor part of the Q material. Lacking evidence that Q was one document, one should make no assumptions about its unity but, along the lines of form criticism, should reckon with several tracts or collections of tradition.

A more important question for interpreting Luke 9 is the "minor agreements" of Matthew and Luke against Mark. B. H. Streeter sought to explain such phenomena as coincidence or textual corruption.[13] But are the agreements so minor, and is Streeter's explanation adequate? In the episodes of Luke 9 the following agreements with Matt occur:[14]

1. 9:1-9:   7 words (2, 5, 7), 2 phrases of 3 words each (1, 5) and one of 2 words (4), partial agreement of one verse (2). All but one agreement are in 9:1-6.

2. 9:10-17: ten words (12, 13, 14, 16, 17), one phrase of four words (11),

---

[9] This does not mean that they are thereby less "Lukan." See n. 19 below.

[10] H. Marsh, "Origin and Composition of Our Three First Canonical Gospels," in J. D. Michaelis, *Introduction to the New Testament,* Cambridge, 1793-1801, IV Appendix, p. 202. Earlier (1794) J. G. Eichhorn had posited written "sources" for the non-Markan material common to Matthew and Luke, and later (1804) he also identified them as one document. Cf. W. G. Kümmel, *The New Testament...Investigation of Its Problems,* Nashville, 1972, p. 78 (German ed., p. 92).

[11] Cf. W. G. Kümmel, *Introduction to the New Testament,* Nashville, 1966, pp. 51f.

[12] Cf. V. Taylor, "The Original Order of Q," *New Testament Essays ... in Memory of T. W. Manson,* ed. by A. J. B. Higgins, Manchester, 1959, pp. 246-69; Fitzmyer, "Priority of Mark," p. 152.

[13] B. H. Streeter, *The Four Gospels,* Oxford, 1927, pp. 179ff., 293-331. Cf. Fitzmyer, "Priority of Mark," pp. 142ff., 155f.

[14] Agreements only in grammar or of a negative character (i.e. absence of words) are not counted.

approximate agreement of one word (10) and of a reference to healing (11).
3. 9:18-27: three words (19, 20), one phrase of two words (20) and one of four words (22). All agreements are in 9:18-22.
4. 9:28-36: two words (31, 35), one phrase of three words (29), approximate agreement of one phrase of three words (34), word order (30).
5. 9:37-45: five words (38, 40, 41, 44), approximate agreement of one phrase of two words (41) and one of four words (42).
6. 9:46-50: none

From this analysis one receives the impression that, with the exception of 9:23-27, 46-50 and perhaps of 9:7-9, Luke has used Q traditions in addition to Mark in composing this chapter. Dr. Tim Schramm in his book, *Der Markus-Stoff bei Lukas,* reaches similar conclusions: Luke 9:7-9, 46-50 is composed of Markan material slightly reworked; the rest of Luke 9:1-50 (with the possible exception of 9:23-27) is Markan material that has been altered under the influence of non-Markan sources.[15] Noting a Lukan tendency to combine traditions, Schramm sought to isolate non-Markan sources from Lukan editorial in the triple tradition. For this task he used several "indicators": agreements of Matthew and Luke against Mark, special Lukan (L) material unlikely to be editorial,[16] semitisms replacing Markan idiom, and certain other divergencies from Mark in style and content. Schramm concludes, justifiably in my judgment, that a rigid two-document hypothesis is an oversimplification of the Synoptic problem.

III

If this conclusion is correct, what effect does it have on the composition criticism of Luke 9, specifically on the Herod pericope and on the christological (and soteriological) emphases following upon it? The title, God's Messiah, and the greater stress upon Jesus' healings (2, 11, 42; cf. 6) are taken from Q material. The same is true of Jesus' glorified countenance in the Transfiguration (29). Other non-Markan elements in the Transfiguration, e.g. Jesus' glory (32) and the disciples' fear (34; cf. 36b), are more difficult to assign; but the presence of semitisms suggests the use of a tradition.[17] In the last episode Jesus' knowledge of the disciples' thoughts (47) and the title "Master" (49)[18] appear to be editorial. The marveling crowd in the second Passion prediction (43ab) may have the same explanation, but it is not necessarily Luke's creation since the element of "marvelling" may have been present in the Q version of the episode (cf. Luke 7:9; 8:25).

---

[15] T. Schramm, *Der Markus-Stoff bei Lukas,* Cambridge, 1971, pp. 29n, 185f.; cf. 70-85.

[16] *Ibid.,* pp. 77f.; cf. J. C. Hawkins, *Horae Synopticae,* Oxford, 1968 (1909), pp. 194-97. Otherwise: H. Schürmann, *Lukasevangelium.* Freiburg, 1969, 1, 521-74, *passim.*

[17] Schramm, *Markus-Stoff,* p. 139.

[18] Of the five NT occurrences (all Lukan), three occur in episodes dependent on Mark and Q, two in L traditions.

It is difficult to make sure distinctions between Luke's use of non-extant traditional material and his variations *de novo*.[19] But the composition of Luke 9 appears to have been achieved by the selection and combination of traditions. Even the placing of Peter's confession after the feeding miracle, the major break with the Markan order, may have a traditional basis. As J. Schniewind and others have shown,[20] Luke has traditions in common with the Fourth Gospel; and that Gospel also connects the feeding miracle and Peter's confession in a somewhat similar fashion (John 6:14, 68-69).

In conclusion we may return to Herod's question. Is it not clearly Luke's creation designed to provide the headline for the following stories? Since Dibelius' essay this view has been widely accepted. It is true that the pericope has a number of Lukan characteristics,[21] and the one Q parallel (*ho tetraarchēs*) may well be coincidental. But it should be noted that Herod's question includes, alongside the christological reference, an allusion to the Passion: Herod wants to *see* Jesus. This points forward to Herod's interview with Jesus in Luke 23:6-12, composed out of Luke's special traditions,[22] where Herod's long-standing desire is explicitly stated (23:8). Luke may infer from that tradition the earlier curiosity of Herod and in this way find traditional support for introducing the question at Luke 9:9. However, other references to the Passion in Luke 9 are dependent on pre-Lukan traditions, including the semitic-styled pericope on the coming "exodus" of Jesus.[23] Episodes mentioning Herod Antipas elsewhere in Luke-Acts[24] also are largely of a literary and traditional character. On balance, Herod's question, like the subsequent episodes, is probably to be ascribed to a Lukan combination and reworking of pre-Lukan traditions. Thus, the Evangelist's contribution turns out to be more editorial organization than creative addition. In Luke 9, at least, his traditions are the matrix of his theology.

---

[19] Cf. E. E. Ellis, *Eschatology in Luke,* Philadelphia, 1972, pp. 1-3.

[20] J. Schniewind, *Die Parallelperikopen bei Lukas und Johannes,* Darmstadt, 1958 (1914). Cf. Ellis, *Gospel,* p. 28. There is also a limited but discernible affinity between Luke and John in the general "model" on which their Gospels are formed: revelation of the Son of God (Luke 1-2; John 1), public works of Jesus, teaching section (Luke 10-19; John 13-17), Passion and resurrection.

[21] Schramm, *Markus-Stoff,* p. 128.

[22] Luke 23 contains traditions in common with the Gospel of John, but the Herod episode is not in the latter Gospel. It was probably composed by Luke himself out of tradition contained in the non-Markan source (V. Taylor, *The Passion Narrative of St. Luke,* Cambridge, 1972, p. 89). Cf. Schniewind, *Parallelperikopen,* pp. 62-85.

[23] Luke 9:31-34. Schramm (*Markus-Stoff,* pp. 133f., 138f.) notes the following semitic constructions: parallelism (34), *egeneto*-clause (33), *en tō* + infinitive (33, 34, 36), *conjugatio periphrastica* (32), parataxis (34, 36). Cf. K. Beyer, *Semitische Syntax im Neuen Testament,* I, Göttingen, 1962; J. H. Moulton-N. Turner, *A Grammar of New Testament Greek,* Edinburgh, 1963, 3, 398.

[24] Luke 13:31; Acts 4:27; cf. Luke 8:3; 13:1. Cf. H. W. Hoehner, *Herod Antipas,* Cambridge, 1972, pp. 224-50. Otherwise, M. Dibelius, "Herodes und Pilatus," *ZNW,* 16 (1915), 113-26, who conjectures that Ps 2:1f. (cf. Acts 4:25) became the occasion for creating the story in Luke 23:6-12. In my judgment the priorities of early Christian ("eschatological") exegesis were just the opposite: the (tradition of an) event was ordinarily the prerequisite from which the search of the

IV

The conclusions above are significant for the christological statements in Luke 9 at a number of points. (1) The two Passion predictions (22, 43-45) of the suffering "Son of man," together with Peter's confession of Jesus as "Messiah" and the command to secrecy (18-21; cf. 44f.), are attested in both Mark and Q. (2) The same appears to be true of the threefold messianic attribution by the divine voice in the Transfiguration (35f.): the royal "Son" (Ps 2:7), the "elect" Servant (Isa 42:1) and the eschatological prophet (Deut 18:15, 18f.: *autou akouete*). For the allusion to the Servant is clearly present only in the Q tradition that is given in (different) part by Matthew and Luke.[25] In contrast to these relatively direct messianic affirmations is the implicit Christology of the Feeding story (10-17), i.e. that Jesus is one like Moses, and the non-messianic speculation about Jesus in the Herod episode (7-9). Thus, the motif of the "messianic secret" is the common property of Mark and Q, and it is implicit within the several episodes quite apart from the express commands to secrecy. That is, the hidden character of Jesus' messiahship, as it appears in Mark and Q, has not been imported into a non-messianic tradition at certain points but is indigenous to the tradition as a whole.[26]

As far as it can take us, the source criticism of Luke 9 does not suggest that Jesus had a non-messianic view of his ministry or that he made public claim to the title Messiah. Of the three messianic predicates in the heavenly voice, two—the suffering servant and the prophet like Moses—are implicitly confirmed in the Feeding story and in the Passion predictions. The third, the royal Son, may find a parallel in Peter's confession. At an early stage in the Gospel tradition, then—at least as early as Q—various messianic images from the OT had been carefully related to one another and set forth in the context of the words and works of Jesus.

How far does this take us toward the preresurrection teaching of Jesus? If one assumes, with some of the earlier form criticism, a caesura between Jesus and the earliest church, it does not take us very far. But if the historical probabilities suggest that there was no caesura and that Jesus

---

Scriptures proceeded. While the chosen text often influenced the *description* of the event, i.e. the "fulfillment," it was not the occasion for creating events out of whole cloth. For example, from the Scriptures one could argue that Messiah was to be born either in Galilee (Isa 9:1f.) or in Bethlehem (Mic 5:2). The early Christian expositors chose the "Bethlehem" passage because they already had a "Bethlehem" tradition about Jesus' birth. .

[25] Namely, *rṣh = eudokein, bhr = eklektos* (Isa 42:1 Theodotion); cf. Matt 17:5; Luke 9:35. The Markan *agapetos* = "only" (cf. Mark 12:7) also may allude to Isa 42; cf. J. Jeremias, *TDNT,* 5, 701. But it is uncertain. Since Q *Vorlage* is reflected in the episode as a whole, Q rather than Mark more likely lies behind the clear allusions to Isa 42 in Matt and Luke. The story of the Transfiguration may have been traditioned originally in the context of a midrash on Exod 34:27-35 in which Ps 2:7, Isa 42:1 and Deut 18:15, 18f. served as supporting texts. If so, in the development of the tradition the OT texts were stripped away, leaving only the allusions incorporated into the voice from heaven.

[26] Otherwise, W. Wrede, *The Messianic Secret,* London, 1971 (1901), p. 145, who attributed to Mark "an important share" in developing an (unhistorical) idea of a messianic secret. But see J. D. G. Dunn in *Tyndale Bulletin,* 21 (1970), 92-117.

himself taught his disciples to read the OT in terms of his mission,[27] a different conclusion will follow. In this case the perceptive use of the OT in Luke 9 would be indebted, as the Evangelist suggests it to be, to the teaching of Jesus, a teaching that like pieces of a puzzle fell into place in the light of the stupendous event of the resurrection.

[27]Cf. C. H. Dodd, *According to the Scriptures*, London, 1953, p. 110; E. E. Ellis, "The Role of the Christian Prophet in Acts," *Apostolic History and the Gospel . . . Presented to F. F. Bruce,* ed. by W. W. Gasque and R. P. Martin, Exeter and Grand Rapids, pp. 58-61.

Wisdom, Torah, Word: The Johannine Prologue and the Purpose of the Fourth Gospel

ELDON JAY EPP

It is no simple matter to state the purpose which the author of the Fourth Gospel had in mind. It is widely recognized, in the first place, that a *single* aim or purpose is not necessarily to be sought nor likely to be found. It is clear, secondly, that the formal statement of purpose in John 20:31 is not as helpful as at first it might appear:

> ... These [signs] are written that you may believe that Jesus is the Christ, the Son of God, and that believing you may have life in his name.

If tenses can be interpreted strictly, the closely divided manuscript evidence for *pisteusēte* ("that you may come to believe") and *pisteuēte* ("that you may continue to believe") makes the author's statement of purpose unclear: was he writing to non-Christians to bring them into the Christian community, or was his aim to strengthen and encourage those already within the group? The third edition of the United Bible Societies' Greek New Testament places the questionable sigma in brackets (*pisteu[s]ēte*) so as not to prejudice its readers as to the purpose of the Gospel by making a choice between the two readings.[1] The author writes, of course, in the interests of belief or faith, with the qualification that he expects belief in Jesus as Messiah and as Son of God, but the Gospel of Mark does almost as much when it announces its theme in 1:1: "The beginning of the gospel of Jesus Christ, the Son of God." We have learned from form criticism that all the Gospels were written from faith and in the interests of faith, and the Fourth Gospel has only stated this more explicitly than the others. In doing so, however, its author has not enlightened us very much as to his more specific purpose.

This diminished utility of 20:31 for determining the aim of John's author means that his purposes must be determined from other portions of the text, and the Prologue (1:1-18) is a natural place to begin, assuming

---

[1] See Bruce M. Metzger, *A Textual Commentary on the Greek New Testament*, London-New York, 1971, p. 256.

Eldon Jay Epp, Harkness Professor of Biblical Literature at Case Western Reserve University, Cleveland, Ohio. B.A., Wheaton College; Ph.D., Harvard University.

quite properly that a formal preface in an ancient writing (as in a modern one) is likely to reveal something of the author's purpose, intentions and interest.

I

Our analysis of certain features of the Prologue will lead to an argument as to one of the purposes of the Fourth Gospel. Our chain of argument begins by referring to the well-known *poetic character* of the Johannine Prologue. Indeed, it has in it instances of Hebrew synonymous parallelism, antithetic parallelism and synthetic parallelism, with particularly striking examples of masterful refinement of the third type, which yields a climactic or concatenation type of parallelism. Notice, for instance, 1:1 (following the Greek order of key words):

> In the beginning was the *Word;*
> And the *Word* was with *God,*
> And *God* was the *Word.*

Or 1:4-5:

> That which had come to be in him was *life,*
> And the *life* was the *light* of men.
> The *light* shines in the *darkness,*
> And the *darkness* did not overcome it [*light=life*] .

The individual links—each bringing a new idea—form a chain that is itself circular, ending on the word or theme with which it began (Word . . . Word; life . . . light=life), building in the meantime a series of steps or a staircase of related thoughts.

All of this is well known, and the point is merely to call attention again to this poetic character of the Prologue so as to show its connection, as far as form is concerned, with OT and related poetic works.

II

A second step or link in our argument is to point to the widely recognized *hymnic character* of the Johannine Prologue. Whether the hymnic Prologue was composed by the author of the Fourth Gospel, was written by someone else within the Johannine circle, or existed independently of and prior to the Fourth Gospel are questions that are not substantive to the present argument, though a consensus seems to be emerging that it was originally an independent poem—perhaps from Johannine circles—which has been taken over by the author of John[2] as a formal, elegant and highly appropriate introduction to his account of the "signs" and the Passion of Jesus Christ.

Furthermore, a comparison of the sequence of ideas, of their content, and of the general form and style of the Prologue with those of recognized Jewish and early Christian hymns (in the NT, notably Phil 2:6-11 and Col

[2] Raymond E. Brown, *The Gospel According to John (i-xii),* Garden City, N.Y., 1966, pp. 19-23.

1:15-20) reveals similarities more than sufficient to show that the Prologue represents or incorporates an early Christian hymn. Again, this conclusion is widely held and, for our purposes, is in no need of further discussion here.

III

The third link in our chain of argumentation is the identification of the probable source of inspiration for the composition of the original Christian hymn of the Prologue and the location of its ideational matrix. Was there a model for its composition that not only provided its form but also informed its context of thought? The clear answer (developed by J. Rendel Harris in 1917) is that such a model was provided by the *Wisdom hymns* of the OT and the Apocrypha. That is, the Johannine hymn to the Logos was inspired, in content and in form, generally at least, by the hymns about or by personified Wisdom, such as those in Prov 8:1-36; Job 28:12-28; Sir 24:1-34; Bar 3:9-4:4; and Wis 7:22-10:21.

Though these OT and Apocrypha Wisdom hymns do not match the Johannine hymn in conciseness, the numerous and obvious parallels clearly place them in the same category, as shown by these excerpts (*RSV*):

PROVERBS 8:22-35 (parts)
(Wisdom is speaking)

8:22 The LORD created me at the beginning of his work,
      the first of his acts of old.
   23 Ages ago I was set up,
      at the first, before the beginning of the earth.
   27 When he established the heavens, I was there. . . ,
   29 When he marked out the foundations of the earth,
   30 then I was beside him, like a master workman.
   34 Happy is the man who listens to me. . . .
   35 For he who finds me finds life
      and obtains favor from the LORD.

In this Proverbs hymn of Wisdom, she, like the Word in John, is pre-existent with God, is active in creation, effects or mediates salvation/life for men, and is associated with truth (8:6-8, not quoted above).

SIRACH 24:3-9; 23-32 (parts)
(Wisdom is speaking through vs. 22, and again in vss. 30-34)

24:3 I came forth from the mouth of the Most High,
      and covered the earth like a mist.
   6 In the waves of the sea, in the whole earth,
      and in every people and nation I have gotten a possession.
   7 Among all these I sought a resting place;
      I sought in whose territory I might lodge.
   8 Then the Creator of all things gave me a commandment,
      and the one who created me assigned a place for my tent.
      And he said, "Make your dwelling (*kataskēnōson*) in Jacob,
      and in Israel receive your inheritance."
   9 From eternity, in the beginning, he created me,

and for eternity I shall not cease to exist.
23 All this is the book of the covenant of the Most High God,
    the law which Moses commanded us as an inheritance for
        the congregations of Jacob.
27 It makes instruction shine forth like light. . . .
32 I will again make instruction shine forth like the dawn,
    and I will make it shine afar.

Here in Sir, Wisdom is God's word (vs. 3), takes up a dwelling in Israel,
exists from eternity and for eternity, is identified with the law of Moses,
and is enlightening.

BARUCH 3:9-4:2 (parts)

3:9 Hear the commandments of life, O Israel;
    give ear, and learn wisdom!
14 Learn where there is wisdom,
    where there is strength, where there is understanding,
  That you may at the same time discern
    where there is length of days, and life,
    where there is light for the eyes, and peace.
29 Who has gone up into heaven, and taken her,
    and brought her down from the clouds?
32 But he who knows all things knows her,
    he found her by his understanding.
35 This is our God;
    no other can be compared to him!
36 He found the whole way to knowledge,
    and gave her to Jacob his servant and to Israel whom he loved.
37 Afterward she appeared upon earth
    and lived among men.
4:1 She is the book of the commandments of God,
    and the law that endures for ever.
  All who hold her fast will live,
    and those who forsake her will die.
 2 Turn, O Jacob, and take her;
    walk toward the shining of her light.

Themes seen in the preceding hymns reappear in that of Bar: Wisdom is the
source of life and light; she dwells with God ("heaven"); she appears on
earth and dwells with men; and she is identified with the law.

WISDOM OF SOLOMON 7:21-9:18 (parts)
("Solomon" is speaking)

7:21 I learned both what is secret and what is manifest,
    for wisdom, the fashioner of all things, taught me.
25 For she is a breath of the power of God,
    and a pure emanation of the glory of the Almighty. . . .
26 For she is a reflection of eternal light,
    a spotless mirror of the working of God, and an image of his goodness.
29 Compared with the light she is found to be superior,
30   for it is succeeded by the night, but against wisdom evil does
        not prevail.

8:3 She glorifies her noble birth by living with God,
   and the Lord of all loves her.
 4 For she is an initiate in the knowledge of God,
   and an associate in his works.
9:1 O God of my fathers and Lord of mercy,
   who hast made all things by thy word (*logos*),
 2   and by thy wisdom hast formed man. . . .
 4 Give me the wisdom that sits by thy throne. . . .
 9 With thee is wisdom, who knows thy works
   and was present when thou didst make the world.
 10 Send her forth from the holy heavens,
   and from the throne of thy glory send her,
   that she may be with me and toil,
   and that I may learn what is pleasing to thee.
 11 For she knows and understands all things,
   and she will guide me wisely in my actions
   and guard me with her glory.
 17 Who has learned thy counsel, unless thou hast given wisdom
   and sent thy holy Spirit from on high?
 18 And thus the paths of those on earth were set right,
   and men were taught what pleases thee, and were saved by wisdom.
[Here follows a summary of Wisdom's teaching and saving work from Adam to Moses (10:1-11:4).]

In the Wisdom of Solomon the figure of Wisdom appears repeatedly as active in creation and is characterized as closely related to God and as reflecting his glory; she is characterized by light and is a means of salvation.

This hasty survey of the Wisdom hymns makes it clear that a number of Wisdom's most characteristic features and functions are closely parallel to the major characteristics and functions of the "Word" as described in the Johannine Prologue—so much so that the Wisdom hymns confidently may be designated as the literary matrix of the Prologue.

A subsidiary argument for the same position may be formed by noting that the hymns in the OT and Apocrypha identify Wisdom with the word of God. For example, Sir 24:3 has Wisdom say, "I came forth from the mouth of the Most High," and Wis 9:1-2, through the employment of synonymous parallelism, makes the identification of Wisdom and God's word: "O God. . . , who hast made all things by thy word, and by thy wisdom hast formed man"; cf. also Prov. 2:6, "For the LORD gives wisdom; from his mouth come knowledge and understanding"; and Job 28:27, which says that God "declared" wisdom. Indeed, with a possible exception or two, the term "Wisdom" could be substituted for "Word" (and its pronouns) in the Johannine Prologue, and the resulting sentences hardly would cause the raising of eyebrows by one familiar with the Wisdom hymn tradition.

IV

This connection of the Johannine Prologue with the Jewish Wisdom hymns has, like the preceding points, long been recognized. Nor will our next contention be any more surprising, for the fourth link in our argument is that both the Wisdom hymns and the Judaism of the time recognized the *equation of Wisdom and Torah*. This equation is explicit in Bar 4:1: "She is the book of the commandments of God, and the law (*nomos*) that endures forever"; cf. 3:9. It is found also in Sir 24:23, following Wisdom's own words in the preceding long discourse: "All this is the book of the covenant of the Most High God, the law (*nomos*) which Moses commanded us"; and it is implied in Prov 8:32-36. The identification of Wisdom and Torah is attested also by 4 Mac 1:17; 2 Apoc Bar 38:2-4; 77:16; and it is not only substantiated but assumed by rabbinical sources. Since the point is not in doubt, no further references or discussion is required here.

If Wisdom and Torah are identified, then there is likely to be an overlap in their respective functions and attributes, and this is clearly the case in the literature and sources of the Judaism of the time. Some of the major categories are the following:

Existence prior to creation:

    a.   Wisdom: See Prov 8:22-30; Sir 24:9; Wis 7:21; 8:5-6; 9:1-2, 9.

    b.   Torah: "[Torah] has been stored up there for 974 generations before the creation of the world" (Zebahim 116a; cf. Sabbath 88b); "The law, because it is more highly prized than everything, was created before everything, as it is said [quoting Prov 8:22]" (Sifrè on Deut 11.10 § 37 [76a-b]); "Seven things were created before the world was created, namely Torah, ..." (Pesahim 54a; cf. Nedarim 39b; Genesis Rabbah 1.2; 8.2; Pesikta Rabbati 46.1; Midrash on Psalms 90 § 12, which quotes Prov 8:30; 72 § 6; 93 § 3, which, like Aboth 6,10, quotes Prov 8:22 as a statement about Torah).

Existence with God/close relationship with God (divinity?):

    a.   Wisdom: See Wis 8:3; 9:4; cf. Prov 8:27-30; Bar 3:29; Wis 7:25; 9:9-10.

    b.   Torah: "The Torah lay on God's bosom" (Aboth of Rabbi Nathan 31 [8b]) or "rested on God's knee" (Midrash on Psalms 90 § 12); in the context of a father speaking of his daughter, "So God says to Israel, 'I have given you my Torah; I cannot be separated from her; yet I cannot say to you, Do not take her. . . .' But God, when he gave the Law to Israel, said, 'With the Torah you, as it were, take also me'" (Exodus Rabbah 33 [94a]). See also Leviticus Rabbah 20.7 (120a); Sanhedrin 101a baraita, where God calls Torah "my daughter."

Role in creation:

    a.   Wisdom: See Prov 8:27-30; 3:19; Wis 7:21; 8:4-6; 9:1-2, 9; Aboth Rabbi Nathan 31 (8b).

    b.   Torah: "God created the world by Torah: the Torah was his handmaid and his tool by the aid of which he set bounds to the deep, assigned their functions to sun and moon, and

formed all nature. Without the Torah the world falls" (Tan-
huma, Bereshit, § 1 [6b]); "Through the first-born, God
created the heaven and the earth, and the first-born is no
other than Torah" (Genesis Rabbah 1.1; also, Torah describes herself as "an architect's apparatus for God"); cf.
Aboth 3.15, where Torah is referred to as "the precious
instrument by which the world was created."

Endurance for eternity:

a. Wisdom: See Bar 4:1; Sir 24:9 (in the contexts of both
passages Wisdom is identified explicitly with Torah); cf. Sir
1:1.

b. Torah: See Ps 119:152, 160; "the eternal law" (1 Enoch
99:2); Bar 4:1; Tob 1:6; " . . . And we may hope that [the
laws of Moses] will remain for all future ages as though
immortal, so long as the sun and moon and the whole
heaven and universe exist" (Philo, *Life of Moses* 2.3.14);
"Our Law . . . remains immortal" (Josephus, *Against Apion*
2.38.277); "Everything has a measure, heaven and earth
have a measure, except one thing which has no measure:
and what is it? The Torah. . . " (Genesis Rabbah 1.1); cf.
Matt 5:18; Luke 16:17.

Related to light/life/salvation:

a. Wisdom: See Prov 8:35; 3:16-18, 22; Sir 24:27, 32; Bar
3:14; 4:1-2; Wis 7:10, 26, 27, 29; 8:13, 17; 9:18; 10:17.

b. Torah: See Pss 19:8; 119:93, 105, 107-8; Prov 6:23; 2 Esdr
(4 Ezra) 14:30; Sir 17:11; "Just as oil is life for the world,
so also are the words of the Torah light for the world"
(Deuteronomy Rabbah 7.3 [204a]); "Whoever is slack about
Torah will not live again. Whoever makes use of the light of
Torah, the light of Torah will revive [after death]; and
whoever does not make use of the light of Torah, the light
of Torah will not revive" (Ketubbot 111b); "on account of
the Torah. . . , which is called 'fountain of life,' I am
destined to enjoy thy light in the time-to-come" (Pesikta
Rabbati 36.1); "Great is the Law, for it gives life to them
that practice it, both in this world and in the world to
come, as it is written [citing Prov 3:16, 18, among other
texts]" (Aboth 6.7); further on Torah as life, see Aboth
2.7; Sanhedrin 88b; 91b; Mekhilta on Exodus 15:26;
Midrash on Psalms 1 § 19; on Torah as light, see Sifrè on
Numbers 6:25 § 41 (referring to Prov 6:23); Numbers
Rabbah 11 (163d); 2 Apoc Bar 59:2; 77:16; Wis 18:4; T
Levi 14:4. (For numerous other texts referring to Torah as
life or salvation, see Str-B, 3, 129-31.)

Appearance in the world/among men:

a. Wisdom: See Sir 24:7-12; Bar 3:36-37; Wis 9:10; cf. Wis
9:17-18; 10:1-21; 1 Enoch 42:2.

b. Torah: See OT, Apocrypha, and rabbinic references to the giving of Torah at Sinai through Moses, etc., where this theme is self-evident. Note also the elaborate and curious story in Pesikta Rabbati 20.4, which tells of the opposition Moses faced from the angels who did not, at first, want to let Torah go to men; God says, "But if Israel does not receive the Torah, there shall be no abiding place—neither for Me nor for you [=the angel Hadarniel]."

Associated with truth:

a. Wisdom: See Prov 8:6-8: "Hear, for I will speak noble things, and from my lips will come what is right; for my mouth will utter truth. . . ; all the words of my mouth are righteous; there is nothing twisted or crooked in them."

b. Torah: See LXX Pss 118:89 (=119:89); 119:142, 151, 160; Neh 9:13; cf. Mal 2:6; 4 Mac 5:18; ". . . truth, by this Torah is meant" (Midrash on Psalms 25 § 11).

Characterized by glory:

a. Wisdom: See Wis 7:25; 9:10-11.

b. Torah: "When the Israelites keep the Torah in their midst, God will cause them to possess the throne of glory" (Numbers Rabbah 11 [on 6:22]); "If thou wouldst see the face of the Presence in this world, then occupy thyself with Torah in the Land of Israel. . . " (Midrash on Psalms 105 § 1); cf. the narrative of the replacement tables of the law and the theme of glory associated with the events described (Exod 33:18-23; 34:29-35). (Cf. the elaborate story in Pesikta Rabbati 20.4, which claims that God appeared face to face in his glory both to Moses and to Israel when Torah was given, hence showing the close connection between Torah and God's glory.)

These conceptions and treatments of Wisdom and Torah show that the two terms not only shared numerous characteristics and functions, but were often interchangeable and that the writer or hearer of a Wisdom hymn could just as well be thinking of Torah as he pondered its phrases. Indeed, on the basis of our previous points—that the Prologue of John is patterned after a Wisdom hymn and that the term "Wisdom," with perfect sense and almost without reservation, properly could be substituted for "Word" in the Prologue, we can now say that the term "Torah" also could properly be substituted for "Word," though with the same few reservations. It is clear, furthermore, that the writer of the Johannine Prologue, and also the hearer of it—if he were familiar with Wisdom hymns—would have Wisdom in mind from the very first lines of the Prologue and, moreover, would move at once in his thoughts to the notion of Torah.

V

This leads directly to the fifth step in our argument, for it calls into prominence the single and otherwise unexpected reference to Torah in the Johannine Prologue, John 1:17:

For the law was given through Moses;
grace and truth came through Jesus Christ.

To the casual reader, this reference to the law of Moses is startling, abrupt and without preparation. Why suddenly this mention of the Mosaic law? The reader familiar with Wisdom hymns, however, is not caught unawares, nor is the writer of John 1:1-18 moving jarringly to a new subject in vs. 17. To the author and to such readers the mention of Torah in this context and in this familiar format is natural, consistent and of a piece with what has preceded. Torah comes naturally to mind in a Wisdom hymn context.

To say this is not necessarily to argue that John 1:17 was part of the original, pre-Johannine hymn to Christ as the Word; that is another question and a difficult one.[3] We shall assume that it was not, though the only essential point for us is that the author (or at least the final author) of the Gospel deliberately and meaningfully interwove the basic poetic elements (i.e. the original hymn—at least vss. 1-5, 10-12, 14, 16) with the final two verses (17-18) in accordance with his own distinctive plan and purpose. This is to say nothing less than (1) that the writer of vs. 17 saw the Prologue as a derivative and semblance of the Wisdom hymn, (2) that he was clearly cognizant of the Wisdom/Torah exchangeability, and (3) that, therefore, his apparently abrupt introduction of the term "law" was actually a subtly tendered, carefully studied and superbly executed climax to the whole Prologue. Moreover, this high point of the Prologue was intended to indicate one of the major themes, if not the chief purpose, of the Fourth Gospel as a whole.

Incidentally, those familiar with Wisdom hymns would be acquainted with another such seemingly abrupt reference to Torah in the Wisdom hymn of Sirach. In the first twenty-two verses of Sir 24, Wisdom describes her attributes and work; then, without warning, vs. 23 declares, "All this is the book of the covenant of the Most High God, the law which Moses commanded us."

Precisely what is the force of the reference to law in John 1:17? We have noted earlier that both "Wisdom" and "Torah" properly might be substituted for the term "Word" (and its pronouns) in the Prologue, and we have suggested that a reader of the Prologue who was familiar with Wisdom hymns and with rabbinic thought would have been reminded at once of the category "Wisdom hymns" and would have thought of Wisdom and Torah as he encountered the various lines: " . . . was in the beginning"; " . . . was with God"; "all things were made through him"; "in him was life and . . . light"; " . . . was coming into the world"; " . . . was in the world . . . and dwelt among us"; "full of grace and truth . . . and glory"; and "from his fulness have we all received." One or two items, of course, might have been marked in his mind for further reflection: the masculine pronoun rather

---

[3] See Brown, *Gospel according to John (i-xii)*, pp. 16, 21-23. Vs. 18 has been construed as poetry (see Brown, p. 17, for examples), though it lacks the *kai* connective found in the more certainly poetic portions of the Prologue. The *kai* connective is lacking also in vs. 17, but could it not equally well be taken as poetic, perhaps as two lines of antithetic parallelism? Our discussion assumes, however, that the author of John has added vss. 17-18 to an earlier Christ hymn.

than the feminine of Wisdom, and the term "Word." Both of these reservations, however, would have been alleviated upon the briefest reflection, for both Wisdom and Torah—especially the latter—were understood explicitly in terms of God's "word" (see above), and when this equation was made, the masculine pronouns (for *ho logos*) would cease to be a problem. Naturally, the reader would ponder other claims of the Prologue in the context of Wisdom and Torah: " ... was God"(?); "his own people received him not"(?); " ... became flesh"(?); and "glory as of the only Son"(?). A further brief reflection, however, would allow for the acceptance of these as claims for Wisdom and Torah, for Wisdom's "divinity" (though not deity) was attested, e.g. by such phrases as "living with God" and "sitting by [God's] throne" (Wis 8:3; 9:4), and Torah was thought of as resting in God's bosom and as inseparable from God as his daughter (see above). Also, as witnessed earlier, the notion of Wisdom and Torah dwelling or tenting on earth or with men was common enough, though incarnation would be too strong an image to use; and the rejection by individuals of both Wisdom and Torah was something easily enough documented from Jewish history and literature (cf. also the following texts on the rejection of Wisdom: Prov 1:24-25, 29-30; 1 Enoch 42:1-3).

Such a reader as we have described could, therefore, have gone along with the Prologue through 1:16. Upon reaching vs. 17, however, he would be greatly puzzled, *not by the mention of law* (for the reasons given earlier), but by the sudden expulsion of Torah from the positive discussion that preceded; whereas until this point he could read "law" into the entire hymn (via the "Wisdom" concept and its identification) and could fill the term "Word" with the meaning "law" (and "Wisdom"), now suddenly and wholly unexpectedly *law is excluded* and "Jesus Christ" is the *only* content that remains for the term "Word":

> For the law was given through Moses;
> grace and truth came through Jesus Christ.

Here is the scandal for the reader acquainted with Wisdom and Torah!

The following verse (18), the final one of the Prologue, makes the point clearer and definitive:

> No one has ever seen God;
> God the only Son,[4] who is in the bosom of the Father,
> he has made him known.

How is the statement that "No one has ever seen God" relevant to the mention of law? Clearly relevant, as a moment's reflection will show, for what did Moses request prior to his receipt of the replacement tables of the law on Mount Sinai? "Show me thy glory" (Exod 33:18). And God replied, "You cannot see my face; for man shall not see me and live" (Exod 33:20). Thus, John 1:18 remains in the context of a discussion of Torah by appealing to an incident involving Moses' receipt of the law and makes the

---

[4] The reading adopted is supported by P^{66}, P^{75}, ℵ, B, *et al.* and preferred by UBSGNT, though the difference in meaning from "the only son" is not significant for our purposes.

point that although the law was given directly from God to Moses, yet the law of Moses is not an unmediated revelation of God—his glory is not seen directly. The Prologue, however, affirms that—in contrast to the law—Christ, who is God the Son, does constitute a direct revelation of God, for the Son resides in the very "bosom" of God and makes him known in a direct and immediate fashion. The Fourth Gospel knows the answer to the Wisdom writer's question in Sir 43:31, "Who has seen (*tis heoraken*) him [i.e. God] and can fully make him known (*ekdiēgēsetai*)? Or who can extol him as he is?" John 1:18: "No one has ever seen (*oudeis heōraken*) God; God the only Son. . . , he has made him known (*exēgēsato*)." Jesus Christ is now the interpreter, the narrator, the exegete of God!

Furthermore, the phrase "bosom of the Father" establishes the point more securely when it is remembered that the Rabbis could say that the Torah "lay on God's bosom" (see reference above). John 1:18 declares, then, that "no one has seen God"—true!—not even Moses did when he received the law from God, but "God the only Son, who is in the bosom of the Father"—the very place where Torah was thought to be located before creation, "he"—not Torah—"has made him [God] known."

The reader of vss. 17-18 now will realize that this line of thought has been anticipated to some extent in vs. 14, where the term "glory" is prominent:

> We beheld his glory,
> glory as of the only Son from the Father.

Moses' request to see God's glory was denied, but the "Word" embodies that very glory which was denied to Moses, the recipient of Torah. Moreover, that "glory as of the only Son from the Father" has been seen and can be seen in Jesus Christ. Henceforth it is in Christ—not in Torah—that the glory of God is open to view.

Verses 14 and 17 are tied together also by the words "grace and truth" (*charis kai alētheia*), which again take us back to the Exod context just discussed; notice Exod 34:6-7:

> The LORD, the LORD, a God merciful (LXX: *oiktirmōn*) and gracious (LXX: *eleēmōn*), slow to anger, and abounding in steadfast love (Hebrew: *ḥsd;* LXX: *polyeleos*) and faithfulness (*'mt;* LXX: *alēthinos*), keeping steadfast love (*ḥsd;* LXX: *eleos*) for thousands, forgiving iniquity and transgression and sin.

Examples of other passages that emphasize these two attributes of God—steadfast love and truth—in the context of Torah are Ps 119:64, 75-77, 88-90, 124, 138, 159-60. It should be noted that "steadfast love" (*ḥsd*) becomes "mercy" (*eleos*) in the LXX, where it means "undeserved favor," that is, "grace"; therefore, *ḥsd* as an attribute of God is quite properly represented by "grace" (*charis*) in the Prologue, since in NT times *eleos* more commonly refers to human compassion (especially in the Gospels), while divine "favor" and "gracious care" are expressed more commonly by *charis*. Hence, the Johannine "grace" (*charis*) represents both the Hebrew "steadfast love" (*ḥsd*) and the LXX "mercy" (*eleos*); the latter, by the way, virtually always in the LXX has the term *ḥsd* behind it. The Johannine "truth" (*alētheia*) stands for the Hebrew "truth" or "faithfulness" (*'mt* or its cognates), and ninety percent of the occurrences of *alētheia* in the LXX have *'mt* or its cognates behind them. (*Charis* never appears again in the Fourth Gospel; it is found four times, all in the Prologue; *eleos* is not used at all in John.)

More importantly, "grace" and "truth" are two of the most distinctive OT attributes of God. The two terms appear together, for example, in the following passages: 2 Sam 15:20 (cf. LXX); Ps 25:10 (quoted also in Tob 3:2); Pss 40:11; 57:10; 89:1, 2, 14, 24, 33, 49; cf. Pss 86:15; 108:4; and Hos 4:1 (which says that "there is no steadfast love or truth or knowledge of God in the land").

The *locus classicus* concerning God's "grace and truth" is Ps 25:10, and it is also in a Torah context:

> All the paths of the LORD are steadfast love (*hsd;* LXX: *eleos*) and faithfulness (*'mt;* LXX: *alētheia*), for those who keep his covenant and his testimonies.

Notice, now, how the Midrash on Psalms 25 § 11 explains this "grace and truth" of God:

> Moses answered them. . . , I shall tell you the paths of the LORD. All the paths of the LORD are grace [*or* mercy] and truth. "Grace," by this is meant the proofs of [God's] love, and "truth," by this is meant the Torah. And to whom did he send them? To those who keep his covenant and his testimonies.

Thus, Torah is closely tied to the notions of God's "grace and truth"; the rabbinic understanding expressed in the Midrash is that grace and truth come to those who keep the law, so it might be said that Torah is "full of grace and truth"; moreover, Torah is itself truth.

In John 1:17 the law is spoken of as given through Moses—calling on the reader to think about Torah—but grace and truth, prime attributes of God that have been associated also with Torah in Jewish tradition, are not mediated by Torah, but by Jesus Christ. This at once calls the reader back to 1:14, where it is the "Word," that is, Jesus Christ, which is "full of grace and truth"—again, not the law. The paths of God may be "grace and truth," and these may have been mediated through Torah to those who observed it, but no more, for now it is the only Son, presently occupying the (former) resting place of Torah in God's bosom, who reveals God. For the author of the Prologue, then, Torah has been displaced—superseded by Jesus Christ!

If the notion expressed in Pesikta Rabbati 20.4 (quoted above) was widely held, that God would have had no abiding place if Israel had not received the Torah, then the force of the Prologue, in such a context, is something like this: The "Word" dwelt among us, which corresponds to Torah having been given to Israel; God found an abiding place in Israel through its acceptance of Torah, but now Torah's place is taken by the "Word," that is, by Jesus Christ, in whom are present the most distinctive attributes of God, grace and truth, and in whom is embodied the very glory of God. Torah has been superannuated, and God has an abiding place among his people only through Jesus Christ.

Finally, the relationship between vss. 17-18 and vs. 14 goes one step farther: the clause, "The Word . . . dwelt among us" (in vs. 14), recalls again a Moses/Exodus context (which is explicit in vs. 17), for the verb "to dwell" (*skēnoō*) is, of course, "to pitch a tent" or "to tabernacle," recalling the instructions to Moses to build the Tabernacle for God's dwelling place (Exod 25-40). This well-known theme needs no discussion here, except to refer to the glory of the Lord that filled the Tabernacle and prevented Moses' entry, as noted in Exod 40:34-35. The Prologue's statement that "the Word ... dwelt among us, full of grace and truth" is followed immediately by "We have beheld his glory." The glory denied to Moses but resident in the Tabernacle is now seen in Christ, who "tabernacled among us."

When the author of the Fourth Gospel has led the reader through vss. 17-18, his intention for the whole Prologue becomes clear: First, the "Word" is extolled in terms not at all uncongenial to a description of Wisdom and Torah as expressions or revelations of God (since, as we have seen, the "Word" shares many of the distinctive features and functions of Wisdom and Torah). Secondly, the "Word" is "full of grace and truth" and associated with the "glory" of God, all apt ways to describe Wisdom and Torah. Yet, thirdly, for the Fourth Gospel neither Wisdom nor Torah is the subject of the Prologue; quite the contrary, for they are excluded and displaced by the real subject, the ultimate, genuine "Word" or expression of God, namely, Jesus Christ, who—rather than Torah or Wisdom—henceforth mediates grace and truth and is the *direct* revelation of the very glory of God himself. Christ the Word now is "instruction" or "teaching" from and about God and has supplanted Torah (which, in its broadest and richest meaning, signifies "instruction/teaching"). Torah, which had been a middle term between God and his people since the momentous, formative exodus-events, has that position usurped, according to John, by the new "Word" from God, Jesus Christ. All of this is not to suggest that John has a "gospel versus law" motif, either in the Gospel as a whole or even in the Prologue. Bultmann (*Commentary,* pp. 17, 78-79), for example, claims that vs. 17 "makes use of the (Pauline) antithesis *nomos-charis* [law-grace], which is otherwise foreign to the Gospel." Clearly, there is a contrast or a sharp line drawn between Torah and Christ in vs. 17 and elsewhere in the Prologue, but this difference should be viewed more in terms of fulfillment and continuity than in terms of opposition or antithesis.

Actually, it seems as much an injustice to Paul as to the Fourth Gospel to ascribe to them an antithesis between Moses and Christ or law and gospel. For Paul, Christ is the "end (*telos*) of the law" (Rom 10:4), and the law was a "custodian until Christ came" (Gal 3:19, 23-24) and served "to increase the trespass" (Rom 5:20; 7:7-9); therefore, the law is not "sin" but "holy" (Rom 7:7, 12; cf. Rom 3:31; Gal 3:21). Thus, for Paul, the law served a timely function, even though the promises of God reach back to a time prior to the law (Gal 3:17-18; Rom 4:13). Paul has, then, a displacement or supersession theme: the law functioned as God's agent from Moses until Christ, when the ancient promises were fulfilled.

The Fourth Gospel has a similar view of law: 1:45 affirms that Moses in the law wrote of Jesus of Nazareth; 5:39 indicates that the Scriptures bear witness to Christ; 5:45-46 says again that "Moses wrote of me";

7:19-23 employs the law to validate the authority and actions of Jesus as sent by God; 7:42 recalls the Davidic messianic expectations in Scripture; 7:49-51 (stressing, especially in vs. 51, civil aspects of the law) speaks of the law's provisions for a fair trial of Jesus when dispute arose whether he was Messiah or not; 8:17 cites the law to show that Jesus' claims were valid; similarly 10:34 employs the law to authenticate Jesus as Son of God; 12:34 refers to a statement of law as it applies to the Messiah; 15:25 affirms that such a prophecy in the law was fulfilled when Jesus was rejected; and 18:31-32 ties in the law with the fulfillment of Jesus' statement about his own death. Cf. 4:22: "Salvation is from the Jews."

There is nothing here that speaks against the law, but what is said about Moses, Torah and the Scriptures fits the displacement theme—the law points or leads to Christ and serves, therefore, a positive and "holy" function as far as the Fourth Gospel is concerned. It is not, then, a matter of opposition or antithesis—in the sense of an either/or—between Torah and Christ, but of Torah leading to Christ and of Christ displacing Torah when the latter has fulfilled its divine role and purpose. It is not so much an either/or as it is a then/now situation. Naturally, the then/now implies the either/or, that is, urges the choice of Christ rather than Torah, and in this sense, though *only* in this sense, there is a negative judgment on law. At the same time, it is clear that John has no positive judgment on law of the kind implied, for example, in Matt 5:18-19, where the present, future, and indeed eternal validity of the details of Torah is delineated:

> For truly I say to you, till heaven and earth pass away, not an iota, not a dot, will pass from the law until all is accomplished. Whoever then relaxes one of the least of these commandments and teaches men so, shall be called least in the kingdom of heaven, but he who does them and teaches them shall be called great in the kingdom of heaven.[5]

Rather, the Fourth Gospel has transferred these eternal and normative characteristics from Torah (and Wisdom) to Jesus Christ, as is evident first from the Prologue and then from the Gospel as a whole.

Incidentally, if it can be assumed that John knew Paul's views on law, then John 15:22 may have a special significance. Paul, in view of Rom 7:7-9, could very well have said, "If Torah had not come, they would not have sin, but now they have no excuse for their sin"; actually, the Fourth Gospel has Jesus say, "If *I* had not come and spoken to them, they would not have sin, but now they have no excuse for their sin" (cf. John 9:40-41).

VI

This theme of the Prologue, that Christ has displaced Torah and has become the fulfillment, the new and direct "Word" or expression of God, reveals itself as a purpose of the entire Fourth Gospel. It will not be feasible

---

[5] M. Jack Suggs, *Wisdom, Christology, and Law in Matthew's Gospel*, Cambridge, Mass., 1970, p. 106, makes the point that in Matt 11:28-30 Jesus speaks as Wisdom and as Torah, but that he is *not* offering there an alternative to Torah. This is another evidence that Matthew and John have different views on law.

or essential to trace this out in fine detail, but some hints and broad strokes of its development will make the point sufficiently clear.

The Fourth Gospel, quite in contrast to the Synoptics, portrays the historical Jesus unambiguously as one who knows himself to be the direct, immediate and full revelation of God the Father. From the beginning to the end of John, Jesus is depicted in that intimate relationship with God which the phrase "in the bosom of the Father" would imply; the most substantial of these passages are John 5:19-47; 6:29-58; 7:14-29; 8:12-59; 10:22-38; 14:1-31; and 17:1-26. It is striking that in these and in some similar, though shorter, contexts the themes of Moses, the law, or God's glory (which earlier we have tied in with the Mosaic law) are present and prominent. These several passages require closer examination.

The lengthy monologue on Jesus' intimate interrelationship with God the Father that occupies 5:19-47 is occasioned by a dispute about Sabbath laws, which in turn arose from Jesus' act of healing at the pool of Bethzatha (5:2-18). In 5:17, as a defensive procedure, Jesus links himself with the Father as one who works; the result seems to be that Jesus places himself above the law, but the rest of the discourse shows more clearly his evaluation of law (as John portrays it). The theme of Jesus' authority for the deeds performed is pursued directly in 5:19-20 and again in 30-47. We are brought into the context of the Prologue by references to John the Baptist as a witness to Christ (5:33-36; cf. 1:6-8, 15) and to God not being visible to men (5:37), but the climax is reached in 39-47 with the mention of searching the Scriptures (i.e. written Torah) to secure eternal life and of placing hope in Moses (i.e. Torah). The theme of the Prologue is brought out clearly by Jesus' claims (1) that life is to be found in him, not in the Scriptures, and (2) that the Scriptures and Moses wrote of him. Both claims imply that Torah, while it had a distinct and sacred task, has been superseded by the one who has "glory that comes from the only God" (5:44). A further reflection of the Prologue is 5:43: "I have come in my Father's name, and you do not receive me"; cf. 5:37-38, where the same charge is made, along with the implication (vs. 37) that Jesus has seen God.

The dialogue in 6:25-58 leads early to a discussion of manna (6:31) and returns to it near the end (6:49). Again, Moses is brought to the center by Jesus' comment, ". . . It was not Moses who gave you the bread from heaven; my Father gives you the true bread from heaven" (6:32). The connection of bread and life is explicit in vs. 33, recalling 1:4, "In him was life," and the Prologue (as well as the Moses/law context) comes into view also in vs. 46: "Not that any one has seen the Father except him who is from God; he has seen the Father"; finally, 6:47-49, as well as the concluding verse 58, complete the cycle of thought by returning to manna and contrasting the mere physical sustenance of manna ("they died") with the eternal life that issues from the "living bread." Hence, the Moses/Christ contrast is repeated here.

The dialogue in 7:14-29 refers back to the Sabbath healing in 5:2-18 and continues Jesus' lengthy defense of his authority in 5:19-47, where—as already noted—Torah, Moses and God's glory were prominent. The same themes reappear in chap. 7: "glory" in 7:18, which portrays Jesus as seeking the glory that is from God (subjective genitive; cf. 5:44) rather than his own; this is consistent with the derivative glory of the "Word" first mentioned in 1:14. Although Torah is not discredited by Jesus in 7:19-24, since he employs a rabbinic argument (7:23) to validate his healing on the Sabbath, yet the net effect—as the narrative portrays it— is to place Jesus in contrast, once again, to the law of Moses and to suggest that he superseded it.

The theme of Jesus' authority and his self-witness is taken up once more in 8:12-59. The bitter interchange with the Jews that develops here does not mention Moses or Torah, but it reaches back—in Pauline fashion (Gal 3:17-18; Rom 4:13-22; cf. John 7:22)—behind the law of Moses to Abraham. The climax of the passage (8:54-58), however, implies the Moses/Torah context in two ways. First, it refers to Jesus' glory in a way that again is a reminder of and consistent with the Prologue (1:14, 18): Jesus' glory is meaningless unless it derives from God the Father (8:54). "No one has ever seen God," says the Prologue, though the "Word" now reveals him; certainly, then, it is significant that twice in vs. 56 the word "see" is used with reference to Abraham: "Abraham rejoiced that he was to *see* my day; he *saw* it and was glad." Secondly, and more pointedly, the Moses context is implied in 8:58, where Jesus claims that "before Abraham was, I AM." The obvious reference is to Exod 3:14-15, where God identifies himself to Moses as "I AM WHO I AM. . . . Say this to the people of Israel, 'I AM has sent me to you.' " The Fourth Gospel has Jesus apply the personal name of God to himself, calling to mind a key Moses passage from the OT. (Cf. also John 6:20; 13:19; the famous Johannine "I am" sayings; and 5:43, "I have come in my Father's name.") Not only does such an expression applied to Jesus attest his deity—"the Word was God"—but it rather signally emphasizes his transcendency to Moses.

The discussion in 10:1-38, particularly vss. 22-38, is a familiar one: Jesus defending his deeds and his claims. In the course of the dialogue, the law of Moses is utilized by Jesus in a rabbinic-type argument to reaffirm the close interrelationship between himself and the Father (10:34-36). The parenthetical statement, "And scripture cannot be broken," adds to the positive evaluation of Torah, but the impact of the entire passage in John 10 is that Torah is the foundation or ground for attesting the claim that Jesus is "the Son of God," "consecrated and sent" by God himself (10:35-36)—in other words, a repetition of the theme, "Moses wrote of me" (5:46).

One of the clearest passages on Jesus' identity with the Father is 14:1-31, especially vss. 6-11, where there is no direct mention of Moses or Torah. It might be argued, however, that the entreaty of Philip, "Lord, show us the Father," parallels Moses' request, "Lord, show me thy glory" (Exod 33:18, discussed earlier). The request of Philip is introduced into the narrative by the rather abrupt reference to having "seen" the Father, which is in the preceding Jesus-Thomas dialogue (14:7). In the case of Moses, the answer to his question was "No"; in the case of Philip, a quite different response came from Jesus: "He who has seen me has seen the Father" (14:9). Again, we are back to the Prologue: "No one has ever seen

God; God the Son, who is in the bosom of the Father, he has made him known."

Finally, the prayer of Jesus in 17:1-26 brings the Prologue strikingly into view when Jesus prays, "Father, glorify thou me in thy own presence with the glory which I had with thee before the world was made" (17:5; cf. 24). The theme of glory is picked up again in 17:22: "The glory which thou hast given me I have given to them." The glory of God, which Moses could not see, but which was the possession of the pre-existent Son, now has been "given" (*dedōka* > *didōmi*) to those who believe, just as Torah once was "given" (*edothē* > *didōmi*) through Moses (1:17). Again, however, the subtle point is that God's glory is not revealed fully by Torah, but by Jesus Christ, and in this respect he has displaced the law of Moses. Notice, too, the statement in 17:17, which, when compared with the Prologue, has an obvious double meaning: "Thy word is truth."

A survey of these "I am in the Father and the Father is in me" passages shows that they nearly always involve or at least are supportive of the theme of Moses/Torah displaced by Christ in the ways in which that theme is developed by the Prologue. The Fourth Gospel in this way reveals one of its purposes: to show that the God of Israel, the "I AM" of the Exodus, the God of glory who gave the law, in spite of his extraordinary steadfast love (grace) and faithfulness (truth), never was revealed fully to humankind until Jesus Christ, full of grace and truth, made him known.

A similar point is made through the much-studied "signs" of the Fourth Gospel. First, all interpreters will agree that most, if not all, of the seven "signs" or miracle stores in John point to Jesus Christ (i.e. both the earthly Jesus as John portrays him and the risen Christ of John's theology) as the giver of life or light, culminating in the last sign, the raising of Lazarus. When Jesus literally restores light (sight) and life (or health), he illustrates what the Prologue has earlier affirmed: "That which had come to be in him was life, and the life was the light of men." Life and light were understood by the Prologue, however, to have come through Jesus Christ in contrast to and as the successor of Torah (and Wisdom) as the mediator of life and light.

This point is made quite nicely in chap. 9 in the "sign" of restoring sight to the man born blind (which illustrates not only the Prologue's references to the "Word" as light, but more immediately Jesus' statement in 8:12, "I am the light of the world; he who follows me . . . will have the light of life," which is repeated in 9:5). The Pharisees who were investigating the healing said to the healed man, "You are his [Jesus'] disciple, but we are disciples of Moses. We know that God has spoken to Moses, but as for this man [Jesus], we do not know where he comes from" (9:28-29). The contrast between Moses and Christ is obvious: it was no longer the disciples of Moses (to whom God had spoken—implying "word"=Torah) who brought light and life through Torah; rather, light and life reside in the "Word," Jesus Christ.

Secondly, the "signs" become significant in another way—viewed in the light of the Prologue—when it is noted that the author conceives of them as manifestations of Jesus' glory (2:11):

This, the first of his signs, Jesus did at Cana in Galilee, and manifested his glory; and his disciples believed in him.

Already in the book of Numbers this connection between "signs" and "glory" had been noted in God's words to Moses, which refer to ". . . the men who have seen my glory (LXX: *doxa*) and my signs (LXX: *sēmeia*) which I wrought in Egypt and in the wilderness" (Num 14:22). In the Johannine account of the first sign (2:1-11), the "six stone jars . . . for the Jewish rites of purification" were filled, and their contents were changed miraculously by Jesus. The customary interpretation is that the Fourth Gospel views Jesus as filling these Jewish ritual jars with new meaning or content, a new way of life. We may say, then, that John here is illustrating his conviction that Jesus has displaced and is the fulfillment of the Mosiac regulations. (Since the jars came to hold wine, is it too farfetched to suggest that the saying in 15:1, 5, "I am the vine," implies that Jesus Christ is the "good wine" which fills these Mosaic jars?—again, a displacement theme.) John, in any case, regards the filling of the Mosaic jars—this supersession of Torah—as an instance of seeing the glory of God as revealed through Jesus Christ.

Furthermore, in the account of the last sign, when Jesus heard of Lazarus' illness, he said, "It is for the glory of God, so that the Son of God may be glorified by means of it" (11:4), and just before the actual resuscitation Jesus said to Martha, "Did I not tell you that if you would believe you would see the glory of God?" (11:40). Finally, at the end of the "Book of the Signs" (John 2:1-12:50), following a summary statement about the "many signs" Jesus had done and yet the lack of belief in him, words of Isaiah are cited, and the author of John comments (12:41): "Isaiah said this because he saw his [Jesus'] glory and spoke of him."

Hence, the "signs," which comprise a notable portion of the Gospel, are present in John (1) so that Jesus' glory, "glory as of the only Son from the Father," can be seen or "manifested" in a direct fashion never attained in Moses' day or through Mosaic regulations, and (2) so that light and life, formerly mediated by Torah, can reach those who believe.

VII

In summary, an analysis of the Prologue, specifically its poetic and hymnic character, its literary and ideational matrix in the Wisdom hymns (along with the Jewish identification of Wisdom with Torah), and its contrast between Moses/Torah and Christ, uncovers at least one of the purposes, not only of the Prologue, but of the entire Fourth Gospel. The general structure and the specific content of the Prologue, the numerous christological passages in the body of the Fourth Gospel, and the narratives of the "signs" indicate, both in explicit and in more subtle ways, that Torah has been superannuated, superseded and displaced by Christ, the direct "Word" or expression of God and the unmediated disclosure of the glory of God. This does not mean that Torah has no positive judgment placed on it, but only that it has served its sacred function as a prelude to Christ. Whereas Torah was a middle term between the God of steadfast love and faithfulness and his people, henceforth Christ mediates these prime attributes of God, grace and truth, to those who believe; whereas Torah conferred life, light and salvation, henceforth Christ is the giver of life and light to those who believe; and whereas Torah brought Moses *nearly* face to face with God, furnished God an abiding place in Israel, and was the "instruction" of God to his people, henceforth Christ is the direct encounter with God, the lodgment of the very glory of God, and the exegesis of God uniquely open to view.

A New English Translation
of Melito's Paschal Homily

GERALD F. HAWTHORNE

In 1940 Campbell Bonner published the first Greek text with notes, and an English translation, of the *Sermon on the Passover* by Melito, Bishop of Sardis (died about 190).[1] Since that time much scholarly attention has been turned in Melito's direction.[2] And no wonder, for in the words of Professor Frank Cross, Melito's Homily "must be regarded as the most important addition to Patristic literature in the present century."[3]

In spite of all this interest, however, no new, and hence no complete translation of Melito's Homily for the English reader has been forthcoming, even though the discovery and publication of a new Greek text of the Homily, and studies focusing on the Latin, Coptic, Syriac and Georgian translations of it now make possible the reading of the sermon in its entirety.[4]

Because of the importance of Melito's Paschal Homily, and because of an abundance of recent available data, I am now offering to the English reader a new translation based on an eclectic critical Greek text prepared especially for it. This text differs in several places from the only published critical text—that prepared by Othmar Perler.[5] But variations from Perler's

---

[1] Campbell Bonner, *Melito of Sardes, the Homily on the Passion, with Some Fragments of Ezekiel,* Studies and Documents, 12, Philadelphia, 1940.

[2] For a full bibliography on Melito's Paschal Homily until 1969, see G. F. Hawthorne, "Melito of Sardis: His Rhetoric and Theology," unpublished doctoral dissertation, the University of Chicago, 1969. From correspondence with Professor S. G. Hall of Nottingham, I learn that he is in the process of compiling a complete bibliography on Melito. It may be in print by the time this translation appears.

[3] F. L. Cross, *The Early Christian Fathers,* London, 1960, p. 104.

[4] The Michigan-Beatty Papyrus, used by Bonner, was mutilated in spots. This made reconstruction necessary, either on the basis of an existing translation, another Greek text, or conjecture. Sometimes reconstruction was totally impossible, and hence lines of text were omitted. Bonner's translation (1940), therefore, was fragmentary and in many places had to be conjectural.

[5] O. Perler, *Méliton de Sardes sur la Pâque et Fragments,* SC, 123, Paris, 1966. This volume includes a French translation and notes.

Gerald F. Hawthorne, Professor of Greek at Wheaton College, Wheaton, Illinois. Th.B., Biola; B.A., Wheaton College; M.A., Wheaton College Graduate School; Ph.D., The University of Chicago.

text have been noted in the margin, as well as many differences from the other major translations of the Homily.[6] I do not presume that this translation is perfect, nor that it will be final.[7] Nor do I claim that it is a "critical" translation since the margin takes note primarily of variants among modern translations, not differences between the Greek texts and ancient versions. But I publish it now in the hope that it will honor a respected teacher and colleague of mine, Professor Merrill C. Tenney, and at the same time benefit any interested English reader until a more adequate translation appears.

If my translation differs frequently from other modern versions, it is because I have adopted a different reading, more for rhetorical reasons than for theological ones. I made no attempt to translate the Homily until I had first completed a detailed analysis of Melito's rhetoric—his vocabulary, grammar, structure, rhetorical figures, manner of quoting Scripture, literary milieu, etc.,[8] believing that an understanding of the Homily's literary form is essential in determining its text. Theology did, however, play some part, for one cannot study a person's writing this closely without forming some idea of how he thinks.

The translation is presented in sense lines to give the reader some feel

[6] In addition to Bonner's and Perler's translations, there is another French translation: M. Testuz, ed., *Papyrus Bodmer XIII, Méliton de Sardes Homélie sur la Pâque,* Geneva, 1960; and one in German: J. Blank, *Meliton von Sardes Vom Passa,* Freiburg, 1963, pp. 101-31.

[7] For one thing, not all of the texts of the Homily known to exist have been used in preparation of the Greek text behind my translation. The Mississippi Coptic Codex I (Crosby Codex, at the University of Mississippi), for example, is not presently available to scholars, and the last half of the Georgian version, published by Professor M. van Esbroeck in *Le Muséon,* 84 (1971), 373-94, did not come to my attention until too late for use here. My text and translation are based primarily on the two major Greek texts—the Michigan-Beatty text (Bonner, *Melito of Sardis*), which includes, in fragmentary fashion, sects. 1-104, and the Bodmer text (Testuz, *Méliton*), which has sects. 6-105 in excellent condition. B. Lohse has prepared an easily accessible Greek text of the Michigan-Beatty MS of the Homily arranged in sense-lines (B. Lohse, ed., *Die Passa-Homelie des Bishofs Meliton von Sardes,* Leiden, 1958). He does not always agree with Bonner's reconstructions. In addition, I have also used a Greek fragment of sects. 57b-63 (P. Oxy. 1600 in B. P. Grenfell and A. S. Hunt, eds., *Oxyrhynchus Papyri,* London, 1898-1919, 13, 19-21); two Syriac translations: S[1], which contains sects. 70-72, 80c-82, 93, 95-98, 99c-100, 104 (W. Cureton, ed., *Spicilegium Syriacum,* London, 1855, pp. 31-33, 49-50, 54-56), and S[2], which has sects. 94-98 (J. B. Pitra, ed., *Analecta Sacra,* 8 vols., Paris, 1876-1891, 4, 433 and 199-200); a Coptic fragment of sects. 12-16 (W. E. Crum and H. I. Bell, eds., *Wadi Sarga: Coptic and Greek Texts,* Hauniae, 1922, 3, 47-49); a Latin epitome of the Homily that contains sects. 1-5, 64-65, 67-82, 84, 86, 99-100, 103-104 (H. Chadwick, "A Latin Epitome of Melito's Homily on the Pascha," *JTS,* 11 [1960], 76-82); the Georgian version of sects. 1-45 (J. N. Birdsall, "Melito of Sardis, Περὶ τοῦ Πάσχα in a Georgian Version," *Le Muséon,* 80 [1967], 121-38), and of sects. 46-105 (M. van Esbroeck, "Le traité sur la pâque de Méliton de Sardes en Géorgien," *Le Muséon,* 84 [1971], 373-94).

[8] See Hawthorne, "Melito of Sardis," pp. 188-256. My thanks to Professor Robert M. Grant of the University of Chicago for sharing with me his immense knowledge of the history of the early church, and for giving unstintingly of his time to help and encourage me in preparing this study which culminated in the present tentative translation of Melito's Homily.

for the highly rhetorical nature of the Homily. Melito lived at the height of the Second Sophistic, a literary movement that was more concerned with *how* something was said than with *what* was said. As far as we know, Melito was the first Christian to adopt this "worldly" form in order to make the gospel relevant to his generation. He, however, was interested in content as well as in form; or to put it another way, he knew the importance of form for content. A reading of the Homily, which now follows, will show Melito did have something to say.

MELITO, "ON THE PASSOVER"

Introduction (1-10)

1. First of all, the Scripture about the Hebrew Exodus has been read
and the words of the mystery have been explained[9]
as to how the sheep was sacrificed
and the people were saved.
2. Therefore, understand this, O beloved:
The mystery of the passover is
new and old,
eternal and temporal,
corruptible and incorruptible,
mortal and immortal
in this fashion:
3. It is old insofar as it concerns the law,
but new insofar as it concerns the gospel;[10]
temporal insofar as it concerns the type,[11]
eternal because of grace;
corruptible because of the sacrifice of the sheep,
incorruptible because of the life of the Lord;
mortal because of his burial in the earth,
immortal because of his resurrection from the dead.
4. The law is old,
but the gospel is new;
the type was for a time,
but grace is forever.
The sheep was corruptible,
but the Lord is incorruptible,
who was crushed as a lamb,[12]
but who was resurrected[13] as God.
For although he was led to sacrifice as a sheep,

---

[9] Much discussion has gone into how this initial sentence should be translated—
as here, or as, "The Scripture about the Exodus has been read in Hebrew, and then
translated." See the discussion in Bonner, *Homily*, pp. 30-36; "A Supplementary
Note on the Opening of Melito's Homily," *HTR*, 36 (1943), 317-19; G. Zuntz, "On
the Opening Sentence of Melito's Paschal Homily," *HTR*, 36 (1943), 299-315; A.
Wifstrand, "The Homily of Melito on the Passion," *VC*, 2 (1948), 217; Perler,
Méliton, pp. 131-32; Testùz, *Méliton*, p. 18. Scholarship is divided. For the many
allusions to the OT in the Homily, see the footnotes to the text prepared by Perler.

[10] Greek: *logos*.

[11] Bonner: world (?); Lohse: time.

[12] Blank, Bonner, Testuz: who, as the lamb, was not broken; Perler: sacrificed as
a lamb.

[13] Blank, Perler, Testuz: who rose up.

yet he was not a sheep;
and although he was as a lamb without voice,
yet indeed he was not a lamb.
The one was the model;
the other was found to be the finished product.[14]

5. For God[15] replaced the lamb,
and a man the sheep;
but in the man was Christ,
who contains all things.

6. Hence, the sacrifice of the sheep,
and the sending of the lamb to slaughter,[16]
and the writing of the law—
each led to and issued in Christ,
for whose sake everything happened in the ancient law,
and even more so in the new gospel.

7. For indeed the law issued in the gospel—
the old in the new,
both coming forth together from Zion and Jerusalem;
and the commandment issued in grace,
and the type in the finished product,[17]
and the lamb in the Son,
and the sheep in a man,
and the man in God.

8. For the one who was born as Son,
and led to slaughter as a lamb,
and sacrificed as a sheep,
and buried as a man,
rose up from the dead as God,
since he is by nature both God and man.

9. He is everything:
in that he judges he is law,
in that he teaches he is gospel,
in that he saves he is grace,
in that he begets he is Father,
in that he is begotten he is Son,
in that he suffers he is sheep,
in that he is buried he is man,
in that he comes to life again he is God.

10. Such is Jesus Christ,
to whom be the glory forever. Amen.

---

[14] Lit.: the truth.

[15] Bonner, Lohse: Son. The Georgian supports this. Three Latin texts have *dominum;* one has *deus.* Hall thinks there is little to be said for "God," and since both "God" and "Lord" would be abbreviated in Greek, there would be too little space for the uncertain word in the mutilated Greek manuscript. It seems, on the other hand, that Melito's theology demands either "God" or "Lord." The whole theme of the Homily is the God-man acting for our salvation. The theme is set here.

[16] Blank, Perler, Testuz: and the celebration of the passover.

[17] Lit.: truth.

I. *The Meaning of the OT Passover* (11-71)

A. The Biblical Setting—Exod 12:11-30 (11-15)

11. Now comes the mystery of the passover,
    even as it stands written in the law,
    just as it has been read aloud only moments ago.
    But I will clearly set forth the significance of the
    words of this Scripture,
    showing how God commanded Moses in Egypt,
    when he had made his decision,
    to bind Pharaoh under the lash,
    but to release Israel from the lash
    through the hand of Moses.
12. For see to it, he says,
    that you take a flawless and perfect lamb,
    and that you sacrifice it in the evening
    with the sons of Israel,
    and that you eat it at night, and in haste.
    You are not to break any of its bones.
13. You will do it like this, he says:
    In a single night
    you will eat it by families and by tribes,
    your loins girded,
    and your staves in your hands.
    For this is the Lord's passover,
    an eternal reminder for the sons of Israel.
14. Then take the blood of the sheep,
    and anoint the front door of your houses
    by placing upon the posts of your entrance-way
    the sign of the blood, in order to ward off the angel.[18]
    For behold I will strike Egypt,
    and in a single night
    she will be made childless from beast to man.
15. Then, when Moses sacrificed the sheep
    and completed the mystery at night
    together with the sons of Israel,
    he sealed the doors of their houses
    in order to protect the people
    and to ward off the angel.

B. Egypt's Calamities (16-29)

16. But when the sheep was sacrificed,
    and the passover consumed,

---

[18] The lines "and anoint ... angel" read as follows in the Coptic (British Museum Or. MS. 9035): "and shall smear it upon the doorposts and the lintels of the doors of your houses for a sign unto the angel." Bonner basically follows this version in reconstructing the Beatty text.

and the mystery completed,
and the people made glad,
and Israel sealed,[19]
then the angel arrived to strike Egypt,
who was neither
initiated into the mystery,
participant of the passover,
sealed by the blood,
nor protected by the Spirit,
but who was the enemy and the unbeliever.

17. In a single night the angel struck and made Egypt childless.
For when the angel had encompassed Israel,
and had seen her sealed with the blood of the sheep,
he advanced against Egypt,
and by means of grief subdued the stubborn Pharaoh,
clothing him,
not with a cloak of mourning,
nor with a torn mantle,
but with all of Egypt, torn,
and mourning for her firstborn.

18. For all Egypt,
plunged in troubles and calamities,
in tears and lamentations,
came to Pharaoh in utter sadness,
not in appearance only,
but also in soul,
having torn not only her garments
but her tender breasts as well.

19. Indeed it was possible to observe an extraordinary sight:
in one place people beating their breasts,
in another those wailing,
and in the middle of them Pharaoh,
mourning, sitting in sackcloth and cinders,
shrouded in thick[20] darkness
as in a funeral garment,
girded with all Egypt,
as with a tunic of grief.

20. For Egypt clothed Pharaoh[21]
as a cloak of wailing.
Such was the mantle that had been woven for his royal body.
With just such a cloak did the angel of righteousness clothe
the self-willed Pharaoh:
with bitter mournfulness,
and with thick darkness,
and with childlessness.

[19] The verbs in sect. 16 to this point are all present tenses.
[20] Lit.: touchable, palpable.
[21] For the most part sect. 20 is missing from the Michigan-Beatty MS due to mutilation of the text.

For that angel warred against the firstborn of Egypt.
Indeed, swift and insatiate
was the death of the firstborn.

21. And an unusual monument of defeat,
set up over those who had fallen dead in a moment,
could be seen.
For the defeat of those who lay dead
became the provisions of death.[22]

22. If you listen
to the narration of this extraordinary event
you will be astonished.
For these things befell the Egyptians:
a long night,
and darkness which was touchable,
and death which touched,
and an angel who oppressed,
and Hades which devoured
their firstborn.

23. But you must listen to
something still more extraordinary and terrifying:
in the darkness which could be touched
was hidden death which could not be touched.
And the ill-starred Egyptians touched the darkness,
while death, on the watch,
touched the firstborn of the Egyptians
as the angel had commanded.

24. Therefore, if anyone touched the darkness
he was led out by[23] death.[24]
Indeed one firstborn,
touching a dark body with his hand,
and utterly frightened in his soul,
cried aloud in misery and in terror:
What has my right hand laid hold of?
At what does my soul tremble?
Who cloaks my whole body with darkness?[25]
If you are my father, help me;
if my mother, feel sympathy for me;
if my brother, speak to me;
if my friend, sit with me;[26]
if my enemy, go away from me
since I am a firstborn son!

---

[22] The text of sect. 21 is defective in the Michigan-Beatty MS, and somewhat corrupt in the Bodmer. Blank, Perler, Testuz give a translation essentially the same as here. Bonner translates: "And a strange trophy was to be seen, raised over the firstborn, dead in one moment, and the saving of Moses became the slaying of those who were condemned."

[23] Perler: to.

[24] Blank, Testuz: the angel.

[25] Blank, Perler, Testuz: What is the darkness that surrounds my whole body?

[26] Perler: Be good (to me); Testuz: Do not harm me.

25. And before the firstborn was silent,
    the long silence held him in its power, saying:
    You are mine, O firstborn!
    I, the silence of death, am your destiny.

26. And another firstborn,
    taking note of the capture of the firstborn,
    denied his identity,
    so that he might not die a bitter death:
    I am not a firstborn son;
    I was born like a third child.[27]
    But he who could not be deceived
    touched that firstborn,
    and he fell forward in silence.
    In a single moment[28]
    the firstborn fruit of the Egyptians was destroyed.
    The one first conceived,
    the one first born,
    the one sought after,
    the one chosen
    was dashed to the ground;
    not only that of men
    but that of irrational animals as well.

27. A lowing was heard in the fields of the earth,
    of cattle bellowing for their nurslings,
    a cow standing over her calf,
    and a mare over her colt.
    And the rest of the cattle,
    having just given birth to their offspring
    and swollen with milk,
    were lamenting bitterly and piteously
    for their firstborn.

28. And there was a wailing and lamentation
    because of the destruction of the men,
    because of the destruction of the firstborn who were dead.
    And all Egypt stank,
    because of the unburied bodies.[29]

29. Indeed one could see a frightful spectacle:
    of the Egyptians
    there were mothers with dishevelled hair,
    and fathers who had lost their minds,
    wailing aloud in terrifying fashion in the Egyptian tongue:
    O wretched persons that we are!
    We have lost our firstborn
    in a single moment![30]
    And they were striking their breasts with their hands,

---

[27] The Georgian version: I am the third son of my mother.
[28] Blank, Perler, Testuz: from a single blow.
[29] Bonner: dead.
[30] Blank, Perler, Testuz: from a single blow.

beating time in hammerlike fashion to the dance for their
dead.[31]

C. Israel's Safety (30-33)

30. Such was the misfortune which encompassed Egypt.
In an instant it made her childless.
But Israel, all the while, was being protected
by the sacrifice of the sheep
and truly was being illumined[32]
by its blood which was shed;
for the death of the sheep
was found to be a rampart for the people.

31. O inexpressible mystery!
the sacrifice of the sheep
was found to be the salvation of the people,[33]
and the death of the sheep
became the life of the people.
For its blood warded off the angel.

32. Tell me, O angel,
At what were you turned away?
At the sacrifice of the sheep,
or the life of the Lord?
At the death of the sheep,
or the type of the Lord?
At the blood of the sheep,
or the Spirit of the Lord?
Clearly, you were turned away[34]

33. because you saw the mystery of the Lord
taking place in the sheep,
the life of the Lord
in the sacrifice of the sheep,
the type of the Lord
in the death of the sheep.
For this reason you did not strike Israel,
but it was Egypt alone that you made childless.

D. Model versus Finished Product (34-38)

34. What was this extraordinary mystery?[35]

---

[31] The Greek for the lines "and they were striking . . . for their dead" is difficult, and results in different translations—Blank: They beat their breasts! They clapped loudly with their hands over the departure of the dead; Perler: And they struck their breasts; they beat with their hands the instruments of bronze in the dance for the dead; Testuz: They beat their breasts, clapping their hands loudly because of the loss of their dead (see the notes in Bonner, *Homily*, p. 104; Perler, *Méliton*, p. 150).

[32] Bonner: was baptized.

[33] Bonner, Perler: Israel; cf. sects. 16, 30.

[34] The Michigan-Beatty MS is corrupt here. Bonner translates, Show me that whereat thou wast confounded.

[35] The Michigan-Beatty MS is more or less defective throughout sects. 34-35.

It was Egypt struck to destruction
but Israel kept for salvation.
Listen to the meaning of this mystery:

35. Beloved, no speech or event takes place
without a pattern or design;
every event and speech
involves a pattern—[36]
that which is spoken, a pattern,
and that which happens, a prefiguration—
in order that as the event
is disclosed through the prefiguration,
so also the speech
may be brought to expression through its outline.

36. Without the model,[37]
no work of art arises.
Is not that which is to come into existence
seen through the model which typifies it?
For this reason a pattern of that which is to be is made
either out of wax,
or out of clay,
or out of wood,
in order that by the smallness of the model,
destined to be destroyed,
might be seen that thing which is to arise from it—
higher than it in size,
and mightier than it in power,
and more beautiful than it in appearance,
and more elaborate than it in ornamentation.

37. So whenever the thing arises
for which the model was made,
then that which carried the image of that future thing
is destroyed as no longer of use,
since it has transmitted its resemblance to that which is
by nature true.
Therefore, that which once was valuable, is now without value
because that which is truly valuable has appeared.

38. For each thing has its own time:
there is a distinct time for the type,
there is a distinct time for the material,
and there is a distinct time[38] for the truth.

Bonner's translation based on a reconstructed text differs considerably from the
translation offered here.

[36] Lit.: encounters a parable; Blank: belongs to the parable; Perler, Testuz:
participates in the symbol.

[37] With Blank and Perler I have adopted for sect. 36 a text reconstructed by
Testuz. In spite of the changes and against the testimony of both the
Michigan-Beatty and Bodmer manuscripts this reconstruction gives a more coherent
text, and one that harmonizes well with the context. The two Greek manuscripts
presuppose a common text already corrupt (see Perler, *Méliton*, pp. 152-53).

[38] This third expression, "and there is a distinct time," is not in the Greek
manuscripts, but is a logical addition suggested by Wifstrand and in harmony with

You construct[39] the model.
You want this,
because you see in it the image of the future work.
You procure the material for the model.[40]
You want this,
on account of that which is going to arise because of it.
You complete the work
and cherish it alone,
for only in it do you see both the type[41] and the truth.

E. Relationship Between OT and NT (39-45)

39. Therefore, if it was like this with models of perishable objects,
so indeed will it also be with those of imperishable objects.
If it was like this with earthly things,
so indeed also will it be with heavenly things.
For even the Lord's salvation and his truth
were prefigured in the people,
and the teaching of the gospel
was proclaimed in advance by the law.

40. The people, therefore, became the model for the church,[42]
and the law a parabolic sketch.
But the gospel became the explanation of the law
and its fulfilment,
while the church became the storehouse of truth.[43]

41. Therefore, the type had value
prior to its realization,
and the parable was wonderful
prior to its interpretation.
This is to say that
the people had value
before the church came on the scene,
and the law was wonderful
before the gospel was brought to light.

42. But when the church came on the scene,
and the gospel was set forth,
the type lost its value
by surrendering its significance to the truth,[44]

Melito's style ("The Homily of Melito on the Passion," pp. 201-23). Omitting it, Bonner and Perler translate this line as follows: of the truth thou makest the type.

[39] After the first line of this sect. the Bodmer MS omits everything to this point and the following line. Blank and Testuz translate accordingly: . . . each thing has its own time. You desire this model. . . .

[40] The verb *prokomizeis* is difficult here. Bonner: Thou helpest on the material by the type.

[41] Blank, Perler, Testuz, following the Bodmer MS, add: the material.

[42] Blank, Perler, Testuz: was (as) the outline of a plan.

[43] Perler, Testuz: and the church the place of its realization.

[44] The Michigan-Beatty MS is defective in much of sect. 42. Apparently, however, it omitted this line and the next three, "by surrendering . . . just as the type lost its significance." Bonner translates accordingly.

and the law was fulfilled
by surrendering its significance to the gospel.
Just as the type lost its significance
by surrendering its image to that which is true by nature,
and as the parable lost its significance
by being illumined through the interpretation,

43. so indeed also the law was fulfilled
when the gospel was brought to light,
and the people lost their significance
when the church came on the scene,
and the type was destroyed
when the Lord appeared.
Therefore, those things which once had value
are today without value,
because the things which have true value have appeared.

44. For at one time the sacrifice of the sheep was valuable,
but now it is without value because of the life of the Lord.
The death of the sheep once was valuable,
but now it is without value because of the salvation of the Lord.
The blood of the sheep once was valuable,
but now it is without value because of the Spirit of the Lord.
The silent lamb once was valuable,
but now it has no value because of the blameless Son.
The temple here below once was valuable,
but now it is without value because of the Christ from above.

45. The Jerusalem here below once had value,
but now it is without value because of the Jerusalem from
above.
The meager[45] inheritance once had value;
now it is without value because of the abundant grace.
For not in one place alone,
nor yet in narrow confines,
has the glory of God been established,
but his grace has been poured out
upon the uttermost parts of the inhabited world,
and there the almighty God
has taken up his dwelling place
through Jesus Christ,[46]
to whom be the glory for ever. Amen.

F. Components of the Mystery of the Passover (46-71)

1. The Passover (46-47a)

46. Now that you have heard the explanation of the type
and of that which corresponds to it,[47]

---

[45] Bonner: new. His text was deficient, however.
[46] Bonner: Christ Jesus.
[47] Bonner: and of the retribution.

hear also what goes into making up[48] the mystery.
What is the passover?
Indeed its name is derived
from that event—
"to celebrate the passover" (*to paschein*) is derived from
"to suffer" (*tou pathein*).
Therefore, learn
who the sufferer is
and who he is who suffers along with the sufferer.
47. Why indeed was the Lord present upon the earth?[49]
In order that having clothed himself with the one who suffers,
he might lift him up to the heights of heaven.

2. The Creation and Fall of Man (47b-48)

In the beginning, when God made heaven and earth,
and everything in them through his word,[50]
he himself formed man from the earth
and shared with that form his own breath,
and himself placed him in paradise,
which was eastward in Eden,
and there they[51] lived most luxuriously.
Then by way of command God gave them this law:
For your food you may eat from any tree,
but you are not to eat
from the tree of the one who knows good and evil.[52]
For on the day you eat from it,
you most certainly will die.
48. But man,
who is by nature capable of receiving good and evil
as soil of the earth is capable of receiving seeds from
both sides,[53]
welcomed the hostile and greedy counsellor,
and by having touched that tree
transgressed the command,
and disobeyed God.
As a consequence, he was cast out into this world
as a condemned man is cast into prison.[54]

3. Consequences of the Fall (49-56)

49. And when he had fathered many children,

[48] Bonner: Hear also the plan (structure, Perler; explanation, Testuz).
[49] The first half of sect. 47 is missing from the Michigan-Beatty MS.
[50] Blank and Testuz take this phrase with the creation of man: He formed man from the earth by (the intermediary of) his word.
[51] Blank and Perler: he.
[52] Bonner and Perler: The tree of the knowledge of good and evil; Blank, Testuz: The tree which knows good and evil.
[53] Bonner and Blank: receiving seed of both kinds.
[54] Bonner, Perler: as unto a prison of the condemned.

and had grown very old,
and had returned to the earth
through having tasted of the tree,
an inheritance was left behind by him for his children.
Indeed, he left his children an inheritance—
not of chastity but of unchastity,
not of immortality but of corruptibility,
not of honor but of dishonor,
not of freedom but of slavery,
not of sovereignty but of tyranny,
not of life but of death,
not of salvation but of destruction.

50. Extraordinary and terrifying indeed
was the destruction of men upon the earth.
For the following things happened to them:
They were carried off as slaves by sin, the tyrant,
and were led away into the regions[55] of desire
where they were totally engulfed
by insatiable sensual pleasures—
by adultery,
by unchastity,
by debauchery,
by inordinate desires,[56]
by avarice,
by murders,
by bloodshed,
by the tyranny of wickedness,
by the tyranny of lawlessness.

51. For even a father of his own accord lifted up a dagger against his son;
and a son used his hands against his father;
and the impious person smote the breasts that nourished him;
and brother murdered brother;
and host wronged his guest;[57]
and friend assassinated friend;
and one man cut the throat of another
with his tyrannous right hand.

52. Therefore all men on the earth
became either murderers,
or parricides,[58]
or killers of their children.[59]
And yet a thing still more dreadful and extraordinary was
to be found:
A mother[60] attacked the flesh which she gave birth to,

---

[55] Bonner, changing the Michigan-Beatty text from *chronous* to *klonous*: turmoils.
[56] Blank, Testuz: omit this line.
[57] Bonner: omits this line
[58] Blank, Testuz: fratricides; Perler conflates: fratricides, or parricides.
[59] Blank, Testuz: omit this line.
[60] Blank, Testuz: father.

a mother attacked those whom her breasts had nourished;
and she buried in her belly
the fruit of her belly.
Indeed, the ill-starred mother became a dreadful tomb,
when she devoured the child which she bore in her womb.[61]

53. But in addition to this
there were to be found among men
many things still more monstrous and terrifying and brutal:[62]
father cohabits with his child,
and son with his mother,
and brother with sister,
and male with male,
and each man lusting after the wife of his neighbor.

54. Because of these things sin exulted,
which, because it was death's collaborator,
entered first into the souls of men,
and prepared as food for him the bodies of the dead.
In every soul sin left its mark,
and those in whom it placed its mark[63]
were destined to die.

55. Therefore, all flesh fell under the power of sin,
and every body under the dominion of death,
for every soul was driven out from its house of flesh.
Indeed, that which had been taken from the earth
was dissolved again into earth,
and that which had been given from God
was locked up in Hades.
And that beautiful ordered arrangement was dissolved,
when the beautiful[64] body was separated (from the soul).

56. Yes, man was divided up into parts by death.
Yes, an extraordinary misfortune and captivity enveloped him:
he was dragged away captive under the shadow of death,
and the image of the Father remained there desolate.[65]
For this reason, therefore,
the mystery of the passover has been completed
in the body of the Lord.

---

[61] The Michigan-Beatty MS is defective for much of this sect. Hence, Bonner's translation is a reconstructed one and differs considerably from the one offered here.

[62] There are difficulties in the text of both Greek manuscripts for the first four lines of sect. 53. Bonner: Many deeds they also did which were accounted most horrible among men; Perler: I am going to stop speaking! Nevertheless one finds many other strange things, still more frightful and more impudent among men; I have followed the reconstruction of Testuz; Blank also.

[63] Bonner: and *all* alike she devoted *to death.*

[64] Bonner: omits beautiful.

[65] Bonner: and the image of the soul (*pneumatos*) was dragged away alone.

4. Predictions of Christ's Sufferings (57-65)

57. Indeed, the Lord
    prearranged his own sufferings
    in the patriarchs,
    and in the prophets,
    and in the whole people of God,
    giving his sanction to them through the law and the prophets.
    For that which was to exist in a new and grandiose fashion
    was pre-planned long in advance,[66]
    in order that when it should come into existence
    one might attain to faith,
    just because it had been predicted long in advance.
58. So indeed also the suffering[67] of the Lord,
    predicted long in advance by means of types,
    but seen today,[68]
    has brought about faith, just because it has taken place
    as predicted.
    And yet men have taken it as something completely new.
    Well, the truth of the matter is
    the mystery of the Lord
    is both old and new—
    old insofar as it involved the type,
    but new insofar as it concerns grace.
    And what is more, if you pay close attention to this type
    you will see the real thing through its fulfillment.
59. Accordingly, if you desire to see the mystery of the Lord,
    pay close attention to Abel who likewise was put to death,
    to Isaac who likewise was bound hand and foot,
    to Joseph who likewise was sold,
    to Moses who likewise was exposed,
    to David who likewise was hunted down,
    to the prophets who likewise suffered
    because they were the Lord's anointed.[69]
60. Pay close attention also
    to the one who was sacrificed as a sheep in the land of Egypt,[70]
    to the one who smote Egypt
    and who saved Israel
    by his blood.

---

[66] For the remainder of this sect. Bonner translates: prepares beforehand the work of faith, *being* seen before from afar.

[67] Blank, Perler, Testuz: mystery.

[68] For the lines "predicted long . . . seen today," Bonner has: manifested of old from afar and seen through a type is thus today fulfilled. After this the Michigan-Beatty MS is defective until the end of the sect.

[69] Blank, Bonner, Perler, Testuz: for the sake of Christ. Greek: *ton christon*. It makes more sense to say that they suffered because they had on them the anointing of the Lord, than to say they suffered because of Christ. Cf. Heb 11:26 where the idea of Moses' suffering because he is God's anointed is quite defensible.

[70] Blank, Perler, Testuz: to the sheep which was sacrificed in Egypt.

61. For it was through the voice of prophecy
that the mystery of the Lord was proclaimed.
Moses, indeed, said to his people:
Surely you will see your life suspended before your eyes night and day,
but you surely will not believe on your Life.   Deut 28:66
62. And David said:
Why were the nations haughty
and the people concerned about nothing?
The kings of the earth presented themselves
and the princes assembled themselves together
against the Lord and against his anointed.   Ps 2:1-2
63. And Jeremiah:
I am as an innocent lamb
being led away to be sacrificed.
They plotted evil against me and said:
Come! let us throw him a tree for his food,
and let us exterminate him from the land of the living,
so that his name will never be recalled.   Jer 11:19
64. And Isaiah:
He was led as a sheep to slaughter,
and, as a lamb is silent
in the presence of the one who shears it,
he did not open his mouth.
Therefore who will tell his offspring?   Isa 53:7
65. And indeed there were many other things
proclaimed by numerous prophets
concerning the mystery of the passover,
which is Christ,
to whom be the glory forever. Amen.

5. Deliverance of Mankind through Christ (66-71)

66. When this one came from heaven to earth
for the sake of the one who suffers,
and had clothed himself with that very one
through the womb of a virgin,[71]
and having come forth as man,
he accepted the sufferings of the sufferer
through his body which was capable of suffering.
And he destroyed those human sufferings
by his spirit which was incapable of dying.
He killed death which had put man to death.
67. For this one,
who was led away as a lamb,
and who was sacrificed as a sheep,
by himself delivered us from servitude to[72] the world

---

[71] Blank, Bonner, Testuz: Through a (the) virgin, Mary. From this point on to
the end of sect. 66 the Michigan-Beatty MS is defective.
[72] Bonner: ruin of.

as from the land of Egypt,
and released us from bondage to the devil
as from the hand of Pharaoh,
and sealed our souls by his own spirit[73]
and the members of our bodies by his own blood.[74]

68. This is
the one who covered death with shame
and who plunged[75] the devil into mourning
as Moses did Pharaoh.
This is the one who smote lawlessness
and deprived injustice of its offspring,
as Moses deprived Egypt.
This is the one who delivered us
from slavery into freedom,
from darkness into light,
from death into life,
from tyranny into an eternal kingdom,
and who made us a new priesthood,
and a special people forever.[76]

69. This one is the passover of our salvation.
This is the one who patiently endured many things in many people:
This is the one who was murdered in Abel,
and bound as a sacrifice in Isaac,
and exiled in Jacob,[77]
and sold in Joseph,
and exposed in Moses,
and sacrificed in the lamb,[78]
and hunted down in David,
and dishonored in the prophets.

70. This is the one who became human in a virgin,
who was hanged on the tree,[79]
who was buried in the earth,[80]
who was resurrected[81] from among the dead,
and who raised mankind up
out of the grave below
to the heights of heaven.[82]

71. This is the lamb that was slain.[83]
This is the lamb that was silent.[84]

[73] Blank, Testuz: blood.
[74] Blank, Testuz: omit this line.
[75] Bonner: bound.
[76] Blank, Testuz: omit the last two lines of this sect.: "and who . . . forever."
[77] Blank inadvertently omits this line.
[78] Blank, Testuz: omit this line.
[79] Bonner: whose *bones* were not broken on the tree.
[80] Bonner: who in burial was not resolved into earth.
[81] Blank, Bonner, Testuz: who arose.
[82] Blank, Perler, Testuz, for the last three lines of this sect. (and who raised . . .
below): who was lifted (taken) up to the heights of heaven.
[83] Blank, Perler, Testuz: the lamb that was silent.
[84] Blank, Perler, Testuz: the lamb that was slain.

This is the one who was born of Mary, that beautiful ewe-lamb.
This is the one who was taken from the flock,
and was dragged to sacrifice,
and was killed in the evening,
and was buried at night;[85]
the one who was not broken while on the tree,
who did not see dissolution while in the earth,
who rose up from the dead,
and who raised up mankind
from the grave below.

II. *The Death of Christ and Israel's Sin* (72-99)

A. Place and Cause of Christ's Death (72-86)

72. This one was murdered.
    And where was he murdered?
    In the very center of Jerusalem!
    Why?
    Because he had healed their lame,
    and had cleansed their lepers,
    and had guided their blind with light,
    and had raised up their dead.
    For this reason he suffered.
    Somewhere it has been written in the law and prophets,
    "They[86] paid me back evil for good,
    and my soul with barrenness,[87]   Ps 34:12
    plotting evil against me,   Ps 34:4; 40:8
    saying, Let us bind this just man
    because he is troublesome to us."   Isa 3:10 (LXX)
73. Why, O Israel, did you do this strange injustice?[88]
    You dishonored the one who had honored you.
    You held in contempt the one who held you in esteem.
    You denied the one who publicly acknowledged you,
    You renounced the one who proclaimed you his own,
    You killed the one who made you to live.
    Why did you do this, O Israel?[89]
74. Has it not been written for your benefit:
    "Do not shed innocent blood
    lest you die a terrible death"?
    Nevertheless, Israel admits, I killed the Lord![90]

---

[85] From this point through the first part of sect. 72 the Michigan-Beatty MS is defective.

[86] Bonner: ye.

[87] Bonner: and [wicked] counsel.

[88] Blank: What wicked injustice, O Israel, have you done?

[89] Blank, Perler: What have you done, O Israel? Bonner: Thou hast done an impious deed.

[90] Bonner: Come, he says, Israel, thou hast slain the Lord.

Why?
Because it was necessary for him to die.
You have deceived yourself, O Israel,
rationalizing thus about the death of the Lord.
75. It was necessary for him to suffer, yes,
   but not by you;
   it was necessary for him to be dishonored,[91]
   but not by you;
   it was necessary for him to be judged,
   but not by you;[92]
   it was necessary for him to be crucified,
   but not by you,
   nor by your right hand.[93]
76. O Israel!
   You ought to have cried aloud to God with this voice:
   "O Lord,
   if it was necessary for your Son to suffer,
   and if this was your will,
   let him suffer indeed,
   but not at my hands.
   Let him suffer at the hands of strangers.
   Let him be judged by the uncircumcised.
   Let him be crucified by the tyrannical right hand,
   but not by mine."[94]
77. But you, O Israel,
   did not cry out to God with this voice,
   nor did you absolve yourself of guilt before the Lord,
   nor were you persuaded by his works.
78. The withered hand which was restored whole to its body
   did not persuade you;
   nor did the eyes of the blind which were opened by his hand;
   nor did the paralyzed bodies
   restored to health again through his voice;
   nor did that most extraordinary miracle persuade you,
   namely, the dead man raised to life from the tomb
   where already he had been lying for four days.[95]
   Indeed, dismissing these things,
   you, to your detriment, prepared the following
   for the sacrifice of the Lord at eventide:[96]
   sharp nails,
   and false witnesses,

[91] This line omitted by Blank and Testuz.
[92] This and the two previous lines omitted by Blank and Testuz.
[93] For the last two lines, Blank, Perler and Testuz: but not by your right hand.
[94] For the last three lines of this section, Blank, Testuz: by people of a different race let him be judged; by strangers let him be crucified; by a tyrannous hand, but not by me.
[95] From this point to the middle of sect. 79 the Michigan-Beatty MS is defective.
[96] For these two lines (You, to your . . . at eventide), Blank, Perler: At the time of the sacrifice of the Lord, towards evening, you prepared (for him). . . .

and fetters,
and scourges,
79. and vinegar,
and gall,
and a sword,
and affliction,
and all as though it were for a blood-stained robber.
For you brought to him
scourges for his body,
and the thorns for his head.
And you bound those beautiful hands of his,
which had formed you from the earth.
And that beautiful mouth of his,
which had nourished you with life,
you filled with gall.
And you killed your Lord
at the time of the great feast.
80. Surely you were filled with gaiety,
but he was filled with hunger;
you drank wine and ate bread,
but he vinegar and gall;
you wore a happy smile,
but he had a sad countenance;
you were full of joy,
but he was full of trouble;
you sang songs,
but he was judged;
you issued the command,
he was crucified;
you danced,
he was buried;
you lay down on a soft bed,
but he in a tomb and coffin.
81. O lawless Israel,
why did you commit this extraordinary crime
of casting your Lord into new sufferings—
your master,
the one who formed you,
the one who made you,[97]
the one who honored you,
the one who called you Israel?
82. But you were found not really to be Israel,
for you did not see God,
you did not recognize the Lord,
you did not know, O Israel,
that this one was the firstborn of God,
the one who was begotten before the morning star,
the one who caused the light to shine forth,

[97]Bonner: omits this line.

the one who made bright the day,
the one who parted the darkness,
the one who established the primordial starting point,
the one who suspended the earth,
the one who quenched the abyss,
the one who stretched out the firmament,
the one who formed the universe,

83. the one who set in motion the stars of heaven,[98]
the one who caused those luminaries to shine,
the one who made the angels in heaven,[99]
the one who established their thrones in that place,
the one who by himself fashioned man upon the earth.
This was the one who chose you,
the one who guided you
from Adam to Noah,
from Noah to Abraham,
from Abraham to Isaac and Jacob and the Twelve Patriarchs.

84. This was the one who guided you into Egypt,
and guarded you,
and himself kept you well supplied there.
This was the one who lighted your route with a column of fire,
and provided shade for you by means of a cloud,
the one who divided the Red Sea,
and led you across it,
and scattered your enemy abroad.

85. This is the one who provided you with manna from heaven,
the one who gave you water to drink from a rock,
the one who established your laws in Horeb,
the one who gave you an inheritance in the land,[100]
the one who sent out his prophets to you,
the one who raised up your kings.

86. This is the one who came to you,
the one who healed your suffering ones
and who resurrected your dead.
This is the one whom you sinned against.
This is the one whom you wronged.
This is the one whom you killed.
This is the one whom you sold for silver,
although you asked him for the didrachma.[101]

---

[98] Bonner, Perler: He who fixed the stars in heaven. The difference is between *hormēsas* and *harmosas*.

[99] From this point to the beginning of sect. 84 the Michigan-Beatty text is defective.

[100] Blank, Testuz: omit this and the previous two lines.

[101] The didrachma was a poll-tax exacted of male Jews to meet the cost of the daily services of the temple (cf. Matt 17:24-27). It was a sign that the one who paid belonged; i.e. Christ belongs to the very ones who sold him out.

B. Israel Brought to Trial (87-93)

87. O ungrateful Israel, come here
and be judged before me for your ingratitude.
How high a price did you place on being created by him?[102]
How high a price did you place on the discovery of your
fathers?
How high a price did you place on the descent into Egypt,
and the provision made for you there
through the noble Joseph?

88. How high a price did you place on the ten plagues?
How high a price did you place on the nightly column of fire,
and the daily cloud,
and the crossing of the Red Sea?
How high a price did you place on the gift of manna from
heaven,
and the gift of water from the rock,
and the gift of law in Horeb,
and the land as an inheritance,
and the benefits accorded you there?

89. How high a price did you place on your suffering people
whom he healed when he was present?
Set me a price on the withered hand,
which he restored whole to its body.

90. Put me a price on the men born blind,
whom he led into light by his voice.
Put me a price on those who lay dead,
whom he raised up alive from the tomb.[103]
Inestimable are the benefits that come to you from him.
But you, shamefully,
have paid him back with ingratitude,[104]
returning to him
evil for good,
and affliction for favor[105]
and death for life—

91. a person for whom you should have died.
Furthermore, if the king of some nation is captured by an enemy,
a war is started because of him,
fortifications are shattered because of him,
cities are plundered because of him,
ransom is sent because of him,
ambassadors are commissioned because of him
in order that he might be surrendered,[106]
so that either he might be returned if living,

[102] Perler: How high a price did you place on his direction?
[103] Blank, Perler, Testuz: add, being there already three or four days.
[104] The first half of this sect. is defective in the Michigan-Beatty MS.
[105] Blank, Perler, Testuz: joy.
[106] Bonner: omits this line.

or that he might be buried if dead.

92. But you, quite to the contrary,
voted against your Lord,
whom indeed the nations worshipped,
and the uncircumcised admired,
and the foreigners glorified,
over whom Pilate washed his hands.
But as for you—
you killed this one at the time of the great feast.

93. Therefore, the feast of unleavened bread
has become bitter to you
just as it was written:
"You will eat unleavened bread with bitter herbs."
Bitter to you are the nails which you made pointed.
Bitter to you is the tongue which you sharpened.
Bitter to you are the false witnesses whom you brought forward.
Bitter to you are the fetters which you prepared.[107]
Bitter to you are the scourges which you wove.
Bitter to you is Judas whom you furnished with pay.
Bitter to you is Herod whom you followed.
Bitter to you is Caiaphas whom you obeyed.
Bitter to you is the gall which you made ready.
Bitter to you is the vinegar which you produced.
Bitter to you are the thorns which you plucked.
Bitter to you are your hands which you bloodied,[108]
when you killed your Lord
in the midst of Jerusalem.

C. Gentiles Are Witnesses of Israel's Crime (94-98)

94. Pay attention, all families of the nations, and observe!
An extraordinary murder has taken place
in the center of Jerusalem,
in the city devoted to God's law,
in the city of the Hebrews,
in the city of the prophets,
in the city thought of as just.
And who has been murdered?
And who is the murderer?
I am ashamed to give the answer,
but give it I must.
For if this murder had taken place at night,
or if he had been slain in a desert place,
it would be well to keep silent;
but it was in the middle of the main street,
even in the center of the city,
while all were looking on,

[107] Bonner: omits this line.
[108] Blank: which you bound (without textual warrant).

that the unjust murder of this just person took place.

95. And thus he was lifted up upon the tree,
and an inscription was affixed
identifying the one who had been murdered.
Who was he?
It is painful to tell,
but it is more dreadful not to tell.
Therefore, hear and tremble
because of him for whom the earth trembled.[109]

96. The one who hung the earth in space, is himself hanged;
the one who fixed the heavens in place, is himself impaled;
the one who firmly fixed all things, is himself firmly
fixed to the tree.
The Lord is insulted,
God has been murdered,
the King of Israel has been destroyed
by the right hand of Israel.

97. O frightful murder!
O unheard of injustice!
The Lord is disfigured
and he is not deemed worthy of a cloak for his naked body,
so that he might not be seen exposed.
For this reason the stars turned and fled,
and the day grew quite dark,
in order to hide that naked person hanging on the tree,
darkening not the body of the Lord,
but the eyes of men.

98. Yes, even though the people did not tremble,
the earth trembled instead;
although the people were not afraid,
the heavens grew frightened;
although the people did not tear their garments,
the angels tore theirs;[110]
although the people did not lament,
the Lord thundered from heaven,
and the most high uttered his voice.

D. Israel Questioned and Sentenced to Death (99)

99. Why was it like this, O Israel?[111]
You did not tremble for the Lord.

---

[109] Bonner: before him who made heaven and earth tremble.

[110] Bonner, Perler: the angel tore his.

[111] The first seven lines of this sect. (why was it . . . your own who were murdered) furnish great difficulties. Even the Bodmer text, which is often the most complete, is not without defects. The Latin translation does not help sufficiently. Along with Bonner, Perler and Testuz I have tried to give a coherent translation consistent with Melito's style. It is based on an emended text. Blank and Testuz translate differently: Why, O Israel, did you not tremble before the Lord, did you not fear before the Lord, did you not lament before the firstborn, did you not rend

You did not fear for the Lord.
You did not lament for the Lord,
yet you lamented for your firstborn.
You did not tear your garments at the crucifixion of the Lord,
yet you tore your garments for your own who were murdered.
You forsook the Lord;
you were not found by him.
You dashed the Lord to the ground;
you, too, were dashed to the ground,
and lie quite dead.

III. *The Final Triumph of Christ* (100-105)

100. But he arose from the dead
and mounted up to the heights of heaven.
When the Lord had clothed himself with humanity,
and had suffered for the sake of the sufferer,
and had been bound for the sake of the imprisoned,
and had been judged for the sake of the condemned,
and buried for the sake of the one who was buried,

101. he rose up from the dead,
and cried aloud with this voice:
Who is he who contends with me?
Let him stand in opposition to me.
I set the condemned man free;
I gave the dead man life;
I raised[112] up the one who had been entombed.

102. Who is my opponent?
I, he says, am the Christ.[113]
I am the one who destroyed death,
and triumphed over the enemy,
and trampled Hades under foot,
and bound the strong one,
and carried off man
to the heights of heaven,
I, he says, am the Christ.[113]

your garments before the Lord? You abandoned the Lord.... S. G. Hall set the
two Greek manuscripts and the Latin version of this passage side by side. On the
basis of this he reconstructed what he considered to be the original text that
underlies all three sources. His emendation continues the antithesis already found in
sect. 98. A translation of his text follows: "Therefore because, O Israel, you did not
tremble at the Lord, you trembled because you were warred upon by your enemies;
(because) you did not fear for the Lord, you are afraid for those who besiege
you; (because) you did not lament for the Lord, you lamented for your
firstborn; (because) you did not rend your garment at the crucifixion of the Lord,
you rent your garments for those of your number who were murdered. You left the
Lord; you were not found by him. You did not show the Lord mercy; you were not
shown mercy by him. You dashed the Lord to the ground; you were dashed to the
ground, and lie there dead...."

[112] Greek: a present tense.

[113] Blank, Testuz: I, says the Christ.

103. Therefore, come, all families of men,
     you who have been befouled with sins,
     and receive forgiveness for your sins.
     I am your forgiveness,
     I am the passover of your salvation,
     I am the lamb which was sacrificed for you,
     I am your ransom,[114]
     I am your light,[115]
     I am your saviour,
     I am your resurrection,
     I am your king,
     I am leading you up to the heights of heaven,[116]
     I will show you the eternal Father,
     I will raise you up by my right hand.

104. This is the one who made the heaven and the earth,
     and who in the beginning created man,
     who was proclaimed through the law and prophets,
     who became human via the virgin,
     who was hanged upon a tree,
     who was buried in the earth,
     who was resurrected from the dead,
     and who ascended to the heights of heaven,
     who sits at the right hand of the Father,[117]
     who has authority to judge and to save everything,
     through whom the Father created everything
     from the beginning of the world to the end of the age.

105. This is the alpha and the omega.
     This is the beginning and the end—
     an indescribable beginning
     and an incomprehensible end.
     This is the Christ.
     This is the king.
     This is Jesus.
     This is the general.
     This is the Lord.
     This is the one who rose up from the dead.
     This is the one who sits at the right hand of the Father.
     He bears the Father
     and is borne by the Father,
     to whom be the glory
     and the power forever. Amen.

[114] Blank, Testuz: I am your baptism.

[115] From this point on the order and content of the two Greek manuscripts do not agree. Blank, Perler, Testuz: I am your life; I am your resurrection; I am your light; I am your salvation; I am your king.

[116] Blank, Perler, Testuz: add, I will raise you up there.

[117] The Michigan-Beatty MS comes to an end here.

The *Peri Pascha* of Melito.
  Peace to the one who wrote,
  and to the one who reads,
  and to those who love the Lord
  in simplicity of heart.

The Weightier and Lighter Matters
of the Law: Moses, Jesus and Paul

WALTER C. KAISER, Jr.

It has become almost a commonplace among biblical scholars to commence any discussion on the topic of law or grace with citations from both testaments that appear to give two completely different evaluations of the Mosaic law.[1]

On the one hand, a positive evaluation of the law is elicited from such references as: "the law of the Lord is perfect, reviving the soul . . . rejoicing the heart, . . . enduring forever" (Ps 19:8-11); the law of God is "holy, just, and good" (Rom 7:12); it is "spiritual" (Rom 7:14); and instead of opposing faith, it is "established" through faith (Rom 3:31).

But an apparently negative note is struck where that same law is called "our custodian until Christ came" (Gal 3:24), from which bondage we have now "been discharged," so that "we serve not under the old written code" (Rom 7:6), or under "statutes that were not good and ordinances by which [we] could not have life" (Ezek 20:25). The contrast could not be more striking.

It is precisely at this point, then, that the Christian interpreter of the OT is faced with a serious dilemma. How should he handle this apparent ambivalence to the law: Must he sharply distinguish the Mosaic law from the gospel promises given to the Patriarchs and David? Did the book of the law *only* serve to bring all men under sin and drive them deeper into sin? Was Sinai addressed solely to sinners, while the provisions of the promise and God's grace were temporarily suspended (at least for Israel) during the reign of the law of God?

Our day deserves the same evaluation that John Wesley gave to his when, in his series of three sermons on "The Original [*sic*] Nature,

---

[1]Norbert Lohfink, "Law and Grace" in *The Christian Meaning of the Old Testament,* trans. by R. A. Wilson, London, 1969, pp. 103-5; C. A. A. Scott, "Paul and the Law" in *Christianity According to St. Paul,* Cambridge, 1966, pp. 41-42; Ernest Kevan, *The Moral Law,* Jenkintown, 1963, pp. 1-4; *et al.*

Walter C. Kaiser, Jr., Professor of Semitic Languages and Old Testament at Trinity Evangelical Divinity School, Deerfield, Illinois. B.A., Wheaton College; B.D., Wheaton College Graduate School; M.A. and Ph.D., Brandeis University.

Property, and Use of the Law,"[2] he stated, "Perhaps there are few subjects within the whole compass of religion so little understood as this."[3] Small wonder, then, that present-day interpreters should express such delight when they read the conclusions set forth by Cranfield.[4] His assessment of the contemporary status of biblical scholarship and teaching on the law is our own also. It is that

> ... the need ... exists today for a thorough re-examination of the place and significance of law in the Bible. .... The possibility that ... recent writings reflect a serious degree of muddled thinking and unexamined assumptions with regard to the attitudes of Jesus and St. Paul to the law ought to be reckoned with—and even the further possibility that, behind them, there may be some muddled thinking or, at the least, careless and imprecise statement in this connection in some of the works of serious New Testament scholarship [not to speak of OT scholarship also!] which have helped to mould the opinions of the present generation of ministers and teachers.[5]

As one contribution in that re-evaluation and as a token of the writer's deep appreciation, Christian esteem and thankfulness to God for Dr. Merrill C. Tenney, this article is dedicated.

I. The Key Issues

Any number of arguments and texts have been advanced over the years as the solution for the relationship of the Mosaic law to the promises given to Abraham and David. But obviously each argument must ultimately rest on a careful analysis of the Scripture writer's own use of his vocabulary.

One class of interpreters elevated a selected key word from the biblical vocabulary as an all-encompassing rubric, such as "Christ is the end (telos) of the law" (Rom 10:4) or "the commandment was ordained to life (zōēn)" (Rom 7:10). Word studies, then, were expected to deliver the major share of the answer.

But does Paul in Rom 10:4 indeed mean that there is a "full stop" or "cessation" of the law?[6] The error of this conclusion can be spotted immediately when its proponents claim that nomos and dikaiosunē in Rom 10:4 "denote the Jewish way of salvation which is set aside in Christ."[7] On the contrary, it was Israel herself who made a law out of righteousness (nomon dikaiosunēs, Rom 9:31) rather than aiming at the righteousness of the law (the text does not say dikaiosunē nomou).[8] The situation is best summarized by Cranfield:

[2] John Wesley, Sermons: On Several Occasions, First Series, London, 1964, pp. 381-415.
[3] Ibid., p. 381.
[4] C. E. B. Cranfield, "St. Paul and the Law," SJT, 17 (1964), 43-68.
[5] Ibid., pp. 43-44.
[6] Gerhard Delling, "τέλος," TDNT, 8, 56.
[7] Ibid.
[8] F. Godet, Commentary on the Epistle of Romans, Grand Rapids, 1883 (repr. 1956), p. 368. Also see George E. Howard, "Christ the End of the Law," JBL, 88 (1969), 334-36.

Those who think that Paul's attitude to the law was predominantly negative are naturally inclined to choose the meaning "termination", as does the N.E.B., which translates: "For Christ ends the law. . . ." This interpretation has many supporters; but, in view of such passages as Rom 7:12, 14a, 8:4, 13:8-10 and of the categorical statement in Rom 3:31, and also of the fact that Paul again and again appeals to the Pentateuch in support of his arguments (specially suggestive perhaps is the fact that he does so in Rom 10:6-8), it seems extremely probable that it should be rejected, and the translation "goal" preferred.[9]

Likewise, the analysis of "life" in Rom 7:10 suffers from a subjective lexicography when its meaning is arbitrarily linked with a "hypothetical offer of salvation" based on perfect obedience to the law.[10] Therefore Rom 10:5 and Gal 3:12 are used as texts to prove that under Sinaitic terms God had said, "He that performs all these things shall live in them." But could it not be that the meaning of life is assumed all too quickly as being equal to *eternal* life or salvation? Certainly Paul's usage of the word life is affected by its connection with obedience to the will of God as reflected in Deut and Pss 1, 19, 40:9 and 119. For example, Ps 119:93 affirmed: "In them [your ordinances] you gave me life." A study of these passages leads to the conclusion stated by Matthew J. O'Connell that life refers to "that inner life which flows from the fulfillment of the divine will."[11] He continues:

> Thus, with the interiorization of the concept of life and the identification of true life with the joyful, liberating fulfillment of the divine will, the vocabulary associated throughout Israelite history with the Promised Land has been interiorized.[12]

The proof that this "life" is not eternal salvation, but rather one's total well-being, inside and out, spiritual and material, is further supported by the preposition *en* (Rom 10:5). J. Oliver Buswell summarized his study of this word in the key passages and concluded that

> The words, *en autē* [Rom 10:5], and the corresponding words in Galatians 3:12, *en autois*, where the same Old Testament passage [Lev 18:5] is quoted, should not be construed as instrumental, but as locative, indicating the sphere or horizon of the life of a godly man. . . . Moses is obviously describing not the means of attaining eternal life, but the horizon within which an earthly godly life ought to be lived.[13]

---

[9] Cranfield, "St. Paul and the Law," p. 49. One of Cranfield's contributions is that "Paul had no word-group to denote 'legalism,' 'legalist,' and 'legalistic.' This means not just that he did not have a convenient terminology to express a key idea, but that he had no definite, ready-made concept of legalism with which to work in his mind" (p. 55). C. F. D. Moule seems to agree in part in his essay, "Obligation in the Ethic of Paul" in *Christian History and Interpretation: Studies Presented to John Knox,* ed. by W. R. Farmer, C. F. D. Moule and R. R. Niebuhr, Cambridge, 1967. He distinguishes, in Paul, "two different attitudes and uses of law—on one hand, the recognition of law as a revelation of God's will and purpose, and, on the other hand, the attempt to use it 'legalistically,' to establish one's rightness."

[10] Alva J. McClain, *Law and Grace,* Chicago, 1967, pp. 17-19; Richard Longenecker, *Paul: Apostle of Liberty,* New York, 1964, pp. 121-22; *et al.*

[11] Matthew J. O'Connell, "The Concept of Commandment in the O.T.," *TS,* 21 (1960), 387.

[12] *Ibid.,* p. 388.

[13] J. Oliver Buswell, *A Systematic Theology of the Christian Religion,* Grand

Indeed, did not Paul clearly state in Gal 3:21 that "If there had been a law given which could have given life, verily righteousness would have been by the law"? But alas, there was not. Surely this approach builds on too narrow a base and often with a faulty lexicography which assumes too much for the author's own meanings.

Another group of interpreters, in a somewhat less atomistic approach, elevates selected biblical phrases to an all-encompassing summary of the relationship between law and grace. Such phrases are: "The righteousness of God is revealed *apart from the law*" (Rom 3:21); "You were made dead to the law" (Rom 7:4); "We serve not the oldness of the letter" (Rom 7:6b); or "We have been discharged from the law" (Rom 7:6a).

But when these clauses and phrases are used as theological summaries, often a full consideration of all the immediate contexts is neglected. Paul's own explanations are frequently not more than a few verses away. "Without the law" (Rom 3:21) is not a Christian slogan against the law; instead Rom 3:28 amplifies the same Greek phrase by saying "without *the works* of the law a man is justified by faith." In fact, Rom 3:21 says that this very righteousness which is known "apart from the law" is witnessed to by the law.

Just so, the notice of our discharge from the law and our death to it in Rom 7:6a is to be linked with only one event: the death of Jesus Christ for all who believe. Therefore, as Rom 8:1 states, "There is now no condemnation [which was the curse of the law] to those in Christ Jesus." Christ has forever removed that.

Likewise, although Paul "did not serve in the oldness of the letter"[14] (Rom 7:6) he went on to affirm that "with the mind" he himself did "serve the law of God" (Rom 7:25).

Hence, the key issues have not been broached in either of these methods. In order to insure a measure of success, (1) the underlying question must be ferreted out of the maze of possible questions, (2) the answer to this question must have the advantage of an authoritative review or pronouncement by some writer of Scripture, and if possible, (3) a large teaching passage on the subject would also be the most ideal situation. These three key methodological considerations need to be faced by all students of the problem.

The underlying question is this: Does Scripture advocate and observe any distinctions in the law of God? Does rabbinic Judaism distinguish between the civil, ceremonial and moral aspects of this one law? Most modern commentators answer this question negatively,[15] but few, if any, have exegetically established what all will agree is a most crucial point: if the law is a monolithic unity, and if we can establish from Heb, Eph (2:15)

Rapids, 1962, 1, 313. See also W. C. Kaiser, Jr., "Leviticus 18:5 and Paul: 'Do This and You Shall Live (Eternally?),' " *JETS,* 14 (1971), 19-28.

[14] See below for a fuller discussion of the "letter."

[15] H. A. W. Meyer, *Commentary on the New Testament,* New York, 1, 120, says, " . . . the distinction between the ritualistic, civil, and moral law is modern." John Knox, *The Ethic of Jesus in the Teaching of the Church,* Nashville, 1961, pp. 98f., says, "There is no evidence that Paul differentiated between various elements within the law—or various kinds of laws—as, for example, between the ceremonial

and Col (2:14-15) that part of the law, namely, the ceremonial, has been terminated by Christ's atoning death and resurrection, then obviously the whole law has been terminated. Hence the problem is solved before it has actually begun. But surely this is solving the problem by imposing categories and externally derived definitions.

Second, in spite of such an array of scholars, whose minds are already made up about this key question, is there any new authoritative review or contrary revelatory opinion to be considered? In my judgment there is. None other than that of Jesus himself. In Matt 23:23, the Lord of the church teaches us to distinguish between the lighter and weightier matters of the law. There are greater and lesser commandments, each demanding appropriate responses for stated durations of time in keeping with explicit and often separate purposes.

Finally, 2 Cor 3:1-18 is certainly one of the largest passages involving this most sensitive question of the duration of the law. If Paul spoke his mind anywhere at length on the subject, it was in 2 Cor. 3:1-18. Here he sets forth a clear contrast between the ministry of Moses and that of Paul. Thus, readers may exegetically test the results and effects of an argument for or against observing distinctions in the law.

II. Judaism on Distinctions
in the Law

The strength of most discussions on the law today lies in their case for the unity of the Mosaic laws. Oddly enough, the argument often rests more on the alleged understanding of later Judaism's espousal of a law of full equivalence than on a careful exegesis of the Old and New Testament.

The unified character of all the laws in the Pentateuch is confidently based on the Jewish assertion that the law consisted of 613 statutes: 365 prohibitions (one for each day of the year) and 248 positive commands (one for each member of a man's body). These 613 laws were further grouped into two sets of twelve different categories: twelve positive families and twelve negative families.[16]

Now I agree that Rabbi Shemšon ben Azzai first referred to the 365 prohibitions ca. A.D. 100 and Rabbi Shimšon ben Eleazar first wrote of the

---

and moral, or the general and the particular. Law, as such, is no longer valid for the Christian." G. B. Stevens, *The Theology of the New Testament,* New York, p. 24, in a footnote affirms, " . . . this distinction is recognized neither in the Old Testament nor in the New. . . ." Also Godet, *Commentary on Romans,* p. 144: "In general, the distinction . . . is foreign to the Jewish conscience, which takes the law as a divine unity." W. R. Nicoll, *Expositor's Greek New Testament,* Grand Rapids, 3, 527, declares this distinction "has no meaning in Paul." Wherever any Scriptures are included in the argument, they are Matt 5:13, "Whoever breaks one of the least of these commandments" and Jas 2:10, "Whosoever shall keep the whole law and yet offend in one point is guilty of all." Cf. McClain, *Law and Grace,* p. 9, and C. C. Ryrie, "The End of the Law," *BS,* 124 (1967), 239-42.

[16] See Ryrie, "The End of the Law," pp. 240-41 for a listing of the contents and a use of this argument. Cf. C. C. Ryrie, *The Grace of God,* Chicago, 1963, p. 96. Cf. also Roy L. Aldrich, *Holding Fast to Grace,* Findlay, Ohio, 1962, pp. 47-51.

complete body of 613 laws ca. A.D. 190.[17] But what I contest is that this shows that Judaism, and thereby OT religion and NT background conceptuality, demand no distinctions in the handling of the law. On the contrary, no less an authority than C. G. Montefiore contends:

> The Rabbis, we may say, were familiar with the distinction between ceremonial and moral commands, and *on the whole* they regarded the "moral" as more important and more fundamental than the "ceremonial." . . . Again, there was some tendency to distinguish "heavy" and "light" commands according to certain punishments or threats. . . . Nevertheless, on the whole the "heavy" commands are the moral commands. The "heaviest" (apart from circumcision) are commands such as the prohibition of unchastity, idolatry, or murder, the honoring of parents, the Sanctification of the Name. The distinction between "light" and "heavy" commands was well known, and is constantly mentioned and discussed.[18]

Gustaf Dalman agrees:

> The Rabbis did not differentiate between the smallest and the greatest commandments but rather between "light" (Hebrew *kallīn*) and "heavy" (Hebrew *hamārīn*). This distinction between commandments is made only in connection with "the words of the (Mosaic) Law", but not with "the words of the Scribes". Moreover, "light" and "heavy" commandments are not those which are in themselves easy or difficult to keep, but such that cause the keeping of other commandments to be either light (*kōl*) or heavy (*hōmer*). . . . The freeing of the mother bird (Deut xxii. 6 is considered to be the "lightest" of all, the "heaviest" of all—the honoring of father and mother (Exod xx. 12). . . . Our Lord's "least" is in the category of these "lightest" commandments of the Rabbis.[19]

Ultimately, however, the whole exegetical tradition which attempts to distinguish between lighter and weightier, smaller and greater must be located in the prophets and the OT itself. This is the conclusion of Israel Abrahams:

> Such attempts to find a basic principle for the whole of the law can thus be traced clearly from Hillel through Aqiba to the days of Simlai. Simlai, it will be observed, quotes the prophets as the authors of attempts in this direction.[20]

It was said that David summarized the 613 precepts in *eleven* principles in Ps 15. Then Isaiah further reduced them to *six* commands (Isa 33:15). Micah was said to establish them as *three* (Mic 6:8), only to have them further narrowed to *two* by Isaiah (Isa 56:1) and to *one only* by Amos in 5:4: "Seek ye me and ye shall live." Habakkuk also made the total law stand on *one* fundamental idea in 2:4: "the righteous man shall live by faith."[21] While this historical progression need not be followed in all its

[17] *TDNT*, 4, 535, n. 31.

[18] C. G. Montefiore, *Rabbinic Literature and Gospel Teachings*, New York, 1930 (repr. 1970), pp. 316-17. I am indebted to my student Gene Bourland for pointing out this reference to me.

[19] Gustaf Dalman, *Jesus-Jeshua: Studies in the Gospels*, trans. by Paul P. Levertoff, London, 1929, pp. 64-65.

[20] Israel Abrahams, *Studies in Pharisaism and the Gospels*, New York, 1917 (repr. 1967), pp. 23-24.

[21] For a discussion of these steps, see *ibid.*, p. 23.

details, the hermeneutical principles displayed by these reductions demonstrate precisely what the prophets and Jesus were attempting to teach. There were priorities to be observed in responding to God's law; indeed, Moses himself was the first to say so.

III. The Mosaic Revelation of Priorities in the Law

The fundamental fact about law in the OT is that it proceeds from the God of the fathers who had chosen them and delivered them from Egypt. Therefore, before any commandments in the Decalogue are given, the basis for any and all divine claims is immediately established: "I am the Lord your God, who led you out of the land of Egypt, out of the house of bondage" (Exod. 20:12). The same basis is laid in the formula repeated over and over again in the holiness teaching of Leviticus: "Be ye holy, for I the Lord your God am holy," or simply: "For I am the Lord your God" (Lev 11:44, 45; 19:2, 3, 4, 10, 12, 14, 16, 18, 25, 28, 30, 31, 32, 34, 36, 37; 20:7, 8, 26; 21:6, 8, 15, 23; 22:9, 16, 32-33, etc.). Nor is it any different in the theological and religious motive clauses supplied for all types of laws throughout the OT law.[22] These clauses plead God's holy character, God's jealousy and his salvific acts on their behalf in history as a basis for obedience.

This evaluation of legal bases, priorities and motivations is substantiated by the very structure of Deut. No stipulations or commandments are laid on Israel until each person fully understands and individually enjoys a proper relationship as indicated by the responses of fearing the Lord and loving him with all his heart, soul, strength and mind. In other words, chaps. 12ff. are not to be considered unless Deut 1-11 has been met, "for in the command to love God, law is carried into the heart to become a transforming force."[23] Thus, obedience to the law must be preceded by obedience to a person: "I command you this day to love the Lord your God, to walk in his ways[24] and to keep his commandments" (Deut. 30:16; cf. 10:12; 11:1, 13, 33; 19:9; 30:20). Since the Lord "is [their] life and the length of [their] days," they should "cleave to him." Clearly, two kinds of obedience are taught: an "evangelical" obedience ("I command you to love the Lord your God") and a "legal" obedience ("I command you . . . to keep his commandments, . . . statutes . . . and his judgments").

It is just such a distinction which serves the former prophets, the psalmists, and the latter prophets as a basis for setting priorities in the law. In fact, Mic 6:6-8 repeats the same question introduced by Deut 10:12: "And now, Israel, what does God require of thee?" The answer was always the same. A genuine heart relationship was God's own prerequisite to obeying his laws.

Nor did the issue change when the ceremonial law was under discus-

---

[22] B. Gemser, "The Importance of the Motive Clauses in Old Testament Law," VTSup., 1 (1953), 50-66, esp. 57-61.

[23] O'Connell, "The Concept of Commandment in the O.T.," p. 377.

[24] See the article "ὁδός," TDNT, 5, 48-56.

sion. Even the holy effects of the grandest day of all, the day of atonement, were not efficacious unless Israel "afflicted their souls," i.e. humbled themselves by confessing their own sins (Lev 16:29, 31). Was not this also the deficiency in Cain's offering in Gen 4? God inspected the man first and then he looked at his offering. So it has ever been. Formal correctness and ceremonial exactness have never been a substitute for true repentance and a heart relationship with God. This was Samuel's cry to Saul in 1 Sam 15:22, David's hard lesson of Ps 51:16-19, and the prophet's stern rebuke of a religiously sterile people in Hos 6:6; Isa 1:11-18; 43:22-24; Mic 6:6-8; Amos 5:21-24; and 7:21-23.[25] If merely doing the law was all that was necessary, then Israel should easily have by then more than fulfilled her ceremonial obligations. But that was precisely what displeased the prophets. Loving God was more important than sacrificing bulls. As Hosea said with a double metonymy, give God "the bulls of [your] lips" (14:2), which Heb 13:15-16 accurately rendered: ". . . offer the sacrifice [bulls] of praise [lips] to God continually . . . with such sacrifices God is well pleased."

IV. Jesus' Authoritative Distinctions

The quest for a *sine qua non*, a fundamental principle or an epitome of the law, was illustrated in two or three situations in the life of our Lord: Mark 12:28-34; Matt 22:34-40; and Matt 23:23-24.

A lawyer (*nomikos*) put the question to Jesus. He asked in Mark 12:28, "Which (*poia*) commandment is the first (*prōtē*) of all?" (Matt 22:36 has, "Which is the great (*megalē*) commandment in the law?"). Such attempts to reduce many commandments to a few chief principles are reflected in Hillel's saying (found also in Tob 4:15), "What is hateful to you, do not do to thy neighbor. This is the whole law; the rest is commentary."[26] Rabbi Aqiba spoke of neighborly love in Lev 19:18 as the *kelāl gādôl battôrāh*, "the greatest principle in the law." Rabbi Ben Azzai used the same term. Abrahams explained that what both men meant by this term *kelāl* was "a general or basic command from which all the other commands could be deduced."[27]

Precisely in the same manner did Jesus respond to the lawyer's question by linking Deut 6:4-5 with Lev 19:18: love for God was first, and this was to be followed by love for one's neighbors. Such an association of texts may already have been in existence in three passages in *The Testament of the Twelve Patriarchs*: T Issa 5:2; 7:6; T Dan 5:3.[28] At any rate, it might appear from Mark 12:32 that the lawyer recognized the truthfulness of the answer just given to him by Jesus. But the most remarkable thing was that this lawyer went on to link Deut 6:4 and Lev 19:18 with 1 Sam

[25] Cf. also the teaching of Prov 15:8; 21:27; 28:9.

[26] Montefiore, *Rabbinic Literature*, p. 319; *Sifra*, Lev 19:18 and *Genesis Rabbah* 24:7. On this "negative golden rule" see *Pirque 'Abot* 1:12, *Shabbat* 31a. Perhaps it is based on Ps 15:3; cf. Rom 13:10.

[27] I. Abrahams, *Studies in Pharisaism*, p. 24. Actually Rabbi Ben Azzai found Gen 5:1 as the greatest principle.

[28] *Ibid.*, p. 18. Cf. also George Foote Moore, *Judaism*, 3, 84-88.

15:22; Hos 6:6; and Mic 6:6-8: loving God and one's neighbor was "much more than all the whole burnt offerings and sacrifices" (Mark 12:33). And did Jesus rebuke this attack on the unified character of the law? Quite the reverse, he commended the man for his wisdom and said, "You are not far from the Kingdom of God," i.e. from being converted.[29] This is exactly what the prophets had been urging and this Jew received their authoritative teachings.

Not only did Jesus approve of this manner of handling the law; he also encouraged it in his own teachings. In Matt 23:23 Jesus condemned the Scribes and Pharisees for their hypocritical actions. Indeed, they should have kept such trifling laws as tithing the herbs and seed of the land (in part as taught in Lev 27:30), but they were not thereby excused from "the weightier matters of the law."

Gottlob Schrenk warns against viewing the contrast here as being between *harder* and *easier* commands. Instead, the emphasis is on the comparative weight, dignity and power of some of those commands.[30]

That part of the law which Jesus taught as being much more crucial was exactly what Mic 6:6-8 had identified as more significant. Matthew identified it as "justice, mercy and faith." Luke 11:42 listed it as "justice and the love of God."

Now this must not be understood as merely an ethical substitute for external, formal religion. In both of the OT contexts where the question of God's primary requirements or demands are discussed, what is strongly urged is more than just another duty. It is duty grounded in the saving action and grace of our God.

In Deut 10:10-12, God's grace is announced after Moses' intercessory prayer on behalf of the calf-worshiping idolaters in Israel (cf. Exod 32:10, 14). With the free and gracious forgiveness of Israel's sins, Moses exclaims: "And now, O Israel, what does the Lord your God require of you, but to fear the Lord your God, to walk in all his ways, to love him, and to serve the Lord your God with all your heart and with all your soul?"

So it was in Mic 6:3-5. How pitiful that God should have to beg, "O my people, what have I done to you? Wherein have I wearied you? Testify against me." Had Israel completely forgotten "the righteousness(es) of the Lord" (6:5)? This rare use of the plural occurs only five times in the OT[31] and together with the context suggests the several free, gracious deliverances of God: the Exodus, the provision of leadership (Moses, Aaron and Miriam), the blessing of God and providential protection against all the potential curses of Balaam. The context of Mic 6:6-8 is totally that of grace. It is exactly like Exod 20:2, which likewise precedes any ethical demands made upon man.

The response of the people to such an impressive listing of God's favors toward them is the pitiful question, "With what [thing] shall we go meet God? Is it quality ('year-old calves') that God wants? Or quantity

---

[29] This equivalence is guaranteed by Scripture in Matt 19:16, 23, 24, 25. Should that appear to be pre-cross terminology, then cf. Acts 20:24b, 25b, 27b.

[30] Gottlob Schrenk, "βάρος," *TDNT*. 1, 558, 554.

[31] The other passages are 1 Sam 12:7; Judg 5:11 (*bis*); Ps 103:6; Dan 9:16.

('thousands of rams or ten thousand rivers of oil')? Or even my oldest child?" Never! The answer has already been given in the law itself. It is "doing justice," a most comprehensive term for a new life-style, living according to God's word. It is *hesed,* "loyal fidelity" to one's friends and neighbors. It is "walking humbly with your God," a life of faith giving God first place. This is equivalent to Moses' injunction to Israel, "Circumcise your hearts" (Deut 19:16; 30:6).

Now, that was Jesus' challenge to the meticulous Scribes and punctilious Pharisees. They must penetrate to the more significant and abiding aspects of the law. In other words, Jesus instructs the Jews of his day to do just what most modern commentators find to be a most difficult, if not impossible, task. Surely the Lord of the church and the living Word himself must be trusted as authoritative in these matters. Our exegesis has shown that the heaviest part of the law was exactly that part described by Moses in Deut 1-11, announced in the prologue to the Decalogue, and preached by the prophets. Jesus made the same point in Matt 9:13 and 12:7 when he instructed the Jews to go home and reflect on Hos 6:6 if they wanted to understand the requirements of the law of Moses: "I desire loyal love [*hesed*] and not sacrifices."

According to Jesus, some things in the law take precedence over others in the proverbial pattern of "this is better than that." One must acknowledge that there are "greater commandments" and "lesser commandments" in the law. But this does not invite anyone to regard the "lesser commands" as unimportant unless and until the lawgiver himself says they are obsolete.[32] Rather it requires a recognition of rank, significance and primacy which more than hints at the character of their permanence or linkage with the person of our Lord.

V. A Key Exegetical Passage:
2 Cor. 3:1-17

Notwithstanding the case that can be made for distinctions and differentiations in the law, one passage still dominates the horizon for present-day Christians. As Charles Ryrie stated the issue:

There is one other passage in the writings of Paul which, because it is more particular, is even more emphatic concerning the ending of the law. In II Corinthians 3:7-11 Paul makes the comparison between what is ministered through Moses and what is ministered through Christ.... Thus, this passage says that the Ten Commandments are a ministration of death; and furthermore, the same passage declares in no uncertain terms that they are done away (vs. 11). Language could not

---

[32] It is to be strictly observed that Jesus does not thereby condone what some call "Ethical Hierarchicalism." I strongly differ with my colleague in his otherwise excellent work on ethics; Norman L. Geisler, *Ethics: Alternatives and Issues,* Grand Rapids, 1971, pp. 103, 107, 114ff. Jas 2:10 denies to all the luxury of arbitrarily or subjectively designating some of God's laws as unimportant, no matter what the human reason is. Matt 23:23 does not argue that the assessment of priorities requires that we do the "weightier" and leave (if necessary or if forced) the "lighter" and the "least" undone. Only when Christ releases us from the "lesser laws" may we jettison our obligation to them; anything less than this leads to ethical latitudinarianism.

be clearer, and yet there are fewer truths of which it is harder to convince people.[33]

Admittedly, all the proper components for making a decisive statement against the permanence and usefulness of the law are present in the vocabulary of this passage: "tables of stone" versus "tables of human hearts," "letter" versus "Spirit," a "ministry of death" and "condemnation" versus a "ministry of the Spirit" and "righteousness," a fading ministry versus an unfading ministry, and a veiled reading of the old covenant versus an unveiled reading of Moses and the old covenant today. The thesis advocated here, however, is that a careful grammatical-syntactical analysis of these items supports the solution already discovered in those texts discussed above which relate to Moses and Jesus.

A. The Tables of Stone and the Tables of Fleshy Hearts[34]

In defending himself against the charge of self-praise Paul responds that his commendation and letters of recommendation are found in the lives of the converts at Corinth; they are letters known and read by all men since they were written by the Spirit of the living God, not in an external fashion ("on tables of stone"), but internally on the heart as promised in Jer 31:33; Ezek 11:19; 36:26.

This is precisely the argument of the whole Bible. In accordance with God's ancient promise, God would write the *same* law (for he has no other law) on their hearts; he would "be their God, and they [would] be [his] people."[35] Thus enabled, they (and we) would walk in God's statutes, keep his judgments and fear him forever (cf. Jer 32:29; 24:7).

Now this was the heart of New Covenant Theology. But can anyone fail to see at least some OT intimations of this provision in Deut 30:6: "And the Lord your God will circumcise your heart and the heart of your seed to love the Lord your God with all your heart and with all your soul that you may live"? Was not this the weightiest matter of the law according to Moses? Without faith, without an internal operation by the living God and a turning to the Lord, it would be impossible to keep the law in any genuine manner.

The contrasts between "ink" and "Spirit," "stones" and "heart" must not be pressed too sharply. Since Paul is using the metaphor to refer to the Corinthian believers as letters written on his [or "their"; cf. textual varia-

---

[33] Ryrie, "The End of the Law," pp. 243-44; essentially the same material is in his *The Grace of God*, p. 102.

[34] For a sampling of the various ways this phrase has been handled in the history of interpretation see B. Ramm, *Special Revelation and the Word of God*, Grand Rapids, 1961, pp. 181-87. Also Philip E. Hughes, *Paul's Second Epistle to the Corinthians*, NIC, Grand Rapids, 1962, pp. 96-102.

[35] For development of this thesis, W. C. Kaiser, Jr., "The Eschatological Hermeneutics of 'Epangelicalism': Promise Theology," *JETS*, 13 (1970), 91-99, esp. 96-99; W. C. Kaiser, Jr., "The Old Promise and the New Covenant," *JETS*, 15 (1972), 11-23, esp. 12-14.

tions here] heart, it was altogether consistent for him to continue that same figure of speech to describe himself as a minister of the Spirit. Exod says nothing about "ink," but it does say that the "tables of stone" were "the work of God" in Exod 31:18; 32:16. The contrast, then, appears to be motivated more by a desire to highlight the emphasis found in the New Covenant promises of Jeremiah and Ezekiel[36] than a desire to demean the Ten Commandments of God's previous work in (ink or) stone. After all, it was not the mode of revelation that was under judgment in this passage; rather it was the blinded response of the people themselves which came under God's indictment.

B. The Letter and the Spirit

Three Pauline passages contrast the letter and the Spirit. In Rom 2:29 Paul compares two types of Jews: the one is a Jew inwardly whose circumcision is that of the heart and the spirit (cf. Moses' word in Deut 30:6); the other is a Jew outwardly in the letter and the circumcision of the flesh. Notice carefully, however, that in *dia grammatos kai peritomēs* (Rom 2:27)

The διά cannot be translated "in spite of", . . . it must be given an instrumental significance. It is precisely through what is written and through circumcision that the Jew is a transgressor. He is to see that his true position involves possession of the γράμμα and περιτομή, but with no genuine fulfillment of the law.[37]

Consequently, it is Rom 2:29 that supplies the real solution to this letter/Spirit contrast. Only when the heart is refashioned for obedience can this false use of the law in *either Testament* be overcome. As in Deut 30:6. what is needed is *peritomē kardias en* (instrumental) *pneumati*. The contrast is total, as shown below.

Not this: *peritomē en* (locative) *sarki en* (instrumental) *grammati*, but this: *peritomē en* (locative) *kardia en* (instrumental) *pneumati.*

Schrenk declares that this theme of a circumcision of the heart dominates all the letter/Spirit passages in Paul.[38] Thus Paul is not speaking so much of the inadequacy of the law or the mere letter as he is stressing the need for that power which alone can produce an obedience to this law. That power comes from turning to the Lord with all one's heart and life. Men actually transgress the law when they outwardly observe all its prescriptions but inwardly remain impervious to it.

In a similar manner, Rom 7:6 is not a discharge notice whereby the

---

[36] For a more detailed statement of the continuity/discontinuity factor between the Mosaic and New Covenants, see Kaiser, "The Old Promise and the New Covenant," pp. 16-23 and the bibliography cited there.

[37] Gottlob Schrenk, "γράμμα," *TDNT*, 1, 765. The *RSV* is guilty of assigning an "in spite of" translation to Rom 2:27: ". . . you who have the written code and circumcision but break the law." So also *JB*. The *NASB* and *NAB* are to be preferred. The latter reads ". . . you who, with your written law and circumcision, break it."

[38] Schrenk, *TDNT*, 1, 765.

older dispensation of the law has now been terminated in order to allow room for the new dispensation of the Spirit. It was not that the *graphē* of the law had ceased, but the *gramma*. For Paul, this meant an outward, fleshly, uncommitted observance of the letter of Moses and a prefunctory circumcision of the flesh. All to no avail. To do all this was only to sin (Rom 2:27); indeed, it was a "serving in the oldness of the letter (*gramma*)." Paul could "serve" the law of God with the mind. But "with [his] flesh" he served "the law of sin." There it is again, Paul's contrast between the heart, which he here calls his "mind," and the flesh. In other words, there are two ways of serving the law of God. People recognize the weightier matters of that law and inwardly respond to God first. In Mosaic vocabulary, they "fear God" and "love him with all their hearts," or "circumcise their hearts." They too have found, with the prophets and Paul, that what God requires is "obedience" (cf. John 3:36, "believing the son" = "obeying"), justice, mercy, faith and love for God.

The same is true in 2 Cor. 3:6. If Paul teaches that the Old Covenant or law *as written (graphē)* was *unto death* in this verse, then he has flatly contradicted himself in Rom 7:10ff., and contradicted also the OT and Jesus. "The commandment," he there had said, "was ordained unto *life!*"[39] But Augustine correctly saw the meaning:

> ... the letter of the law, which teaches us not to commit sin, kills, if the life-giving Spirit be absent.[40]

R. Bultmann also assessed the problem accurately:

> The reason why man's situation under the law is so desperate is not that the Law as an inferior revelation mediates a limited or even false knowledge of God. What makes [man's] situation so desperate is the simple fact that prior to faith *there is no fulfilment of the law*. . . . That is why the "ministration of the Law" is a "ministration of death" or of "condemnation" (II Cor 3:7, 9); that is why "the written code kills" (II Cor 3:6); that is why the Law is "the law of sin and death" (Rom 8:2). The reason why man under the law does not achieve [justification] and life is that he is a transgressor of the Law, that he is guilty before God.[41]

The problem then is not that the law of God is B.C. in time, but it is B.C. in faith. Man must set his priorities and turn by faith to Christ, or his reading of Moses and his obeying of the law will be veiled.

---

[39] See O'Connell, "The Concept of Commandment," pp. 384-89 for a discussion of "life" in the commandments according to Deut and Ps 119. Cf. meanwhile Deut 32:47; Ps 119:93, 114.

[40] Augustine, *De Spiritu et Littera*, 5, as quoted in Hughes, *Paul's Second Epistle to the Corinthians*, p. 99. One must not dismiss the regenerating work of the Holy Spirit from the OT too quickly, or he too will be puzzled and publicly rebuked as Nicodemus, a teacher of the Jews, was rebuffed by Jesus for not knowing and teaching about the work of the Spirit and the need of a new birth in a pre-cross conference (John 3). See the programmatic study by Geoffrey W. Grogan, "The Experience of Salvation in the Old and New Testaments," *Vox Evangelicum* (1967), ed. by Donald Guthrie, esp. pp. 12-17.

[41] Rudolf Bultmann, *Theology of the New Testament*, 1, 262-63, as quoted in Hughes, *Paul's Second Epistle to the Corinthians*, p. 100.

C. The Ministry of Death and the
Ministry of the Spirit

The subject of 2 Cor. 3:7-11 is the contrast between the two ministries: that of Moses and Paul. Cranfield was the first to so put it:

> The key to the true understanding of this whole passage is to recognize that it is really the two ministries which are being contrasted rather than the two covenants themselves; when this is recognized the connection between verses 7-11 and verses 4-6 and 1-3 becomes clear.[42]

The ministry of Moses is not called one of "death" and "condemnation" (vss. 7, 9) because it "was engraved on stones in letters." Paul has just made plain what he intended by his use of letter, ink and stone. He had no desire to demean the written word of God, a literal interpretation of the Scriptures, or the law of Moses in the Old Covenant, else he would be a two-faced liar when he affirmed the opposite in Rom 3:31; 7:12, 14a; 8:4; 13:8-10. Do not the Scriptures also teach that the "gospel" itself may be an "odor of death unto death" to some (2 Cor. 2:16) and that Christ may be a "rock of offense" and a "stone of stumbling set for the ruin of many" (1 Pet 2:8)?[43] And yet no one, for this reason, dares to make an accusation against Christ and the gospel. Hughes, quoting Chrysostom, warns:

> And mark too what great caution he uses in the comparison, so as to give no handle to the heretics; for he did *not* say "which *causeth* death," but "the ministration of death"; for it ministers unto, but *was not the parent of death; for that* which caused death was sin; but the law brought in the punishment and showed the sin; it did not cause it.[44]

Consequently, the ministry of Moses was one of death only when viewed comparatively (with Paul's ministry) and relatively (with the condition of the doer's heart).

D. The Fading Glory and the Abiding Glory

Paul does indeed carefully circumscribe his argument in vs. 10. It is only in comparison with the newly added ministry which Paul represents that the older ministry represented by Moses may be said to be passing away. It was only "in this respect" and "on account of" the surpassing glory. The repeated comparative phrase "how much more" (vss. 8, 9, 11) and the supporting words "abounding" and "surpassing" contribute to the same conclusion.

What was it, then, that was fading? The answer is clear in vs. 7:

---

[42] Cranfield, "St. Paul and the Law," p. 58. Notice that Paul's ministry is still under discussion in 2 Cor 4:1. This shows that it was the uppermost thought in Paul's mind.

[43] John Calvin, *Commentary on the Epistles of Paul the Apostle to the Corinthians,* trans. by John Pringle, Grand Rapids, 1948, 2, 177. However, Calvin gave too much ground and misses part of Paul's point in his discussion which follows.

[44] P. E. Hughes, *Paul's Second Epistle to the Corinthians,* p. 102 (italics mine).

"which glory was to be done away." The external glow on Moses' face which appeared each time he met with God was "that which was fading away" or disappearing. That is what happened in Exod 34:29-35. Even though Moses was at first unconscious of the tremendous glory that glowed from his face as a result of his personal communion with God on Mount Sinai (and subsequently whenever he went into the tabernacle), the people were aware of it. Out of deference to their fear of approaching him personally (a very unnecessary fear), Moses acted *on his own* initiative and wore a veil whenever he finished speaking to the people. Customarily, then, he would remove the veil whenever he approached the Lord's presence [45] and leave it off until he had completed speaking God's word to the people. Only then would Moses replace the *humanly* devised veil on his face and talk with the people.

Thus Paul also notes in vs. 7 that the people could not "look intently on Moses' face" because of the brightness (glory) on his face. Moreover, without contradicting himself in vs. 13 (for he does not assign a totally different motive there), he noted that Moses used to put[46] this veil on so that the Jews would not "look intently to the end of what was fading away." The *telos* here cannot mean the "termination" or "full stop," for the Mosaic and Jewish administration was just beginning and there was no danger of the people gazing on it right up to the end of its duration. Rather, Paul meant the "ultimate significance," or "goal."[47] Thus, not as a subterfuge, a mystical symbol, a *pesher* illustration or for midrashic purposes—or any such thing—did Moses place the veil over his face. Rather, it was as a prophetically enacted parable that he did it. He wanted the people of Israel to realize that their iniquities had rendered them unable, and unworthy, to behold such glory in its "ultimate significance." They, like Moses, would need to turn to the Lord if they were to look intently at the glory of the Lord.

In contrast to Moses' veil, the apostle spoke to the Corinthians with "great boldness" (*parrēsia*). W. C. van Unnik has suggested that the word Paul used for "boldness" is an Aramaic loan word. In fact, the expression "to uncover the face or head" is used synonymously in the Syriac liturgies with *parrēsia*. Therefore, "to unveil the face" meant openness, confidence and boldness.[48] Paul's ministry was, on that basis, very different from Moses' ministry. Even though Moses' glory was from God, it was temporary and reflective. Further, it was hindered, since "the understanding" of Israel "was blocked" (vs. 14). Indeed, up to the *present day* "the same veil

---

[45] Does this mean that Moses would seldom (if ever) speak to the people as God's prophet until he had first spoken to the Lord and the Lord had spoken to him?

[46] *Etithei,* iterative imperfect; so Hughes.

[47] Jean Héring, *The Second Epistle of Saint Paul to the Corinthians,* trans. by A. W. Heathcote and P. J. Allcock, London, 1967, p. 25, n. 16, suggests, " '*Telos*' can also mean 'the full' development of, 'the consummation of' (cf. Plato, *Symposium* 210E and 211B)." Cf. Jas 5:11 for a possible parallel. For the meaning "aim," cf. 1 Tim 1:5.

[48] W. C. van Unnik, " 'With Unveiled Face', an Exegesis of II Corinthians 3:12-18," *NovT,* 6 (1963), 161.

remains" whenever the Old Covenant or Moses is read! Nothing has changed in this respect, if the hearts of the people have remained where they were in Moses' day: the same blindness, the same condemnation and death persist.

How can this situation be remedied? Only one way. Not by declaring that we have finished with all our service to all the law or the ten commandments. Moses' veil is "lifted," and the glory (temporary and in need of renewal as it was) is revealed in its "ultimate significance" (and subsequent permanence in the contrasted ministry of Paul) whenever men "turn to the Lord." Only then is the veil "removed" (vs. 14). The law itself is not "done away with" or "annulled" at that time, for Paul had asked that question about the law's relationship to the promise and grace of God in Rom 3:31: "Do we therefore make void the law through faith?" His clear answer abides for all of eternity and for all theologies everywhere—"No! Not at all!" Therefore, it is the *veil* that is "abrogated," or better "removed," according to Paul. The *NEB* is totally out of line when it gives this translation: " ... because only in Christ is the *Old Covenant* abrogated" (italics mine). The subject of this verb surely is the same as that for "lifted up" in vs. 14. "It is the same veil."[49]

Once again, we have come full circle. Only when one meets God's prior conditions of "fearing him" and "loving him with all one's heart," can Moses' law be read and the glory that is fading be viewed in its full significance. Thus, as vs. 17 implies,[50] to turn to the Lord is to be introduced into the spiritual realm spoken of in vss. 6 and 8.

Conclusion

The case for a single, monolithic law of God, which refuses to recognize Jesus' ranking of the "weightier" and "the least" within that law, must now be totally re-evaluated. Further, the claim that the law of the Lord, in all its parts, has now been ended *en toto* due to Christ's perfect fulfillment of that one (i.e. ceremonial) law and due to Paul's allegedly unequivocal statement that even the Ten Commandments have been abrogated (2 Cor 3) (?), must now itself be abandoned in light of Paul's teaching in that very passage and elsewhere.

Instead, what is needed now for the reading of the law of the Lord is the same thing that was needed in Moses' day. We must turn to the Lord and by means of the Spirit of the Lord, together with the single truth-inten-

[49] Gerhard Delling, "καταργέω," *TDNT*, 1, 454, at first concedes that the subject of the verb "abrogated" is the veil, but then arbitrarily turns around and declares, "On the other hand, we get a clearer sense if we take *palaia diathēkē* as the subject here. This is invalidated or devalued in Christ. . . ." This illustrates almost every other interpreter's dilemma who concurs with this conclusion. The grammar says "veil," but a "clearer sense" (what must that mean in this context?) is obtained if we just slip in "the old covenant."

[50] There is a huge literature on this verse. See the more recent literature by J. D. G. Dunn, "II Corinthians 3:17–'The Lord is the Spirit,' " *JTS*, 21 (1970), 309-20; David Greenwood, "The Lord is the Spirit: Some Considerations of 2 Cor 3:17," *CBQ*, 34 (1972), 467-72; and van Unnik, "With Unveiled Face," pp. 153-69.

tion that Paul indicated in the Greek grammar and syntax of Scripture, *graphē*, have the veil lifted from our eyes as well. Anything less than this will still be a "letter" (*gramma*) reading of the law, which according to Rom 2:27 is a felony before God. However, whenever reading of the law is preceded by true conversion, and the proper priorities are observed in one's own life, there is no more bondage to the "letter," but great liberty in the "word" of the Lord (2 Cor 3:17), even the perfect law of liberty (Jas 1:25; 2:12).

Bultmann's Law of Increasing Distinctness

LESLIE R. KEYLOCK

I

Bultmann is the most prominent contemporary exponent of what may be called the "law" of increasing distinctness. Stated in its most general form, this literary law maintains that

> whenever narratives pass from mouth to mouth the central point of the narrative and general structure are well preserved; but in the incidental details changes take place, for imagination paints such details with increasing distinctness.[1]

First developed by classical scholars in Germany who studied popular oral literature, this law was later applied to similar materials in rabbinical and Hellenistic literature.

I have neither the training nor the talent for evaluating the existence of such a law in general; the more modest aim of this essay is to outline the ways in which Bultmann applies this general law to post-canonical literature and to the Synoptic Gospels, to test the validity of its application to the Synoptic Gospels by an analysis of the relevant material, and in a quite preliminary way to suggest reasons for differing with Bultmann's conclusions.

Bultmann maintains that the post-canonical literature follows the same law of increasing distinctness that can be observed in all popular orally transmitted material:

> In the later legends it is to be observed, for example, that names are sought for

[1] Rudolf Bultmann, "The New Approach to the Synoptic Problem," *Existence and Faith*, selected, translated and introduced by Schubert M. Ogden, Cleveland and New York, 1960, pp. 41-42. This article originally appeared in *JR*, 6 (1926), 337-62. Others who have held this theory in various forms include Dibelius, Weiss, Köster, Bussmann, Schmid and Nineham. See summaries of their views in E. P. Sanders, *The Tendencies of the Synoptic Tradition*, Cambridge, 1969, pp. 88ff. For Streeter's interesting view, see *ibid.*, pp. 89-90.

Leslie Robert Keylock, Assistant Professor of Religious Studies at the College of Mount St. Vincent, New York, New York. B.A. and B.Ed., University of Alberta; M.A., Wheaton College Graduate School; doctoral studies, University of Iowa; Th.D. candidate, General Theological Seminary.

many people whom the gospels mention without naming them. What was the name of the woman with the issue of blood whom Jesus healed? Who were the thieves crucified with Jesus? What was the name of the captain of the guard over the grave of Jesus? Later legends undertake to tell us.[2]

Bultmann finds evidence of a similar tendency at work in the NT:

Such legendary creations of the imagination are also to be observed in the gospels. Who were the two disciples mentioned in Mark 14:13 whom Jesus sent on before to prepare the Passover meal? In Luke 22:8 we have their names: Peter and John. *Imagination always portrays in more precise and vivid form what it receives.*[3]

Four further examples from the Gospels are then given.

Where Mark 9:17 narrates that a father brought to Jesus his deranged son, we read in Luke 9:38 that it was his only son. Mark says simply that the thieves crucified with Jesus reviled him (15:32). Luke tells us that only one of them did this, while the other acknowledged Jesus and received from him a gracious answer (23:39-43). The scene in which Judas betrayed Jesus with a kiss is narrated in Mark without any accompanying words (14:45). It is easy to understand that people later should ask: "What did Jesus say to him?" Matthew puts into the mouth of Jesus the words, "Friend, why hast thou come?" (26:50). According to Luke, Jesus said, "Judas, betrayest thou the Son of Man with a kiss?" (22:48). According to Mark 15:37, Jesus died uttering a loud cry. What did he say? What were his last words? Luke 23:46 puts in the mouth of Jesus the quotation from one of the Psalms, "Father, into thy hands I commend my spirit"; while the Gospel of John later represents Jesus as saying, "It is finished" (19:30).[4]

In his earlier and more important work *The History of the Synoptic Tradition,* Bultmann also hints at such an application to the first three Gospels of the general literary law of increasing distinctness in the incidental details of an oral narrative. In discussing the Transfiguration, Bultmann says that the two figures who appear with Jesus may originally have been unidentified heavenly beings who, "following a law of folklore," were later identified as Moses and Elijah.[5] But in a footnote he adds:

It remains a question of whether the two heavenly beings, as Goetz and Meyer suppose, can be identified as the two escorts who, in Iranian belief, took the souls of the pious into the world of light.[6]

He also suggests that details in miracle and pronouncement stories (apothegms) are secondary.[7]

[2] Bultmann, "New Approach," p. 42.
[3] *Ibid.* Italics mine.
[4] *Ibid.*
[5] Rudolf Bultmann, *History of the Synoptic Tradition,* New York and Evanston, 1963, p. 260. The date is rather deceptive, however, for the original German edition was published in 1919. The English translation was based on the third revised edition, published in Germany in 1958.
[6] *Ibid.,* n. 3. The authors mentioned reflect the ideas of the *Religionsgeschichtliche* or History of Religions School of German biblical criticism. The amazingly thorough research on which their conclusions were based is unfortunately not very well known in America—not as well known as it should be, largely because most of it has never been translated into English.
[7] *Ibid.,* pp. 241ff. On the other hand see his observation that Matthew is often less detailed than Mark (*ibid.,* p. 353). Sanders, *Tendencies of the Synoptic Tra-*

Although in 1926 Bultmann asserted that tradition *always* follows the law of increasing distinctness, in 1930, in "The Study of the Synoptic Gospels," he appears to have modified his position somewhat:

> The laws governing the formulation of popular narrative and tradition may be studied in detail in the material which the Synoptists hand down.... As such narratives pass from mouth to mouth, *or when one writer takes them over from another,* their fundamental character remains the same, but the details are subject to the control of fancy and are *usually* made more explicit and definite.[8]

We may then summarize Bultmann's expression of the law of increasing distinctness as follows: in their oral stages and in the redactional process the pericopes of the Synoptic Gospels tend to retain their basic outline but in their details to become increasingly concrete and distinct. Bultmann's position remains relatively constant, although at no time does he carry out his own investigation of the validity of the law. Rather he seems to accept uncritically the conclusions of the History of Religions School of German biblical criticism.

II

That there is a tendency in the post-canonical or apocryphal literature to identify characters that are not named in the Gospels cannot be denied. Bultmann himself mentions the woman with the issue of blood. She is identified as Bernice in the Greek Acts of Pilate, Veronica in the Latin versions of the work and in the Gospel of Nicodemus, and a princess of Edessa in Macarius Magnes.[9] The two thieves crucified with Jesus are identified as Zoatham and Camma or Chammatha, or as Joathas and Maggatras in the Latin versions.[10] And the captain of the guard who watched over Jesus' sealed tomb is called Petronius in the Gospel of Peter.[11] The Christmas carol "We Three Kings of Orient Are" gives us three traditional names for the astrologers or "wise men" who followed a star to the Bethlehem manger. A fragment of the Gospel of the Nazaraeans from the Middle Ages mentions that it was actually a large crowd of pilgrims who came to visit the baby Jesus, "even if, according to some, the foremost leaders of this crowd were named with the definite names Melchus, Caspar

---

dition, p. 146, n. 3, observes, "He seems never to have reconciled his claim that the Synoptic material became more detailed with the statement that Matthew frequently lacks Mark's details, nor to have investigated just how often details are added and omitted in the later Synoptic tradition."

[8] Bultmann's essay appears in an English translation along with another by Karl Kundsin as *Form Criticism: Two Essays on New Testament Research,* New York, 1962. The earlier English hardback edition was published in 1934. In the quote (p. 32), Bultmann extends an oral law to written materials (perhaps unjustifiably) and allows for exceptions. (Italics are mine.)

[9] See Edgar Hennecke and Wilhelm Schneemelcher, *New Testament Apocrypha,* 2 vols., Philadelphia, 1963-64, 1, 457; and Bultmann, *History of the Synoptic Tradition,* p. 241.

[10] See the notes to Matt 27:38; Mark 15:27; and Luke 23:32 in D. Eberhard Nestle and D. Irwin Nestle, *Novum Testamentum Graece,* Stuttgart, 1952[21]. See also Alfred Plummer, *The Gospel According to Luke,* Edinburgh, 1922, p. 530.

[11] Hennecke-Schneemelcher, *New Testament Apocrypha,* 1, 185.

and Phadizarda."[12] The familiar names Caspar, Melchior and Balthazar are first mentioned in the sixth-century *Excerpta Latina Barbari.*[13] The expansion of the Protevangelium of James, known as the Armenian Infancy Gospel, speaks of three royal brothers named Melqon, Balthasar and Gaspar.[14]

The variety of names given to the rich man of the parable of the rich man and Lazarus further serves to confirm the fact that tradition liked to give specific names to those who are not named in the Gospels. He is most often identified as Dives, but in the Sahidic Version and in the recently discovered Bodmer papyrus he is called Ninevah, and the fourth-century Priscillian knows him as Finees.[15] Luke himself rather provocatively gives the name Cleopas to one of the men going to the village of Emmaus. Who was the other one? The margin of the tenth-century manuscript identifies him as Simon, but the margin of the ninth-century codex (V) says he is "Nathanael, as the great Epiphanius said in the Panarion." The same codex also adds that "Cleopas was the cousin of the Savior, the second bishop of Jerusalem."[16]

From even such a selective list it may easily be seen that later tradition often did give names to the nameless characters of the NT.[17] Furthermore, few would argue that these names were produced after rigorous historical research revealed that they were in fact the names used by the individuals during their lifetimes or by Jesus in narrating the stories in which they appear.

III

Has a similar tendency taken place, then, within the Synoptic tradition? There are those who would argue a priori that such a tendency is inconsistent with a high view of inspiration. I see no reason, however, for not adopting a more open outlook, while still maintaining the integrity of the Scriptures. Certainly it cannot be denied that such a development *could* have taken place in the Gospel tradition, especially in the oral stages prior to the actual writing of Mark, Luke and Matthew. If it can be demonstrated that such a tendency did occur in the literature of the time, there would seem to be no valid evidence for the conclusion that the NT authors consciously resisted it. But the question still remains as to whether the

[12] *Ibid.,* 1, 151.

[13] *The Oxford Dictionary of the Christian Church,* ed. by Frank L. Cross, London, 1958, p. 842.

[14] Hennecke-Schneemelcher, *New Testament Apocrypha,* 1, 405.

[15] Nestle, *Novum Testamentum Graece,* p. 200, the note referring to Luke 16:19. See also F. W. Danker, *Multipurpose Tools for Bible Study,* St. Louis, 1966[2], p. 21.

[16] Bruce Metzger's perceptive review of the first volume of Hennecke-Schmeemelcher's *New Testament Apocrypha* in *TT,* 21 (1964), 139-41, contains much of the relevant information, and notes the unfortunate omission of A. Meyer's "Namen der Namenlos" from the English translation.

[17] For further examples of this and related tendencies in the post-canonical tradition, see Sanders, *Tendencies of the Synoptic Tradition,* pp. 96-146.

Synoptic tradition actually did follow this tendency. The purpose of this article is to answer that question.

Before analyzing the Synoptic materials, however, we need to make a few remarks about what, to our knowledge, is the only thorough analysis dealing specifically with increasing detail as a possible tendency of the Synoptic tradition, i.e. E. P. Sanders' *The Tendencies of the Synoptic Tradition.*

The purpose of Sanders' book is to analyze three possible tendencies in the Synoptic tradition—increasing length, increasing detail, and diminishing Semitism. For each of these possible tendencies he presents the evidence from the post-canonical tradition, and then the Synoptic evidence. In the Synoptic section of the chapter on increasing detail (pp. 88-189), Sanders breaks down all the examples of change from each Synoptic Gospel into eighteen different categories—subjects, objects, adjectives, prepositions, explanations, conclusions, results, emotions, miscellaneous details, and other types found in one Gospel but not in another. Finally, he tabulates the frequencies where each Gospel is more detailed in each of these categories than in either of the other two Gospels, and suggests conclusions that may be drawn from the data.

Sanders is to be commended for being the first to treat such an important question so extensively and objectively. His presentation of the views of Bultmann, Streeter, Taylor, Cadbury, Bussmann, Farmer and Nineham on the whole question of oral and redactional changes in the first three Gospels is excellent. Sanders rightly concludes that Bultmann has not explicitly noted or dealt with the inconsistency that results in his thought because he accepts the fact that Mark is more detailed than the other two Synoptics, and at the same time espouses the law of increasing distinctness. He would also seem to be right in stating that the post-canonical tendencies cannot be correlated with the evidence from the Synoptics as directly as one might hope, possibly because the redactional history of the canonical Gospel genre is so different from that of the post-canonical writings. Sanders' conclusion that the criterion of detail should not be used too quickly to establish the relative antiquity of one document over another would also seem to be sound.

The book is nevertheless surprisingly unsatisfactory in several ways. The most serious weakness of Sanders' analysis is its excessively statistical handling of the material, coupled with a seriously deficient sensitivity for literary quality. To give just one example, the suggestion that the substitution of "he" for "Jesus" is evidence of decreasing distinctness, which Sanders makes time and again, is possible only by neglecting the elementary fact that pronouns are used to avoid excessive repetition of a given noun. Numerous similar examples could be cited to substantiate our conclusion that Sanders' results are seriously distorted by trivial differences which do not really have much, if anything, to do with a possible law of increasing distinctness.

Also missing is a thorough statement of the implications of the results and suggestions as to why certain tendencies occurred. Instead of analyzing in detail the impact, for example, of theology on literary change (Conzelmann is not even mentioned once in the whole book!), Sanders tends to get sidetracked on the secondary question of the chronological sequence of the writing of the Gospels. The reason for the division of the Synoptic material into eighteen categories is not sufficiently clear or justifiable. Nor does the writer compile a table that would bring together all the individual tables into one overall summary of the tendencies of each Gospel as a whole. Individual charts are also distorted by a failure to consider Q; the result is that what may seem to be an example of decreasing distinctness is in fact merely a preservation by one author of Q and a tendency of the other author to increasing precision.

Although the following analysis is more limited, it is hoped that the weaknesses of Sanders' study have been avoided and that the problem has been carried one step further toward solution.

IV

To test Bultmann's hypothesis we have placed certain limitations on our analysis. We have limited ourselves almost totally to the Synoptic Gospels, although the Fourth Gospel could often have been cited as further evidence of a tendency. Only occasional references will be made to patristic and apocryphal materials, since they are a major study in themselves.

The following tables are a fairly thorough sampling of the significant changes that occur in the Synoptic Gospels. These changes have been grouped into five distinct tables representing five different tendencies. In a concluding section each table will be analyzed and some specific conclusions will be drawn.

TABLE 1.* LUKE MORE PRECISE THAN MARK

PERIC-OPE	MARK	LUKE	REASON FOR CHANGE
1	1:4 wilderness	3:2, 3 and all the region about the Jordan	Luke's theology
6	1:10 the Spirit	3:22 the Holy Spirit	Stylistic peculiarity
12	1:21 Capernaum	4:31 Capernaum, a city of Galilee	Explanatory addition
13	1:30 a fever	4:38 a high fever	Heightening
52	2:1 many	5:17 Pharisees and teachers of the law . . . who had come from every village of Galilee and Judea and from Jerusalem	Luke's theology (Conzelmann)

*Notes to the tables: The pericope number is from the Gospel parallels as found in A. Huck, *Synopsis of the First Three Gospels,* New York, 1935; Caird = G. B. Caird, *The Gospel of St. Luke,* Baltimore, 1964; Conzelmann = Hans Conzelmann, *The Theology of St. Luke,* New York, 1961; Flender = Helmut Flender, *St. Luke, Theologian of Redemption,* trans. by R. H. and I. Fuller, Philadelphia, 1967; McNeile = A. H. McNeile, *The Gospel According to St. Matthew,* London, 1915; PCB = *Peake's Commentary on the Bible,* rev. and ed. by M. Black and H. H. Rowley, London-New York, 1962.

TABLE 1.   LUKE MORE PRECISE THAN MARK

PERIC-OPE	MARK	LUKE	REASON FOR CHANGE
54	2:22 wine	5:37 new wine	Improvement of style
58	3:18 Andrew	6:14 Andrew his brother	Explanatory addition
69	2:24 the Pharisees	6:2 some of the Pharisees	Improvement of style
70	3:1 hand	6:6 right hand	Increasing distinctness
70	3:2 they	6:7 the scribes and the Pharisees	Improvement of style
71	3:7 a great multitude from Galilee	6:17 a great crowd of his disciples and a great multitude of people	Luke's theology (Conzelmann)
83(=232)	14:3 a woman	7:37 a woman of the city, who was a sinner	Explanatory addition or Luke's theology
83(=232)	14:4 some	7:39 the Pharisee (Simon)	Increasing distinctness (John 12:4 says Judas)
90	4:4 birds	8:5 birds of the air	Stylistic peculiarity
93	4:14 the word	8:11 the Word of God	Improvement of style
97	4:31 upon the ground	13:19 in his garden	Cultural adaptation
106	5:2 a man	8:27 a man from the city	Increasing distinctness?
106	5:9 we are many	8:30 many demons had entered him	Improvement of style
107	5:23 little daughter	8:42 only daughter, about twelve years of age	Increasing distinctness
107	5:31 his disciples	8:45 Peter	Increasing distinctness
107	5:37	8:51 and the father and mother of the child	Luke's theology (compassion)
108(=10)	6:1 his own country	4:16 Nazareth where he had been brought up	Improvement of style
120	8:15 leaven	12:1 leaven . . . which is hypocrisy	Explanatory addition
122	8:28 one of the prophets	9:19 one of the old prophets has risen	Luke's theology (Flender, p. 50).
122	8:29 the Christ	9:20 the Christ of God	Stylistic peculiarity
124	9:2 a high mountain	9:28 the mountain	Luke's theology (Conzelmann)
126	9:19 O faithless generation	9:41 O faithless and perverse generation	Stylistic peculiarity from Q
189	10:17 a man	18:18 a ruler	Increasing distinctness
193	10:48 many	18:39 those who were in front	Improvement of style
196	11:4 those who stood there	19:33 its owners	Improvement of style
196	11:9 those	19:37 the whole multitude of the disciples	Inference from Mark
196	11:10 he	19:38 the King	Luke's theology (Conzelmann, p. 139)
204	12:12 they	20:19 the scribes and the chief priests	Improvement of style
206	12:14 pay taxes	20:22 give tribute	Stylistic peculiarity (synonymous)

TABLE 1. LUKE MORE PRECISE THAN MARK

PERIC-OPE	MARK	LUKE	REASON FOR CHANGE
216	13:14 the desolating sacrilege	21:20 Jerusalem surrounded by armies	Historical influence
220	13:29 he	21:31 the Kingdom of God	Improvement of style
233	14:10 chief priests	22:4 chief priests and captains	Luke's theology; anticipates 22:52
234	14:12 his disciples	22:9 they (Peter and John)	Increasing distinctness
234	14:13 two of his disciples	22:8 Peter and John	Increasing distinctness
236	14:24 the covenant	22:20 the new covenant	Influence of Paul (I Cor. 11:25)
240	14:47 his ear	22:50 his right ear	Increasing distinctness
240	14:48 them	22:52 the chief priests and captains of the temple and elders who had come out against him	Inference from Mark (Conzelmann, p. 83)
241	14:62 power	22:69 power of God	Improvement of style
241	14:65 cover his face	22:64 blindfolded him	Improvement of style
251	15:43 Joseph of Arimathea	23:50 a man named Joseph from the Jewish town of Arimathea	Explanatory addition
251	15:43 a respected member of the Council	23:50 a member of the Council, a good and righteous man	Luke's theology
253	16:5 a young man	24:4 two men	Heightening? Increasing distinctness?

TABLE 2. LUKE LESS PRECISE THAN MARK

PERIC-OPE	MARK	LUKE	REASON FOR CHANGE
4	1:7 stoop down and untie	3:16 untie	Condensation of Mark
12	1:28 region of Galilee	4:37 region	Luke's theology
13	1:29 house of Simon and Andrew	4:38 Simon's house	Condensation of Mark
13	1:29 with James and John	4:38 —	Luke's theology (cf. Luke 5:10-11)
15	1:36 Simon and those who were with him	4:42 the people	Luke's theology (cf. Luke 5:1-11)
52	2:1 Capernaum	5:17 —	Luke's theology?
52	2:3 four men	5:18 men	Decreasing distinctness
53	2:14 Levi the son of Alphaeus	5:27 Levi	Condensation of Mark
58(=109)	3:17 James the son of Zebedee	6:14 James	Condensation of Mark
58(=109)	3:17 John the brother of James	6:14 John	Condensation of Mark

TABLE 2. LUKE LESS PRECISE THAN MARK

PERIC-OPE	MARK	LUKE	REASON FOR CHANGE
69	2:26 when Abiathar was high priest	6:4 —	Condensation of Mark?
70	3:6 with the Herodians	6:11 with one another	Simplification of Mark
85	3:22 scribes who came down from Jerusalem	11:15 some of them (the people)	Luke's theology?
106	3:20 in the Decapolis	8:39 throughout the whole city	Luke's theology
110	6:14 John the Baptizer	9:17 John	Condensation of Mark
112	3:39 upon the green grass	9:14 —	Condensation of Mark?
123	8:34 the multitude with his disciples	9:23 all	Condensation of Mark
189	10:26 they were exceedingly astonished and said	18:26 (They) . . . said	Condensation of Mark
193	10:46 Bartimaeus, a blind beggar, the son of Timaeus	18:35 a blind beggar	Name unknown to Luke's readers
202	11:27 the scribes and the elders	20:1 the scribes with the elders	?
206	12:13 some of the Pharisees and some of the Herodians	20:20 spies who pretended to be sincere	Simplification of Mark
212	12:42 two lepta which make a quadrans	21:2 two lepta	Condensation of Mark
213	13:1 one of his disciples	21:5 some	Luke's theology (Conzelmann, p. 79)
213	13:3 Peter, James, John, Andrew	21:7 they (some)	Luke's theology (Conzelmann, p. 79)
231	14:1 two days before the Passover and the feast of unleavened bread	22:1 the feast of unleavened bread drew near	Luke's theology (Conzelmann, p. 199)
232	14:3 ointment of pure nard	7:37 ointment	Condensation of Mark
232	14:5 more than 300 denarii	7:37 —	Condensation of Mark
234	14:14 my guest room	22:11 the guest room	Improvement of style
239	14:37 Peter	22:46 them (disciples)	Improvement of style
241	14:66 one of the maids of the high priest	21:5 a maid	Condensation of Mark
241	14:69 the maid	22:58 someone else	Stylistic peculiarity
241	14:69 the bystanders	22:59 still another	Stylistic peculiarity
248	15:21 the father of Alexander and Rufus	23:36 —	Names not known to Luke's readers
249	15:39 centurion who stood facing him	23:47 centurion	Condensation of Mark
250	15:40 Mary Magdalene and Mary the mother of James the younger, etc.	23:49 women	Simplification of Mark

TABLE 2. LUKE LESS PRECISE THAN MARK

PERIC-OPE	MARK	LUKE	REASON FOR CHANGE
251	15:47 Mary Magdalene and Mary the mother of Joses	23:55 the women who had come with him from Galilee	Simplification of Mark
253	16:1 Mary Magdalene and Mary the mother of James	24:1 they (the women)	Simplification of Mark

TABLE 3. MATTHEW MORE PRECISE THAN MARK

PERIC-OPE	MARK	MATTHEW	REASON FOR CHANGE
1	1:4 wilderness	3:1 wilderness of Judea	Improvement of style
1	1:6 camel's hair	3:4 a garment of camel's hair	Improvement of style
6	1:10 the Spirit	3:16 the Spirit of God	Stylistic peculiarity
11	1:16 Simon	4:18 Simon who is called Peter	Explanatory addition
51(=106)	1:14 people	8:34 all the city	Heightening
58(=109)	6:6 the villages	9:35 all the cities and villages	Heightening
58(=109)	3:18 Andrew	10:2 Andrew his (Peter's) brother	Explanatory addition
58(=109)	3:18 Matthew	10:3 Matthew the tax collector	Explanatory addition
70	3:5 restored	12:13 restored, whole like the other	Heightening
93	4:14 the word	13:19 the word of the kingdom	Explanatory addition
97	4:31 upon the ground	13:31 in his field	Cultural adaptation
106	5:2 a man with an unclean spirit	8:28 two demoniacs	Heightening
106	5:13 the herd	8:32 the whole herd	Heightening
114	6:53 the people	14:35 the men of that place	Improvement of style
115	7:17 his disciples	15:15 Peter	Increasing distinctness
118	8:9 about 4000 people	15:38 4000 men, besides women and children	Heightening
122	8:28 one of the prophets	16:14 Jeremiah or one of the prophets	Matt's theology (PCB, p. 787)
122	8:29 Peter	16:16 Simon Peter	Explanatory addition
122	8:29 the Christ	16:16 the Christ, the Son of the Living God	Heightening
122	8:31 the Son of man must suffer	16:21 Jesus . . . must go to Jerusalem and suffer	Historical influence
124	9:2 John	17:1 John his brother	Explanatory addition
124	9:7 a cloud	17:5 a bright cloud	Heightening

TABLE 3. MATTHEW MORE PRECISE THAN MARK

PERIC-OPE	MARK	MATTHEW	REASON FOR CHANGE
126	9:19 O faithless generation	17:17 O faithless and perverse generation	Stylistic peculiarity from Q
187	10:1 there	19:1 Galilee	Improvement of style
189	10:17 a man	19:16, 20, 22 one, the young man	Increasing distinct-ness? Heightening?
191	10:34 scourge	20:19 scourged and cruci-fied	Historical influence
196	11:2, 4 a colt	21:2 an ass . . . and a colt	OT influence
196	11:9 those	21:9 the crowds	Improvement of style
198	11:11 the temple	21:12 the temple of God	Stylistic peculiarity
199	11:12 in the distance	21:18-19 by the wayside	Improvement of style
204	12:1 a man	21:33 a man, a householder	Explanatory addition
204	12:2 the time	21:34 the season of fruit	Improvement of style
204	12:2 a servant	21:34 his servants	Matt's theology (McNeile, p. 309)
204	12:9 others	21:41 other tenants	Improvement of style
206	12:13 some of the Pharisees	22:16 their (Pharisees') disciples	? (cf. Mark 2:18; Luke 5:33)
216	13:14 desolating sacrilege	24:15 desolating sacrilege spoken of by the prophet Daniel	Explanatory addition
216	13:18 it	24:20 your flight	Improvement of style
216	13:14 set up where it ought not to be	24:15 standing in the holy place	Improvement of style
216	13:19 tribulation	24:21 great tribulation	Heightening
217	13:22 signs	24:24 great signs	Heightening
219	13:26 in clouds	24:30 on the clouds of heaven	Stylistic peculiarity
231	14:1 scribes	26:3 elders of the people	Matt's theology
232	14:4 some	26:8 the disciples	Increasing distinctness?
233	14:11 money	26:15 thirty pieces of silver	OT influence
238	14:43 crowd	26:47 great crowd	Heightening
240	14:49 scriptures	26:56 scriptures of the prophets	Stylistic peculiarity
241	14:53 they	26:57 those who had seized	Improvement of style
241	14:53 the high priest	26:57 Caiaphas the high priest	Increasing distinctness
241	14:65 spit on him	26:57 spat in his face	Increasing distinctness?
242	15:1 Pilate	27:2 Pilate the governor	Stylistic peculiarity
246	15:6 them	27:15 the crowd	Improvement of style
246	15:7 a man	27:16 a notorious prisoner	Improvement of style
246	15:12 the man whom you call the king of the Jews	27:22 Jesus who is called Christ	Improvement of style
247	15:16 soldiers	27:27 soldiers of the governor	Stylistic peculiarity
250	15:40 women (cf. also vs. 41)	27:55 many women	Improvement of style
251	15:46 a linen shroud	27:59 a clean linen shroud	Heightening
251	15:46 a tomb	27:60 his own new tomb	Heightening
251	15:46 a stone	27:60 a great stone	Heightening

TABLE 4. MATTHEW LESS PRECISE THAN MARK

PERIC-OPE	MARK	MATTHEW	REASON FOR CHANGE
1	1:4 John the baptizer	3:4 John (the Baptist, 1:1)	Condensation of Mark
9	1:14 preaching the gospel of God	4:17 preach	Condensation of Mark
11	1:20 with the hired servants	4:22 –	Condensation of Mark
13	1:29 house of Simon and Andrew	8:14 Peter's house	Condensation of Mark
13	1:29 with James and John	8:14 –	Condensation of Mark? Not in Q?
45	1:44 offer for your cleansing	8:4 offer	Condensation of Mark
52	2:1 Capernaum	9:1 his own city	Stylistic peculiarity (cf. Matt 8:5)
52	2:3 four men	9:2 they	Matt's or Q's style
53	2:16 scribes of the Pharisees	9:11 Pharisees	Condensation and/or simplification of Mark
55(=107)	5:22 Jairus	9:18 a ruler	Condensation of Mark? Decreasing distinctness
69	2:26 when Abiathar was high priest	12:4 –	A later gloss in Mark? Not in Q?
70	3:6 with the Herodians	12:14 –	Condensation of Mark
71	3:7 a great multitude from Galilee	12:15 many	Condensation of Mark
85	3:22 scribes who came down from Jerusalem	12:24 Pharisees	Condensation of Mark; Matthew's theology
106	5:7 Jesus, Son of the Most High God	8:29 O Son of God	Condensation of Mark? Matthew's theology?
112	5:39 green grass	14:19 grass	Condensation of Mark
113	5:45 to Bethsaida	14:22 –	Condensation of Mark
115	7:21 heart of man	15:19 heart	Condensation of Mark
117	7:31 through the region of the Decapolis	15:29 –	Condensation of Mark
120	8:19 baskets full of broken pieces	16:9 baskets	Condensation of Mark
123	8:38 the holy angels	16:27 his angels	Condensation of Mark
123	8:34 the multitude with his disciples	16:24 his disciples	Improvement of style
187	10:1 there	19:1 Galilee	Improvement of style
188	10:13 them	19:13 the people	Improvement of style
192	10:35 James and John	20:20 the mother of the sons of Zebedee	Matt's theology?
192	10:41 James and John	20:24 the two brothers	Matt's theology?
193	10:46 Bartimaeus, etc.	20:30 two blind men	Condensation of Mark; decreasing distinctness; heightening
196	11:1 Bethphage and Bethany	21:1 Bethphage	Improvement of style
196	11:2 colt on which no one has ever sat	21:2 colt	Condensation of Mark; decreasing distinctness
201	11:20-21 they . . . Peter	21:20 the disciples	Condensation of Mark
202	11:27 the scribes and the elders	21:23 the elders of the people	Matt's theology
209	12:36 Holy Spirit	22:43 Spirit	Matt's theology

TABLE 4. MATTHEW LESS PRECISE THAN MARK

PERIC- OPE	MARK	MATTHEW	REASON FOR CHANGE
213	13:1 one of his disciples	24:1 his disciples	Matt's theology
213	13:3 the Mount of Olives opposite the temple	24:3 the Mount of lives Olives	Condensation of Mark
213	13:3 Peter, James, John, Andrew	24:3 the disciples	Condensation of Mark; decreasing distinct- ness? Matt's theology?
216	13:20 the elect whom he chose	24:22 the elect	Condensation of Mark
217	13:23 all things	24:25 –	Improvement of style
232	14:5 more than 300 denarii	26:9 a large sum	Matt's or Q's style
238	14:31 said vehemently	26:35 said	Condensation of Mark
239	14:33 James and John	26:37 the two sons of Zebedee	Matt's theology
239	14:40 very heavy	26:43 heavy	Condensation of Mark
240	14:43 chief priests and the scribes	26:47 chief priests	Matt's theology
241	14:53 elders and the scribes	26:57 elders	Matt's theology
241	14:66 one of the maids of the high priest	26:69 a maid	Condensation of Mark
241	14:69 the maid	26:71 another maid	Stylistic peculiarity
242	15:1 elders and scribes	27:1 elders of the people	Matt's theology
244	15:2, 5 Pilate	27:11, 14 the governor	Stylistic peculiarity
246	15:13 cried out	27:22 said	Stylistic peculiarity
248	15:21 the father of Alexander and Rufus	27:32 –	Condensation of Mark
249	15:39 centurion who stood facing him	27:54 centurion	Condensation of Mark
251	15:47 Mary the mother of Joses	27:61 the other Mary	Simplification of Mark
253	16:1 Mary the mother of James	28:1 the other Mary	Simplification of Mark
253	16:6 Jesus of Nazareth	28:5 Jesus	Condensation of Mark
253	16:7 his disciples and Peter	28:7 his disciples	Improvement of style

TABLE 5. MATTHEW MORE PRECISE THAN LUKE

PERIC-OPE	LUKE	MATTHEW	REASON FOR CHANGE
2	3:7 multitudes	3:7 many of the Pharisees and Sadducees	Matt follows Q? Luke generalizes
8	4:5 up	4:8 to a very high mountain	Heightening? OT influence?
26	6:29 cheek	5:39 right cheek	Heightening
35	12:25 a cubit	6:27 one cubit	Stylistic peculiarity
43	6:48 a man	7:24 a wise man	Stylistic peculiarity
43	6:49 a man	7:26 a foolish man	Stylistic peculiarity
58	10:12 that day	10:15 the day of judgment	Improvement of Q's style by Matt
58	10:12 Sodom	10:15 Sodom and Gomorrah	OT influence
65(=82)	7:28 John	11:11 John the Baptist	Stylistic peculiarity
87	11:29 the crowds	12:28 some of the scribes and Pharisees	Matt follows Q; Luke generalizes
87	11:29 the sign of Jonah	12:39 the sign of the prophet Jonah	Stylistic peculiarity; explanatory addition
204	20:19 the scribes and chief priests	21:45 the chief priests and the Pharisees	Matt's theology
210	11:49 apostles	23:34 wise men and scribes	Matt follows Q; Luke reflects early church
210	11:49 kill	23:34 kill and crucify	Heightening; historical influence
210	11:51 Zechariah	23:35 Zechariah the son of Berachiah	Explanatory addition
210	11:51 Abel	23:35 righteous Abel	Stylistic peculiarity
226	12:45 servant	24:48 wicked servant	Stylistic peculiarity

TABLE 6. MATTHEW LESS DISTINCT THAN LUKE

PERIC-OPE	LUKE	MATTHEW	REASON FOR CHANGE
50(=105)	8:25 they were afraid and they marveled	8:27 the men marveled	Matt follows Q?
73(=19)	6:23 their fathers	5:12 men	Matt follows Q
77(=86)	6:45 treasure of his heart	12:35 treasure	Matt follows Q
82(=65)	7:33 John the Baptist	11:18 John (cf. 11:12!)	Stylistic peculiarity
226	12:42 steward	24:45 servant	Stylistic peculiarity (synonymous)

V

Before summarizing the comments contained in the tables provided above, certain qualifications and limitations in the above analysis need to be indicated. First, a single phrase of commentary on each of the changes listed in the tables obviously does not do justice to all the study scholars have made of almost every one of the changes listed. Thus, although it was felt that short comments of the kind that have been made were warranted in testing the law of increasing distinctness, we are also aware that the topic requires a much more thorough treatment, one we hope to give at a later date.

Second, the various categories listed under the heading "Reason for Change" may not be as different from one another or from the tendency to increasing or decreasing distinctness as we have made them. It might be argued, for example, that an explanatory addition could be a form of increasing distinctness. We would insist, however, that such additions are probably redactional, whereas Bultmann seems rather clearly to be thinking primarily of trends in the oral tradition that lie behind the actual writing of the Gospels.

The influence of historical events such as the crucifixion and the fall of Jerusalem could admittedly have been felt during the oral stages of the kerygma, and could therefore conceivably be viewed as an example of increasing distinctness. But once again we have kept it separate from that tendency because Bultmann's law of increasing distinctness involves the role of imagination or fancy rather than historical accuracy in producing the change in detail.

Theological presuppositions, stylistic peculiarities such as synonyms, cultural adaptations, heightening, condensations or simplifications of Mark, elimination of names familiar only to Mark's readers, and especially OT influences could also reflect developments during the oral stages of the Synoptic tradition, in which case they too could be considered subdivisions of the tendency to increasing distinctness. In most of these cases, however, we feel a better case can be made for attributing them directly to the redactional phase, and to a conscious revision on the part of the later Synoptic evangelists.

Finally, our analysis is incomplete in at least three additional ways: (1) The lists we have compiled could easily have been lengthened, although the majority of the relevant changes made by Luke and Matt have undoubtedly been included and further examples would not change the conclusions of this paper. (2) Particularly inadequate is our analysis of the Q materials and the way Luke and Matt have treated them. To keep this study within manageable limits the decision was made to focus on the extant Synoptic documents; even with this limitation, however, our study of the tendencies in material common to Luke and Matt is less thorough than it could be. (3) One kind of change not included in this paper is the tendency of the later Synoptic writers to answer the question, no doubt often raised by those who first heard the oral proclamation, especially in its Markan form, "What did Jesus say?" What did Jesus say, for example, to Judas in Gethsemane, or to those who were gathered around the cross at Calvary?

Analysis of Table 1. The most significant result observable in our analysis of the changes Luke makes in Mark's version is that most of the changes are not fanciful changes belonging to the oral stages of the Gospel tradition at all. They are most often patent efforts to improve Mark's often rather awkward or unclear style (twelve cases). Conscious theological presuppositions (ten), stylistic peculiarities (five) and explanatory additions (five) account for the majority of the remaining changes.

There are, however, eight apparent cases of increasing distinctness that might be seen as proof of Bultmann's law. The sampling is admittedly rather small, and inevitably involves us in a brief discussion of Luke's understanding of historical research.

Although it is contrary to much current scholarship to do so, it would appear that we may be forced by the empirical evidence to take Luke's preface somewhat more seriously than we have done.[18] After Conzelmann, of course, we all take Luke more seriously as a theologian. But there are some indications that we might be able to take Luke's preface more seriously in the area of character identification at least. Van Unnik remarks that Luke's role as a historian is a "point that has not received sufficient attention in the present phase of the Luke-Acts debate."[19] Luke *is* a highly sophisticated theologian; but his efforts to produce "an authentic account" (Luke 1:3-4) may just possibly have led to the discovery of several pieces of information, among them names and places, which had previously been unknown. We would not argue that all eight cases of increasing distinctness were the result of such a concern for authentic knowledge, but most of them would seem to be explicable in such terms with a high degree of probability.

Analysis of Table 2. The single most impressive conclusion that may be drawn from this table is that Luke has just as many examples of what might be called decreasing distinctness as he does of what has been called increasing distinctness. Nowhere to my knowledge does Bultmann, or those who have, like him, adopted the law of increasing precision, suggest such a "law of decreasing distinctness." Yet the evidence assembled in this table clearly indicates that some of the differences between Mark and Luke could be considered to move in the direction of imprecision, just as Table 1 showed an equal number of differences to have moved in the direction of greater precision.

Once again, however, we discover that most such changes are probably

---

[18] See, for example, Reginald H. Fuller, *Interpreting the Miracles,* London and Philadelphia, 1963, p. 24: "Matthew's and Luke's alterations to Mark are important clues to their own theology, but are rarely of direct historical value." See also Bultmann, *Form Criticism,* p. 70: "Luke betrays the effort to write as a historian and to find points of contact for his narrative in various world-historical dates (i.5; ii.1-3; iii.1-2). Yet this is not really based upon a genuine historical interest, but is only the endeavor to bring home to educated Gentiles the universal significance of the gospel story."

[19] W. C. van Unnik, "Luke-Acts, a Storm Center in Contemporary Scholarship" in *Studies in Luke-Acts,* ed. by Leander E. Keck and J. Louis Martyn, p. 27. He goes on to say, "A decision can be reached here only if the relations, if there be any, between Luke and historiography in antiquity, both in its theory and its practice, have been investigated properly. Far too little study has been given to this

redactional rather than social products. The most frequent changes seem to have been efforts to condense Mark's frequently prolix or redundant style (fifteen cases). But Luke's theological presuppositions once again account for a number of apparently less precise expressions (nine). This suggests that perhaps a more fruitful way of studying the alterations of Mark and Q made by the later Synoptic writers might be in terms of style and theology rather than increasing or decreasing precision.

Analysis of Table 3. The tendency to greater precision also occurs in Matt's handling of his Markan material. As was true of Luke, Matt is sensitive to what appear to be hasty infelicities of Mark's Gospel. He therefore tries to improve Mark's style (sixteen cases). Although on a rare occasion Luke will heighten a "fever" (Mark 1:30) to a "high fever" (Luke 4:38), heightening is especially characteristic of Matt's adaptations of Mark (fourteen cases; note esp. Matt's use of "all" in 8:32, 34 and 9:35, and "great" in 24:21, 24; 26:47; and 27:60). Explanatory additions (seven) and stylistic peculiarities (six) account for the bulk of the remaining changes.

There are three examples of what could be considered a tendency to increasing distinctness as Bultmann describes it (15:15; 26:8; and 26:57). Although it is hazardous to draw conclusions from such a small number of examples, it does not seem beyond the realm of reasonable probability that historical and theological rather than purely imaginative factors have been at work in these cases. The identification of Caiaphas as the high priest at the time of the trial of Jesus is a clear case of increasing precision based on historical accuracy. It is probably impossible to determine whether the identification of Peter as the disciple who asked for an explanation of Jesus' remarks on what defiles a man has a historical or theological origin, but either possibility would seem to be more probable than an identification based on fancy and the tendencies of folklore. Matt's identification of the disciples as the ones who criticized the "waste" of expensive ointment on Jesus' head is probably theologically motivated,[20] especially since a strikingly similar story in each of the other three Gospels attributes the identical criticism to three other individuals or groups.

Analysis of Table 4. In an overwhelming number of cases (thirty) what seems to be less precise in Matt than in Mark can best be explained as a desire on the part of the author to condense Mark rather than as the result of oral transmission. Matthean theology and style have also resulted in a number of changes (thirteen) which ensue in an apparently less precise word or phrase. Simplification and other improvements in Mark's style account for a number of other changes (eight).

Once again the sheer number of changes in the direction of "less precision" is an impressive contradiction of the dogma that details are usually made more explicit and definite.[21]   Based on the tables, two

---

aspect of the case.... A thorough study comparing him to well-known historians of his own times is missing." This section of our paper underscores the pleas of van Unnik's article.

[20] See G. Barth's discussion of discipleship in G. Bornkamm, G. Barth and H. J. Held, eds., *Tradition and Interpretation in Matthew*, Philadelphia, 1963, pp. 105-24.

[21] See Bultmann, *History of the Synoptic Tradition*, p. 241.

opposite tendencies seem in general to have been operative in the Synoptic tradition, neither of which reflects the kind of "novelistic" interest of which Bultmann speaks.

Analysis of Tables 5 and 6. The study of tendencies that may be observed between Luke and Matt broadens the scope of our study in a number of ways. These two Gospels are believed to depend also upon a source other than Mark, a sayings-source, called Q. Given what Luke says in his preface (Luke 1:1-4), a thorough study of our problem would properly have to include indications of dependence by Mark or Q on oral traditions, or, perhaps, on some kind of written traditions, which Mark and Q then altered according to patterns similar to those alterations of Mark made by Luke and Matt. Important as this kind of study may be, it is highly speculative and difficult, and will not be pursued in the present article.

Although some scholars have seen Luke as more conservative in his handling of Q materials,[22] it is interesting to notice that a good case can be made for the position that Matt follows more closely, while Luke, by his more frequent changes, is both more and less precise in his handling of Q materials. Given the incompleteness of our analysis of these materials, however, our conclusions remain highly tentative.

Several stylistic peculiarities, however, closely related to heightening, also characterize Matt and might tend to support the thesis that Matt is more liberal in his handling of the Q materials.

VI

With the limitations noted earlier in the article, therefore, we can now, with some degree of confidence, conclude that a study of the relevant data from the Synoptic Gospels does not indicate the existence of a tendency or "law" of increasing distinctness, at least not in the form in which it is stated in the writings of Rudolf Bultmann quoted earlier. In no instance did we note a clear-cut case of imaginative or fanciful, "novelistic" interest such as is apparently common in the apocryphal NT literature and other post-apostolic writings. In fact, wherever a question of whether a given change was purely imaginative or historical/theological arose, an equally valid or even stronger argument could be made for a historical/theological modification. Instead of a single tendency of the traditions to develop definition, in fact, there appears to have been a dual tendency at work in which some materials tended to become more distinct and others tended to become less precise. So mixed is the evidence, in fact, that future studies of the question might rather classify tendencies as theological, historical, stylistic, etc., and see the results of such tendencies as being in the direction of greater precision in some cases and lesser precision in others.

Whatever may be said about a "law of folklore" in regard to other oral and written materials in general and non-biblical Christian literature in particular, it is clear at least that with respect to the Synoptic Gospels, Bultmann's law of increasing distinctness should be put permanently to rest.

---

[22] For example, Caird, *Saint Luke,* pp. 166, 179.

The Holy Spirit in Galatians*

GEORGE ELDON LADD

Modern biblical theology has discovered the eschatological orientation of the NT perspective. Cullmann has convincingly argued that the NT authors take over the two-age system of Judaism—this present evil age vs. the Age to Come of eternal life. However, the Christian understanding of time modifies the Jewish time line by making the Christ-event the center of the time line instead of the Day of the Lord.[1] Many years before this, C. H. Dodd had expounded his "Realized Eschatology," arguing that the early Christian kerygma proclaimed that "The prophecies are fulfilled, and the New Age is inaugurated by the coming of Christ."[2] While there is a striking similarity between Cullmann and Dodd, there is also a profound difference. Dodd proclaimed a *fully realized* eschatology. "All that prophecy and apocalypse has asserted of the supernatural community was fulfilled in the Church."[3] "All that the Church hoped for in the second coming of Christ is already given in its present experience of Christ through the Spirit."[4] "All that the prophets meant by the Day of the Lord is realized."[5] While Dodd admits that a residue of eschatology remains which is not exhausted in realized eschatology,[6] he makes little use of it.

---

*On December 11, 1930, I turned in to Professor Merrill Tenney, then at Gordon College, my first term paper on a biblical subject. The course was on Galatians, and I wrote a paper on "The Holy Spirit in Galatians." Dr. Tenney wrote a comment on my paper which was the instrument God used to call me to a career of Bible study, teaching and writing. I dedicate this essay on the same subject to him with a sense of great indebtedness. He stimulated in me my initial love for the study of the Word.

[1] Oscar Cullmann, *Christ and Time,* Philadelphia, 1964.
[2] C. H. Dodd, *The Apostolic Preaching and Its Developments,* London, 1936, p. 28.
[3] *Ibid.,* p. 145.
[4] *Ibid.,* p. 174.
[5] *Ibid.,* p. 214.
[6] *Ibid.,* p. 231.

George Eldon Ladd, Professor of New Testament Exegesis and Theology at Fuller Theological Seminary, Pasadena, California. Th.B., Gordon College; B.D., D.D., Gordon Divinity School; graduate studies, Boston University and Episcopal Theological Seminary; Ph.D., Harvard University; post-doctoral studies, University of Heidelberg and University of Basel.

For Cullmann, while the Christ-event puts a new center in redemptive history, the Day of the Lord remains an essential element in the time line. The present author has felt that Cullmann would have been theologically more accurate if he had said that the Christ-event places two pivotal points instead of one in the time line: the Christ-event and the Day of the Lord.

This theology of proleptic or inaugurated or realized eschatology has been even more adequately expounded by the great evangelical scholar, Geerhardus Vos. Instead of a new center in the time line or realized eschatology, Vos argues for an overlapping of the two ages, as follows:[7]

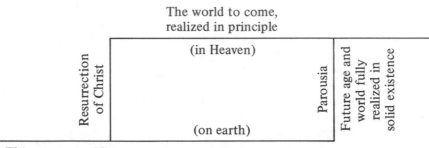

The world to come,
realized in principle

(in Heaven)

(on earth)

Resurrection of Christ

Parousia

Future age and world fully realized in solid existence

This age or world

The result is that the great redemptive realities are "eschatological"; that is, they belong to the Age to Come but have been unexpectedly (from the OT point of view) experienced in Christ.

The present author has become convinced that this scheme represents the core of NT theology. Some years ago, I published an essay in which I defended this position.[8] In the Synoptic Gospels, the Kingdom of God is an eschatological blessing belonging to the Age to Come (Mark 10:23-30); but in the mission of Jesus, this same Kingdom *has come* among men (Matt 12:28). In John, eternal life is the life of the Age to Come (John 12:25); but in Jesus, this life has come to men as a present experience. In Paul, justification is essentially the verdict of acquittal at the Day of the Lord (Rom 8:33); but because of the death of Christ, justification-acquittal is already pronounced upon believers (Rom 3:21-22). Furthermore, the gift of the Spirit is an eschatological gift. Two metaphors used of the Spirit are *aparchē* and *arrabōn*. The present gift of the Spirit is an *aparchē*—first fruits of our eschatological inheritance. Although we anticipate the eschatological redemption, we groan inwardly from the pain and evil in the world, even though we have the first fruits of the Spirit (Rom 8:23).[9] First fruits is the actual beginning of the harvest. It is not promise or hope; it is experience-realization. The same is true with *arrabōn*—down-payment. The possession

[7] Geerhardus Vos, *The Pauline Eschatology,* Grand Rapids, 1952, p. 38.
[8] G. E. Ladd, "Eschatology and the Unity of New Testament Theology," *ExpT,* 68 (1956-57), 268-73.
[9] The genitive is clearly an appositional genitive.

of the Spirit is the *arrabōn* "of our [eschatological] inheritance until we acquire possession of it" (Eph 1:14). Clearly, the gift of the Spirit is an eschatological blessing. This is why Paul describes the resurrection body as a "spiritual" (*pneumatikon*) body (1 Cor 15:44): not a body consisting of spirit but a body completely transformed by the Holy Spirit.[10]

The thesis of this essay is that there are numerous indications in Galatians which support the view that the gift of the Spirit is an eschatological gift and can only be fully appreciated from this perspective.

The first and most explicit reference to Paul's eschatological outlook is found in the first lines of the epistle: "Christ gave himself for our sins to deliver us from the present evil age" (Gal 1:4). Here is a clear reference to the eschatological perspective that underlies Paul's theological thought. We do not need here to recite the passages where the two-age idea occurs in Paul, although it is a theme that has been singularly neglected by evangelical scholars. This verse tells us that the present age is evil (see 2 Cor 4:4). However, the work of Christ suffices to *deliver* men from the evil powers of this present age; and this can be accomplished only by the inbreaking of the powers of the future age. The death of Christ, as well as the gift of the Spirit, is an eschatological event.

It is interesting to note that while the older commentaries adequately discuss the doctrine of the two ages,[11] they do not interpret this verse in terms of experienced eschatology. Lightfoot approaches it when he says, "The Apostles speak of themselves and their generation as living in the frontier of two aeons, the Gospel transferring them as it were across the border."[12] Recent commentaries have been more explicit. Schlier says, "Since Jesus gave himself to blot out our sins, he created the situation in which we, in anticipation of the future aeon, are freed from the present aeon. The Christ event, in the sacrifice that bears our sins, causes the future age to break in upon us."[13] Beyer expresses the same idea: "The final redemption, the new world order (*Weltzeit*), has broken in with Christ."[14] Shires goes too far when he says, "For the believers, therefore, the old age has gone."[15] The old evil age will pass away only with the Parousia of Christ and the coming of the Day of the Lord. As Vos points out, Paul sees an overlapping of the two ages. The old evil age remains, and believers, like unbelievers, are subject to its evil powers. Yet something has happened in the Christ-event which radically modifies the situation for the believer. He is delivered from the evil powers of the present age.[16] And this is achieved

[10] E. Schweizer, *TDNT*, 6, 421.

[11] See J. B. Lightfoot, *Saint Paul's Epistle to the Galatians*, London, 1890, pp. 73-74; E. D. Burton, *A Critical and Exegetical Commentary on the Epistle to the Galatians*, New York, 1920, pp. 13-14; and Excursus on *Aiōn*, pp. 426-31. See also H. N. Ridderbos, *The Epistle of Paul to the Churches of Galatia*, Grand Rapids, 1952, pp. 43-44.

[12] J. B. Lightfoot, *Epistle to the Galatians*, p. 74.

[13] H. Schlier, *Der Brief an die Galater*, Göttingen, 1949, p. 10.

[14] H. W. Beyer, *Das Neue Testament Deutsch, 8. Die kleineren Briefe des Apostel Paulus*, Göttingen, 1965, p. 5.

[15] H. M. Shires, *The Eschatology of Paul*, Philadelphia, 1966, p. 146.

[16] "*Exeletai* denotes not a removal from, but a rescue from the power of." E. D. Burton, *Galatians*, p. 13.

only by experiencing the power of the future age. The believer lives, as it were, in two ages at once.

The gift of the Spirit is the gift of the Age to Come. "He who sows to the flesh will from the flesh reap corruption; but he who sows to the Spirit will from the Spirit reap eternal life" (Gal 6:8). Flesh—Spirit; corruption—eternal life. Eternal life is here an eschatological blessing; it is the life of the Age to Come. "The reaping of eternal life follows from the sowing *into* the Spirit because the Spirit and eternal life belong together through identity of content. . . ."[17] Since eternal life is created by the Spirit, those who in this age direct their lives to the Spirit will reap the life that the Spirit gives.

The eschatological orientation of the Spirit is again seen in the affirmation, "For through the Spirit by faith we wait for the hope of righteousness" (Gal 5:5). It is because the Spirit dwells in us and because we rely on the Spirit rather than on the flesh that we have the hope of divine vindication at the day of eschatological consummation.

The eschatological character of the Spirit is further seen in the gift of the Spirit as the fulfillment of promise. ". . . That in Christ Jesus the blessing of Abraham might come upon the Gentiles, that we might receive the promise of the Spirit through faith" (Gal 3:14). This verse places us back in an OT perspective. The prophets frequently refer to the day when "I will pour my Spirit upon your descendants, and my blessing upon your offspring" (Isa 44:3). One of the most vivid promises is that of Ezek 36:26-27: "A new heart I will give you, and a new spirit I will put within you; and I will take out of your flesh the heart of stone and will give you a heart of flesh. And I will put my spirit within you, and cause you to walk in my statutes and be careful to observe my ordinances." Again in 37:14, "And I will put my Spirit within you, and you shall live"; and in 39:29, "And I will not hide my face any more from them, when I pour out my Spirit upon the house of Israel, says the Lord God."

Such prophecies in the OT look forward to the messianic salvation that will be experienced in the Day of the Lord. From the OT perspective, the promise of the Spirit is an eschatological promise, and is one of the blessings of the establishment of God's rule on the earth. This is most vividly illustrated in the prophecy of Joel 2:28ff., where the outpouring of the Spirit is associated with the Day of the Lord.

On the day of Pentecost, Peter made it clear that the outpouring of the Spirit was the fulfillment of the Joel prophecy. Furthermore, he asserted that Christ at his resurrection and ascension was enthroned upon the throne of David (Acts 2:30-35), and had therefore entered in upon his messianic reign as Lord and Christ (Acts 2:36). In other words, Peter affirmed what is implicit in Paul: that the messianic salvation had come to men while the Day of the Lord remained yet in the future. It is clear that Paul views the reception of the Spirit as a blessing enjoyed by all believers (Gal 3:2, 3; 4:6; 5:25).[18]

---

[17]G. Vos, "Eschatology and the Spirit in Paul," *Biblical and Theological Studies,* New York, 1912, p. 226.

[18]Schmithals seems to be far afield in interpreting such verses to mean that Paul is adopting the emphasized self-assertion of Gnostic Galatians to already have

The fruit—the manifestation—of the Spirit is love, joy, peace, patience, kindness, goodness, faithfulness, gentleness, self-control (Gal 5:22). These are the characteristics of the life of the new aeon; and those who realize such a life of the indwelling Spirit will enter the eternal life of the Age to Come (Gal 6:8).

Another eschatological perspective in Galatians, closely associated with the Spirit, is the affirmation that in Christ Jesus, "the blessing of Abraham might *come upon the Gentiles,* that we might receive the promise of the Spirit through faith" (Gal 3:14). The promise to Abraham included the blessing of the Gentiles (Gen 12:2). The prophets often refer to the blessing of the Gentiles, but again, it is an eschatological hope that will occur in the Day of the Lord. Isaiah sees a time "in the latter days" when all nations will come to Jerusalem to worship the God of Israel and to learn his will. God will rule over them, and peace will prevail (Isa 2:2-4). Zephaniah anticipates the coming of the Day of the Lord when all nations will speak a single language that they may call upon the name of the Lord (Zeph 3:9). At that time Israel will be praised among all the peoples of the earth (Zeph 3:20).

Paul affirms that the blessing of Abraham has already come upon the Gentiles, in the mission of Jesus Christ (Gal 3:8). This means that "Israel" has received a new definition; all men of faith are the sons of Abraham (Gal 3:7). In the light of this, it is probable that the "Israel of God" in 6:16 refers to the church. The point is that this blessing of the Gentiles, from an OT perspective, is an eschatological blessing, which has been fulfilled, unexpectedly, in history.

However, this life of the Spirit is not easy to achieve, for even the Spirit-indwelt believer lives in the old evil age, one of whose characteristics is *sarx.* The connection between *sarx* and the evil aeon is seen in a comparison of 5:24 and 6:14. The only solution for the flesh is its crucifixion. "Those who belong to Christ Jesus have crucified the flesh with its passions and desires" (5:24). To quote the most recent study on the subject, "The 'flesh' is Paul's term for everything aside from God in which one places his final trust. . . . *Sarx* for Paul is not rooted in sensuality but rather in religious rebellion in the form of self-righteousness which was in his terms a 'boasting in one's own flesh.' "[19] "Spirit" is not the "pneuma-self" as Schmithals describes it,[20] but the Holy Spirit. That *sarx* is an evil power of this present age is seen in the fact that not only the *sarx* but also the world[21] must be crucified.

Here we meet a difficult tension. How can one live out the life of the new age while still living in the old evil age? Paul's answer is twofold. First, both the flesh (5:24) and the world (6:14) *have been* crucified to the

---

become Spirit-possessed men—*pneumatikoi.* See W. Schmithals, *Paul and the Gnostics,* Nashville, 1972, pp. 46f.

[19] Robert Jewett, *Paul's Anthropological Terms,* Leiden, 1971, pp. 103, 114. Jewett works out the eschatological perspective of flesh-spirit.

[20] Schmithals, *Paul and the Gnostics,* p. 49.

[21] I do not need recall that Paul can use *aiōn* and *kosmos* interchangeably. See 1 Cor 1:20; 2:6, 8, 12; 3:18, 19.

believer, and the believer *has been* crucified both to the flesh (2:20) and to the world (6:14). This crucifixion, which occurred in the death of Christ, is, however, no mechanical fact, no statistical event, which operates in and of itself. It is incumbent upon the believer not only to recognize that the flesh has been crucified, but, in the light of this fact, to put the flesh to death. This fact is not expressed in Galatians, but it appears clearly in Rom 8:15 and Col 3:15. Here is the heart of the Pauline ethic: the indicative and the imperative.[22] Because the flesh has been crucified, the Spirit-indwelt man is to reckon the deeds of the body to be dead and walk in the Spirit. Because he has been crucified to the world, he is not to be conformed to the age but be transformed by a new indwelling power.

This new life is not achieved without struggle. "For the desires of the flesh are against the Spirit, and the desires of the Spirit are against the flesh, for they are opposed to each other, to prevent you from doing what you would" (Gal 5:17).[23] Here is an unambiguous statement of the apostle. The Christian life is one of conflict, and so long as one lives in this age, he can never be all that he wants to be. Perfection awaits glorification in the Age to Come.

Nevertheless, one must always endeavor to live out the imperative in the light of the indicative. "If we live [i.e. have entered into life] by the Spirit, let us walk by the Spirit" (5:25); and "walk by the Spirit and you will not fulfill the desires of the flesh" (5:16).[24] In the light of the verse that follows, I can only take this to mean "insofar as you walk by the Spirit, you will not fulfill the desires of the flesh."

In conclusion, a beautiful practical devotional thought emerges from this study. The believer has already received the life of the Spirit which is the life of the Age to Come (5:25), and he is to show forth by his life in this present evil world the character of the new age, however imperfectly. This thought applies especially to Christians in their relationship one to another. A Christian fellowship is not a social organism or institution—although it is both. It is an eschatological community. Its mission is not only to proclaim the gospel, but to demonstrate by life and fellowship the life of the Age to Come.

---

[22] This has been admirably expounded by Victor Furnish, *Theology and Ethics in Paul,* Abingdon, 1968, pp. 224-27. Furnish also recognizes the eschatological perspective of Pauline ethics in which *sarx* is a power of this present evil age. See pp. 115-18.

[23] I view the *hina* clause as consecutive, not final. See C. F. D. Moule, *An Idiom Book of New Testament Greek,* Cambridge, 1953, p. 142.

[24] The Greek is much stronger than the translation of the *RSV.* It is the emphatic negative, *ou mē.*

Literary Criteria in Life of Jesus Research:
An Evaluation and Proposal

RICHARD N. LONGENECKER

Life of Jesus research has fallen out of favor in many circles and taken new directions in others. Karl Barth, Paul Tillich and Rudolf Bultmann, to mention only three of the most illustrious theologians of the past half century, have taught the fraternity of biblical scholars to think in ways inimical to such an enterprise.

Bultmann, in particular, has convinced a number of NT interpreters that, in opposition to a so-called "positivistic" historiography, (1) the meaning of history (*Geschichte*) lies not in events themselves (*Historie*) but in the interpreter's own self-understanding; (2) the adjective "historical" refers not to accounts given of ancient personages but to one's own existence in history; (3) writings claiming to relate events in history tell us more about the authors who wrote them than about the events they purport to relate (the so-called "New Hermeneutic"); and (4) a proper historiography must always be "existential" (i.e., a "demythologizing" of the purely culturally conditioned narrative and message in order to arrive at the underlying faith that impelled the proclamation) rather than "positivistic" (i.e. a laying out of details, together with their causes and nexuses, from some feigned "neutral" perspective and in "objective" fashion in order to arrive at a comprehensive picture of what actually took place and was proclaimed).

In opposition to all interpreters of the Christian religion who, whether liberal or orthodox in their commitments, assume that some type of explicit and propositional continuity must surely have existed between Jesus and the Christian church that followed him, Bultmann also has carried the day in many quarters in asserting that (1) the Jesus of history was not the basis for the church's faith but the occasion for it; (2) the message of Jesus did not become a part of the theology of the NT but is a presupposition for it; and (3) the faith of modern Christians, while in continuity with the "selfhood" of Jesus and the faith of the early disciples,

Richard N. Longenecker, Professor of New Testament at Wycliffe College, University of Toronto, Ontario, Canada. B.A., Wheaton College; M.A., Wheaton College Graduate School; Ph.D., The University of Edinburgh.

is not mediated by the specific details of the apostolic message but rather arises instead of them.

Not everyone, of course, has followed Bultmann in all of his conclusions. Among those who share with him a common philosophic and historiographic stance, a number have attempted to do what he insisted was impossible: to spell out the basic features of continuity between the Jesus of history and the Christ of the church's proclamation (or, at least, to explain how such a continuity was presumed by the early Christians), which endeavor inevitably involves them in Life of Jesus research of a type. Martin Dibelius, for example, who published in concert with Bultmann an explication of the "form-critical" method and who coined the term *Form-geschichte* for this new approach to the biblical materials, saw his work as a basically constructive effort to identify certain critically assured elements in the portrayals of Jesus, in opposition to the scepticism of classical liberalism.[1] And Ernst Käsemann in his 1953 Marburg address on "The Problem of the Historical Jesus" gave voice to a concern among many of Bultmann's own students to moderate the historical negativism of their teacher and to bridge the gap in the Bultmannian system between Jesus and the church's proclamation, lest they become enmeshed in some new form of docetism.[2]

On the other hand, a number of scholars holding to a more objective historiography and having a more positive (though not "positivistic") appreciation of the NT's historicity have worked in basic continuity with older approaches in Life of Jesus research—though all the while refining the tools of their discipline by newer data and more recent insights, and have disassociated themselves in the main from Bultmann's conclusions—though without disavowing what each believes to be a "proper" employment of the critical methodologies of *Formgeschichte* and *Redaktionsgeschichte,* which Bultmann in large measure inspired and succeeding generations have developed. Most prominent among this latter group of scholars are Oscar Cullmann, Joachim Jeremias, Harald Riesenfeld and Charles F. D. Moule, each of whom has influenced in his own way a cluster of students to carry on his own particular type of approach and study.

In such a matrix of stances and concerns (as alluded to above so very briefly), the modern complex of literary criteria in Life of Jesus research has been developed. While many voice their agreement as to the validity of the criteria themselves, there is widespread disagreement as to their employment. Generally speaking, Neo-Bultmannians (if we may call them that) tend to use the criteria negatively, to focus on criteria having to do with content more than form, and to presume that the burden of proof for any individual unit of biblical material rests with those who would accept

---

[1] M. Dibelius, *Die Formgeschichte des Evangeliums,* Tübingen, 1919.

[2] Now published in English in E. Käsemann, *Essays on New Testament Themes,* trans. by W. J. Montagne, London, 1964, pp. 15-47. The clearest description of the resultant endeavor is provided by J. M. Robinson, *The New Quest of the Historical Jesus,* London, 1959. Three prominent examples of the task in practice are G. Bornkamm, *Jesus of Nazareth,* trans. by I. and F. McLuskey with J. M. Robinson, New York, 1960; R. H. Fuller, *The Foundations of New Testament Christology,* New York, 1965; and N. Perrin, *Rediscovering the Teaching of Jesus,* New York, 1967.

authenticity;[3] non-Bultmannians, on the other hand, tend to approach the Gospel records with an expectation of basic reliability, to focus on criteria having to do with form more than content, and to employ the criteria more positively, though without being adverse to expressing their doubts or ruling negatively in individual cases where they feel the evidence is contrary.[4] In scope, however, both tend to restrict the investigation in the Gospels to the words of Jesus, concentrating mainly on the parables and those features of his teaching that can be critically acclaimed to have been distinctive.

I. The Criteria and Their Employment Today

The task of delineating precisely the various literary criteria currently in vogue in Life of Jesus research, and of assigning the proper nomenclature in their regard, is somewhat formidable, for the lines of demarcation and the terminology employed vary considerably from scholar to scholar. Nevertheless, five basic criteria can be singled out as being widely employed today: two having to do with form ("formal criteria") and three having to do with content ("material criteria"). While these could be arranged according to some order of increasing or decreasing importance, they are probably most easily presented and best understood historically—i.e. as they have arisen to prominence in scholarly discussion during the past century.

The first criterion is most commonly known today as *multiple attestation* (or, "the cross section method") and arose in conjunction with the discipline of source criticism. It argues that our assessment of the authenticity of any particular saying of Jesus can be heightened when that saying appears in more than one tradition (i.e. Q and Mark), in all or most of the Gospels in the same manner, or within one tradition or Gospel in more than one form (e.g. a parable and an aphorism). F. C. Burkitt, for example, traced thirty-one sayings back to both Q and Mark, and declared that these may therefore be assumed to have originated no later than ten or fifteen years after Jesus himself.[5] C. H. Dodd invoked this criterion to argue that

---

[3] Käsemann asserts that "our questioning has sharpened and widened until the obligation now laid upon us is to investigate and make credible not the possible unauthenticity of the individual unit of material but, on the contrary, its genuineness" (*Essays on New Testament Themes,* p. 34). N. Perrin argues that "the burden of the proof must lay [sic] on the claim to authenticity, and the difficulties of establishing that claim become very great—very great indeed, but not impossible" (*What is Redaction Criticism?,* Philadelphia, 1969, p. 70).

[4] Jeremias insists that "the linguistic and stylistic evidence . . . shows so much faithfulness and such respect towards the tradition of the sayings of Jesus that we are justified in drawing up the following principle of method: In the synoptic tradition it is the inauthenticity, and not the authenticity, of the sayings of Jesus that must be demonstrated" (*New Testament Theology,* Vol. 1: *The Proclamation of Jesus,* trans. by J. Bowden, London, 1971, p. 37). O. Cullmann employs form criticism with the expectation of finding authentic sayings of Jesus (*Salvation in History,* trans. by S. G. Sowers, London, 1967, pp. 189-92); and C. F. D. Moule argues that "in a sense, the post-Easter *interpretation* was only a *re-discovery* of what had been there in the teaching of Jesus himself" (*The Phenomenon of the New Testament,* London, 1967, p. 46).

[5] F. C. Burkitt, *The Gospel History and Its Transmission,* Edinburgh, 1911[3], pp. 147-83.

where the same application of one of Jesus' parables appears in more than one Gospel, it probably appeared in the source or sources employed by the Evangelists; but where it appears in only one of the Gospels, it may be considered the work of that writer himself.[6]

The second criterion focuses on the *semitic features* (or, "Aramaic and Palestinian forms") in the teaching of Jesus. It argues that the retention of such elements in Gospels written in Greek—particularly in Luke's account—"is of great significance for the question of the reliability of the gospel tradition."[7] Pioneer work in identifying the semitic features of expression and structure in Jesus' teaching was done by Gustav Dalman at the end of the nineteenth century.[8] Since then—particularly with the rising interest in Judaic studies among Christian scholars—almost everyone has employed this criterion to some extent. The overzealous endeavors of C. F. Burney and C. C. Torrey to find Aramaisms everywhere in the Gospels tended to discredit such an approach during the second quarter of the present century.[9] But the careful and moderate application of this criterion to the Gospels by Matthew Black and Joachim Jeremias has brought it back into currency in recent days.[10]

A third criterion commonly, though not universally, employed in critically determining authentic elements in Jesus' teaching is that of *eschatological context and temper*. Many listings of criteria in Life of Jesus research do not, it is true, include any specific reference to such a criterion. Nevertheless, a decisive factor in judging authenticity is very often whether or not an individual saying appears, or originally appeared, in a futuristic context or reflects a "proleptic" (i.e. anticipated) eschatological temper. Rudolf Bultmann and Joachim Jeremias, to take the leaders of two somewhat competing systems of NT interpretation as examples, agree in this: that a criterion for authenticity is whether or not the words in question are set in the context of or reflect a "proleptic" type of eschatology. The *magnum opus* of each of these scholars invokes this criterion repeatedly— often as the final and overriding consideration.[11] Bultmann's work avowedly begins on such a premise with a study of "The Eschatological Message."[12] Historically, the criterion came to prominence in conjunction with the "consistent" or "thorough-going" type of eschatology advocated by Johannes Weiss and Albert Schweitzer at the turn of the century. [13]

---

[6] C. H. Dodd, *The Parables of the Kingdom*, London, 1936, pp. 26-29; cf. also *History and the Gospel*, New York, 1938, pp. 91-103.

[7] Jeremias, *New Testament Theology*, 1, 8.

[8] G. Dalman, *Die Worte Jesu mit Berücksichtigung des nachkanonischen jüdischen Schrifttums und der aramäischen Sprache erörtert*, Leipzig, 1898 (ET = *The Words of Jesus*, Edinburgh, 1902). Dalman had earlier produced a grammar of Palestinian Aramaic (1894) and a lexicon to the Aramaic of the Palestinian Targum and the Mishnaic Hebrew of the Talmud and Midrash (1897).

[9] Cf. C. F. Burney, *The Poetry of Our Lord*, Oxford, 1925; C. C. Torrey, *The Four Gospels*, New York, 1933.

[10] Cf. M. Black, *An Aramaic Approach to the Gospels and Acts*, Oxford, 1946, 1967[3]; Jeremias, *New Testament Theology*, 1, 3-37, *passim*.

[11] R. Bultmann, *Theology of the New Testament*, 2 vols., trans. by K. Grobel, London, 1951; Jeremias, *New Testament Theology*, 1.

[12] Bultmann, *Theology of the New Testament*, 1, 4-11.

[13] Cf. J. Weiss, *Die Predigt Jesu vom Reiche Gottes*, Göttingen, 1900; A.

Modern-day proponents of "proleptic" eschatology, however, do not credit Weiss or Schweitzer for their stance; probably because, for varying reasons, they hesitate to attribute to Jesus all of the details of Jewish apocalypticism or to join in Schweitzer's portrayal of Jesus' messianic consciousness. Nevertheless, Bultmann and Jeremias, together with those who at this point have been influenced by them, are heavily indebted to Weiss and Schweitzer in requiring a "proleptic" eschatological context and temper for authentic sayings of Jesus—though, of course, Dodd with his "realized" eschatological position and Cullmann with his "inaugurated" eschatology, and those influenced by them, are not ready to judge matters in quite the same fashion.

The fourth criterion is most widely known as the criterion of *dissimilarity* (or, "distinctiveness"). Rooted in the *formgeschichtliche* schemata of Martin Dibelius, Karl L. Schmidt and Rudolf Bultmann, it has come to most vocal expression in the programmatic studies of Reginald H. Fuller and Norman Perrin on early Christology and the teaching of Jesus.[14] It proposes that while individual sayings may or may not pass the first two criteria as to form, "material [as to content] may be ascribed to Jesus only if it can be shown to be distinctive to him, which usually will mean dissimilar to known tendencies in Judaism before him or the church after him."[15] In applying this criterion, some, like Bultmann, require a saying to be in opposition to all previous Jewish teaching and piety as well as not a part of later Christian theology before accepting it as authentic. Others, like Fuller, prefer to speak along the lines of Jesus transforming Jewish teaching in terms of his own distinctive message and of the church failing to catch the essence of this transformation as signalling authenticity. Both types of employment, however, presuppose a fairly accurate knowledge of first-century Judaism and at least "a provisional picture of the primitive community and its history"[16] by which to make comparisons.

The fifth criterion is that of *coherence* (or, "consistency"), and parallels the fourth in its origin and development. It argues that "material which is consistent with or coheres with material established as authentic by other means may also be accepted."[17] At times the criterion of coherence is employed in a manner that relates it only to the criterion of dissimilarity, so that only those elements consistent with features found to be dissimilar in Jesus' teaching are taken to be also authentic. At other times, however, it is employed more broadly. James M. Robinson, for example, works from the premise that the parables of Jesus (minus their allegorical features, *à la* Jülicher, Dodd, Jeremias, *et al.*) substantially

---

Schweitzer, *The Quest of the Historical Jesus,* trans. by W. Montgomery, London, 1910, and *The Mystery of the Kingdom of God,* trans. by W. Lowrie, New York, 1914.

[14] Fuller, *Foundations of New Testament Christology;* Perrin, *Rediscovering the Teaching of Jesus.*

[15] Perrin, *What is Redaction Criticism?*, p. 71; cf. *Rediscovering the Teaching of Jesus,* p. 39.

[16] R. Bultmann, *The History of the Synoptic Tradition,* trans. by J. Marsh, Oxford, 1963, p. 5.

[17] Perrin, *What is Redaction Criticism?*, p. 71; cf. *Rediscovering the Teaching of Jesus,* p. 43.

preserve the original message of Jesus, since they can be validated as to form by the criteria of multiple attestation and semitic features and as to content by eschatological temper and dissimilarity. He then measures other sayings of Jesus by the critically established teaching in the parables, and judges them accordingly.[18]

II. *An Evaluation of the Criteria*

The issue regarding the proper criteria to be employed in Life of Jesus research is hotly debated today and of great concern. This is as it should be, for the question deals with matters lying at the very heart of Christianity both as a subject of scientific inquiry and as a religion. What, then, can we say to the question, particularly in light of the proposals that have been made?

To begin with, it must be insisted that if in the outworking of human redemption and its culmination in Jesus of Nazareth God truly entrusted himself to the historical process—which, admittedly, neither those on the extreme left nor on the extreme right of the theological spectrum really believe he did, though that is part-and-parcel of the NT proclamation—we must be prepared to do the same. Both "issues of history" and "issues of faith" are involved in any assessment of Jesus, requiring us to think both historically and theologically in our appraisal of the Gospels wherein he is portrayed. Yet while history and theology are inextricably intertwined in the study of the Gospels, and while decisions made in one area invariably affect those made in the other, the two disciplines can for purposes of analysis be treated to some extent separately. It is for this reason that the various literary criteria have been formulated, for without the framing of such criteria one would be in no position to ask many of the necessary historical questions—which questions, in turn, are productive of critically founded historical answers.

The endeavor to develop such a set of criteria, therefore, must be judged to be absolutely essential to the scientific study of the biblical narratives, and can hardly be faulted *per se*. Having said this, however, it must still be kept firmly in mind that the particular criteria proposed must be constantly reviewed to see that they pose their questions in a manner appropriate to the genre of material under consideration, are not too inclusive to be unserviceable, or so exclusive as to negate the possibility of rendering fair judgments. Only as the questions are pertinent and proper will the answers be appropriate and significant.

In evaluating the proposed literary criteria, at least three observations need to be made. In the first place, *each of the criteria considered separately falls short of its intended demonstration, though in concert with other criteria the degree of probability is heightened.* The criterion of multiple attestation evidences a consistency at certain points in the tradi-

---

[18] J. M. Robinson, "The Formal Structure of Jesus' Message," *Current Issues in New Testament Interpretation,* ed. by W. Klassen and G. F. Snyder, New York, 1962, pp. 96f.

tion, but does not assure us that the tradition itself stems directly or even ultimately from Jesus. The criterion of semitic features suggests that the material in question probably circulated among Aramaic believers, but cannot tell us how their recounting of the teaching of Jesus corresponds to Jesus' own utterances. In some cases, even, the Aramaic and Palestinian forms to which the criterion points may have arisen under septuagintal influence or because of a Jewish-Greek idiom current in the day, and would not therefore indicate an earlier semitic tradition.[19] The criterion of eschatological context and temper puts its finger on one feature in the eschatological message of Jesus, but fails to explicate the fullness of that message (particularly if the adjective "inaugurated" better describes Jesus' own eschatological consciousness than does "proleptic"). It may, in its exclusivism, even distort it. The criterion of dissimilarity provides us with what was distinctive in the proclamation of Jesus, but only in the sense of what was "unique" and not at all of what was "characteristic"[20] —which, ultimately, is what we really want to know from our historical study and why the various literary criteria were originally formulated. And the criterion of coherence operates effectively only if the essential message of Jesus is already known; but if any or all of the other four criteria have been misapplied, this fifth criterion only compounds the error. Such difficulties, of course, are inherent in any historical investigation. But they need to be kept in mind lest we begin to confuse "issues of history" with "issues of faith" and to attribute to the probability-arguments of history an aura of psychological certainty associated with faith.

Second, it needs to be observed that *the criteria are hardly able to be employed negatively because of the paucity of data available by which to make comparisons and our lack of adequate knowledge as to the Evangelists' respective purposes.* Neo-Bultmannians, it is true, often speak of elminating the unauthentic elements in the Gospels by means of one or more of these criteria.[21] But this assumes a knowledge of data and of purposes far beyond what is historically justifiable at present. C. F. D.

[19] Cf. E. P. Sanders, *The Tendencies of the Synoptic Tradition,* London, 1969, pp. 194ff., though without negating the general thrust of the evidence marshalled by Black and Jeremias, and their protégés.

[20] In opposition to Perrin's claim that "if we are to seek that which is most characteristic of Jesus, it will be found not in the things which he shares with his contemporaries, but in the things wherein he differs from them" (*Rediscovering the Teaching of Jesus,* p. 39), Miss Hooker rightly observes: "Use of the principle of dissimilarity, it is claimed, gives us what is distinctive in the teaching of Jesus. But the English word 'distinctive' can have two senses—it can mean 'unique' (what makes it distinct from other things, the German *verschieden*), or it can mean 'characteristic' (the German *bezeichnend*). In what sense is it being used here? Clearly the method is designed to give us the former—but what we really want is the latter; and the two are by no means necessarily the same" ("Christology and Methodology," *NTS,* 17 [1971], 481).

[21] Robinson speaks of "the helpless ambiguity of the old term 'unauthentic,' " since a saying Jesus never spoke "may well reflect accurately his historical significance, and in this sense be more 'historical' than many irrelevant things Jesus actually said" (*New Quest of the Historical Jesus,* p. 99; cf. Bornkamm, *Jesus of Nazareth,* p. 21). To this, D. G. A. Calvert correctly responds: "Ambiguity, however, is avoided if the word 'authentic' is reserved for those words which Jesus actually spoke. All other material is unauthentic" ("An Examination of the Criteria for Distinguishing the Authentic Words of Jesus," *NTS,* 18 [1972], 209).

Moule rightly warns against such a negative use of the criterion of multiple attestation in commenting upon the John the Baptist traditions in the Synoptics and the Fourth Gospel: "After all, selection is often at work on the traditions; and I see no reason to reject a tradition merely because it appears in only one stream, provided it is not intrinsically improbable or contradicted by the other."[22] And this is true as well for the criterion of semitic features; for much that was originally spoken in Aramaic and structured along Hebraic lines would invariably have been transformed into more appropriate Grecian dress in the proclamation to the Jewish diaspora and among Gentiles, either by early Greek-speaking believers or by the Evangelists themselves, so that while semitic elements in Gospels written in Greek may be suggestive of an earlier stratum of tradition the lack of such elements cannot be said to indicate the reverse.

While this second observation is true of these more formal criteria, it is especially true for the criterion of content most employed today: the criterion of dissimilarity. Many applications of the criterion of dissimilarity not only presuppose a fairly accurate knowledge of first-century Judaism and a fairly extensive understanding of early Christian theology, but also seem to assume that such knowledge, unlike the portrait of Jesus gained from the Gospels, has come about in some direct and unmediated fashion. Bultmann, for example, readily confesses that he begins with "a provisional picture of the primitive community and its history, which has to be turned into a clear and articulated picture in the course of my inquiries,"[23] and he and his students have drawn up comprehensive expositions of what was undoubtedly believed in the Judaism of Jesus' day and in the Christian communities that followed him—both as to what was positively affirmed and what would have been unthinkable.[24]

But while "a provisional picture" is certainly necessary in any inquiry, such a picture must be constantly tested by the data and cannot be allowed to dominate the results. While our knowledge of first-century Judaism is enormously extended and diversified over what it was in previous generations, it is still very far from being complete. Likewise, our knowledge of the earliest days of the Christian church is only sketchy and partial—and all of it derived from primary source materials that have as their thesis the essential unity that existed between Jesus of Nazareth and the earliest body of his followers. To invoke the criterion of dissimilarity in negative fashion, therefore, is to lay claim to both a fullness of knowledge and a type of knowledge regarding first-century Judaism and the early church such as is impossible to vindicate on a scientific basis. And since this is so, it must still be insisted that to recognize the currency of a saying or tradition in the church it is not necessary to exclude it from our picture of Jesus; nor to find its parallel in contemporary Judaism is it essential to assert its impossibility on the lips of Jesus.[25] There must have been at least some continuity

[22] Moule, *Phenomenon of the New Testament,* p. 71.

[23] Bultmann, *History of the Synoptic Tradition,* p. 5.

[24] Cf. R. Bultmann, *Primitive Christianity in Its Contemporary Setting,* trans. by R. H. Fuller, London, 1956; H. Conzelmann, *Geschichte des Urchristentums,* Göttingen, 1971.

[25] Cf. M. D. Hooker, *The Son of Man in Mark,* Montreal, 1967, pp. 6f. R. S. Barbour observes that among many more radical form critics, "the belief, which is

between Jesus and his contemporaries in Palestine—both those who opposed him and those who accepted him—for "the wholly unique would be the totally incomprehensible."[26]

In the third place, *the criteria as proposed today have a positive value in establishing a critically assured minimum of authentic material in the Gospels, and no more.* To determine such "a critically assured minimum"[27] by means of probability arguments, taking the literary criteria individually or in concert, is of real significance historically. But to reduce the portrait of Jesus in the Gospels to such a minimum, while critically "safe," is to produce a picture of Jesus so historically unbalanced and theologically distorted as to be disastrously misleading. What is required to go beyond the critically assured minimum as it is presently drawn up in Life of Jesus research is (1) an expansion of the literary criteria to include various divergent patterns of thought and expression that appear in the Gospel narratives for both circumstantial and redactional reasons (as developed in the discussion below), (2) the development of a set of historical criteria that will take into account recent archaeological data on first-century Palestine and recent studies of Pharisaic and non-conformist Judaism of the day, and (3) the development of a set of theological criteria that will give guidance in those areas beyond the province of the purely literary and historical criteria.

The problem with the literary criteria is not that they provide only a critically assured minimum of authentic material, but that they are often being employed too exclusively and in a manner to preclude further inquiry. Many contemporary critics, for example, stress almost exclusively the criteria of content over the criteria of form (which, to some degree, makes them more "content critics" than "form critics") and then proceed to employ the criteria of eschatological temper, dissimilarity and coherence in such a way as to settle all issues. Scholarly research into the life of Jesus has undoubtedly been advanced in determining by means of such literary criteria a certain assured critical minimum. But the literary criteria themselves must be perfected and must be combined with other criteria of an historical and theological nature if we are to characterize aright, and not merely caricature, Jesus of Nazareth.

III. A Proposed Sixth Criterion

Literary criteria in Life of Jesus research, as we have argued, cannot be employed in any monolithic, exclusivistic or ham-fisted manner. They

doubtless correct, that most of the material in the Synoptic Gospels has a *Sitz im Leben* in the concerns of the early Church and is not simply remembered because Jesus said it or did it and for no other reason, is turned into the different and much more questionable assumption that because the material has a *Sitz im Leben* in the early Church, therefore the early Church may plausibly be assumed to have composed it" (*Traditio-Historical Criticism of the Gospels*, London, 1972, pp. 10f.).

[26] Barbour, *ibid.*, p. 8, citing D. Daube's argument on the presence of "Amen" in the Gospels, in *The New Testament and Rabbinic Judaism*, London, 1956, p. 388.

[27] The expression comes from N. A. Dahl, "The Problem of the Historical Jesus," *Kerygma and History*, ed. by C. E. Braaten and R. A. Harrisville, New York, 1962, p. 156.

are of value in the scientific endeavor to establish a critically assured minimum of authentic material in the Gospels, but their results must be incorporated into a larger body of conclusions drawn from more directly historical and theological sets of criteria in order for a true scholarly appraisal to emerge. Nevertheless, while not the final determining factors, literary criteria are important in the scientific study of the NT—though attention must be constantly given to their proper formulation and application.

In a recent article, D. G. A. Calvert argues: "Form-criticism has played too exclusive a role both in determining the criteria and in their application. The literary and source-criticism that preceded form-criticism has often been ignored, and redaction-criticism that succeeded form-criticism has not yet been given its place."[28] Calvert then proceeds to suggest a redactional criterion that he proposes ought to be employed in conjunction with the criteria of multiple attestation and dissimilarity:

> If each of the gospel writers is expressing his own point of view through the stories he selects and the way his material is presented, the inclusion of material which does not especially serve his purpose may well be taken as a testimony to the authenticity of that material, or at least to the inclusion of it in the tradition of the Church in such a clear and consistent way that the evangelist was loath to omit it. The material asserts itself even though it does not particularly suit the purpose of the storyteller. For instance, it is well recognized that Matthew and Mark take different attitudes to the disciples of Jesus. Mark seems anxious to show their lack of understanding and their lack of faith, whereas Matthew takes a much more sympathetic view. A saying in Mark which did not fit in with his criticism of the disciples would seem to be authentic; a saying in Matthew which was critical of the disciples would seem to be authentic.[29]

We need not here get into the sticky issue as to whether redaction criticism is a development from form criticism or form criticism arose out of redaction criticism; both are inherent in the *formgeschichtliche* schemata of Dibelius, Schmidt and Bultmann. Advocates of each discipline, however, are renowned for their confidence that the development of their own particular type of approach is the apex of modern critical achievement. What is significant in Calvert's proposal is the question: Is there a further literary criterion of a redactional nature that should be employed in Life of Jesus research? The question may seem somewhat academic, since distinctions of this nature are what redaction criticism is all about. But Calvert has gone beyond most redaction critics to suggest the application of redaction criticism to *Das Leben Jesu* as well as to *Das Leben Kirche*.

C. F. D. Moule has long been employing redaction criticism as a tool not only for determining the individual outlooks of the Evangelists and explicating their respective theological tendencies but also for identifying certain features within their writings that are at variance to some degree with their stances and that thereby unintentionally witness to a persistent tradition within the church—which features, because of their durable qual-

---

[28] D. G. A. Calvert, "An Examination of the Criteria for Distinguishing the Authentic Words of Jesus," *NTS*, 18 (1972), 219.
[29] *Ibid.*

ity within the tradition taken over by the Evangelists, may be assumed to be rooted in some manner in Jesus himself. It is an argument based upon divergent patterns of thought and expression, which lays emphasis upon both development and continuity (employing the one to explicate the other), and which has been worked out by Moule along both circumstantial and redactional lines. Moule's articles on "The Influence of Circumstances on the Use of Christological Terms"[30] and "The Influence of Circumstances on the Use of Eschatological Terms"[31] are programmatic explications of his position along circumstantial lines, while chapter four of his *The Phenomenon of the New Testament*[32] is his fullest statement along redactional lines. In effect, what he is proposing is an additional criterion in Life of Jesus research, a sixth criterion as we have enumerated them: the criterion of *divergent patterns of thought and expression* that appear in the Gospels for both circumstantial and redactional reasons and which unintentionally signal a note of authenticity.

In applying the criterion, Moule focuses on two types of patterns in particular. The first has to do with distinctions that appear in Luke-Acts between the pre-resurrection portrait of Jesus and the post-resurrection presentation, the first in the Third Gospel and the other in the Acts of the Apostles (both, of course, assumed to be by the same author). This complex of unintentioned distinctions "gives the lie to the notion that the Church's estimate of Jesus is something which Christians unconsciously adopted in the course of time, and then simply assumed as having obtained from the beginning."[33] The second has to do with "certain features in the story of Jesus, the retention of which can scarcely be explained except by their genuineness and durable quality, since everything else was hostile to their survival."[34] The instances where Moule applies this criterion are numerous, and the argument is cogent. Yet, sadly, as Robin Barbour points out, "arguments of this kind from unintentional data are not common among New Testament scholars."[35]

I have myself applied this criterion elsewhere in explicating the Christological convictions and expressions of early Jewish Christianity, and the results are particularly significant in this regard for such titles as "Messiah," "Son of Man," "Son of God," and "Lord."[36] One further example, however, could be given here—an example of a purely formal kind—for it illustrates quite well the application of this sixth criterion.

Much has been made of late of the fact that the eleven fulfillment-formulae quotations from the OT in Matthew's Gospel reflect a definite

---

[30] C. F. D. Moule, "The Influence of Circumstances on the Use of Christological Terms," *JTS*, 10 (1959), 247-63.

[31] C. F. D. Moule, "The Influence of Circumstances on the Use of Eschatological Terms," *JTS*, 10 (1959), 247-63.

[32] Moule, *Phenomenon of the New Testament*, pp. 56-76.

[33] *Ibid.*, p. 75.

[34] *Ibid.*, p. 62. Moule's argument here confessedly runs parallel to that of P. W. Schmiedel in the article on the "Gospels" in *Encyclopedia Biblica*, and draws from the work of such scholars as G. B. Caird, D. Daube and E. Stauffer.

[35] Barbour, *Traditio-Historical Criticism of the Gospels*, p. 27.

[36] R. N. Longenecker, *The Christology of Early Jewish Christianity*, London, 1970, pp. 63ff., 82ff., 93ff., 120ff.

semitic influence in their text-forms, whereas the quotations in the common narrative of this same Gospel—and also in the Gospels of Mark, Luke and John—are quite septuagintal in form. The observation is extremely pertinent, incorporating within it several significant implications for a redactional understanding of the First Gospel and illuminating the Evangelist's own distinctive treatment of Scripture.[37] But while the Hebraic nature of the text-forms in the editorial material of Matthew's Gospel has significance for an understanding of Matthean theology and practice, the septuagintal text-forms of the common narrative have something to say with regard to the Evangelist's employment of earlier traditions.

It will not do, as is commonly asserted today, to say that the septuagintal nature of Jesus' biblical quotations in Matthew's Gospel only indicates that they are part-and-parcel of a Hellenistic *Gemeindetheologie,* and therefore are probably not dominical. This may be argued for the Fourth Gospel, where the difference in text-form between the Evangelist's own citations and those he claims to report is not too distinct, or in the cases of Mark and Luke who report the use of Scripture by others but seldom (if ever) directly quote the OT themselves in their editorial comments. But it will hardly serve as an explanation for the phenomena in the First Gospel, where the Evangelist's own eleven fulfillment-formulae quotations are dominantly semitic in character while those reported of Jesus are strongly septuagintal.

An extended application of the criterion of dissimilarity (i.e. the sharp distinction in text-form between the two sets of quotations) and of the criterion of multiple attestation (i.e. the pattern is consistent in Matthew throughout a large number of samples) prohibits any such easy equation. Nor can it be said that Matthew simply assimilated Jesus' biblical citations to the LXX for the sake of a Greek-speaking audience. If the Evangelist made no attempt to assimilate the fulfillment-formulae quotations in his avowed editorial comments, but allowed his Hebraic text-forms to manifest themselves quite clearly, why should it be thought he would have done this for Jesus? Editorial assimilation may be an explanation for the text-forms elsewhere in the NT, but it is inadequate as a solution for the form of Jesus' quotations in the First Gospel.

A great deal of research, admittedly, remains to be done on such matters as the languages employed in Palestine during Jesus' day, the form of the biblical texts in the first century, and Christian compilations of sayings of Jesus (which, presumably, would include his biblical citations). Nonetheless, this difference in text-form between Matthew's fulfillment-formulae quotations and those of his common narrative suggests that the form of Jesus' quotations in Matthew's Gospel is not just a product of *Gemeindetheologie* nor a result of editorial assimilation by the Evangelist, but must be accounted for in some other manner. It may be that an early Greek sayings-compilation (or, compilations), which not only translated Aramaic into Greek but also assimilated Hebraic text-forms to their septua-

---

[37] Cf. K. Stendahl, *The School of St. Matthew,* Uppsala, 1954, 1967[2]. See also my "Can We Reproduce the Exegesis of the New Testament?" *Tyndale Bulletin,* 21 (1970), 3-38.

gintal counterparts, circulated widely in the church and gained a status of quasi-sanctity because it stemmed ultimately from Jesus. Matthew could have employed such a compilation (or, compilations) in his reproduction of the biblical citations of Jesus without disturbing the septuagintal form of the quotations, even though he personally preferred to work from a more semitic text in his own biblical citations. Or it may be that in his use of Scripture, Jesus, who normally spoke a Palestinian form of Aramaic but could also employ Greek and Mishnaic Hebrew to some extent, at times engaged in textual selection among the existing versions then current, and that therefore some of the septuagintal features in the text-forms attributed to him actually stem directly from him. The mixed text-form of Isa 61:1f. in Luke 4:18f. would seem to support such a view in at least this one case, for the quotation defies all explanations along the lines of assimilation, whenever such assimilation may be supposed to have been employed. Or, perhaps, the septuagintal nature of Jesus' quotations in the First Gospel (and, perhaps, in the others as well) lies in postulating both the employ- ment of an early Greek sayings-compilation (or, compilations) and textual selection on the part of Jesus himself.

But however explained, such a divergent pattern in this very formal matter of text-forms in the biblical citations within one Gospel points up in unintentional fashion a difference between Matthew's own editorial materi- al and his handling of what may be presumed to be more traditional material. And it is this type of literary observation and application that must be made in order to complement the current and more usual literary criteria in Life of Jesus research.

Sins Within and Sins Without:

An Interpretation of 1 John 5:16-17

DAVID M. SCHOLER

I

Difficult texts of Scripture have, by their very nature, always been intriguing. One such problematic passage is 1 John 5:16-17[1] in which a distinction is made between a "sin not unto death" (*hamartia ou pros thanaton*) and a "sin unto death" (*hamartia pros thanaton*).[2] The meaning of these designations concerning sin and the consequent instruction (the last sentence of 1 John 5:16), which appears to forbid prayer (*erōtan*) for the "sin unto death," are major unresolved difficulties.[3]

This text is related to a major theme in 1 John: the relationship of sin to the Christian believer, which is in view in 1:5-2:2, 3:4-10 and 5:16-18. From these passages another question emerges: the relationship between the very clear statements that the believer not only does not sin (3:9; 5:18)[4] but is not able to sin (3:9), and the equally clear recognition that the believer does sin (1:8; 2:1; 5:16).[5]

---

[1] I would like to note that my first teacher in Johannine studies in my graduate work was Merrill C. Tenney. In the development of this article I have profited from the comments of Krister Stendahl and especially from those of J. Ramsey Michaels. An earlier, and briefer, draft of this article was given at the 1967 New England Section meeting of the Evangelical Theological Society.

[2] In this article the text of the NT used is that of K. Aland *et al., The Greek New Testament,* United Bible Societies, 1968². English translations of the NT are my own.

[3] E.g. note the comments of E. J. Cooper, "The Consciousness of Sin in 1 John," *Laval Théologique et Philosophique,* 28 (1972), 247, " . . . the exact nature of this sin [unto death], which appears in the Bible only in this text of the First Epistle of John, remains unknown," and of R. Bultmann, *The Johannine Epistles: A Commentary on the Johannine Epistles,* trans. by R. P. O'Hara, L. C. McGaughy, and R. W. Funk, ed. by R. W. Funk, Philadelphia, 1973, p. 87, "a decision can scarcely be taken, as the diverse efforts of exegetes indicate."

[4] Note the similar thought in Ign Eph 14:2: "No man who professes faith sins (*hamartanei*), nor does he hate who has obtained love."

[5] For a thorough discussion of sin and the Christian in 1 John, cf. R. Schnacken-

---

David M. Scholer, Assistant Professor of New Testament at Gordon-Conwell Theological Seminary, South Hamilton, Massachusetts. B.A., Wheaton College; M.A., Wheaton College Graduate School; B.D., Gordon Divinity School; Th.D. candidate, Harvard Divinity School.

Various attempts have been made to reconcile these apparently contradictory statements that believers do not sin and that they do. One attempt argues that the conflict is resolved by seeing the inability to sin as the conduct of the "new nature" (= *sperma*, 3:9) and the fact of sinning as that of the "old nature."[6] However, it is the person born of God, not the *sperma*, who does not sin. Further, neither the "old nature/new nature" terminology nor the concept is expressed or implied in 1 John.

Perhaps a more common solution is to argue that the present tense of *hamartanein* in 3:9 and 5:18 means that the believer does not habitually sin, while the aorist tense in 2:1 shows that the sin of the believer is to be understood as an occasional sin.[7] This argument breaks down completely, however, because of the use of the present tense of *hamartanein* in 5:16 with reference to the sinning of a believer as well as the use of the present tense in 1:8.[8]

Another type of solution is to see the two aspects of the believer's sinning and not sinning as two levels in the Christian life, in which the second (not sinning) is the actualization of perfection.[9] There is not, however, any such "progression" for the believer indicated at any point in 1 John; rather, both statements are asserted equally and at all times for all believers.

A more satisfactory solution for the problem of relating these two statements—that believers do sin and that believers do not sin—is that which recognizes the polemical character of 1 John. The statements that believers do sin are directed against the opponents of 1 John, who, it is assumed because of the strong counterstatements of 1 John (1:8, 10), must be contending that believers never (or are beyond) sin. Nevertheless, to the believing community 1 John stresses the ideal of a life without sin for one who is a child of God.[10]

---

burg, *Die Johannesbriefe*, HTKNT, Freiburg, 1970[3], 13, 281-88 (an excursus on the subject); cf. also K. Wennemer, "Der Christ und die Sünde nach der Lehre des ersten Johannesbriefes," *Geist und Leben*, 33 (1970), 370-76; and Cooper, "Consciousness of Sin in 1 John," pp. 237-48 (who, incidentally, does not sufficiently stress the emphasis in 1 John on believers not sinning).

[6] E.g. S. Cox, "The Sin Unto Death: 1 John V. 16," *Expositor*, 2:1 (1881), 429. Another form of this view is that the statements that the believer does not sin refer to the inner divine principle which a believer can follow, but may neglect; e.g. cf. Wennemer, "Der Christ und die Sünde nach der Lehre," pp. 370-76.

[7] E.g. A. T. Robertson, *Word Pictures in the New Testament*, Nashville, 1933, 6, 222-23. A. H. Dammers, "Hard Sayings—II. 1 John 5:16ff," *Theology*, 66 (1963), 371, argues for this, not on the basis of tense distinctions, but on the grounds of Christian experience.

[8] For a critique of this commonplace solution cf. S. Kubo, "1 John 3:9: Absolute or Habitual?" *AUSS*, 7 (1969), 47, 51. Some commentators (e.g. A. E. Brooke, *A Critical and Exegetical Commentary on the Johannine Epistles*, ICC, Edinburgh, 1912, p. 17; B. F. Westcott, *The Epistles of John: The Greek Text with Notes and Essays*, London, 1892[3], p. 22; Cooper, "Consciousness of Sin in 1 John," p. 240) argue that *hamartia* refers to a "sinful principle" rather than "sinful acts," thus attempting to maintain some type of solution that distinguishes between occasional and habitual sinning. For the unacceptability of this view of 1 John 1:8 cf. Kubo, "1 John 3:9," pp. 51-53, and Bultmann, *Johannine Epistles*, pp. 20-22.

[9] E.g. O. D. Lovell, "The Present Possession of Perfection in First John," *Wesleyan Theological Journal*, 8 (1973), 38-44.

[10] Cf. Kubo, "1 John 3:9," p. 56, who identifies the opponents as gnostic

II

This solution, however, can be given a more precise character in terms of all the evidence on 1 John.[11] It is the thesis of this article that the problem of reconciling the statements in 1 John that believers do and do not sin is solved by an interpretation of 1 John 5:16-17 in which, it will be argued, the "sin not unto death" is one which a believer can and does commit and the "sin unto death" is one which a believer does not and cannot commit. It should be noted that 1 John 5:16-17 does not state, contrary to common assumption, that the "sin unto death" is committed by believers.

1 John 5:16-17 is part of a section (5:14-17) that deals with confident, effective prayer, a theme already mentioned in 1 John (3:21-22; 4:17). The general instruction concerning prayer (5:14-15) introduces the specific case of prayer for a sinning brother (5:16-17). 1 John 5:16-17 is followed by three affirmations (5:18, 19, 20), the first of which repeats the assertion of 3:9 that believers do not sin and thus, by its immediate juxtaposition to 1 John 5:16-17 and its content, is significant for understanding the matter of the relationship of sin and the believer in 1 John. 1 John ends (5:21) with the warning "little children, keep yourselves from idols," which probably is a warning against false teachers/teaching,[12] and thus, as will be shown, would tie in with the mention of the "sin unto death" (5:16).

1 John 5:14-21, including 5:16-17, is assumed here to be part of the text of the document known as 1 John and not, as argued by Bultmann, an appendix added to 1 John by a later ecclesiastical redactor.[13] Among the several arguments advanced by Bultmann[14] for viewing 1 John 5:14-21 as a later appendix, the most important one seems to be his assertion that the distinction of two types of sin in 1 John 5:16 abandons the dialectical

---

heretics, and Bultmann, *Johannine Epistles,* pp. 20-22, 51-53, who also sees the opponents as gnostic heretics.

[11] Kubo does not mention 1 John 5:16-17 in his article, and Bultmann views 1 John 5:14-21 as an appendix to 1 John added by an ecclesiastical redactor in which 5:16-17 contradicts previous statements on sin and the believer (*Johannine Epistles,* pp. 86-87); for further discussion of Bultmann on this matter, cf. below. Further, the solution as posed by Kubo and Bultmann still finds the statement that the Christian is not able to sin (3:9) a problem (Kubo, "1 John 3:9," p. 50, identifies 1 John 3:9 as an idealistic comment; Bultmann, *Johannine Epistles,* p. 53, says that the statement that the believer is not able to sin " . . . is . . . to be understood as the possibility of not sinning. . . .").

[12] So Bultmann, *Johannine Epistles,* p. 90.

[13] There is no textual question concerning 1 John 5:14-21; it is found in every manuscript containing 1 John. The legitimate question of Bultmann has to do with redactional history not reflected in textual history.

[14] Bultmann's main argument for his position is given in "Die kirchliche Redaktion des ersten Johannesbriefes," *In Memoriam Ernst Lohmeyer,* ed. by W. Schmauch, Stuttgart, 1951, pp. 192-96, in which he notes, in addition to the point described above, that 1 John 5:13 is a conclusion (cf. John 20:31); that the literary structure of 1 John is a rhythm of christological and parenetical material into which 1 John 5:14-21 does not fit; that *kai hautē estin* in 1 John 5:14 points forward, but otherwise in the Johannine letters this expression always points back; and that 1 John 5:21 is wholly un-Johannine.

understanding of Christian existence reflected in 1:5-2:2 and 3:4-10 and reflects the church's interest in regulations concerning repentance as reflected in Heb and Herm.[15] It is clear that 1 John 5:13 does indicate a breaking point in the composition and that 1 John 5:14-21 is a separate section,[16] but this does not in itself establish 1 John 5:14-21 as a later appendix by a different author. Nauck has given a fairly comprehensive linguistic and structural analysis of 1 John 5:14-21 in which he argues against Bultmann that the passage belongs integrally to 1 John.[17] What is most important here, however, is that the point at which Bultmann finds the greatest difficulty, namely, 1 John 5:16-17, is precisely the issue that this article proposes to solve by its interpretation of the "sin not unto death"/"sin unto death" and the correlation of these expressions with the rest of 1 John.[18]

III

Some have sought the solution to the problems of the "sin not unto death" and the "sin unto death" in 1 John 5:16-17 in terms of OT and intertestamental Jewish distinctions regarding sin. Num 15:27-31 draws a line between sins committed unwittingly,[19] which can be forgiven by a priest's atonement, and sins done with a high hand, which bring complete exclusion from God's people.[20] This same distinction, using the same terminology, is found in Qumran's Manual of Discipline (1QS 8:21-9:2), although with a stiffer penalty for a sin of inadvertence. The one who sins inadvertently is excluded from participation in the community life for two years, during which time he is on probation. At the end of the probationary period, he is reinstated in the community if he has maintained good conduct during that time. The one who sins deliberately or through slackness is permanently expelled from the community.

This type of distinction seems to be the background to the sin

[15] This is discussed in Bultmann's article, "Die kirchliche Redaktion des ersten Johannesbriefes," pp. 192-94. In "Johannesbriefe," *RGG*, Tübingen, 1959[3], 3, col. 837, Bultmann mentions only this reason and the first item listed in the preceding note. Bultmann in his commentary gives attention to analysis of many details in 1 John 5:14-21 (pp. 85-91), but especially focuses on the problems of 1 John 5:16-17 (pp. 86-88) as clear indication that the appendix is the work of a later ecclesiastical redactor.

[16] This point of Bultmann, as indicated in the two preceding notes, is certainly to be recognized.

[17] W. Nauck, *Die Tradition und der Charakter des ersten Johannesbriefes: Zugleich ein Beitrag zur Taufe im Urchristentum und in der alten Kirche*, Wissenschaftliche Untersuchungen zum Neuen Testament, Tübingen, 1957, 3, 133-46.

[18] Thus, the solution proposed here obviates any necessity for viewing 1 John 5:14-21 as an appendix and, in fact, argues strongly for the unity of 1 John 5:14-21 with the rest of 1 John.

[19] The unwitting sins are also in view in Lev 4:2; 5:15.

[20] Another type of distinction between sins is in view in 1 Sam 2:25 in which a sin against man is forgivable, but one against the Lord is not. (According to Westcott, *Epistles of John*, p. 212, both Origen and Jerome appealed to this text as an aid in understanding 1 John 5:16.) For a treatment of sin in the OT cf. J. Pedersen, *Israel: Its Life and Culture*, London, 1926-1940, 1-2, 411-52; 3-4, 264-375, 611-69.

problem of Heb. The discussion of Heb 10:26-31 concerns deliberate sin for which the only prospect is the judgment of the living God. Evidently for the author of Heb the sin of apostasy and rejection of the Son of God (6:4-6; 10:29) is a deliberate sin in the OT-Qumran tradition for which there is no repentance (cf. 12:16-17) or forgiveness.

This distinction between inadvertent and deliberate sins presents an attractive approach to the problems of understanding the "sin not unto death" and the "sin unto death" in 1 John 5:16-17.[21] This solution should be rejected, however, for nowhere in 1 John, in distinction from Heb, is it expressed or implied that the two types of sin in 5:16-17 are to be understood as inadvertent and deliberate. Further, an implicit assumption of this view is that the "sin unto death" is one committed by believers. This, however, is not stated in 1 John 5:16-17 and, as will be argued later, is in fact not the case.

It should be noted that the OT and intertestamental literature also speak of a sin unto death. The LXX text of Num 18:22 uses the terminology *labein hamartian thanatēphoron* (in a warning to the Israelites not to come near the tabernacle of the congregation). A closer parallel to the language of 1 John 5:16-17 is found in the T Issa 7:1 (*hamartia eis thanaton*)[22] and in Jub in which a "sin unto death" is mentioned (21:22; 26:34; 33:18; cf. 33:13).[23] All of these references apparently speak of a sin that results in physical death. These texts, because they provide only formal parallels to the expression of the "sin unto death" in 1 John 5:16, do not give any insight into the meaning or significance of the expression in the Johannine context.[24]

In this connection another solution to the terminology of 1 John 5:16-17 can be noted. It is argued that the expression "sin unto death" in 1

---

[21] This solution for 1 John 5:16-17 is endorsed by both Nauck, *Die Tradition*, pp. 144-46 (he argues that there is here not a distinction between two classes of sin, but a differentiation of two attitudes of community members toward sin; this appears, however, to avoid the direct statement of the text) and Schnackenburg, *Die Johannesbriefe*, p. 278. In this solution, there is no prayer for the "sin unto death" (cf. the last phrase of 1 John 5:16) because those who commit it are expelled from the community, the only place of effective prayer. For a different analysis of the relation of the Qumran text to the NT cf. K. Stendahl, "Hate, Non-Retaliation, and Love: 1QS *X*, 17-20 and Rom. 12:19-21," *HTR*, 55 (1962), 343-55.

[22] This expression is not in all MSS, but is in β and A; cf. R. H. Charles, *The Greek Versions of the Testaments of the Twelve Patriarchs . . .*, Oxford, 1908, p. 114. The problems of the date of the T 12 Patr need not be discussed at this point. In the context of this passage Issachar is speaking of his long life in which no sin led to his death.

[23] The only complete version of Jub is in Ethiopic (a few fragments exist in Greek Christian authors); cf. A.-M. Denis, *Introduction aux pseudépigraphes grecs d'ancien testament*, Studia in Veteris Testamenti Pseudepigrapha, 1, Leiden, 1970, 150-62, for details. The contexts of these passages vary, but they all refer to heinous sins that lead to death (Jub 26:34 concerns Esau; 33:13, 18 concerns incest) or could lead to death (21:22 is a warning against offending God).

[24] The same is true of the phrase *hoi en oligō hamartēsantes* in T Gad 4:6. The context here concerns the desire of "hatred" to see the death even of those who sin "in a little way."

John 5:16 is a reference to a sin that results in literal physical death.[25] It is mentioned in order to make clear that no prayers for the dead should be made.[26] This view should be rejected primarily because it fails to understand the meaning of *thanatos* within the context of 1 John.[27] Further, there is nothing in the context of 1 John that indicates any relationship between sin or acts of sin and consequent physical death.

Other attempts to explain the terminology of 1 John 5:16-17, especially the phrase "sin unto death," have been made in terms of comparisons with other texts of early Christian literature. The "sin unto death" is commonly related to or equated with the blasphemy against the Holy Spirit (Matt 12:31-32 and parallels).[28] Usually associated with this passage is Heb 6:4-6 (cf. 10:29), which speaks of some type of apostasy.[29] However, neither of these texts provides a solution for understanding the "sin unto death" in 1 John 5:16, for nowhere in 1 John are the specific concepts of either Matt 12:31-32 or Heb 6:4-6 discussed.[30]

Another possible parallel to 1 John 5:16-17 is Herm Sim 6.2.1-4. In

[25] This view is summarized, but not actually endorsed, by F. F. Bruce, *The Epistles of John: Introduction, Exposition and Notes*, Old Tappan, 1970, pp. 124-25. Bruce refers to Acts 5:1-11 (the death of Ananias and Sapphira), 1 Cor 5:5 (assuming that "destruction of the flesh" indicates physical death) and 1 Cor 11:30 (the death of believers who misused the Lord's Supper). Again note that the assumption is made that the "sin unto death" is committed by believers. This interpretation is strongly endorsed by S. M. Reynolds, "The Sin Unto Death and Prayers for the Dead," *Reformation Review*, 20 (1973), 130-39 (this article refers to an earlier draft of my own article which was shared with S. M. Reynolds within the context of a faculty discussion group). S. M. Reynolds cites the *pros thanaton* in John 11:4 as Johannine proof of his interpretation. However, the context of John 11:4 is so different from that of 1 John 5:16 that it offers no genuine solution.

[26] Such is this solution's interpretation of the last phrase of 1 John 5:16—*ou peri ekeinēs legō hina erōtēsē*. The major thrust of Reynolds' article (cited in the previous note) is concerned with theological arguments against prayers for the sins of the dead.

[27] Cf. R. Law, *The Tests of Life: A Study of the First Epistle of St. John*, Edinburgh, 1909, pp. 139-40. The meaning of *thanatos* in 1 John taken in this article is developed below.

[28] Cf. Law, *ibid.*, p. 140; Bruce, *Epistles of John*, pp. 125, 132 n. 21.

[29] Cf. Law, *Tests of Life*, p. 141; Bruce, *Epistles of John*, pp. 125, 132 n. 21.

[30] For a rejection of this solution cf. e.g. Schnackenburg, *Die Johannesbriefe*, p. 277; Brooke, *Commentary on the Johannine Epistles*, p. 147; R. Seeberg, "Die Sünden und Sündenvergebung nach dem ersten Briefe des Johannes," *Das Erbe Martin Luthers und die gegenwärtige theologische Forschung*, Festschrift für D. Ludwig Ihmels, ed. by R. Jelke, Leipzig, 1928, p. 27. C. H. Dodd, *The Johannine Epistles*, London, 1946, p. 136, holds that the author of 1 John is thinking in terms of apostasy in a manner similar to Heb (1 John 4:2-5) and may have associated it with the sin of blasphemy against the Holy Spirit (1 John 2:22-23); cf. also H. Windisch, *Die Katholischen Briefe*, HNT, Tübingen, 1951[3], p. 135. There is no evidence in 1 John of the concept of the sin of blasphemy against the Holy Spirit. 1 John 4:2-5 does deal with the subject of Christians' confession of Christ, but is different from Heb in that the latter deals with the apostasy of Christians, whereas 1 John 4:2-5 deals with Christians who believe and people of the world who do not. The thesis to be developed in this article will associate the "sin unto death" with a type of apparent "apostasy," but it will be a different concept from that of Heb.

this text there are two sins, one to corruption and one to death. Those who commit the sin to death (*eis thanaton*) are those who have given themselves up to the lusts of this age (cf. 1 John 2:15). They have no repentance because they have blasphemed against the name of God. Those who sin to corruption are those who are guilty of luxury and deceit, but not of blasphemy. Therefore, they have hope of repentance and thus life. Although the sin "unto death" (*eis thanaton*) in Herm Sim 6.2.1-4 bears a formal similarity to the "sin unto death" (*pros thanaton*) of 1 John 5:16, the Herm Sim text differs from 1 John in that it is dealing with apostasy, and that in terms of a sin from which there is no repentance. Thus Herm Sim 6.2.1-4 is parallel to Heb 6:4-6 and 10:29 and not to 1 John 5:16-17.[31]

Another explanation of the terminology of 1 John 5:16-17 is that which identifies the "sin unto death" with the sins associated with the "way of death" as described in Did 5:1-2 (cf. 1:1). These coarse heathen sins are represented in 1 John 2:16. Those who commit such sins are Christians who practice these abominations before the Christian community without any shame or repentance.[32] This view is attractive in that it attempts to specify the content of the "sin unto death," but it should be rejected because it imposes from another context (Did 5:1-2) a structure and a situation that is neither expressed nor implied in 1 John or, more particularly, in 1 John 5:16-17.[33]

The last solution[34] for the terminology of 1 John 5:16-17 to be reviewed here is that of Tertullian, which in a sense became the classic view of the 1 John 5:16-17 passage.[35] In his *De pudicitia* Tertullian twice cites 1

---

[31] Cf. the discussion of Heb 6:4-6 and 10:29 above. It should be noted that both Herm Sim and Heb specify a sin for which it is expressly stated that there is no repentance. This is not said concerning the "sin unto death" in 1 John 5:16; cf. Schnackenburg, *Die Johannesbriefe,* p. 278.

[32] This view is that of Seeberg, "Die Sünden und Sündenvergebung," pp. 28-29. Seeberg holds that prayer for such a sinner is discouraged (the last phrase of 1 John 5:16) because any type of involvement with such a sinner would be dangerous (cf. Gal 6:1-2). Note that 1 John 2:16 does not include the religious sins of *eidōlolatria* and *mageia,* which are mentioned in Did 5:1.

[33] Seeberg understands the confession of sin in 1 John 1-2 in a baptismal setting that strengthens the parallel with the Did. However, it is very doubtful that 1 John 1-2 is baptismal-confession material. Further, Seeberg also assumes that the "sin unto death" is committed by Christians; this is not stated in the text of 1 John 5:16-17.

[34] The view of N. Lazure, *Les valeurs morales de la théologie johannique* (Evangile et Epîtres), Paris, 1965, p. 312, that the "sin unto death" is a homicide (he refers to 1 John 3:15) misunderstands the Johannine meaning of "death" (and the meaning of 1 John 3:15). The suggestions of Cox, "The Sin Unto Death," p. 422, that the "sin unto death" is any act that separates a man from Christ, and of Dammers, "Hard Sayings," pp. 371-72, that the "sin unto death" is impenitence, are too general to be helpful and, further, make no use of the context of 1 John itself. (I have been unable to consult A. Zahn, *De notione peccati, quam Iohannes in prima epistola docet, commentatio,* Halle, 1872.)

[35] For a convenient and brief summary of some views of and references to several patristic authors (including, in addition to Tertullian, Clement of Alexandria, Origen, Ambrose, Jerome, Augustine, Chrysostom, Gelasius and Oecumenius) on 1 John 5:16-17 cf. Westcott, *Epistles of John,* pp. 211-14.

John 5:16-17 for its distinction between a "sin not unto death" and a "sin unto death" for the development of his own argument.[36] In developing this argument, which is to show that adultery and fornication are sins that the church should not pardon, Tertullian early (2.12-15) develops the distinction between remissible and irremissible sins. Tertullian cites 1 John 5:16 as his proof: a "sin not unto death" is remissible; a "sin unto death," for which prayer is denied, is irremissible. "Accordingly, where there is room for prayer there is also room for remission. Where there is no room for prayer there, likewise, is no room for remission."[37] Later, Tertullian returns to a discussion of several passages from 1 John (*De pudicitia* 19.10-28) in which he notes that 1 John contains both statements that believers do sin and statements that believers do not sin. Tertullian rejects the idea that the author of 1 John is confused; rather, he turns to 1 John 5:16 for his solution. The "sin not unto death" refers to the type of sin that daily besets the believer; the "sin unto death" refers to graver and deadlier sins—murder, idolatry, injustice, apostasy, adultery and fornication—for which there is no pardon. "He who has been born of God will not commit them at all; if he should commit them, he will not be a child of God's."[38] Tertullian continues by introducing 1 John 5:16 with these words:

> Thus an explanation of the apparent contradiction in John will be found in the fact that he is making a distinction between classes of sins when he asserts, in one place, that sons of God *do* sin, and in another, that they *do not*. For he was looking forward to the close of his epistle and, with this in mind, he first composes these passages, intending to say very clearly in his conclusion [here he quotes 1 John 5:16] ....[39]

Tertullian's view is a helpful prelude to the development of the solution proposed in this article because he solved the problem of the apparently contradictory statements that believers do sin and do not sin by reference to 1 John 5:16. Apart from this insight, Tertullian's interpretation suffers from a weakness common to other solutions reviewed. Tertullian defines the "sin unto death" in terms of specific sins, most of which are not mentioned or even implied in 1 John. There is no contextual evidence that the author of 1 John understood the "sin unto death" in the way in which Tertullian describes it. Tertullian also assumes, in a way, that

---

[36] The quotations occur in *De pudicitia* 2.14 and 19.27. For the Latin text see E. Dekkers, "De pudicitia" in *Tertulliani Opera*, Pars 2: *Opera Montanistica*, Corpus Christianorum, Series Latina 2, Turnholti, 1954, pp. 1280-1330. For an English translation cf. W. P. Le Saint, *Tertullian, Treatises on Penance: On Penitence and On Purity translated and annotated*, ACW, 28, Westminster, 1959. Le Saint gives a good explanation of his English title *On Purity* for *De pudicitia* on p. 198, n. 1.

[37] *De pudicitia* 2.15; Le Saint, *Tertullian, Treatises on Penance*, p. 59.

[38] *De pudicitia* 19.26; Le Saint, *Tertullian, Treatises on Penance*, p. 114.

[39] *De pudicitia* 19.26-27; Le Saint, *Tertullian, Treatises on Penance*, p. 114. For a discussion of Tertullian on sin in reference to this passage cf. Le Saint, *Tertullian, Treatises on Penance*, pp. 273-75, nn. 591-95, and H. Windisch, *Taufe und Sünde im ältesten Christentum bis auf Origenes: Ein Beitrag zur altchristlichen Dogmengeschichte*, Tübingen, 1908, pp. 427-28. Note especially in addition to Tertullian on 1 John 5:16, Origen, *On Prayer* 28.10 (which Westcott, *Epistles of John*, pp. 211-14, does not include).

believers commit the "sin unto death," which is not stated in 1 John 5:16, but he does indicate that if one commits a "sin unto death" then he would not be God's child. This, as will be argued, points in the direction of a proper understanding of 1 John 5:16-17.

IV

As already indicated, the thesis to be presented here is that the "sin not unto death" refers to the sins of believers and the "sin unto death" refers to the sins of nonbelievers. In terms of the proposals reviewed above, this solution, it will be argued, has the advantages of recognizing that 1 John 5:16-17 does not say that the "sin unto death" is a believer's sin. Moreover, it utilizes directly and exclusively the context and patterns of thought of 1 John to provide an interpretation for 1 John 5:16-17.

There can be no question that the believer, according to 1 John, can and does commit sin. Not only is this indicated in 1:8 and 2:1, but it is reiterated in 5:16-17.[40] That the believer is in focus in this text is clear from the use of the term "brother" (1 John 5:16).[41] The sin that the believer commits is designated twice in 5:16 and once again in 5:17 as a "sin not unto death."[42] In 5:17b the declaration that there is a "sin not unto death"[43] is emphasized by the author (*kai* here is an adversative)[44] in the face of the statement (5:17a) that "all unrighteousness is sin."[45] Thus the author's interest is focused sharply on the "sin not unto death" committed by believers, rather than on the "sin unto death." In fact, the

---

[40] The sin of the believer in 5:16-17 should certainly be identified with the sins of the believer presupposed in 1:8-2:2, even though the sin of this latter passage is not specified as a "sin not unto death"; cf. Schnackenburg, *Die Johannesbriefe*, p. 279.

[41] "Brother" is used in 1 John at 2:9-11; 3:10, 12-17; 4:20-21 (note 3:13 in which "brother" is put in opposition to "world").

[42] In 5:16 the negative is *mē*; in 5:17 it is *ou*. Any distinction between the *mē* and the *ou* at this point is questionable if the declaration of N. Turner in reference to 1 John 5:16-17 is accepted: "there can be no difference . . .," *Syntax*, Vol. 3 of J. H. Moulton, *A Grammar of New Testament Greek*, Edinburgh, 1963, p. 281. It may well be that the *mē* is due to the use of *ean* and/or the participle and that the *ou* occurs in a simple indicative sentence; cf. Brooke, *Commentary on Johannine Epistles*, p. 146, and Westcott, *Epistles of John*, p. 191.

[43] In some MSS (including 33, some Old Latin MSS and the Vulgate, the Harclean Syriac, Tertullian) the phrase in 5:17 does not have the *ou*. Such texts undoubtedly represent the thought that the logic of the passage required its absence, which it does not; cf. Schnackenburg, *Die Johannesbriefe*, p. 278. Another change based on the thought that 5:17b is not logical in its present position is that suggested by Windisch, *Die Katholischen Briefe*, p. 135, who argues that the order should be either 17b, 16c, 17a or 17b, 16a-c, 17a.

[44] For *kai* as an adversative here cf. Schnackenburg, *Die Johannesbriefe*, p. 279; cf. also F. Blass and A. Debrunner, *A Greek Grammar of the New Testament and Other Early Christian Literature*, trans. and rev. of the 9th-10th German ed. incorporating supplementary notes of A. Debrunner by R. W. Funk, Chicago, 1961, 442 (1).

[45] Cf. 1 John 3:4: "sin is lawlessness." For an intensive study of this text cf. I. de la Potterie, " 'Sin is Iniquity' (I Jn 3, 4)," in I. de la Potterie and S. Lyonnet, *The Christian Lives by the Spirit*, trans. by J. Morriss, Staten Island, 1971, pp. 37-55; cf. also the comments of Bultmann, *The Johannine Epistles*, p. 50.

immediate context, as previously indicated, is concerned with confident, effective prayer within the believing community (5:14-15), which is then focused on the very serious problem of what to do when a sinning brother is observed.[46] The "sin unto death" actually receives, in comparison with the totality of 1 John 5:16-17, scant attention.[47]

1 John 5:16-17 deals with believers' sins as a community phenomenon. This is indicated by the indefinite pronoun, which includes anyone (i.e. everyone), the term "brother" (discussed above), and the *idein* and the *aitein* (reflecting the plural *aitōmetha* of 5:14-15). The community aspect is also stressed by the use of the plural participle[48] (*hamartanousi*, 5:16) used in apposition to the *autō* to generalize the application of the prayer and its answer to all brothers who "sin not unto death."

Any believer who observes a brother committing a "sin not unto death" should pray for him.[49] Such a prayer will result[50] (cf. "we have the requests which we ask of him," 5:15) in the giving of life to the sinning brother, indicating that it is a prayer "according to his [God's][51] will" (5:14).[52]

Two minor problems arise in this analysis of a believer's effective prayer for a sinning brother (5:16). First is the identification of the subject of "he will give" in the phrase "he will give him [the sinning brother] life."

[46] Cf. Windisch, *Taufe und Sünde,* pp. 271-72, for an excellent statement on the seriousness of the problem of sinning believers for 1 John. 1 John stresses that all lawlessness and unrighteousness is sin, that all sin leads to a rupture of a believer's relationship with God and that all sin needs intercession, confession and forgiveness.

[47] This scant attention is explained by the author: *ou peri ekeinēs legō hina erōtēsē* (5:16), on which there is discussion later in this article.

[48] A singular participle is found in some MSS (206, 255, 383, 614, 1518, 1758) and the Vulgate, according to H. F. von Soden, *Die Schriften des Neuen Testament in ihrer ältesten erreichbaren Textgestalt hergestellt auf Grund ihrer Textgeschichte: Text und Apparat,* Göttingen, 1913, p. 652.

[49] Schnackenburg, *Die Johannesbriefe,* pp. 275-76, gives an extensive list of passages from the OT and the literature of Judaism that illustrate the intercession of the righteous for the sinner. The difference between these texts and 1 John, as Schnackenburg notes, is that in Judaism only the great saints and martyrs intercede, whereas in 1 John any believer can intercede. Cf. also the early Christian statement of concern in 1 Clem 56:1: "Let us then also intercede for those who have fallen into any transgression. . . ."

[50] Prayer is effective only within the believing community; cf. Nauck, *Die Tradition,* pp. 144-46. The connection between the power of prayer and sinning brothers is seen elsewhere in the NT, e.g. Mark 11:25; Matt 6:12, 14-15 (cf. the Coptic Gos Thom 48). These passages make effective prayer dependent on forgiveness between brothers; 1 John has effective prayer used to obtain forgiveness for a brother.

[51] It is not clear to whom the *autou* refers—God or Christ; cf. Bultmann, *Johannine Epistles,* p. 85.

[52] Some other NT passages that deal with community handling of sinning brothers are Matt 18:15-22; John 13:1-18; 1 Cor 5:1-5; 2 Cor 2:6-11; Gal 6:1-2; 2 Thess 3:14-15; 1 Tim 1:20; and Jas 5:15-20; cf. also Herm Man 4.3.1-7; Herm Sim 6.2.1-4; Herm Vis 2.2.4-5. Of these, Jas 5:15-20 (esp. 5:16, 19-20) provides the closest parallel to 1 John 5:16-17 because it mentions prayer. None of the other texts noted here suggests a method of treatment for the problem similar to that of 1 John 5:16-17.

In spite of the difficulty in the change of subject from "he will ask" (the praying believer is the subject here), God rather than the interceding brother should be understood as the subject of "he will give."[53] Second, the matter of the sinning brother's being given "life" is problematic since the believer has already been transferred out of death into life (3:14) and thus possesses life (5:11-13). The "life" that is given to the sinning brother, in the context of 1 John, must be understood as a renewal or reconfirmation (cf. 1:6-10) of the life already possessed (3:14; 5:11-13).[54]

As already indicated, the mention of the "sin unto death" (1 John 5:16c) is very brief and is not at all developed. In an attempt to define the "sin unto death" in Johannine terms, it should be noted first that both types of sin mentioned in 1 John 5:16 are defined in terms of "death." [55] In 1 John death is the state in which one is before he becomes a believer and out of which he is transferred into life (3:14; cf. John 5:24). The one who does not love the brothers (= believers) remains in death (3:14). Those who do not love (i.e. unbelievers; cf. 3:9-10; 4:7-8) are not of God (3:10), are in darkness (2:11; cf. 1:5) and do not know God (4:8; cf. 4:7). Thus it is clear that a "sin unto death" is one which signifies the complete absence of any fellowship with God.

1 John associates the one who is in death with the devil. In contrast to the one who is born of God and who is, therefore, a child of God (3:9-10), the one who commits sin is of the devil (3:8, 10). The devil is the prototype and fount of such persons because he has been sinning from the beginning (3:8). 1 John 3:8 is significantly paralleled in the literature of the Johannine school by John 8:44.[56] John 8:44 has Jesus say to the Jews:

---

[53] The main arguments for the interceding brother being the subject are the parallel with Jas 5:20 and the apparently abrupt change in subject in the two verbs *aitēsei* and *dōsei*; cf. Brooke, *Commentary on the Johannine Epistles,* p. 146; Bultmann, *Johannine Epistles,* p. 87 n. 16. Windisch, *Die Katholischen Briefe,* p. 135, gives 2 Clem 19:1 as a parallel text for this view. That God is the subject is supported by the Johannine view that God gives life (5:11) and the believer possesses it (5:12) rather than distributes it; cf. also John 5:26; 10:28; 17:2; cf. Schnackenburg, *Die Johannesbriefe,* p. 276, and Westcott, *Epistles of John,* p. 191, for this view. In support of God as subject cf. the long note, which discusses both the grammar and the Jas 5:20 parallel, in A. Buttmann, *A Grammar of the New Testament Greek,* trans. by J. H. Thayer, Andover, 1873, p. 133 n. 1.

[54] So Schnackenburg, *Die Johannesbriefe,* p. 276, and Seeberg, "Die Sünden und Sündenvergebung," p. 277. Schnackenburg, *Die Johannesbriefe,* p. 277, refers to Rev 3:1-2 as a parallel idea.

[55] The phrase "not unto death" occurs in John 11:4 in reference to the sickness of Lazarus. In that context "death" has both a physical and a theological connotation, but the situation is so different from that of 1 John 5:16-17 that the John 11:4 phrase offers no help in determining the meaning of the 1 John text.

[56] The legitimacy of using the Gospel of John in the exegesis of 1 John is partially dependent on the unity of authorship, which is accepted here. Even if unity of authorship is not the actual state of affairs, 1 John certainly stems from the same "school" as the Gospel of John. Thus, comparisons between the Gospel of John and 1 John are legitimate wherever the ideas are not in conflict. For a discussion of the authorship question cf., for the case against unity, C. H. Dodd, *Johannine Epistles,* pp. xlvii-lvi, and "The First Epistle of John and the Fourth Gospel," *BJRL,* 21 (1937), 124-56, and cf., for the case for unity, W. F. Howard, "The Common Authorship of the Johannine Gospel and Epistles," *JTS,* 48 (1947),

"You are of your father the devil,[57] and you wish to do the desires of your father." Two designations are then given to the devil: first, he is a "murderer from the beginning" (cf. the expression "from the beginning" in 1 John 3:8); and second, he is a "liar and the father of it" and "there is no truth in him." Thus the devil's sinning from the beginning noted in 1 John 3:8 may be understood to consist primarily of two kinds: murder and lying.

Since the unbeliever is a child of the devil, his sinning can be expected to follow the pattern of his father. That this is in fact the case is confirmed by noting that the two most heinous sins in 1 John are murder and lying. As already noted, one who does not love is not a child of God. 1 John equates a brother-hater with a murderer (3:15) and declares that a murderer does not have eternal life abiding in him. 1 John emphasizes the importance of loving one another as a primary evidence of being a child of God (cf. esp. 4:7; cf. also 2:10; 3:10-11, 14, 16-18, 23; 4:8, 11, 12, 16, 19-21; 5:1-3). Thus one who does not love (i.e. a murderer) is showing himself to be in the grasp of death.

Further, in 1 John a liar is an antichrist, of whom there are many (2:18), who denies both the Father and the Son and that Jesus is the Christ (2:22; 4:3; 5:10). In 1 John 4:2-3 the theme of the lying spirit of the antichrist who does not confess Jesus but denies him is contrasted with the Spirit of God who does. Since belief in Jesus is a criterion of being a child of God (5:1-5, 10-13; 4:15; 2:23), one who is a liar (i.e. denies rather than believes Jesus) shows himself to be in the grasp of death (cf. John 8:24).[58]

Thus "sin unto death" is in 1 John composed of hating the believers (murder) and not confessing Jesus (lying).[59] The "sin unto death," there-

---

12-25, and W. F. Wilson, "An Examination of the Linguistic Evidence Adduced against the Unity of Authorship of the First Epistle of John and the Fourth Gospel," *JTS*, 49 (1948), 147-56. Cf. also the summary in Schnackenburg, *Die Johannesbriefe*, pp. 34-38.

[57] Cf. Blass-Debrunner, *Grammar*, 268(2), for a discussion of the translation of *tou patros tou diabolou*.

[58] Is Judas in the Gospel of John an example of one who commits the "sin unto death"? The devil is mentioned in John only at 8:44 (discussed above) and at 6:70 and 13:2. In the first of these texts Judas is called a devil and in the second the devil is said to have entered Judas' heart. Judas certainly denied Jesus and hated the brothers in the context of the Gospel of John.

[59] Other interpreters, of course, have reached similar (but not exactly the same) conclusions, but by different routes. My interpretation is prefigured, but not developed, in the virtually neglected article of A. Klöpper, "Zur Lehre von der Sünde im 1. Johannesbrief, Erläuterung von 5, 16-fin.," *Zeitschrift für wissenschaftliche Theologie*, 43 (1900), 585-602. He argues that for 1 John the "sin unto death" refers to the false teachers (1 John 2:19) who broke with the believing community in their denial of Jesus as the Christ and in their rejection of love (pp. 589-90). He does not distinguish this situation sharply enough from that of Heb 6:4-6 with which he compares 1 John 5:16-17. Often others include either denial of Jesus or hating the brothers or both in a list of several other items in the definition of the "sin unto death." J. Herkenrath, "Sünde zum Tode," *Aus Theologie und Philosophie: Festschrift für Fritz Tillmann zu seinem 75. Geburtstag*, ed. by T. Steinbüchel and T. Müncker, Düsseldorf, 1950, pp. 135-36, identifies the "sin unto death" as a denial of the messiahship and sonship of Christ, a practice of idolatry and a hatred of the brethren. Windisch, *Die Katholischen Briefe*, p. 136, in addition to

fore, as previously indicated, is not a sin committed by a believer in the community. Actually, it is somewhat of a tautology for 1 John to suggest that believers do not "sin unto death." By definition, the "sin unto death," which is to hate believers (murder) and to deny Jesus (lying), is that which makes one an unbeliever (cf., e.g., 3:23-24; 3:10). In 1 John one is either a believer or an unbeliever; there is no reference to apostasy. This is made very clear in 1 John 2:19, an important text for understanding the whole problem. After stating that many antichrists, already present and active (2:18; cf. 4:1-5), have come from the Christian community (2:19), the statement is modified in such a way as to negate it. In actuality the antichrists were not from the Christian community, for if they really had been, they would not have left it. The fact that antichrists left the community was a good thing: it showed conclusively that they were never real members of it in the first place; they had been pretenders only.

Thus the opponents of the believing community represented by 1 John had masqueraded as believers, but were actually unbelievers who committed the "sin unto death" of hating the brothers and denying Jesus. They evidently claimed a spiritual stance that put them, from their point of view, beyond sin (cf. 1:8-2:1; 3:4; 5:17).[60] 1 John asserts that they, however, actually do "sin unto death" in that they are outside the believing community that knows life. Those within the believing community are not guilty of "sin unto death"; however, they should not, as their opponents do, make false spiritual claims in regard to sin. Believers are guilty of "sin not unto death," that is, they do break fellowship with God (1:6-2:1), but without participating in hating the brothers or denying Jesus.

Because the "sin unto death" is for 1 John a sin of those who are actually disruptive, heretical outsiders, there is no concern at this point (in 5:14-17 where the concern is effective prayer for sin within the believing community) for prayer for the "sin unto death." The "sin unto death" is mentioned as an aside in contrast to the "sin not unto death," which does in fact occur within the believing community. The mention of the "sin unto death" is not developed: "I speak not concerning that ["sin unto death"] [61]

---

noting Matt 12:31-32, includes murder and idolatry. Brooke, *Commentary on Johannine Epistles,* pp. 146-47, suggests that the "sin unto death" is any deliberate rejection of the claims of Christ. Westcott, *Epistles of John,* pp. 209-10, mentions, along with other items, both the hatred of brethren and the denial of Christ; cf. also W. Grundmann, *TDNT,* 1, 307. Law, *Tests of Life,* p. 141, identifies the "sin unto death" as, among other suggestions, the sin of the antichrists in 1 John.

[60] A precise identification of the opponents is not possible. Not only did they claim a spiritual stance beyond sin (cf. 1:8-2:1; 3:4), but they also had christological deviations from the perspective of 1 John (4:1-5; 2:22-23) that fall into the broad category of "docetism." Probably these opponents noted in 1 John are early Christian gnostics of some type; cf. R. McL. Wilson, *Gnosis and the New Testament,* Philadelphia, 1968, pp. 40-42, 44, 46, 59, for a good discussion of the matter. Wilson identifies the heresy combatted in 1 John as incipient Gnosticism.

[61] 1 John "plays down" the "sin unto death" by not speaking about it. The *peri ekeinēs* should be understood with the *legein* rather than the *erōtan* (with Schnackenburg, *Die Johannesbriefe,* p. 278, and against Westcott, *Epistles of John,* p. 192). This is indicated by the position of the *peri ekeinēs* between the *ou* and the *legō* and by the suggestion (of Schnackenburg) that one prays for the sinner, not the sin. One MS (614) reads *hyper* for *ou peri,* which is probably the result of the omission of the first (*o*) and last (*i*) letters in the grouping.

in order that (*hina*) anyone [any member of the believing community] should pray (*erōtēsē*)[62] [about it]" (5:16). Prayer is not absolutely forbidden concerning the matter,[63] nor is it said that one who commits the "sin unto death" is forever beyond the hope of becoming a member of the believing community.[64] But throughout 1 John there is a radical separation between the believing community and the unbelieving world so that prayer for the unbelieving world would not be a "normal" or "effective" practice.[65] This would be especially true of prayer for those of the world who had deceptively and without reality been within the believing community (1 John 2:19) but who were actually liars and haters belonging to the world.[66]

It has been argued, however, that the intent of the last sentence in 1 John 5:16 is not to discourage prayer, but rather to rule out discussion of the "sin unto death." In this view, the meaning of *erōtan* is taken as "to ask a question."[67] The most careful development of this view[68] is that of P. Trudinger, who paraphrases this sentence: "I am not speaking about that

[62] Attempts are made by Westcott, *Epistles of John*, p. 192; G. Stählin, *TDNT*, 1, 193; and H. Greeven, *TDNT*, 2, 806, to make a clear distinction between *aitein* (5:14-15) and *erōtan* (5:16), the latter term indicating a more intimate relationship between the one praying and the one addressed. Westcott, then, concludes that such intimate prayer should not be used for one committing a "sin unto death." But why, it may be asked, would the less intimate term be used for prayer for the believer? On the whole, it would be better to make no distinction between the terms in 1 John 5:16 (so Brooke, *Commentary on the Johannine Epistles*, p. 147).

[63] So, e.g., Brooke, *ibid.*, p. 147.

[64] This is recognized by Schnackenburg, *Die Johannesbriefe*, p. 278, who notes that 1 John 5:16 says nothing about the possibility or impossibility of reversal for one involved in the "sin unto death." The term "unto death" does not necessarily mean that inclusion in the realm of death is final (with Westcott, *Epistles of John*, p. 210, and against Law, *Tests of Life*, p. 139). In fact, 1 John 2:2 may be the guarantee that one who commits the "sin unto death" may still have hope.

[65] A parallel to this may be seen in the prayer of Jesus in John 17:9 in which Jesus prays for the ones given to him (the believers) but not for the world (*erōtan* is used). Cf. again on effective prayer as occurring only within the believing community Nauck, *Die Tradition*, pp. 145-46.

[66] Klöpper, "Zur Lehre von der Sünde in 1. Johannesbrief," pp. 590-91, stresses that the "sin unto death" in 1 John is associated with these false teachers who disrupt the believing community. In 1 John this sin and group are sharply distinguished, with prayer concerning them discouraged, from believers and their sin so that no believer will through a sentimental attachment pray for disruptive heretics. Such association should be rejected (cf. 2 John 10). Klöpper makes the important observation that the discouragement of prayer is directed against these community disrupters who have proven to be heretical outsiders and not against those who have never made any profession or pretense of association with the believing Christian community.

[67] This view is foundational to the interpretations of E. H. Sugden, "Critical Note on I John v. 16," *Expositor*, 2:3 (1882), 159; O. Bauernfeind, "Die Fürbitte angesichts der 'Sünde zum Tode,'" *Von der Antike zum Christentum: Untersuchungen als Festgabe für Victor Schultze zum 80. Geburtstag*, Stettin, 1931, pp. 43-54; and P. Trudinger, "Concerning Sins, Mortal and Otherwise: A Note on 1 John 5, 16-17," *Bib*, 52 (1971), 541-42.

[68] The view of Bauernfeind, "Die Fürbitte angesichts der 'Sünde zum Tode,'" pp. 43-54, is rather distinctive. He argues that the 1 John passage is a cautious attempt to regulate community life and prayer. In the past, certain (pneumatic) persons, impelled by the Spirit, dared to pray for the ultimate "sin unto death." 1

(that is 'the sin unto death' in contrast to 'the sin not unto death'), in order that one should question or debate it."[69] Trudinger's main argument[70] is that *erōtan* usually means "ask a question" and thus it should have that meaning in 1 John 5:16. However, as he notes, *erōtan* in the Johannine material in John 13-17 does mean "prayer to God." It would be unlikely that in a context about prayer (1 John 5:14-17) *erōtan* is to be understood otherwise.[71]

If the "sin unto death" represents the sin of the unbeliever/outsider, the "sin not unto death" represents the sins of believers (cf. 1 John 1:5-2:2). These sins of believers are the focus of attention in the passage as a matter of serious concern for effective community prayer (5:14-16b). After the aside concerning the "sin unto death" (5:16c), the point is reaffirmed that there are believers' sins which, although very serious ("all unrighteousness is sin"), are in the category of "sin not unto death" (5:17). Then, immediately after this discussion of believers' sins (5:14-17), it is asserted that believers do not sin (5:18; cf. 3:4-10).

It is at this point that the meaning of the terms "sin not unto death" and "sin unto death" in 1 John 5:16-17 applies to the solution of the larger problematic in 1 John in which it is stated that believers both sin (1:5-2:2) and do not (and cannot) sin (3:4-10). For the author to say that believers do not sin (5:18) immediately after a discussion of believers' sins (5:14-17) can mean only that two different concepts of sin are in view. The believer does "sin not unto death" but does not and cannot "sin unto death." He has been transferred out of death into life (3:14), and therefore his sin can be described only as "sin not unto death." The believer's relationship to God is contrasted with the statement that the whole world is in the grasp of the devil (5:19). The world is the designation for that which is the very opposite of the believing community. Thus the world does not know either believers or God (3:1). It hates believers (3:13) and is the source and support of deniers of Jesus Christ (4:5). Believers are commanded to love not the world (2:15) but fellow believers. In fact, believers have overcome the world (5:4-5), which is to say that they have overcome the Evil One in

---

John is attempting to control this pneumatic prayer, but does not go so far as to forbid it. Thus, Bauernfeind, p. 52, paraphrases 1 John 5:16c: "There is, however, a sin unto death. Intercession for it, as you know, is a work which will take place only through the direct work of the divine Spirit himself. I naturally do not speak of this work so that anyone should dispute it" (translation my own). Apart from the problem of Bauernfeind's interpretation of *erōtan* (cf. below), this view simply assumes a controversy concerning pneumatic and regulated prayers that is not indicated in 1 John.

[69] Trudinger, "Concerning Sins," p. 542; i.e. a believer is to pray for sinning brothers, not to worry about gradations of sin.

[70] *Ibid.*, p. 541. He also states that the traditional interpretation of 1 John 5:16c (i.e. discouragement of prayer) does not make sense in view of 1 John 5:17 and that the *hina* clause is taken as an objective rather than a final clause. The interpretation offered in this article does take the *hina* clause in a final sense. As noted earlier, 1 John 5:17 (with the adversative *kai*) resumes the main point of concern, believers' sins, after the aside concerning the sin of outsiders.

[71] Trudinger, *ibid.*, p. 542, acknowledges that a difficulty with his own view is that he makes both *legein* and *erōtan* intransitive, which is not the usual case in the NT.

whose grasp the world is (2:13-14). A believer (*pas ho gegennēmenos ek tou theou*), therefore, does not "sin unto death"; indeed, he cannot "sin unto death" because the Son of God (*ho gennētheis ek tou theou*) keeps him (*auton*) from it; the believer is beyond the grasp of the Evil One (5:18).[72]

V

1 John 5:16-17, then, is one of several texts that deal with the problem of the "sins of the righteous" ("sins within"), but which notes the fact of the "sins of the unrighteous" ("sins without") as well.[73] It is unlike Matt 12:31-32 (and parallels), Heb and Herm in that it does not speak of sin(s) for which there is absolutely no repentance. It is similar to such passages as Matt 18:15-22, John 13:1-18, 1 Cor 5:1-5, 2 Cor 2:6-11, Gal 6:1-2, 2 Thess 3:14-15 and 1 Tim 1:20 in that it deals with the problem of sins within the Christian community, but it differs from all of them both by the way in which the sin problem is handled (in 1 John 5:16-17 by effective prayer) and by the setting in which the problem is discussed (in 1 John 5:16-17 by reference to two types of sin, one of which believers do not commit). The Jas 5:15-20 passage is the closest parallel to 1 John 5:16-17 in that it relates community sins to prayer, but its context is quite different from that of 1 John.[74]

[72] This analysis of 1 John 5:18 interprets the *ho gennētheis* as a reference to the Son of God (Jesus Christ) and the *ho gegennēmenos* as a reference to the believer (note the *pas*; cf. 3:9), and accepts the textual reading *auton* rather than *heauton* as the object of "keeps." The view that *ho gennētheis* refers to the Son of God is supported by the change from the perfect to the aorist participle; by equating the *auton* of 18b with the *autou* of 18c; by the fact that the Son of God is the opposite of the Evil One (cf. 1 John 3:8); and by the Johannine parallel of John 17:12 and Rev 3:10 (cf. Schnackenburg, *Die Johannesbriefe*, p. 281). (Note that the alternate text of John 1:13 gives the title *ho gennētheis* to Christ; cf. also Philo, *De conf lingu* 63 where the one who is undifferentiated from the image of God is called *ho gennētheis*.) With respect to the textual problem of *auton/heauton*, cf. B. M. Metzger, *A Textual Commentary on the Greek New Testament*, London/New York, 1971, p. 719, for a defense of *auton*. Not only does *auton* have better MSS support, but the internal argument demands *auton* if *ho gennētheis* is the Son of God. The *auton* would be easily changed to *heauton* if the *ho gennētheis* was misunderstood to refer to the believer (the change could be accidental as well, since *auton* occurs following *tērei*, which ends in *-ei*). This misunderstanding was present also in texts that read *auton*; cf. the *hē gennēsis* for *ho gennētheis* in 1852, 2138 and the complete Latin tradition. Schnackenburg, *Die Johannesbriefe*, pp. 280-81, understands the *ho gennētheis* to refer to the believer and the *auton* to God. The expression, *tērein ton theon* is equated with *echein ton theon* (1 John 2:23; 5:12; 2 John 9).

[73] For the Jewish background of this distinction, cf. especially Pss Sol, but also 1 Enoch, 4 Ezra and 1QS.

[74] Not all texts on community discipline have been mentioned here (cf. e.g. Acts 5:1-11). For a broader discussion of discipline texts in early Christianity cf. the recent works of G. Forkman, *The Limits of the Religious Community: Expulsion from the Religious Community within the Qumran Sect, within Rabbinic Judaism, and within Primitive Christianity*, ConNT, 5, Lund, 1972, and C. J. Roetzel, *Judgement in the Community: A Study of the Relationship between Eschatology and Ecclesiology in Paul*, Leiden, 1972.

In 1 John the believer does not and cannot "sin unto death" (3:4-10; 5:18), for such sin belongs to the devil and his children from whom believers have been released. Believers do, however, "sin not unto death" (1:5-2:2; 5:16-17). In these cases it is the responsibility of the believing community to exercise effective prayer for the sinning brother and thus bring to him, through the work of God, a reconfirmation of life (5:14-16).

The best summary of this exegetical study would be a fully developed, interpretive paraphrase of 1 John 5:16-18:

[16] If any member of the believing community sees a fellow believer committing any one of the "sins of the righteous," i.e. those which do *not* preclude membership in the believing community, he should pray for him, and God will give to the sinning brother reconfirmation (cf. 1 John 1:6-10) of his transfer from the realm of death to the realm of life (cf. 1 John 3:14). Indeed, this will be done for any and all brothers who sin in this way. There is, of course, sin which *does* preclude membership in the believing community (i.e. murder = hatred of believers and lying = denial of Jesus); it is sin in the realm of death. I do not speak concerning that sin unto death in order that anyone should pray about it. [17] All unrighteousness is sin; however, there is sin which does *not* preclude membership in the believing community. [18] We know that every one who has been born of God (i.e. believers in the community) does not sin in any way which precludes membership in the believing community. The Son of God keeps each believer, and therefore the devil is not able to hold him.

Multiple Meanings in the Gospel of John

RUSSELL SHEDD

Introduction

Scientific hermeneutics characterized by scholarly exegesis has rendered the student of the Bible a great service by providing a relative assurance that the meaning derived from the Scripture is solely that which the author intended.[1] So it should be. All honest biblical hermeneutics must eschew the unwarranted temptation, ancient and modern, to confuse exegesis with any possible number of applications.[2] However, despite the disfavor into which typological hermeneutics has fallen, the pendulum of late has been swinging back in Johannine studies.[3] The "new look" should not be confused with a search for ingenious connections between the text of the Gospel of John and the fertile imagination of the interpreter; rather, there is an increasing awareness that the Evangelist intended his readers to grasp two or more meanings subtly intertwined. This is John's way of presenting both his and Jesus' two-world outlook. By giving more than one meaning to selected key words, the spiritual reality is allowed to shine through. Long ago Clement of Alexandria perceptively called John's masterpiece a "spiritual gospel."

[1] E. C. Blackman, "The Task of Exegesis," in *The Background of the New Testament and Its Eschatology*, ed. by W. D. Davies and D. Daube, Cambridge, 1964, p. 5.

[2] Andrés Kirk, "A Bíblia e Sua Hermenêutica," *Tópicos do Momento*, São Paulo, 1973, pp. 4ff.

[3] E.g. O. Cullmann, *Early Christian Worship*, London, 1953; A. Guilding, *The Fourth Gospel and Jewish Worship*, London, 1960; T. F. Glasson, *Moses in the Fourth Gospel*, London, 1963; J. Crehan, *The Theology of St. John*, London, 1965, to list but a few. Blackman asks if Newman was "completely wrong to insist that 'mystical interpretation and orthodoxy stand or fall together'" ("The Task of Exegesis," p. 6). O. Cullmann, "Der johanneische Gebrauch doppeldeutiger Ausdrüke als Schlüssel zum Verständnis des vierten Evangeliums," *TZ*, 4 (1948), 360-72.

Russell Shedd, Professor of New Testament and Greek Exegesis in the Faculdade Teológica Batista de São Paulo, São Paulo, Brazil. B.A., Wheaton College; M.A., Wheaton College Graduate School; B.D., Faith Seminary; Ph.D., New College, University of Edinburgh.

Nevertheless, when looking for clues to the author's intention we must be ever cautious. "How easy it is for us to attribute to the original speaker or writer ideas which never entered his mind when he uttered the expression which is being interpreted."[4] Right at the outset we are forced to ask ourselves how we are to recognize the indications that John wishes his readers to perceive more than the literal and obvious meaning in a word, phrase or extended passage. The answer can be found in peculiarities and hints provided by the author's explanations buried in the context, near or distant. We begin by examining the "signs" and continue with some specific examples of words and phrases.

Multiple Meanings in the Signs

If John was concerned to convey more in the miracle of the transformation of water to wine than the wondrous power of Jesus, what was his further purpose? No declaration of specific significance is brought out either by Jesus or the author. However, the striking phrase, "my hour has not yet come" (2:4), is tantalizing. "My hour" is surely not intended to be taken in one sense alone, for Jesus does in fact perform the miracle suggested by Mary's request. Repeated uses of the same or a corresponding phrase in 7:30, 8:20, 13:1 and 17:1 show that Jesus refers to a more decisive "hour" than that in which he performs his first miracle. Outside of this passage, "the hour" of Christ denotes the time in which his life blood will be poured out in redeeming love. Many naturally would have understood that the appointed time for working miracles had not begun. But Jesus' reply shows that Mary and he are thinking on two distinct wavelengths. The embarrassment created by a failing wine supply at an oriental wedding feast cannot be compared to the universal disaster of sin's corrupting power (Jesus' basic concern). Even a seemingly unlimited supply of pure water for Jewish ceremonial cleansing is incapable of diminishing the eternal effects of sin's contamination. So the Lamb of God that comes "by water" must also come "by blood" that he might take away the sins of the world (John 1:29; 1 John 5:6). In the Synoptic parable, the "new wine" is better, coming as it does after the old has failed (2:10; cf. Matt 9:17 and parallels). We may well be persuaded that John relates the first miracle to emphasize the same truth. By this means the historically actual event of the Cana miracle is transformed from seeing to believing, from facts to an apprehension of their eternal salvific intent.

For John, Jesus' miracles are "signs" (*sēmeia*, "omens," "portents"), not primarily in the fact that they point to the contrast between the present and the future but in distinguishing external event from internal truth.[5] To a degree, we may be correct in seeing John's "signs" taking the

---

[4] A. B. Mickelsen, *Interpreting the Bible*, Grand Rapids, 1963, p. 56. C. H. Dodd, *The Old Testament in the New*, Philadelphia, 1963, p. 8, contrasts the NT as a whole with Philo's writings in the paucity of allegorical use of OT history.

[5] R. H. Lightfoot, *St. John's Gospel*, London, 1960, p. 22. The signs serve also as credentials to authenticate the divine commission of the Messiah (5:36; 10:25, 30, 37; 14:10; 20:21).

place of the parables in the Synoptics,[6] although there is an important difference. The events of a parable do not generally draw significance from being actual occurrences. The Johannine miracle, on the other hand, to constitute a sign must be rooted in history, just as the gospel cannot be cut off from the saving events of the life and death of Christ. Neither were the signs selected, as were the parables, to explicitly "make intellectual concepts easier to understand by means of concrete illustrations from familiar fields."[7] John's miracles provided visual perception and consequent assurance for faith in Christ as the unique Savior of the world.

The "signs" by their peculiar twofold nature provoke the crisis of belief and unbelief;[8] consequently John says that through this "sign" Jesus "manifested his glory; and his disciples believed in him" (2:11). The incredulous Jews sought signs that conformed to the popular messianic expectation (2:18) but failed to see the inner light thrown by faith upon the Person of Jesus and the nature of his work.[9] For this reason "many believed in his name when they saw the signs which he did" (2:23), but "Jesus did not trust himself to them, since he himself knew what was in man" (2:24).

In other words, where belief does not penetrate beyond intellectualized wonder in the presence of observable divine power (note Nicodemus' admission in 3:2) we are faced with truncated faith. John's concern is to warn his readers against a belief that is not fully operative on both levels—the sensate and the transcendent worlds apprehensible by the mind and the spirit. Mental assent alone is insufficient for the saving knowledge of God (17:3), but it is still essential.[10] Lying at the heart of the Son's revelation of the invisible Father (1:18) are the events of the Incarnation (1:14; 1 John 1:1-3) and the operation of the work which he was commissioned to do (17:4). Jesus chided Philip for failing to see through the outward reality to the inward truth (14:8-11).

It is conceivable that Thomas in his post-resurrection encounter with Jesus might have seen and touched the raised body of the Lord. Trusting his senses and the evidence, he would have identified him with the historical Jesus in whose company he had walked for so many months. Such intellectual faith established on sufficient evidence, however, was not complete in itself. It did prepare the ground for full belief shown through a heart moved to worshipful confession and obedience—"My Lord and my God" (20:28). Outward seeing and inward believing combined to bring about the experience of transforming trust. Equally blessed are all who

[6]This does not deny that John has some parables, although they are less in the nature of the *parabolē* and more in that of the *paroimia* corresponding to the Hebrew term *mashalim*, i.e. allegorical comparisons such as are found in John 10 and 15.

[7]Hauck, *TDNT*, 5, 756.

[8]M. C. Tenney, *John: the Gospel of Belief*, Grand Rapids, 1948, p. 177.

[9]R. V. G. Tasker, *The Gospel According to St. John*, London, 1960, pp. 61-62.

[10]There can be little doubt as to what the Fourth Evangelist's reaction would be to the existentialist theologians' asseverations that faith cannot be grounded in dogmatic or historical propositions! Faith, for John, most certainly must be grounded in facts before it can grow into commitment.

similarly ground faith in history and manifest it in worship and life (20:29).[11]

This understanding of the necessary historical demonstration of the work and person of the Son in signs may throw some light on those difficult words, "except ye see signs and wonders, ye will not believe" (4:48). Over against a negative expression of disappointment with the Jews or Herod's entourage, as Knox would have it,[12] Jesus simply asserts a fact: without the mighty works of God in history, culminating in the central sign of the death and resurrection of Christ, there can be no faith at all (cf. 5:17; 9:4; 7:31; 10:37-38; 14:10-11). Further confirmation can be found in 2:18 where the Jews' quest for a sign does not bring a negative reaction from Jesus as it does in the Synoptics (cf. Matt 12:38-40; Luke 11:29-32): he simply points them specifically to the greatest miracle of all, the sign of the resurrection (2:19, 20).

The twofold nature of the "signs" is confirmed by the meaning Jesus himself gives to the multiplication of the loaves.[13] The selection of the miracles by John, far from being chosen with a view to supplementing the Synoptic record,[14] is made with the purpose of portraying the unity of material and spiritual reality in Christ. To the Jews' challenge, "What sign therefore do you perform so that we might believe on you?" (6:30), Jesus' answer is incisive, tearing the ground from anyone who would see him as merely a notable miracle worker in the order of a Moses or Elijah. The sign that uniquely produces and alone can substantiate faith is none other than the cross.[15] The broken bread of the miracle anticipates the true bread (i.e. Jesus' flesh) "broken" on the cross that gives life to the world (6:32-33). Accompanying the broken bread, Jesus announces that his shed blood slakes spiritual thirst (6:55). The words *alēthēs*, "true" (6:55), and *alēthinon*, "genuine" (6:32), furnish a key to the deeper understanding of the physical terms "bread," "blood" and "flesh," just as Jesus' claim to be the Bread of Life.

The material bread, signifying Christ's historical flesh crucified, gains its life-giving and sustaining power through the Spirit. The flesh alone, whether in Jesus' messianic fulfillment of Jewish expectations that omitted Isaiah's Suffering Servant and Daniel's humiliated Son of Man, or in later Christian formal participation in eucharistic celebrations, "profits nothing" (6:63). "Yet the evangelist has endeavoured more than any other to avoid the misleading conclusion which could be drawn from this that the flesh, the *sarx*, as a medium of the working of the Spirit, is therefore really not to be taken seriously."[16]

---

[11] Rom 10:9 makes salvation's requirement twofold: inward belief accompanied by confession with the lips.

[12] Tasker, *The Gospel According to St. John*, p. 82.

[13] Cf. Cullmann, *Early Christian Worship*, p. 84, for a discussion of the symbolic meaning of the healing sign at the Pool of Bethesda.

[14] Cf. D. M. Smith, "The Sources of the Gospel of John," *NTS*, 10, no. 3 (1964), 349.

[15] See Glasson's chapter on the serpent in the wilderness, *Moses in the Fourth Gospel*, pp. 33-35.

[16] Cullmann, *Early Christian Worship*, p. 100.

Before Jesus heals the man born blind, he prefaces his work with the declaration, "When I am in the world, I am the light of the world" (9:5). By healing physical eyes, Jesus not only provided grounds for belief in his supernatural power to transform material reality but also to remove scales from the eyes of the heart.[17] The performance of this sign is part of the necessary finishing of the works that the Father has ordered before the approaching night closes in (9:4). The "night" points forward to the hardening rejection of Christ and his word by Jewish authorities, culminating in the crucifixion.

The details analogously signify the saving illumination that Christ as the world's light brings to men born in sin (9:1). Perhaps Jesus intended the mud on the eyes to represent conviction of sin and the washing to symbolize repentance in baptism.[18] Be that as it may, Jesus' dramatic action answers the crowd's question, "How opened he thine eyes?" (9:10, 26).[19] But the gateway to seeing the glory of God cannot be found without belief. That glory shines dimly through the "sign" (9:3). The healed man's new spiritual vision brought with it expulsion from the synagogue (9:22, 34). Nor should excommunication surprise anyone, since Judaism blinded men by giving the illusion of vision. As Jesus put it, "Ye say, 'We see.' Therefore your sin remaineth" (9:41b).

The delegation of Greeks who desired to "see Jesus" were not really ignored or sidetracked by Jesus' answer to Andrew and Philip (12:21-22). The "seeing" that will eternally benefit the beholders is the glorification of the Son of Man. Such glory is that seen in the grain of wheat planted in death and which through resurrection bears much fruit. The salvation coming equally to Jews and Gentiles through the release of the divine life of the Spirit in true disciples of Christ depends on that double perception (12:24-26). Otherwise, the prophecy of Isa 6 that followed his vision of the glory of the Lord (12:40-41) will be fulfilled in blinded eyes and hardened hearts (12:39-40). The Evangelist precedes this evaluation of the general Jewish rejection of Christ with a citation from Isa 53 (12:38). The "report" that too often has been disbelieved is the redemption historically fulfilled in Christ's death demanding faith of the hearer. We are reminded by the Baptizer's words, "*Look* at the Lamb of God which taketh away the sins of the world" (1:29), so that we might believe.[20]

The raising of Lazarus is specifically declared to be a "sign" (12:18).[21] But to what did it point? Jesus' affirmation, "I am the resurrec-

[17] Cf. Mark 2:5-12 for a similar connection between healing and the annulling of sin's effects.

[18] Cf. Cullmann, *Early Christian Worship*, pp. 102-5. There is hardly any doubt that the word "bathed" in 13:10 refers to baptism, while the washing of the feet points to the daily cleansing of the Christian in his walk through confession and restoration both by Christ and his followers (13:14). See further on "water" in Glasson, *Moses in the Fourth Gospel*, pp. 57-59.

[19] Cf. the New Scofield Bible's note on 9:10 which delineates the progress in the healed man's apprehension of the Person of Christ.

[20] Limits on space do not allow for discussion of John's use of "light" as essential to faith-vision. See Crehan, *The Theology of St. John*, pp. 60-62.

[21] Rengstorf, *TDNT*, 7, 246, reminds us that "Raising the dead and healings are typical wonders of the Messianic age."

tion," can most fully be understood in the context of John's characteristic hermeneutic. Christ's effective power to counteract the effects of death in the physical realm gave ample basis to his claim to be the life-giver on the spiritual plane to all who believe.[22] The raising of Lazarus' physical body palpably shows by analogy the invisible raising of believers with their Lord (cf. Rom 6:4-5; Eph 2:5; Col 2:12, 13; etc.). However, this often observed evidence of realized eschatology is by no means limited to the spiritual reality, to be grasped only by faith's apprehension. A future, physical resurrection, a frequent theme in the Fourth Gospel, must not be excluded (cf. 5:21-29; 6:40, 45; 11:24-26; 12:48). "He that believeth in me, though he were dead, yet shall he live" refers to the future visible resurrection; while "whosoever liveth and believeth in me shall never die" signifies the present invisible reality of the new age (11:25b, 26). In Jesus' self-affirmation, "I am the resurrection," we are not supposed to see a mere figure of speech or a metaphor; on the contrary the Lord propounds that in his person ("I am") and work (atoning passion) two realities, the physical and spiritual, are telescoped into one. To all who believe in him, Christ guarantees life, through the twofold nature of his life: (1) the eternal invisible Logos that was with God and was God and (2) the human life visible in the flesh have united in the incarnate Son that we might all partake of his fullness (1:1ff., 14, 16).

In the signs John calls for us to see a demonstration of the infusion of the new age into the old. In the operation of the miracle something in the familiar world of the senses changes. Through the divine meaning we are brought into contact with God's eternal realities. Just as the sign participates in both aeons, it is John's thesis that faith must also be rooted in the uncreated and the created worlds.[23]

Multiple Meaning in Words and Phrases

The Apostle John wrote against an intellectual and religious background that readily imbibed gnostic dualism. Irreconcilable separation between light and darkness, flesh and spirit, God and man, and time and eternity has impressed some interpreters of the Gospel with the gnostic influence on the Evangelist. However, the more closely we look, the more sure we are that "The resemblances between John and Gnosticism . . . are a verbal bridge by which John expresses his essential antagonism to gnostic-type thought."[24] For matter is not despised, nor is salvation attained by esoteric "gnosis" limited to the privileged few. The manifestation of the never-seen God by the Son through incarnation in human flesh is the new

[22] Cf. J. H. Bernard, *Gospel According to St. John,* ICC, Edinburgh, 1928, 2, 388.

[23] C. S. Lewis in "Transposition," *Transposition and Other Essays,* Portuguese ed., Lisboa, 1964, pp. 15-16, calls for more than symbolism in the Incarnation. Rather we are to recognize an elevation of the inferior reality to the superior. The spiritual reality lends significance to natural reality, and in some measure transforms it. Such is the case in an ordinance like the Lord's Supper.

[24] E. E. Ellis, *The World of St. John,* New York and London, 1965, p. 23.

and living way back to the Father. We might say that John displaces gnostic dualism with his doctrine of the Logos (1:1, 14; 1 John 1:1; Rev 19:13).

John is completely out of step with Greek philosopical speculation in which the Logos is divine reason, or Stoic dogma that affirmed the Logos to be the mind behind the pattern and order of the universe such as Cicero's "soul of the world." The Logos in John is a person, true deity in the full Hebraic conception of a personal God.[25] It is he, the Logos, who lightens every man by his coming into the world. By him life on a new plane is offered to all men (1:4, 9), but not silently or immaterially. The Logos was and is a message both in life and words. "My sayings are spirit and life" (6:63) makes the identification clear. Although *rhēmata* ("words") is the term here, *logos* is used in 12:48: " . . . the word (*logos*) that I have spoken will be his judge on the last day." More striking still is the concept of Jesus "abiding" in the believer (15:3) explained in 15:7: "If ye abide in me and *my sayings* abide in you, ask what you will. . . ." Plainly, Christ abides in his followers along with his word. "Jesus embodies in Himself both God's creative Word and God's communicative Word."[26] This is in keeping with the Hebrew designation of the Holy Place in the Temple of Solomon as $d^e b\hat{\imath}r$ ("word"). The term $d\bar{a}b\bar{a}r$ has a dual significance. On the one hand it refers to the hinterground of meaning, the inner reality of the word, but on the other hand it refers to the dynamic event in which that inner reality becomes manifest."[27] It is most likely, then, that John's use of Logos should be understood in just such a Hebraic thought world.

What are we to make of *ta idia*, "his own," "his home" (1:11)? This may offer still another example of the intentional ambiguity in John. John's emphasis on the Jewish rejection of Christ suggests that "his own" refers to the Holy Land and its covenant people. On the other hand, the meaning may include all men in the world created through the agency of the Logos (cf. 1:3). Maybe the Evangelist does not wish for us to choose between the broader meaning or the narrower. Both are true. Both "homes," Israel and the world, ironically reject their Creator-redeemer. Nevertheless, some welcome him and thereby are granted the right to share the sonship of God (1:12).

One of the clearest examples in John of "double reference" is found in the imperative, "Destroy this temple" (2:19). The plain meaning would denote the temple rebuilt by Herod over a period of forty-six years. But lest the reader miss Jesus' intention, vs. 21 states plainly that "he spoke of the temple of his body." But who would have been likely to have captured the hidden meaning behind those words of Christ? The most natural understanding of his challenge would have looked forward to the judgment

---

[25] In the Targum of Jonathan the "Word of God" is used as a periphrasis for "God" because of the ever present Jewish concern to avoid the use of the divine name.

[26] Ellis, *The World of St. John*, p. 27. C. F. H. Henry put it this way, "The fountain and content of revelation converge and coincide in the incarnate Logos," in a lecture presented at the Faculdade Teológica Batista de São Paulo, Aug. 2, 1973.

[27] T. F. Torrance, "Royal Priesthood," *SJT*, Occasional Papers no. 3 (1955), p. 1.

to be meted out on the entire system of Jewish worship, especially following the destruction of Jerusalem in A.D. 70. On the deeper spiritual level, the whole community of God's redeemed form a temple which is the "Body of Christ." And that temple grows directly out from Jesus' death and resurrection (12:24). It is not likely that the rank and file of Christians would have been unfamiliar with the Pauline and Petrine teaching regarding this new temple preserved in several of their letters (cf. 1 Cor 3:16; 2 Cor 6:16; Eph 2:21; 1 Pet 2:4-6).[28]

In this same vein, "the house of my Father" (2:16) means the temple. Such a periphrasis arises naturally from the citation of Ps 68:10 (LXX), "The zeal of your house . . . ," referring to God. When Jesus changed the tense from the past to the future (*kataphagetai* versus *katephagen*, LXX), the disciples were given grounds for a messianic reference.

In the only other use of the phrase "my Father's house" (14:2)[29] a similar temple typology may be included in Jesus' discourse. The Lord states the necessity of his departing to prepare a place, a possible hidden reference to the cross, for he declares that he will leave the disciples for only a "little while" (16:16). On a distinct level of meaning Jesus speaks of the ascension, "I came forth from the Father . . . and go to the Father" (16:28).[30] This latter conception fits the generally accepted understanding of the Father's house as God's heavenly abode. But this meaning does not exhaust its intended significance, for the resurrection, the ground of the formation of the universal church, is also the Father's house.[31] It too has many *monai* ("abiding places"), that is, congregations or individuals that worship God in Spirit and truth (4:23). Such worship depends neither on race nor geography but only on the receiving of the Holy Spirit which the raising and glorifying of Christ make available (7:39).

Further hints that this meaning lodged in the mind of the Evangelist are found in the context. The Spirit of truth comes to dwell (*menei*) with and "be in" the believing individual and community (14:17b). This is explained as being equivalent to Christ himself coming to his disciples (14:18). Still more significant is the declaration that both the Father and the Son will come and make their "abode" (*monēn*, 14:23; *monai*, 14:2) with the disciple who loves Christ and keeps his words. To the Jewish mind, where God dwells is the temple and his Shekinah glory is manifested in it. The coming of the Paraclete in John 14-16 fulfills the new covenant promise of the pouring out of the Spirit to indwell the new temple composed of God's people both on earth and in heaven. The extended

[28] R. H. Lightfoot, *St. John's Gospel*, p. 114, sees a triple meaning: (1) condemnation of the temple service; (2) a sign of the destruction of the old order and the replacement with God's new order, the Christian church; (3) the death and resurrection of Christ making possible the inauguration of the new order. Cf. E. C. Hoskyns, *The Fourth Gospel*, London, 1947, p. 195.

[29] Just prior to 14:2, Peter is insisting that he will follow Christ to death and also to glory (John 13:36-37; 17:24; 21:18-19).

[30] See Bernard, *Gospel According to St. John*, 2, 533, for discussion.

[31] Paul in 2 Cor 5:1 also assures us that the New Temple composed of the true people of God exists on the earthly plane as well as the heavenly. See E. E. Ellis, *Paul and His Recent Interpreters*, Grand Rapids, 1961, pp. 41-43.

metaphor of the Vine and the Branches teaches the same truth. The True Vine is equivalent to the Father's House (2:19, 21; 14:2) while the "branches" are equivalent to the "abiding places" (14:2). John 14 is cast in the context of worship and protection, while the key to John 15 is the obedience and discipline of the fellowship. But in both Christ through the Holy Spirit is living out his resurrection life.

Since the Father dwells both in heaven (16:28; 17:5; 20:17) and in his House (15:23) on earth, free access to him through Christ must be understood in two ways. First, the way to him in our present human life is following and obeying Jesus (cf. 8:12), believing on him as the truth, and receiving his life through birth from above (14:6). Second, it is no less true that the way to the Father in glory at the end of this physical life is through Christ, who transforms death into full life (11:25-26). In sum, John says that Jesus Christ continues to be the living bridge between God and man, time and eternity, creation and Creator. The point of convergence in time is at the cross and the empty tomb; in space he joins two or three gathered "in the name" of their Lord. For Christ is at one and the same time on earth in intimate fellowship with his followers (cf. Matt 28:20) even while he is at the right hand of the Father in glory (13:36; 17:5; 1 John 2:1).[32]

Evidently John's futurist and present (realized) eschatology are both present in one and the same terminology, forming yet another example of the multiple meanings the Evangelist intends for us in his Gospel. No one is supposed, therefore, to be confused by Jesus' declaration that the future hour is already present ("now is") in which the dead spiritually (see the immediate context of 5.24 where believers pass from death unto life) and the dead physically are in view. "The hour is coming in which all that are in the graves shall hear his voice and shall come forth . . ." (5:25, 28). Temple is right, but he does not go far enough in perceiving that "Death is used throughout (5:19-27) in both its senses—physical and spiritual. The Son raised some who were physically dead during His earthly mission. This was a *sign* of the quickening of the multitudes spiritually dead."[33]

When Nicodemus came to Jesus to discuss God's truth with "the teacher come from God," he was caught quite off guard by distinct meanings within words such as *anōthen*, "again" (Gal 4:9), "from the beginning" (Luke 1:3), "from above" (John 3:31; 19:11, 23), and *pneuma*, "spirit," "wind" (3:5, 6, 8). Since Nicodemus was thinking solely on the earthly level, he gives the term the natural meaning of "again" and skeptically objects to a return to his mother's womb for rebirth. But Jesus meant more than "again"; all men must be born from above, that is, from the Spirit. Nicodemus' myopia leads him to construe rebirth on horizontal terms alone. The Jews that reject Christ are "from below" while Christ is "from above" (8:23). Christ's coming from above, from the "bosom of the Father," has manifested and offered the new life of the Kingdom. However,

---

[32] Cf. R. E. Brown, *The Gospel According to John*, Garden City, 1970, p. 627. See also R. H. Gundry, "In My Father's House Are Many *Monai* (John 14:2)," *ZNW*, 58 (1967), 68-72.

[33] W. Temple, *Readings in the Gospel of John*, London, 1942, p. 113.

we must not overlook the earthly dimension. The new birth from above is also out of water (*ex hydatos*), a probable reference to the baptismal confession and repentance of the novice believer (cf. Rom 10:9; Ezek 36:25-27). Both the Spirit from above, invisible in his action as the wind, and the visible human participation, symbolized in the dying and rising again with the Mediator who shares the life from God, must be operative in regeneration. Nicodemus, along with all men, heard the challenge to accept the twofold reality of the one essential salvation experience, involving as it does human response in the world and God's action through the Spirit.

Similarly, *hypsōthēnai*, "lifted up," "exalted" (3:14; 8:28; 12:32, 34), bears a double meaning in the Fourth Gospel. Glasson has already noted that this term is used with a dual reference, "or rather it includes as in a single concept the crucifixion and the glorification of Jesus."[34] The Johannine usage of the term "lift up" or "exalt" corresponds precisely to the use of the key Johannine concept of "glorification." That is why in 1:14 the verb "beheld" (*etheasametha*) is used with reference to the glory of the Incarnate Logos. This term *theasthai* is never used in the NT of spiritual vision, yet over twenty times it denotes "seeing" through bodily eyes. [35] The glory with which John is concerned in 1:14 is the manifestation of the presence of God in the life of the Messiah, perceived by disciple-eyewitnesses. The crisis of this glorification had its denouement in Jesus' passion, i.e. his lifting up (7:30; 12:16, 23), and was consummated in the resurrection and ascension to glory (17:5; 13:32).[36]

Jesus predicts plainly that the Jews will "lift up" the Son of Man (8:28). And on the middle cross of Golgotha that prediction was fulfilled. Nevertheless, Jesus continued, "Then you will know that I am he" (8:28, lit. "I am," a probable reference to the hidden divine name). Certainly the cross in and of itself would never persuade Jesus' Jewish opponents that he was the Messiah, but the ascension to glory (cf. Acts 2:33; 5:31) and return in power would convince not only Jews (Rev 1:7) but all men (John 12:32). Being voluntarily pinned to the raised cross (12:33 makes this physical meaning inescapable) means that inevitably the Father will exalt him to the position of glory at his right hand (17:5; this same cause-effect relationship between the Suffering Servant's humiliation and exaltation is found in Phil 2:9-11).[37] It is therefore our conclusion that the four uses of *hypsoō* in John are intended to bear both earthly and heavenly frames of reference.

The fundamental demand upon the disciple is "to follow." In keeping with numerous other concepts in the Gospel of John, "following," too, is employed with distinct dimensions of meaning. First of all, we are informed of two disciples of the Baptist (Andrew and his unnamed companion) who "followed" Jesus as he walked. Upon turning, Jesus asked them what they were looking for; their response was, "Where do you

---

[34] Glasson, *Moses in the Fourth Gospel*, p. 35.

[35] Bernard, *Gospel According to St. John*, 1, 21.

[36] *Ibid.*, 2, 525.

[37] G. A. Turner and J. R. Mantey, *The Gospel of John*, Grand Rapids, n.d., p. 254, see still another meaning: "When Christ is extolled in thought, sermon or song, people are attracted to His person and message."

abide?"[38]   Jesus thereupon extended to them the invitation to come and see (1:35-39), but doubtless not merely on the material level with a view to satisfying their curiosity over his street address, but more cogently on the plane of eternal verities (cf. 12:35).

It is evident that discipleship in the typical oriental style requires physical accompaniment of a rabbi. But in John, Jesus walks and talks on his way to Jerusalem and the cross.[39] The two levels of significance in "following" became critical in Perea. There Jesus invited them to accompany him back to Judea (11:7). The disciples objected strenuously in view of the perils of stoning they had only recently escaped. Then Jesus told them that to remain behind would be to walk in the night and to be certain of stumbling (11:9, 10). None but he walks by his own light. As the disciples follow they have light (present tense), for Jesus is their Guide, but as they see him sacrificed and exalted for them, they are promised a share in the light of life (see the future tense "shall have" in 8:12). Their future physical presence at the cross and the empty tomb is essential to their personal assurance and subsequent witness to all those that will "follow" in spiritual commitment.

The way in which the sheep are to follow their shepherd (10:4-5) is not expounded. The shepherd "going before" may well point to the cross. In any case, the sheep recognize his voice and obey his directions, which is equivalent to following. It is because the disciples have "heard" the historical Jesus and become convinced that he is the Messiah, the Son of God, that they will be able to guide other sheep into following the one shepherd and thereby create the one true flock of God made up of Jew and Gentile together (10:16, 27).

Following Christ demands faith-commitment. Where such submission and confidence are lacking, followers "stumble" (*skandalizei*, 6:61; cf. 64) and "walk no more with him" literally and spiritually (6:66). Asked whether the twelve would also go away, Peter answers by defining the true disciple's objective: (1) proximity, "To whom shall we go?", and (2) obedience, "Thou hast the words of eternal life" (6:68). Thus we are made aware that in the context of the earthly ministry of Jesus, following meant physical identification and spiritual commitment. Further still lies the possibility of imitation in his death. "Whither I go, thou canst not follow me now; but thou shalt follow afterwards" (13:36). This prediction is confirmed by 21:18-19. Peter will indeed die for his Master as a direct consequence of his "following" (21:19, 22). The Beloved Disciple on the other hand is depicted as "tarrying," which initiated the rumor that he would remain alive until the return of Christ. There may be some significance in the fact that only Peter is asked to follow, while John (assuming him to be the disciple whom Jesus loved) died a natural death according to tradition.[40]

---

[38] "Abide" (*menō*) bears the characteristic twofold meaning in John. Here "abide" means a physical place (as in 4:40; 7:9; 11:6; 19:31; 21:22, 23), but in the discourse on the Vine and the Branches the "abiding" refers to spiritual fellowship and obedience (15:10) similar to the use of "follow."

[39] See E. Schweizer, *Lordship and Discipleship*, London, 1960, pp. 81ff.

[40] Cf. *ibid.*, p. 12.

The preceding discussion is no more than an initial attempt to get behind the terminology of the Fourth Gospel to the fuller intention of the writer. There is surely much more to be culled from reflecting on the inspired Evangelist's choice of words and signs. We do well to quote from the *Jerusalem Bible,* "The absorbing concern of the evangelist is the *meaning* of those events which were at once both divine and human, events which were at one and the same time both historical and theological; events which flowered in time but were rooted in eternity."[41] We make no plea for importing types or a spiritual sense where none was originally intended by the author. Our contention remains, however, that having labored for and not despised the literal sense, our exegetical task is incomplete. John's thesis claims that God the Son came in the flesh. Much that he said and did, therefore, partook of the two dimensions in which he lived and moved. Rich reward belongs to him who can penetrate and unravel the full significance of what John has to say.

[41] *Jerusalem Bible,* Garden City, 1966, p. 143.

The Limits of Ecstasy:
An Exegesis of 2 Corinthians 12:1-10

RUSSELL P. SPITTLER

Despite the continuing disagreement about the integrity of 2 Cor,[1] the section comprising chapters 10-13 is generally regarded as (at least part of) an authentic Pauline polemic against recent intruders at Corinth. The opening words (*autos de egō Paulos,* 10:1) already betray the strongly personal and controversial tone of 10-13, which is not only markedly sharper than earlier portions of 2 Cor but also is not easily paralleled elsewhere in any of Paul's letters. Gal, for example, dealt with attacks on Paul's gospel (Gal 1:9); 2 Cor 10-13 included that also (11:4), but met charges of the severest sort against Paul's own person as well (e.g. 10:1, 10; 11:6; 12:17).

The narrower context of the "paradise pericope" (as 2 Cor 12:1-10 may be called) has been identified by Windisch[2] as the "fool's speech" (*Narrenrede*) spanning 11:1-12:13. The major significance of this "fool's speech" lies in Paul's use of it as a polemic instrument:[3] he engages in self-praise only as a fool, but then he (and by designed implication, they) no longer speaks *kata kyrion* (11:17). The issue of apostolic authority that thus emerges may, with Käsemann,[4] be taken as the major underlying theme in 10-13, and that theme (as will be shown below) figures prominently in the paradise pericope.

Before he reached 12:1-10, the "Klimax im Gedankengang des

---

[1] Within the last few years the unity of 2 Cor has been affirmed by P. Hughes (1962), J. Jeremias (1962), J. Munck (1960), and A. Wikenhauser (1953), and contested by G. Bornkamm (1961/2), R. Bultmann (1963), E. Dinkler (1960), and J. Héring (1958). For a review of the problem and a newly proposed solution see D. Georgi, *Die Gegner des Paulus im zweiten Korintherbrief*, WMANT, Neukirchen-Vluyn, 1964, pp. 16-29.

[2] H. Windisch, *Der zweite Korintherbrief*, Göttingen, 1924.

[3] Georgi, *Gegner*, p. 228 n. 6.

[4] E. Käsemann, "Die Legitimität des Apostels," *ZNW*, 41 (1942), 33-71. However, "Der um Paulus geführte Kampf hat totale Ausmasse: Richtet er sich zentral gegen sein Apostolat, so gilt er darüber hinaus auch seiner gesamten Existenz" (p. 36).

Russell Paul Spittler, Dean of the College, Southern California College, Costa Mesa, California. B.A., Florida Southern College; M.A., Wheaton College Graduate School; B.D., Gordon-Conwell Theological Seminary; Ph.D., Harvard University.

Briefes,"[5] Paul had already responded to certain other charges (e.g. inconsistency [10:2, 11]; unimpressive speech [10:10; cf. 11:6]; lack of proper apostolic authority attested by refusal to accept salary [11:7]; inferiority as a servant of Christ [11:22ff.]) and at the same time lodged some counter-charges of his own (they are false apostles [11:13], who misuse their authority [10:8; cf. 13:10], love to commend themselves [10:12], and in fact preach a different Jesus [11:4]).

In the passage immediately preceding the paradise pericope (i.e. in 11:21b-33), Paul, reflecting the *Peristasenkatalog* form,[6] recounted the hardships of his ministry. His recital of these hazardous experiences is not so much an attempt to outdo the opponents as it is a polemic shift to a totally different ground for *kauchēsis,* namely, personal sufferings—*astheneiai.* And this in turn implies a qualitatively distinct Christology[7] — one keyed to the *astheneia* motif[8] rather than a superficial view of Jesus as a *theios anēr,* a miracle-monger.[9] As if to end with a consummate example of one species of *astheneia,* Paul completes the catalogue of (adverse) circumstances with the over-the-wall incident in Damascus (11:32-33)—an escape both cowardly in conception (*ekpheugein!*) and undignified in execution (*dia thuridos en sarganē*).

With the use of the programmatic *eleusomai de* (12:1), Paul takes on a new charge—his alleged ecstatic or visionary deficiencies. The topic he now treats in 12:1-10 is announced as *optasias kai apokalypseis,* anarthrous and thus implying competitive claims of the opponents to similar experiences.[10] The apostle is no stranger to visionary experiences[11] —one may even speak of an ecstatic stratum in his Christian experience[12] —but it

---

[5] Georgi, *Gegner,* p. 297.

[6] Details in A. Fridrichsen, "Zum Stil des paulinischen Peristasenkatalogs 2 Kor. 11.23ff.," *Symbolae Osloenses,* fasc. 7 (1928), 25-29.

[7] *Allon Iēsoun . . . hon ouk ekēryxamen,* 11:4. Even their understanding and use of ecstasy implied a different Christology. See Georgi, *Gegner,* pp. 297-99.

[8] *Kai gar estaurōthē ex [!] astheneias* (13:4).

[9] For elaboration see Georgi, *Gegner,* pp. 295 (on 11:23ff.) and 282ff. (on "Jesus als *theios anēr*").

[10] The plural may suggest also a genre of personal experiences of the apostle, one of which is recounted here. At any rate it was the *hyperbolē tōn apokalypseōn* (12:7) which had to do with the giving of the *skolops.*

[11] Notably Gal 1:12, 16; 2:2, not to mention the frequent references in Acts (e.g. 9:17, Damascus; 18:9, Corinth; 23:11, Jerusalem). Public sharing of an *apokalypsis* might be one component of a divine service, according to Paul (1 Cor 14:26, 30). The apostle does not elsewhere use *optasia.*

[12] Of major significance is the statement in 2 Cor 5:13: *eite gar exestēmen theō.* If this sentence disguises a charge that he has lost his right senses, the apostle does not deny it, but asserts that such ecstatic states as he may occasionally reach are personal, *theō*—and not for propagandistic enticement as his spectacle-loving opponents engaged in. The private character of spiritual ecstasy also appears in the apostle's use of glossolalia: to the surprising assertion, *eucharistō tō theō, pantōn hymōn mallon glōssais lalō* (1 Cor 14:18), he immediately adds that *en ekklēsia* he prefers five words in the vernacular to ten thousand in glossolalia (14:19). The glossolalic *ouk anthrōpois lalei, alla theō* (14:2), and so the whole of 1 Cor 14, is essentially a plea for the vernacular in public assembly (whether by straight *prophēteia* or by interpreted glossolalia, *dihermēneuein*), not denying the private

doubtless goes too far to speak of *Paulus als Visionär* as E. Benz does.[13] At no time does the apostle attach any enduring ecclesiastical or communal value to the experience: apparently he had never (in the fourteen years[14] since it occurred, 12:2) mentioned it before to the Corinthians—despite his stay with them as pastor for a year and a half (Acts 18:11) and despite the highly charismatic orientation of that congregation.

The paradise rapture would not even have been mentioned now but for the fact that Paul was forced to do so (*dei*, 12:1; *hymeis me ēnangkasate*, 12:11), that is, he was forced to respond to attacks on his apostolic authority based on charges (whether expressed, or implied in the extravagant ecstatic claims of the opponents) of his ecstatic or pneumatic deficiency. The thrust of his polemic is by no means an attempt to outdo the opponents by detailing a superior ecstatic experience. Rather, and still speaking "as a fool,"[15] he inverts the very criterion of his opponents by saying in essence that ecstasy is no proper cause for *kauchēsis* nor does it provide any adequate apostolic accreditation. He had been to the third heaven, to paradise, and for the glory of it all he received the implacable *skolops*. In this experience he has come to know strength in weakness, to locate *kauchēsis* in *astheneia* and not in pneumatic *dynamis*. The opponents boasted as pneumatic demonstrationists; Paul could and would only boast "as a fool," and even then—paradoxically—only in various sorts of "weaknesses" (one of which was the paradise rapture tempered by the *angelos satana*). The folly of self-praise and the legitimation of *kauchēsis* either *en kyriō*, or *en tais astheneiais* are themes basic to Paul's thought and frequent in both Corinthian letters (1 Cor 1:29, 31; 3:21; 4:6-10, 18; 5:2, 6; 8:1; 13:4; 2 Cor 10:8, 13, 15-17; 11:30; 12:5, 9).[16]

---

values of (uninterpreted) glossolalia. However one understands Paul, he must be recognized as one who experienced such spiritual ecstasies as glossolalia, visions and revelations, and a *Himmelsreise* to paradise.

[13] E. Benz, *Paulus als Visionär: Eine vergleichende Untersuchung der Visionsberichte des Paulus in der Apostelsgeschichte und in den paulinischen Briefen*, Wiesbaden, 1952, p. 45. Pre-occupation with the theme, it appears, prompts Benz to take *kyriou* (12:1) as an objective genitive rather than (with, e.g., Georgi, Plummer, Wendland) a subjective genitive. On the other hand, I may only mention here the text Käsemann somewhere calls "an interesting question": *ouchi Iēsoun ton kyrion hymōn heōraka* (1 Cor 9:1; = Damascus Road?).

[14] Reluctantly J. Knox, *Chapters in a Life of Paul*, New York, 1950, p. 78 n. 3, surrendered his earlier identification of the paradise rapture with the reference in Gal 2:1. Equating the Jerusalem visit of Acts 11 with Gal 2, L. Dieu reads in Gal 2:1 "four years" in place of fourteen ("Quatorze ans ou quatre ans?" *ETL*, 14 [1937], 308-17). I have thus far been unable to locate a written source for the suggestion that the vision of 2 Cor 12:2 occurred during the stoning at Lystra (Acts 14:19), in which case it could have tallied with martyrological visions such as that of Stephen (Acts 7:55f.). Windisch is right after all: "Wir müssen uns damit bescheiden, dass Paulus es nicht für angebracht gehalten hat, uns nähere Andeutungen zu geben" (*Der zweite Korintherbrief*, p. 373, where he also notes that provision of the date is reminiscent of OT prophetic style).

[15] *Gegona aphrōn*, 12:11a.

[16] In 2 Cor Paul includes as subjects of his boasting his good conscience (1:12), his congregation (1:14; 7:14), his authority (10:8), his unpaid preaching (11:7), and his weaknesses (11:30; 12:5, 9).

It is in fact the paradoxical linkage of *kauchēsis* to *astheneia* that structurally binds the unit 12:1-10.[17] Not only is the passage introduced with the phrase *kauchasthai dei, ou sympheron men* (v. 1) and concluded with the words *hēdista oun mallon kauchēsomai en tais astheneiais* (vs. 9b), but in the very middle of the passage—separating, or rather uniting, the rapture (vss. 2-4) and the *skolops* (vss. 7b-9a)—the principle is laid down *hyper de emautou ou kauchēsomai ei mē en tais astheneiais mou* (vs. 5; cf. 11:30).

The paradise pericope thus continues and sharpens—one may say consummates—the same argument as that of the *Peristasenkatalog* (11:21b-33): the physical hardships endured in the ministry and the *skolops*-tempered, superlative revelations of paradise are no mere quantitative proofs of apostolic superiority or even of legitimacy. They rather function as qualitative inversions to a wholly new ground for *kauchēsis* (cf. 11:30 with 12:5b and 12:9b). While the apostle had earlier (1 Cor) strictly opposed boasting for personal aggrandizement, that is now exactly what the intruders at Corinth were doing. Paul himself is thus forced to boast (12:1, 11), does it only with reluctance (11:1, 16), "as a fool" (11:17, 21), and indicates that he of all people should least be required to boast among his own Corinthians (12:11; cf. 3:1-2). The opponents authenticate their apostolic authority by pneumatic demonstration; Paul paradoxically accredits his own authority by a recital of weaknesses, thus aligning himself with his Lord, who "was crucified from a position of *astheneias*" (13:4).

This overall statement of the tone and function of 12:1-10 within its context may now be supported by certain exegetical observations.

The vision[18] Paul recounts consists of a snatching up into the third heaven, to paradise.[19] What is involved here is a *Himmelsreise*,[20] a (round)

---

[17] The passage 12:1-10 structurally divides into five units: vs. 1, introduction of the subject; vss. 2-4, the paradise/third heaven rapture; vss. 5-7a, character and grounds for boasting; vss. 7b-9a, the *skolops* and its persistence; vss. 9b-10, strength in weakness.

[18] Psychological aspects of this and similar visionary experiences may be studied with the aid of G. Widengren, *Literary and Psychological Aspects of the Hebrew Prophets*, UUA, 1948:10, Uppsala. The same author, in *The Ascension of the Apostle and the Heavenly Books*, UUA, 1950:7, Uppsala, sets down roving researches tracing—from early Mesopotamia to Mohammed—a broad historical background. He shows the widespread Near Eastern motif of an ascended "apostle," who, upon enthronization, received marvelous heavenly books that are now readable by him (or translated for him; cf. *arrēta rhēmata*, 2 Cor 12:4).

[19] Paradise is placed in the third heaven also in T Levi 2 (oldest form); 2 Enoch 8; Life of Adam and Eve 37; and Apocalypse of Abraham. H. Bietenhard, *Die himmlische Welt im Urchristentum und Spätjudentum*, Tübingen, 1951, presents a thorough survey of Hellenistic cosmology. Particularly relevant is I. du Vippens, *Le paradis terrestre au troisième ciel: eposé historique d'une conception chrétienne des premieres siècles*, Paris, 1925. One of the striking parallels to Paul's experience is the famous Talmudic tale of the "four who entered paradise" (= R. Akibah and three of his pupils, b. Hagigah 14b-15a). I owe to my colleague, Arnold Levine, the observation that this account may be taken as a rabbinic polemic against Gnosticism (since only R. Akibah survived—the others died, went mad, and turned heretical, respectively—one endangers himself to toy with gnostic speculations). Is it possible that the infrequency and potential dangers involved in an ascent to paradise may in themselves have given weight to Paul's claim to have been there—and back?

[20] It is useful to observe R. Meyer's distinction ("Himmelfahrt," *RGG* [1959³],

trip to heaven, an experience widely claimed in the ancient world, whose major attraction, according to G. Scholem,[21] lay in the disclosure of knowledge ordinarily obtained after death to a living venerated figure. Such trips were made as an ascent of the soul either with or without the body. Jewish apocalyptic, notably the Enochic cycle (Enoch himself had ascended, according to Gen 5:24), abounds with such disclosures of esoteric lore received from the angelic guide. From such roots, in part, developed both the Merkabah speculation current in certain Jewish (even Rabbinic) circles during NT times as well as the subsequent (ca. fourth to tenth centuries) Hekhaloth speculations.[22]

The single detail Paul furnishes about the revelation itself indicates its esoteric character: while there he heard *arrēta rhēmata,* which he could not and should not retell (12:4).[23] Although Windisch speaks of *arrēta rhēmata* as "ein technischer Ausdruck den Paulus mit Bewusstsein aus der Kultsprache der Mysterien entnomen haben muss,"[24] not one of the texts he supplies—nor any of those provided by Lietzmann[25]—contains the specific combination *arrēta rhēmata. Arrēta* often appears by itself (or with the article) substantively.[26] One meets such expressions as *arrēta mystēria, arrēta hiera, arrēton epos,* even *arrēta* as the predicate of *ta eirēmena* (Plato, *Symposium,* 189B). While *arrētos* doubtlessly comes from the vocabulary of the mystery cults, the compound expression *arrēta rhēmata* appears to be unique with Paul. It is really an oxymoron:[27] how can "words" be "unutterable"? Both terms in this compound warrant closer attention.

Even if *rhēmata,* following the generalized use of the Hebrew *debārîm,* means only "things" or "matters," there still must have been some audible quality to the revelation. For not only did Paul hear (*ēkousen*) something; he was also charged not to tell (*lalein*) what he heard, a charge incomprehensible if *arrēta* meant here strictly "not capable of being put into words." Moreover, when the apostle wished to describe the

---

3, 333-35) between a *Himmelfahrt* (permanent ascension) and a *Himmelsreise* (round trip).

[21] G. Scholem, *Jewish Gnosticism, Merkabah Mysticism, and Talmudic Tradition,* New York, 1960, pp. 17-18.

[22] These matters may be approached in the works of G. Scholem. To his volume cited in the previous note, add *Major Trends in Jewish Mysticism,* New York, 1961, and *Von der mystische Gestalt der Göttheit,* Zürich, 1962.

[23] Naturally this regretful lapse of the apostle was soon to be compensated by subsequent apocryphal literature; see the Apocalypse of Paul in M. R. James, *The Apocryphal New Testament,* Oxford, 1924, pp. 525ff. An apocalypse of Paul has been found in the library uncovered at Nag Hammadi (W. van Unnik, *Newly Discovered Gnostic Writings,* Naperville, 1960, p. 17).

[24] Windisch, *Der zweite Korintherbrief,* p. 378.

[25] H. Lietzmann, *An die Korinther I, II,* HNT, Tübingen, 1949, p. 154.

[26] "Saepissime ea quae in mysteriis traduntur ἄρρητα esse dicuntur. . . . Eiusdem significationis est vox ἀπόρρητος." O. Casel, *De philosophorum graecorum silentio mystico,* Giessen, 1919, p. 6.

[27] E. Repo, *Der Begriff 'Rhema' im biblisch-Griechischen,* Vol. 2, *Rhema im NT,* Helsinki, 1954, p. 84. Vol. 1 of this work treats *Rhema in der Septuaginta* (1951). Repo distinguishes "die Sprech-, Sach- und Befehlsbetonungen als Spezialakzente" (Vol. 1, p. 186), thinks *arrēta rhemata* in 2 Cor 12:4 is a semitic expression in part at least, and suggests the apocalyptic notion of divine (Deut 4:12) or angelic voices (Dan 10:9) as the proper background for the expression.

unambiguously wordless quality of a sign, he could choose another *hapax legomenon: stenagmois alalētois* (Rom 8:26).

The word *arrētos* basically means "inexpressible," but it vacillates between texts where it means clearly "inexpressible by nature" (as generally in the mystery religion vocabulary, also as a description of God, e.g., *Poimandres* 31) and other texts where it means clearly "inexpressible by prohibition" (as Philo, *Quod deterius potiori* 175, where just men bit off their own tongues to avoid disclosing *ta arrēta*).[28] The latter shade of meaning seems preferable in 2 Cor 12:4 in view of its juxtaposition with *rhēmata* and its use with the verbs *akouein* and *lalein*. What is involved is a paradisaical audition, the disclosure of which was forbidden.[29]

It is precisely this esoteric disclosure in paradise (vss. 2-4) which illumines both the third-person character of vss. 2-4 and the force of vs. 5, which are interrelated. One must recall the interest of the opponents in ecstasy[30] and observe the propagandistic use of esoteric traditions that would be prompted by their interests. By casting his (autobiographical![31]) report in the third person, Paul thus distinguishes his present self (= the challenged apostle) from his ecstatic self ("14 years ago"). About his ecstatic self (*hyper tou toioutou*, vs. 5) he will not boast (except in the *astheneiais*).[32] This involves no idea of an ontological or psychological split, but is a device Paul uses to mark himself off from the demonstrational, propagandistic uses of ecstasy (and esotericism[33]) utilized by his opponents. Both Paul and his opponents experience ecstasy; the difference lies in the use they make of it. For Paul, such experiences are *theō* (1 Cor 14:2 and 2 Cor 5:13[34]). For the opponents, ecstasy serves not only for propagandistic enticement, but as well for apostolic accreditation. Once again the issue of apostolic authority emerges: by his refusal to capitalize on the *arrēta rhēmata*, Paul rejects apostolic accreditation by ecstasy as well as the ecstatic conception of Jesus such a view presupposes.

---

[28] W. Bauer, *A Greek-English Lexicon of the New Testament and Other Early Christian Literature*, trans. by W. Arndt and F. Gingrich, Chicago, 1959, p. 109.

[29] It remains a lexical possibility (to me unlikely) that *akouein tōn arrētōn rhēmatōn* may mean something like "to witness ineffable matters." Even so, the force of Paul's argument (= his refusal to exploit ecstasy) remains unchanged.

[30] 2 Cor 5:13; 12:1. Cf. Georgi, *Gegner*, pp. 296-99.

[31] Any doubts that the paradise pericope details Paul's own experience are removed by vs. 7, where the thorn was given to prevent *his own* undue exaltation as a result of the rapture. For possible solutions to the curiously placed phrase *kai tē hyperbolē tōn apokalypseōn* at the beginning of vs. 7, see especially Lietzmann, *An die Korinther I, II*, p. 155.

[32] There is a certain tension in the use of *kauchasthai* in 12:1-10. Boasting is necessary but unprofitable (vs. 1) and Paul *will not* engage in it (vs. 5). Yet he will "boast" in and over his weaknesses (vs. 5), even gladly so (vss. 9-10) once he has learned the paradox of strength in weakness.

[33] Paul of course has his own brand of esotericism, as 1 Cor 2:9 indicates. But he immediately adds: *hēmin gar apekalypsen ho theos dia tou pneumatos* (vs. 10). Paul's secrets are open secrets, mediated by the Spirit. The esoteric motif of 1 Cor 2:9 recurs in the Gos Thom, logion 17, slightly expanded. Cf. 1QS 11:3ff. The wide usage of this quotation, attributed by Origen (*Comm Matt* 17:9) to an unknown Apocalypse of Elias, may be studied with the aid of P. Prigent, "Ce que l'oeil n'a pas vu, 1 Cor. 2:9: histoire et pré-histoire d'une citation," *TZ*, 14 (1958), 416-29.

[34] Käsemann, "Legitimität," p. 68.

In vs. 6 Paul observes that if he held it advisable to boast, he could do so, and would not in the process be using the persiflage of a fool but would be telling the truth. He refrains from such straightforward, factual boasting for a reason that confirms his rejection of exterior criteria of apostolic accreditation: *mē tis eis eme logisētai hyper ho blepei me ē akouei ex emou.* J. Cambier has argued that the *blepein—akouein* couplet is an equivalent of *astheneia* and that the phrase refers exactly to "l'aspect d'humilité et de faiblesse extérieure de son ministère qui appelle normalement le mépris du monde . . . mais qui, in fait, sout le signe de l'acceptation par l'âpotre de son rôle de serviteur fidèle."[35]

Thus in vss. 5-7a[36] Paul presents for authentication of his apostolic authority not the ecstasy of a half-generation ago but the humiliating weaknesses lived out before the Corinthians.

The *skolops* given to Paul, which persisted despite the thrice-repeated prayer (vss. 7b-9a),[37] has never been adequately identified.[38] Whatever it was, it (or he) surely had the effect of a "thorn in the flesh" as that phrase is now understood. Where earlier interpretations preferred physical disability of some sort, there has been a recent trend to interpret the *skolops* more existentially, even if to stress the *astheneia* character of the physical malady. The *angelos satana*,[39] as J. Thierry observes,[40] could be taken as the grammatical subject of *edothē.* Thierry conjectures Paul was labeled an *angelos satana* by his opponents and that the shame of bearing this epithet constituted the *skolops.* T. Mullins,[41] on the other hand, takes *hyper*

---

[35] J. Cambier, "Le critère paulinien de l'apostolat en 2 Cor. 12:6s," *Bib,* 43 (1962), 504-5.

[36] For convenience I here retain the punctuation of the Nestle text. Cf. n. 31.

[37] "Ce texte est sans doute le seul passage paulinien attestant expréssement une prière adressée au Christ et non à Dieu le Père. Mais l'expression οἱ ἐπικαλούμενοι τὸ ὄνομα τοῦ κυρίου ἡμῶν Ἰησοῦ Χριστοῦ montre que son invocation n'etait pas inhabituelle (voir par exemple Acts 9.14)," J. Héring, *La seconde Epitre de St. Paul aux Corinthiens,* CNT, Neuchatel, 1958, p. 96 n. 4.

[38] Some earlier guesses: eye trouble (Renan), epilepsy (Lightfoot), malaria (Ramsey), physical disability of one sort or other (most interpreters, including Bultmann, Deissmann, Goodspeed, Knox, Lietzmann, Schweitzer). Itemized interpretations *s.v. kolaphizō,* and guide to literature *s.v. skolops,* both in W. Bauer, ET. This English translation (1957) of Bauer's fourth German edition (1952) supplies several important bibliographic items not included in his fifth German edition (1958). On the other hand the fifth German edition supplies an additional ancient textual reference. All of which suggests use of both the German and the English Bauer!

[39] Is it at all conceivable that the phrase *angelos satana* as an appropriate designation of the *skolops* arose in Paul's mind as an alternate to the *angelos tou kyriou,* who may have been the angelic guide during the *Himmelsreise?* If an angel of the Lord was instrumental in exaltation, would it not be appropriate for an angel of Satan to be the instrument of humiliation? I offer this only as a possibility. It is at any rate clear that the angelic interpreter is a familiar figure in the *Himmelsreise.* The *arrēta rhēmata* may well have been spoken by angels.

[40] J. Thierry, "Der Dorn im Fleische (2 Kor. 12.7-9)," *NovT,* 5 (1962), 303f.

[41] T. Mullins, "Paul's Thorn in the Flesh," *JBL,* 76 (1957), 303. In addition to Mullins and Thierry as examples of this trend may be added two essays in *Studia Paulina,* Festschrift for J. de Zwaan, Haarlem, 1953: H. Clavier, "La sante de l'apotre Paul," pp. 66-82 (= the endurance of physical weakness); H. Menoud, "L'echarde et l'ange satanique (2 Cor 12.7)," pp. 163-71 (= the vision of Acts 22:17-21).

toutou (vs. 8) as masculine and concludes that the *skolops* is some un-named but specific personal enemy.

The interpersonal, polemic character of 12:1-10 provides slight con-firmation of some personal identification of the *skolops*, but the identifica-tion remains conjectural. What is more certain is the result of the buffeting thorn: the tension issuing from the continuing encounter, unrelieved by prayer, brought Paul a personal revelation from the Lord: *arkei soi hē charis mou· hē gar dynamis en astheneiā teleitai* (vs. 9). If 12:1-10 is the climax of the argument of 10-13, this word from the Lord is the climax of 12:1-10. Where the opponents presumed a Christology of might (*dynamis*), Paul operated with a Christology of weakness (*astheneia*).

The conclusion (vss. 9b-10) shows how thoroughly Paul had assimi-lated this principle. From it he developed a personal motto: *hotan gar asthenō, tote dynatos eimi* (vs. 10). On it he based the defense of his ministry: paradoxically he now takes pleasure in insults, calamities, perse-cutions, moments of anguish—all varieties of *astheneiai*. This he did *hyper Christou,* and found that *hē dynamis tou Christou* "took up quarters"[42] within him.

In 12:1-10 Paul thus agrees reluctantly to "boast" and to speak of his revelations (vs. 1). Though he had experienced a *Himmelsreise* and heard *arrēta rhēmata,* he could not "boast" (in the way the opponents were boasting) in his present self (vss. 2-5). He could truthfully "boast" but would not, for he rested his authority on his life and not his claims (vss. 6-7a). The thorn in the flesh taught him the adequacy of divine grace (7b-9a), which in turn yielded as a (paradoxical) ground-principle the perfection of strength through weakness—a principle presupposing a weak-ness-Christology (cf. 13:4). It is this principle which reflects the signifi-cance of 11:23-33 and overturns the demonstrationist claims and charges of Paul's opponents.

---

[42] So translated by Bauer, *s.v.* ἐπισκηνόω. The word is used only here in the literature, and it may be compared with the similar thought in Luke 1:35: *dynamis hypsistou episkiasei soi.*

Charismatic Theology

in the Apostolic Tradition of Hippolytus

JOHN E. STAM

Introduction

Hippolytus of Rome probably wrote his *Apostolic Tradition* (Ap Tr) "within a year or two either way of A.D. 215,"[1] near the end of the episcopacy of Zephyrinus. Hippolytus, the contentious and somewhat pedantic presbyter, was resolutely hostile toward Zephyrinus and his archdeacon, Callistus. Upon the death of Zephyrinus and the choice of Callistus as bishop of Rome, Hippolytus and his followers established their own true Church of Rome in opposition to the "sect" of the "Callistians." Hippolytus thus became history's first "anti-pope."

The Prologue and Epilogue of Ap Tr reveal clearly that the cantankerous presbyter composed his Church Order with a very specific polemical purpose: to "hold fast to that tradition which has continued until now" (1.3) and denounce "that apostasy or error which was recently invented out of ignorance and [because of certain] ignorant men" (1.4; cf. 38.3). Zephyrinus and Callistus would hardly miss that reference! Yet precisely this polemical furor helped make Hippolytus a staunchly conservative witness who amassed every possible shred of second-century tradition against his bishop and rival. With only a few quite obvious exceptions (e.g. the bishop as High Priest, the eucharist as propitiation), his Church Order is

---

[1] G. Dix, *The Treatise on the Apostolic Tradition of St. Hippolytus of Rome*, London, 1937, 1968[2], p. xxxvii. Dix provides an excellent introduction, plus the critical English edition cited throughout this article. For a summary of the historical and literary problems see J. E. Stam, *Episcopacy in the Apostolic Tradition of Hippolytus*, Basel, 1969, pp. 7-14. The document has survived in an incomplete Latin translation (Verona Palimpsest), in the so-called "Egyptian Church Order" (Ethiopic, Arabic, and Sahidic), in the "Canons of Hippolytus" (H. Achelis, 1891) and the "Testament of Our Lord" (I. Rahmani, 1899), plus Book VIII of the "Apostolic Constitutions" (Funk, 1891). The derived Egyptian versions are given in G. Horner, *The Statutes of the Apostles*, 1904.

John Stam, Professor of Evangelical Theology, and Director of the Department of Christian Thought at the Seminario Biblico Latinoamericano, San Jose, Costa Rica. B.A., Wheaton College; M.A., Wheaton College Graduate School; B.D., Fuller Theological Seminary; D. Theol., University of Basel.

a remarkably faithful mirror of second-century doctrine and practice in the Roman Church.

Gregory Dix has with good reason described Ap Tr as "the most illuminating single source of evidence extant on the inner life and religious polity of the early Christian Church."[2] Its unique value has been widely acclaimed with regard to the history of the early Roman Church's doctrine, liturgy, daily life and church order. But one significant aspect of its thought has until now received surprisingly little attention, namely, Hippolytus' theology of the Holy Spirit and his gifts in the church. The general neglect of this theme is all the more remarkable because the document itself begins with a reference to a now-lost treatise of Hippolytus entitled *peri charismatōn* ("On Charismatic Gifts"). In fact, the Church Order itself quite possibly constituted the second half of a single work on "The Apostolic Tradition concerning Charismatic Gifts" (cf. Ap Tr 1.1-2).[3]

"Charismatic Theology" can be understood simply as a theology of the free grace-gifts (*charismata, pneumatika*) of the Holy Spirit in the Body of Christ. This allows for the "irregular," non-hierarchical or unstructured gifts and manifestations of the Spirit. But charismatic theology also interprets the structures (Acts 20:28) and functions (Acts 15:28) of the "official" ministry as inspired by, and subject to, the living Spirit. Such a theology will necessarily involve a dynamic concept of the laity.[4]

I. The Holy Spirit in the Holy Church

Like his master Irenaeus, Hippolytus links the Spirit and his work very emphatically to the church, and in turn understands the church as the organ and sphere of the Spirit's action. In some passages he relates this specifically to the episcopal-presbyteral hierarchy which through the decades has preserved sound doctrine against all innovation and perversion (e.g. *Philosophumena* 1, preface, 6, 8.19.2). But in total perspective, his writings show a decisive tendency to associate the work of the Holy Spirit with the entire church rather than with any specific hierarchical office. In a uniquely beautiful figure, he urges all the faithful to hasten to the daily Assembly "where the Spirit blossoms" (*ubi floret spiritus,* 31.2). This congregational morning Bible study is "the place where the Holy Spirit abounds" (35.3). The derived Egyptian versions interpreted this in highly colorful terms: "the place where the Holy Spirit breaks forth" (Sahidic, Horner, p. 328) or "rises (like the sun)" (Ethiopic, Horner, p. 182).

---

[2] Dix, *Treatise on the Apostolic Tradition*, p. ix.

[3] The historical significance of this charismatic emphasis is even greater if Ap Tr in fact conserves three distinct theological and stylistic strands of tradition (episcopal, presbyteral, and charismatic). See Stam, *Episcopacy in the Apostolic Tradition,* pp. 43-44, 47, 65, 96; cf. A. Ehrhardt, *The Apostolic Succession in the First Two Centuries of the Church,* London, 1953, p. 113, regarding Irenaeus.

[4] For the background of charismatic and prophetic theology in the early church, see H. von Campenhausen, *Kirchliches Amt und geistliche Vollmacht,* Tübingen, 1953, esp. chap. 8, "Propheten und Lehrer im zweiten Jahrhundert," pp. 195-233; Ehrhardt, *Apostolic Succession,* esp. chap. 4, "The Prophetic and Other Extraregular Ministries," pp. 83-106; and J. V. Bartlet, *Church Life and Church Order During the First Four Centuries,* Oxford, 1943.

This view of the Spirit and the church is clearly expressed in Hippolytus' almost invariable doxology "glory to the Father and to the Son with *the Holy Spirit in the Holy Church*" (6.4). Similar doxological formulas occur in the eucharistic prayer (4.13), the consecration of the presbyter (8.5), the baptismal confession (21.17) and the confirmation prayer (22.1).

The charismatic concept of the laity, correlative to this view of the Spirit and the church, is central to the thought of the Prologue and the Epilogue. The Prologue opens with a reference to his *peri charismatōn*, on "spiritual gifts such as God has from the beginning bestowed on men according to His own will in presenting to Himself that image which had gone astray" (1.1). Lately, however, the entire church has gone astray through the ignorance and disobedience of her leaders (1.4-5; 38.2-3). Nevertheless, "the Holy Spirit bestows the fulness of grace (*perfectam gratiam*) on those who believe rightly that they may know how those who are at the head of the Church should teach the tradition and maintain it in all things" (1.5; cf. 38.2).

This most remarkable passage suggests a number of far-reaching implications, which are probably representative of the charismatic theology of the now-lost *peri charismatōn*:

(1) Hippolytus, faithful to his second-century traditions, clearly recognizes the gifts of the Spirit and accentuates their importance both in Ap Tr and in his other writings.

(2) The Spirit bestows these gifts in the sovereignty of his divine will to those who believe rightly (1.1, 5), without distinction of hierarchical rank, theological refinement or ecclesiastical endorsement. In fact, while those at the head wander blindly and rebelliously (1.3-5; 38.3), "those who believe rightly" (and are clearly not ecclesiastical authorities) receive *perfectam gratiam* from the Spirit.

(3) Therefore, faithful laymen have the charismatic right and duty of setting straight the bishops! It must be observed that Hippolytus is here demanding this right not for himself but for his readers, the Spirit-gifted laity. Hennecke, Botte and others have suggested that this right of the laity to judge and counsel the hierarchy, and reprimand them as necessary, constitutes a kind of corporate gift of discernment (*diakrisis pneumatōn*, through their *teleia charis*).

(4) This charismatic judgment and correction by the laity is part of—in fact, the central principle of—the continuity of the apostolic tradition in the church (1.3, 5; 38.1-4). Although it is the solemn task of the clergy to guard the tradition (cf. also *Philosophumena* 1, preface, 6), it is in fact the laity who, in the Holy Spirit, must guard the clergy! Thus both central principles in the theology of Irenaeus and Hippolytus, the apostolic tradition and the incipient concept of apostolic succession, are fundamentally charismatic in nature.[5]

---

[5] See E. Hennecke, "Hippolyts Schrift 'Apostolische Überlieferung,'" in *Harnack-Ehrung*, Leipzig, 1921, pp. 159-82; B. Botte, *La tradition apostolique*, Münster, 1946, p. 26; A. Hamel, *Kirche bei Hippolyt von Rom*, Gütersloh, 1951, pp. 105-6.

The final sentence of the Epilogue underscores these perspectives: "And, beloved, if we have omitted anything, God will reveal it to those who are worthy, steering the Holy Church to its moorings in the quiet haven" (38.4). The "worthy" (*axioi*) here mentioned are identical with "those who believe rightly" (*recte credunt,* 1.5; cf. *axiōs pisteuomenoi, Philosophumena* 9.31.2) and have received *perfectam gratiam* from the Spirit. The fullness of grace-gifts among the charismatically *axioi* will include all necessary revelation for the steering (*kybernan*) of the good ship church. The *charismata* of revelation and strategic leadership (*kybernēsis,* steersmanship or pilotry, 1 Cor 12:28) accompany the apostolic tradition on its way through history and guide the church to its destined port.

Similarly, the Egyptian versions conclude the long list of baptismal requirements (Ap Tr 16.1-24) with a final instruction to the lay catechists: "If we have omitted anything, decide ye as is fit; for we all have the Spirit of God" (Ap Tr 16.25, probably an interpolation based on 38.4). In the same vein, another Egyptian interpolation adds that "there is no man who believed God through His holy Son, who does not receive a spiritual grace or gift from Him" (Horner, pp. 188, 334-35).

Ap Tr 15, "Of a Gift," deals with the "gift (*charisma*) of healing by a revelation," or according to the Egyptian versions, "healing and revelation" (*Testament of Our Lord:* "or revelation"). Although the use of *charis* in Ap Tr 3.2 and 8.2, 4 seems to refer to "grace" rather than grace-gifts, its use in the Confirmation prayer probably has the charismatic sense (22.1, see below).[6] It is also possible, but less than certain, that "the gift (*dōron*) of the Spirit" in 36.11 may refer to charismatic endowment. In his *Commentary on Daniel* 3.16.3-4, Hippolytus complains that in his time, as in Daniel's, "when some man becomes worthy (*axios*) to receive a special grace (*charis*) from God," all begin to view him with jealous suspicion. Elsewhere he accuses the Montanists of magnifying themselves "above the Apostles and every *charisma,*" and even above Christ himself, because they claim gifts and wisdom greater than those found in the church catholic (*Philosophumena* 8.19.2; cf. also 6.39-41; *Blessing of Jacob* 49.11).

The prayer of Confirmation for the newly baptized is worthy of special attention: "O Lord God, who didst count these (Thy servants) worthy of (deserving) the forgiveness of sins by the laver of regeneration, make them worthy to be filled with Thy Holy Spirit and send upon them Thy grace, that they may serve Thee according to Thy will" (Ap Tr 22.1). Confirmation is viewed here entirely as a charismatic action whose significance is realized in the fullness of the Holy Spirit and his grace, besought from God in prayer. True to the sense of this petition, the Egyptian version adds, "make him a Temple of Thy Holy Spirit" (Horner, p. 171). And from this fullness of the Spirit will flow the fullness of grace-gifts (cf. 1.5) that will qualify believers and make them worthy (*axios*) to serve God. Thus the prayer of Confirmation is, in its own way, a prayer of "ordination" to ministry in the Holy Spirit.

Two passages on the sign of the cross provide a curious reference to the Holy Spirit. If the believer catches his breath in his hands and signs

[6] Stam, *Episcopacy in the Apostolic Tradition,* pp. 74, 93.

himself with spittle (*spm* can abbreviate either *sputum* or *spiritum*), then "the gift of the Spirit and the sprinkling of the font, drawn from the heart of the believer as from a fountain, purifies him who has believed" (36.11). The adversary then beats a hasty retreat, "pursued by the Holy Spirit who indwells him who makes place for Him within himself" (37.2). Since all believers possess the indwelling Spirit, Ap Tr never speaks of a believer's being exorcised by the clergy. The breath and moisture of life within his heart assure him certain victory over the enemy.

In summary, Hippolytus (like Irenaeus) uses the terms *charis, charisma,* and *dōrea* interchangeably for any gift of divine grace, including the Holy Spirit himself. The Holy Spirit indwells the believer (37.2), fills him (eucharistic prayer [4.11], confirmation prayer [22.1]), and imparts *virtutem spiritus* to defeat Satan (37.2).

II. The Spirit and the Word

In Ap Tr the Spirit and the Word are closely linked. The high concept of the charismatic endowment of all believers, qualifying them for spiritual and doctrinal discernment, implied the responsibility of all Christians to persist in careful and constant Bible study. All the faithful are to engage regularly in daily personal prayer (Ap Tr 26, 26) and private study of the "holy book," especially on those days when there is no morning assembly (36.1). Laymen should instruct one another in the traditions and encourage the catechumens to perform them, so that no one will be tempted or perish (36:15-16).

Great importance was clearly ascribed to the weekday morning assembly (31.2; 33.1-2; 35.2-3):

> But if there should be any instruction by the word, he shall put this first, to go and hear the word of God for the strengthening of his soul. And they shall be zealous (*spoudazein*) to go to the assembly where the Spirit abounds (31.2).

> But if there should be an instruction in the word let each one prefer to go thither, considering that it is God whom he hears speaking by the mouth of him who instructs. For having prayed with the Church he will be able to avoid all the evils of that day. The God-fearing man should consider it a great loss if he does not go to the place in which they give instruction, and especially if he knows how to read (35.2).

Though the bishop apparently did not need to attend, he appointed the presbyters and deacons to lead the teaching in each place. Sometimes, however, the "instruction in the Word" was assigned to lay teachers from whom the people did not entertain great expectations:

> If there is a teacher there, let none of you be late in arriving at the assembly at the place where they give instruction. Then indeed it shall be given to him who speaks to utter things which are profitable to all, and thou shalt hear things which thou thinkest not to hear and thou shalt be profited by the things which the Holy Spirit will give to thee by him who instructs and so thy faith will be established by what thou hearest. And further he shall tell thee what thou oughtest to do in thine own house. And therefore let each one be careful (*spoudazein*) to go to the assembly to the place where the Holy Spirit abounds (35.3).

To Hippolytus these sometimes-despised instructors were a noble "choir of teachers" (*Commentary on Daniel* 1.17.8), an independent charismatic fellowship in the ministry of the Word, and the daily congregational Bible study was a highly charged encounter with the living Spirit through the Word.

III. The Holy Spirit and Church Order

Ap Tr is of unique historical value because of its very extensive and detailed exposition of the Christian ministry in Rome at the beginning of the third century. Yet its consistent emphasis on Church Order is in fact also profoundly charismatic in character.

Bishop. To begin with, the bishop's popular election, *hypo pantos tou laou,* was quite clearly understood as a charismatic indication of the divine will manifested through God's people as the instrument of his Spirit. Thus the *electus ab omni populo* (2.1) becomes, in the ordination prayer, *quem eligisti ad episcopatum* (3.4): God himself, through his Spirit-directed people, has chosen the bishop (cf. Acts 1:24; 20:28). Thus the later text of *The Testament of Our Lord* (1.20) makes explicit the charismatic implications of Ap Tr 2.1 with "eligendus ab universo populo secundum placitum Spiritus sancti." (Cf. Cyprian, *Epistles* 43.1; 55.8.)

Curiously, the episcopal ordination rite in Ap Tr calls for two impositions of hands upon the candidate. The first is a corporate act by all the bishops present, during which nothing at all is said but "the presbytery stand by in silence. And all shall keep silence praying in their hearts for the descent of the Spirit" (2.3-4). This corporate episcopal-presbyteral rite, undoubtedly derived from a presbyteral tradition based on the synagogue, marked with high dramatism the collegial nature of ordination, the solidarity of clergy and laity in the act, and the mystery and power of (silent!) prayer. The corporate prayer of the church and the "descent of the Holy Spirit" constitute thus the very essence of ordination itself.

After the silent prayer, one of the bishops "chosen at the request of all" (2.5) lays his hand upon the ordinand and pronounces the ordination prayer (2.1-6), which contains two significant references to the Spirit. The first petition supplicates God to "now pour forth that Power which is from Thee, of 'the princely Spirit' which Thou didst deliver to Thy Beloved Child Jesus Christ, which He bestowed on Thy holy Apostles who established the Church . . ." (3.3).

Significantly, the bestowal of the Spirit is seen in this petition, and throughout Ap Tr, as the free gift and act of God in answer to prayer. The dynamically vertical quality of the verb "pour out" and the "from Thee" parallel the verticality of the "descent of the Spirit" prayed for during the first imposition of hands. This pentecostal-patterned understanding of the charismatic gift from above represents a long and consistent line of Roman tradition (1 Clem 46.6; Justin, *Dialogue* 49.3, 87-88; Irenaeus, *Adversus haereses* 3.1.1; 3.12.1; 5.8.1-2; cf. in Alexandria, *Barn* 1.2-3; Clement, *Paedagogus* 1.6).

Some Roman Catholic scholars (J. Lécuyer, H. Elfers) have sought to find in the "princely Spirit" an authoritative official *charisma* of the episcopacy transmitted by ordination. B. Botte has wisely judged that "la demostration est loin d'etre convaincante."[7] Irenaeus clearly refers the "princely Spirit" of Ps 51:12 to the Holy Spirit who descended upon Jesus at his baptism and upon the nascent church at Pentecost (*Adversus haereses* 3.17.2).

The second reference to the Spirit occurs in Ap Tr 3.5:

> And that by the high priestly Spirit he may have authority "to forgive sins" according to Thy command, "to assign lots" according to Thy bidding, to "loose every bond" according to the authority Thou gavest to the Apostles. . . .

The adverbial phrase, *tō pneumati tō archieratikō*, which introduces this list of episcopal *exousiai*, is clearly related to Hippolytus' emphasis on the high-priesthood of the bishop (cf. *Philosophumena* 1, preface, 6). Hippolytus, the unbending enemy of innovation, seems here to have consciously or unconsciously absorbed into his Church Order a recent change, the specific designation of the "clergy" as priests and the bishop as "high priest."[8]

Hippolytus is clear, however, that all the pastoral and priestly functions of the bishop can be validly exercised only in the Holy Spirit. Although the term "high-priestly Spirit" has no patristic parallels, the language of the petition has clear echoes of John 20:22-23. There is every reason also to believe that this term, like the "princely Spirit" of 3.3, refers specifically to the Holy Spirit whom Christ bestowed upon the apostles. Only the Spirit of God can empower and qualify men for priestly ministry.

Presbyter. The bestowal of the Holy Spirit is likewise central to the ordination prayer for presbyters: "Look upon this Thy servant and impart to him the spirit of grace and counsel. . . . As Thou didst look upon the people of Thy choice and didst command Moses to choose presbyters whom Thou didst fill with the Spirit which Thou hadst granted to Thy minister, so now, O Lord, grant that there may be preserved among us unceasingly the Spirit of Thy grace" (8.3, 4; cf. Isa 11:2; Zech 12:10). In Num 11:25-29 the Spirit granted the seventy elders was the Spirit of prophecy, which was later also communicated to Joshua (27:18-19). Justin Martyr also quotes these passages, along with Mal 4:5, to demonstrate the effusion of the Spirit upon prophetic men such as Joshua, Elijah and John the Baptist. Here again the thought is clearly vertical and charismatic rather than the horizontal concept of a transmission of the Spirit through successive layings-on-of-hands.

Although the rubric for presbyteral ordination specifies that the bishop shall pray over the presbyter the same prayer as for episcopal ordination, the article proceeds immediately to furnish a prayer totally different in style and thought from the preceding episcopal prayer of 3.1-6.

---

[7] *Bulletin de Théologie ancienne et Médiévale*, 6 (1953), 588. Cf. Stam, *Episcopacy in the Apostolic Tradition*, pp. 23-29, 59-63.

[8] A. Harnack, *History of Dogma*, Boston, 1901, pp. 128-31, and *The Constitution and Law of the Church in the First Two Centuries*, trans. by F. L. Pogson, ed. by H. O. A. Major, New York, 1910, pp. 117-21; Longs-Hasselmans, "Un Essai de théologie sur le sacerdoce catholique," critical remarks by Y. Congar, *Revue des Sciences Religieuses*, 25 (1951), 187-99, 270-304.

Some (J. V. Bartlet, A. Hamel) have sought to resolve the contradiction by eliminating the presbyteral prayer as an interpolation, but in fact both the rubric and the prayer are well attested textually. In 1915 C. H. Turner proposed, on the basis of an analogy to the Gregorian Sacramentary, that the rubric directs the bishop to pray the first part only of the episcopal prayer, up to the key words "praise of Thy name" (the common phrase in 8.2 and 3.3), after which the properly presbyterian petitions of 8.2-3 should replace the uniquely episcopal *potestates* of 3.4-5.[9] If the theory is correct, the conflate presbyteral prayer must have also besought "the power of the princely Spirit which is from Thee" for the presbyter.

Deacon. The deacon's ordination prayer also consists basically of a petition for the gift of the Spirit: "grant the Holy Spirit of grace and earnestness and diligence upon this Thy servant whom Thou hast chosen" (9.11). The deacon, however, is ordained by the bishop alone and not by the corporate presbyterate, because he does not share "the similar Spirit common to all the clergy" (i.e. the bishop and presbyters; 9.1, 4, 6). The entire discussion of ordination in Ap Tr 9 reveals clearly a unique charismatic basis for the collegiate episcopal-presbyteral office, in contrast to the deacon. But the crucial charismatic difference between them was not understood as a consequence of the deacon's ordination by the bishop alone rather than by the "sealing" of the co-presbyters, but as the theological difference that finds its appropriate expression in the contrasted rites of ordination.

The entire passage underlines the correlation between ministerial function and charismatic endowment. The "spirit of grace and solicitude and industry" (9.11) corresponds most appropriately to the diakonic functions, in personal submission to the bishop. In contrast the "Spirit of grace and counsel" (8.2) refers to the Spirit by whose fullness and power alone the bishops and presbyters could be charismatically qualified to guide and govern the People of God and to fulfill their liturgical-sacerdotal ministry. The "high-priestly Spirit," however, was invoked only in the prayer of episcopal consecration.

Confessor. "But if a confessor has been in chains in prison for the Name, hands are not laid on him for the diaconate or the presbyter's office. For he has the office [*timē*, "honor"] of the presbyterate by his confession. But if he be appointed bishop, hands shall be laid on him" (10.1). This mysterious clause has produced a jungle of textual corruptions and variants, but one phrase at least is almost surely original: the confessor "has the honor of the presbyterate by his confession" without any ordination. The fact that Hippolytus was a confirmed anti-Montanist, and that his arch-rival Callistus was in fact a confessor, makes it very unlikely that he would have invented this provision.

Although patristic literature offers no other direct statement of *de facto* presbyteral rank for confessors, much evidence confirms this clause indirectly. In Vis 3.1.8 Hermas asserts the right of martyrs and prophets to

---

[9] C. H. Turner, "The Ordination Prayer for a Presbyter in the Church Order of Hippolytus," *JTS,* 16 (1915), 542-47. Turner's solution has been widely accepted (Frere, Müller, Dix, Elfers, Lécuyer *et al.*).

a place among the presbyters, at least in the heavenly church. Origen calls the martyrs "the priests of whom Christ is High Priest" (*Exhortatio ad martyrium* 30), and for Clement the charismatic Christian gnostic is "a presbyter of the Church, a true minister of the will of God, not as being ordained by men" (*Stromata* 6.13). According to Karl Müller, martyrs, prophets and some other charismatics (virgins, ascetics) sat among the presbyters.[10] Did 10-13 confirms this thesis with regard to Syria.

Many passages indicate that confessorship was a recognized claim to clerical office or function. Around the year 200, Tertullian reports that someone "in an inferior place" can manage to "have a more important one, if he has made some upward step by enduring persecution" (*Adversus Valentinianos* 4; *De fuga* 11; cf. Eusebius, *Hist Eccl* 5.28.8-12). Even Cyprian, several decades later, clearly implies the same claim (*Epistles* 5, 13, 14, 38-40). The charismatic authority of the confessors was especially evident in the common practice of their reconciling penitents and restoring them to communion (Eusebius, *Hist Eccl* 5.2.5, 5.18.6-7, 6.42.5-6; Tertullian, *Ad martyras* 1; *De pudicitia* 21-22; *Adversus Praxean* 1; Cyprian, *Epistles* 15-20, 23, 27, 33, 36, 55). Tertullian and others indicate the charismatic basis of this practice. Origen, influenced by John 20:22-23, made the power to bind and loose depend on the gift of the Spirit (*De oratione* 28.8-10).

New Testament passages such as Matt 10:18-20; Acts 7:55-57; 1 Cor 2:9-10; 2 Cor 1:5; Col 1:24; 1 Pet 4:13-14; and Rev 1:10; 2:7, 11, 17 provided a biblical basis for the charismatic interpretation of martyrdom. As "God's prisoner," Ignatius claimed to speak "with God's own voice" (Phld 7.2-3), since the prophetic Spirit in him gives supernatural knowledge and cannot be deceived. "I am in bonds and can understand heavenly things, and the places of angels and the gatherings of principalities, and 'things seen and unseen' " (Trall 5.2). "At the hour of their torture," according to Mart Pol 2.2-3, "the noble martyrs of Christ were absent from the flesh, or rather the Lord was standing by and talking with them," showing them "things which ear hath not heard nor hath eye seen." The *Paraklētos* is abundantly present in the martyrs, for the Risen Lord suffers and triumphs in their flesh (Eusebius, *Hist Eccl* 5.1; cf. Irenaeus, *Adversus haereses* 4.33.9).

It is the Holy Spirit who trains the martyrs for mortal combat (Tertullian, *Ad martyras* 1, 3; *De fuga* 8, 10, 14; *De pudicitia* 22). Thus, according to Cyprian, "the uncorrupted and unconquered might of the Holy Spirit broke forth by their mouth," so that "the Spirit of God our Father . . . Himself both speaks and is crowned" in them (*Epistles* 58.5). Hippolytus also asserts that the Spirit teaches the martyrs to despise death and conquer through divine power (*Commentary on Daniel* 2.21.1-2). He viewed the "choir of martyrs" as a distinctly charismatic band, which he characteristically correlates with the apostles (also charismatic in nature) and the prophets (*Commentary on Daniel* 1.17.8-9; 4.14.3; *De antichristo* 59).

---

[10] Karl Müller, *Kirchengeschichte*, 3rd ed. by H. von Campenhausen, 1941, 1.1, 119-20, 274. Cf. Ehrhardt, *Apostolic Succession*, pp. 92-94.

This continuous line of patristic evidence converges with the charismatic thought of Ap Tr especially as revealed in the ordination prayers and the argument over the ordination of deacons. We have seen that the "princely Spirit" and the *communis praesbyterii spiritus* refer to the Holy Spirit charismatically manifested in the corporate presbyterate. Since martyrdom was an undeniable and transcendently glorious manifestation of this same pneumatic *dynamis,* it would be natural to conclude that the confessors also shared, by virtue of their confession, in the "Spirit of the presbyterate." But on the other hand the confessors, like all presbyters, must be ordained by imposition of hands in order to receive the high-priestly office and *potestates* of a bishop.

Conclusion

The thought of Hippolytus of Rome, especially as recorded in Ap Tr, places significant emphasis upon the gifts of the Spirit and their spontaneous manifestation, and also understands Church Order and Church Office in a charismatic way. This is especially evident in the Prologue and Epilogue, the passages on the daily assembly, and the *de facto* presbyteral status of confessors. His charismatic theology very probably had deep roots in the second-century traditions of the Roman Church.

"Love" in the Old Testament: Some Lexical Observations

LARRY L. WALKER

Introduction

Emblazoned in gas lights behind the pulpit in the Moody Tabernacle in Chicago was "God is Love" (1 John 4:8, 16). Such an abstract theological statement is alien to the character of the OT and not found there. The words for "love" in the OT do not carry the romantic and sentimental nuances found in modern life and literature.

The nature and character of God is reflected in many expressions in the OT: Holy One,[1] true God,[2] high God (Mic 6:6). He is referred to as "my strength" (Ps 18:2) and "my maker" (Job 36:3). He is called protector, refuge, fortress, rock, strength, tower and shield. Names like the rider of a cloud (Isa 19:1) and the rider of heaven (Deut 33:36; Ps 68:4)[3] are ascribed to him. But the important concept of "love" is not used in these titles and references to God. We do not find titles like "my lover" or "the one who loves." It is true that most of these titles describing God are concrete (rock, tower, shield), but there are a few abstract ones as well (holy, true, exalted). We would therefore expect to find the basic theological idea of "love" in those expressions referring to God. But the names, titles and other such references to God noticeably omit "love" vocabulary.

Why is this basic theological concept of "love" not expressed in names of God? Names such as El Shaddai, LORD of Hosts, Most High and other compounds of El and LORD reflect God's power, majesty and glory, but words for "love" are not used. T. Noldeke, in his outstanding study of personal names in the Bible, gives a detailed discussion of names that reflect

[1] Very often in Isa; also Pss 71:22; 78:41; 89:18.
[2] 2 Chron 15:3. Cf. "God of truth" (Ps 31:6). Biblical references in this article follow the versification of the Hebrew text.
[3] But in Ps 68:4 this should read "rider of the clouds," as in the *RSV*. Cf. M. Dahood, *Psalms*, AB, 17, Garden City, New York, 1966, 2, 136.

Larry L. Walker, Associate Professor of Semitic Languages and Old Testament at Southwestern Baptist Theological Seminary, Fort Worth, Texas. B.A., Bob Jones University; B.D., Northern Baptist Theological Seminary; M.A., Wheaton College Graduate School; Ph.D., Dropsie College.

the various attributes of God.[4] Theophoric names, he says, reflect God as one who gives, increases, is gracious, is merciful, blesses, helps, is good, strengthens, delivers, comforts, heals, redeems, preserves, protects, builds, knows, sees, hears, answers, speaks, dwells (among his worshippers), lives, makes glad, judges, rules, is high, is glorious, is perfect, is incomparable, and many more.[5] But names reflecting the love (*'hb, ḥsd*) of God are noticeably missing.[6]

God's "love" in the OT is revealed in the course of salvation history through his compassion, mercy and kindness.[7] A specific aspect of "love" in the OT is revealed in God's fidelity and loyalty expressed through the covenant. It is in the covenant idea that we find "love" defined in terms of election, grace and faithfulness. The key word used in expressing this covenant love is *ḥsd*.

Confusion in the study of "love" in the OT has been caused by the use of the same stock of words to express both the general idea of love and the more specific concept of covenant love. The same words were used to express divine love as well as human love in all its aspects. Semantic imprecision results from the lack of separate words to express different kinds of love. Greek—and other languages—have particular words to express various categories of love: sexual, family (various social relationships) and divine (religious).[8]

The Hebrew word *'hb*[9] may express erotic love,[10] human relationships[11] or divine relationships.[12] It is interesting to note that this basic

[4] *Encyclopedia Biblica*. London, 1902, 2, 3271-3307.

[5] Space here does not permit a full discussion of his examples and categories, but his survey is most instructive.

[6] The only personal names possibly reflecting "love," according to Noldeke, are from the root *ydd:* Jedidah (2 Kgs 22:1), Eldad (Num 11:26-27) and Jedidiah (2 Sam 12:25). But this is uncertain. According to W. L. Holladay, *A Concise Hebrew and Aramaic Lexicon of the Old Testament*, Grand Rapids, 1971, p. 128, this verb means "to throw." M. Noth, *Hebraisches und Aramaisches Lexikon zum Alten Testament*, ed. by L. Koehler and W. Baumgartner, rev. by B. Hartmann and E. Y. Kutscher, 1967[3], p. 49, takes it from a root meaning "to love"; F. Gröndahl, *Die Personennamen der Texte aus Ugarit*, Rome, 1967, p. 122, finds this same root in some Ugaritic names; H. B. Huffman, *Amorite Personal Names in the Mari Texts*, Baltimore, 1965, p. 181, also finds it among Amorite names. *The Chicago Assyrian Dictionary*, A, lists *dādu* with the meaning of "love-making" and "darling." Cf. Isa 5:1 where "my lover" (root, *dādu*) seems to refer to God.

[7] These aspects of "love" are expressed in such words as *'hb, ḥnn, ḥsd* and *ḥšq*.

[8] Cf. the well-known divisions in Greek: *eraō, phileō, agapaō* and their derivatives. (These categories are not rigidly distinguished, but the very fact that such different words exist in a language says something.)

[9] In the Septuagint all three Greek terms for love are used to express this one Hebrew word. Cf. V. Warnach, *Encyclopedia of Biblical Theology*, ed. by J. B. Bauer, London, 1970, 2, 518.

[10] Gen 34:3. For more examples, cf. the article by E. Jenni in *Theologische Handwörterbuch zum Alten Testament*, ed. by E. Jenni and C. Westermann, München, 1971, p. 63.

[11] Love of father for child (Gen 22:2); husband for wife (Gen 24:67); personal friends (1 Sam 18:1, 3); neighbors (Lev 19:18); strangers (Lev 19:34); and slave for master (Exod 21:5).

[12] Love of man for God (Exod 20:6; Deut 6:5; 7:9; 10:12; 11:1), and love of God for man (Deut 4:37; 7:13; 10:15; 15:16; 23:5).

word for "love" is not used in any Hebrew personal names,[13] or proper names of any kind, nor is it attested in any Canaanite (Ugaritic, Phoenician) personal names.[14] For some reason this root was avoided in personal names. It is interesting to note that in Canaanite this one word carries both the sexual and divine usage simultaneously—something unthinkable in the Hebrew Scriptures. (By this we mean that a deity is the subject of the verb when it is used for sex.) For example, we read of the Canaanite god Baal: "He *loves* a cow of DBR// a heifer in the field of SHHLMNT."[15] Despite the two unknown geographical terms used here, the meaning is quite clear. The passage continues, "He lies (*škb*) with her seventy-seven ... times eighty-eight. She conceives and gives birth to Mt."[16] The word *'hb* is not common in Ugaritic (which seems to be weak in words for "love") and does not have cognates in the other Semitic languages outside of Canaanite.[17]

Confusion is also caused in the study of God's "love" by making too sharp a distinction between God's love (*'hb*) and his faithfulness (*hsd*).[18] Such a distinction is unwarranted because *hsd* may clearly refer to either "love" (kindness, mercy, favor) or "faithfulness."

Hsd[19] may refer to love or mercy in a very general sense or be used of loyalty or faithfulness to the covenant in a formal sense. It is used of ordinary human relationships in the sense of loyalty or faithfulness between son and dying father (Gen 47:29), wife and husband (Gen 20:13), relatives (Ruth 2:20), guests (Gen 19:19), friends (1 Sam 20:8), king and people (2 Sam 3:8). It is never used of sexual love, and its meaning becomes strongly influenced by its association with the covenant. Its etymology remains, to use Stoebe's word, "dunkel,"[20] and the word remains unattested in our extant Canaanite sources. More important than etymology, however, is its usage and association in Scripture.

Snaith[21] helpfully notes the use of *hsd* 43 times in close association with other nouns—an association so close it may be termed hendiadys.

---

[13] See M. Noth, *Die Israelitischen Personennamen im Rahmen der Gemeinsemitischen Namengebung,* Stuttgart, 1928.

[14] See F. L. Benz, *Personal Names in the Phoenician and Punic Inscriptions,* Rome, 1972; Grondahl, *Personennamen,* Rome, 1967.

[15] Cf. *Ancient Near Eastern Texts,* ed. by J. R. Pritchard, Princeton, 1955, p. 139.

[16] *Ibid.*

[17] Aramaic uses the roots *hbb* and *rhm*; Arabic, *hbb* and *wdd*; Akkadian, *rāmu*. For a full discussion, including the semantic cognates in Sumerian and Egyptian, see *Theological Dictionary of the Old Testament,* ed. by G. J. Botterweck and H. Ringgren, Grand Rapids, 1974, *s.v. 'hb.*

[18] Thus E. Jacob, *Theology of the Old Testament,* New York, 1958, pp. 103-12, devotes one chapter to the "love" of God and discusses *'hb* and *hšq,* and uses a separate chapter to discuss God's faithfulness (*hsd*).

[19] H. J. Stoebe, *Theologische Handwörterbuch zum alten Testament,* p. 60, finds the word 245 times in the OT—including 11 times in Genesis and 127 times in Psalms.

[20] Stoebe, *Theologische Handwörterbuch,* p. 600.

[21] N. H. Snaith, *The Distinctive Ideas of the Old Testament,* New York, 1964, p. 100. N. Glueck, *Hesed in the Bible,* Cincinnati, 1967, p. 102, also wrote, "God's *hesed* and *emet* are to be considered a hendiadys in which *emet* has the value of a descriptive adjective."

Twenty-three times it is used with *'mt* and *'mûnh* (fidelity, firmness, truth),[22] and 7 uses are with *brît* (covenant). Of the remaining 13 cases, 4 are used with the two words for righteousness, *ṣdqh* and *mšpṭ*; 1 with *ṭôb* (prosperity); 1 with *mṣûdh* (stronghold); 1 with *ḥn* (kindness); and 6 with *rḥmîm* (compassion).

Snaith also notes the cases of Hebrew parallelism where *ḥsd* is involved. Of the 18 cases examined, 9 involved a parallel with *'mt* or *'mûnh*, the two fidelity-terms; 4 are involved with *ṣdqh* or *mšpṭ*, the two terms for righteousness; and 3 times *ḥsd* was paralleled with *ḥnûn, ḥn,* and *rḥmîm.* Snaith concludes his study of the contexts of *ḥsd* with the statement that in 8 cases it has the idea of "keeping faith, being firm, covenant," and in 9 cases it has the idea of "kindness." These examples reveal the basic meaning of "kindness" closely linked with "firmness."

While the idea of "loving-kindness" in *ḥsd* is not excluded, this translation does not render adequately the idea of persistence and firmness innate in the word—a concept clearly noted when it is studied in the light of the terminology employed in ancient treaty documents.[23]

Stoebe finds this word in such personal names as Hesed (1 Kgs 4:10); Hasadiah (1 Chron 3:20) and Jushab-hesed (1 Chron 3:20),[24] but this fundamental theological term is not common in Hebrew names. Huffman suggests the root may be attested in Amorite personal names,[25] and Stack lists the root in his study of Palmyrene personal names,[26] but the evidence given appears inconclusive. If used at all, it was rare.

A word reflecting God's loving concern or compassion is *rḥm*, often translated "mercy" in the *AV*. It is also found in Ugaritic[27] (*rḥm*) and Akkadian (*rêmu*). It may be found in both Israelite[28] and Akkadian[29] personal names. A noun-form of this root literally means "womb," which is used to express the seat of emotions.[30] God's love and concern is also vividly expressed by this anatomical term. It is used of the feeling of a father for his child (Ps 103:13), and of the feeling of God for his own children. It is used with great significance in the names Ruhamah and Lo-Ruhamah—the names of Hosea's children (Hos 1:6, 8; 2:1 [3], 23 [25]).

The verb *ḥšq*, which is used of the yearning of a man for a woman (Gen 34:8; Deut 21:11), is also used of God's love for man (Deut 7:7; 10:15; Ps 91:14).

---

[22] The references for these and the following observations may be found in Snaith, *Distinctive Ideas,* p. 100.

[23] This will be discussed in connection with the usage of this word in Deut.

[24] Stoebe, *Theologische Handwörterbuch,* p. 600; cf. also Noth, *Die Israelitischen Personennamen,* p. 183.

[25] Huffman, *Amorite Personal Names,* p. 201. But he also thinks it may be related to the word for "stork."

[26] J. K. Stack, *Personal Names in Palmyrene Inscriptions,* Oxford, 1971, p. 89.

[27] J. Aisleitner, *Wörterbuch Der Ugaritischen Sprache,* Berlin, 1963, p. 219. He lists only one example.

[28] "Raham" (1 Chron 2:44) and "rehum" (Ezra 4:8-9, 17, 23). Cf. Noth, *Die Israelitischen Personennamen,* p. 187.

[29] Stamm, *Die Akkadische Namengebung,* pp. 103, 122, 193, 239.

[30] Gen 43:30; 1 Kgs 3:26 (translated "bowels" in the *AV*).

Another basic word revealing God's nature as "loving" or "gracious" is *ḥnn*. It often refers to concrete favor rather than affection. The verb is used about 78 times, and the noun (*ḥn*) about 69 times.[31] It has wide usage and appears also in Ugaritic, Phoenician-Punic and Akkadian. In addition, it is attested as a West Semitic word in the Amarna letters (*EA* 137:81; 253:24).[32] It is found in many Canaanite personal names,[33] and appears compounded with the Canaanite deity Baal in the well-known Punic general's name, Hannibal. It also shows up in the NT name of Ananias. It is compounded in Israelite theophoric names with El (Elhanan, Hananeel) as well as with Jehovah (Jehohanan). Still another usage is in Ugaritic personal names: *yḥnb'l* ("May Baal be gracious"), *ḥnnb'l* ("Baal has been gracious").[34] The root is often used in Akkadian[35] personal names, including names in the Amarna tablets. In fact, this root was widely used throughout the Semitic onomasticon—including Syriac, Elephantine Aramaic and Old South Arabic.[36]

We thus find a rather striking contrast between "love" (*'hb*), which appears to have been purposely avoided in Canaanite names, and "grace" (*ḥnn*), which was widely used.

I. Love in Genesis

The very first occurrence of the word "love" (*'hb*) in the English OT (*AV*) is in Gen 22:2, which refers to the love of Abraham for Isaac. Immediately following this we find a series of passages in the patriarchal narratives referring to family love: Isaac's love for Rebekah (24:67); Isaac's for Esau (25:28); Rebekah's for Jacob (25:28); Jacob's for Rachel (29:18, 20, 30); Leah's for Jacob (29:32); Israel's for Joseph (37:3, 4; 44:20).

God's "gracious" (*ḥnn*) character is expressed in Gen 33:5, 11, where Jacob referred to the children and the wealth God had "graciously" given him.

The word that became the term for a certain important kind of "love," *ḥsd*, makes its first appearance in the Bible in Gen 19:19 where Lot experienced God's "mercy" (*AV*; "kindness," *RSV*) in being delivered from the destruction of Sodom. The next appearance of this word (Gen 20:13) concerns the "favor" Sarah was to show Abraham by saying he was her brother. But soon the word picks up even stronger nuances of "loyalty" (cf. Gen 21:33), and by the time we reach Gen 24:27 we find the significant expression "steadfast love and faithfulness" (*RSV*, *ḥsd w'mt*), concerning God's relation to Abraham. Thereafter in the OT we often find *ḥsd* coupled with *'mûnh* or *'mt* in a kind of hendiadys to express "fixed love."

[31] Stoebe, *Theologische Wörterbuch*, p. 588.
[32] Cf. *CAD*, E, p. 164.
[33] Cf. the many examples collected from Phoenician-Punic by Benz, *Personal Names*, pp. 313-15.
[34] Cf. Gröndahl, *Personennamen*, pp. 135-36.
[35] The root in Akkadian is *enēnu*. For examples, cf. Stamm, *Die Akkadische Namengebung*, p. 182. In West Semitic cuneiform texts (Mari, Amarna, Alalakh) the root appears as *hanānu*, and is found in personal names in all these places. See Huffman, *Amorite Personal Names*, p. 200.
[36] For examples in Palmyrene, cf. Stack, *Personal Names*, p. 89.

The term *ḥsd* is used of God in Jacob's prayer for deliverance from his brother Esau when he exclaims to God, "I am not worthy of the least of all thy mercies (Gen 32:10, *AV*; "steadfast love," *RSV*) . . . thou hast shewed." It is next used of God when the "LORD showed mercy" (*AV*; "steadfast love," *RSV*) to Joseph in prison (Gen 39:21).

The same word is used of human relations, where it sometimes denotes more the idea of doing a "favor": Sarah for Abraham (Gen 20:13), the butler for Joseph (40:14)[37] and Joseph for Jacob (Gen 47:29). In other cases of human relations it expresses more the idea of "loyalty": Abimelech (Gen 21:23), Laban and Bethuel to Abraham (Gen 24:49).

Sexual love (*yd'*) is first referred to when Adam "knew" his wife (Gen 4:1, 25). Then it is used in reference to Lot's daughters (Gen 19:8), Lot's male guests (Gen 19:5), Rebekah (Gen 24:16) and Tamar (Gen 38:26). Sexual love has also been found by some[38] in the word *ṣḥq*, which in Gen 39:14 is translated "mock" in the *AV*; the same verb is used in Gen 26:8 where we read of Isaac "fondling" (*RSV*; "sporting with," *AV*) his wife. (The reason this particular verb was used here is probably because of the play on the word "Isaac" [*yṣḥq*].) Elsewhere this word seems to mean "entertain" (Judg 16:25), "joke" (Gen 19:14) and "laugh" (Gen 18:13).

The idea of sexual lust or desire may also be found in the word *ḥšq* [39] in Gen 34:8 where Shechem "longed for" Dinah. The same word carries a similar meaning in Deut 21:11 where the Israelite warriors have a "desire" for captive women. This word has not yet been found in Canaanite (Ugaritic and Phoenician).

II. Love in Exodus, Leviticus and Numbers

The word "love" (*'hb*) is found in the *AV* of Exod, Lev and Num at Exod 20:6 (in connection with the prohibition of graven images, where God is said "to visit the iniquity of the fathers upon the children unto the third and fourth generations of them that hate him but show mercy unto those that love [*'hb*] him"). It is found also in connection with the love of a servant for his master, wife and children (Exod 21:5), of one's neighbor (Lev 19:18) and of the stranger among Israel (Lev 19:34).

The idea of God's "favor" or "grace" (*ḥnn*) toward Israel is found in Exod 3:21; 11:3; 12:36, and is used in reference to Moses in Exod 22:12, 13, 16, 17; 34:9; Num 11:11, 15. The same word used in these passages is found in the adjective form in Exod 34:6, where the LORD passed before Moses on Mount Sinai and described himself as "gracious." The verb *ḥnn* is used in Exod 33:19 where the LORD declared, "I will be gracious to whom I will be gracious."

The word *ḥsd* is found in Exod, Lev and Num only four times. In Exod 15:13 we read of God who in his "mercy" (*AV*; "steadfast love,"

---

[37] This example could also perhaps illustrate the "loyalty" of the butler to help his fellow-prisoner. (There appears to be a semantic overlapping of "favor" and "loyalty" in all these examples.)

[38] See E. Speiser, *Genesis,* AB, Garden City, New York, 1964, 1, 201.

[39] It should be noted that this verb sometimes is used of divine love. It takes God for its subject in Deut 7:7; 10:15; and Ps 9:14.

RSV) led the people which he had redeemed. Exod 20:6 speaks of God showing *ḥsd* "to the thousands who love me and keep my commandments." In Exod 34:6 we read of the LORD passing before Moses and identifying himself as merciful (*rḥûm*), gracious (*ḥn*), longsuffering, and abundant in goodness (*ḥsd*) and truth (*'mt*), and in the next verse that the LORD has "mercy" (*ḥsd*) for thousands. In the one passage in Lev (20:17) it is translated "wicked thing" (*AV*; "shameful thing," *RSV*) and seems unrelated to our discussion here.

The concept of sexual love (*yd'*) is expressed in Num 31:18, 35.

III. Love in Deuteronomy

The doctrine of God's love for the people of Israel (and the response expected from them) is only implied in the first four books of Scripture, but it becomes explicit in Deut. Here God's love for Israel is viewed as a result of his election manifested in covenant (Deut 7:7-8).

It is in Deut that divine love first comes to the forefront in OT revelation. In this book the *AV* uses "love" 19 times[40] to translate *'hb* and once for *ḥbb* (Deut 33:3). Specific references to God's love are found in Deut 4:37; 7:8, 13; 10:15; 23:5. It is also used of man's love for God (Deut 5:10; 6:5; 7:9; 10:12; 11:1, 13, 22; 13:3; 19:9; 30:6, 16, 20). All these are passages where the word "love" is found in the *AV* of Deut, but the concept of divine love or favor or kindness is expressed by other terms as well.

The love of God is expressed in Deut with *ḥšq*·[41] "the LORD did not set his love upon you, nor choose you, because ye were more in number . . ." (7:7). The same verb is used in Deut 10:15: "the LORD had a delight (*ḥšq*) in thy fathers to love (*'hb*) them, and he chose their seed after them."

The term *ḥsd* is found only three times in Deut (5:10; 7:9, 12), where the *AV* always translates it as "mercy," but the *RSV* always as "steadfast love."

The concept of divine love in Deut appears to be strongly colored by the use of "love" in the extra-biblical covenant and treaty-texts.[42] In these texts from the eighteenth to the seventh centuries B.C., "love" is used to describe the friendship and loyalty of the parties involved. A servant of the king of Mari calls himself servant and *ra'imka*[43] ("the one who loves you"). By the Amarna period "love" is used in the terminology of international relations. The Pharaoh is expected to "love" (*rêmu*) his vassal (*EA* 121:61; 123:23), and the vassal must "love" the Pharaoh. The use of "love" in such

---

[40] Deut 4:37; 5:10; 6:5; 7:9, 13; 10:12, 15, 18, 19; 11:1, 13, 22; 13:3; 15:16; 19:9; 23:5; 30:6, 16, 20. *'hbh* is used in Deut 7:8.

[41] This verb is also used to express human love in Deut 21:11 where it refers to the "desire" of the Israelite warrior for a captive woman.

[42] W. Moran, "The Ancient Near Eastern Background of the Love of God in Deuteronomy," *CBQ*, 25 (1963), 77-87.

[43] The root *'hb* is not used in Akkadian, which uses *rêmu* as the semantic equivalent of Hebrew *'hb*. (Akkadian *ḥâbu* [B] = *râmu* as listed with some West Semitic words in one text. Cf. *CAD*, H, p. 21.)

contexts certainly means more than affection; it denotes faithfulness and loyalty. A good example of this is *EA* 138:71-73 where the king of Byblos writes, "Behold the city! Half of it loves the sons of 'Abd-Asir-ta (who fostered a rebellion) and half of it (loves) my Lord." In such a context, "to love" equals "to be loyal."

Moran gives additional examples where subjects must "love" ("be loyal to") their king. Rib-Addi's "loyal" subjects are those who love him and are opposed to the rebels (*EA* 83:51; 137:47). Such concepts and expressions are not limited to the Amarna and the Mari letters. In an Assyrian text of later date, the author writes, "The King of Assyria, our Lord, we will love" ("be loyal to").[44]

Another parallel to the Akkadian treaty-texts is the biblical expression "with all your heart" (Deut. 6:5). This expression is used in requiring the vassal to be faithful and to fight "with all your heart."[45]

In the OT we also have some examples where "love" seems to equal "loyalty." In 1 Sam 18:16 we read "all Israel and Judah loved David" ("were loyal to" David). In 2 Sam 19:6-7 Joab protests David's grieving over Absalom a rebellious son, while showing no concern for "those who love you" (*'hbk*). This surely contrasts the one who was rebellious to those who were "loyal." The same Hebrew word (*'hb*) is used in 1 Kgs 5:15 where Hiram of Tyre is called David's "lover," which in view of the context, and the history between Solomon and Phoenicia, must be considered the language of treaty relationship.

All this indicates that in some cases in the OT "love" refers to "loyalty," an attitude and action that could be commanded, rather than to a psychological feeling. Love and obedience are blended; one author says they are inseparable.[46] Deut 6:5 is a prime example of this command "to love" ("be loyal to") the LORD. This command is most intimately connected with the service of God and keeping the rest of the requirements of the covenant law (Exod 20:6; Deut 6:2-9; 7:9; 10:12ff.; 11:1, 13; 30:10, 16; Josh 22:5; 23:6-16). Furthermore, the love of God is intermingled almost inextricably with the fear of God in Deut 10:12; 13:4. However, man's love for God was to be far from sheer legalism or external observance only. It was to engage the whole man (Deut 4:29; 6:5; 10:12; 11:13; 13:3; 30:6), and must lead to a "cleaving to" God (Deut 10:20; 11:22; 13:4; 30:20; Josh 22:5; 23:8).

IV. Love in the Prophetic Proclamation

The prophets, utilizing a rich religious heritage, proclaimed a manifold love of God. The entire range of Hebrew vocabulary for love, loyalty, mercy, kindness and grace is used in preaching the message of God to the heirs of the covenant promises. It is in the prophetic books that the love of God is made vivid, being preached with great force and conviction.

[44] L. Waterman, *The Royal Correspondence of the Assyrian Empire*, Ann Arbor, Mich., 1930-36, p. 266.

[45] Akkadian uses *ina kul libbi* and *ina gammurti libbi*. For examples, cf. Moran, "Ancient Near Eastern Background," p. 83.

[46] C. Lehman, *Biblical Theology*, Scottdale, Pennsylvania, 1971, 1, 182.

One of the earliest writing prophets, Hosea, preached (and lived) a message that was a bold portrayal of God's love. Some eighteen times he used forms of *'hb,* in addition to related love-words such as *rhm* [47] ("mercy, compassion") and *hsd,* which the *A V* translates "lovingkindness" in 21:19 (21), "goodness" in 6:4, and "mercy" in 4:1; 6:6; 10:12; 12:6 (7). [48]

Isaiah described divine love revealed in grace and mercy, a love made more meaningful against a background of justice. Isaiah is rich in setting forth the love and mercy of God: "For a brief moment I forsook you, but with great compassion *(rhm)* I will gather you. In overflowing wrath for a moment I hid my face from you, but with everlasting love *(hsd)* I will have compassion *(rhm)* on you. . . . My steadfast love *(hsd)* shall not depart from you, and my covenant of peace shall not be removed, says the LORD, who has compassion on you" (Isa 54:7-10).

Love and kindness do not exist as isolated graces in the nature of God, but rather form, along with his holiness, one grand unity of his Being, and they are expressed in relation to his people. Jeremiah, for example, speaks of God's covenant love.

Jeremiah preached that God's covenant love *(hsd)* endures forever (33:11), even though it is complemented by justice (9:24; 32:18). "I have loved *('hb)* you with an everlasting love *('hb);* therefore I have continued my faithfulness *(hsd)* to you" (Jer 31:3). In other prophets this love is often associated with compassion *(rhm)* [49] that is abundantly ready to pardon, [50] though of course only when the sinner has repented and been converted. [51]

The prophets proclaimed that the love of God for men is not only the love of a Creator for his work (Isa 43.1-7, 21) but also the love of a father for his child (Hos 11:1-4; Isa 1:4; 30:1, 9; Jer 3:19; 31:20); it is greater than the love of a mother for her own infant (Isa 49:15; 66:13; Mal 1:6). The prophets use *'hb* to express these traits of warm affection (Hos 9:15; 11:1, 4; 14:4; Mal 1:2).

The prophets did more than bring into focus the various facets of God's love for man, however. They made clear what God expected in response from man. As an essential element in their proclamation, they emphasized that man's love for God means in essence faithfulness to God's covenant, which is shown by keeping his commands (Jer 2:2; Isa 56:6; Jer 11:1-5; 26:3; 31:31).

And yet the prophets denounced mere mechanical externalism and superficiality as a response to God's love (Isa 1:10-15; 29:13-14; 58:1-5; Jer 7:21-28; Ezek 33:10-20; Hos 6:6; Mic 6:6). They demanded genuine piety or loyalty *(hsd)* in its place (Hos 4:1; 6:4-6; 10:12; 12:7). Again and

[47] Hos 2:23 (25); 1:6, 7, 8; 2:1 (3), 4 (6), 23 (25); 14:3 (4). This is the term employed in the names of his children: Ruhamah (*AV* mg., "having obtained mercy") and Lo-ruhamah (*A V* mg., "not having obtained mercy").

[48] The *RSV* also used a variety of words (kindness, steadfast love, love) to translate this term.

[49] Hos 2:21 (19); Isa 54:8; 60:10; 63:7; Zech 1:16.

[50] Isa 55:7; Mic 7:19.

[51] Hos 1:6; Jer 18:8; 21:4-7; Ezek 18:27.

again they called for true conversion of the heart (Isa 1:16-20; 55:6-7; Jer 3:12-13; Ezek 18:30-31; Amos 5:14-15; Joel 2:12-13; Jonah 4:2). In all this, love for God continues to mean, in essence, faithfulness to the LORD's covenant, which must be made real by keeping the commandments (Jer 2:2; Isa 56:6; Jer 11:1-5; 26:3-4; 31:31ff.).

Daniel, in his great intercessory prayer, referred to the LORD as the one who "keepest covenant and steadfast love (ḥsd) with those who love ('hb) him and keep his commandments" (Dan 9:4).

V. Love in the Psalms

The Psalms, in accordance with their literary character as prayer-chants, speak chiefly of a love expressed by thankfulness and gratitude toward God (5:12; 31:24; 97:10; 116:1; 138:2; 145:20). The inner depths of this love are brought out by the use of rḥm (18:1) and ḥšq (91:14). Moreover, the idea of love is reflected in the LORD's unwavering kindness and covenant faithfulness toward his people (Pss 89:4; 103:17). But beyond this, we find reference to the LORD's love for individual men (Pss 4:1; 25:6ff.; 119:76ff.; 143:12; 146:8).

It may be surprising for some to learn that 'hb is used only twice in the Pss. One passage speaks of God's love for Jacob (47:4), and the other states that the LORD loves the righteous (146:8).

On the other hand the word ḥsd is found many times, and is a key word for understanding God's love as portrayed in the Pss. This word is translated by a variety of words as the translators attempted to capture the richness of its meaning: love, grace, mercy, steadfast love, kindness, covenant love, and loving-kindness. But it usually stands primarily for covenant love, as in Ps 89:28: "My steadfast love I will keep forever and my covenant will stand firm for him." Repeatedly, the psalmist clearly brings together the close relationship between God's steadfast love and his covenant with Israel. The most glorious presentation of the ever enduring quality of God's steadfast love shines forth in Ps 136. Here the psalmist brings into view God's mighty acts in creation, in delivering his people from Egypt, and in giving them the land of Canaan. In response to each of these great manifestations of what the LORD did the psalmist responds, "For his steadfast love (ḥsd) endures forever!"

VI. Love in the Wisdom Literature

In the Wisdom Literature of the OT, theological vocabulary is not as developed as in later literature. Words like ḥsd have not yet taken on theological significance. In the book of Job, ḥsd occurs only three times (37:13; 6:14; 10:12), and none of these refers to any special covenant love. The same is true in Prov where there is also no explicit reference to covenant love, or any divine love, in the use of ḥsd.[52] This word does not occur in Eccl.

---

[52] The ten occurrences are Prov 3:3; 11:17; 14:22, 34; 16:6; 19:22; 20:6, 28; 21:21; 31:26.

The common word for love, *'hb*, occurs only once in Job (19:19) and seems to denote the idea of loyalty. This word is also found in Eccl in the well-known verse "there is a time to love and a time to hate" (3:8). It is further used in Eccl for the "love of silver" (5:10 [9]), and for the "love of [your] wife" (9:9). It is used often in Prov but rarely of God's love.[53] Its meaning is in fact quite varied in Prov.[54]

The common noun *ḥn*, "grace," is not found in Job, but the root word is.[55] It is used in connection with God, however, only in Job 33:24. The noun *ḥn* occurs in Eccl 9:11; 10:12, but not in connection with God. The verb *ḥnn* occurs six times in Prov,[56] but again not in reference to God. One characteristic of Wisdom Literature is the absence of theological formulation, and we find this to be true concerning the teaching of God's love.

The root *rḥm*, "mercy," is found in Prov 28:13: "whoso confesseth and forsaketh [his sins] shall have mercy." It is also found in Prov 12:1 but with no theological significance. This root (*rḥm*) in the sense of compassion or mercy is not found in Job, although the word from which it is derived, *rḥm* ("womb"), is.[57]

Conclusion

God's elective love is not conditioned by any covenant,[58] but only by the will or nature of God himself, the one who loves. The verb *'hb*, according to one commentator, represents the "ultimate category of God's beneficent sovereignty."[59] It results, however, in God's making a covenant with his chosen people.

That election is related to love is clearly seen in the many associations of the word "love" with the word "choose": "Because he loved (*'hb*) your fathers and chose (*bḥr*) their descendants after them" (Deut 4:37). In Deut 7:7, 8 we read, "It was not because you were more in number than any other people that the LORD set his love (*ḥšq*) upon you and chose (*bḥr*) you ... but it is because the LORD loves (*'hb*) you. ..." The frequent occurrence of "choose" (*bḥr*) with words for love is significant. Many commentators have noted the place given to the love-concept in Deut. It is also noteworthy that 20 of the 153 occurrences of "choose" (*bḥr*) in the OT are found in Deut.[60]

It should be noted, too, that the verb "know" (*yd'*), which is used of the sexual relations between man and woman, and represents what may be

---

[53] The only references to God's love seem to be 3:12; 15:9. The word is used in connection with "wisdom" in 8:17, 21; 29:3.

[54] See Prov 8:36; 4:6; 1:22; 9:8, 13, 24; 15:12; 16:13; 20:13; 14:20; 17:17, 19; 18:21, 24; 19:8; 21:17; 22:11; 27:6.

[55] Job 8:5; 9:15; 19:16, 21; 33:24.

[56] Prov 14:21, 31; 19:17; 21:10; 26:25; 28:8.

[57] Job 3:11; 10:18; 24:20; 31:15; 38:8.

[58] Cf. the comments by Snaith, *Distinctive Ideas of the Old Testament*, p. 95.

[59] J. B. Payne, *The Theology of the Older Testament*, Grand Rapids, 1962, p. 163.

[60] L. Koehler, *Old Testament Theology*, London, 1957, p. 82.

considered the most intimate kind of love, is also used in the sense of election in the OT. Payne writes, " 'To know' carries the idea of elective grace and is equivalent to saying 'choose'."[61]

The connection between love and election in the Bible is also reflected in verses like Mal 1:2, 3: "I have loved (*'hb*) Jacob but I have hated Esau." In this passage "love" = "elect" and "hate" = "reject." (Such an Hebraic mode of thought is undoubtedly behind a verse like Luke 14:26.)

The close relationship that exists between *'hb* and *yd'* is found not only in the sexual sphere (Gen 4:1) but in the religious one too.[62] So we find significant semantic overlapping in Hebrew between love (*'hb*), know (*yd'*) and choose (*bḥr*).

In contrast to elective love, covenant love (*ḥsd*) strongly suggests steadfastness and determined loyalty. Payne[63] describes *ḥsd* according to the three categories of strength, loyalty, and faithfulness. Although some verses speak of God's love for the righteous (Ps 146:8; Prov 15:9) and his love for all creatures (Ps 145:9), the OT primarily develops the theme of God's covenant love for his chosen people. The word *ḥsd* was used to express the enduring quality of God's love and the loyalty involved in the covenant relationship.

> God was the God of love because he was the God of the covenant; the establishment of the covenant and the giving of the law had been the supreme expression of his love.[64]

---

[61] Payne, *Theology of the Older Testament*, p. 179. Cf. Exod 1:8; 33:12; Hos 13:5; Amos 3:2.

[62] Cf. the examples collected by V. Warnach in *Encyclopedia of Biblical Theology*, p. 526.

[63] Payne, *Theology of the Older Testament*, p. 162.

[64] A. Nygren, *Agape and Eros*, trans. by P. S. Watson, Philadelphia, 1953, p. 48.

The Greek "Verbal Genitive"[1]

G. HENRY WATERMAN

It has long been recognized that the genitive case in Greek has a variety of uses. A. T. Robertson called it "the specifying case" or "the case of genus (*genos*) or kind."[2] He distinguished thirteen uses of the true genitive and seven uses of the ablative, which even in his day, he admits, was called an "ablatival genitive" by some grammarians.[3] Blass and De-Brunner, combining the old genitive and ablative, give twenty-two uses of the genitive case.[4] Nigel Turner says: "The relationship expressed by the genitive is so vague that it is only by means of the context and wider considerations that it can be made definite. For practical purposes perhaps the only real division is that between subjective and objective."[5] He proceeds to list twelve additional uses of the case, distinguishing between the true genitive and the ablatival genitive.[6] Zerwick notes the "various usages into which grammarians have classified the immense variety of the genitive."[7] He takes note of a book by O. Schmitz published in 1924 under the title, *Die Christusgemeinschaft des Paulus im Lichte seines Genitive-gebrauchs*, of which Zerwick says: "This book shows how the grammarian's classification of the uses of the genitive, useful as it may be, is inadequate and may become misleading."[8]

---

[1] A Paper Presented to the Midwestern Section of the Evangelical Theological Society at Trinity Evangelical Divinity School, March 30, 1973.

[2] A. T. Robertson, *A Grammar of the Greek New Testament in the Light of Historical Research*, Nashville, 1934[4], p. 493.

[3] *Ibid.*, pp. 494-520.

[4] F. Blass and A. DeBrunner, *A Greek Grammar of the New Testament and Other Early Christian Literature*, trans. and ed. by R. Funk, Chicago, 1961, pp. 89-100.

[5] James H. Moulton, *A Grammar of New Testament Greek, Vol. 3: Syntax*, Edinburgh, 1963, p. 207.

[6] *Ibid.*, pp. 207-18.

[7] Maximilian Zerwick, *Biblical Greek Illustrated by Examples*, English Edition Adapted from the Fourth Latin Edition by Joseph Smith, S.J., Rome, 1963, p. 12.

[8] *Ibid.*, p. 12.

G. Henry Waterman, Professor of New Testament Interpretation at Wheaton College Graduate School, Wheaton, Illinois. B.A., Houghton College; M.A. and B.D., Wheaton College Graduate School; Ph.D., New York University.

This paper concurs with Zerwick's conclusion. It confines itself, how-ever, to the uses of the genitive in noun-noun phrases, i.e. in phrases in which the word in the genitive case is a noun (or a pronoun or an adjective functioning as a noun) and is dependent on another noun. The subjective and objective uses of the genitive, with which both Zerwick and Turner (following Zerwick) begin their discussion of this case, are examples of the genitive used in noun-noun phrases. *hē ptōsis autēs*, "its fall," in Matt 7:27 (the house falls) and *gongysmos tōn Hellēnistōn*, "murmuring of the Hellenists," in Acts 6:1 (the Hellenists murmur) are clearly subjective. On the other hand, *hē de tou pneumatos blasphēmia*, "but the blasphemy of the Spirit," in Matt 12:31 and *apothesis rhypou*, "removal of dirt," in 1 Pet 3:21 are clearly objective. There are other places where the genitive may be either subjective or objective, such as in Phil 1:3, where *epi pasē tē mneia hymōn* may be subjective, "whenever you remember me," or objective, "whenever I remember you."

It is apparent, however, as Zerwick points out, that these two uses of the genitive do not exhaust the uses of this case in noun-noun phrases. They simply form a convenient starting point to discuss its various uses. In addition to the subjective and objective uses, there are the following: the possessive genitive, e.g. *pōlēson sou ta hyparchonta*, "sell *your* posses-sions";[9] the genitive of relationship, e.g. *Iōannēn ton Zachariou huion*, "John the son *of* Zechariah";[10] the qualitative or descriptive genitive, e.g. *ton oikonomon tēs adikias*, "the *dishonest* steward";[11] the appositional genitive, e.g. *elegen peri tou naou tou sōmatos autou*, "he was speaking about the temple *which was his body*";[12] the genitive of material or content, e.g. *alabastron myrou nardou*, "an alabaster jar *of nard per-fume*";[13] and the partitive genitive, e.g. *dōsō soi heōs hēmisous tēs basileias mou*, "I will give you as much as half *of my kingdom*."[14]

All of these genitives a e dependent in some way or another on a substantive. Most grammarians classify these uses under the heading of adjectival genitive[15] or adnominal genitive.[16] Robertson seems to have been somewhat hesitant about using this classification, although he admits that "the genitive does indeed resemble the adjective" and that "the function of the case is largely adjectival."[17] He goes on to explain that his hesitancy was due to the influence of some of his contemporaries who preferred to make the verb the starting point for explaining the genitive.[18] Dana and Mantey accept Robertson's view that the genitive is in function adjectival, and go on to say that it "usually limits a substantive or substan-tival construction, though its use is not infrequent with verbs, adjectives,

[9] Matt 19:21.
[10] Luke 3:2.
[11] Luke 16:8.
[12] John 2:21.
[13] Mark 14:3.
[14] Mark 6:23.
[15] E.g. Moulton-Turner, *Grammar*, p. 207.
[16] E.g. Blass-DeBrunner, *Grammar*, p. 89.
[17] Robertson, *Grammar*, p. 493.
[18] *Ibid.*

and adverbs. Its adjectival nature is very pronounced and quite obvious."[19]

The present writer, while in essential agreement with other grammarians that the genitive is a case that is used primarily to show attribution,[20] is not convinced that the uses given under this general classification cover all the uses of the genitive case in noun-noun phrases. How does one classify the genitive construction used in Eph 1:13, *esphragisthēte tō pneumati tēs epangelias tō hagiō*, "you were sealed with the Holy Spirit of the promise"? In this passage the genitive expression, *tēs epangelias*, is neither subjective nor objective. In fact, it does not fit any of the usages mentioned above. The clear meaning of the verse is that the Christian believers had been sealed with the Holy Spirit whom God had promised.[21]

The present writer suggests that, in trying to sort out the various uses of the genitive in noun-noun phrases, some valuable insights may be gained from "transformational grammar." This relatively new approach to grammar was introduced by Noam Chomsky less than twenty years ago.[22] It is now accepted as a distinctive but legitimate approach to grammar by a number of present-day linguists,[23] and a number of books have been written to describe how to write such a grammar.[24] A transformational grammar seeks to describe a language by constructing a series of formulas by which one may generate all the possible grammatical structures of the language from certain "kernel" sentences. (Hence, this type of grammar is also called a "generative" grammar.)

This method of analyzing a language has one very important advantage over other methods: it enables the student to distinguish among expressions that have the same formal structure but obvious differences in meaning. For example, in English the expressions "his fine car," "their beloved ruler," and "his aged helper" all have the same form, i.e. they each consist of a possessive pronoun, an adjective and a noun. It is obvious, however, that they have very different meanings. The first phrase, "his fine car," means that "he has a car" and "the car is fine." The second phrase, "their beloved ruler," means that "they love him" and "he rules over them." The

---

[19] H. E. Dana and Julius R. Mantey, *A Manual Grammar of the Greek New Testament*, New York, 1927, p. 72.

[20] *Ibid.*, p. 74.

[21] Cf. Acts 1:4 where Jesus, in speaking of the coming of the Holy Spirit, commanded his disciples to wait for "the promise of the Father," and Acts 2:38-39 where Peter, after exhorting the multitude at the feast of Pentecost to "repent and be baptized, each of you, in the name of Jesus Christ, so that your sins will be forgiven, and you will receive the gift of the Holy Spirit" (vs. 38), says, "for the promise [of the Holy Spirit] is to you and to your children and to all who are far away, to as many as the Lord our God may call" (vs. 39).

[22] Noam Chomsky, *Syntactic Structures*, The Hague, 1957.

[23] Henry A. Gleason, *An Introduction to Descriptive Linguistics*, rev. ed., New York, 1961, pp. 171-94; Robert A. Hall, Jr., *Introductory Linguistics*, Philadelphia, 1964, pp. 224-27; Eugene A. Nida, *Toward a Science of Translating*, Leiden, 1964, pp. 59-69.

[24] E.g. Emmon Bach, *An Introduction to Transformational Grammars*, New York, 1964; A. Koutsoudas, *Writing Transformational Grammars: An Introduction*, New York, 1966.

third phrase, "his aged helper," means that "the man is aged" and "he helps him."[25]

If one applies this technique to the uses of the Greek genitive in noun-noun phrases, one may distinguish the following uses:[26] (1) In Eph 1:1 *thelēmatos theou*, "the will of God," is equivalent to *thelei ho theos*, "God wills," and is therefore a subjective genitive. (2) In Eph 1:7 *tēn aphesin tōn paraptōmatōn*, "the forgiveness of trespasses," is equivalent to *aphiēsin [ho theos] ta paraptōmata*, "[God] forgives trespasses," and is an objective genitive. (3) In Eph 1:13 *ton logon tēs alētheias*, "the word of truth," is equivalent to *ho logos alēthēs*, "the word is true," and is a descriptive or qualitative genitive. (4) In Eph 1:11 *tēn boulēn tou thelēmatos autou*, "the counsel of his will," is equivalent to *hē boulē autou estin to thelēma autou*, "his counsel is his will," and is an appositional genitive. (5) In Eph 1:3 *patēr tou kyriou hymōn*, "Father of our Lord," is equivalent to *ho kyrios hymōn echei patera*, "our Lord has a Father," and is a genitive of relationship. (6) In Eph 1:23 *to sōma autou*, "his body," is equivalent to *echei sōma*, "he has a body," and is a possessive genitive. (7) In Eph 1:13 *tō pneumati tēs epangelias tō hagiō*, "the Holy Spirit of the promise," is equivalent to *[ho theos] epēngeilato to pneuma to hagion*, "[God] promised the Holy Spirit," and is what this writer proposes to call a "verbal genitive."

The genitive in a noun-noun phrase may, then, function as (1) the subject of the idea expressed in the noun on which it depends; (2) the object of the idea expressed in the noun on which it depends; (3) a predicate nominative adjective describing or characterizing the noun on which it depends; (4) a predicate nominative noun in apposition with the noun on which it depends; (5) a noun denoting someone to whom the noun on which it depends is related (in a familial sense); (6) a noun denoting someone who possesses the noun on which it depends; and (7) a verb indicating the action or state of the noun on which it depends. In other words, this kind of genitive construction may be regarded as a "transform" from "kernel" sentences, in which the genitive replaces any of the basic parts of the sentence: subject, object, predicate nominative adjective, predicate nominative noun, object of the verb *echei* (both to express relationship and possession), and even the verb itself.

All of these uses of the Greek genitive have been recognized by Greek grammarians except the last one. The term "verbal genitive" has been coined by the present writer. To show that this usage is not confined to the first chapter of Ephesians, the following additional examples are submitted:

Eph 2:2: *en tois huiois tēs apeitheias*, literally, "among the sons of disobedience," i.e. "among people who disobey God."

Matt 9:38 = Luke 10:2: *tou kyriou tou therismou*, "the Lord of the harvest," i.e. "the Lord who is harvesting."

---

[25] Nida, *Toward a Science of Translating,* p. 61.
[26] For the reader's convenience, all of the examples are taken from Ephesians.

Matt 13:38: *hoi huioi tēs basileias*, "the sons of the kingdom," i.e. "those who will reign as kings."

Luke 9:51: *tas hēmeras tēs analēmpseōs autou*, "the days of his ascension," i.e. "the days when he will ascend."

John 6:35: *ho artos tēs zōēs*, "the bread of life," i.e. "the bread which gives life."

III. THEOLOGICAL

The Deity of Christ in the Writings of Paul

WALTER ELWELL

For many years now it has been a basic assumption of liberal theology that in the NT God and Christ are never really identified. A distinction is usually made, we are told, between God, who is referred to as *Theos*, and the status to which Jesus was exalted by virtue of his death and resurrection (however that be explained), which is defined by the title *Kyrios*. God (*Theos*) is one being and Jesus (*Kyrios*) is another. Jesus may be the Lord of the church or the Lord of the cult, but he is certainly not the one eternal God, who is the maker and ruler of all things. C. J. Cadoux, in his updated *Pilgrim's Progress*, put it this way: "P[ilgrim] : Did Paul assert that Christ was God? I[nterpreter] : Not explicitly. Passages like Rom 9:5b (which is a parenthetical doxology, and possibly an early gloss), Acts 20:28 (which is ambiguous), and Tit 2:13 (which is probably not from Paul's hand) are inconclusive. Paul habitually differentiates Christ from God."[1] Later, Cadoux wrote, "Some modern Christians take it for granted that the full worship of Christ as God was a uniform practice of the whole church from the early days of the Apostles onwards. That, however, is an error. The attribution of full Deity to Christ and the regular custom of praying to Him were the results of a long development of thought."[2] Harold DeWolf argues in much the same fashion in his *A Theology of the Living Church*. He says, "If Jesus be regarded simply as God, then we encounter his own emphatic contrary teaching, as recorded in the Gospels, even, or rather specifically, in the Fourth Gospel."[3] DeWolf goes on to speak of Jesus' distinctiveness as that of being the locus of God's work, the place where others may find God, or his having the same purpose as God, but this in no way implies that

---

[1] C. J. Cadoux, *A Pilgrim's Further Progress*, London, 1945, pp. 40-42. Cf. also V. Taylor, "Does the New Testament Call Jesus God?" *ExpT*, 72 (1961-62), 116-18; cf. also R. E. Brown, "Does the New Testament Call Jesus God?" *TS*, 26 (1965), 545-73.

[2] Cadoux, *A Pilgrim's Further Progress*, p. 45.

[3] L. Harold DeWolf, *A Theology of the Living Church*, New York, 1953, p. 243.

Walter Elwell, Associate Professor of Bible and Chairman of the Department of Bible at Belhaven College, Jackson, Mississippi. B.A., Wheaton College; M.A., Wheaton College Graduate School; graduate studies, The University of Chicago and Tübingen University; Ph.D., The University of Edinburgh.

he is God. He was exalted above other men to a much higher status, but this shows no favoritism on God's part because "it is an obvious fact that God does differently endow and call to different vocations the various ones of his children. Not everyone is endowed or called to be a DaVinci or a Bach. Not everyone is equally endowed with Jesus for all-pervasive, filial God-consciousness."[4] It is this God-consciousness which was Christ's "deity."

More recently Martin Werner has suggested that "the ascription of the title *Kyrios* to Christ . . . constitutes a remarkable piece of evidence indicative of the fact that, in terms of the Primitive Christian conception, related as it was to the apocalyptic doctrine of the Messiah, Christ was a high heavenly being of angelic kind."[5] So whether Christ was habitually differentiated from God, or a highly God-conscious man, or an angelic being of some sort, he is not to be identified with God because, in fact, he was not qualitatively the same as God either by right or by attainment.

However, the teaching of the NT runs directly counter to this assessment of the evidence. One does not need to probe very deeply beneath the surface to see that in the minds of the writers of the NT Christ and God were indeed more than simply equals, they were *equal* to each other, that is to say, Christ was distinct from God the Father, but was in some mysterious way equal to him. God and Christ were one.

It is the purpose of this article to examine the evidence as it appears in the writings of Paul in order to establish this thesis. This will at the same time show the inadequacy of the prevailing liberal opinion that such an identification between God and Christ was not made (or at best only vaguely hinted at) in the NT. It was not possible to examine all of Paul's writings exhaustively, but books were selected from each phase of his writing ministry and every reference to Christ and God was tabulated in order to determine what specific use was made of each. The books examined were: Gal, 1 Thess, 2 Cor, Phil, Col and Phlm; however, references were taken from all of Paul's writings when appropriate. No use was made of the Pastorals out of deference to critical opinion, even though in this writer's thinking they are Pauline. That the Pastorals identify Christ with God is almost universally acknowledged (this is, in fact, one of the reasons for making them post-apostolic), so that point does not need to be established here.[6] What emerged from all this is that Paul reflected his feelings concerning Christ's deity in at least five different ways, thus giving us five different lines of evidence that may be pursued.

I

The first thing that draws our attention is the way in which Paul ascribes to Christ qualities that are specifically God's in the OT. In the OT

---

[4] DeWolf, *A Theology of the Living Church*, pp. 253-54.

[5] Martin Werner, *The Formation of Christian Dogma*, Boston, 1965, p. 124.

[6] Even Bultmann is willing to accept this. Rudolf Bultmann, *Theology of the New Testament*, New York, 1951, 1, 129.

the name of God is occasionally linked together with a qualifying idea to give a compound idea. For example:

> Jehovah Mekaddaschem—The Lord our Sanctifier (Exod 31:13).
> Jehovah Shammah—The Lord (is) present (Ezek 48:35).
> Jehovah Shalom—The Lord our Peace (Judg 6:24).
> Jehovah Tsidkenu—The Lord our Righteousness (Jer 23:6).
> Jehovah Nissi—The Lord our Banner (of victory) (Exod 17:8-15).
> Jehovah Rapha—The Lord our Healer (Exod 15:26).

It is significant that in Paul's writings all of these ideas are directly ascribed to Christ. So for Paul:

> Christ is our Sanctification (1 Cor 1:30).
> Christ is Present in us (Col 1:27; Eph 2:5, 6; cf. Matt 28:20).
> Christ is our Peace (Eph 2:14).
> Christ is our Righteousness (1 Cor 1:30).
> Christ is the one in whom we have victory (1 Cor 15:57).
> The Body of Christ is given the gift of healing (1 Cor 12:9; cf. Acts 3:6 where Peter heals in the name of Jesus).

Paul would hardly have done this had he thought that God was distinct from Jesus and that Jesus had a lesser status than God.

Paul also takes OT quotations or ideas that refer to God and refers them to Christ. In 2 Cor 10:13-18 Paul is speaking of his own ministry and his "boast" in what he is doing, but he does this in order to be commended by the Lord (Christ), so that his boast will not be in vain—indeed, "Let him who boasts boast of the Lord" (quoting Jer 9:24). In Jeremiah, the quote refers to God; in Paul it refers to Christ. (See also Phil 1:26; 3:3 where Paul boasts in Christ.) Another place where Paul does this is in Phil 2:10-11. Here he says that every knee shall bow and every tongue confess that Jesus is Lord, using the words of Isa 45:23. In Isaiah the words refer to God, but as they are used by Paul here they refer to Jesus. We will bow our knees to him as Lord of all. Paul uses these same words elsewhere (Rom 14:11; Eph 2:14) to refer to God. However, this created no problem for Paul. To him God and Christ were one.

II

A second line of evidence which shows that Paul identified Christ with God can be found in a series of objective statements that he makes about each one. It is not that Paul is attempting to prove Christ's deity by these statements, but simply that the identity of the two was so deeply imbedded in his mind that it never occurred to him to speak otherwise. Consider the following examples:

Gospel. Paul frequently speaks of the gospel in absolute terms, being the message that he preached, and from which none may deviate, except under the anathema of God (Rom 2:16; 2 Cor 4:3; Gal 1:8, 9). It is also God's gospel (1 Thess 2:2, 6, 9), one that he preached in the ages past to Abraham, which brought about Abraham's salvation (Gal 3:8). Because this gospel is the power of God (Rom 1:16), Paul is not ashamed to defend it. But it is also Christ's gospel, because it belongs to him and concerns him (1 Thess 3:2; Gal 1:7; Rom 1:16), and God will take vengeance on those who are not obedient to the gospel of the Lord Jesus (2 Thess 1:8).

Church. Paul writes that the churches in Christ greet the Roman believers (Rom 16:16), but these churches are also the church of God (Gal 1:13; 1 Cor 15:9). The church is further defined as being "the Church . . . in God the Father and the Lord Jesus Christ" (1 Thess 1:1) and the church of God in Christ (1 Thess 2:14). In these references, it is quite clear that Paul makes no distinction between the church as being in God or in Christ; they may be in either or in both, because it amounts to the same thing.

Love. The transcendent message of the NT is that God is love and that his love moved him to provide mankind with a redeemer; hence Paul tells the Thessalonians that they are loved by God, and that this secures their election (1 Thess 1:4). The same idea is found in Eph 1:3-5 where we read that God has predestinated us unto the adoption of children in love. But this love is also seen as supremely Christ's love. Who may separate us from it? (Rom 8:35). Christ loved us and gave himself for us, thus making us his own (Gal 2:20). This love may also be defined as the love of God in Christ (Rom 8:39). Thus like the church, which is in both Christ and God, love, the greatest of all God's gifts to men, is the love of Christ, and of God as well.

Kingdom. The Kingdom of God that Jesus preached is for Paul the Kingdom into which we are called (1 Thess 2:12) and the ultimate inheritance of the saints (Gal 5:21). It is also the Kingdom of Christ, God's beloved Son (Col 1:13) or the Kingdom of God and Christ (Eph 5:5).

Word of God. Jesus, quoting Deut 8:3, tells us that we are not to live by bread alone but by every word that proceeds out of the mouth of God (Matt 4:4). Paul echoes this by saying that his ministry is to fulfill the word of God (Col 1:25), and he thanks God that the Thessalonians have accepted the message which they heard as God's word, because that, in truth, is what Paul preached (1 Thess 2:13). But in the same epistle, Paul thanks God that from them has sounded out the word of the Lord (Christ) (1 Thess 1:8), and he, Paul, speaks to them by the word of the same Lord (1 Thess 4:15). This word is further defined as the word of Christ that dwells in us richly, providing wisdom and grace in our hearts (Col 3:16).

Spirit. In Gen 1:2 the Spirit of God broods over the waters; in 1 Thess 4:8 the Spirit of God is the possession of the believer; in Phil 1:19, the Spirit of Jesus Christ is supplied to effect Paul's release from prison. The Spirit is both the Spirit of God and the Spirit of Christ. (One finds this elsewhere in the NT as well. See, for example, 1 Pet 1:11 and 1 John 4:2.)

Power. According to Paul, the gospel is the power of God (Rom 1:16) and we all live through it. But we also live by the power of God that works in us as it worked in Christ (2 Cor 13:4), holding this power in earthen vessels (2 Cor 4:7) and showing it forth to men (2 Cor 6:7). But if this transcendent power belongs to God, it also belongs to Christ, for Paul glories in his weakness, so that the power of Christ might rest upon him (2 Cor 12:9).

Mystery. Paul says he preaches the long-hidden, but now revealed, mystery (Eph 3:8, 9), which mystery is the mystery of Christ (Col 4:3; Eph 3:4). However, it is also the mystery that belongs to God, the content of which is Christ (Col 2:2) or the unsearchable riches of Christ (Eph 3:8).

Peace. The fruit of the Spirit (who is of God or of Christ) is peace (Gal 5:22), and Paul prays that the God of peace may be forever with the Philippians (Phil 4:9). He concludes his first Thessalonian letter with the prayer that the God of peace may sanctify them wholly (1 Thess 5:23). However, in Col 3:15 it is the peace of Christ that rules in their hearts and this peace comes from both God and Christ (Col 1:2; Phil 1:2; 1 Thess 1:1). In Phil 4:7 the peace of God guards our hearts and minds through Christ Jesus and in Eph 6:15 we preach a gospel of peace (this gospel being either Christ's or God's). When we believe this gospel of peace, we find that Christ is our peace (Eph 2:14).

Day of the Lord. The Day of the Lord, promised as God's awful judgment upon sin in the OT (Isa 21:2; 13:6; Ezek 13:15; Zeph 1:14), is in Paul the day of the Lord indeed (1 Thess 5:2), but this is understood by him to be the day of Christ (Phil 1:6, 10; 2:16; 1 Cor 1:8). It is the day of God Almighty in Rev 16:14. With this eschatological note in mind, it is well to observe that Paul says we "stand" before God (Gal 1:20) but we also stand before Christ on that awful day (1 Thess 2:19).

In summary, it is abundantly clear that when Paul speaks of the great facts of the gospel and of life in general, he is governed by the proposition that God is at work because Christ is at work and that both are engaged, to the same degree, in all that is taking place. There is no distinction made as to the work of either. They are separate in being, but somehow wondrously the same.

III

A third line of evidence is where Paul speaks of what God is doing in the lives of men. This is not wholly separate from who God is, for God cannot do anything on any other basis than what he is, but for our purposes the two may be separated to provide a clearer picture of how Paul thought. Here, as above, the evidence shows that in Paul's mind Christ and God are equal.

Grace. The heart of Paul's preaching is the grace of God, which is the foundation for the salvation of man (Eph 2:8, 9). We live by the grace of God (Col 1:6) and are called by the grace of God (Gal 1:15). But this grace comes from both God and Christ (Col 1:2; Phil 1:2; 1 Thess 1:1) and is defined by Paul as being the grace of Christ (1 Thess 5:28; Gal 1:6; 6:18). So closely is Christ identified with the grace of God that Paul argues that to fall from grace is to be cut off from Christ (Gal 5:4). However, so closely is God identified with this grace that when the grace of Christ is with our spirits (Phil 4:23) we are then moved to worship God with our spirits (Phil. 3:3).

Salvation. Men cannot save themselves; it must be God who saves—yet in Eph 5:23 and Phil 3:20 Christ is called our Savior and salvation is specifically defined as coming through Christ (1 Thess 5:9). God rescues us from the power of darkness in Col 1:13, but it is Christ who rescues us in 1

Thess 1:10. God redeems us (through Christ) in Gal 4:4, but it is Christ who redeems us in Col 1:14 and Gal 3:13. God forgives us our sins in Col 1:13, but it is the Lord (Christ) who forgives us in Col 2:13. Finally, as a result of our being saved, God takes up his residence in us according to Eph 4:6, but it is Christ who takes up his residence in us in Gal 1:20 and Col 1:27. The result of this is that we may be filled with the fullness of God, according to Eph 3:19, or, according to Eph 4:13, filled with the fullness of Christ. If a person refuses God's salvation, he is lost, that is, separated from Christ, and this person Paul defines as an atheist (Eph 2:12).

The Life of Man. We must all live according to God's will, because it is God who works all things according to the counsel of his will (Eph 1:11); our lives, therefore, should conform to what he desires (1 Thess 4:3; Gal 1:4). But the will of God is made known to us in Christ (1 Thess 5:18), and we need to know what the will of the Lord (Christ) is for us (Eph 5:17). Our own insights are not enough to provide us with the wisdom we need, for God only is wise, who providentially rules the world in his wisdom (1 Cor 1:21), and Christ *is* himself the wisdom of God (1 Cor 1:24, 30). When we need help God reveals to us what we need to know (Phil 3:15), but it is Christ who revealed to Paul the gospel of God that he preached (Gal 1:12). Our lives then must conform to the revealed will of God, but when we do this, we are fulfilling the law of Christ (Gal 6:2), although, as we all know, God is the one who gave the law on Mount Sinai (Gal 3:19, 20).

IV

The fourth line of evidence pointing to the identity of Christ with God is in the attitude that Paul adopts toward each. Paul clearly would not offer worship due God alone to a mere man or an angel, because he specifically rejects this in Col 2:17-19, yet he offers to Christ exactly the same homage that he offers to God. More than that, the full range of religious experience is related to Christ in precisely the same way as it is to God, just as Paul spoke of the being and works of God and Christ as though they were the same.

Slave. Paul considered himself to have been purchased by the death of Christ and thus enrolled into Christ's service as his slave. He habitually refers to himself as Christ's slave (Rom 1:1; Gal 1:10; Phil 1:1) and as one who is serving Christ (Col 3:24). He also serves the living and true God (1 Thess 1:9), and as his servant (1 Thess 3:2; 2 Cor 6:4) he will be judged by God for the deeds done in the flesh (1 Cor 4:5) at the judgment seat of *Christ* (2 Cor 5:10), or God (Rom 14:10-12).

Glory. Man lives in hope of the glory of God (Rom 5:2), which will be his eternal reward, and here on earth he lives his life in such a way that God will be glorified (Gal 1:24), because glory is due him forever (Phil 4:20). God extends grace to us so that we may live to his glory (2 Cor 4:15). But the glory of God is seen in the face of Christ (2 Cor 4:6), and the glory of Christ, who is in the likeness of God (2 Cor 4:4), shines out upon the world. Hence, we labor for the glory of the Lord (2 Cor 8:19) and wish to be workers to the glory of Christ (2 Cor 8:23). When we confess that Jesus is the Lord, we do this to the glory of God (Phil 2:11), because Christ is, indeed, the Lord of glory (1 Cor 2:8).

Boast. Because we glory in God, we may boast in the glory that will someday be ours, and the OT makes it clear that such a boast may be extended toward God alone (Jer 9:23, 24), because there is only one God. Yet Paul says we are to boast in Christ (Phil 1:26; 3:3), and he labors so that he may boast in the Lord and be commended by him (2 Cor 10:17-18). We do this in the sight of the Lord (2 Cor 8:31), but also in the sight of God (2 Cor 4:2; 12:19) who sees our lives and will judge them.

Faith. Abraham believed God and this was counted to him as righteousness (Gen 15:6), and Paul says that we are to do the same (Gal 3:6-7). That a man must have faith in God is axiomatic; in fact, faith in God is what God requires of us for a right relationship with him (1 Thess 1:8-9; Rom 4:1-5). For Paul, this faith in God is faith in Jesus Christ (Gal 3:22). He is the one in whom we believe and for whose sake we suffer (Phil 1:29). It is by faith in Jesus Christ that we are justified in the sight of God and are allowed to live with respect to God (Gal 2:16-19), and we pray to him as the expression of our dependence and faith (2 Cor 13:7; Phil 1:3, 4).

Knowledge. Closely allied to faith in God is the knowledge of him. When we believe what he has revealed we know him and that what he says is true. Indeed, to know God is to be saved and not to know him is to be lost (Gal 4:8; 1 Thess 4:5). Yet it is the truth of Christ that is in Paul (2 Cor 11:10), and he tells us that it is the knowledge of Christ that surpasses all (Phil 3:10). At the same time, however, Paul prays that the Colossians might bear fruit in every good work and increase in the knowledge of God (Col 1:10). In line with this, when Paul wishes solemnly to affirm that what he says is true, he appeals to the source of truth, God, as his witness (Phil 1:8), yet he also adjures the Thessalonians by the Lord to follow his instructions (1 Thess 5:27).

Worship, Thanks and Prayer. We worship God because he is our Lord and the praise of men is due him (Phil 3:3). We thank him for what he has done on our behalf (Phil 1:3; 1 Thess 1:2; 2:13), and we pray to him as the expression of our dependence and faith (2 Cor 13:7; Phil 1:3, 4). But Paul also directed his devotion to Jesus (2 Cor 11:3), defines his praise as being specifically through Christ Jesus (Rom 1:8; 7:25), and earnestly prays to Christ that he may be relieved of the thorn in his flesh that Satan had inflicted upon him (2 Cor 12:8).

A Worthy Life. Paul admonishes the Thessalonians to live in a manner worthy of God, because God has called them into his Kingdom (1 Thess 2:12). In order to accomplish this, we are to live in Christ (Col 2:6), being taught by him, that our lives may be worthy of Christ (Col 1:10). When we do this we will also be living in a way worthy of the gospel of Christ (Phil 1:27).

When one surveys this evidence of Paul's religious feelings and how he blended together his worship of God and Christ, it comes as no surprise that he concludes his Philippian letter with a doxology to God (Phil 4:20), followed immediately by the benediction of Christ (Phil 4:23). He concludes his second Corinthian epistle with a threefold benediction, this time including the Holy Spirit (2 Cor 13:14). But to Paul such a thing would have implied no blasphemy, for he was speaking of one and the same God, the only one that exists.

V

The final line of evidence consists of a series of more or less unconscious reflections on the part of Paul that God and Christ are one. Here it will be seen that the acts of the two are so closely linked together that it is often difficult to determine who, in fact, is performing the act. Either that, or the acts or references to the two are so closely united that it is difficult to decide to whom Paul is referring. This, of course, shows the identity of the two in Paul's mind, at the deepest possible level. He simply made no effort to sort out what God was doing and what Christ was doing. In his mind it was all the same thing.

Let us observe first two grammatical constructions where this is borne out. In Col 1:18-20 Paul begins the sentence with Christ clearly as the subject. Christ is the head of his body, the church, the beginning, the firstborn from the dead, that he might be pre-eminent. He ends the sentence with Christ clearly as the subject, "having made peace through the blood of his cross." However, the middle section can refer only to God, although no indication is given that any change is made or that Paul considered such a shift of subjects—Christ to God to Christ—in the middle of a sentence as being unusual. The clause runs (vs. 19): ὅτι ἐν αὐτῷ εὐδόκησεν πᾶν τὸ πλήρωμα κατοικῆσαι (20) καὶ δι' αὐτοῦ ἀποκαταλλάξαι τὰ πάντα εἰς αὐτόν, "that in him, he was pleased to cause all the fulness to dwell and to reconcile all things unto himself through him." The question is, Who was pleased to do this? It can hardly refer to Christ, for he could not have caused the fullness to dwell in himself. Not only that, but when one reads on to Col 2:9 the same words are used, and here it is clearly the divine fullness that dwells in the incarnate Christ.

It might be thought that *plērōma* could be the subject here as it is in 2:9, but this is not likely either. In 2:9 *plērōma* is an abstract idea that is described simply as dwelling in Christ. Here in 1:19 there is personal action on the part of the subject of *eudokēsen*, and it is difficult to imagine the *plērōma* being pleased to dwell in Christ and also to reconcile *ta panta* to himself (itself?) *di' autou*. Nowhere in the NT do we read of such an extraordinary action on the part of this abstract idea. However, it is wholly in keeping with the being of God the Father, who was pleased to allow his fullness to reside in the incarnate Christ, and who did in fact reconcile the world to himself through Christ, to be spoken of in this fashion. He was pleased to cause his own divine fullness to dwell in Christ so that he could indeed bring about the great reconciliation of *ta panta* to himself (*eis auton*) through Christ (*di' autou*). This makes perfectly good sense and is consistent with other references in Paul, 2 Cor 5:13, for example. However, taken in this way, it shows that in Paul's mind the great act of God's salvation was the act of God in Christ, or God and Christ, because Christ was God. Paul saw no need to sort it all out.

A second passage where the grammar shows this shift from Christ to God is Col 2:8-15. In this long sentence Paul begins with Christ as the main subject, but shifts over to God in 12b where the power of God raises Christ from the dead and makes us alive together with him and forgives us our trespasses. Then 14a continues by saying that the bond with its legal demands was taken away when it was nailed to his cross. This can hardly refer to God the Father, yet no shift is indicated in the subject at all. The clause runs (14): ἐξαλείψας τὸ καθ᾽ ἡμῶν χειρόγραφον τοῖς δόγμασιν ὃ ἦν ὑπεναντίον ἡμῖν, καὶ αὐτὸ ἦρκεν ἐκ τοῦ μέσου προσηλώσας αὐτὸ τῷ σταυρῷ. One could solve this by making Christ the subject of the participle exaleipsas, but this creates other problems, not the least of which is that no such switch is indicated. However, even if this were done the point can still be made that here in the midst of a long sentence dealing with what is clearly God's prerogative, providing salvation to man, Paul shifts from Christ to God to Christ without any indication that he is doing this and in such a way that it is difficult to tell who is doing what. Once again, the unity of the action of the two, God and Christ, is so deeply engraved in Paul's mind that he unconsciously reflects it, even in the grammar he uses. It could be that this is also the case in Acts 20:28 where Paul says God obtained the church with his own blood. It was God's blood that was shed upon the cross when Christ died for the sins of the world, but quite obviously it was the incarnate Christ who died. Was it "the blood of his own" or "his own blood"? A choice is not really necessary, theologically speaking, following the line of Col 1:18-20 and 2:8-15.

Another place where Paul reflects the identity of God and Christ is when he speaks of the actions of God relative to men and in the very same sentence includes Christ as a co-actor. In 1 Thess 3:11 Paul says, "Now may our God and Father himself and our Lord Jesus direct our way to you." No distinction is made whatsoever. God and Jesus do the directing.[7] Or again, in 1 Thess 3:12-13, the concerted actions of the two may be seen. Christ causes us to abound in love so that we may stand before God when Christ comes again. Both are deeply involved in the lives of men, to such an extent that the actions of God and Christ are virtually inseparable.

Finally, one might refer to such verses as Col 3:3 where Paul blends God and Christ together in such a way that they can hardly be separated. Paul says, "Your life has been hidden with Christ in God." How else can one take this except as Paul's affirmation that we are in Christ in God? Or consider this series of ideas: God is a God of peace (Phil 4:9; 1 Thess 5:23), and peace comes from Christ and God (Phil 1:2). This peace of God guards our hearts and minds in Christ (Phil 4:7). But Paul also says the peace of Christ controls our hearts (Col 3:15), because he (Christ) *is* our peace (Eph 2:14) and we preach a gospel of peace (Eph 6:15), Christ, of course, being the content of the gospel (1 Cor 15:1-5). Whence comes this peace, then? From God only? From Christ only? Can one really separate out what God does and what Christ does respecting peace? Clearly, both God and Christ

---

[7] In fact, with a singular verb (*kateuthynai*) made to follow a compound subject, could not this verse (1 Thess 3:11) be translated grammatically, "Now may our God and Father himself, even our Lord Jesus, direct our way to you"? (Ed.).

are so intimately involved in providing peace to man that no distinction either can or needs to be made.

VI

So far nothing has been said regarding the *loci classici* where Paul *affirms* the deity of Christ. This was done intentionally in order to show that these verses are not simply isolated passages unrelated to the rest of Paul's writings. Rather, they are distillations upward of the essential core of what Paul says, epitomizing the whole of his thought on this subject. The teaching that pervades the writings of Paul is crystallized in brief and infrequent statements where the deity of Christ is unequivocally affirmed. So when Paul says in Rom 9:5: ὁ Χριστὸς τὸ κατὰ σάρκα ὁ ὢν ἐπὶ πάντων θεὸς εὐλόγητος εἰς τοὺς αἰῶνας, there is no need to translate it, as does the *RSV*, "to them belong the patriarchs, and of their race, according to the flesh, is Christ. God who is over all be blessed forever. Amen." It would be better grammatically and theologically to take the *RSV*'s footnote as the translation, "Christ, who is God over all, blessed forever" (note the translation of the *NIV*), because this is precisely what Paul believed and said. Christ *is* God, blessed forever. The same is the case in Phil 2:5-11. Jesus was in *morphē theou*, being *isa theō*. He took on the *morphēn doulou* to become obedient unto death. Paul's point in this passage is the amazing condescension of Christ and his humiliation for the salvation of men. God became man in order to save him. This is exactly the same idea as expressed in Rom 5:8 where *God* shows *his* love for us in that while we were yet sinners Christ died for us. Christ dies as an expression of God's love, and this because Christ is God incarnate and could thus express God's love by his act of obedience unto death. What could be clearer than that Paul looked upon Jesus as very God of very God?

Conclusion

Although the foregoing material is only a selection from the writings of Paul, it nevertheless provides us with a cross-section of what he believed and from it a number of important conclusions may be drawn. First, there is no essential difference in the mind of Paul between God and Christ. When he writes of either, he is willing to say anything that could be said of the other and no restriction is made on what God could do and what Christ could do. This is not to say that God did not do some things that Christ did not do or that the incarnate Christ did not submit to God and will not yet do what is required of him, but simply that it is not a matter of essential nature that is in question, rather one of function. Anything could have been decided a priori in the counsel of God and this would not have touched the fundamental unity of the Father and the Son. As it stands, however, the overwhelming impression created by Paul is that when he speaks of the Father and the Son he is speaking of the one eternal God, no matter how jarring that might have sounded to the strict monotheists of his day or to the modern theologians who take the same unitarian position.

For Paul, Jesus is all that God is, and all that God is Jesus is, as far as their essential nature is concerned.

Second, it is difficult to detect any fundamental difference in Paul's attitude toward the deity of Christ from an earlier to a later period. He is not any more convinced of it later than earlier, nor is more divine activity ascribed to Christ later than earlier, nor is some fundamentally new thing ascribed to him later that was not either implied or stated earlier. The full deity of Christ is accepted from the very beginning. One interesting thing did emerge in this context, however, and that is how increasingly christological Paul's orientation becomes. It is not really a development in his thought as far as Christ's deity is concerned so that he becomes more christologically oriented as time progresses, but he certainly does become more Christ-centered toward the end of his ministry. Consider the following totals:[8]

	Galatians	1 Thessalonians	Philippians	Colossians	Philemon
Christ	57	41	71	79	11
God	41	40	25	34	2

Perhaps the explanation for this lies in the fact that as time passed the full meaning of Paul's own statement that the glory of God was to be seen in the face of Christ became increasingly more apparent to him. At any rate, the vision of Christ became more luminous to Paul with the passing of the years until to live meant Christ and to die meant more of Christ. It should not be forgotten, however, that in Gal Christ was said to live in Paul, and in 1 Thess it was Paul's earnest expectation "to ever be with the Lord" (1 Thess 4:17). So, of development as far as Christ's deity is concerned, there is none; but of variations on earlier themes with increasing crescendo, there is much.

Third, there is no essential difference with regard to the work of God and of Christ. Both are said to save, to direct, to hear prayer, to love, to provide grace, to dwell in the believer and much more. Once again, this is not to say that no differences exist, but that whatever differences do occur must be seen in the light of the essential unity that exists elsewhere.

Fourth, as human beings our relationship to God and Christ must be the same. Both are to be worshipped, thanked, prayed to, asked forgiveness of, given glory to, and served. We are to walk so as to be worthy of both, preach the gospel of both, rely on the Spirit of both, accept the grace of both, have the peace of both, live our lives in the sight of both, and ultimately appear before the throne of both, there to give an account of ourselves for our eternal gain or loss. It is conceivable that at this point

[8] This chart represents the number of times each is mentioned, every part of speech being counted separately. When there was a verb form, however, it and its subject were counted only once. For example, in Col 1:13 God is mentioned three times (*hos errysato ... metestēken ... autou*) and Christ once (*tou huiou*).

Cadoux, DeWolf and Werner have their greatest theoretical problems. Perhaps in their desire to worship God alone, the thought that a mere man could receive such divine worship would be a scandal to them. But it would have been to Paul as well. To worship a mere man would be blasphemy. However, the solution to this problem does not lie in denying that Paul offered such homage to Jesus, but in recognizing that to Paul Jesus was not a mere man, but God incarnate for us. When we worship Jesus, we are worshipping God, none else. In its own way, this, too, is a scandal, but of a different kind. It is a scandal of the mystery of godliness, of God manifest in the flesh, the scandal of God being in Christ for the purpose of reconciling the world to himself. This scandal, however, we must preach and glory in, for such glory is due God who condescended to become Man for us men and our salvation.

Some Reflections on the Mission of the Church

DAVID M. HOWARD

World mission is not a concept unique to the NT. The worldwide responsibility of the church to make Jesus Christ known to the nations is rooted in the doctrine of creation. While the world mission of the church is brought into focus by Christ in his Great Commission and by the Holy Spirit in his empowering of the church, it is nevertheless true that the foundation of this outreach is the OT.

J. H. Bavinck highlights this when he says, "Genesis 1:1 is obviously the necessary basis of the great commission of Matthew 28:19-20."[1] Johannes Blauw makes the same point by saying:

> Therefore for an understanding of the universal purport of the Old Testament, it is necessary to have the Old Testament begin where it begins. As long ago as 1936 K. Hartenstein pointed out (albeit in another connection) that the first chapters of Genesis are of special significance for a theology of mission.[2]

We will therefore look first at the OT roots for the NT understanding of world mission.

I. The Old Testament Foundation of World Mission

1. Creation

By the very act of creation God was expressing his interest in the world. Everything that he made was good and belonged to him. "The earth is the Lord's and the fulness thereof, the world and those who dwell therein" (Ps 24:1). By placing man, made in the image of God, in the midst of his creation and giving him dominion over it, he was showing his interest in man. No man has ever fallen outside the scope of God's concern.

[1] J. H. Bavinck, *An Introduction to the Science of Missions*, Grand Rapids, 1960, p. 12.
[2] Johannes Blauw, *The Missionary Nature of the Church*, New York, 1962, pp. 17-18.

David M. Howard, Missions Director of Inter-Varsity Christian Fellowship, formerly of the Latin America Mission, Colombia and Costa Rica. B.A., Wheaton College; M.A., Wheaton College Graduate School; LL.D., Geneva College.

The first command God gave to man was, "Be fruitful and multiply and *fill the earth* and subdue it . . ." (Gen 1:28). Why fill the earth? Because the whole earth was the realm of God's concern, and he wanted to reveal to man his worldwide designs.

But it was not long before man disobeyed God and turned from him. Because of man's rebellion God finally decided to wipe out almost the entire human race and get a fresh start.

2. Renovation

Following the Flood, the first command God gave to Noah as he came out of the ark was, "Be fruitful and multiply, and *fill the earth*" (Gen 9:1). God's plans had not changed. He still intended to carry out his designs in the whole earth, and man was told to start over with the same command given to Adam.

Roman Catholic missionary-theologian John Power comments, "The biblical story of the origins and early days of humanity is studded with unmistakable statements of universality—God's love for all men, and his plans to translate that love into action."[3] Commenting on the covenant made with man, as found in Gen 9:12-16, Power says:

> Notice the almost monotonous repetition of the universality theme in these verses, and in the surrounding ones: "every living creature for all generations." It is highly significant that the first mention of covenant in the Bible should occur in such a universalist context, long before any covenant made with the Patriarchs or with Israel as a people. Surely the essential message of this is that the original and enduring divine plan is concerned with the salvation of all men.[4]

3. Dispersion at Babel

The sinful nature of man in rebellion against his Creator came to the fore again at the Tower of Babel. God had told man to "fill the earth," but man decided to stay put. "Let us build ourselves a city, and a tower with its top in the heavens, and let us make a name for ourselves, *lest we be scattered abroad upon the face of the whole earth*" (Gen 11:4). Man refused to do the first thing God had told him to do. But again God's plans would not be thwarted. He intervened and confused man's language, thus forcing him to move out across the face of the whole earth in fulfillment of that command.

4. Call of Abraham

God chose one nation through whom he would develop his redemptive plans for the world. In his first words to Abraham he made it clear that what he would do in and through Abraham and his descendants was on behalf of the whole world: "By you *all families of the earth* shall bless themselves" (Gen 12:3). While Israel often did not understand this truth

---

[3] John Power, *Mission Theology Today,* Maryknoll, N.Y., 1971, p. 63.
[4] *Ibid.,* p. 64.

(that God would work through them to reach the whole world), the foundation was nevertheless laid in God's call to Abraham. It could never be said that God had had a limited vision of his creation or of his people.

5. Historical Development

Throughout the history of Israel God worked for Israel, to meet immediate needs in the life of that nation, but always so that he could fulfill his purposes in the world. Joshua saw this when he reviewed for Israel God's great works in the Exodus from Egypt:

> For the LORD your God dried up the waters of the Jordan for you until you passed over, as the LORD your God did to the Red Sea, which he dried up for us until we passed over, *so that all the peoples of the earth may know that the hand of the LORD is mighty* (Josh 4:23-24).

David caught a glimpse of this in his challenge to Goliath:

> This day the LORD will deliver you into my hand, and I will strike you down, and cut off your head; . . . *that all the earth may know that there is a God in Israel* (1 Sam 17:46).

Solomon sensed that the great temple he had built could have worldwide significance.

> Likewise, when a foreigner, who is not of thy people Israel, comes from a far country for thy name's sake (for they shall hear of thy great name, and thy mighty hand, and of thy outstretched arm), when he comes and prays toward this house, hear thou in heaven thy dwelling place, and do according to all for which the foreigner calls to thee, *in order that all the peoples of the earth may know thy name and fear thee* . . . (1 Kgs 8:41-43).

Hezekiah had the same vision when he prayed for deliverance from Sennacherib.

> So now, O LORD our God, save us, I beseech thee, from his hand, *that all the kingdoms of the earth may know that thou, O LORD, art God alone* (2 Kgs 19:19).

6. Poetic and Prophetic Declaration

Both the poets and the prophets of the OT expressed with some frequency the understanding that the God of Israel was for all nations and that his redemption was to be for all men. Just a few examples will suffice as illustrative of this fact.

> May God be gracious to us and bless us and make his face to shine upon us, *that thy way may be known upon the earth, thy saving power among all nations* (Ps 67:1-2).
> Sing to the LORD, bless his name; tell of his salvation from day to day. *Declare his glory among the nations, his marvelous works among all the peoples!* (Ps 96:2-3).

Of all the prophets Isaiah probably had the clearest picture of the fact that God intended that his redemption should reach beyond Israel. He even exhorts Israel to declare this fact when redemption comes to them, whether it be deliverance from captivity or ultimate deliverance from sin.

> Go forth from Babylon, flee from Chaldea, declare this with a shout of joy, proclaim it, send it forth to the end of the earth, say, "The LORD has redeemed his servant Jacob!" (Isa 48:20).

Isaiah also saw that the people of Israel were to be a witness to other nations.

> I will give you as a light to the nations, *that my salvation may reach to the end of the earth* (Isa 49:6).

While this may appear to be an attempt at using "proof texts," it is in reality a presentation of the universal emphasis in the OT. From the story of creation on through the entire history of Israel God wanted it known that he loved all nations and all men. He chose Israel as his instrument through which to reach the nations, and he declared through her that he loved the world.[5]

II. Christ and World Mission

In spite of the universal emphasis in the OT Israel conceived of her mission as primarily centripetal. She saw the nations coming to Zion for salvation. The centrifugal outreach in the mission of the church did not get its full development until the NT. But the groundwork was laid in the Old. Thus when Christ came, he could build on a foundation that spans the entire history of the human race.

1. Universal Emphasis in His Coming

The announcements of the birth of Christ contain in them the seed of universality. The shepherds at Bethlehem heard the angel pronounce "good news of great joy which will come *to all people*" (Luke 2:10). This child was not to be limited to Israel. He was for all people. Simeon saw this when he thanked God and said, "For mine eyes have seen thy salvation which thou hast prepared *in the presence of all peoples, a light for revelation to the Gentiles,* and for glory to thy people Israel" (Luke 2:30-32).

2. Universal Pattern in His Ministry

During Jesus' ministry on earth he did not travel very far geographically from the place where he was born. But in his outreach he showed his concern for every level of society and every class of people. He started with the Jews and ministered to the Pharisees, the religious élite. But this did not keep him from reaching also to those who never could get into the inner circle of religious leaders. He reached out to the sick, the diseased, the lepers—the outcasts of Israel.

Beyond that he reached out to those who were spurned because of their way of life. He was known as "a friend of tax collectors and sinners" (Luke 7:34), and he even had a tax collector among his disciples. He

---

[5] For a detailed study of the missionary theology of the OT see George W. Peters, *A Biblical Theology of Missions,* Chicago, 1972, Pt. 1.

brought salvation to the home of Zacchaeus, a hated tax-collector (Luke 19:1-10). He allowed a woman known publicly as a sinner to anoint his feet, and in the process he ministered to her by forgiving her sins (Luke 7:36-50).

While the average Jew of Jesus' day had no dealings with the Samaritans (cf. John 4:9), Jesus did not hesitate to reach out to them. He ministered to the woman at Jacob's well (John 4:1-42). He told a story to illustrate the real meaning of "neighbor" and chose to make the hero of the story a Samaritan (Luke 10:29-37). He healed ten lepers, only one of whom thought to return and thank him. This one was a Samaritan, and that fact is recorded as being significant (Luke 17:11-19).

If the Samaritans, who at least had some connections with Israel, were not worthy of salvation (in the view of the Jews of Jesus' time), how much less worthy were the Gentiles! Even the early Christians in Acts could not conceive that God's redemption reached that far. The universal emphasis of the OT had not penetrated their understanding.

Yet Jesus did not omit the Gentiles from his loving concern. He went to Tyre and Sidon, Gentile cities, and ministered to the Syrophoenician woman (Mark 7:24-30). He responded to the faith of a Roman centurion in Capernaum by saying, "Truly, I say to you, not even in Israel have I found such faith" (Matt 8:10). Thus there was not one strata of society nor one type of person who fell outside the sphere of his concern.[6]

Geographically Jesus set an example for his disciples that laid the foundation for his Great Commission given later. Early in his ministry in Capernaum the people urged him not to leave them. He had barely begun a fruitful ministry in that city, teaching and healing, when he started to move on. When they tried to keep him from going, he said, "I must preach the good news of the kingdom of God to the other cities also, for I was sent for this purpose" (Luke 4:43).

3. Universal Emphasis in His Commission

Volumes have been and will yet be written on the Great Commission Christ gave to his disciples. The limitations of space here require only a passing glance at these passages, which are so full of meaning. Taking them chronologically, the first to be noted is Luke 24:44-49. Here Christ met his disciples on the evening of the resurrection day, his first encounter with them as a group since the crucifixion. Turning to the OT he showed them how he had fulfilled all that the law of Moses, the prophets, and the psalms had said of him. Moving on he summarized the contents of the gospel message. He then pointed out that the message of repentance and forgiveness of sins must be preached among all nations. Finally, and possibly pointing his finger directly at them, he said, "You are witnesses of these things." Thus he told them that they were responsible to make the message known *among all nations.*

John 20:19-23 records the same incident but with different words.

---

[6] For an expansion of this concept see Ferdinand Hahn, *Mission in the New Testament,* London, 1965, chap. 2.

Here Jesus told his disciples that he was sending them in the same way that he had been sent by his Father, which means to all mankind.

Matthew records another incident which took place in Galilee in a mountain some days after the resurrection. When Jesus came to his disciples he told them of his authority, and then proceeded to commission them with their responsibility to "make disciples *of all nations*" (Matt 28:16-20).

While the ending of Mark's gospel (Mark 16:9-20) does not appear in the earliest manuscripts, the contents of the commission as given there coincide perfectly with the whole tenor of Jesus' teachings to his disciples in the post-resurrection appearances. The responsibility to "preach the gospel to the whole creation" gives a completeness to the message that is in keeping with the other Gospels.

In Acts 1:8 the last words that Jesus spoke to his disciples are recorded. It is significant that he chose for his final moment the emphasis that must have been uppermost in his mind at that point—the responsibility of his followers now to be witnesses "in Jerusalem and in all Judea and Samaria and *to the end of the earth.*"

In summary of these passages it is notable that Jesus gave this commission at least three times, if not more. He spoke it on the day of the resurrection in his first encounter with his disciples. He repeated it in Galilee on a mountain. And he chose to leave this as his final word to those men who were to lead the church in its first outreach. The significance of this repeated emphasis must not be lost to the church. It shows how vital this command was to Christ in the fulfillment of his redemptive plans for the world. The simple yet profound truth that "God so loved *the world* that he gave his only Son" is beautifully illustrated in the life, ministry and commands of his Son.

III. *The Holy Spirit and World Mission*

In his final words Jesus promised the necessary power to carry out the task that he was leaving with the church: "But you shall receive power when the Holy Spirit has come upon you; and you shall be my witnesses in Jerusalem and in all Judea and Samaria and to the end of the earth" (Acts 1:8). This promise was fulfilled on the day of Pentecost. The book of Acts illustrates how the Holy Spirit moved the church out to witness to the world.

1. The Fullness of the Holy Spirit

In the book of Acts there are nine cases where individuals or groups were filled with the Holy Spirit. Space does not permit a study of each of these incidents, but such may be found elsewhere.[7] Suffice it to say that there is one common factor in all of them, and it is of great importance in understanding the world mission of the church. Every time an individual or group was filled with the Spirit, he (or they) gave forth the message of the

---

[7] See David M. Howard, *By the Power of the Holy Spirit,* Downers Grove, Ill., 1973, chap. 3.

gospel with power and some came to the Lord. Thus, the key to outreach with the gospel is the fullness of the Holy Spirit.[8]

2. The Leading of the Holy Spirit

In addition to filling believers with the power to carry out their task, the Spirit was also directing the strategy of outreach by his clear leading.

Sometimes the Spirit led *to an individual,* so that through him the gospel might go to others. A classic example of this is his guidance of Philip to the Ethiopian eunuch in Acts 8. When the eunuch had received and understood the word of God and had been baptized in the name of Jesus Christ, he "went on his way rejoicing." There is every reason to believe that he shared the good news of salvation with others in his homeland. In fact, the Coptic church today claims that its spiritual roots can be traced to that eunuch.

At times the Spirit led *to an ethnic group,* thus directing the expansion of the church beyond the limitations of Judaism. This was true when Peter was led to Cornelius. The Jewish Christians had not yet grasped the full significance of the Great Commission nor of the OT teaching that they were to be a light to the Gentiles. It was only when the Spirit intervened dramatically that Peter, and subsequently the other apostles, recognized that Gentiles could also be saved. It took two visions, one to Cornelius and one to Peter, to effect this crossing of ethnic boundaries.

Also the Spirit led *to diverse geographical locations.* To study Acts without a map is to miss some of the most profound implications of the book. Let me comment at this point by way of tribute to Dr. Tenney. I shall never forget two consecutive assignments given by him in a study of Acts. One was to study all the references in Acts to the Holy Spirit (there are well over fifty of them) and correlate their meaning for the book. The other was to study all references to geography in Acts and discover the strategy of the Holy Spirit in terms of geography. These two assignments, each of which took many hours to complete, opened up whole new horizons of understanding about the early church and its world outreach.

Acts 16:6-10 is a key passage in noting the geographical guidance of the Spirit. Paul had faithfully preached the gospel in Phrygia and Galatia (the eastern part of Asia Minor). He had been forbidden by the Holy Spirit from going to Bithynia (northern part). Therefore, he went west to Troas, a seaport. Now where was he to go? At this point, when he had used all human efforts to fulfill the Great Commission in terms of geographical outreach, the Spirit gave him a vision of Macedonia and led him across into Europe. His "Macedonian call" came only when he had been obedient to the limits of his ability. He did not get this call by sitting comfortably at home waiting for lightning to strike. He got it as he moved out in obedience to Christ's commands under the promptings of the Holy Spirit.

A study of the cities mentioned in Acts will also show the strategic

---

[8] For a scholarly and up-to-date study on the Holy Spirit see Frederick Dale Bruner, *A Theology of the Holy Spirit,* Grand Rapids, 1970.

place that these centers played in the Roman Empire and in the outreach of the church. But this leads to the next point.

3. The Response of the Church to the Holy Spirit

The church in the NT was "not disobedient to the heavenly vision" (as Paul put it to Agrippa [Acts 26:19]). It was sensitive to the promptings of the Spirit and obedient in outreach. The church was obedient even when it was not the easiest thing to do. Philip probably did not want to go down to the Gaza road when he was having great success in Samaria. Ananias definitely did not want to go to Saul of Tarsus in Damascus. Peter never would have gone to Cornelius on his own initiative. Yet each of these men obeyed the Spirit, and the gospel was spread not only to the individuals involved but to whole groups of people.

The church also responded by every believer becoming involved in witness. They did not leave the task of preaching the gospel only to the apostles. When they were scattered abroad by persecution, they went everywhere preaching the gospel (Acts 8:1-4). This was a primary key in the rapid expansion of the church.

The use of strategic centers as a base of operations for outreach to the entire empire was also important. After Paul spent two years in Ephesus it could be stated that "all the residents of Asia heard the word of the Lord, both Jews and Greeks" (Acts 19:10). To the Christians in the key city of Thessalonica Paul could write, "For not only has the word of the Lord sounded forth from you in Macedonia and Achaia, but your faith in God has gone forth everywhere, so that we need not say anything" (1 Thess 1:8).

The church in its obedience was also a praying church. References to prayer in Acts and in the epistles are too numerous to mention here, but it would be impossible to read the NT without seeing the vital part that prayer played in the life and outreach of the church.

Another factor in their witness was the recognition of the gifts of the Spirit. Again and again Paul speaks of individuals who became like hands and feet to him in helping him reach others with the gospel. His whole concept of the body of Christ, developed so vividly in 1 Cor 12-14, demonstrates how the gifts are indispensable to witness.

The unity of the church is related to its recognition of the gifts of the Spirit. As the Spirit gives many gifts within the body, he also emphasizes that the body is one. Christ prayed for this unity "so that the world may believe that thou hast sent me" (John 17:21).

Thus the early church responded to the work of the Holy Spirit in its midst by reaching out to others with the message of salvation. Harry Boer shows how the Great Commission as given by Christ actually received its significance and was applied by the church because of the coming of the Holy Spirit.

> The Great Commission played a powerful role in the missionary witness of the early church from the day of Pentecost to the present. It can be said that it always has been, is now, and always will be the heart and soul of all true missionary witness.

But its meaning for and place in the life of the missionary community must, we believe, be differently construed than is customarily done. The Great Commission . . . derives its meaning and power wholly and exclusively from the Pentecost event.[9]

Witness began not with the receiving of the Great Commission, but with its *internal effectuation* at Pentecost . . . . Pentecost made the Church a *witnessing Church*.[10]

Conclusion

The missionary enterprise of the church in the NT is not an isolated teaching unrelated to the rest of Scripture. It is, rather, an integral part of God's whole plan of redemption as revealed from Gen to Rev. It is not like a pyramid built upside down with its point on one text. No, it is based on all of Scripture. Its foundations go back to Gen 1:1, and its structure is developed throughout the entire Bible.

God showed his people Israel that his redemption was to be for all mankind, and they were to be his light to the Gentiles. Jesus Christ in his own ministry set the pattern for world outreach. He confirmed this by his commands, which were given credence by the example of his life. The Holy Spirit empowered the church and then directed it in its outreach through Jerusalem to Judea and Samaria, and to the end of the earth.

The NT leaves no doubt that every Christian must become involved in God's plan for the world. The ministry of reconciliation has been committed to us (2 Cor 5:18-20). As the church becomes involved in world mission it does so with the great assurance that the day will come when it can be said, "The kingdom of the world has become the kingdom of our Lord and of his Christ, and he shall reign for ever and ever" (Rev 11:15). The church also knows that when we stand before the Lamb upon his throne there will be some from every tribe and tongue and people and nation in that great throng which numbers myriads of myriads and thousands of thousands joining in the song, "Worthy is the Lamb who was slain, to receive power and wealth and wisdom and might and honor and glory and blessing!" (Rev 5:6-14).

[9] Harry Boer, *Pentecost and Missions*, Grand Rapids, 1961, p. 43.
[10] *Ibid.*, pp. 128-29.

Some Reflections on Evangelism in the New Testament

PAUL E. LITTLE

While the work of evangelism is central in the NT, there is no exact equivalent for the word "evangelist." The words "gospel" and "evangel" represent the Greek *euangelion,* and the verbs "preach" (the gospel) and "evangelize" represent the Greek *euangelizomai.* The term "evangelist" (*euangelistēs*) occurs only three times in the NT. The study of what an evangelist says and does, however, is most instructive in understanding what evangelism is.

What Is the Message?

Jesus came preaching the gospel of the Kingdom of God and announced, "the time is fulfilled and the kingdom of God is at hand. Repent and believe in the gospel." According to Mark 1:15 a moral change was to take place through repentance based on a belief in Jesus and the message that he presented. Paul and the apostles, after the death and resurrection of our Lord, amplified this message, and included the facts "that Christ died for our sins according to the Scriptures, that he was buried, and that he rose again the third day according to the Scriptures" (1 Cor 15:3-5). The gospel here is clearly seen to involve facts of history, i.e. the death and resurrection of Christ, and an interpretation of those facts, namely, that he died for our sins and that his death and resurrection were in accordance with the Scriptures. Paul was at pains to make clear that this message was not his idea, nor that of any other man, but that he was taught it supernaturally by revelation through Jesus Christ (Gal 1:12). Evangelism, then, is proclaiming a message that comes by revelation from God.

The message clearly calls for decision. Our Lord said in Luke 9:23, "If any man will come after me, let him deny himself and take up his cross daily and follow me." He never hid the fact that to embrace the gospel was costly. He rebuked those who believed that he was a miracle worker and

Paul E. Little, Assistant to the President of Inter-Varsity Christian Fellowship, and Associate Professor of Evangelism at Trinity Evangelical Divinity School, Deerfield, Illinois. B.S., The University of Pennsylvania; M.A., Wheaton College Graduate School; Ph.D. candidate, New York University.

who enjoyed the benefits of that power through receiving food, but who were not prepared to follow him (John 6:66). Peter, on the day of Pentecost, in answer to the question, "What shall we do?" after he had proclaimed Jesus as Messiah, said, "Repent and be baptized every one of you in the name of Jesus Christ for the forgiveness of sins" (Acts 2:38). Paul was always reasoning with his hearers from the Scriptures about the truth of the gospel, clearly implying that his objective was to elicit from them a decision in favor of it (Acts 17:2; 18:4, 19; 24:25).

There is an intellectual content to the gospel to which one must respond personally. Paul talks of the judgment of those who do not love or believe the truth (2 Thess 2:10, 14), and of those "who do not obey the truth" (Rom 2:8) or the gospel (2 Thess 1:8).

The message of evangelism is an exclusive one. Jesus very clearly says, "I am the way, the truth, and the life; no man comes to the Father but by me" (John 14:6), and Peter unequivocally declares this same idea in Acts 4:12: "there is salvation in no one else [than Jesus], for there is no other name under heaven given among men by which we must be saved." It is not the Christian only who says this, but our Lord as well. In fact the Christian has no option but to declare it faithfully. Dr. Radhakrishnan, the Hindu philosopher who became President of India, saw this clearly and made this comment about the exclusiveness of Christ: "The Christian has no choice. That is what your Scriptures say; you cannot say less. You are saved from arrogance when you say it in the spirit of Jesus Christ."[1]

To Whom Is Evangelism Directed?

Since Christ is the only way, it is clear that the message is to be communicated to everyone. "God so loved the world" (John 3:16). Our Lord in Matt 28:20 says we are to go and make disciples of all nations, and in his ascension farewell he makes clear that we are to go to the uttermost part of the earth. The gospel is not exclusively for the Jews, as the early church learned with some difficulty. It was "to the Jew first, but also to the Greek" (Rom 1:16). Christ and his message are not Middle Eastern or Western, but for all men everywhere.

Who Is to Be Involved in Evangelism?

The apostles themselves were clearly to do the work of evangelists, by virtue of our Lord's commandment (Matt 28:20). It is clear, too, that the gift of an evangelist was given to the church (Eph 4:11, 12). But it seems an unwarranted inference that because this special gift and ministry was given to some, though not all, in the church, that therefore evangelism is to be the work of the apostles alone. In Acts 8:1-4 we learn that when the persecution arose against the church in Jerusalem, all were scattered throughout the region of Judea and Samaria, *except* the apostles. And we are told that those who were thus scattered went about preaching the word.

---

[1] Cited by Samuel H. Moffatt, "What is Evangelism?", *Christianity Today*, 13 (Aug. 22, 1969), 5.

It would seem, then, that the so-called full-timers and those who were officially commissioned to the ministry of evangelism were kept in Jerusalem, and the "non-professionals" were scattered, in the providence of God, and effectively spread the gospel.

One of the first signs of new life seems to be desire on the part of the convert to share the message of the gospel. Many in Samaria believed as a result of a woman's testimony about Christ (John 4:39). Paul commended the Thessalonians for the fact that the word of the Lord had sounded forth from them in Macedonia and Achaia and that their faith in God had gone forth everywhere so that he did not need to say anything (1 Thess 1:8).

Each Christian, then, it would seem, has both the privilege and responsibility of bearing testimony to what he has personally experienced of Christ and of sharing the message of the gospel as he has opportunity.

Why Evangelism?

Jesus declared the clearest, most powerful motivation for evangelism in quoting the prophet Isaiah in the synagogue in Nazareth when he said, "The spirit of the Lord is upon me . . . he has anointed me to preach good news to the poor. He has sent me to proclaim release to the captives and recovering of sight to the blind, to set at liberty those who are oppressed, to proclaim the acceptable year of the Lord" (Luke 4:18, 19). In other words, he was compelled by the Spirit, and in this he becomes the model for all would-be evangelists.

Paul was very conscious of the fact that the ministry of reconciliation had been given to him (2 Cor 5:18, 19). Love for one's fellow man, too, is a clear motivation for evangelism (Matt 22:37, 38). Again, Paul indicates that he considers himself to be "under obligation both to the Greeks and the barbarians, both to the wise and to the foolish." How could one keep silent about the greatest thing he has found in life if he had any love for his neighbor. The supreme motivation, however, is the response of love. Paul says in 2 Cor 5:14 that love for Christ constrains or compels him. There is no more powerful motive possible than our response in love to the prior love of God in Christ.

How Was Evangelism Done?

How are we to evangelize? It is clear from both the record of Jesus' ministry and that of the apostles that there was both a public and private proclamation of the message. Jesus spoke to the multitudes on numerous occasions, but he also spoke to individuals—a woman who had been ill for twelve years, a corrupt tax-collector and many others. Paul, like Jesus, spoke at every opportunity. He preached in the synagogue and in the open air. But he also spoke to individuals like the Philippian jailer, the Roman guard and Lydia. Philip left a public meeting to speak to a particular Ethiopian.

Frequently, there is tension between Christian presence and proclamation: "Are not my presence in the world and my conduct as a Christian sufficient in themselves without verbalizing, without proclaiming, my faith?" Jesus answered this question as follows: "Let your *light* so shine before men that they may see your *good works* and give glory to your Father who is in heaven" (Matt 5:16). By "light," I suggest, Jesus meant the proclamation of the message. Through this proclamation, the hearers are able to identify the moral quality of the lives (i.e. the good works) of those who proclaim it as coming from God. Good works are a necessary preparation for the proclamation; but good works without proclamation might never be traced back to God as their source. Proclamation and good works belong inseparably together.

Various metaphors are used in the NT to describe the evangelist and his work. Among them are that of sower (Matt 13), fisherman (Mark 1:16, 17) and ambassador (2 Cor 5:20). Each has practical implications and instruction. In Matt 13, where Jesus gives the parable of the sower, it is clear that he sees response as not dependent on the sower or the seed, both of which are assumed to be of good quality, but on the receptiveness of the ground on which it falls. As a fisher of men in Mark 1, presumably one must go where fish are in order to catch them, must know how to attract them, and must "draw the net" (i.e. invite a response). An effective ambassador (2 Cor 5:20) must be highly motivated and enthusiastic about his message. He must know how to win the friendship of those to whom he is sent and how to introduce his message. He must clearly understand it, be able to answer questions about it, and invite response to it.

The "how" of evangelism in the NT clearly involved the primacy of God as *the* Evangelist who chooses to use human instrumentality. Paul says with passion, "*God* makes his appeal through us, and *we* beseech you on behalf of Christ to be reconciled to God (2 Cor 5:20).

Paul speaks of planting the seed and Apollos watering, but of God giving the growth (1 Cor 3:5, 6). Jesus, in John 4:36, 37, refers to the disciples as reapers. These passages would imply that planting or sowing has to do with an initial hearing of the word, watering with encouraging the growth of that which has been sown or planted, and reaping with the invitation for people to respond positively to what they have heard. God is operative in all three aspects. Jesus says in John 6:37, "All whom the Father gives me will come to me; and him who comes to me I will not cast out." It is clear, too, that "no one can say Jesus is Lord except by the Holy Spirit" (1 Cor 12:3), and yet God is pleased to draw men through the message we preach and the witness we give.

An understanding of God's role and ours in evangelism delivers us from fear. We come to realize that no one is beyond the reach and power of the Holy Spirit. On the other hand, it delivers us from pride. If we are the last link in the chain to introduce someone to the Savior, we are not so foolish as to think it has been because of our own cleverness or wisdom. Rather, we realize we have been privileged to be God's messengers. Our Lord told his disciples, "He who hears you hears me" (Luke 10:16). He went on to point out that "he who rejects you rejects me, and he who rejects me rejects him who sent me." A negative response to our proclamation, then, if we have communicated the message clearly and in love, should not cause us to feel threatened but to realize that the recipient in reality is rejecting Christ. A positive response should not puff us up with pride because in reality it is Christ they have received.

The evidence from the NT shows that the natural man, unaided by the illumination of the Holy Spirit, considers the gospel to be foolishness (1 Cor 2:14). We are involved in a spiritual battle. The God of this world has blinded the minds of unbelievers to keep them from seeing the light of the gospel of the glory of Christ who is the likeness of God (2 Cor 4:4). We are to present the gospel as cogently and as relevantly as possible. Having done this, however, the gospel may still be rejected. The reason for this is not that the gospel is trivial or nonsense, but rather that man is morally intransigent. Jesus, addressing the Pharisees, said to them, "you refuse to come to me that you may have life" (John 5:40). It must always be borne in mind that "the word of the cross is folly to those who are perishing, but to us who are being saved, it is the power of God" (1 Cor 1:18).

The Results of Evangelism

The NT sees the consequences of man's response to the gospel or lack of it as enormous in their implications. Jesus promised rest (Matt 11:28), light (John 8:12), salvation (John 10:9). He promised that he would be for men the bread and water of life (John 6:35), and a good shepherd for his sheep (John 10:14). He also promised eternal life to those who believe in and follow him (John 11:25). Response to Jesus Christ makes one a child of God (John 1:12). Certainty about having eternal life is also the privilege of the believer (1 John 5:11, 12).

All of this comes as a response intellectually, on the one hand, to the facts of the gospel and morally, on the other, to the Lordship of Jesus Christ. Our Lord combines the two clearly in Matt 11:28, 29. Here Jesus appeals to people in their need and offers to meet it. "Come to me," he says, "all who labor and are heavy laden, and I will give you rest." But he then goes on to say, "Take my yoke upon you, and learn of me; for I am gentle and lowly in heart, and you will find rest for your soul. For my yoke is easy, and my burden is light" (Matt 11:28-30). One cannot have the rest without the yoke. Jesus also promised to receive in heaven for eternity those who trust in him (John 14:3).

The consequences of rejecting the gospel are equally enormous. Jesus, while speaking to the unbelieving Jews, said, "I go away and you will seek me and die in your sins. Where I am going you cannot come." The writer to the Hebrews points out that "men are destined to die once, and after death comes their judgment" (Heb 9:27). Clearly one's eternal destiny hinges on his response to the message of the gospel.[2]

---

[2] For a full discussion of evangelism in its NT background, see Michael Green, *Evangelism in the Early Church,* Grand Rapids, 1970.

Summary

The church came into being as a result of evangelism. The message includes facts such as the death and resurrection of Christ and the interpretation of these facts as the basis for salvation.

The message demands a decision, a decision that has great consequences for the hearer. A positive response brings one into personal and vital relationship with Jesus Christ. A rejection of the message results in eternal separation from God.

While the message is exclusive in that Christ is the only way to God, it is comprehensive in its audience. The gospel is for all men.

God has given the gift of evangelism to particular persons within the church, but all Christians are involved to some degree in the privilege and responsibility of sharing their faith.

The command of Christ, love for one's neighbor and love for Christ are the compelling motivations for evangelism. The hand of the Spirit of God on the individual in moving him to proclaim the message is the overarching motive.

The methods of evangelism are varied. There is public proclamation and personal witness. There is the interplay of divine initiative and human instrumentality. All response is clearly the result of the work of the Holy Spirit who removes blindness from human eyes so that they might see the truth and who urges men to submit to the authority of Christ. We must communicate the message, but its effectiveness depends on God and the response of the hearer.

We ourselves are the result of those who have been faithful in carrying out the NT mandate for evangelism. We in turn must discharge our responsibility to this present generation.

Christology and "The Angel of the Lord"

WILLIAM GRAHAM MACDONALD

One of the most engaging unsolved problems of Christology is that of how our Lord Jesus is to be regarded with reference to the OT. Both before and after his resurrection Jesus set forth and sanctioned the hermeneutic of using the OT as a source of information about himself and his redemptive work (John 5:39; Luke 24:27). There its "promise" character confronts us on all sides in anticipation of NT fulfillment. More specifically, it contains precise prophecies that, after Jesus came, were seen to have anticipated him accurately. Moreover, in the subspecies of prophetic promise known as typology, holy objects, offices and sacrificial animals were used to fore-shadow the coming Christ.

It is another question entirely, however, whether, under the old covenant with Israel, God chose to actually reveal himself *in Christ* there and then by multiple appearances as a human being under the form and label of an angel. Was God acting like the lad who could not resist showing his friends their Christmas presents beforehand, so that when Christmas finally came—literally—there were no surprises? The question being raised in this essay must not be misconstrued as dealing with minor issues of typology or angelology, though the latter is pertinent for necessary clarifications. Here, explicitly, basic Christology is on trial—the doctrine of the reality of Jesus' humanity. If one can locate dozens of manifestations of Jesus in the OT—or even one concrete preview of his humanity—the implications are devastating for the doctrine of his humanity.

Since this is a sensitive subject radiating from the christocentric core of the Christian faith, my own christological presuppositions must be made clear. With the fathers of the Creed of Chalcedon I cling to these certainties: (1) the true and full deity of Christ; (2) the true and full humanity of Christ. It is the reconciliation of these two orthodox principles that compels a restudy of the most fascinating of the supposed *vestigia Christi* in the OT, "the angel of the Lord."

William Graham MacDonald, Professor of Biblical and Theological Studies at Gordon College, Wenham, Massachusetts. B.A., Florida Southern College; M.A., Wheaton College Graduate School; S.T.M., Concordia Seminary; Th.D., Southern Baptist Theological Seminary.

From each of these major presuppositions a correlative subproposition follows. First, the doctrine of the deity of Christ would demand that as God he was present in or related to the OT era *ibi et ubi* God was active. Whenever God's Word or Spirit was heard or sensed or interacted with men, there was Christ—not separately or incarnately, but spiritually, invisibly, eternally one God. Furthermore, I regard as altogether valid the classical formula for theologizing about the Trinity: *opera trinitatis ad extra indivisa sunt.* It should guard us from expecting there a single trinitarian "person" isolable for solitary inspection.

Second, if our Lord had true humanity, his human nature (mind and body) had a temporal beginning *and* continuous existence. Transporting Jesus' humanity into the preparatory era, or even, as Karl Barth has done, to a pretemporal eternity before the creation of Adam,[1] unhitches from history that which makes Christianity a faith grounded in history—the conception in Nazareth and the birth in Bethlehem. Without there being a precise point of a man's beginning there is no finitude, and *without finitude there is no real humanity.* If Jesus' *human* history did not originate when he was "born of a woman," then the docetists win the day. If the man of Galilee had appeared before on the earth—repeatedly—his sojourn there in the first century would be presumed to be but another protracted appearance in a series of illusory apparitions.

No more forceful denial of the angel-Christ view can be found anywhere than in the first two chapters of Hebrews. They teach that as "God," Christ Jesus was above all angels (1:4-14), and as man he was a little lower than the angels (2:5-17). Hereby Hebrews closed the door on the possibilities of a superangel view with such finality that this may have been a decisive reason why Hebrews was so long in making its way into full acceptance in the canon of the Western churches.

Just as sound Christology gives no ground for a worldly view of Jesus as a superstar (a heightened human, but only a human), so it will be the thesis defended here that neither does a biblical Christology support a view of Jesus as a superangel, either as an Angel/man or a God/Angel/man.

I

There being no hint of an angel-Christ view in the NT, we must search elsewhere for its provenance. It is not to be found in the writings of the apostolic fathers. Only Hermas made reference to *ho angelos tou Kyriou.* But he used the term when writing of "the great and glorious angel, Michael."[2]

In the post-apostolic period Christian apologists scrambled for all available materials to defend Christ's authority and deity before Jews and pagan intellectuals. Justin Martyr, who wrote in the middle of the second century, pioneered the way for succeeding apologists[3] to find "a second

---

[1] Karl Barth, *Christ and Adam,* New York, 1956, p. 35, *passim.*

[2] Herm Sim 8.2.3. In this text he also referred to "the Son of God," not as an angel, but as "the law of God," like a tree casting a shadow over all the earth.

[3] Cf. Pierre Prigent, *Justin et l'Ancien Testament,* Etudes Biblique, Paris, 1964, p. 126.

God" in the OT under the title of "an angel" as well as under other names, e.g. the glory of the Lord, firstborn, power, Logos, Son, man. Justin elaborated four instances (i.e. with Abraham, Gen 18; with Jacob, Gen 28; with Moses, Exod 3; with Joshua, Josh 5) that he interpreted as pre-incarnate appearances of Christ under the guise of an angel.[4] For succeeding angel-Christ advocates these episodes became standard proofs. Could Justin have derived his angel-Christ hypothesis from Hellenistic Judaism? Philo generally regarded the *logos* as impersonal reason, but he once hypostatized the *logos* as God's senior archangel: *ton prōtogonon autou logon, ton angelōn presbytaton, hōs an archangelon*.[5]

It was but the next short step in the development of this view to expand Justin's *Logos*-"angel" into the biblical expression "the angel of the Lord" [*Yahweh*] or "the angel of God" [*Elohim*], equating the angel with the second factor in the synonymous expressions. Ironically, however, the three classic episodes of Justin's proofs where the angel/ messenger appears in the form of a "man" all lack the term "the angel of the Lord/God" in the texts. The one instance having it, featured Moses at the burning bush (Exod 3:2); the NT account, based most likely on the LXX, used only *angelos* (Acts 7:30). Martin Buber's interpretation of what was seen contains all that the Hebrew idiom requires there: "Moses actually sees the messenger *in* the flame [itself], he sees nothing other than this."[6]

Clement of Alexandria fueled the allegorical minds of North Africa with his crisp identification of the angel who wrestled with Jacob as "God, the Word, the Instructor."[7] Tertullian, the North African theologian, contended for the true and solid substance of the "unborn" flesh in Christ's supposed visits to the patriarchs.[8] Novatian, the noted Roman presbyter, supplied the notion that the Son was "accustomed to descend and be seen" as an angel prior to the incarnation.[9]

Hilary of Poitiers represented the literalist's attempt to pinpoint the reference of Jesus' words, "Abraham saw my day" (John 8:56), as the occasion of Abraham's hospitality to the three angels, one of whom was supposed to be Christ.[10] (Actually Jesus said, "my day," and not "me"; Abraham's parabolic experience on Mt. Moriah with Isaac would satisfy the full intent of Jesus' words.)

The development of the angel-Christ view seemed to strengthen the case for Arianism. If the human body of Jesus was not created at his birth but pre-existed, then surely this condition as a creature can be presumed always to have been true. Arian creaturism denied his full deity as un-created God. Athanasius countered by teaching that the Word only took

---

[4] Justin, *Dial* 56-61 and a parallel section, 126-29.
[5] Philo, *Confusion of Tongues* 28.146.
[6] Martin Buber, *Moses, the Revelation and the Covenant*, New York, 1958, p. 41.
[7] Clement of Alexandria, *The Instructor* 1.7.
[8] Tertullian, *Against Marcion* 2.27; 3.9; and *Against Praxeas* 13, 14, 15.
[9] Novatian, *Concerning the Trinity* 17.
[10] Hilary, *On the Trinity* 4.27.

the clothing of an angel as an external form, but in nature he was not homogeneous with angels.[11]

Of all the fathers Augustine was most acutely aware of the dangers implicit in the doctrine. He argued for the invisibility and incorporeality of the Trinity in the OT,[12] but nevertheless favored the Athanasian position, saying that the angel was not called "Lord" but the God living in him. [13] He broadened the use of "angel" (messenger) so that it could apply to the Holy Spirit as well, and stoutly opposed any idea of subordinationism on the basis of this term. The Formula of Sirmium in the mid-fourth century had included two anathemas (15, 16) against anyone who denied that it was the Son who appeared to Abraham and Jacob respectively. Augustine's calm view tended to dissipate this hyperorthodox position for over a millennium. Significantly, Aquinas did not pursue it in the Middle Ages.

Not being Hebrew scholars for the most part, the Church Fathers were forced to handle sharp-edged biblical affirmations such as those that said "no one can see God and live," and others that told of people testifying of seeing God and living, e.g. Hagar (Gen 16:13), Jacob (Gen 32:30), Manoah and his wife (Judg 13:22). They found a solution of a sort by stressing the last name in the expression "the angel of the Lord," and by identifying "the Lord" with the incarnate Lord of the NT and the eternal Logos. But the price was high; it deprived Jesus of the dimensions of true historicity. What is more, it worked on the false assumption that in the incarnation only the Son was "seen," and not the Father and the Spirit (John 12:45; 14:7-11, 17b; Col 1:19; 2:9).

Another concern that ignited the angel-Christ theorists was that of extending to the OT worthies the nearness of a NT Christ with all the benefits of one who was readily seen and touched. Calvin in the *Institutes* committed himself to a descent of the not-yet-incarnate Christ "in a mediatorial capacity, that he might approach the faithful with greater familiarity."[14] For the Lutherans, issues not covered by the Formula of Concord were decided by A. Calovius in his *Consensus repetitus fidei vere Lutheranae* (1664). The *Consensus* deemed it heresy to deny that "the angel of the Lord" was Christ.[15] Calvin in his list of accusations against Servetus indicted him for heresy in not holding that the angel was Christ.[16]

In the battles over the deity of Christ the nineteenth century heard a number of big guns booming away again in support of the angel-Christ view. Perhaps the most influential of these was E. W. Hengstenberg in his

[11] Athanasius, *Three Orations Against Arius* 1.56; cf. J. Daniélou, "Trinité et angelologie dans la théologie judéo-chrétienne," *RSR*, 45 (1957), 41.

[12] Augustine, *Ad Paul.* 44.287, 345; *City of God* 16.29; for a thorough treatment see Joseph Barbel, *Christos Angelos*, Bonn, 1941, pp. 163-74.

[13] Augustine, *Sermo* 7.3-6; cf. *De trinitate* 2.12, 13.

[14] John Calvin, *Institutes* 1.13.10; cf. 14.5. H. Beveridge in the Eerdmans edition of 1953 has "intermediate form" for "mediatorial capacity" (John Allen's translation of 1909), which changes the picture somewhat but keeps it in the same gallery.

[15] O. W. Heick, *A History of Christian Thought*, Philadelphia, 1965, 2, 60.

[16] Calvin, *Institutes* 1.13.10.

three-volume *Christology of the Old Testament,* first published in 1836. [17] H. C. Leupold, the well-known commentator on Genesis, followed Hengstenberg in claiming the mediator of both testaments must be the same. H. P. Liddon's influential Bampton Lectures at Oxford in 1866,[18] passing through several reprintings, stoutly affirmed the deified-Angel view as one of the pillars of the doctrine of the deity of Christ. Franz Delitzsch was one of the few outstanding nineteenth-century conservative scholars to question this angelomorphic christophanology. Because Delitzsch equivocated on the issue, his position was considered unsatisfactory by Hengstenberg.

The century-old journal, *Bibliotheca Sacra,* has published six articles advocating the angel-Christ view,[19] and none favoring the angel *qua* angel. John F. Walvoord, in one of these articles, reiterated the view as if it were ready for creedal formulation: "It is the teaching of Scripture that the Angel of Jehovah is specifically the Second Person of the Trinity."[20] Most of the other theological journals have registered little or no interest in the subject in the twentieth century. Recent literature indicates that the view continues to draw some supporters. Noteworthy are these: Don Brandeis, *The Gospel in the Old Testament,* 1961; Anthony T. Hanson, *Jesus Christ in the Old Testament,* 1965; and H. Harold Kent, *The House of Christmas,* 1964, in which Kent amazingly concluded, " . . . in this context [Luke 1] the angel Gabriel is God the eternal Son."[21]

One common characteristic pervades the literature that advanced the angel-Christ view over the past century. All theophanies are constricted into christophanies! W. M. Baker's 1883 treatise, *The Ten Theophanies,* is typical. Furthermore, virtually every angelophany in which the angel appears *by himself* turns out to be a christophany, except in Daniel and the apocryphal Tobit where names of individual angels occur.

II

The case for the angel-Christ position would hardly have been heard for so long had it no plausible supports. For the moment I will become "the angel's advocate" and summarize the angel-Christ defense without critique.

1. The terms *malak Yahweh* (henceforth, *m-Y*), "the angel of the

---

[17] Later editions omitted some of the shakier angel-of-the-Lord exegetical arguments. More recently Walter Kaiser, a contributor to this *Festschrift,* has edited a one-volume Kregel edition of the work. Purposefully, he did not include any of the angel-Christ sections.

[18] H. P. Liddon, *The Divinity of Our Lord and Savior Jesus Christ,* London, 1872.

[19] *BS,* 32 (1875), 421-52; 36 (1879), 593-615 (the most definitive article); 103 (1946), 348-62; 104 (1947), 154-69, 282-89, 415-25.

[20] J. F. Walvoord, "The Preincarnate Son of God," *BS,* 104 (1947), 166.

[21] H. H. Kent, *The House of Christmas,* Grand Rapids, 1964, p. 39. Kent's view is strangely reminiscent of a statement attributed to Christ in a post-resurrection appearance as recorded in *Epistula Apostolorum* (Coptic) 14: "I became an angel among angels. . . . I took the form of the angel Gabriel; I appeared to Mary. . . . I formed myself and entered her womb; I became flesh." See E. Hennecke, *New Testament Apocrypha,* ed. by W. Schneemelcher, trans. by R. McL. Wilson, 2 vols., Philadelphia, 1963-64, 1, 198-99.

Lord," and *malak Elohim* (*m-E*), "the angel of God," should be translated into English with the definite article indicating a specific personage. The article sets this one off from others within its class; therefore, the *m-Y* must be a special personage actually above the ordinary angels.

2. The *m-Y* spoke ambiguously in the third and first persons on numerous occasions, that is, "for" and "as" God. In response to the *m-Y* or *m-E*, people dialogued with him or Yahweh indiscriminately. Therefore, this double identity, "angel" and "God," must be resolved by understanding the Christ great enough to encompass both.

3. Divine honor and worship are accorded the *m-Y*. He accepted both petitions and praise, and even a sacrifice on the altar on occasion. Since the NT forbids the adoration of angels—an act regularly practiced in the OT, the *m-Y* must be Christ, or the worshippers would not have been accepted.

4. Divine knowledge and attributes are ascribed to the *m-Y*, and divine acts identical with all God's redemptive actions in the world prior to the cross are accomplished by him. Hence he must be the Christ.

5. The palpable humanity of one of those "men" who visited Abraham was a partially realized anticipation of the incarnation. "Does it not seem more congruous that a human soul should actuate that human body which ate and drank with Abraham under a tree, and should actuate those human limbs when a man wrestled with Jacob?"[22] "And here [Dan 3] is the first showing of himself by Christ to any of the race outside the Hebrew Church; his first showing, not his last."[23]

6. If the mediator of the two testaments is not the same in name, form and substance, then the unity of the testaments is broken. If the angelophanies are not christophanies, then the redeemer is not the same. When it is conceded that the mediator is the same, our storehouse of historical data on the incarnate Christ found in the Gospels burgeons with large blocks of material from the OT.

7. Because the OT itself interprets the fourth "man" in Nebuchadnezzar's furnace as "the Son of God" (*KJV*—Dan 3:25),[24] the angel-Christ identification is corroborated.

III

These seven arguments will now be examined in order from an exegetical perspective. Theologically, I contend that it is inadmissible to defend the doctrine of the deity of Christ at the expense of his humanity and hazardous to suspend his deity from appeals to angelology. There are two dozen angel-of-the-Lord/God clusters of texts in the OT if one includes the special ones often cited but without the terms.[25] Moreover, the

---

[22] H. L. Kendall, "Dr. Watts' Theory of Christ's Pre-existent Human Nature," *BS*, 32 (1895), 437.

[23] W. M. Baker, *The Ten Theophanies*, New York, 1883, p. 194.

[24] The *RSV* has the rendering: "A son of the gods."

[25] Gen 16:7-14; chap. 18; 21:17; 22:9-18; 24:7, 40; 28:12; 31:11; 32:24-31 and Hos 12:4; Exod 3:1-6; 14:19; 23:20-24; 32:34; 33:2; Num 20:16; 22:21-35; Josh 5:13-6:5; Judg 2:1-5; 5:23; 6:11-24; 13:1-25; (1 Sam 29:9); 2 Sam 24:15-17; 1 Chr 21:15-30; 1 Kgs 19:5-7; Ps 34:7 (Heb 34:8); Isa 63:9; Zech 1:11-12:8.

equivalent term "angel of the Lord/God" occurs a dozen more times in the NT and must be accounted for as well.[26] My detailed exegesis of all these passages cannot be included here, but my comments, covering the whole range of texts, constitute a summary of the specific exegesis of every passage.

First. It is reading too much into the first article in the expression, "*the* angel of the Lord," to infer that a special angel within the class is intended and that all instances of this title have the same personage (should we rather say "angelage"?) in mind. Because Hebrew has no indefinite article some ambiguity always attends the translation of an expression like *malak Yahweh* (*m-Y*), "angel of Yahweh," into English. *Malak* is in the Hebrew construct state. As such its determinateness (whether it is articular or anarthrous) is decided by the determinateness of the noun with which it is constructed, in this case, "*Yahweh.*" Now every proper noun is determinate per se.[27] This would in itself authorize us to translate "*the* angel of [the] Yahweh" for the anarthrously literal, "angel of Yahweh." But the inclusion of the article before angel is by no means necessary to translation. "In a few instances," wrote the grammarian Gesenius, "the nomen regens appears to be used indefinitely notwithstanding a following determinate genitive; . . . *it is often so before a proper name* as in . . . a feast of the Lord . . . an abomination unto the Lord . . . a virgin of Israel . . . a man of Benjamin," etc.[28] One may therefore translate *m-Y* correctly as "*an* angel of the Lord" or "*an* angel of Yahweh," and *m-E* as "*an* angel of God."

Of course, the grammatical rule of "second mention" would always make it proper on the second use to translate, "*the* angel of Yahweh." The LXX does this for *angelos Kyriou* (the linguistic equivalent of *m-Y*) in Judg 2:4, following the anarthrous use in Judg 2:1. Justification for including the article might also be theological as is done in the *RSV* for all instances except one (1 Sam 29:9). Much as translators have been prone to keep "thee" and "thou" in referring to deity, so they are inclined to designate with the article anything that belongs to God. For instance, to the reverent ear "the finger of God" sounds more majestic than "a finger of God."

Concerning "an angel" sent by God to guard and direct Israel, the text says: "My name is in him" (Exod 23:20, 21). Can one legitimately use this saying to justify the equation of "the angel of God" with God the Son? Hardly, for the term and its counterpart, "the angel of Yahweh," are not to be found in the context here, just as they are missing in all the most *sensational* of the christophanic episodes, namely, the incidents of the one—actually there were three—who ate veal and yogurt with Abraham, Jacob's opponent clinched in a night of wrestling, Joshua's strategist for taking Jericho, and the fourth "man" in Nebuchadnezzar's blazing furnace. Instead of looking for a divine name cryptographically hidden in Israel's *malak* who led them through the desert, it is far more Hebraic to understand "my name is in him" by the idiomatic paraphrase: "he has my full

[26] Matt 1:20, 24; 2:13, 19; 28:2; Luke 1:11 (Gabriel); 2:9; Acts 5:19; 8:26; 12:23; 27:23; Gal 4:14.

[27] E. Kautzsch and A. E. Cowley, eds., *Gesenius' Hebrew Grammar,* Oxford, 1910[2], p. 410, 127a(a).

[28] *Ibid.,* p. 412, d 3 (my italics).

authority." The cultural rationale for this will be set forth when I discuss the question of how the *m-Y* can speak in the first person as God.

Furthermore, both *m-Y* and *m-E* are non-specific enough as terms to be used also of men, e.g. of David, *m-E* (1 Sam 29:9), of Haggai the prophet, *m-Y* (Hag 1:13), in fact, of all the prophets (2 Chr 36:15), including the last before John the Baptist, known only as *malaki* (lit. my [God's] angel, Mal 1:1), and of a priest, *m-Y* (Mal 2:7).

The linguistic argument for the christological identification of *m-Y* reaches its nadir in the NT. The terms *angelos Kyriou* (henceforth, *a-K*) and *angelos tou Theou* (*a-Th*) are Hebraisms paralleling *m-Y* and *m-E* respectively. The Greek language, like Hebrew, lacks the indefinite article. These terms occur without the definite article generally in the NT and might well be translated that way in both testaments. Action by the *a-K* occurred *before, during* and *after* the incarnation. Who was the *a-K* who spoke with Joseph while Jesus' human embryo was already lodged in the womb of Mary? Once, before the incarnation, the *a-K*, having been ruffled by the incredulous Zechariah, identified himself as "Gabriel." The biblical texts disclose parallel terms whose continuity is at stake. According to traditional angelology, *m-Y* and *m-E* are used congruously with *a-K* and *a-Th*. According to the angel-Christ view, there is a glaring incongruity. The *onus probandi* must rest with anyone who would deny the parallelism.

Second. That "a" or "the" *m-Y* spoke both "for" God and "as" God must not be regarded as strange. The function of a *malak* in patriarchal times has been illuminated in a perceptive study by Aubrey R. Johnson.[29] In Hebrew thought a patriarch's personality extended throughout his entire household to his wives, his sons and their wives, his daughters, servants in his household, and even in some sense to his property. The "one" personality was present in the "many" who were with him. In a specialized sense when the patriarch as lord of his household deputized his trusted servant as his *malak*, the man was endowed with the authority and resources of his lord to represent him fully and transact business in his name. In Semitic thought this messenger-representative was conceived of *as being personally*—and in his very words—the presence of the sender.[30] Abraham's servant who swore fidelity "with his hand under the thigh of Abraham" illustrates the seriousness with which both men took the *malak* relationship.

The Joseph narrative demonstrates how the *malak* can speak alternately in the third and first persons. The *malak* of Joseph mentioned Joseph (in the third person) as the one whose cup was stolen, but (in the first person) he spoke of making the culprit "my slave" and releasing the rest. Even more graphic is a quotation from Moses, since for all practical purposes he too filled the continual role of a *m-Y* to Israel. The following passage from Deut 29:2-6 illustrates the familiar pattern of subtle shift in speaker from third to first person, i.e. from Moses to Yahweh:

And Moses summoned all Israel and said to them: "You have seen all that the LORD did before your eyes . . . but to this day the LORD has not given you a mind

[29] A. R. Johnson, *The One and the Many in the Israelite Conception of God,* Cardiff, 1961, pp. 4-32.
[30] Millar Burrows, *An Outline of Biblical Theology,* Philadelphia, 1946, p. 120.

to understand.... I have led you for forty years in the wilderness; your clothes have not worn out upon you ... that you may know that I am the Lord your God."

Disregard of the *malak* idiom would lead to one of two literal absurdities: (1) that Moses was claiming to be their God; (2) that Moses was a *vestigium Christi* in whose shell the true Christ was hiding (cf. John 1:17).

The Semitic *malak* idea was perfectly adaptable to the monarchical order. One is not surprised to find in the celestial court of Yahweh an array of angels waiting like royal ministers to magnify his presence throughout the earth. A dispatched angel would arrive anonymously (in terms of his own name), because coming in the name of God, i.e. as *m-Y* or *m-E*, his sole concern was to speak or act for God as the situation required and to receive man's response to God.

Third. The angel-Christ view does not reckon with the true intermediary character of angels as capable of communicating all man's responses—even worship—to God. It is my firm conviction that the NT does not create the insoluble dilemma of either condemning the old covenant worthies who "worshipped" angels or, on the other hand, of denying that the angels so addressed were really angels, since they did not forbid it. Col 2:18, 19, the plausible proof text, warns against being duped by a self-inaugurated seer who puts on the act of humbling himself and worshiping before angels for having received "visions" that are manifestly not from Christ. If the "angels" Paul had in mind here have any objective reality at all, they would in context have to be satanic, or similar to the *angelos phōtos* he alluded to in 2 Cor 11:14, the equivalent of a "false apostle" (2 Cor 11:13).

The only other NT prohibition of adoration of angels is found in the last chapters of the last book of the Bible (Rev 19:10; 22:9). And, of all wonders, it was given to the most knowledgeable of living Christians, the grand old apostle who had been—no less—a Jewish Christian for half a century. Two important considerations color our understanding of this prohibition: (1) The term *angelos* is transliterated "angel" but it is every bit as proper to translate it "messenger." (In a similar way *malak* could consistently be translated "messenger" throughout the OT, since in Hebrew this one term was used for the emissaries of both God and men.) John's interpreting-*angelos* may have been "one of the [twenty-four] elders" seated on thrones around God's throne (Rev 5:5). He described himself in terms that could easily be taken as identifying him as a glorified saint, a fellow servant with the believers and prophets (Rev 19:10; 22:8, 9). (2) Regardless of how we construe John's guide, his command to "Worship God" must be seen as indicative of a whole new order in which the physical dimension of separation between God and man has been overcome. The immediacy of the presence of God precluded any further use of angelic mediation for those like John who were already (by vision) *in heaven.* We must infer that either the beloved apostle was shamefully ignorant of proper protocol in matters of reverencing God or that the coming of the eternal order brought about a change in the old proprieties.

Fourth. Throughout the OT God's angels effected the intervention of

God in the affairs of men (wherever God was not working through anointed men). Divinely conceived and executed actions in the world, therefore, afford no proof that the "angel"-actor was, indeed, Christ, being present incognito as an angel.

A major biblical principle that differentiates between the old and new covenants merits consideration here. In the OT God is always the one *to be served* as the supreme monarch (Deut 6:13), and he himself never *serves* except indirectly by an intermediary (Gal 3:19; Heb 1:14). The NT opens with the most stupendous humiliation of God taking place. He who existed in the form of God, having taken "the form of a servant," *served*—a most profound reversal of roles for the Almighty (Luke 22:27). Jesus' untiring service and his refusal to be served by the world as a superstar (Mark 10:45) concealed his identity completely to all but the eyes of faith.

The angel-Christ view founders on the sharp distinctions between the indirect and the direct service of God in the two successive testaments. Was the Son the chef who served up two meals for the famished Elijah? Did the Son locate water for Hagar and Ishmael in the desert? (Did Ishmael, therefore, get to "see" the Son while Isaac, the son of promise, only got to hear him?) Who was the *m-Y* sent to foil and tame and mate and kill all those diverse animals—Balaam's donkey, Darius' lions, Laban's goats, the firstborn cows in Egypt? The angel-Christ theory would necessitate that God so acted "personally," while angels were held in readiness for group activities.

Fifth. The seeming reality of the humanlike manifestation of Abraham's three visitors, one of whom the view supposes to be Christ, does not require such an identification. In the first place it burdens our credulity too much to assume that the eternal Word had to become an "angel"—whether in form or substance—on the way to becoming a man. Did God "devolve" through the angel state in becoming incarnate? In the second place, anyone, youth or scholar, reading the NT narratives gets the all-pervading impression that the incarnation was *unique*. The virgin conception, the congregating of heaven's multitudinous angels to glory in Jesus' birth, the historical implications of his secret name (to be known only by those of faith, "Immanuel" [lit. "God with us"]), all point to something really new in God's economy. If Jesus had appeared full grown on the earth two dozen times or even once, his advent as a child in Bethlehem would be somewhat anticlimactic. But to the contrary Jesus himself points us to the proper interpretation. A favorite parable of his was that of the absentee king who, after sending many servants to his vineyard estate, finally sent them his son (Mark 12:1-12).

If the incarnation is cut adrift from its moorings in first-century history, all history—both biblical and universal—will lose its significance eventually. To dislocate the humanity of God the Son from its origin in 4 B.C. and its manifestation until A.D. 29 is to undermine the reality of that humanity. If it was eternal flesh, it is not like our humanity. If it was temporal but prenatal, it was still not like our humanity. If it was intermittent, appearing and disappearing without continuity, it was not like our humanity. *If its inception and its conception coincide, it was like our humanity.*

Sixth. Must the mediator of the Old and New Testaments be the same in name, form and substance in order to maintain the unity of the Bible?

Christ as the eternal Word of God was certainly the mediator of the creation of the world, and as the firstfruits of the resurrection mediates the new creation emanating from his resurrection. But both the old and new covenants had their earthly administrators. The contrast of law and grace, Moses and Christ, is stark in the NT (John 1:17). The chain of command under the old covenant moved down from the triune God via angels to Moses, who spoke on behalf of God to Israel, and to the priests, like his brother Aaron, who mediated man's response to God ceremonially.

The NT cut the chain of intermediaries. The God-man established the new covenant himself at Jerusalem and promised the continued divine administration by his resident *paraklētos* while he was physically absent; but both the inaugurator and administrator are God—the Son and the Spirit. The OT's *Deus absconditus* and angelic intermediaries (LXX Deut 33:2; Acts 7:53; Gal 3:19-24; Heb 1:5-2:3) were superseded by the NT's *Deus revelatus* of Christ and the Spirit (Acts 2:17, 32, 33; Gal 4:4-7; Heb 2:3-9). This contrast is as basic (in the texts) as that of kindergarten and graduate school, and no amount of allegorizing can bring the former to the independent level of the latter.

Christology, however, is not inimical to true typology. The NT writers identify Christ with the God of the old covenant and also find him typologically prefigured in Adam, in the office of the high priest, in the water-yielding rock of the wilderness and in even more elusive types. Never once, however, does any writer state or obliquely imply that he was seen or spoke—or was typified—in the form of a *m-Y, m-E* or Angel/man. Although this observation rides on an argument from silence, in view of the praxis of the NT itself that silence could not be more resounding and eloquent.

Seventh. Finally, shall we go to the pagan Nebuchadnezzar, the man who could not make sense of his own providential dream imagery, for our understanding of God's *malak*? Dare we presume that this Babylonian was conversant with the evangelical subject, "the Son of God," and could distinguish him from a seraphic angel? Should we interpret his exclamation about the fourth man in the furnace as an observation based on inspiration? His consternation was expressed in terms fit to indicate a supernatural being, and nothing more need be implied (Dan 3:25, 28).

True Christology necessitates the doctrine of the Trinity. Only by a false separation within God, isolating one "person," does the angel-Christ equation take its form.[31] Such a theory, held by devout scholars whose motives cannot be impugned, nevertheless discredits the very doctrine of the deity of Christ it attempts to demonstrate. Again and again its advocates have written, "Christ was seen, but not the Father who is invisible." But in the incarnation Jesus said that if one had seen him, he had seen the Father (John 12:45; 14:8-11). If the invisibility of the Logos, like that of God (John 1:18; 1 Tim 1:17), is not maintained in the OT, *then neither can*

---

[31] By applying the same isolating methodology to Num 22:35-38; 24:1, 2 and Isa 63:9, 10 one would determine that the *m-Y* in the former and "the angel of his face" in the latter were "personally" the Spirit!

we maintain his true and full deity there (Exod 33:20; John 1:18; 1 John 4:12, 20).

IV

What relationship, therefore, does the Christ of the NT have with the OT beyond that inherent in prophecy and typology? We may say categorically that he was there *however* and *whenever* and *wherever* God was. But he is not to be sought there by peeps and squints at visions and visitors so much as in the long, steady vision of the progressive unfolding of God's faithful word and works. He does not lurk there either corporeally or chimerically, as human fact or angelic apparition. But he pervades the old era as the covenant-keeping Yahweh Elohim, who prepares salvation history for the absolutely unique event that will forever demarcate it into two great contrasting eras.

The doctrine of the divinity of Christ demands that he be acknowledged as one with the eternal God in the OT; and the doctrine of his humanity demands that he not be physically present in that era to create suspense or for any other reason. The belief that Christ was present there as "the angel of the Lord" ranges from Tertullian's "true flesh" idea to the opposite pole of phantom flesh, but in all cases Christ's humanity suffers the loss of a true historical existence.

The argument for the angel-Christ view proves too much, finding Jesus retroactively in every nameless angel the Lord sent. It also falls prey to the Arian arguments for creaturism and essential subordinationism. Additionally, it places the most serious docetic question marks after the incarnation.

Angelomorphic christophanology is threatened by three main factors: the linguistic phenomena, the cultural understanding of a patriarchal and monarchical *malak,* and the theology of the NT that stresses: (1) the uniqueness and historicity of the incarnation; (2) the teaching of the *supra-*angelic character of the Son—not as a superangel but in consonance with Heb 1:1-14; and (3) the methodology of building Christology without ever capitalizing upon some great secret of angelic identities in the OT.

The deity of Christ is preserved throughout the Bible because God is Spirit. Its unity is not "in the flesh" with a continuity of human mediators (a chimerical Christ preceding a substantial one), but in the one God who worked in both testaments first mediately and then immediately to deliver men according to his covenantal promises. The God who intervened in ancient Israelite history by his law and powerful angels, at a precise moment in history, became incarnate to share man's finitude and to bring, by his Spirit, believing men to share his everlasting glory.

A Study of the New Testament Concept of the Parousia

W. HAROLD MARE

The views of many modern NT scholars raise several questions regarding the doctrine of the Parousia. For example, what kind of influence was exerted on this doctrine by OT Judaism? How clearly is such a doctrine set forth in the NT? What are the ranges of meaning to be seen in the use of this concept in the NT? Are there really antithetical views about the Parousia expressed by the various NT writers? Is the Parousia only encountered personally in "God's eternal rule," or does it involve historical events as well, including a series of future events at Christ's Second Coming?

In order to deal with such questions we will first briefly discuss the contribution of the OT and Judaism toward the meaning of Parousia. Second, we will consider the uses of Parousia and other parallel words as they occur in the NT. Finally, we will discuss some of the theological questions raised above.

The Background of Old Testament Judaism

A brief look at Parousia in Liddell-Scott's *A Greek-English Lexicon* shows that this word was used from the Homeric period down through that of the NT, with meanings ranging from the *presence* of persons to their *arrival* or *advent*. Liddell-Scott attributes this latter meaning to Parousia in Matt 24:27.[1] In the Hellenistic period Parousia is used to indicate the visit of a ruler, whether human or divine, or to designate the presence of the gods who bring help to men.[2] Although the word Parousia does not occur in the LXX translation of these OT books originally written in Hebrew, other expressions are used that convey the same idea. *Erchomai,* for example, translates the Hebrew *bō'* ("come" or "go") in the messianic

[1] H. G. Liddell and Robert Scott, *A Greek-English Lexicon,* Oxford, 1951, *s.v.* παρουσία.
[2] Albrecht Oepke, *TDNT,* 4, 859-60.

W. **Harold Mare**, Professor of New Testament at Covenant Theological Seminary, St. Louis, Missouri. B.A., Wheaton College; M.A., Wheaton College Graduate School; B.D., Faith Theological Seminary; Ph.D., The University of Pennsylvania.

statement of Gen 49:10: "until Shiloh come" (*KJV*) or "until he comes to whom it belongs."

The idea of the coming of God and of the Messiah, as illustrated in Gen 49:10, is clear in many other places in the OT. Compare, for example, God's coming to Hagar (Gen 16:13), to Jacob (Gen 28:16-18), to Samuel (1 Sam 3:10), etc. God's "coming out of Seir" is certainly an expression of God's coming and acting in power on the earth, and is of equal significance with *erchomai*. (*Erchomai* was used by Jesus in his statement regarding his coming in the clouds of heaven with power and great glory, Matt 24:30; cf. also *parousia* in Matt 24:27.)

Parousia is also used in literature written during the intertestamental period and the first century A.D., namely, that by Josephus and the literature found in the Dead Sea caves.[3] Josephus speaks of the Parousia of God at Sinai (*Antiquities* 3.80), and describes how God made his presence felt when he made the tabernacle his dwelling place (*Antiquities* 3.202). He even says that God showed his presence to Petronius the heathen governor (*Antiquities* 18.284).

In the Dead Sea community, there is evidence of messianic expectancy. Its people anticipated the coming of two Messiahs, one from Aaron and one from Israel (IQS 9.11; Zadokite Document 12.23; 14.19), who were to be the anointed high priest and the anointed king of Israel.[4] In this apocalyptic period yet to come God in his avenging wrath was to bring destruction upon the doers of wickedness—this is the final "visitation" (IQS 3.18; 4.18-19, 26).[5] The Scrolls speak of a prophetic forerunner of the messianic age (IQS 9.11), of the messianic "star out of Jacob" and of "a sceptre that shall rise out of Israel" (Zadokite Document 7.18; cf. Num 24:17). In this apocalyptic period a faithful shepherd will arise (New Covenant 3.2.8).[6] This language, if not in the exact words, is like that expressed in the NT regarding the first and second events of Jesus Christ.

The Parousia Concept in the New Testament

Most NT occurrences of Parousia refer to Jesus' activity and are related to the Second Coming.[7] Four of these uses are in Matthew's account of the Olivet Discourse (chaps. 24-25). The disciples question Jesus

[3] *Ibid.*, p. 864. Oepke notes that there is no use of Parousia in Philo, which he feels may be due to the influence of Hellenism, which almost obliterated the expectation of the Messiah.

[4] Theodore H. Gaster, *The Dead Sea Scriptures*, rev. ed., Garden City, New York, 1964, p. 400.

[5] *Ibid.*, p. 407.

[6] *Ibid.*

[7] Paul uses Parousia in the sense of "physical presence" when referring to his own presence (or absence) from one of his churches (2 Cor 10:10; Phil 2:12), to the past coming (and presence) of others to be with him (1 Cor 16:17; 2 Cor 7:6-7) or to some future coming (Phil 1:26). These uses of Parousia with persons other than Jesus indicate that the word can convey the idea of a concrete presence of persons in an historical situation, of a person's coming in the past or in the future. In the Philippian passage (1:26) Paul's future coming is confidently expected, and expected soon, but its exact time is not known. These usages of the word Parousia have bearing on Jesus' ministry—past, present and future.

as to the sign for his *coming* (*parousia*), and thus indicate their confidence in his Second Coming, a confidence instilled in them by Jesus himself (cf. Matt 13:24-30, 36-43). Their question, which includes the expression "the consummation of the age," throws the whole matter, including Jesus' Parousia, to the end of the age, to a time when, as the disciples expect, there will be a change in the order of things (Acts 1:7). The same definite article qualifies both "coming" and "consummation," indicating that they refer to aspects of the same event.[8] The word *sign,* singular in form, suggests that the disciples were expecting some important physical historical event that would begin the end times. In his answer Jesus describes his coming as a definite historical event, just as definite as the flashing of thunder in the sky (Matt 24:27). How concretely historical this Second Advent is, is seen in Jesus' comparison of it with the catastrophic flood that occurred when Noah entered the ark (Matt 24:37, 39).[9]

Paul, more than anyone else, uses the word Parousia of Christ. He does so particularly in those letters where he is dealing with the subjects of the future bodily resurrection and of the events of the Second Coming. He does not use Parousia simply to describe a *presence*. Rather, his usage of the word has a dynamic force—Jesus will come and be present in resurrection power and glory (cf. 1 Cor 15:23).

The rest of Paul's uses of the word occur in the Thessalonian letters. Here he has much to say about rewards, resurrection, the end time and eternal judgment. In 1 Thess 2:19, for example, Paul talks about the hope and joy he expects to have when Jesus comes again (lit. "at his coming," 1 Thess 2:19). He also expresses his desire that God will preserve his people in love until the time they stand blameless in his presence at the Second Coming of Christ (1 Thess 3:13).

Paul teaches that those living until the time of Christ's Second Advent—"unto the coming of the Lord"—will also be taken to be with the Lord when he comes from heaven (1 Thess 4:15; cf. Acts 1:11). Then he prays that the Lord will preserve the Christians blameless until the time of the *coming* of Christ (1 Thess 5:23).

The Thessalonians had been bothered by claims that Jesus had already come a second time. Paul persuades them that this is not so (2 Thess 2:1-10), and assures them that this event cannot occur until the lawless one is revealed and destroyed at Christ's appearance (lit. "at the appearance of his coming").

James, too, speaks of Christ's Second Coming and urges the Christians to exercise long-suffering until the time of the Parousia (Jas 5:7). In urging this he comforts them by saying that the coming of the Lord is near (5:8), that he as judge is standing right at the door (5:9). But when he calls them to long-suffering, he implies that the exact time of the Second Coming is uncertain.

Peter also discusses the Second Coming. He does so in terms of the revelation and appearance of Jesus Christ (1 Pet 1:7; 5:4), and in terms of

---

[8] A. T. Robertson, *A Grammar of the Greek New Testament,* Nashville, 1934, pp. 785-86.

[9] The word Parousia does not occur in Mark, Luke or the Fourth Gospel.

the power and coming (Parousia) of the Lord Jesus (2 Pet 1:16).[10] He declares that in the last days men will scoff at "the promise of Christ's coming" (Parousia, 2 Pet 3:3-4), and he shows that his *coming* is not spiritual but historical by associating it with the past historical catastrophe of the flood in Noah's time, and with the future end time when the heavens and the earth will be destroyed by fire (3:3-7). John's reference to the Parousia (1 John 2:28 where *ean* with the subjunctive is used) suggests that the exact time of the coming of the Lord is uncertain.

This summary of the testimony to the Parousia certainly points to a widespread belief in the future advent of Christ, a hope that no doubt came from the Savior himself (Matt 24-25, etc.).

An important synonym of Parousia is *epiphaneia* ("appearing, appearance"). It was often used as a religious technical term meaning "a visible manifestation of a hidden divinity, either in the form of a personal appearance or by some deed of power by which its presence is made known."[11] Josephus' many uses of *epiphaneia* are sufficient to illustrate this particular meaning (*Antiquities* 1.255; 2.339; 3.310; 3.60; 18.75).

The verb *epiphainō* describes Jesus' first advent in terms of a light shining on those in spiritual darkness (Luke 1:79; cf also 2 Tim 1:10; Tit 2:11; 3:4). Paul used the noun *epiphaneia* of Christ's Second Coming and its accompanying events. He said that Christians are to keep God's commands until the "appearance" of Christ (1 Tim 6:14), when he will destroy the lawless one (2 Thess 2:8). He urged Timothy to be faithful in his ministry because he will stand before Christ who will judge the world at his "appearance" (2 Tim 4:1) He himself looked forward to being rewarded at Christ's "appearance" (2 Tim 4:8). For Paul *hē epiphaneia* was "the appearing in glory of our great God and Savior Jesus Christ" (Tit 2:13).

Peter quotes from Joel in speaking of the *epiphanēs*, "the appearing," of the great day of the Lord (Acts 2:20). There can be no doubt, then, that the NT uses the word *epiphaneia* and its cognates for the glorious, visible, physical appearance of Jesus, both at the time of his incarnation and of his Second Advent at the end of the age.

Phaneroō, "reveal," "appear," is also used to refer to both comings of Christ—to his first coming (John 21:1, 14; 1 Tim 3:16; 2 Tim 1:10; Heb 9:26; 1 Pet 1:20; 1 John 1:2; 3:5, 8; 4:9), and to his Second Coming (2 Cor 5:10, Col 3:4; 1 Pet 5:4; 1 John 2:28; 3:3).

Although the word Parousia occurs only in Matt in the Gospels,[12] the idea of the Second Coming is clearly indicated elsewhere by different words with essentially the same meaning. Mark (and its parallels) uses *erchomai* to describe the Son of Man coming in the clouds of heaven with power and

---

[10] Parousia here (2 Pet 1:16) could refer to the first coming of Christ. But since it is coupled with the word "power"—the same article used with both "power" and "presence" (*tēn dynamin kai parousian*) shows how closely the two words are related—Peter seems to have in mind the Second Coming, a coming in power foreshadowed in the transfiguration (cf. 2 Pet 1:17, 18). See J. E. Huther, *The General Epistles*, New York, 1881, p. 391, and H. Alford, *The Greek New Testament*, London, 1866, 4, 397.

[11] Arndt and Gingrich, *A Greek-English Lexicon*, Chicago, 1957.

[12] Parousia is not used in Acts and only once in 1 John (2:28).

great glory (Mark 13:26=Matt 24:30=Luke 21:27; cf. also Matt 16:27; 25:31; 26:64).

In the Fourth Gospel Jesus promises to come again and take his people to be with him (14:3; cf. John 21:23). The Book of Acts uses *erchomai* to state that Christ will come to the earth again in the same way he left it (1:11). His coming will begin the great day of the Lord (2:20). Jesus, the great ruler, will then restore all things (3:21), will completely subdue his enemies (2:34-35) and will judge the whole inhabited world (17:31).

Paul urges the Corinthians to avoid making biased judgments by waiting for the Lord to decide the case when he "comes" (1 Cor 4:5). Paul also reminds believers that in celebrating the Lord's Supper they actually remember the Lord's death "until he comes" (1 Cor 11:26). At this coming the Lord will appear unexpectedly like a thief in the night (1 Thess 5:2) to bring his wrath on all who practice wickedness (Col 3:6) and to share his glory with his redeemed people (2 Thess 1:10). He who comes will not delay (Heb 10:37); the Lord is coming, and myriads of his holy people with him (Jude 14).

John strikes the same note in the Revelation: "Behold, he comes with clouds" (1:7). When he comes, the great day of his wrath will also have come (6:17). So in the light of this "coming" men should fear God (14:7; 16:14, 15). The concluding message from the Lord to the Christian is, "Look, I come quickly" (22:7, 20) and "my reward is with me" (22:20).

The verb *hēkō*, "come," is also used to describe the Second Coming of Jesus. Like *erchomai,* it is a synonym for Parousia in contexts where the bodily return of Christ is intended (Matt 8:11; 24:14, 50; Luke 12:46; Rom 11:26; Heb 10:37; 2 Pet 3:10; Rev 2:25; 3:3).

An examination of the phrases "day of judgment," "the last day," "day of the Lord," "the day of Christ" and "the day of God" also increases our understanding of the Parousia. More than once Jesus is quoted as saying that it will be more tolerable for Sodom and Gomorrah and for Tyre and Sidon in the day of judgment than for enlightened sinners who have rejected the message of Christ (Matt 10:15; 11:22, 24; cf. Luke 10:13-14). Jesus also says that on the judgment day men must give account for every idle word they speak (Matt 12:36), and on that day he will raise to life again those who believe in him (John 6:54; cf. 11:24). Peter describes it as a day of judgment and destruction of ungodly men (2 Pet 2:9; 3:7). It is the great day of God when nations will be gathered for the final battle (Rev 16:14-16).

Accompanying this day are signs in the heavens and on earth (Acts 2:20; cf. 2 Pet 3:10). Although it is yet future (2 Thess 2:1, 2), Christians are nevertheless to live in the present in a manner worthy of that day, anticipating and standing in awe of it (Phil 2:15, 16). They are to love one another and thus be without offense when that day finally comes (Phil 1:10). That day is also a day when believers can be proud of the results of their witness for Christ (2 Cor 1:14).

From this survey it is evident that the Parousia of Christ is the great day of God's final judgment. It is evident, too, that the term Parousia and its synonyms are used many times over in the NT, indicating that the general concept of the physical return of Christ was widespread and not the idea of one writer alone.

But what of the questions raised earlier? Did Jesus actually teach this doctrine, or did the church put the words into his mouth? To what extent is the Parousia a future event? It is to these types of questions that we now address ourselves.

Theological Problems Involving the Concept of the Parousia[13]

A basic question asked by scholars today is whether the idea of the Parousia originated with Jesus himself, or with the Christian community. Another has to do with the nature of the Parousia: Is it imminent or remote, i.e. does it refer only to that time near his resurrection and ascension, or to a much more distant time?

J. A. T. Robinson is one scholar who claims that Jesus never taught that he would come again but that this doctrine of the Parousia was read back onto his lips by the early church.[14] Glasson, too, believes there is little evidence for Jesus teaching anything about the end of the world. He says the Parousia did not form a part of the original gospel, because the gospel was concerned "with events which had already happened and of which the Apostles were witnesses." Rather, he says, the teaching about the Parousia developed in the period between the death of Christ and the time of the Thessalonian epistles.[15]

But any view that claims the Gospel had to do only with what happened and what was witnessed by the apostles really argues for the authenticity of what Jesus did and said. And these things his disciples, in a rabbi-disciple relationship, would be careful to preserve.[16] Such accurate and careful preservation of the words and actions of Jesus is implied, if not explicitly stated, in John's remark that the disciples had fully heard Jesus'

---

[13] I presuppose the doctrine of verbal inerrancy of Scripture (cf. 2 Tim 3:16) and do not accept the statement, "A Gospel is not the same thing as history. . . . It is saving truth" (R. H. Lightfoot, *The Gospel Message of St. Mark*, Oxford, 1958, pp. 29-30). I understand history to mean "the record of past events, especially in connection with the human race" (*The Random House Dictionary of the English Language*, New York, 1967, *s.v.* "History"), and in this connection I believe that the Bible qualifies as an accurate record of history so defined (2 Pet 1:21).

[14] See Robinson's remarks in J. Reumann, *Jesus in the Church's Gospel*, London, 1970, p. 275. See also J. A. T. Robinson, *Jesus and His Coming: The Emergence of a Doctrine*, New York, 1957. It is difficult for me to believe Robinson is correct here, if for no other reason than that Jesus was a bona fide rabbi whose disciples were closely attached to him and to his teaching. Gerhardsson has shown something of the infinite care pupils took in preserving the teachings of their rabbis and the exactness with which these teachings were handed on. It is quite likely that Jesus' disciples treated his words with the same care and exactness. See B. Gerhardsson, *Tradition and Transmission in Early Christianity*, Lund, 1964; W. H. Mare, "The Role of the Note-Taking Historian and His Emphasis on the Person and Work of Christ," *JETS*, 15 (1972), 107-21. See also the conservative scholarly discussion of these and other critical questions in C. C. Anderson, *The Historical Jesus: A Continuing Quest*, Grand Rapids, 1972.

[15] T. F. Glasson, *The Second Advent*, London, 1947, pp. 149, 155-56.

[16] See W. Harold Mare, "The Role of the Note-Taking Historian," pp. 113-14.

words and had seen and handled his person (1 John 1:1). This tends to argue for the validity of other NT accounts about Jesus' words and works, including his teaching about the Parousia (Matt 24). Thus, the early church's hope for the return of Christ can be grounded in his own promise.

It is argued, on the other hand, that Jesus did teach about his return, but that he took this teaching over from contemporary Judaism and then applied it to himself.[17] There is truth in this argument. It is true, for example, that the NT presents the view that first-century Jews had a hope in the coming of Messiah. Simeon and Anna illustrate this (Luke 2:29-38), as well as Peter (Acts 2:24-36; 3:22, 23) and Paul (Acts 13:26-37). And the NT assumes Jesus believed he was that coming Messiah (Matt 22:41-44). But one thing many Jews, even early Christian Jews, did not fully sense was that there were to be *two* comings of Christ (Acts 1:6-7). Jesus, however, made this distinction. His first coming he saw as bringing redemption for his people (Matt 20:28), and he said his Second Advent was to be in power and great glory (Matt 24:30).

At this point it is necessary to discuss the meaning of the Parousia concept in the teaching of the NT. It is commonly stated in theological circles today that in dealing with the Scriptures we should not ask the question, What happened? but rather, What does it mean? Presupposing a verbally inspired record, we believe it is proper to ask both questions. We have already asked, What happened? Now we are ready to ask the second question, What did Jesus and the writers of the NT mean when they taught about the Parousia?

What Jesus taught regarding this concept, although sometimes only in bare outline form, the Apostle Paul and the other writers of the NT received, amplified and developed. But they did not twist or change Jesus' concept of the Parousia. Jesus described the Parousia in terms of the consummation, with physical disturbances and human indifference. But did he conceive of a time interval between his resurrection and the Parousia? If so, did he think of this interval as an extended period of time or as an extremely brief one? How, if at all, does Paul's view of the Parousia and that of the other writers differ from the view expressed by Jesus?

It is to be observed, first of all, that Luke 17:20-25 discusses both Jesus' suffering and his Parousia. But this does not preclude an extended interval between the two events. In fact, the illustration Jesus used here of Noah's time, when people were eating and drinking before the Flood (Luke 17:26-27), suggests that he understood a lapse of time to take place between his resurrection and his Parousia (cf. also Gen 5:32; 7:11; 1 Pet 3:20). Furthermore, after his resurrection Jesus spoke explicitly of a period of time when the gospel would be preached prior to the "consummation of the age" (Matt 28:18-20).

But what of those passages where Jesus seemingly predicted his Parousia as immediately at hand? We need now to examine these texts to see if they are to be taken as referring to the *time* of Jesus' generation or to a more distant time.

---

[17] Glasson, *The Second Advent*, p. 10.

In one of these texts, examined by Kümmel,[18] Jesus says, "the harvest is near" (Mark 13:28-29; cf. Matt 24:32-33; Luke 21:29-31). But he does not say how near. Mark 13:24-26, with its emphasis on "those days" and on the dramatic disturbances to occur in the heavens at the time when the Son of Man will come, suggests that the "harvest" is not meant to be interpreted as near. The emphasis on being watchful so as not to miss the *future* signs of the Parousia (Mark 13:28), signs that herald the nearness of the harvest, indicates also that it was conceived as being some distance away.

Mark 13:30, "This generation shall not pass away until all these things shall come to pass," is undoubtedly one of the more difficult eschatological passages. In context, "all these things" quite naturally refer to such things as the physical disturbances attendant upon the gathering of God's elect (Mark 13:24-29). But then, what do the words "this generation shall not pass away" mean? Beasley-Murray feels that *hē genea hautē*, in the light of its reference to Jesus' contemporaries (Matt 11:16; 12:39, 41, 42, 45; 23:36; Mark 8:38; Luke 11:50-51; 17:25), must mean the same thing here.[19] If so, then this whole passage with its heavenly signs would have to be taken as fulfilled in the death and resurrection of Jesus or in the events leading up to the fall of Jerusalem. But this sounds strange in the light of Mark 13:31, which implies the destruction of both the heavens and the earth. This, however, did not occur at A.D. 70. The word "generation" may just as well be taken to mean "family" or "race" in the more general sense, as is its meaning in Luke 16:8.[20] Jesus may be interpreted here as teaching that people of the *family of faith* will still be here on earth when "all these things" come to pass.

Mark 8:38 and 9:1 similarly teach that some people then standing in the presence of Jesus would see the Kingdom of God accomplished with power. But this remark is followed by the transfiguration (Mark 9:2-8), which can be interpreted to fulfill the basic meaning of that prediction. Plummer comments that the parallel expressions in Mark and Luke (9:27), "before they see the kingdom of God," may "refer to the transfiguration regarded as a foretaste of Christ's glory in the future Kingdom."[21]

Matt 10:23 is the most difficult of the eschatological passages. It is used to show that Jesus had no concept of a distant Parousia. For many scholars this verse confirms the idea that Jesus counted on the coming of the Kingdom and of the Son of Man in glory within his lifetime and the lifetime of his hearers.[22] However, this verse could simply mean that Jesus, the Son of Man, having sent his disciples on a preaching itinerary through

[18] W. G. Kümmel, *Promise and Fulfillment*, London, 1967, pp. 70-71.

[19] G. R. Beasley-Murray, *A Commentary on Mark Thirteen*, London, New York, 1957, p. 100.

[20] Arndt and Gingrich, *Lexicon*, interpret *genea* (Luke 16:8) to mean "the children of this age are more prudent *in relation to their own clan* (i.e. people of their own kind)."

[21] Alfred Plummer, *The Gospel According to St. Matthew*, London, 1915, p. 236.

[22] See Kümmel, *Promise and Fulfillment*, p. 64.

the cities of Israel, would meet them at a designated place before they finished their job. It is a saying warning them not to loiter because the task was so great and his time so short.[23]

In the light of these alternate but viable interpretations of difficult texts, we posit that Jesus did make a distinction between his resurrection and the Parousia, and that he did conceive of an interval of time in between—a period of time he did not describe in detail.

Another question asks whether Jesus divested Jewish eschatology of its political and literal character by putting the active and ethical elements in the foreground.[24] Do passages like Matt 25:14-46, for example, support such a view? In my judgment Jesus does not divest the Second Advent of its political and literal character in Matt 25. Rather, he is merely teaching human accountability to God without either denying or affirming the political implications of the Parousia. Matt 19:28 (cf. Luke 22:30), however, with its message about "regeneration," calls attention to the fact that Jesus' disciples will have a place in judging the twelve tribes of Israel when the Son of Man comes in glory. Here the future political and literal aspects of Jewish eschatology are clearly taught.[25]

The term Parousia is absent from the Fourth Gospel and is found in the Johannine Epistles only in 1 John 2:28 (cf also John 21:22, 23 and 1 John 3:2). Does this minimal use of the word Parousia suggest that the Johannine eschatology is a timeless possession of eternal life devoid of any future events?[26] We must answer in the negative and point out that John's concept of judgment carries historical-eschatological as well as spiritual-eternal meanings (cf. John 3:17, 18; 5:24, 45; 8:15; 9:39; 12:31, 47; 1 John 3:14). Certainly the words "resurrection unto judgment" (John 5:29) imply a final period of reckoning. In addition, Jesus' expression "the last day" (John 6:39, 40, 44, 54; 12:48; cf. 11:24; 1 John 2:18) also argues for a future eschatological emphasis in Johannine writing.

It goes without saying that the Second Coming judgment theme is stressed in Paul (cf. Rom 12:19; 1 Thess 5:3; 2 Thess 1:7-9; see above).

In our study it has been observed that OT Judaism's view of eschatology contributed significantly to the development of the Parousia concept of the NT. Though the term Parousia is not used with great frequency, nor in every NT book, to indicate the Second Advent, yet where it is used it adds significantly to our understanding of the future Advent of Jesus. It has been noted that in books where Parousia is not used, or is used infrequently, there are other parallel concepts and synonyms that convey the same thought.

In discussing a selected number of problems raised about the theological implications of the Parousia, we have argued that the church faithfully preserved the teachings of Jesus, and therefore the remarks about his Second Advent are to be taken as his own. We posited that what Jesus

---

[23] See John A. Broadus, *A Commentary on the Gospel of Matthew*, Philadelphia, 1886, pp. 227-28.
[24] See Oepke, *TDNT*, 4, 867.
[25] Contrast Robinson, *Jesus and His Coming*, p. 57.
[26] Oepke, *TDNT*, 4, 869.

taught about the Parousia, even when it was in bare outline, was received, amplified and developed further by the apostles.

We argued, too, that Jesus distinguished between the events of his resurrection and his future Parousia and that there was an indefinite period of time between these two events. We stated, further, that Jesus did not divest Jewish eschatology of its political and literal character. He included this in his teaching as well as man's future judgment before God.

Finally, we argued that in such Christian philosophically-oriented works as the Johannine writings, mixed in with their Christianity of "timeless possession," there is to be found the doctrine of the Parousia with its "last day" events and final judgment. We observed that this theme of future judgment is also prominent in other parts of the NT.

The Metaphorical Language of Theology:
Its Experiential Base — Biblical and Contemporary

A. BERKELEY MICKELSEN

In the debates about the nature of theological language, one must never forget its purpose. The purpose of theological language ancient or modern is not just *talk* about God. Nor is it just *truths* about God. Rather, theological language brings understanding so that men can have *a growing involvement* with the Living God himself. Today we talk about God in a particularly secular age. Langdon Gilkey has made clear the four concepts that are characteristic of this secular spirit of our time.

1. *Contingency.*—All that exists is the result of causes that are neither necessary, rational, or purposive.
2. *Relativity, relativism.*—Nothing in itself is unchanging, self-sufficient, capable of existing in and by itself, with an essence that is underived.
3. *Temporality, transience.*—Reality *as a whole* is becoming, changing, mortal. Since everything in this reality is cut off in the process of becoming, finiteness and limitedness are the hallmarks of existence.
4. *Autonomy, freedom.*—Man has the innate capacity to know his own truth, to decide about his own existence, to create his own meaning, and to establish his own values.[1]

Gilkey insists that this secular spirit touches all of us. If we think that secularism does not leave any imprint on us, Gilkey reminds us that the secular spirit is a mood. This mood infiltrates all areas. It is an atmosphere in which men live.[2] We can be influenced by secularism without being a secularist. Gilkey attacks this secular spirit by showing that the secular man has a serious disjunction between his *secular self-understanding* (and *world understanding* as seen in these four characteristics) and *his lived experience.*[3]

[1] Langdon Gilkey, *Naming the Whirlwind: The Renewal of God-Language,* Indianapolis and New York, 1969, pp. 39-61.
[2] *Ibid.,* p. 181.
[3] *Ibid.,* p. 248.

A. Berkeley Mickelsen, Professor of New Testament Interpretation and Chairman of the Department of New Testament Studies at Bethel Theological Seminary, St. Paul, Minnesota. B.A., Wheaton College; M.A. and B.D., Wheaton College Graduate School; Ph.D., The University of Chicago.

In his *creed* the secularist asserts contingency, relativity, temporality; in his *living* or *existence* he comes face to face with ultimacy. Whence come values? The very whence of existence haunts him. The answers the secularist gives to these probing questions of ultimacy do not make the questions go away.[4]

In his creed the secularist asserts his freedom and autonomy. He believes that man, freed from external authorities, can control himself. But lived experience so often disagrees with this naive assumption. Does man, free and autonomous, control the stream of history? At some points he can influence that stream, but he does not control it. Man is not the master of his own fate at all.[5]

If secularism has a gulf between its self-understanding, its world understanding and its lived experience, we as Christian thinkers must be sure that our lived experience does not refute our lofty assertions or theological discussion about a reality that we may be involved with only in an intellectual manner.

Metaphorical language about God is *not* abstract. From Calvin to Barth—over four hundred years—Christian thinkers have certainly given their God-talk an abstract form. When Calvin discusses the Trinity, he says:

> What I denominate a Person is a subsistence in the Divine essence, which is related to the others [Persons, members of the Trinity], and yet distinguished from them by an incommunicable property. By the word subsistence we mean something different from the word essence.[6]

On the same theme Barth says:

> The doctrine of the Trinity means on the one hand, as the denial of subordinationism, the express statement that the three moments do not mean a more and a less in the Godness of God. . . . Father, Son, and Spirit are the one, single, and equal God. . . .
>
> But on the other hand, the doctrine of the Trinity means, as the denial of *modalism,* the expressed declaration that those three elements are not foreign to the Godness of God. The relationship is not that we should have to see the proper God beyond these three elements, in a higher being in which He was not the Father, the Son, and the Spirit.[7]

When the truths of God are put in such philosophical, abstract language, they show how much rigor of thought is necessary at this level of communication. But this is not where theological language begins (ancient or modern), and it is not the only form that serious thought can take to polish off its careful reflections.

Metaphorical language certainly begins in the here and now. It has an experiential base. It usually involves ordinary, customary, finite existence. But this is where it starts. From this well-known experiential base, metaphorical language moves out to involve man with the Ultimate, with the Living God, Maker of heaven and earth.

[4] *Ibid.*, pp. 252-55
[5] *Ibid.*, pp. 255-60.
[6] Calvin, *Institutes* 1.13.6.
[7] Karl Barth, *Church Dogmatics,* trans. by G. T. Thomson, Edinburgh, 1936, 1, 1, 437-40. Italics mine.

This ability to take significant earthly experiences and to move them into a higher realm makes metaphorical language about God effective. Military situations or those involving natural disasters often find men resorting to language about "deliverance," "rescue" or "salvation." These experiences become the base for a far higher deliverance or rescue. In family language, places of security give rise to the metaphorical language of "dwelling place," "refuge" and "fortress." Political language supplies the vehicle for the metaphorical use of "king," "ruler," "judge," "act of reigning." Useful as this kind of language is to carry men into a higher realm, it did not do so for all. Men could not celebrate deliverance in a higher key until they knew first their inability to solve their own dilemmas. They could not speak of God as a Dwelling Place unless they knew that they had here no place to abide permanently. They could not talk of God and Christ as King, of God reigning, unless they saw first the chaos and anarchy that follows when man is his own lord or king. Individually and collectively, man dreams of a golden age (happy years of retirement; a generation without war, poverty, ghettos, industrial strife and inflation) when somehow each person is king. But when a man reaches the age of retirement, he is not king because the ominous threats to existence hang as storm clouds in the sky.

Many modern religious men, members of Christian churches, look to the past for a reality that they do not have in their own actual existence. Gilkey sees this situation as existing among all groups.

> Among our most conservative groups, this elusiveness of God expresses itself strangely but pervasively: in nostalgia for old-time religion, for the religion of father and even of grandfather. We call this *nostalgia for another time* rather than real religion because the suburban layman who wants this kind of religion has no intention of living the rest of his existence in terms of this old-time faith, as his small-town forebears surely did. He maintains his big car, his modern house, his conventional habits, and his drinks on the back patio throughout the week—as his religious grandfather, *who lived in this faith's terms,* never would have. His religion is thus the one place where his life, his thinking, and his standards reflect this old small-town existence out of which he came. He actually exists, therefore, in another world, in the modern suburban, commercial world—and he has no intention of *relinquishing that world!* So he merely "hankers" after this religion his predecessors had possessed, and would not dream of living within its terms or within its set of meanings.[8]

Here we have a too frequently occurring dilemma. The language about God is known. But a genuine, vital relationship with the Reality that the language talks about is not known. Mere language without the relationship to the reality of God is exactly what Gilkey says: "nostalgia for the past." Commitment in the present means fellowship with God because the emptiness and void of a secular life has been felt. In its place has come a growing experience of the reality of God—not just the idea of God.

The experiential base for the metaphorical language about God transforms ideas about God into a genuine awareness and relationship with God. Men have encountered firsthand both literal, earthly experiences and the

---

[8] Gilkey, *Naming the Whirlwind*, pp. 105-6.

higher experience with God that is described in this ordinary kind of language. Because we are stressing the crucial role that experience plays in theological language, we must explain: this emphasis has nothing in common with the religious experience emphasis of Schleiermacher. Rather, the experiential base gives metaphorical language its authentic quality. This kind of language is involved with lived existence.

We will examine three areas where the metaphorical language about God was first experienced in an earthly, ordinary experience. Even if some of these experiences were extraordinary, they were still part of life in the here and now. From this realm, the language moves into a higher realm while at the same time it transforms the earthly to be descriptive of this realm. God thus reveals himself through the experienced reality of the finite to bring man to the experienced reality of the Infinite.

I. The Deliverance Theme in the Bible
Emphasizes Man's Desperate Predicament

The metaphorical nature of this kind of language becomes clear when we see what the customary, socially acknowledged meaning of the term deliverance is in the small and big crises of life. The extensiveness of the vocabulary of deliverance in the OT is imposing.[9]

Salvation from External Evils

This idea of "salvation from external evils" is clearly illustrated in Judg 6. Israel was suffering oppression from the Midianites. Gideon was addressed as a mighty man of valor. The angel of the LORD told him that the LORD was with him. Gideon became perplexed. His actual, lived, historical situation did not seem to indicate that the LORD was with his people: "Why has all this befallen us?" (Judg 6:13). Gideon wanted to know where the LORD was who had brought them out of the land of Egypt. Then the LORD himself addressed Gideon: "Go in this might of yours and *deliver* Israel from the hand of Midian; do not I send you?" (Judg 6:14). In the light of who Gideon was, and the weakness of his clan, he responded: "Pray, Lord, how can I *deliver* Israel?" (Judg 6:15). The famous fleece-test of Gideon was to increase his confidence and knowledge that God would *deliver* Israel (Judg 6:36-37). By God's help, with the faithful three hundred Gideon delivered Israel from a foreign oppressor. Here is salvation in a common earthly setting—one group freed from the tyranny of a stronger power.

War and its accompanying evils is not the only disaster from which men need deliverance. Paul was caught in a hurricane that came from the

[9] John F. A. Sawyer, *Semantics in Biblical Research: New Methods of Defining Hebrew Words for Salvation*, SBT, second series, 24, Naperville, 1972. Sawyer makes clear the importance of integrating a number of procedures before one has confidence that he has an adequate basis for meanings. Although this is a highly technical linguistic study, the various words for salvation with their own different, established meanings illustrate the varied kinds of experiences that give rise to these meanings.

northeast over Crete. Instead of moving along the coast to a bigger harbor in which to winter, the ship was driven westward and finally broke up on the rocks at Malta. During this period the passengers came almost to despair: "And all hope of our being saved was gradually abandoned" (Acts 27:20). But Paul brought hope. He told all of his fellow passengers that he had a message from God: He (Paul) would stand before Caesar and God had granted him all those who sailed with him. As they came near Malta, certain sailors had lowered the small boat to get to land by it. Paul warned against this: "You are not able to *be saved* or rescued if these do not remain on the ship" (Acts 27:31). When the ship finally hit the rocks, some swam, some came on planks and pieces of the ship, but "in this fashion it happened that all *were brought safely through* to land" (Acts 27:44). Here is rescue from almost sure death at sea. The fire that they provided and the unusual hospitality of the natives on Malta showed how they recognized the surprising turn of events—no lives lost in a horrible shipwreck. Here again is an earthly, experiential base for the analogous transfer of meaning from a physical deliverance to a spiritual one that includes this life and the next. A limited earthly experience serves as a means of making real a far more important and extensive salvation.

Salvation: Personal, National, and Cosmological

Whether it be military oppression or physical catastrophe, salvation comes after the awareness of a genuine threat to living or existence. After God's judgment that brought Israel to Assyria, Isaiah talks about God's anger being turned away (Isa 12:1). Then the prophet gives his own testimony that salvation is a lot more than an event. "Behold, God is my salvation; I will trust, and will not be afraid; for the LORD God is my strength and my song, and he has become my salvation" (Isa 12:2). God is clearly the reality. He is joy. He is strength. He is salvation. This is an experienced reality that goes far beyond the ordinary, earthly kind of salvation. Of course, this is a reality experienced on earth. But in being caught up with ultimate Being such a reality transcends every ordinary, earthly experience.

Ezekiel addresses the house of Israel in the time of the Babylonian captivity. God's judgment had fallen. In the picture of God's restoration the verb "to deliver or save" is found in a most fascinating context: "And I will deliver you from all your uncleannesses" (Ezek 36:29). This climaxes a vivid descriptive narrative of God giving them a new heart and putting within them a new spirit; God removes a heart of stone and gives a heart of flesh (Ezek 36:26). Here deliverance or salvation is a predicted reality. What set the stage for it was the experienced judgment. Hence the metaphorical language of salvation or deliverance has the ring of genuineness because the One who will deliver in the future is described as the One who has just acted in judgment. The grounds for the experienced judgment are bloodshed and idolatry. The ground for the coming deliverance or salvation is God-centered: "It is not for your sake . . . that I am going to act, but for the sake of my holy name" (Ezek 36:22). Salvation in these higher levels of meaning is the effect of God's transforming action.

The NT likewise builds personal deliverance or salvation on God's action, what he has already done. Calvary and the resurrection were known and experienced by certain disciples. They participated in what for them was a momentous discovery. This was followed by earnest proclamation. Men are to confess with their mouths the Lordship of Jesus Christ. They must have the conviction in their heart that God raised him from the dead. The outcome of this confession and conviction is that the individual *will be saved, rescued, delivered.* He will *attain salvation.* A Christian constantly makes confession with a view to salvation (Rom 10:9-10). The experiential side of analogical language involving salvation is a response to a reality that is so sure to the confessor that he makes this confession with a customary regularity. He has salvation; he has the prospect of final, total and complete deliverance.

Interestingly enough, both God the Father and Jesus the Son are called "Savior" in Tit 1:3-4. God promised eternal life and manifested it in his word or message. This message Paul proclaimed. He did so at the command "of God, our Savior" (Tit 1:3). Grace and peace come from God the Father and from Jesus Christ "our Savior" (Tit 1:4). This God who is the Savior never lies. The truthfulness of God is based on the long record of God's dealings with his people. Grace and peace are not ideas but realities known and felt by God's people. Hence the saviorhood of God and of Christ is not just a title but a meaningful term that is based on the actions of both. Furthermore, God's people have known firsthand these actions. They have certainty that they will experience more of these actions.

Christians were saved for the hope, i.e. the redemption of their bodies (Rom 8:23-24). This latter objective is part of a far larger one. When Christians receive new bodies, *the creation itself* will be freed from slavery to decay into the freedom of the splendor that belongs to the children of God (Rom 8:21). Here is good news. Physical creation is included in salvation. The experience that anticipates this final state is the eager expectation on the part of all aspects of creation for the revelation of the sons of God. This expectation is due to creation being subject to futility. A realistic picture of things as they are is coupled with a conviction about what lies ahead. This hope centers in the reality of God—his past, present and future action that insures monumental change and complete deliverance.

II. The Habitation Theme in the Bible
Emphasizes Man's Need for Security

Homes where men dwell, refuges and fortresses where men go when under attack by an outside foe are capable of being treasured, hallowed spots. Because of the depth of meaning in this kind of experiential base, the metaphorical language about God that employs this emphasis can point to a far more profound kind of dwelling.

Where God's People Dwell

The opening verse of Ps 90 describes an experienced reality: "Lord, you are a dwelling place for us in generation after generation." But before all generations, "from everlasting to everlasting thou art God" (Ps 90:2). Here is a magnificent picture of fellowship with God in this earthly scene. How profound is this type of dwelling and this kind of fellowship. Modern man is lonely because he has not found this kind of dwelling place. Even though he may have an ideal home and family life with superb physical surroundings, modern man finds such a kind of dwelling just too cramped and too narrow. Unless he dwells with the Lord, a cosmic loneliness will settle in, and he will not know abiding or permanent fellowship.

Ps 91 begins with a similar theme. "The one who dwells in the shelter (i.e. the Most High), who lodges himself in the shadow of the Almighty, will be constantly saying to the LORD: 'My refuge and my fortress; my God, I trust in Him' " (Ps 91:1-2). Trust or committal, which is the essence of the faith spoken about in the NT, is the response of one who dwells in God. Additional metaphors of God as a fortress or refuge are also found in Ps 71:1-3. There the psalmist also takes refuge in the LORD. He prays that God will be for him a rock as a dwelling place. He asserts that God is his rock and fortress (Ps 71:3). How clear it is that for OT believers who speak in Pss 91 or 71 there was no place of security but in God.

The final picture of security involving the Holy City that comes down from heaven (Rev 21:2) is of God as both a camper and city dweller! "Look, the tent or dwelling of God is with men, and he will tent or dwell with them; further, they will be his people or peoples, and God himself will be with them, their God" (Rev 21:3). Only because we have experienced in earthly situations the reality of camping at its best, and home life in a helpful key, can we project these experiences freed from all the limitations of earthly life to the final realm.

Where the Spirit of God Dwells

The heart of the New Covenant is the dwelling of the Spirit of God in his people (Rom 8:9, 11). With this assumed as a fact, Christians are not to be in the flesh, i.e. in a self-centered kind of existence. Further, God will raise us from the dead through his Spirit that is dwelling in us. Not only do we dwell in God, but much more, he dwells in us. His Spirit brings a whole new life and a whole new walk. How powerful is this metaphor to express the closeness of God to his believing people.

Where God Dwells Transcendently

Immanence is not the only picture of God in Scripture. God, the one who is Sovereign alone, is also the one who alone has immortality and dwells in unapproachable light, whom no man has ever seen or can see (1 Tim 6:15-16). The figure of dwelling in unapproachable light was powerful for ancient readers. It is even more powerful in our day when we understand more vividly the damaging effects of infrared light, of cosmic rays and of many other forms of light. This metaphor—God dwelling in unapproachable light—says clearly that man cannot control God. Man cannot reach God except on his terms and invitation. The God who reveals himself is also the God who hides himself. Where God dwells, man cannot go. But this is not the final word. God comes to man; God camps and dwells with his people; he brings them to himself.

III. The Sovereign Ruler Theme in the Bible
Emphasizes Man's True Dependence

The True Judge, Ruler and King

After Israel had been devastated by invasion, after foreigners had gone through with their strange speech, Isaiah talks about peace, of tents that will not be plucked up and of cords that will not be broken. What is the guarantee of this? "But there [in this situation of peace] the LORD in majesty will be for us" (Isa 33:21). Who is this Lord? "For the LORD is our judge, the LORD is our ruler, the LORD is our king; he will save us" (Isa 33:22). The Judge of Israel is the one who judges all the earth (Gen 18:25). The ruler is the one who has the commander's staff (Gen 49:10; cf. Ps 60:10=108:11). The king who will save is not only the king of Israel (cf. Isa 33:17; 41:21; 43:15; 44:6), but he is also the King of the nations (Jer 10:7). Today there is a great longing for peace, but peace seems to be so elusive. If we get peace in one part of the world, hostility breaks out some place else. Only in the True Ruler, Judge and King, who will be able to do what no earthly ruler, judge or king has the power to do, will there be lasting peace.

The Final Acquisition of Power

In Rev 11:17 the twenty-four elders give thanks to God because he has taken his great power and begun to reign. Similarly God's people praise him because the Lord God, the Almighty, has begun to reign (Rev 19:6).

Revelation also pictures Christ as King. The lamb who conquers and defeats all his foes is Lord of lords and King of kings (Rev 17:14). The one who comes to rule with a rod of iron, to bring both retribution and rest for his people, has upon his garment and upon his thigh a name written: "King of kings and Lord of lords" (Rev 19:16). It was Handel who took this metaphor and made it even more powerful by his music. The experiential base here is that men have known powerful rulers. But these are broken pieces of flax alongside the Commander of the Nations.

Summary

The language of theology, then, is a language with a firm experiential base. It comes out of the realities, agonies and perplexities of human existence. With experienced reality at one level of understanding, it takes us far beyond this level. By the vehicle of metaphorical or analogous language we transcend our finite limitations. We not only discover reality; we have a vital relationship with it. Without this Ultimate Reality, the Living God of the Bible, language is dead. With this experienced Reality, language is living because it becomes the gateway to Life Eternal.

We communicate with God; he communicates with us. God's people engage in the miracle of dialogue with him. In such communication there is communion. After communication and communion there is continued discourse. We talk about God—the language of theology—as the true result of a growing fellowship. Our talk shows clearly both our temporal finiteness and our tremendous destiny. We are citizens of two worlds, and our language shows the demands of this dual citizenship.

Some Comments on Hebrews 6:4-6
and the Doctrine of the Perseverance
of God with the Saints

ROGER NICOLE

The passage that occupies us is one that has captivated the attention of Christians probably ever since it was written. Intimately tied to its interpretation are difficult questions to which perhaps no definitive answer may be forthcoming here on earth: Who are the people to whom the author refers? What is the sin that they have committed and which places them beyond recovery? How can such a situation be diagnosed with certainty in this world, so that Christians would be justified in ceasing to make any effort to retrieve these apostates?

Early church history provides us with salient examples of the misuse of this passage. The Novatians and the Donatists rather hastily applied it to the case of church members who in times of persecution had the weakness to engage in idolatrous worship or had fallen into gross and manifest sin. This very passage should have warned them that their interpretation was faulty, for there were many of these sinners who did sincerely repent of such failing, so that the text was clearly not applicable to them! But this abuse of Heb 6:4-6 (and 10:26-29) was one of the considerations that caused the church of the West to withhold for some time its recognition of the canonicity of the Epistle to the Hebrews. Such serious mistakes surely should prompt us to special caution as we undertake to interpret this text.

I. To Whom Does the Text Refer?

We notice at once five characteristics that describe the people in view prior to their fall:

1. They have been once-for-all enlightened, vs. 4.
2. They have had a taste of the heavenly gift, vs. 4.
3. They have become partakers of, sharers in (*metochoi*), the Holy Spirit, vs. 4.
4. They have tasted the good Word of God, vs. 5.

Roger Nicole, Professor of Systematic Theology at Gordon-Conwell Theological Seminary, South Hamilton, Massachusetts. B.A., Gymnase Classique, Lausanne, Switzerland; M.A., The University of Paris, Sorbonne; B.D., S.T.M., Th.D., Gordon Divinity School; Ph.D., Harvard University.

5. They have tasted the powers of the world to come, vs. 5.

To these must be added a sixth one:

6. They have had an experience of repentance (which it would be essential to renew), vs. 6.

If we conceive that Heb 10:26-29 refers to the same type of case we might add yet a seventh, and perhaps an eighth, characteristic:

7. They have received a knowledge of the truth, 10:26.

(8. They were sanctified in the blood of the covenant, 10:29.)[1]

A. The most immediate impulse would be to interpret this cluster of statements as describing regenerate persons, especially since the epistle is addressed to Christians and in chap. 10 the author even uses the pronoun "we." There are very great difficulties in this course, however, which may account for the fact that its supporters are not agreed among themselves.

1. In order to relate the passages to the impressive witness of Scripture concerning God's persevering grace with those to whom he has once given new birth, some, for instance Westcott, Loane, Hewitt and Griffith Thomas, suggest that the warning of Heb relates to a sin that it is impossible to commit. The author of Heb, they aver, analyzes what would be the consequences of such a sin, but does not affirm that anyone has committed it, or even can commit it. This warning, they hold, is one of the means God uses to prevent Christians from apostatizing. But, without wanting to minimize the significance of scriptural admonitions and their effectiveness in God's plan, it would appear odd that this one, and it alone, should be entirely efficacious, when other divine exhortations and warnings are in fact occasionally disregarded by man. This would be a very strange phenomenon.

If, in fact, the sin contemplated in Heb 6 simply cannot be committed, it would seem absurd for the author to dwell on it precisely at the time when he avows that he will "press on." When there is an insuperable barrier there is no need to give warning concerning dangers on the other side! This type of interpretation shows a wholesome regard for the strength of the scriptural doctrine of perseverance, but it tends to artificiality.

2. Not a few interpreters are of the opinion that these texts, by themselves alone, but even more forcibly when viewed in connection with other passages of Scripture, spell the doom of the doctrine of the infallible perseverance of the regenerate. God indefatigably supplies grace to those who are trusting him, they say, but the final perseverance of any saint must perforce depend upon the cooperation of the saint's free will, and God will not exercise any influence that would interfere with the proper liberty of free agents. Therefore any Christian on this earth, whatever his spiritual advancement, is still capable of defecting and the epistle to the Heb gives us solemn and meaningful warnings against this fearful eventuality.

[1] The propriety of this last item depends on the interpretation of the phrase "wherewith he was sanctified." Grammatically it may refer to the apostate and thus constitute an additional description, but it may equally well—and in our judgment, preferably—apply to Christ, who offered himself through the blood of the covenant, so that the text may be paraphrased: "Who has despised and counted as common the precious blood of the covenant, the blood which manifests that Christ gave himself in sacrifice for us and was consecrated priest unto God." Cf. John 17:19; Heb 2:10; 5:7, 9; 9:11, 12; as suggested by John Owen, *Works*, 23, 545.

Besides the problem of perseverance, which we shall consider more fully below, this approach seems at once open to two serious difficulties, one exegetical and the other theological.

a. Heb 6 and 10 both assert that people who commit this sin are beyond recovery. But these interpreters—in virtue of what we might call a happy inconsistency—are not willing to treat people who are deemed to have lost their salvation as beyond the pale of redeeming grace. In public meetings as well as privately they admonish them to repent and to return to God who will forgive, and frequently backsliders respond to these entreaties, proving thereby that their case was not that described in Heb 6. Yet how can we think that someone, whose sin has been great enough to set at naught God's grace in his life and to disannul the regenerating work of the Holy Spirit, is really less guilty than those whom Heb 6 and 10 describe?

If Heb 6 proves anything about losing salvation, it proves too much! A wise Arminian might do well not to quote this text, since before the end of the discussion he may have to concede that he does not understand it, and that he is unable to point to concrete cases where it applies. This, we should think, would be better than to abandon to damnation all those who are viewed as apostates.[2]

b. The theological difficulty relates to the nature of free will in its relation to the sovereign purpose of God. Just about everyone grants that in heaven there will be no more danger of apostasy. Does this mean that in glory men will be deprived of that freedom which constitutes the distinguishing characteristic of humanity, the gift that stands so high that even the sovereign purpose of God must be viewed as subordinate to it? Surely not. But if in glory perseverance is not inconsistent with freedom, why should it be thought incompatible on earth?

c. Undoubtedly, the greatest difficulty with this type of interpretation lies in its repudiation of the doctrine of God's perseverance with the

---

[2] How heavily this difficulty burdens the position may be perceived in the suggestion made by some that the text does not assert that it is forever impossible to renew such people to repentance, but merely that they cannot be renewed as long as they continue to crucify afresh the Son of God. The following comments at once come to mind.

(1) If this is what the author of Heb has in view, it is difficult to see what is in any way unusual in the case of those apostates whose privileges he takes such care to describe at length. Nobody can repent at all, let alone be renewed to repentance, while he persists "in crucifying to himself the Son of God." This is a truism too obvious to warrant statement, not to speak of the awesome solemnity of Heb 6.

(2) On this assumption, the author of Heb should take time to get these apostates to desist from crucifying afresh the Son of God, since then they might well be renewed to repentance and be reclaimed to the faith. But he does not do this, and in the context surely appears to say that all efforts in this direction are bound to be futile. The Novatians and Donatists, wrong as they were otherwise, at least understood this point well.

(3) This explanation does not avail for Heb 10:26-29, which includes no qualification but spells inescapable judgment and doom for the apostates. Of course, the comment is offered in relation to Heb 6, not to Heb 10, but what is the value of a partial solution of Heb 6 that leaves intact the whole difficulty in Heb 10? And what probability is there that these two parallel cases are in fact wholly dissimilar?

saints. And this doctrine is powerfully grounded both in its close relationship to other aspects of God's sovereign purpose of grace and in very specific scriptural affirmations.

Scripture asserts that "He who has begun a good work . . . will perfect it until the day of Christ" (Phil 1:6; cf. Luke 14:28-32).

Scripture asserts that "life" shall not separate believers from the love of God in Christ (Rom 8:38, 39).

Scripture asserts that the golden chain of God's purpose is not thinning out toward the end, but that the very people who are known, foreordained, called and justified *are also glorified* (Rom 8:29, 30).

Scripture asserts that believers are "kept by the power of God through faith unto final salvation and for an incorruptible inheritance" (1 Pet 1:4, 5; cf. Jude 24, 25; 2 Tim 1:12).

Scripture asserts that true believers are "sealed by the Spirit unto the day of redemption" (Eph 4:30).

Scripture asserts that apostates were never true members of Christ because otherwise they would not have fallen away (1 John 2:19).

Scripture asserts again and again that the new life in Christ is "eternal" (*aiōnios*). What kind of eternity would that be which could be brought to an end in our own life-span?

Jesus asserts that it is impossible "to lead the elect astray" (Matt 24:24).

Jesus asserts that "every one who beholdeth the Son and believeth on him will have eternal life, and he will raise him up at the last day" (John 6:40; cf. 54).

Jesus asserts, "I know my sheep, and they follow me; and I give them eternal life, and they shall never perish, and no one shall snatch them out of my hand" (John 10:27-28). The emphasis in this combination of statements appears to us irresistible.

Now these passages, although admittedly chosen and brought together for good effect, constitute only a fraction of the scriptural support for perseverance. Is it conceivable that the author of Heb would contradict all this? It is true, of course, that the epistle contains impressive admonitions against drifting (2:1), neglecting salvation (2:3; 4:1; 12:25), disobedience (3:12, 18; 4:6, 11), hardening in sin (3:13), weariness (12:3), falling short of God's grace (12:15), besides the warnings contained in chaps. 6 and 10. But none of these texts asserts that defectors were ever true believers, and some of them are based on cases of people like Esau (12:16, 17) and disobedient Israelites (3:16, 17; 12:25), who can scarcely be viewed as such.

Furthermore, the epistle emphasizes the persevering character of true faith (3:6, 14; 4:14; 6:11, 15; 9:28; 10:23) and exhorts believers to faithfulness in terms of it, but this does not imply that there are genuine believers who will not hold fast.

The plain fact is that Heb contains a wealth of materials oriented toward perseverance.

Heb describes God as all-powerful (1:3; 2:10) and fulfilling the designs of his will (2:4). His counsels are immutable (1:12; 6:17, 18) and his faithfulness is the ground of the confidence of believers (2:17; 6:10; 10:23; 11:6, 11). These are precisely the divine perfections in evidence in the doctrine of sovereign grace!

Heb describes the ministry of Christ, not in terms of what it might perform if only men should be willing, but rather in terms of what it does and will certainly accomplish. Christ is viewed as one who leads his sons to glory (2:10), who brings to naught the devil (2:14), who delivers all . . . the seed of Abraham (2:15), who propitiates for the sins of his people (2:17; 12:24) so that no divine wrath remains against them. He is the surety of the better covenant (7:22; 12:24), the perfecter of the faith (12:2), the shepherd of the sheep (13:20—and what shepherd worthy of the name would feel that all his job entails is to protect the sheep from enemies on the outside, but that he is not responsible for sheep slipping away from the flock?), the High Priest, representing his people and interceding for them (7:25—and what kind of intercession would this be that would not even protect them from ultimate apostasy?).

Heb describes believers in terms that imply permanent status: those who shall inherit salvation (1:14), God's sons (2:10; 12:5-11), Christ's brethren (2:12, 17; 3:1), God-given children (2:13; cf. John 17:2, 6, 9, 11, 12, etc.), the seed of Abraham (2:16), God's people (2:17; 4:9; 8:10), the partakers of the heavenly calling (3:1) and of Christ (3:14), Christ's house (3:6), the heirs of the promise (6:17; 8:6; 9:15), those who have been sanctified once for all (10:10, 14; 13:12, 21), the assembly of first-born enrolled in heaven (12:23).

Heb describes salvation in terms that do not admit of defection or termination: the sons are brought to glory (2:10), the people of God enter God's rest (4:3, 9), the hope is well grounded (6:18, 19), the new covenant is one where members do not fail (8:10; cf. 10:15-17), the saints are perfected forever (10:14; 12:2), the Kingdom cannot be shaken (12:28), the salvation is to the uttermost (7:15), eternal (5:9; 9:12) and marked by endless life (7:16).

Even in connection with his most solemn warnings, the author of Heb hastens to indicate that this tragic apostasy will not happen to true Christians: 6:9—"We are persuaded better things of you" (the whole end of chap. 6 is full of most comforting reassurance); 10:39—"We are not of them that shrink back unto perdition; but of them that have faith unto the saving of the soul."

B. Under these circumstances it is not surprising that a number of commentators have chosen the view that the people described in Heb 6:4-6 were not true believers. Rather, it is urged, they must be viewed as men and women who have received an exceptionally thorough exposure to the gospel and all that it entails, and who may have made an external profession of acceptance of it, so that for a season they shared in the blessings and the fellowship of God's people, but who at a later point have made spectacular shipwreck as to the faith, renouncing their earlier profession, and manifesting such opposition to the gospel of grace as to make it evident that they have placed themselves beyond the range where God will reach them.

Those who advocate this view are under obligation to account for all the elements of the description as consistent with something short of genuine salvation. They do not need to prove that the expressions used cannot apply to real Christians—indeed, in most cases, they readily concede that these may so apply—but they must be prepared to show that none of them singly, nor all of them jointly, necessarily implies true regeneration. Let us review each of the eight characteristics to see the range of spiritual conditions that they may properly describe.

1. "They have been once-for-all enlightened." At the one end of the spectrum light is characteristic of God himself (1 John 1:5; 1 Tim 6:16) and is often connected in Scripture with the experience of salvation (1 Pet 2:9; 1 John 1:7; Eph 1:18; 5:8; 2 Cor 4:6; John 8:12, etc.). But Scripture also speaks of people who receive an exposure to the light, and fail to respond in faith (John 1:9-11; 3:19; 9:39-41; Matt 4:16, 17; 2 Cor 4:4). This group may range all the way from those whose blindness makes them totally impervious to light, to some who for a season show some external acceptance of the light but who are not truly irradiated by it.

In our text the presence of the word "once for all" indicates something especially decisive in this exposure to the light. The Peshitta Syriac translation interpreted this as referring to baptism, which was called "enlightenment" in the early church, although not demonstrably as early as the time of composition of Heb. Without being quite so specific, we might say that Heb 6:4 may well refer to people who have been in close contact with the gospel, who may have taken some significant steps in professing acceptance of it, and who have then renounced their allegiance to it (cf. 2 Pet 2:19-21).

2. "They have had a taste of the heavenly gift." It is not essential for our present purpose to explore whether the "heavenly gift" here refers to Christ himself, to the Holy Spirit, or to the blessings associated with salvation. The crux of the matter appears to reside in the meaning of the word "taste." One meaning of this word is "to ingest," "to have a deep experience of a thing such as one may gain by swallowing" (cf. Heb 2:9 and other passages where the expression "taste death" is found). More commonly, however, it refers to taking a small amount of food or drink so as to test whether it is suitable or pleasing (John 2:9). Metaphorically, it means "to make a trial or experiment" (Owen). This manifestly may remain so far short of a true commitment that in some cases it may not even imply an external profession of allegiance.

3. "They have become partakers of the Holy Spirit." This expression, perhaps even more than the others, appears to lend support to the view that true Christians are described here. The English "partaker" is stronger than the Greek metochoi, but metochoi and its cognates are sometimes used to refer to a very close connection, such as ingesting food (5:13), belonging to a certain tribe (7:13), Christ's sharing in human nature in the incarnation (2:14), or the Christian's relation to Christ and his calling (3:1, 14). On the other hand, the term may apply to mere companionship (1:9), or to external participation (12:8; 1 Cor 10:21). Those who are "sharers in the Holy Spirit" may have received him in personal indwelling (which would imply regeneration), but they may also have been simply exposed to the

benefits that accrue to the whole congregation because of the Spirit's presence,[3] or again, they may be people who have received for a season some spiritual gifts without being renewed unto salvation.[4]

4. "They have tasted the good Word of God." This expression is so clearly compatible with a mere exposure to the preaching of the gospel that no further comment is needed. We note that the word "taste" is used here again, as well as in the next characteristic, and that it may well connote intentional restraint in the description.

5. "They have tasted of the powers of the world to come." This designation could refer to people who have received "eternal life," but it may equally well describe people who had been in contact with the supernatural power of the gospel (cf. Matt 11:20; Mark 9:1; Luke 17:21), or some who had accomplished miracles (*dynameis*) in Christ's name without bearing true allegiance to him (Matt 7:22, 23).

6. They experienced repentance of a sort that it would be desirable, though impossible, to renew. This characteristic, although frequently by-passed even by those who do claim that this passage refers to regenerate people, appears to confront us with greater difficulties than any of the other seven descriptions. For if the repentance that these apostates had experienced were not truly godly sorrow (2 Cor 7:10), it is hard to see why it would be desirable to renew it. And if this repentance is the genuine sorrow of the penitent believer, as the word *metanoia* ordinarily denotes, then regeneration appears presupposed as the only adequate fountain for such an attitude.

Two explanations have been advanced, however, not wholly distinct from one another, which would account for the language used here without assuming that the persons in view were regenerate.

a. John Owen distinguishes between real, internal repentance (which is invariably the fruit of regeneration) and outward repentance, publicly professed and accompanied by the pledge of renovation sealed in baptism. It is this latter, he holds, which the apostates in our text had experienced, and emphatically not the former. And Heb asserts that they cannot even be renewed to this standing of external repentance, let alone be led to real internal repentance. This is the position of the majority of Reformed interpreters, notably F. W. Grosheide and Philip Hughes.

b. William Gouge suggests that the state from which the apostates fell is here described in terms of what they professed to be. And this is taken at face value according to the judgment of charity.

Neither of these explanations appears entirely free of difficulty, although one may prefer to have recourse to them rather than to be forced to the conclusion that regenerate individuals may be lost.

7. "They have received knowledge of the truth" (10:26). While the verb "know" and its cognates may denote union and intimacy of a high

---

[3] Israelites who were not spiritually renewed appear to be cases in point: they had an external participation in the benefits of the covenant (Rom 9:4, 5), betokened by circumcision, but ultimately this does not avail unto salvation (Rom 3:1-4).

[4] The people mentioned in Matt 7:22, 23 would appear to be cases of that nature. Cf. also Matt 13:20-22.

order (Matt 1:25; John 8:32; 17:3; Phil 3:10), they may also refer to intellectual cognition not accompanied with a wholehearted commitment of personality (Luke 12:47; John 14:31; 17:23; Rom 1:21; cf., for *epignōsis*, Rom 3:20; 1:32; 2 Pet 2:21).

8. "They were sanctified in the blood of the covenant" (10:29). It may be doubted whether this is in fact a characteristic (cf. above, n. 1), but if the question is resolved in the affirmative, the language used may well at one extreme describe a true Christian, regenerate, sanctified in God's sight, and rightly partaking of the Lord's Supper, but it may also refer to a man professing to belong to Christ and sharing in the worship of the covenant community, even to the extent of participating in the Eucharist, but whose heart is not renewed and who desecrates the Lord's Supper by his unbelief (1 Cor 11:27-29; 1 John 2:19). Such a one may be stated to be "sanctified" because of the claim he makes, rather than on account of his actual spiritual condition. His profession is taken at face value in the judgment of charity.

Our examination makes it apparent that the elements of the description given in Heb, while not incompatible with true salvation, do not, nevertheless, either singly or jointly, necessarily imply regeneration. They may have been chosen by design to describe those who have received the greatest possible external exposure to the truth, including a temporary profession of allegiance to it, and whose subsequent rejection must be seen as irremediable precisely on account of the privileges they enjoyed.

It is noteworthy that the author of Heb does specify some characteristics that differentiate those whom he addresses from the apostates in view in 6:4-6 and 10:26-29: (a) They had things that accompany salvation (6:9), that is to say, they gave evidence of true salvation. (b) They fulfilled duties of obedience and bore fruits of faith, which God would not forget (6:10; 10:39).

Now these statements do not provide us at once with infallible criteria that would enable us to determine with certainty whether a given person is truly regenerate, or merely professing the faith. Yet they make it fairly apparent that the author was making a distinction, and that he postulated a group of believers who would not be subject to a fall such as he described in verses 4-6. It seems a natural interpretation here to assume that this group includes all who are regenerate and them only.

II. What Is the Sin That Places Apostates Beyond Recovery?

It is interesting to juxtapose the teaching of Heb 6 and 10 with two other scriptural statements where mention is made of an unpardonable sin. We refer to Matt 12:31-32 (Mark 3:28-29; cf. also Luke 12:10) and 1 John 5:16. John gives us no further description of the character of the sin in view,[5] but the Synoptic setting may help us to grasp something of its nature. The Pharisees had just witnessed Jesus' manifest exercise of divine

---

[5] Although the passage in 1 John 5:16 does not specify the nature of the "sin unto death," we must note that in the same context John appears to say that no

power in miraculous healing, but rather than concede that God's blessing was upon Christ, they preferred to ascribe the miracle to the agency of Satan. It was this deliberate resistance to the shining light of Christ's activity and testimony that led our Lord to pronounce his awesome verdict: "Every sin and blasphemy shall be forgiven unto men, but the blasphemy against the Spirit shall not be forgiven."

The Pharisees whose attitude elicited this judgment may be seen to fit rather closely the elements of the description given in Heb 6:4-6. They had been enlightened by their contact with Christ, his teaching and his person (John 3:19; 9:39, 41); they had had a taste of the heavenly gift by being confronted with the ministry of Jesus; they had been sharers in the power of the Holy Spirit by witnessing this miraculous deliverance, this signal victory over evil spirits gained by virtue of the Spirit of God (Matt 12:28);[6] they had tasted of the good word of God both in their acquaintance with OT revelation and with the teaching of our Lord; they had tasted of the powers of the other world in their witnessing the signal miracle enacted before their eyes. But in spite of all these blessings, they chose to close their hearts and alleged that the miracle was the work of Satan rather than of God. This was an irretrievable affront to the Holy Spirit, a sin indicative of total alienation in darkness, even when confronted by overwhelming light.

It is not evident that these men had ever had a form of repentance, but even this is possible, since some of them may well have been exposed to the ministry of John the Baptist. In any case, since the description of Heb 6:4, 5 fits them so aptly, even though they never seemed to profess being disciples of Christ, it is fairly apparent that it is not necessary to assume that Heb 6:4-6 points indubitably to regenerate Christians. Both in the case of the Pharisees and in that of the apostates of Heb 6 and 10, the sin in view appears to be man's willful rejection of God under conditions of full exposure to the light.

The case of Judas the betrayer naturally comes to mind as that of a man who sank into this deep pit of sin. Probably all eight of the characteristics given in Heb 6 and 10 would readily apply to him.[7] Yet how can we imagine him to be, or ever to have been, truly regenerate, whom our Lord called "a devil" (John 6:70), "the son of perdition" (John 17:12), one for whom it "were good not to have been born" (Mark 14:21)? His true spiritual condition, although known by Jesus from the start, remained hidden from the apostles to the end, for on the last day of our Lord's life they were abashed to hear that one of them would betray him, and they were unable to determine who this might be (Mark 14:18-20; Luke 22:21-23).

---

regenerate person (πᾶς ὁ γεγεννημένος ἐκ τοῦ θεοῦ) may ever commit this sin because of the divine safekeeping (1 John 5:18). This same truth appears to be the point of 1 John 3:6-9. These passages, far from teaching sinless perfection, should properly be listed in emphatic support of perseverance. Cf. further the essay of David Scholer in this *Festschrift*.

[6] The importance of this element in the description is increased by the fact that Christ characterizes their sin as "blasphemy against the Spirit."

[7] The aptness of the eighth characteristic depends on whether or not Judas did partake of the Lord's Supper. Cf. P. E. Hughes, "Hebrews 6:4-6 and the Peril of Apostasy," *Westminster Theological Journal*, 35 (1973), 137-55.

III. How Can This Sin Be Diagnosed?

The case of Judas stands as a warning that it is not easy to discern the kind of apostasy envisioned in Heb 6. To the very last Judas was indistinguishable from the true apostles.

The case of David, on the other hand, makes it clear that a believer may fall into very aggravated forms of sin, and yet find recovery. The Novatians and Donatists, in the early church, made inadequate identification of this sin, and their diagnosis was proved erroneous in some cases by the genuine repentance of the culprits. Apparently the author of Hebrews, and possibly the recipients of the letter, had some concrete cases in view, perhaps people of Jewish race who had made a drastic disavowal of Christianity after having shared in the life of the church for some time. John also seems to have recognizable cases in mind, since refraining from prayer implies concrete identification of persons.

In spite of this it remains very precarious to attempt to designate anyone as having committed this sin. It might be better to offer prayer for one who is already beyond the range where God will reach for him, than to surrender to death and damnation one whom God may yet be willing to retrieve. In this area the injunction to refrain from judging (Matt 7:1) may well control our approach, as we attempt to relate to once professing Christians who appear to have abandoned the faith.

Inasmuch as there are some sensitive souls who torment themselves with the thought that they have committed this sin, it may be wise to point out that their concern about this indicates that they are not immune to the grace of God nor incapable of repentance. Those who have committed the unpardonable sin are blissfully unconcerned about it.

The presence in Scripture of these passages and of other solemn warnings against apostasy is certainly calculated to encourage an attitude of constant watchfulness on the part of Christians: there are enough promises in the Bible so that the believer who is frightened by his own propensity to sin may gain comfort and confidence in the safekeeping perseverance of God with his saints; and there are enough warnings so that the Christian who might be inclined to presume on his own strength and security may flee instead, in holy abhorrence of sin and fear of God, to the sanctifying and keeping power of the Holy Spirit.

Historical Explanation and Barth on Christ's Resurrection

STANLEY R. OBITTS

Since the appearance of Barth's *Römerbrief* the central historical claim of traditional Christianity, namely, the resurrection of Jesus Christ, has received more theological and exegetical attention than at any other time, except during the second and third centuries.[1] In his recent survey of the current debate over the original explanatory context of the resurrection Hans-Georg Geyer describes three main positions. The first is taken by Rudolf Bultmann and Karl Barth "insofar as both regard the context which constitutes the meaning of the resurrection of Jesus Christ as lying in its relationship to the cross." Willi Marxsen and Gerhard Ebeling are leaders in the second camp. As Marxsen sees it, "the decisive and defining context for the event of the resurrection is formed by going back to the words and deeds of the historical Jesus." Rounding out the number of competing approaches is one represented by Ulrich Wilckens and Wolfhart Pannenberg. The basic point here is that the resurrection must be explained in terms of "the apocalyptic expectation of the general resurrection of the dead and the judgment at the end of the world."[2]

An equally vigorous debate among philosophers of history on the nature of historical explanation was occasioned by the appearance of Carl Hempel's classic essay.[3] Hempel's article, forcefully articulating the positivistic or covering-law theory of explanation in history, eventually brought forth by way of response William Dray's presentation of the non-positivistic, humanistic or rational theory of historical explanation.[4] The point at

[1] Gerald O'Collins, S.J., "Karl Barth on Christ's Resurrection," *SJT*, 26, No. 1 (Feb. 1973), 85.

[2] W. Marxsen, "The Resurrection of Jesus Christ: A Survey of the Debate in Present Day Theology," *The Significance of the Message of the Resurrection for Faith in Jesus Christ*, ed. by C. F. D. Moule, London, 1968, p. 105.

[3] Carl Hempel, "The Function of General Laws in History," *Journal of Philosophy*, 39 (1942).

[4] W. Dray, *Laws and Explanation in History*, Oxford, 1957. R. G. Collingwood's later thought, particularly as expressed in *The Idea of History*, published post-

Stanley R. Obitts, Professor of Philosophy at Westmont College, Santa Barbara, California. B.A., Wheaton College; B.D., Wheaton College Graduate School; Ph.D., The University of Edinburgh.

issue between the opposing sides of the debate is the conceptual one, not the empirical one, of whether past instances of intentional action can be reduced to behavior operationally described.

Anyone familiar with the current philosophical discussion of the nature of historical explanation occasionally finds the theological debate on the historical dimension of the resurrection of Jesus Christ confusing, if not at times confused. In the present essay attention will be focused on what may be a conceptual confusion in Barth's treatment of this issue. First, an attempt will be made at ascertaining what he understands himself to be saying about the resurrection as far as this touches on the problem of historical explanation. Second, by extrapolation his position will be located *vis-à-vis* the philosophical discussion of historical explanation. Finally, his view will be criticized accordingly.

It must be granted that the early writings of Barth are not at ease with the notion of an historical resurrection. For example, in Barth's *Römerbrief* Kierkegaard's antithetical dialectic between God and man shines through clearly. Unlike Hegel's dialectic, Barth's is not mediated by history, or anything else, for that matter. God alone is seen as the transcendental subject of historical reality. The historical process becomes, for Barth, an unfolding of the revelation of God's glory, the last phase being the resurrection of the dead. Hence, the resurrection of Jesus Christ is construed to be the eschatological realization of this possibility lying before the absolutely sovereign subject of history, namely, God. Of human history Barth will speak only of its sinfulness, "nothingness," meaninglessness and purposelessness. God is the *eschaton* and absolute *telos* of creation. To put it in Barth's words,

> it must not be supposed that . . . resurrection is a contingent happening, and that God is bound to the contradiction between "here" and "there." God is pure negation. He is both "here" and "there." He is the negation of the negation in which the other world contradicts this world and this world the other world. He is the death of our death and the non-existence of our non-existence. . . . This God, and the transformation of all things in Him—*I saw a new heaven and a new earth*—is the faith of Abraham, the radiance from light uncreated, the Genesis narrative, and the LOGOS of all history.[5]

This "non-historical factor which forms the veritable substance quality of all history" renders the methods of historical analysis irrelevant, Barth points out. That which makes history relevant "precedes its critical investigation," "for its value lies in the KRISIS within which all history stands." When the historian recognizes this, he knows that history stands "before the same commanding necessity of a synthesis which is the starting point of

humously in 1946, provided the impetus for the current group of analytic opponents of positivistic historiography. But as Alan Donagan observes, no other description of Collingwood "is so little misleading" as "idealist," in spite of the latter's repudiation of that name (*The Later Philosophy of R. G. Collingwood,* Oxford, 1962, p. 18, n. 1). Consequently, one also finds considerable disagreement with Collingwood's standpoint by those analytic philosophers who take a non-positivistic approach to historiography.

[5] Karl Barth, *The Epistle to the Romans,* trans. from 6th ed., 1928, by Edwyn C. Hoskyns, London, 1933, pp. 141-42.

the Book of Genesis." There really is no other way of writing history. The method of analysis is useless, for, as in the case of the book of Genesis, all it can do is "pronounce Abraham's personality to be unhistorical." But by adopting the method of synthesis we become "involved in a contemporary intercourse between the past and the present." Only then does resurrection become possible and the "union of 'here' and 'there' become believable."[6]

Critical, analytical history has never known the supremacy of death to be challenged. Indeed, this is fortunate, according to Barth.

> Were there a *direct causal connexion between the historical "facts"* of the Resurrection—the empty tomb, for example, or the appearances detailed in I Cor. XV—and the Resurrection itself; were it in any sense a "fact" in history, then no profession of faith or refinement of devotion could prevent it being involved in the see-saw of "Yes" and "No," life and death, God and man, which is characteristic of all that happens on the historical plane.

This means to Barth that "if the Resurrection be brought within the context of history, it must share in its obscurity and error and essential questionableness." But the risen Christ has set behind him "the whole relativity of historical and time-enveloped things . . . because His Resurrection is the non-historical event [*kat' exochēn*]."[7]

Thus it is that for the early Barth, in *The Epistle to the Romans*, religious faith is "unimpeded by historical occurrence" in the analytic sense of "historical"; and the theme of history in the synthetic sense is God, or the glory of God. Or, stated with reference to historiography, the early Barth knows of two methods: the analytic, which critically discovers the factual occurrences in a meaningless series of human events, and the synthetic, which, as "a work of art," "emerges from what has occurred" with the "non-historical" as its subject.[8]

But what of the later Barth? Self-allegedly, and obviously, there is much less dependence upon dialectical and existential thought patterns and forms of expression. Has the essential logic of his position on the nature of historical explanation and its relation to the resurrection of Jesus Christ changed accordingly?

Although he began to shift noticeably in his 1931 study of Anselm (*Fides Quaerens Intellectum*), Barth exhibits his greatest degree of interest in the historicity of Jesus and the resurrection in Volume 4 of *Die Kirchliche Dogmatik*. We shall now look at a few passages in Part Two, which appeared in 1955.

It is important to notice, first of all, that the later Barth persists in conflating the "ontic" and "noetic" aspects of revelation. Speaking of the "divine act of majesty . . . in the incarnation of the Word" as having "not merely the character of objective being and occurrence, but also, as an event within the world and therefore in the sphere of human cognition, [as having] a subjective character as well—in a word, the character of revelation," Barth points out that this act is "a single and unitary action." It is "one and the same fact, His [Jesus Christ's] ontic character being reflected

---

[6]*Ibid.*, pp. 146-47.
[7]*Ibid.*, pp. 204-5 (italics mine).
[8]*Ibid.*, pp. 146-47.

in a noetic." Assuming then "the truth that the fact created by the divine act of majesty has also the character of revelation, that its ground of being is also its ground of cognition . . . there is no other ground of cognition." Hence, asks Barth rhetorically, "What authority, even if it is that of an infallible Church or the apostles, can guarantee it if it does not guarantee itself in their witness?" If we know, it is only on the ground that this fact is not merely a fact, but that as such it speaks for itself, that it makes that self-disclosure, that from its maintained objectivity there springs the fact that it makes itself known, that it *therefore includes in itself a subject which knows it as such.*" There can thus be no "claim to . . . know" by "appealing for our authorization . . . to a knowledge of revelation . . . transmitted to us institutionally . . . [like] the [appeal of the] 'fundamentalists' to the biblical texts."[9]

Next, turning our attention to the resurrection, we find Barth describing it, along with the ascension, as the "once for all and all-sufficient event of revelation—the event of His self-declaration, and therefore the event in which the basis of the knowledge of Jesus Christ . . . was laid and is laid." What it reveals is that Jesus' "being and work . . . are completed in His death on the cross." The resurrection is "in time and space," "in the body," witnessed "not only inwardly but outwardly, by certain men." But because the witnesses were "chosen before by God," there is "no demonstration of the event which has apologetic value" in 1 Cor 15 or anywhere else. Indeed, "the event is not perhaps 'historical' [*historisch*] in the modern sense," even though "it actually happened among men like other events."[10] Yet, being a miracle by virtue of its being "a divine act of majesty as the revelation of God . . . it has no parallel in other events."

The Easter-narratives, stating that Christ is risen, imply the return to life of a dead man and the emptiness of his tomb. But even if these implications were affirmed " 'historically' in the sense of the remarkable investigation of H. F. von Campenhausen, *Der Ablauf der Osterereignisse und das leere Grab,* 1952," they remain "irrelevant for an understanding of the texts and their witness." Because knowledge of God brought about by the revelatory event of the resurrection comes "only from the One who is revealed in it," the "majesty of the will and act of God" determines the nature of that knowledge. That knowledge, "a genuine and fruitful knowledge of love for God," has as its necessary "introduction" or "presupposition," however, a " 'historical' knowledge" of the event of revelation "in the sense of one which can be maintained neutrally and with complete objectivity," Barth points out.

This latter knowledge, to be attained, will demand

> the most impartial and painstaking investigation of the *texts* which speak of this event. . . . If it is to be meaningful as an introduction, the "historical" element to which it addresses itself will have to be the attestation of this event [*stattfindende Bezeugung dieses Ereignisses*—lit., presently occurring attestation of this event] as we have it in the New Testament texts. . . . It will not be "the historical facts"

[9] Karl Barth, *Church Dogmatics,* trans. by G. W. Bromiley, Edinburgh, 1958, 4, 2, 120, 122-24 (italics mine).
[10] *Ibid.,* 4, 2, 142-43.

which we have to find . . . somewhere behind the texts, and which we then claim as objective reality . . . [for in such an improper investigation] "there is no attestation of this event, and . . . [there is] nothing to do with the knowledge of this event."[11]

It appears, then, that the later Barth, while feeling more fully the need to affirm the historicity of the resurrection, still maintains his earlier conception of God's revelation as being an unmediated self-disclosure to which the biblical texts serve as attestations or testimonies (*Bezeugungen*) only. He now talks about the role of the historico-critical method in investigating the texts, but the real purpose of this investigation is not clear, for "genuine" knowledge of God comes not through becoming aware of the historical facts but as a result of being a "chosen" one to whom Jesus Christ reveals himself directly. Still limiting revelation to being an event only, Barth must describe the revelation-status of the resurrection as being constituted by the content of the revelatory event, which is the person Jesus Christ. This means that until the investigator "encounters" Jesus Christ personally, he will use the historico-critical method to no avail. In Barth's words, "because . . . the event of revelation . . . takes place in the majesty of the will and act of God, the knowledge of it . . . [can] derive . . . only from the One who is revealed in it." The value of historical investigation, therefore, comes after, not before, one has "a genuine and fruitful knowledge of love for the God who reveals Himself" in the "event of revelation," which in this case is the resurrection. Faith is not based on historical evidence but on a personal encounter with God in Christ.

Why, then, bother with the apostolic witness in the biblical texts? The reason Barth gives is that our knowledge of the resurrection "will necessarily be ordered by" the apostolic "witness" because "the resurrection is an event that took place for the apostles in their encounter with the living Christ."[12] But, again, it is not clear how this ordering could take place, for Barth does not allow an initial cognitive dependence in our knowledge of the risen Lord upon the apostolic witness.

Is there either a conceptual or a causal connection at all between the " 'historical' " knowledge of the resurrection event, which Barth declares to be a "presupposition" of a "genuine" knowledge of that event, and the "genuine" knowledge, which "comes only from the One revealed in it"? Or is Barth, particularly in his later period, simply confused in thinking that either kind of link does exist?

The first question, we contend, must be answered negatively and the second affirmatively. There is no logical or conceptual connection because the two kinds of knowledge are independently identifiable. That there is no causal connection can be seen in the light of the difference in the truth-conditions upon which each kind of knowledge of the resurrection event depends. The "historical" knowledge is one whose falsifiability is assured by its being "maintained neutrally and with complete objectivity." On the other hand, "genuine" knowledge, having for both its cause and its content "the One who is revealed" in the resurrection event, is self-authenticating and, thus, inconceivably false. Apparently, therefore, Barth is simply con-

[11] *Ibid.*, 4, 2, 147-50.
[12] *Ibid.*, 4, 2, 149.

fused in thinking a necessary link does exist between the two kinds of knowledge.

If this be the case, then in the light of his unrelenting limitation of revelation to an event of self-disclosure by God, Barth's earlier lack of interest in an historical resurrection was a more consistent position for him to take. Why, then, did he gradually move into the more inconsistent position of stressing an historical resurrection? The contributing psychological and theological factors are manifold and beyond the scope of this essay.[13] But it may be pointed out that such a move could possibly have been prevented or at least greatly impeded if Barth had delved deeper into the issues figuring in the current debate on the nature of historical explanation.

We saw the earlier Barth distinguishing between the historiographical methods, which he termed "analysis" and "synthesis." By analysis he meant an objective, natural-science-like search for historical "facts" and the "direct causal connexion" between them. Not finding the resurrection to be such an historical fact, he placed it under the purview of the synthetic method. This latter method involved the interpretation of historical facts by means of an existential apprehension of the "non-historical," dialectically conceived, non-contingent "substance and quality of all history." Although Barth gradually lost interest in touting such a "synthetic" method, there is no evidence in his later writings indicating a modification of his understanding of what he earlier called the "analytic method" and later called the "historical method."

The search for historical "facts" and a "direct causal connexion" between them mentioned in *The Epistle to the Romans* becomes in *The Church Dogmatics*, Vol. 4, " 'historical' knowledge . . . maintained neutrally and with complete objectivity" through a "painstaking investigation of the *texts*." Likewise just as the "synthetic" method figures by contrast to the "analytic" method earlier, so also we read later that "historical" knowledge and its "historical" implications are "irrelevant for an understanding of the texts and their witness" as far as the resurrection is concerned.

The "analytic" or "historical" method as Barth seems to grasp it corresponds most directly with what is now commonly called the covering-law theory of historical explanation, the application in the field of history of the hypothetical-deductive model of explanation typically used in the natural sciences and striving for acceptance in the social sciences.[14] The historian employing this theory of explanation regards the data with which he works as discrete, objective units of historical reality, otherwise known as "historical facts." His goal is to explain them causally, which to him, as to the natural scientist, means empirically. Assuming regular patterns of behavior in all natural phenomena, including human behavior, the covering-law theorist seeks inductively for generalizations of this behavior to serve as laws under which individual occurrences may be subsumed for explanation.

---

[13] A good starting point for the pursuit of this question is the treatment by Gisbert Greshake, *Auferstehung der Toten,* Essen, 1969, pp. 52-95, 163-69.

[14] See Alan Ryan, *The Philosophy of the Social Sciences,* London, 1970. Cf. Peter Winch, *The Idea of a Social Science,* London, 1958.

Although a natural corollary of classical empiricism—it was explicitly formulated in that context in J. S. Mill's *System of Logic* (1843)—this approach to scientific explanation, including scientific historical explanation, took the shape it has today at the hands of logical positivists whose goal was the standardization of all scientific methodology. In their estimation a successful explanation had to meet three requirements, as expressed in a well-known article by Carl Hempel and Paul Oppenheim: First, there is the formal requirement of the conclusion statement being entailed by the premises containing the statements of the law(s) and initial conditions. Second, there is the material requirement of the truth, or at least strong corroboration, of the premises. Finally, there is the requirement of the empirical falsifiability of the *explanans*.[15]

The protagonists of this view admit that historical explanations cannot usually specify all the general regularities they presuppose because the latter are either tacit or too difficult to formulate. Reduced in these instances to the use of probability hypotheses, the historian's explanation would be probabilistic rather than causal. But the goal held before the historian is always a causal explanation based on universal conditionals, i.e. deterministic laws.[16] Hempel prefers to call the historian's usual probabilistic explanation just an "explanation Sketch," in order to distinguish it from a proper explanation.[17]

While it is recognized that human history involves human reasons and intentions, these are treated as objectively as possible in order to facilitate the appeal to the uniformities of behavior upon which genuine explanation is said to depend. Morton White puts it bluntly: "No attempt [by the historian] to distinguish persons from natural objects is defensible if it implies that there are different realms of entities—some natural, some nonnatural."[18] However, philosophers of history taking the positivistic position argue that the causally deterministic view of human behavior they are assuming is not incompatible with human responsibility and freedom *re-defined*.

The non-positivists or humanists in the philosophy of history are not uniform in the manner of their opposition to this claim. Some, like Collingwood, the mentor of the present generation of believers in the autonomous character of historical thought, resolutely affirm with idealist overtones that "historical thought," because it concerns "thought about rational activity," is "free from the domination of natural science."[19]

Reflecting the current reformulation among analytic philosophers of the problem of the freedom of the will into the problem of the freedom of action,[20] Frederick Olafson presents a more recent type of opposition to

[15] C. Hempel and P. Oppenheim, "Studies in the Logic of Explanation," *Philosophy of Science*, 15 (1948), 136f.

[16] W. Dray discusses six types of modification of the covering-law model of historical explanation to be found in recent philosophy of history in his "The Historical Explanation of Actions Reconsidered," *Philosophy and History*, ed. by Sidney Hook, New York, 1963, pp. 110-30.

[17] C. Hempel, "The Function of General Laws in History," reprinted with alterations in his *Aspects of Scientific Explanation*, New York, 1965, p. 238.

[18] M. White, *Foundations of Historical Knowledge*, London, 1965, p. 215.

[19] Collingwood, *The Idea of History*, p. 318.

[20] Ted Honderich, ed., *Essays on Freedom of Action*. London, 1973, p. vii.

covering-law theorists in the philosophy of history. He attacks Arthur Danto and Morton White, two leading covering-law theorists who are unusual in that they, particularly Danto, set out their theory of historical explanation through an examination of the narrative structure of historical writing. This approach is normally associated with the non-positivists, particularly W. Dray and W. B. Gallie.[21] Olafson thinks Danto is unsuccessful in his argument for the "subsumability of . . . narrative sentences under universal causal laws" because he fails to take cognizance of the "limits on the degree to which the description of an action can deviate from the one that would be provided by or be intelligible to the agent if that action is to be imputed to him as it typically is in an historical narrative."[22] Against White, Olafson argues that the "decisive cause" of an historical event is "the action rather than the underlying conditions."[23] Contrary to Danto and White who advocate the application of the "deductive law-based type" of explanation for historical events, Olafson thinks historical explanation is actually similar to the "way we explain actions." That is, it is " 'rational' or 'teleological,' in which the major premise expresses not a universally valid law but the desire of some person or persons to realize a particular goal."[24]

Yet others remain within the framework of the free-will controversy, notably William Dray, as much as anyone the present leading advocate of interpreting historical events in terms of human reasons. It should be noted that he does not think "that the giving of a rational explanation . . . entails indeterminism." He claims himself to hold a "libertarian position" and for that reason finds the "rational model of explanation" attractive, i.e. "because it shows a way in which explanation can be given in history which is logically *compatible* with indeterminism regarding human actions." However, he goes on to point out that his argument for the rational model of explanation is not dependent upon "libertarian metaphysics" but upon the "conceptual grounds that there is a meaning of 'explain' which is already current in history, as well as everyday affairs, which does not entail determinism."[25] The meaning of "explain" in history to which Dray refers is described as follows: "To achieve understanding, what he [the historian] seeks is information about what the agent believed to be the facts of his situation, including the likely results of taking various courses of action considered open to him, and what he wanted to accomplish: his purposes, goals, or motives." In other words, what an historical explanation establishes is "a conceptual connection between understanding a man's action and discerning its rationale," says Dray.[26]

---

[21] See W. B. Gallie, *Philosophy and the Historical Understanding,* London, 1964, the classic example of this stress on historical narrative.

[22] F. Olafson, "Narrative History and the Concept of Action," *History and Theory,* 9 (1970), 272.

[23] *Ibid.,* p. 284.

[24] *Ibid.,* p. 289.

[25] It should be noted that the non-positivists commonly accuse the positivists of taking a prescriptive, rather than a descriptive, approach to historical explanation (Dray, "The Historical Explanation of Actions Reconsidered," p. 108). See John Passmore, "Explanation in Everyday Life, in Science, and in History," *History and Theory,* 2, No. 2 (1962), 105-23.

[26] Dray, "The Historical Explanation of Actions Reconsidered," p. 108.

One response to the kind of view Dray takes is to propose that the covering-law model applies on the theoretical level, while the rational model is better on the practical level of historical explanation. This response is made by Robert Stover.[27] But Patrick Gardiner argues that "in their respective attitudes toward determinism" the positivists and anti-positivists must "come into conflict with one another."[28] And Alan Donagan argues that there would be no point to rational explanation if a law-covered account could be given of the same thing.[29]

Alan Donagan's approach, eclectically manifesting the influence of both Collingwood and Karl Popper,[30] is to deny the covering-law thesis by showing that causal explanations are scientifically established by historians through their appealing to the "logic of the situation." Historians are methodologically sceptical about accounting for an agent's actions in terms of psychological, sociological or neuro-psychological covering laws. And, obviously opposing Michael Scriven, Donagan feels the historian is equally sceptical about a covering-law use of laws derived from "common-sense."[31] Although unable to rule out a priori the possibility of such accounts, historians, as a matter of fact, proceed on "the presupposition of individual choice" which "states simply that, in a situation of a given kind, a man's intentions must not be assumed to be the same as those of any other man, whatever their psychological or sociological similarities; or the same as his own intentions in other situations of the same kind." This is not to assume the uniqueness of an agent's behavior, however. "Historians presuppose neither that individuals of a certain kind act alike nor that they do not, but only that it is *possible* that they do not," i.e. "that a man ultimately has an unconditional power to choose how he will act."

The historian's methodological affirmation of the traditional doctrine of free will does not keep his explanation of an agent's actions from being acceptable scientifically, however. At this juncture disagreeing with Dray, Donagan claims that historical explanations can be deductive without using empirically falsifiable laws, contrary to what the covering-law theorists believe, and can satisfy "the two conditions which underlie the covering law thesis, viz., that they must admit of scientific corroboration, and that they must exhibit a connection between the initial condition and the event

---

[27] See R. Stover, *The Nature of Historical Thinking*, Oxford, 1963, chap. 8. That Dray would not oppose such a response may be inferred from his statement that "the two sorts of explanations [rational and covering-law] are better regarded as belonging to different logical and conceptual networks, within which different kinds of puzzlement are expressed and resolved" ("Historical Explanations of Actions," p. 131).

[28] P. Gardiner, "The Concept of Man as Presupposed by the Historical Studies," *The Proper Study*, The Royal Institute of Philosophy Lectures, London, 1971, 4, 31.

[29] A. Donagan, "Explanation in History," *Mind*, 66 (1957), 153.

[30] See, e.g., R. G. Collingwood, *An Essay on Metaphysics*, Oxford, 1940, pp. 290-95; *The Idea of History*, pp. 213ff.; Donagan, *The Later Philosophy of Collingwood*, pp. 192-96, 289, 297, and Karl Popper, *The Poverty of Historicism*, London, 1960², pp. 149f.

[31] See Michael Scriven, "Truisms as the Grounds for Historical Explanation," *Theories of History*, ed. by P. Gardiner, Glencoe, Ill., 1959, pp. 443-75.

to be explained." In order for historical explanations to be deductive without using empirically falsifiable laws all they need are hypothetical statements of an analytic truth about an agent's intentions, together with a statement of the initial conditions.[32] By the "scientific corroboration" of an historical agent's intentions Donagan means the formulation of an hypothesis about those intentions, the deduction of falsifiable statements about the hypothesis and, finally, the investigation of whether all the statements, except the *explanandum,* are actually falsified. As far as the exhibition by historical explanations of "a connection between the initial condition and the event to be explained" is concerned, Donagan sees no difficulty except one caused by the denial that such connections can be exhibited by statements about an agent's intentions. But such a denial would depend upon "some naturalist or materialist metaphysical doctrine, according to which deciding, intending, and other mental acts are somehow reducible to 'natural events,' which are in principle explicable according to the laws of the natural sciences." He thinks this doctrine is refutable, and is not accepted in practice by historians anyway.[33]

Now, it is our contention that Barth has simply taken over a positivistic, i.e. covering-law understanding of analytical history and has construed it in terms of scientific determinism.[34] The result is the radical conceptual break he makes between what he calls the "historical facts" of the resurrection, which not only do not yield "genuine knowledge" but also have no logical connection with it, on the one hand, and the real resurrection event, which, "being a miracle . . . has no parallel in other events," on the other hand. Because of this utter discontinuity between what can be explained historically and what happens in a revelatory event, Barth sees no problem in affirming that even if there be " 'historically' " the return to life of a dead man and an empty tomb, as the Easter-narratives, he admits, imply, such matters are "irrelevant for an understanding of the texts and their witness." For Barth the analytical or critical historian is investigating "facts" whose "direct causal connexion" is to be deterministically explained. Hence, the incursion into history of the supernatural is accounted

---

[32] An example of the kind of analytical truth Donagan has in mind, stated as a singular hypothetical, is the following: "If Brutus judged that to preserve the Republic it was necessary to perform a certain act, he would perform that act." This hypothetical, along with a statement of the initial conditions, such as, "Brutus judged that to preserve the Republic it would be necessary to join Cassius' conspiracy," yields deductively the *explanandum* that "Brutus joined Cassius' conspiracy."

[33] A. Donagan, "The Popper-Hempel Theory Reconsidered," *History and Theory,* 4 (1965), 17-25.

[34] By "scientific determinism" is meant a key naturalist tenet of the subsumability under general natural laws of all past actions as in principle the only means of their explanation. This is, of course, not equivalent to positivism. There is no reciprocal entailment between scientific determinism or naturalism, on the one hand, and positivism, on the other hand. For example, the essential doctrine of logical positivism is its empirical criterion of meaning, but not determinism or naturalism. And William Kneale's *Probability and Induction,* Oxford, 1949, accepts both naturalism and scientific determinism while advocating a non-positivistic view of natural law.

for in terms of a Humean-like notion of miracle as constituting a contradiction of natural law.[35]

Moreover, Barth gives no evidence that he knows how to meet on its own grounds the objection that even if a violation of natural law were granted, it could not be defined as a miracle, for God's causal relationship to it is still unknowable. Patrick Nowell-Smith, writing within the Humean tradition on miracle, asks of his opponent the following:

> Let him consider the meaning of the word "explanation" and let him ask himself whether this notion does not involve that of a law or hypothesis capable of predictive expansion. And then let him ask himself whether such an explanation would not be natural, in whatever terms it was couched, and how the notion of "supernatural" could play any part in it.[36]

Rather than rebut this kind of reasoning, Barth apparently capitulates to it, while trying to outflank its implications by an appeal to *Heilsgeschichte* and the work of the Holy Spirit.

It is the "work of the Holy Spirit done in" a person, says Barth, which makes possible "the recognition that the history of Jesus Christ is his own salvation history (*Heilsgeschichte*)." In getting at what Barth means by this statement it is important to remember that he does not regard the resurrection as part of Jesus' history. The resurrection is "the manifestation" of Jesus' history. What God wanted Jesus to do he did "perfectly in the temporality, spatiality and personality . . . in His existence in this world, in the history which took place there and then." The resurrection, by way of contrast, was "the beginning of the manifestation of what He was and did perfectly there and then . . . [a manifestation, that is] in all other human history."[37]

Keeping this in mind, we read next that "The work of the Holy Spirit is concerned with the Word which manifests . . . [Jesus'] history in its access and entry into the hearts and consciences of specific men." The "history of Jesus" then becomes "internal" to those men as "a Word which is accepted, affirmed . . ." This is what is meant by saying "the divine change effected and being effected in the history of Jesus Christ" . . . [is] "the event in which the foundation of the Christian life takes place." In saying this, Barth notes that he presupposes "the resurrection of Jesus Christ from the dead as the act of God in which His history was and is revealed as most properly the salvation of all men." In sum, "the *one* act of God is the disclosure of His history to all men in the resurrection of Jesus Christ and the opening up of specific men for His history in the work of the Holy Spirit."[38]

If we understand Barth correctly here, he seems not only to have

---

[35] See David Hume, *An Enquiry Concerning Human Understanding,* ed. by L. A. Selby-Bigge, Oxford, 1902, pp. 114ff.

[36] P. Nowell-Smith, "Miracles," *New Essays in Philosophical Theology,* ed by A. Flew and A. MacIntyre, London, 1955, p. 253, quoted in Richard Swinburne, *The Concept of Miracle,* London, 1970, p. 20.

[37] Barth, *Church Dogmatics,* 4, 4, 24.

[38] *Ibid.,* 4, 4, 28-30 (italics mine). See also 4, 2, 140-42.

removed into the "spiritual" realm the truth-conditions for the belief that God, through the Holy Spirit, is the cause of the resurrection, but also to have eliminated any natural or empirical grounds for arriving at that belief. That there are no such grounds a sceptic like Nowell-Smith fully agrees. Hence, when he reads Barth referring to the witness of the NT or of the church to the resurrection, he has no alternative but to construe this as having a subjective reference only.

In sum, our criticisms of Barth are two. First, by taking a positivist view of analytic history, with the corresponding Humean theory of miracle, and at the same time affirming the importance of the return to life of a dead man and an empty grave as "historical" implications of the Easter-narratives Barth is facing opposite directions at once. Second, by ultimately depending completely upon non-objective, *heilsgeschichtliche* truth-conditions for his faith that the resurrection is the "manifestation" of the meaning of Jesus' history as the meaning of all history, Barth in effect disengages his faith from historical criticism. This means for him, as we have seen, that empirical grounds are neither sufficient nor necessary for belief that Jesus rose on Easter morning. The historical events of the empty tomb and the post-resurrection appearances are not logically necessary conditions of the assertion of the resurrection, for Barth.

Granting his conception of historical explanation and his limitation of the nature of revelation to events that are acts of self-disclosure by Jesus Christ, Barth had more reason to continue his earlier expression of faith in terms of Kierkegaardian paradoxes than later to develop an interest in the historicity of the events on Easter. A theoretical justification for that interest might be possible by combining a non-positivistic conception of historical explanation with a theory of revelation expanded to allow an appeal to the apostolic eyewitnesses. But such a system awaits development.

The substantiation of the truth of the eyewitness reports through historical criticism is not what we are proposing. But what is being proposed is the establishment of a necessary conceptual link between the Christian theological claims about Jesus Christ and the historically validated claims by the apostles to have seen Jesus' empty tomb and to have been appeared to by Jesus after his crucifixion. Such a link is obviously beyond the scope of historical criticism to forge. But that it was forged by the apostolic eyewitnesses is for history to disclose upon critical investigation.

Willi Marxsen has observed that the eyewitnesses of the empty tomb did not have it as an "object of faith," for they perceived it directly. If belief played no role for them, neither can a non-eyewitness have faith in the empty tomb. Supposing someone did imagine he ought to have "faith *in* the empty tomb," he should realize, explains Marxsen, that "faith (today) is not directed towards the empty tomb itself, but 'trusts' the eyewitnesses for the reliability of their account in historical terms." Granting the validity of "this 'faith' in the reliability of the narrative in historical terms," that person would still have been "led only to the fact of the empty tomb." But the "interpretation in historical terms" that "the tomb was empty because Jesus is risen" must remain forever outside the province of history, Marxsen concludes.[39]

While there may be no critical method of historical explanation whereby the *interpretation* that the empty tomb means "Jesus is risen" may be turned into a factual resurrection event, that interpretation, *if apostolic,* could function as revealed historical theological evidence for Jesus' resurrection. In this case, the immediate object of the Christian's faith would be the authority of the apostolic eyewitnesses. Such authority, however, is always vulnerable to the historical denial of the empty tomb and the resurrection appearances, contrary to Barth, because the resurrection event is an historical event inferred by the apostolic eyewitnesses as the explanation *for* the historical empty tomb and appearances. The Christian's faith concerns the apostles' interpretation of some real historical events. If these events did not actually exist to be interpreted, then the Christian's faith in the apostles' interpretation of them is not meaningful.[40]

That the resurrection as an inferred historical event is acceptably inferable is something a non-positivistic theory of historical explanation could countenance. That such an event was inferred must be established historically. That such an inferred event actually occurred depends upon the authority of the apostolic eyewitnesses in whose explanation of the Easter events reference to the resurrection as an historical event first appears.

Summary

The first point made in this essay is that the later Barth is confused in thinking that he has established either or both a conceptual and a causal connection between what he calls the " 'historical' " knowledge of the resurrection event, on the one hand, and what he calls the "genuine" knowledge of that event, on the other hand. Next, a survey of current thought on the nature of historical explanation finds Barth adopting a positivistic, i.e. covering-law understanding of analytical history, which he construes in terms of scientific determinism. Finally, it is claimed that an *apostolically* interpreted, factual, resurrection event could function as revealed, historical, theological evidence. But in that case, a non-positivistic view of historical explanation must be taken.

[39] Marxsen, "The Resurrection of Jesus as a Historical and Theological Problem," p. 25.
[40] That is to say, the apostles' interpretation would have no point or function. It would, of course, still have a meaning in the sense of a cognitive status. Indeed, that status theoretically may even be descriptive, for we are not implying that the meaning of a theological statement, in this case the apostles' interpretation of the empty tomb, is equivalent to empirical expectations by which it could be falsified.
On the distinction between meaning and meaningfulness see Paul Helm, *The Varieties of Belief,* London, 1973, pp. 24ff.